the ARTS as MEANiNG MAKERS

Integrating Literature and the Arts Throughout the Curriculum

Claudia Cornett
Wittenberg University

Katharine Smithrim
Queen's University

Consultants

Chapters 3 & 4
Sylvia Pantaleo
Queen's University

Chapters 5 & 6
Jeri Harmsen
Queen's University
Angela Solar
Queen's University

Chapters 7 & 8
Aynne Johnston
Queen's University

Chapters 9 & 10
Mary-Elizabeth Manley
York University

Prentice Hall
Toronto

Canadian Cataloguing in Publication Data

The arts as meaning makers: integrating literature and the arts throughout the curriculum

Canadian ed.
Includes bibliographical references and index.
ISBN 0-13-087380-2

1. Arts — Study and teaching. 2. Literature — Study and teaching.
3. Interdisciplinary approach in education. I. Smithrim, Katharine. II. Title.

LB1591.C67 2000 372.5 C00-930487-8

Quotations from Walter Pitman, *Learning the arts in an age of certainty* (North York, ON; Arts Education Council of Ontario, 1998), p. 116, reproduced with permission from Walter Pitman; quotations (p. 7) from The National Symposium on Arts Education of Canada reproduced with permission from Eleanor Newman.

ISBN 0-13-087380-2

Vice President, Editorial Director: Michael Young
Acquisitions Editor: Kathleen McGill
Marketing Manager: Christine Cozens
Development Editors: Laura Paterson Forbes, Marta Tomins
Production Editor: Susan Adlam
Copy Editors: Ilana Weitzman and Rosanne Green
Production Coordinator: Peggy Brown
Page Layout: Janette Thompson (Jansom)
Art Director: Mary Opper
Design: Sarah Battersby
Cover Design: Sarah Battersby
Cover Image: Picture Book – Photonica

1 2 3 4 5 05 04 03 02 01

Printed and bound in Canada.

Contents

Foreword

The publication of the Canadian edition of the *The Arts as Meaning Makers* could not come at a better time. Just as the research evidence about the importance of the arts to brain development, academic achievement in other subject areas, and success in school is mounting, support for arts education is declining in many parts of our country. To the extent that teachers enrich their teaching "with, in, about, and through" the arts as described in this book, they will be at the forefront of the reversal of this unfortunate trend. For while it is true that meaningful arts experiences are likely to yield higher scores in mathematics and reading, the ultimate and most worthwhile effects of an education rich in the arts are even more crucial than internationally competitive mathematics scores. The arts are about beauty, soul, and joy. And this book will help teachers experience much more beauty and joy in their teaching while helping feed their souls and the souls of the children they teach. It will inspire great things in elementary schools across the country, humanizing our teaching and our lives.

This is indeed a wonderful and important book. Like other fine books of its type, there are many ways to read it. One could, of course, read it from cover to cover, but most readers are unlikely to do that. Rather, I can imagine that some teachers will begin by reading all of the classroom vignettes, imagining how their own classrooms could be enhanced or, as Maxine Greene would say, imagining the "as if worlds" that are made possible by the arts. Or one could read the sections in each chapter that begin with the simple phrase "why should?"—especially teachers who have embraced the arts in their teaching and are seeking justification for their approach when speaking with skeptical parents and administrators. Or one could begin with the chapters describing "seed strategies"—a natural beginning point for preservice teachers who are eager to learn about curriculum activities that "work." With the approach in this book, there is little danger of the seed strategies serving as a pale substitute for responsive teaching. They are, just as named, seed strategies—not a series of "canned recipes," but rather, a series of suggestions and skeletal outlines that provide enough direction for teachers to develop their own ideas, their own art. Regardless of how this text is approached on first reading (and on many subsequent readings), the results are guaranteed to be both delightful and meaningful for the readers.

Although every chapter will yield new ideas for even the most experienced teachers of the arts, there are some chapters (such as the one that describes ways of integrating literature throughout the curriculum) that are especially strong. Indeed, the depth of integration of the finest children's literature into all of the curriculum subjects makes it the best overview of its type that I have ever encountered. Not only is it rich with resources (as are all of the other chapters—there are enough ideas and references in this book to fill a lifetime of teaching), but these resources are presented in the context of well-researched and accessible theoretical frameworks.

By taking the text of the American author, Claudia Cornett, and making sensitive changes and valuable additions for Canadian teachers, Katharine Smithrim has done much more than provide us with a Canadian edition. She has reinforced for us how the arts are neither American nor Canadian, but universal in their appeal and importance for the development of a child's physical, emotional, intellectual, and spiritual strengths.

It is my fervent hope that this book will be adopted by every faculty of education in Canada. This text alone will aid immeasurably in the preparation of the finest beginning teachers for our elementary schools.

Rena Upitis
Dean of Education, Queen's University
President of the Canadian Association of Deans of Education

Preface

The Purpose of This Book

Art is the imposing of a pattern on experience, and our aesthetic enjoyment in recognition of the patterns.

Alfred North Whitehead

It is an exciting time to be a teacher. Never before have we known so much about how the brain grows and develops. Never have there been so many proposals for instructional alternatives to meet children's diverse needs. But never have we needed to use our powerful creative problem-solving abilities as much as we do now. Will teachers be able to digest the growing mountain of research on learning, convert it to thoughtful, artful practice, and engage children who are used to barrages of television images in seven-second bursts? How can teachers compete for the attention and allegiance of students accustomed to ready emotional and physical stimulation from provocative videos and concert-quality CDs? The entertainment and garment industries have successfully educated our youth to expect stunning designs and hard-impact drama—with special effects produced by creative geniuses. They are way out in front of educators, who squeeze vitality out of learning when they segregate thought from emotion and body from mind, cramming young bodies into rows of desks—all facing forward. School can seem a cold, dim, lifeless place compared to the outside world of compelling stories, alluring songs, cunning images, and opportunities to move in creative ways.

Humankind has always been at its best when painting, potting, dancing, singing, and pretending. The most important aspects of civilization and culture are preserved, not in standardized tests or on report cards, but in imaginative literature, art, drama, dance, and music. And these are the ancient learning rhythms that draw contemporary children. The arts were, and remain, the most basic and most essential forms of human communication. The arts are ways we *make meaning* about our deepest feelings and most significant thoughts. To ignore or minimize their value by compartmentalizing them into "specials" on Tuesday or an annual class play is to deny the power of the piper.

This is an introductory text for preservice and practising classroom teachers. The goal of the book is to help teachers *meaningfully* integrate literature, art, drama, dance, and music throughout the curricular area by providing a basic arts knowledge base, clear reasons for integration, and specific arts integration principles. Teaching *with, about, in,* and *through* the arts implies an alternative approach to the traditional role of classroom teachers who teach science, social studies, math, and language arts/reading and use the arts only as enjoyable add-ons. The book is written from the perspective of a general classroom teacher, for classroom teachers, not specialists—although specialists will find the book valuable in understanding the point of view of a generalist. It is designed to be accessible to novices, so it includes actual teacher stories, lesson plans, tools to plan *original* lessons and units, compendia of *seed* starter strategies in chapters for each art and a separate chapter on integrating the arts with other arts. A special emphasis is placed on active reader engagement through Take Action inserts and the Activities sections at the end of chapters, which invite readers to transform information. Finally, differentiated instruction is addressed throughout the text (to meet the diverse needs of students).

How the Text Is Organized

The book is organized into fifteen chapters. The first two provide necessary historical and theoretical background to understand WHAT is included in arts integration, WHY the arts are important in education, and HOW teachers can use the research and experiences of others to structure an integrated arts program. These two chapters introduce basic frameworks, which are applied in the remaining arts chapters, including implications from brain research, a levelled concept of arts integration (teaching *with, about, in,* and *through* the arts), the *creative problem-solving process,* four unit structures, a two-pronged integrated lesson plan, ten principles of integration, and strategies for differentiating instruction.

Next come ten chapters on integrating the five arts of literature, art, drama, dance, and music—a pair for each art form. One chapter of each pair deals with WHY, WHAT, and HOW the art form should be integrated. WHY includes an overview of the theories, beliefs, and research that support the art's use, as well as a discussion of the art form's unique contribution to student learning. In the WHAT section, the necessary knowledge base for a classroom teacher is discussed, with focus on basic content such as elements (literary elements like plot and theme; art elements such as colour, line, and shape). The HOW section is the bulk of the chapter and consists of general principles of integration applied to each art area. HOW is organized around a model for integration built on daily arts routines, types of integrated units, and other specific structures for making meaning through the arts in science, social studies, math, reading, and language arts. Following each of these introductory chapters is a chapter containing *seed* strategies adaptable for most elementary and middle school age and stage levels. These are brief idea *starters,* offered in the belief that teachers must choose and adapt *all* teaching activities to meet unique student needs. The seed strategies are organized into (1) energizers and warm-ups, (2) strategies to teach arts concepts and elements, and (3) strategies to integrate the arts in science, social studies, math, and reading/language arts.

Chapter 13 is a separate compendium of strategy seeds for integrating the arts with one another in ten combinations.

Chapter 14 is a discussion of the problems and possibilities in assessment and evaluation in the arts.

The final chapter is a series of common questions that classroom teachers ask as they begin to integrate the arts. Topics include censorship, worries about materials, and concerns about diluting the arts through integration.

Special Features

The following features are intended to activate prior knowledge, establish the importance of particular information, engage readers in cognitive, affective, and kinesthetic ways, and structure response and reflection opportunities.

Quotes

The powerful words of artists and teachers are presented to provoke thought and give rhythm to the reading material. These can be culled for classroom use as "quotes of the day."

Classroom Vignettes

Stories have always been the best of teachers. There is a story of one teacher's journey to open chapters and make the possible more personal. A basic principle of arts integration is to experience the art first and then isolate its components for study. These vignettes are *whole* art forms that show how creative teachers craft lessons that meaningfully mingle art and math, science and drama, literature and dance, and social studies and art.

Pictures

The faces of students and teachers tell the integrated arts story throughout the book.

Children's Literature

Children's literature is both an art form and one of the basic integration principles used in all arts chapters. In every chapter there are recommendations about specific books and strategies for using children's literature to integrate art, music, drama, and dance. Poetry writing and sharing and storytelling are given special emphasis in special sections of chapters.

Take Action Notes

These *notes* are inserted throughout the text and invite readers to pause and "do." For deep learning to happen, there is no substitute for acting on information. The notes provide some ways to do so. They are numbered so that they can more easily be assigned or chosen by students.

Post It Pages

These are one- or two-page summaries that pull together information that teachers will need to use over and over to integrate the arts. For example, *News Bulletins* give a quick look at research and current school programs that integrate the arts across the curriculum. *Post It Pages* are summary pages set up so that they can be photocopied for personal ready-reference use.

Teacher Resources

At the end of each chapter, teachers can preview resources for special materials or information for arts integration. These include videos, internet addresses, addresses of organizations and sources for music, computer software, and multicultural information. In addition, there are more comprehensive resources listed in the appendices.

Activities

The activities sections at the end of chapters 1, 2, 3, 5, 7, 9, and 11 offer suggestions for individual readers or class members to "act on" what they have read by reflecting, writing, and doing. Some activities are also appropriate for class assignments.

Appendices

Special items in the appendices include the following:

Arts-based Bibliography of Children's Literature. An extensive bibliography of children's literature, grouped by arts areas, is included to help locate appropriate books, stories, and poems related to visual art, drama, dance, and music.

Awards Bibliography. A bibliography of literary award winners is provided because these books have been judged to be high-quality literature and are usually available in collections of public libraries and schools. For beginning teachers, these bibliographies are useful for finding fine picture books to use for arts integration and powerful fiction and nonfiction with arts connections. The books are labelled by genre and approximate age level to help select books for genre units.

Arts Organizations, Addresses, and Web Sites on the Internet. Find everything from lesson plans to chat rooms on arts integration using these specific addresses.

Interest Inventory. One of the most important assessments that teachers can do is finding out students' interests. A sample inventory helps teachers mesh arts integration efforts with current interests, identify emerging interests, and create new ones.

Bibliography of Recommended Reading and Videos about Arts Integration. This is a resource for specific teaching ideas and materials, as well as locating additional research on arts integration. In this appendix, books, articles, and videos are categorized by relevant topics in integrating the arts.

Creating a Positive Classroom Environment. Because classroom discipline is always one of the top concerns of beginning teachers, I've included a summary of the most common strategies that veteran teachers use to create a positive classroom environment. In addition, there are basic ways to deal with problems that are bound to occur during instruction.

American National Standards for the Arts. There are no official national standards for the arts in Canada. The American National Standards for the Arts are included for reference.

Preface to the Canadian Edition

The Arts as Meaning Makers by Claudia Cornett was the first textbook sent by a publisher that caught my interest enough to consider prescribing a textbook in a course. It was a practical resource for preservice and practising teachers alike and offered broad enough perspectives on arts education to be useful across the diverse provincial arts curricula and practice in Canada. *The Arts as Meaning Makers* offered a wealth of resources to teachers in elementary school and almost all of them were materials produced in the United States. Raffi, Dennis Lee, and Susan Hammond (ClassicKids recordings) are some of the few Canadian artists to gain wide enough recognition across the border to be included in a text for teachers in American elementary schools. This is of course understandable, yet regrettable, because the quality of Canadian recordings and literature for children has equalled and indeed surpassed the best of American production for children for three decades. This Canadian edition has substituted and added Canadian material and resources whenever possible. Other important revisions reflect Canadian sensibilities regarding Aboriginal people, persons with disabilities, and use of language.

Acknowledgments

To Claudia Cornett, author of the original book, my appreciation for your enormous contribution to arts education in classroom across North America in your writing of *The Arts as Meaning Makers.*

The idea of writing a Canadian version of this book came from Aynne Johnston at the Faculty of Education, Queen's University, so my first thanks and the first thanks of all those who benefit from this book go to Aynne, a "haver" of great ideas. The book owes much of its richness to the contribution of those I asked to Canadianize the chapters outside my area of expertise: Sylvia Panteleo in Literature, Jeri Harmsen and Angela Solar in Visual Arts, Aynne Johnston in Drama, and Mary-Elizabeth Manley in Dance. Many of my colleagues at the Faculty of Education at Queen's University have informed, guided, and supported this project. I wish to thank Rena Upitis, Lyn Barclay, Nancy Hutchinson, Andrea Martin, Nathalie Sinclair, Martin Schiralli, Larry O'Farrell, Gary Rasberry, Larry Miller, Jan LeClair, Sandra Casey, and Brenda Reed. A special thanks to my research assistant Crystal Lehtimaki for her hours of research, errand running, and reading, and for her encouragement, clear thinking, and eye for detail.

Many others across the country have responded to my requests for resources and ideas. This book reflects their knowledge and experience. Thanks to Dr. Robert S. Brown, Academic Accountability, Toronto District School Board; Susan Annis, ArtsSmarts; Michael Wilson, University of Ottawa; Bernie Andrews, University of Ottawa; Jane Thurgood Segal, Saskatchewan Education; Brian Roberts, Memorial University of Newfoundland; Sharon McCoubrey, British Columbia Arts Teachers Association; Harry Murphy, St. Patrick Catholic School, Kingston; Elizabeth Morley and Robin Shaw at the Institute of Child Study, University of Toronto; Rita Irwin, University of British Columbia; Gordon Smith, Department of Music, Queen's University; Sherry Johnson, York University; Bob deFrece, University of Alberta; Wendy Newman, ArtStarts in Schools; Hayden Trenholm, Calgary Arts Partners in Education Society, Roger Clark, University of Western Ontario; Bill Zuk, University of Victoria and the Early Childhood Centre, Faculty of Education, New Brunswick.

I also thank reviewers David Booth and Bob Phillips, OISE/University of Toronto; Herb Katz, University of Winnipeg; Wendy Kellet of Malaspina University College and JoAnn Sommerfield of the University of Alberta for their valuable suggestions.

I am grateful to Dawn Lee, Kathleen McGill, Laura Paterson Forbes, Matthew Christian, and Susan Adlam at Prentice Hall and Pearson Education for their support and guidance.

I am in debt to Robin Shaw of the Institute of Child Study for the photographs that appear on pages 133 and 215, and to Sarah Bennett and Angela Solar for the Canadian and American Classroom photos that illustrate this book. I also thank the principals and teachers of the participating schools.

Finally, and most importantly, my thanks and gratitude to Sandy and Clara, for more than words can say, and in particular, for one sliced pear and the Gavotte for Mignon.

About the Authors

Claudia Cornett is a professor in the Education Department at Wittenberg University, where she teaches undergraduate courses in literacy pedagogy and integrating literature and the arts throughout the curriculum. She also teaches graduate courses at Antioch College and Wright State University. Before moving to the college level, she was a classroom teacher in grades 1–8 and a reading specialist.

Claudia is the author of both books and articles about bibliotherapy, children's literature, learning styles, humour, integrated arts, and the teaching of reading. She also developed and is featured in the instructional television series *Sounds Abound* broadcast on PBS stations. She regularly gives keynote talks and staff development sessions for educators throughout the United States, Canada, and Europe, including ongoing work with *Arts Alive,* a Kennedy Center School Partnership. Her most popular program is "Learning through Laughter" presented on the lecture circuit for Phi Delta Kappa.

Claudia received her Ph.D. from Miami University. In 1989 she was recognized with the Distinguished Teaching Award from Wittenberg University.

Katharine Smithrim is a professor in the Faculty of Education at Queen's University, where she teaches curriculum courses in elementary music and graduate courses in arts education. Before completing her Ph.D. at the Eastman School of Music, she taught Grades K–6 at the Institute of Child Study at the University of Toronto, private Music with your Baby, Music with your Toddler and Orff classes, and the Music in Early Childhood Programmes at several community colleges in Ontario.

Katharine sits on the six-member international Music in Early Childhood Commission of the International Society for Music Education which vets international research for presentation and publication. Her current research focuses on arts education for teachers and students, the role of singing in women's lives and the relationships between rhythm and cognition.

In order to keep in touch with the real world of teaching and learning in schools while she is involved in teacher education at the university, she continues to teach music in elementary schools on a volunteer basis, a different grade every year.

An Introduction to Teaching With, About, In, and Through the Arts

1

The arts are not an educational option; they are basic.

John Goodlad

Introduction

The Sense and Soul of the Curriculum

Any school system that fails to open up the spirit of the arts to its students is unworthy of support.

For the Love of Learning
Ontario Royal Commission
on Education, 1994

During the last decade North American schools, from Regina to Los Angeles, have been devising new curricula using the arts as content centres and teaching tools. Called "arts based," "arts integrated," "arts infusion," "Arts PROPEL," "interdisciplinary instruction," "Learning Through the Arts™" "ArtsStarts," "Arts Partners," and a dozen other names, these programs share a common belief: literature, visual art, drama, dance, and music have the power to energize and humanize the curriculum. "The arts and humanities are poised to become leading contenders in the school-reform sweepstakes" (Larson, 1997, p. 91). Why? In North America, rising academic and social expectations for students have met with declining test scores, causing educational leaders to be desperate for solutions. The "transforming power of the arts" has always been there, but mounting research connecting the arts with particular school goals has finally reached attention-getting proportions. Schools with strong arts programs regularly incur the benefits of increased student motivation to learn, better attendance among students and teachers, increased graduation rates, improved multicultural understanding, revitalized faculty, greater student engagement, growth in use of higher-order thinking and problem-solving skills, and increased creative capacities (Larson, 1997, p. 97). The potential for the arts to invigorate learning is demonstrated in the academic superiority of students in schools that devote 25 percent or more of the curriculum to arts courses (Perrin, 1994).

> The arts contribute to an overall culture of excellence in a school. They are an effective means of connecting children to each other and helping them gain an understanding of the creators who preceded them. They provide schools with a ready way to formulate relationships across and among traditional disciplines and to connect ideas and notice patterns. Works of art provide effective means for linking information in history and social studies, mathematics, science and geography . . . opening lines of inquiry, revealing that art, like life, is lived in a complex world not easily defined in discrete subjects. (The Power of the Arts to Transform Education, J. Paul Getty Trust, 1993)

As changes have happened on the school front, voices calling for modifications in teacher preparation have become more strident. Escalating world and national problems, along with technological revolutions occurring at breakneck speed, have prompted school boards and the provincial education ministries to prepare numerous educational reform documents in an attempt to address current and future needs. Unfortunately, the arts are often not included in discussions of "what matters most" and "core knowledge." Maxine Greene, professor emeritus at Columbia University's Teachers College, argues that "it is difficult to accept a call for excellent teaching and 'teaching for America's future' that pays no heed to the awakenings the arts make possible . . . to teach for the future requires a break from the routine and the ordinary, from the merely repetitive. And the arts, of all forms, may awaken teachers-to-be from the 'anesthetic' . . ." (1997). Indeed, while initiatives like Learning Through the Arts™ partnerships with schools are assisting districts and arts agencies to work cooperatively with in-service teachers—with particular emphasis on the use of artists in the classroom—little is being done in some provinces to prepare practising teachers and *preservice* education majors to see the arts as integral instructional content and bodies of strategies to use on a *daily* basis. A new concept of arts integration goes beyond using media, singing, and drama for self-expression *solely*, important as these are. Instead, a broader conception depicts the arts as indispensable sources of cultural and historical information, diverse perspectives, and values.

Throughout history, literature, art, drama, dance, and music have been ways that humans made meaning. They are "fundamental to what it means to be an educated person. To lack an education in the arts is to be profoundly disconnected from our history, from beauty, from other cultures, and from other forms of expression" (Larson, 1997, p. 99).

The school arena is not the only context in which the arts are being examined for their problem-solving relevancy. Communities across the country are tapping into the magnetic power of the arts to pull diverse groups together and offer hope. Why? For thousands of years the arts have brought people together in celebration, worship, festivals, and weddings. Story, art, drama, dance, and music uniquely engage our senses and sensibilities, making us active participants in ways of knowing impossible through other domains. For a thoughtful and uniquely Canadian view of the presence and possibilities of the arts in education, see Pitman's (1998) *Learning the Arts in an Age of Uncertainty.*

The Arts as Remarkable Meaning Makers

From their earliest beginnings, humans have been compelled to express ideas and feelings through the arts. Thirty thousand years ago paintings were made on a cave wall in southern France (Chauvet et al., 1996). Folk tales from every culture are testaments to the importance of the arts in human history and to our commonalities, as well as our cultural differences; there are more than 300 versions of just the "Cinderella" story, and Mother Goose rhymes have been traced back to sacrifice rituals used hundreds of years ago. What has driven peoples in all times to use the arts to answer questions, to explain, to console, to create meaning? The answer has much to do with trying to do the impossible—define art. No one can offer a definition agreeable to all. We can, however, consider unique aspects of the arts and the kinds of special contributions the arts have to make—how literature, music, art, drama, and dance *are* remarkable meaning makers.

Consider an example from visual art. Visual art has the potential to communicate ideas *and* feelings, but without words. The conveyance of visual images, left open to interpretation, causes fine art, or even decorative art, to engage us intellectually and emotionally. Visualize da Vinci's *Mona Lisa* and, for contrast, the red and white label of a Campbell's soup can. Both pieces include the art elements of colour/hue, shape, size, and texture in their compositions. Campbell's Soup Company undoubtedly works hard to use art to get attention and create a design associated with "m-m-m good" feelings. Red is a warm colour, is set off with white, and is even faintly patriotic. The touch of gold adds a classy feel. Consider the emotional and intellectual engagement with the label and how response to Andy Warhol's *paintings* of soup cans might be different. Many think Warhol's paintings, and most believe Leonardo da Vinci's painting, are pieces of *fine* art because they provoke a different kind and degree of cognitive and affective involvement than advertisement art, for example. Perhaps these works are not as accessible and may confuse, disconcert, or give cognitive dissonance. People ask about the *Mona Lisa,* "How did he do that?" "Why is she smiling?" "Who is she?" "Why did he use those colours?" "How did he get that expression on her face?" The mystery has mesmerized millions for four centuries, so much so that it is one of the few paintings in the world shielded with special glass.

A teacher using the arts as meaning makers can take advantage of this unique power of literature, music, art, drama, and dance to deeply affect students intellectually and emotionally. In arts-infused classrooms, students can be more *productively* active, physically and mentally, because the arts offer additional learning modes, have special motivational properties, and celebrate interpretation of the world in multiple ways. For example, students could learn important science concepts in an arts-based plant unit; insights about processes, such as photosynthesis, and knowledge about what makes a plant a plant and not an animal, can be developed using music, dance, and poetry. Textbooks, worksheets, and traditional tests need not be central to learning. Instead, the arts can become the vehicles. Students can consider artistic properties of any topic and *transform* subject matter through paintings, songs, poems, and dances. Imagine a fourth grade showing what they know and *feel* about converting sunshine and water into energy, using pantomime and dance. Imagine a teacher who knows how to assess science goals and objectives from courses of study by using criteria to *observe* student presentations. Imagine students eager to come to school and doing homework to prepare for presentations voluntarily and happily. Imagine this and you've grasped the core of the integrated arts concept.

Waldorf schools and schools modelled after the Reggio Emilia schools in Italy are some of the richest examples of schools in which the arts are fundamental. Some Waldorf schools offer workshops open to the community. For information about Waldorf schools in your area, contact the Association of Waldorf Schools of North America (3911 Bannister Rd., Fair Oaks, CA 95620 USA. Tel: (916) 961-0927. e-mail: awsna@awsna.org). For descriptions of the Reggio Emilia approach see C. Edwards, L. Gandini, & G. Forman, (1993), *The Hundred Languages of Childhood: the Reggio Emilia Approach to Early Childhood Education.*

Teaching *With, About, In,* and *Through* the Arts

> *Because of the mounting evidence linking the arts to basic learning, some researchers refer to the arts as the "fourth R."*
>
> Murfee, 1995, p. 4

Arts specialists have long known that the arts offer a distinctive means for meaning making; now increasing numbers of elementary and middle school classroom teachers are exploring the potential of the arts to inject science, social studies, and math with energy and relevance. However, debate is still hot among groups who argue *for* "arts for arts sake" and *against* the use of the arts as a practical means of communicating. Harvard arts educator Rudolf Arnheim insists on a "rapprochement" between applied and fine arts, declaring the distinction between the two to be pernicious, leading to

> the notion that crafts like architecture are not quite art and that painting and sculpture are privileged to exist for no other purpose than their own sake, that is, for the mere pleasure of their appearance. . . . the arts . . . are an indispensable means of making us cope with the challenges of human experience. This is the entirely practical function of the arts, and unless it is lived up to, they cannot claim as much of a right to exist as other human activities. In other words, unless art is applied art, it is not truly art at all. (1989, p. 54)

Fortunately, many partnerships have formed to create balanced and realistic perspectives on arts education. The worth of the arts as special disciplines, requiring teachers trained in each discipline, needs to be acknowledged; but a *balanced* perspective includes preparing classroom teachers to include the arts as content disciplines and *means* of learning—as alternative modes for expressing and understanding self, others, and the world. This entails teaching *with, about, in,* and *through* the arts. It is the role of classroom teachers in arts integration that is the focus of this book. This role is addressed through sections in each chapter on WHAT should be taught, WHY and HOW by generalists who plan to work at elementary and middle school levels.

Why Integrate the Arts?

In each chapter, *Post It Pages* summarize newsworthy research that teachers need to know and share about arts integration. The first *News Bulletin* summary appears in Post It Page 1–1.

Reasons to Integrate the Arts

1. **The arts are fundamental components of all cultures and time periods.** The arts are our cultural legacy, our *collective memories.* The history of the human species is told most eloquently through its stories, art, drama, dance, and music. By studying the subject matter of the arts, we can connect culture to culture and see and feel the joys and sorrows of our ancestors—think of the impact of *Les Miserables* in increasing public *understanding* of a period in French history and giving vicarious experience with the pain of poverty.

   Demographic projections for the next forty years predict that minorities, with their diverse cultures, will become the majority in the United States. In Toronto and Vancouver over a hundred languages are now spoken by schoolchildren. To live in harmony, we all must gain an understanding and appreciation of the valuable contributions of each culture. One source for such understanding is the arts. They are natural components of interdisciplinary and integrated learning, providing a neutral ground to learn about varied and multiple communication symbols, content disciplines, skills, histories, values, and beliefs. The arts are our heritage, standing as monuments to the creativity and resiliency of the human spirit.

2. **The arts teach us that all we think or feel cannot be reduced to words.** The arts were the first and remain the *primary* forms of human communication—how we understand each other and look inward to understand ourselves. They give voice to ideas and feelings in ways no other communication vehicle can, because they are driven by emotions and passions. The arts engage intellect, heart, and body. They are unique means of knowing, thinking, and feeling *based in* imagination and cognition.

3. **When students engage in the arts they have the opportunity to "be smart in different ways."** (Howard Gardner, 1993). The arts allow perspectives to be shared that could not be made as clear in other ways, because they require us to enter into a shared view with another person. Think of the cliché "a picture is worth a thousand words." For many people it is not words, but paint or a slab of marble that is used to solve problems and to show that they are indeed intelligent. Moreover, because the arts are hands-on, experiential, and problem focused, students in arts-based classes develop creative problem-solving and higher-order thinking skills that are essential "smarts"; life in the 21st century demands citizens who have diverse approaches—people who will readily use intuition, as well as analysis, synthesis, and evaluation to make judgments with moral ramifications.

4. **The arts develop the brain.**

The potential for greatness may be encoded in the genes, but whether that potential is realized . . . is etched by experience in those critical early years.

Nash, 1997, p. 56

The brain has unrivaled power to make meaning from the messages it receives. But there are doors to development that remain open only during childhood; once shut, the doors are forever locked. For example, research on the emotional system now shows that it is wired up by puberty. Frontal brain lobes responsible for cognitive understanding develop until about age sixteen, and, unfortunately, missed chances to develop brain capacities can account for lifelong handicaps. The experiences of childhood build the brain's circuits for music, art, language, math, and emotion. Children who have limited arts experiences are likely to have poor access to the power of the arts to give solace and ecstasy.

5. **The arts provide avenues of achievement for students who might otherwise not be successful.** Imagine Leonardo da Vinci in an average Canadian school. "This illegitimate son of a poor woman, a left-handed writer who loved to draw and challenge conventional thought, would be labeled an at-risk special education candidate . . ." (Murfee, 1995). Just as sports have encouraged many to stay in school, the arts can provide motivation to learn. A special sculpture project in social studies class or learning to play the recorder in music class can be a reason to come to school. The great teachers from children's literature come to mind here: Jess's music teacher, Miss Edmunds, in *Bridge to Terabithia,* who gave him hope by helping him find beauty in his dismal life; Miss Stacey in *Anne of Green Gables,* who encouraged Anne to let her imagination soar.

6. **The arts develop a value for perseverance and hard work.** The self-discipline required to master an instrument or learn lines for a school play can transfer to academic learning. Students involved in the arts learn to value sustained work and understand its connection to excellence. Unlike extrinsic rewards provided by teachers or parents, the rewards from the arts are intrinsic—a good feeling of having done it yourself and the pride of *independent* problem-solving. Indeed, as Pitman says, "We accept incompetence on our shopping trips, mediocrity in any number of services we request at the gas pump or the bank counter, but we demand excellence when we attend a theatre, a concert hall, a dance performance or an art gallery." (Pitman, 1998)

7. **The arts are a necessary part of life.** Why shouldn't the arts be as prominent inside school as they are outside? Imagine a day without the arts—no musical wake-up, no framed art in the home, no drama on television or in theatres, no dancing, no singing. The arts are an enormous part of our lives. In Canada, the arts is a $40 billion industry, replete with career opportunities, ranging from interior decorating to teaching.

Involvement in the arts prepares students for a world that wants artistic thinkers and creative problem solvers. Aristotle observed, "Art loves chance. He who errs willingly is the artist." In the real world of work, questions and problems seldom have but one answer, and the arts help prepare students to attend to multiple solutions, to take risks, and to capitalize on mistakes. Our economy depends on individuals who can imagine and produce products sought around the globe. The unique language, special symbol systems, and variety of technologies that students must master to become successful in the arts prepares them for a world in which change is guaranteed. Through drama/theatre, dance and music, art, and literature experiences students learn to cooperate and work as a team in ways critical to the success of corporations and family unity. Through the arts, students have chances to come to respect unusual points of view and learn that *relationships* matter, and they learn how important the *form* of ideas and feelings are to the content conveyed—Marshall McLuhan's the "medium is the message" idea.

Students who create and respond to the arts also have opportunities to make unique conceptual leaps by learning to focus on the whole, as well as the parts, to achieve understanding. Teachers frequently decry students' lack of attention to detail and undeveloped concern for others; we should not neglect the potential of the arts to develop student sensitivity and responsibility. A poignant life-connected lesson is that *quality* matters, as much if not more than *quantity.* Blessed with so many *things,* we may be losing sight of how the small nuance creates a large difference. A word or single gesture has tremendous potential to uplift another or to devastate. Spock's raised eyebrow speaks volumes. As Elliot Eisner put it, "the subtle is significant."

8. **There is a strong positive relationship between the arts and academic success.** The participative nature of the arts can counter the passive observation habit that television and computers can develop. Active engagement is a key to academic suc-

Post It Page • 1-1

News Bulletin Research You Can Use

- SAT scores for students who studied the arts were 59 points higher on the verbal and 44 points higher on the math portion than for students with no experience in the arts (The College Board, Profile of SAT and Achievement Test Takers, 1995).
- An integrated arts curriculum called "Learning to Read through the Arts" yielded an improvement of one to two months in reading skills for each month students participated. Writing skills also improved. Numerous schools and districts across the country have adopted the program (Zamdmer, 1994).
- Some 3,500 students participated in a program that integrated the arts into literature and social studies in Los Angeles. These students wrote higher-quality essays, showed more conceptual understanding of history, and made more interdisciplinary references than nonparticipating students (Aschbacher & Herman, 1991).
- Elementary students who were a part of the SPECTRA arts program in Hamilton, Ohio, made the most gains in reading vocabulary, comprehension, and math comprehension as compared to a control group. Creativity measures were four times higher for the SPECTRA group and gains continued during a second-year evaluation (Luftig, 1994).
- Stereotypical views toward minority cultures were decreased through arts instruction centred around Native American music and culture in Arizona (Edwards, 1994).
- In the arts-based "Different Ways of Knowing" program in Los Angeles, Boston, and Cambridge (Massachusetts), 920 elementary students in 52 classrooms had significant gains in achievement and motivation. Students increased their beliefs in the value of personal effort and were more engaged; there were more student-initiated discussions, and more time was devoted to literacy activities and problem-solving. High-risk students who had been in the program only one year gained 8 percentile points on standardized language arts tests, and those with two years gained 16 points. Participating students also had significantly higher report card grades in language arts, math, reading, and social studies. Nonparticipating students showed no gains (Catterall, 1995).
- A growing number of Canadians will be employed in arts-related occupations in the future. The economic impact of the arts and cultural industries sector in Canada, in terms of gross domestic product (GDP), was some $29.6 billion in 1993–94, or 4.8 percent of the total economy. When both direct and indirect economic impacts are taken into account, it is almost $40 billion. The sector's labour force grew by 5.5 percent between 1989–90 and 1993–94; in contrast, total employment in Canada decreased slightly over the same period (Statistics Canada).

Note: There is no published Canadian research on the relationship between arts and academic success. A Canadian national research project is underway to study the effects of Learning Through the Arts™ (a model described in Chapter 2) on teacher practices, school principal practices, school board or district policies and practices, and student interest and motivation toward the arts and learning. To ensure continued financial and administrative support for these types of programs, it will be important to demonstrate the links between academic achievement and the arts. As such, student achievement in language and mathematics will also be considered. This is the first-ever national arts education research project in Canada, involving twenty schools at each of the six sites, with an overall population of more than 20,000 students, from which a sample of approximately 6,000 students has been selected (www.rcmusic.ca/itta/index.asp).

cess. See the *News Bulletin* in Post It Page 1–1, especially the statistics on SAT scores for students who participate in the arts.

9. **The arts offer alternative forms of assessment and evaluation.** Quality and quantity of progress in the arts have long been measured by exhibitions, portfolios, and performances. These forms are now being examined by educators as alternatives to tests to more effectively document student growth throughout the curriculum.

10. **The arts can be a "feel good" alternative for students who turn to drugs and other destructive means to "get high."** Tom Stang, a twenty-year veteran teacher in an art-based program for troubled youth at Phoenix Academy/Drug Rehabilitation Center, believes "if there is one thing I have learned as a teacher, it is that the arts are the soul of the education program" (Larson, 1997, p. 94). The arts can uplift and elevate us to soar spiritually and emotionally from the hope that comes from a good laugh, a beautiful song, or a satisfying painting. Enthusiasm is sparked by playing with ideas and creative discovery, and the arts release creative energy—motivational energy to fuel progress toward productive goals. The potential effects of this motivation? Higher attendance rates, decreased dropout rates, fewer discipline problems, and happier students and teachers (Aschbacher & Herman, 1991).

11. **The National Symposium on Arts Education of Canada calls for arts education for all children.** The Symposium's vision is based on the following principles:
    - That participation in the arts is a fundamental right of all citizens,
    - That all Canadians should have access to quality arts education through publicly financed education programs,
    - That arts education programs should be delivered by teachers who have the capacity to deliver quality programs,
    - That communities should promote and support participation in the arts (Articipaction), and
    - That the arts are vital to life and learning.

    The National Symposium on Arts Education also agreed that the following should be government policy:

    - That the arts be recognized and validated as integral to all provincial education curricula so that the arts become part of the lives of all our citizens, and
    - That the arts become a significant component of national and provincial policies in cultural, health, and economic sectors as well as in education and training.

Specialists alone will not be able to help children meet these goals, partly because of the small number of specialists in schools and because of the limited time specialists have to teach the arts. When classroom teachers become arts collaborators, children benefit from increased time spent with the arts and have the opportunity to view the arts as learning tools used throughout the curriculum, and life, on a daily basis.

Preliminary research findings "demonstrate that arts experiences in early childhood help prepare children for their first years of school" (Welch, 1995, p. 157). How do arts experiences make children ready to learn? Children who have heard and sung nursery rhymes (literature and music) have a language foundation on which teachers can build reading and writing skills. This literary heritage invites children to move as parents and teachers sing "Ring Around the Rosie" or "London Bridge is Falling Down." Children dance, sing, laugh, and learn to love language and school. Children who have had opportunities to explore the art media of chalk, paint, collage materials, and clay learn to take risks, experiment, and problem-solve. The delight in manipulating colour, line, shape, and texture can last a lifetime, be the start of an avocation in the arts, or lead to one of the hundreds of arts-related careers, from designing automobiles, furniture, or clothes to making picture books for children.

Children who start school expecting success and who continue to enjoy learning have a greater chance of staying in school; "arts programs are related to dropout prevention and staying in school" (Welch, 1995, p. 157). One stellar example of how the arts motivate students to be successful is the Boys Choir of Harlem. Founded in 1969 by Dr. Walter Turnbull, the choir was formed to share the joy of music with African American children. Turnbull's vision of providing musical, academic, financial, and emotional support for his choir members, many of whom come into the choir off the streets, has been so successful that 90 percent of the participants in the Boys Choir of Harlem go on to college (Gregorian, 1997). But the signs of being at risk develop early, so we can't wait until high school to make learning relevant and exciting. As Gardner showed in his book *Creating Minds* (1993), it is often those unconventional "creative spirits" like Einstein and Freud who make the breakthroughs in science and math; we cannot afford to lose creative thinkers who may dismiss science and math as dismal piles of dates, facts, and graphs. Instead, students can be shown how to learn math and science using musical intelligence, by kinesthetic means (dance/drama), or through the visual arts, giving them more means to enjoy learning and more reasons to return to the arts in the future. Teachers need not only teach *to* interests, but can develop interests by presenting subject matter in new ways.

Research studies also link arts education to a safe and orderly school environment (Welch, 1995). Consider self-discipline and the arts. Anyone who ever learned to play an instrument knows the hours of practice necessary to "become good." College and university students who remember the "forced lessons" by well-meaning parents are often thankful that they persisted. One student's journal entry speaks for so many others: "At first I just wanted to make my parents proud and I loved the applause at recitals. Eventually I found out I could get so much out of just playing—for myself. I could relax, escape, and really just change from a negative mood to a positive frame of mind by sitting down and playing for an hour or so. Other kids got high or zoned out with drugs or booze. I guess I just got high on music!" We can't "just say no." Children need to experience the healing alternative to a chemical high: their own creativity.

What Do Teachers Need to Know and Do to Teach *With, About, In,* and *Through* the Arts?

In February 1997 arts advocate Jane Remer spoke to The Kennedy Center school partners at an annual conference on using the arts as teaching tools. At that Washington, D.C., meeting, she discussed the concept of teaching *with* and *about* the arts. Remer's idea was expanded to teaching *with, about, in,* and *through* the arts and is used as a paradigm to organize integration in this book. Teachers can begin at a modest level and teach *with* the arts by adding daily arts routines or centres. More integration happens when teachers plan lessons *about* arts content so that students are involved *in* the arts in more mindful ways. The fullest integration is teaching *through* the arts and involves creating an aesthetic classroom environment in which substantial content units are planned using the arts as both learning tools and unit centres. But to derive instructional implications for teaching *with, about, in,* and *through* the arts, planning needs to be grounded in respected teaching and learning theories. The next section provides an overview of essential knowledge relevant to arts integration, including trail-blazing *brain research,* Gardner's *multiple intelligence,* Erikson's *life stages,* Piaget's *developmental stages,* Maslow's *hierarchy of needs,* Vygotsky's *social development,* and the *creative problem-solving process.*

Brain Research and Changing Views of Intelligence

Nearly every time one visits a bookstore there's another new book on being smart. Multiple intelligences theory has ignited interest in a nascent field that now includes emotional intelligence (Daniel Goleman's, *Emotional Intelligence: Why It Can Matter More Than IQ,* Bantam, 1995, was a best seller), moral intelligence, creative intelligence, practical intelligence (see Yale University's Robert Sternberg's new book), and Gardner's new addition to his magnificent seven, "naturalistic intelligence."

How do these expanded, more inclusive views of intelligence connect to arts integration? New views consider cultural, social, and environmental factors that raise or lower intellectual capabilities—factors that include significant arts experiences, such as learning to play keyboards. Pioneering brain research, like T. Berry Brazelton's, supports this perspective. Hidden links between brain activity and how the brain comes to be structured are now made visible through microscopic analyses of children's brains (autopsies, PET scans, and MRIs). Studies during childhood show that the brain actually grows like a budding and branching tree, depending on which areas are "sparked." By adulthood the connections in the brain number more than 100 trillion.

Brain Pruning. Neurons start as a spaghetti-like mass. In early childhood they begin to hook up according to sensory input. Music is heard and a link is forged, beautiful colours and shapes surround a child and connections are made, a baby is rocked or cuddled and another circuit is wired. The key is not exposure, but a pattern of repeated stimuli that sculpt the brain. "Deprived of a stimulating environment, a child's brain suffers . . . children who don't play much or are rarely touched develop brains 20% to 30% smaller than normal" (Nash, 1997, p. 51).

Windows of opportunity to develop particular abilities begin to close as early as age ten as a "draconian pruning" of excess brain synapses starts (Nash, p. 50). Some neurons may actually die; children born with cataracts became permanently blind in affected eyes if the clouded lens was not removed by age two. The window for human visual acuity development only lasts until about age eight; we cannot ignore the power of the environment to form neural connections. Use them or you lose them.

What we eventually do and become depends on how each of the brain's billions of neurons links to thousands of other neurons. Each child's brain can form quadrillions of connections, but the number and strength depend on the transformative power of repeated experience. "Each time a baby tries to touch a tantalizing object or gazes intently at a face or listens to a lullaby, tiny bursts of electricity shoot through the brain, knitting neurons into circuits as well defined as those etched onto silicon chips. . . . When the brain does not receive the right information—or shuts it out—the result can be devastating" (Nash, p. 54). Emotionally deprived babies develop "sad brains" when the centre for joy and happiness (left frontal lobe) does not receive stimulation to "get on line."

How Can Teachers Use the Brain Research to Accomplish Arts Integration?

1. **Make the arts an integral part of the elementary curriculum.** Some windows of the mind close before we are out of elementary school. If schools were structured on brain research, there would be *daily* music and movement. Student passivity during lectures would be replaced with hands-on art and drama activities.

2. **Use the power of emotions to release memory proteins.** How? Engage students in experiences that call for feelings to be felt and expressed. For example, literature and art discussions, hands-on art making, working with background music, and dance and creative movement all trigger emotional as well as intellectual responses. Dramatic play and exploration of art materials have the potential to alter brain chemistry, creating a feeling of optimism and well-being because play taps into brain chemicals involved in pleasure: dopamine causes elation and excitement, and endorphin and norepinephrine heighten attention (Brownlee, 1997).

3. **Use music to develop math reasoning.** The window for developing the brain area for music is from three to ten years of age, and the exposure to music rewires neural circuits (research at University of Konstanz in Germany): "the amount of somatosensory cortex dedicated to the thumb and fifth finger of the left hand was significantly larger [in string instrument players] than in non players" (Begley, 1996, p. 57). There is evidence that these circuits endure for life; consider those who successfully return to an instrument later in life after childhood exposure (Begley, citing work of Shaw at the University of California–Irvine). What's more, the circuits for math reside in the brain near those for music, possibly accounting for the correlation between music exposure and math performance. Preschoolers who received keyboard instruction for eight months scored 34 percent higher in spatial–temporal ability than other preschoolers. (They were tested with mazes, patterns, and geometric figures.) (Rauscher et al., 1997). One author concluded that "when children exercise cortical neurons by listening to classical music, they are also strengthening circuits used for mathematics." He believes the "Mozart Effect" may be a result of exciting "inherent brain patterns [used] in complex reasoning tasks" (Begley, p. 57).

4. **Develop a love and command of words early.** It is now clear that children are capable at younger ages to use language, music, art, movement, and drama to make meaning; the optimum learning "window" is ten years, beginning at birth. We should tap into these capacities and not teach down to children. Instead of back to the basics, we need to move forward to a future rich in arts-based learning, including daily poetry sharing, reading aloud, singing, storytelling, and dramatic conversations to stimulate growth in the auditory cortex.

5. **Create a nonthreatening environment.** Stress and threats cause the brain's amygdala to flood the brain with chemicals potentially harmful to development of the cortex, which causes problems with understanding. The arts have the power to relax and calm; for example, playing music at certain times of the day in the classroom can create a few minutes of restorative tranquility.

6. **Give opportunities to move during learning.** Restricted physical activity inhibits brain and development (Begley, 1996, p. 61). For example, a child in a body cast until age four never learns to walk smoothly. Drama and dance are possible avenues to allow students to learn kinesthetically—to use movement essential to development.

7. **Provide a synapse-stimulating environment.** This implication is from research on animals raised with playmates, toys, and hands-on stimuli. Privileged animals grew 25 percent more synapses than rats deprived of stimuli. Since the brain is a malleable mass with infinite potential, teachers and parents need to do what's necessary for children to be all they can be. Childhood experiences stimulate "which

Take Action • 1

Your Brain?

Stop for a few minutes and reflect on the experiences that made you the person you are today. What arts experiences did you have as a child? How did they affect you? What do you remember about teachers who used the arts?

neurons are used, that wire the circuits of the brain as surely as a programmer at a keyboard reconfigures the circuits in a computer. Which keys are typed—which experiences a child has—determines whether the child grows up intelligent or dull, fearful or self-assured, articulate or tongue-tied" (Begley, 1996, p. 56). Bruer (1999), however, suggests that Begley's claim is not substantiated in the research. The research, according to Bruer, shows that most environments, even poor ones, provide sufficient stimulation for brain growth and that only drastic deprivation results in impaired brain function.

Multiple Intelligences Theory

Strong support for arts-based learning comes from the work of researcher Howard Gardner, who developed the theory that we don't have one fixed intelligence, but at least seven separate ones (see Post It Page 1–2). His work with normal and gifted children, as well as brain-injured adults, led him to dispute the prevalent view of intelligence as a single general capacity used to deal with life situations (Blythe and Gardner, 1990). Instead, Gardner defines intelligence as the capacity to solve problems and create products that would be valued in a cultural setting. Four of the seven intelligences (verbal, visual, musical, and kinesthetic) are parallel to the arts domains of literature (verbal), visual art, music, and dance and drama (kinesthetic). The other three intelligences are linked: logical, interpersonal, and intrapersonal are necessary for working with problem-solving in all arts areas, working with people, and doing self-examination. Thus, Gardner's theory views the arts as distinct modes of thinking that fall under the umbrella of intelligence.

Monet Mural

While Gardner posits that we have capacities in all seven domains, he believes we usually have strengths in certain ones. Unfortunately, American schools tend to teach mainly to and through verbal and logical intelligences. Gardner believes it is "educational malpractice to continue to serve education in the same

Post It Page • 1-2

Gardner's Seven Intelligences

	LIKES, NEEDS, GOOD AT
Verbal: "Word lovers" • T. S. Eliot,* Margaret Laurence	Seeing and hearing words, talking and discussing, telling stories, reading and writing (e.g., poetry, literature), memorizing (places, names, facts), using or appreciating humour, using word play, doing word puzzles
Visual: "Imagers" • Emily Carr, Pablo Picasso*	Thinking in pictures and seeing spatial relationships, drawing, building, designing, and creating, daydreaming and imagining, looking at pictures, watching movies, reading maps and charts, doing mazes and puzzles
Musical: "Music lovers" • Igor Stravinsky,* Glenn Gould	Singing, humming, and listening to music, playing instruments, responding to music (likes to tap out rhythms), composing music, picking up sounds, remembering melodies, noticing pitches and rhythms, timbre
Interpersonal: "People–people" • Muhatma Gandhi,* • Jean Vanier	Lots of friends, joining groups, talking out or mediating and resolving conflicts, empathetic and understanding, sharing, comparing, relating, cooperating, interviewing others, leadership and organizing
Intrapersonal: "Loners" • Sigmund Freud,* • James Baldwin	Aware of inner self (feelings, intentions, and goals), working alone, having own space and self-pacing, focuses on own feelings and dreams, pursuing own interests and goals, original thinking, self-reflecting
Logical: "Reasoners" • Albert Einstein,* Marie Curie	Experimenting, asking questions, problem-solving, figuring out how things work, exploring abstract relationships and discovering patterns, categorizing and classifying, reasoning and using logic (inductive and deductive), math, playing logic games
Kinesthetic: "Body Movers" • Martha Graham,* • Karen Kain	Moving and using body to communicate, touching and using nonverbal communication, e.g., hands, face, gestures, hands-on learning; kinesthetic–tactile learning, sports, dancing, drama, and acting

*The seven exemplars that Gardner uses in *Creating Minds* each expressed *extreme* "intelligence" in at least one of the seven areas, but all used capabilities from all seven. None of these "artists" was particularly successful in a traditional school environment.

Take Action • 2

How Are You Smart?

Use the information from the previous and following sections to decide your strongest "intelligences."

way to all consumers" and urges teachers to draw on students' stronger intelligences as vehicles for working in less dominant areas.

Gardner further argues that *real* understanding does not happen unless a person transforms ideas and skills from one domain to another. Indeed, "intelligences seldom operate in isolation" (Blythe and Gardner, 1990, p. 33). Such a view of understanding is an important reason to use the arts, since they are ways of *transforming* ideas and feelings using verbal and nonverbal modes.

How Can Teachers Apply MI Theory?

Here are a few practical ways to use multiple intelligences theory.

Assess Intelligences Informally. Use the information in Post It Page 1–2 to construct a self-assessment checklist or ask students to raise their hands as you ask, *How many of you*

1. Can draw? See pictures in your head? Enjoy TV, movies, art? (visual)
2. Like to read? Listen to stories? (verbal/word smart)
3. Like sports? Like to make things with your hands? (body/kinesthetic)
4. Like to do math and science experiments? (logical/math)
5. Like to listen to music, sing, or play an instrument? (musical)
6. Like to have many friends? Enjoy being with groups? (interpersonal/people–person)
7. Like to work alone? Like to sit and think about yourself? (intrapersonal)

Plan to Use All Seven Intelligences. Set up seven centres or stations that give students alternative ways to "show they know" in the seven different ways to learn skills and content. Code lesson plans to note which intelligences are the focus. Use the ideas in the following chapters to present lessons in new ways, and structure alternative response options for students. (See HOW strategies sections of all chapters.)

Use the Seven-minute Energizer (Armstrong, 1994). Give one minute to each intelligence area as a classroom routine:

1. *Visual:* Make pictures in your head: places, colours. Take a fantasy journey.
2. *Verbal:* Write down all the words you can think of that start with a letter or rhyme (pick a category). Make up a poem or riddle.
3. *Musical:* Hum or sing together. Play a piece of music and move to it.

PLANNING	***Monday***	***Tuesday***	***Wednesday***	***Thursday***	***Friday***
Verbal/words					
Visual/art					
Music					
Inter/group					
Intra/individual					
Logic/math					
Kinesthetic/drama/dance					

4. *Intrapersonal:* Think about a goal. What would you like to do and how could you do it? How could you be a better person or student?
5. *Interpersonal:* Get a partner and give each other honest compliments.
6. *Logical:* Do quick math (e.g., add, subtract, multiply in your head).
7. *Kinesthetic:* Do toe touches, waist stretches, sky reaches, jumping jacks.

Use Clear Assessment and Evaluation Criteria. Present criteria for evaluation in advance so that (1) students can explore many ways to meet the criteria and (2) any product can be examined by the teacher or students to determine its quantity and quality. Evaluation criteria can be jointly developed and applied to performances, portfolios of work, written materials, and other products. The key is deciding what goals or competencies are to *be achieved* in any learning event, not just describing what students will *experience.* It is preposterous to grade any project unless students know, *in advance,* the concepts and skills that the project should show. This emphasis on clear criteria liberates creative thinking by giving focus to the problem-solving process and is a preparation for life, in which time, materials, money, and who you work with are limitations that force you to work with what you have.

Inform Parents about the Seven Intelligences. Use the Post It Page in Post It Page 1–2 to have parents evaluate themselves. Plan presentations and newsletters to let them know about this and other research on learning.

Help Students to Set Goals. Teach lessons or a unit on the different ways to be smart. Create a form with goal blanks under each category so that students can fill in seven goals. Ellison (1992) found it useful to include a sentence description for each intelligence. Invite students to think of how to achieve goals in different ways and encourage the use of all intelligences by taking time each week to discuss what's been tried in each.

Locate People Resources. Find authors, artists, athletes, or fictional characters (Charlotte in *Charlotte's Web* is verbal and kinesthetic) or use Gardner's seven exemplars from *Creating Minds* (see Post It Page 1–2) to study the different intelligences. "Career Day" can be organized around invited guests from each of the seven intelligences to exemplify diverse strengths.

Make Apprenticeships Available. Visual students can be mentored by local artists and musical students by community members involved in the music industry. A combination of shadowing a mentor, discussing, and being coached on projects forms powerful learning opportunities.

Use Project Work. Students can be given the choice of a topic or interest and whether to work alone or with a group as means of encouraging the use of their strengths. Ask students to think of ways to respond or *show they know* using different intelligences, and offer options, besides traditional reports, to present information (writing stories, poems, songs, constructing games from information, making charts, drawings, sculptures, miming, and creative dance).

Team Plan with Teachers Who Have Strengths Different from Your Own. Plan with the art or music teacher to discover alternative means of achieving lesson goals.

Field Trips Can Be Taken to Places That Focus on a Particular Intelligence. Plan a trip to the symphony for music, an art museum for art, a library for verbal, or a dance concert for kinesthetic.

Erikson's Stages

Erik Erikson was a brilliant psychologist who spent his early years studying art. At an invitation from Sigmund Freud to study psychoanalysis, he changed his direction and in 1950 published *Childhood and Society,* a classic book about the influence of culture on child development. He concluded that all cultures place common demands on individuals, and each person develops a sense of self and relationships to others in response to *crises.* Erikson organized these crises into eight stages. The first crisis is faced when a child must learn to *trust* to become *hopeful.* During the toddler period the child must resolve the conflict between *autonomy* and *shame and doubt.* If autonomy and independence are developed, the child will have a sense of *will.* During the preschool years thc child struggles with *initiative versus guilt* and develops a strong *sense of purpose* if he is supported in attempts to take initiative. When a child starts school, she is usually struggling with the conflicts between *industry* and *inferiority.* If this crisis is successfully resolved, there is a growing sense of *competence.* During the adolescent years the crisis is between *self-identify* and *role confusion,* with successful resolution leading to what Erikson termed *fidelity* or a kind of being true to yourself. The final crises are beyond the scope of this book, but involve *intimacy versus isolation* (young adults) to gain acceptable love relationships; *generativity versus rejectivity* (adults) to learn caring; and *integrity versus despair* (mature adults) to gain wisdom (Erikson, 1950).

How Can Teachers Use Erikson's Stages?

The arts can play important roles in the successful crisis resolution encountered in each stage. In general, teachers need to (1) create a safe classroom climate that encourages risk taking, and not publicly humiliate or embarrass children by using methods like writing names on the board for bad behaviour, (2) give adequate think time so that more students try to answer questions, and (3) dignify incorrect responses to signify respect for efforts that are sincere (e.g., if the student sincerely responded "limestone and granite are minerals" when asked "What do you know about minerals?" a teacher might say, "You have given me two good examples of rocks. Can anyone give me two good examples of minerals?" This gives accurate information and allows the child to save face). Finally, children, like adults, struggle to feel competent and want to have a sense of purpose. Here are examples of how arts integration can contribute to developing a sense of industry and competence (the two major crises for primary and intermediate children).

- During early childhood (ages two to six) the crisis of *initiative versus guilt* is successfully confronted by building on the independence (autonomy) developed in the previous stage. The arts offer opportunities for children to actively pursue activities that are intrinsically rewarding and involve use of the imagination. The ability to make and act on individual choices develops as students are invited to engage in dramatic play. Drama and dance help children explore grown-up roles and ways of moving without having to feel uncomfortable about making mistakes. Through arts experiences children learn that not every activity in school has to yield a "correct" product that, when done "wrong," produces feelings of shame and guilt.
- The arts enable students to discover the pleasure and pride resulting from being productive, working hard, and not giving up, which support the developmental crisis about *industry versus inferiority* during the elementary years. The arts allow students to create their own unique products through which they can feel that they are conquering the materials and skills of the world. Teachers can promote a sense of industry through the arts by allowing students to choose individual and group projects, to compose stories and perform poems, and to produce art responses such as sculptures and paintings in social studies and science units. In addition, through group work in drama, dance, music, and art, students have opportunities to develop feelings of competence in peer interactions. Difficulty with any of these challenges can lead to damaging feelings of inferiority. *Note:* A thirty-five year study of 450 males found a correlation between willingness to work hard in childhood and later success in life in both personal relationships, adjustment, and income (Valliant and Valliant, 1981).

Piaget's Stages of Cognitive Development

Jean Piaget, a Swiss biologist and epistemologist, is famous for a four-stage theory based on observing children. He reasoned that the key stimulus for development was interaction with the environment. Piaget thought that, along with genetically programmed biological changes, touching, seeing, hearing, tasting, smelling, and moving and interacting with people cause children to make discoveries that alter world perceptions. In other words, children develop intellectually by experimenting—which appears to be play to adults. He believed children mentally organize reality into psychological structures used to understand. Piaget called these cognitive structures *schema.* A person either *assimilates* new information into schema or through the process of *accommodation* creates new or modifies old cognitive structures—thinking is adjusted based on new information. For example, a child might not recognize a bean bag chair as a chair and call it a "ball" because he is trying to understand using old schema. Once the child is shown how to sit in the chair, this new information is assimilated. Accommodation occurs if new information is added about the category of "furniture." In most learning there is both assimilation and accommodation.

Piaget thought these stages were natural and sequential, building on one another in a progression toward more complex thinking (see Post It Page 1–3). Since part of our genetic predisposition toward cognitive development involves continually trying to achieve an equilibrium when something is not understandable, we are motivated to make sense. But Piaget cautioned against trying to hurry up development, because he believed it took too long to teach something to a child who was not ready to learn, and he offered general flexible age guidelines to gauge readiness (Piaget, 1980). While Piaget believed a child's thinking

Post It Page • 1-3

Piaget's Stages of Cognitive Development

Sensorimotor Intelligence: birth to two years

- Uses all senses to explore the world. Non-verbal communication.
- Gains understanding that objects exist even when not seen. (Remove a toy from a very young child and it won't be missed because she can't see it. Once the child gains *object permanence,* she remembers the toy and will cry to get it back.)
- Moves from mere reflex actions to the ability to direct actions toward a goal. *Example:* Sees something and tries to get it by crying and crawling.

Preoperational: two to seven years

- Begins to carry out mental actions or operations that require forming and using images and symbols. *Example:* Uses symbols for objects and people. Likes fantasy and imaginative play, makes mental images and likes to pretend.
- Rapid language and concept growth occurs (2,000-word vocabulary by age four is common).
- Trouble reversing actions or understanding how objects can change shape but still be the same object (doesn't think a tall glass of milk poured into a short fat glass is still the same amount; being able to think about something from more than one perspective comes later).
- Understanding other points of view is difficult since the child is egocentric (centred on his or her own experiences). May happily talk to his or herself. Thinks everyone thinks, feels, and sees as he or she does.

Concrete Operation: seven to eleven years (hands-on thinking)

- Basic concepts of objects, numbers, time, space, and causality are developed.
- Reversibility (two-way thinking) develops. Can classify by different categories. Understands how a group can be a subset of another (animals and plants are both "living things").
- Uses concrete objects to draw conclusions. Basic logic develops but is tied to physical reality; abstract and hypothetical problem solving is not attainable.

Formal Operation: eleven to fifteen years

- Can make predictions, think hypothetically, do meta-cognition (think about own thinking process and self-question).
- Understands sarcasm, puns, argumentation, and abstract thinking. Generates diverse possible solutions for problems and can evaluate alternatives based on many criteria (e.g., moral, legal, economic). Can form and test hypotheses; uses scientific method.

Data for chart from Piaget, 1950, 1952, and 1954.

would be consistent with his or her developmental stage across situations, more recent research has demonstrated that children show characteristics of one stage in certain situations and then think at a higher or lower stage in other situations. For example, Gelman (1979) reported incidences of four-year-olds speaking in simpler sentences when they talked to two-year-olds, indicating they considered the needs of the younger child. This behaviour was thought by Piaget to not develop until around age seven. Finally, it is worth noting that many individuals never reach the final stage of development called *formal operations.*

How Can Teachers Use Piaget's Theory for Arts Integration?

When teachers work with school-aged students in preoperational and concrete operational stages, they should:

Provide Hands-on Experiences. Visual aids, such as overhead transparencies, charts, timelines, diagrams, pictures, objects, and drama and dance strategies make learning more concrete. It is important to show and use examples, but *not* provide models to copy.

Give Short, Focused Explanations, Followed by Application. Teachers can use five- to seven-minute mini-lessons and then involve students right away in applying what was taught. For example, a mini-lesson on mime can show how to use the face, body, and in-place movements to "become" a character. Students may then think of real-life or fictional characters and, in pairs, become "frozen statues" of characters. Characters can be tapped to come alive and do in-place moves. Teachers can coach with descriptive feedback during mime to stretch creative thinking and ask students to discuss observations about themselves and others to promote depth of understanding. This is effective guided instruction that leads to thoughtful participation.

Start with Shorter Assignments and Engage Students. Gradually increasing length and complexity causes students to feel successful. Arts activities can start with short energizers to activate experiences related to upcoming lessons. For example, open questions like *"What do you know about museums?"* or *"What do think of when I say the word* dance?" can be used. Before assemblies and arts performance, *preview* or give *cue sheets* (Kennedy Center strategy) to teach about what is to be experienced. By giving *listen fors* (a character's line or a musical segment), students are more likely to be actively engaged and can then make more discoveries during performances.

Take Field Trips and Invite Guests to Give Rich Concrete Experiences. Museums, concerts, and plays are all examples of rich experiences that can extend the curriculum, especially if pre-trip and post-trip activities are planned to cause students to be active meaning makers. Guest artists, storytellers, and musicians can give students direct experiences, and students can prepare interview questions, in advance, to develop language arts skills.

Coach Students Before and During Arts Experiences. When children are given specific language to understand basic arts elements, they can use these concepts to create new personal meaning. For example, a teacher can give labels to concepts that children exhibit: *"Yes, when you draw one figure on top of another it looks like the one on top is closer. That is called* overlapping."

Create a Life-centred Curriculum. Life is a series of problems, and school learning using the arts uses the creative problem-solving process so important to success in life. Post It Page 1–5 summarizes the process.

Provide Opportunities to Explore Ideas and Think in a Variety of Forms. Literature, art, drama, dance, and music all have distinct ways of thinking, including special language and symbol systems. Each permits different ways of expressing and receiving information and gives students many opportunities to use the important skill of grouping or classifying. By teaching basic arts elements, we expand capabilities to think in different categories. For example, once students know that dance includes the use of locomotor and nonlocomotor movements, they can brainstorm some of each and experiment with a greater range of movement than before.

Encourage Students to Construct Their Own Meaning. Fat or open questions like *"What makes you think that?" "How do you know that?" "What do you see?" "What have you discovered?"* and *"Why?"* cause students to do more thinking than closed ones requiring yes or no answers. Active learning strategies that engage independent thinking, like *Think–pair–share* after questions, get students to first think of their own answers, then partner and share. Another active learning strategy, *every pupil response,* can be used in every lesson: Ask for "thumbs up" or a signal for all to *show* they have a response; wait for everyone to signal on an important question before calling on anyone. Riddles, jokes, mind bogglers, question of the day, and other puzzles challenge students to use logic and leaps of imagination to "get it." In addition, humour is intrinsically motivating, requires no grade, points, or outside reward to engage students, and may trigger further creative problem-solving, such as students writing their own arts riddles.

Maslow's Hierarchy of Needs

In the 1970s, Abraham Maslow proposed a theory of motivation that has helped educators understand why children do what they do—or don't do. Maslow observed that his subjects seemed to be motivated by what they *needed*. He proceeded to categorize the needs people sought to fulfil and organized them into a hierarchy, with the basic needs for surviving, like food, clothes, and a place to live, on the bottom (see Post It Page 1–4). He believed that once lower-level survival needs and safety needs are met, people move up the ladder. He thought the three top levels, including the need for beauty, represent needs that are *never* filled, so people continue to always seek more in these areas, unlike the low-level needs that are ignored once fulfilled.

How Can Teachers Use Maslow's Hierarchy?

Maslow's information on needs-based motivation suggests that children who are hungry, thirsty, too hot (un-air-conditioned schools), afraid, or worried about their home life have difficulty engaging in arts activities requiring focus on higher-order aesthetic needs. Teachers can help children get lowest needs met through school breakfast and lunch programs and referrals to social agencies. Comfort and safety needs (second level) can be met through strategies such as telling students that mistakes are okay, giving second chances after genuine effort, and offering choice, such as where to sit to learn. Humour in the form of appropriate riddles, gentle teasing, and the teacher making fun of his or her own mistakes can relax students. While we strive for students to think they are individuals with unique and different ideas, the need for group approval is very powerful (third level). Many seek to conform and copy ideas from peers. This is a particular problem in the arts, where uniqueness is highly valued, but where students often feel fearful about being different. Teachers can share stories about artists who have taken risks by being different (e.g., cubism was thought ridiculous by many of Picasso's contemporaries) and celebrate novel responses with clear descriptive feedback: *"Joe painted his sky with orange and red in it."* The need for group approval can also be met by forming *learning circles* to allow students to collaborate on projects, such as writing songs or poems.

Children are not easily pigeonholed and may have needs operating simultaneously at many of Maslow's levels. Stories about artists who deny themselves survival and safety needs to pursue intellectual achievement, aesthetic needs, and self-fulfilment can help students think about the motivational power of higher-order needs. For example, students might discuss why Monet and other Impressionists made paintings others thought looked unfinished. (See short biographies of artists, writers, and musicians by Kathleen Krull in the arts-based bibliography in the appendix.)

Post It Page • 1-4

Maslow's Hierarchy of Needs

↑
- Self-fulfilment
- Aesthetic needs for beauty and order
- Knowledge and intellectual needs
- Approval and recognition from others
- Belonging, love, acceptance by others
- Physical and psychological safety
- Survival needs: food, clothes, water, shelter

Chart based on Maslow, Abraham (1970), *Motivation and Personality.* New York: Harper & Row.

Finally, while we are motivated to *get* some things, many activities are motivating in and of themselves. Teachers can design a classroom around arts experiences that require no extrinsic rewards (food, candy, stickers) because they are *intrinsically* motivating. Just being in a beautiful room can be emotionally and intellectually satisfying. With the help of students, teachers can make the classroom beautiful with plants, artwork, and background music. Another powerful intrinsic motivator is interest, which can be developed through the allotment of regular times to work on interest-based projects and by offering choice whenever possible. Intellectual achievement is encouraged by allowing time and other opportunities to pursue independent projects involving the arts; students might study a person or topic in the arts that connects to units. Teachers can make it a habit to encourage being curious and wondering by having a "Wonder Box" to drop questions and topics that students would like to learn about or information they would like to share (facts about artists or artworks can cause otherwise apathetic students to become excited about learning).

Vygotsky's Social Development

Russian psychologist Lev Vygotsky is another researcher who has given educators a theory from which important arts integration strategies can be derived. Unlike Piaget, Vygotsky thought teachers and other mentors could and should intervene in children's learning and act as *scaffolds* to bridge the gap between where a child *was* functioning and a stage just out of reach, but attainable. He called this developmental position the *zone of proximal development* and demonstrated how students can often solve problems with some help (cues, suggestions, steps, encouragement) from others when they cannot do so independently (Vygotsky, 1994).

How Can Teachers Use Vygotsky's Zone of Proximal Development

The critical idea is to observe students to determine when they can proceed independently, when others might offer some assistance to expedite success, and when the problem or activity is not appropriate at all for a child. Determining this match involves teachers in *instructional* creative problem-solving, estimated to occur thousands of times each day in each teacher's classroom. Vygotsky believed social interactions with others boosted intellectual growth, and the implication is to plan arts experiences in which students can work in pairs, triads, quads, and as a whole group. By listening to each other tell what they see in a piece of art or hear in a piece of music, everyone has the chance to get another perspective and make new connections (*peer scaffolding*). For example, literature discussions can start with an open question that the questioner *really* wants to discuss because the answer is unknown. For example, *"Why did Jack go up the beanstalk the third time when he already had all the money he would ever want?"* While there are clues in the story, there is not *one* answer, so students must interpret based on text clues. This co-construction of meaning leaves everyone, including the teacher, with ideas beyond individual realms of meaning.

Creativity and Creative Problem-Solving

Many problems confront us. How can we feed everyone on the planet? Who is to do this creative problem-solving? Our children, of course, and to prepare them with facts and books and nasty teacher looks is not a strategy for success. In this section, information about creativity and creative problem-solving is provided to offer ideas for success. Moreover, integration of the arts rests on the ability to use the creative problem-solving process; the arts, in turn, advance creativity.

One of our most pressing societal needs is to determine what aspects of creativity can be influenced and what might even be directly taught. Presently, we're not sure where creativity comes from, what it is, or how it develops. We could just sit back and wait for Plato's muses to visit us or, taking a cue from behaviorist B.F. Skinner, wait for it to happen and then reinforce it with stamps and stickers. Neither waiting nor rewarding is wise. We can start work mindful that the known "truths of the universe" were born of personal struggle and honed by ancient practices like noticing *patterns*. Creativity emerges from time spent looking closely at details and listening intensely to gather data that yield *realizations*. These gifts of the mind can be intentionally used and taught. By teaching creative thinking we do more than "disturb the universe"; we create it and, in some sense, control it. Of course, using the creative process without considering the consequences can be frightful, as the Jewish folk tale of the Golem reminds us: human creativity, mindless of morality, is a destroyer. (One version, *The Golem* by David Wisniewski, won the Caldecott Medal for picture books in 1997).

Enhancing creativity through the arts rests on developing habits that include celebrating differences of mind, spirit, and body; inviting students to choose within moral limits; and using the motivational power of personal interest that can change the world—think of Alexander Graham Bell, whose interest in communication developed through living with his deaf mother. We can begin with a cultivation of creative thinking strategies and a commitment to depth of knowledge in domains where creative work is to be done. We can acknowledge that no one creates in a vacuum or without building on foundations others laid. And we can begin by valuing creativity and using it as a high-placed criterion for sorting out what goes in and should come out of curricula—curricula currently too jam-packed to allow substantive creative meaning making. Author and teacher Alane Starko believes that

> the most reasonable course of action is to support and encourage characteristics associated with creativity whenever possible. At the very least, our classrooms should be more flexible, responsive, attuned to the wonder around us. At best, we may make a difference in the creativity of a young person who may one day bring greater knowledge or beauty into the world. (1995, p. 93)

Creative Problem-Solving and Real Life. It is common to associate creative thinking with artists. The arts invite all of us to explore the unusual and create something different, even if it's just another interpretation of a movie. But creative thinking is also an everyday survival skill, a kind of thinking crucial for success in the twenty-first century. Whether we are deciding how to stretch a budget and still have interesting meals or attempting to deal with global warming, we use innate abilities to creatively solve problems. Indeed, the most troublesome problems will only be solved by creative thinking—divergent, original thinking that examines issues from new perspectives. We cannot just recall how the paper-thin ozone layer can be made whole again. Remembering facts and rote skill application, too often the focus in elementary math, science, and social studies, are not sufficient to help children become successful adults in a future promising multitudes of new problems. Therefore, a major part of the school day needs to be spent developing student creativity; the arts provide fertile ground for growing creative thinking skills.

What Is Creativity? It seems as if the most important things in life are hard to define: love, happiness, art. Creativity is no exception. This doesn't mean that many haven't tried. Perkin's definition implies that everyday people have what it takes to be creative. He believes creativity is simply "using ordinary resources of the mind in extraordinary ways" (1988). To use one's experiences, thinking skills, and knowledge of a field in novel and appropriate ways to produce something new, at least new to the individual, seems doable. But context is very important in arts experiences, and this is especially apparent with regard to what is considered creative. Societies value original products used by specific groups and cultures. What is thought creative in one culture or time is not valued in another; for example, restickable mini-notes probably wouldn't have been hot among preliterate people; and common twentieth-century conveniences like the paper clip are no longer considered creative, but must have amazed first users.

Four Creativity Theories or Models. Researchers have tried to make sense out of the elusive concept of creativity through four angles of research: (1) examining characteristics of creative people, (2) the stages or process of creativity, (3) influences on creativity, and (4) interacting elements. Characteristics of creative people, especially adults, have been studied by researchers such as MacKinnon, Torrance, Tardif, and Sternberg. The stages in the development of creativity and the process of creative problem-solving interested Plato, who thought creativity to be a mystical process resulting from a kind of divine intervention and manifested in bursts of insight. Aristotle believed creativity was explainable by natural laws, just like any other thinking process. Aristotle's theory was later used by Perkins, Guilford, and Weisberg. Other notable theorists using the stages and process approach are Wallas, Csikszentmihalyi, Maslow, and Vygotsky. B.F. Skinner observed creativity to be a function of behavioural influences: creativity naturally occurred and, if reinforced, was repeated. Finally, an interactive theory presents creativity as an interaction among (1) individuals using cognitive processes like divergent thinking, (2) their functioning in particular domains or fields (e.g., math or science), and (3) the environment (culture and time period). Sternberg, Gardner, Csikszentmihalyi, and Amabile are all proponents of variations on this last theory.

How Can Teachers Use the Research on Creativity?

This section provides an overview of theories and possible arts integration strategies.

Characteristics of Creative Persons: The Creative Spirit Profile

> *Creative children look twice, listen for smells, dig deeper, build dream castles, get from behind locked doors, have a ball, plug in the sun, get into and out of deep water, sing in their own key.*
>
> Paul Torrance, 1973

When a teacher says, "I am not creative," she stops herself and limits her students in their use of innate creative capabilities. Belief in the ability to be creative and valuing creativity are key attitudes needed to increase the likelihood that creativity will happen. Teachers don't go around saying, "I am not able to do math" or "I can't read." If they did, we would question their competence and find it absurd for them to be employed as professionals. Isn't it just as absurd for a teacher to claim that she or he does not have important real-life creative thinking skills that students need to be taught? And creative problem-solving *is* an essential real-life skill.

While it is hard to settle on a definition of creativity, there is agreement about processes commonly used to arrive at creative products (Post It Page 1–5) and there is a collection of attributes associated with creativity. Studies of highly creative children and adults (the bulk of the studies) yield a profile to use to observe students and plan a classroom environment to encourage creative thinking (Post It Page 1–6). No one person has the same "profile of attributes" and there is no "generic creative person," but we all possess degrees of most of the characteristics.

Find out what researchers have discovered in studies of people who have produced highly creative work. Teachers may choose to encourage some of the characteristics in themselves and their students, while others may seem to be undesirable qualities. To become familiar with the characteristics, take time to rate the level you believe you have of each characteristic. There is no "right" or "better" profile, but perhaps the characteristics will help teachers and students realize the many dimensions of creativity and that all people have creative attributes.

Creative characteristics often emerge in childhood and there are high frequency patterns of:

- first born
- childhood trauma, such as loss of a parent
- estranged relationships with family
- a family that values learning and a pattern of clear expectations and few rules
- early successes
- likes school, books, collections
- creative products emerge in ten-year groupings (Gardner)
- benefits from role models, mentors
- has a supportive person who understands person's work
- may have strong social peer group or be marginal, i.e., somewhat of an outsider
- parents had own interests
- problem finders*

The Process and Stages of Creative Thinking. While there is no agreement on what exactly creativity is or where it comes from, a common creative problem-solving process has emerged from the work of researchers such as Csikszentmihalyi (1990) and Wallace (1926). Here is an example of the process at work.

> "It takes an enlightened stubbornness to produce anything," declared a man with a British accent.
>
> Trevor Baylis was being interviewed about an invention he created. It all started when he had been watching a TV program on the AIDS problem in Africa. Baylis became "aware" of the ballooning disease statistics and the efforts to educate the African population by radio. The part of the problem that intrigued Baylis was the inability of people to afford or obtain batteries—it cost about a month's salary to buy batteries and some people were actually giving up their rice to buy them. Baylis began to visually imagine being in Africa in a pith helmet with a monocle and glass of gin. This input triggered the image of a wind-up radio.
>
> "It just popped into my head," he laughed. He said it seemed so simple he was sure someone else must have already thought of it. But he investigated and his inquiries showed no one had!
>
> "Everyone has a good original idea, but most don't come to fruition because we worry about humiliation, e.g., people laughing, or that our idea is not new," he explained.
>
> So Baylis experimented with different springs and was able to make a radio that would play for 40 minutes with 20 seconds of winding. Now the Third World has a cheap way to use mass communication and the rest of the world is interested, too. (August 27, 1995 @ 5:30 p.m. on National Public Radio)

Baylis's story illustrates the common *stages* people go through when they do creative problem-solving. What's interesting is how we can *manage* our own processes by knowing the conditions necessary to "prime the pump" of imagination. The process begins consciously with an awareness that a problem exists or a desire to do *problem finding*—a personal decision to look for new uses, products, and so on. Next, an unconscious or idle period happens, called *incubation* by some theorists. An "ah-ha" problem solution brings a person back

*(Dacey, 1989; Tardif and Sternberg, 1988; Gardner, 1993; Getzels and Jackson, 1962; and Csikszentmihalyi, 1990.)

to conscious focus on the problem, followed by testing and evaluation of ideas or solutions. Another way of describing the process is by thinking about the brain hemispheres taking turns working on the problem: left (conscious), right (unconscious), left–right (insight on problem), and finally left again (evaluation).

Think about Baylis and your own experiences as you examine the *creative problem-solving process* in Post It Page 1–5. Use the process to spur yourself as you engage in arts experiences and plan lessons and experiences for students. Display the process (in simplified form) for students to refer to as they work. Take time to talk to students about the processes, do mini-lessons on strategies, and when kids get stuck refer to ways to propel thinking forward (e.g., data gathering, brainstorming, etc.).

Creativity Killers and Squelchers

"To engender creativity, first we must value it."

Sternberg and Lubar, 1991

Unfortunately, parents and teachers often do not look favourably on behaviours peculiar to creativity. Just like Leo Lionni's main character in *Frederick,* children who are loners and want to "do their own thing," rather than conform to adult expectations, may be looked on as troublemakers. It is frightening to read reports detailing how creative thinking declines in children as they move through school. Some studies have even concluded that fourth grade is the peak of creativity for many students.

Creativity Squelchers

- Assessment and evaluation: too much, too soon, too often. The cake falls if you open the oven too soon or too often. Even positive evaluations can inhibit next efforts at creative work.
- Hovering over students as they work so that they feel watched.
- Extrinsic rewards like stamps, stickers, and praise that block risk taking and focus on "getting things," rather than the worth of the activity itself.
- Worry. Fear. Not feeling safe enough to take risks and make mistakes.
- Competition, especially when knowledge and skills are great enough to hope for success.
- Too much emphasis on the product rather than the process.
- Too little choice, especially of how to do an assignment or reach a goal.
- Too much emphasis on order, neatness, and following directions.
- Preponderance of teacher questions that ask for literal answers.
- Lack of incubation time.
- Insufficient information to incubate.
- Rush to judgment about value of ideas. Saying "That won't work" right off the bat.
- Adults doing for children what they could do, or do partially, themselves (leads to learned helplessness).
- Lack of independent study time to pursue ideas of personal interest.
- Taking everything too seriously. Teachers that rarely laugh, play, or express a sense of humour.
- Stereotyped or dictated art activities like colouring books. Emphasis on "staying in the lines" (called "predigested activities that force youngsters into imitative behavior and inhibit their own creative expression"). (Lowenfeld & Brittain, 1975)

Classroom Strategies That Boost Creativity

I have no special gift. I am only passionately curious.

Albert Einstein

If we are to facilitate creative thinking, we must teach content in ways that support, rather than threaten, habits and mindsets that allow creative ideas to blossom. Any subject can be the basis for creative thinking if we provide students with opportunities to learn information, methods, and strategies and then teach how to use them in new ways. Traditional content teaching that emphasizes facts and single correct answers is not going to help students learn flexibility or originality. However, it is not enough for children to just play with creative puzzles and games. They must know enough about something to question it, change it, elaborate on it, or do something new with it, and they must have been taught strategies to accomplish these tasks. Post It Page 1–6 lists strategies to boost creative thinking.

How Can a Teacher Put Research and Theories Together to Coordinate Arts Integration?

A dramatic revolution in cognitive understanding began in the 1970's. Research now substantiates what some teachers and parents already knew intuitively—that the arts are critical to learning.

Murfee, 1995

Conditions for Learning: Basic Beliefs

This chapter has presented much information about the research and theories that support the concept of arts integration. All of us can "stand on the shoulders of the greats" as we put theory into practice, but only individual teachers can convert these ideas into classroom reality. Every teacher must use her or his own experiences, creativity, and desire to help children, as forces behind a workable philosophy or set of beliefs—a work forever in progress. Basic beliefs about what students need to be successful are best set out *before* beginning to teach. It is often easier to work from a draft, so here is one to use to synthesize a model for creating a classroom for student meaning making *with, about, in,* and *through* the arts. Try using statements starting with **"I believe in . . ."**

Immersion. People need to be in a stimulating, accepting environment. This is shown in an aesthetic physical environment full of books, posters, fine art, music, and opportunities to move and pretend. Students need to be around others who are in the process of creating meaning with, about, in, and through art forms.

Expectation. People need to *expect* to be creative and successful. This expectation is made strong when teachers support student risk taking through their comments and actions.

Freedom to fail. All students experience failure, and they should be helped to see mistakes as opportunities. Classrooms should have an environment, created mostly by teacher attitude, that encourages risk taking and allows students to feel comfortable learning from mistakes.

Meaningfulness. People want to be involved in important and purposeful work that will contribute to their own happiness and the happiness of others. This means goals need to be clear. Learning is most successful when it is focused on solving life problems with life-centred materials and strategies, such as focus on *discovering patterns* in all disciplines. To paraphrase John Dewey, school is not preparation for life—it *is* life. Each person must *create* personal meaning using all meaning-making tools available, including reading, writing, speaking, listening, drama, music, art, literature, dance, taste, touch, and smell.

Demonstration. We all need examples, but children do not need teachers to *do* tasks *for* them. Demonstrating strategies and techniques is crucial to learning and gets learning started. (Chuck Novak's *"I do–we do–you do"* process.)

Active learning. People remember more, are more satisfied, and achieve mastery of ideas and skills sooner when they are active mentally and/or physically. Active learning includes starting with the known and building on that knowledge and skill base. Passive listening to a lecture or watching a video is not effective. Hands-on learning is powerful: If you don't act, you don't learn.

Application and practice. Repeated practice of what has been introduced helps students to own the new skill or idea. One of the greatest problems in our schools is not giving students adequate amounts and numbers of *meaningful* practices. Until each of us practises, it is almost impossible to achieve competence; it is competence that allows us to be in control of our own lives.

Independence. Human beings want to be in charge of themselves and need to learn how to work independently. We are proud of ourselves when we can function using our own resources. Teachers can help students move toward independence by teaching independent problem-solving strategies and providing time to work independently. It is important for us to have role models of people who are hard-working and persist at overcoming obstacles to achieve independence. Independence is gained only through much hard work to obtain a knowledge and skill base in the areas we need to work in.

Responsibility. People become responsible when they are taught how to make good choices and are given second chances. There is a story about how Thomas Edison had just finished an early prototype of his light bulb. He called a boy to take it to the factory, and the boy dropped it on the way. Edison had to start all over. When he had another light bulb made—many days later—he called the same boy to come and take it to the factory.

Progress and success. We progress when we have goals that are clear and can gauge our progress by self-evaluation and feedback from respected others (hopefully teachers). We all need concrete progress indicators to feel like we are getting better.

Motivation. Among other things, people can be motivated by a pleasant environment, the possibility of success, working partners, and the opportunity to pursue something of personal inter-

Post It Page • 1-5

Creative Problem-solving Process

Preparation (conscious)

1. Problem presented or found (first notion that a problem exists).
2. *Motivated attitude:* "Can do, will do, want to do!" Emotion causes motion. (Rearrange the letters in "motivate" to spell "move at it.") motivation is movement directed at a goal—an "it"! To get energy to move, attitude is critical.
3. *Problem described:* What is the problem, specifically and exactly? *"A problem well defined is half solved."* Charles Kettering (General Motors electrical wizard).
4. *Data gathering:* Input of facts by reading, researching, interviewing. Use all senses and put in hard work. *"We can have facts without thinking, but we cannot have thinking without facts."* Educator, John Dewey.

Creative Thinking

5. *Divergent thinking* (Alex Osborne's "brainstorming"): Quantity first! *"The best way to have a good idea is to have lots of ideas"* (Linus Pauling, scientist). Generate as many ideas as possible. Use webbing and clustering to record ideas.

   - *Withhold judgment:* Do *not* evaluate or analyze ideas yet or risk shutting down right-brain thinking.
   - *Be fluent:* Generate lots of ideas.
   - *Be flexible:* Try different perspectives or categories; examples/non-examples.
   - *Be original:* Never take the first idea. Stretch until you feel there are no more ideas. Sometimes the idea right after you seem to run out of ideas is the best idea. Think of what no one else will think of.
   - *Elaborate:* Add details and examples to ideas.
   - *Play with ideas and relationships:* Experiment! Ask "What if . . . ?"
   - *Use SCAMPER* (Eberle, 1971; Osborne, 1963):
     Substitute—change characters, setting, time, place, ...
     Combine—force relationships; e.g., "How are a computer and a tree related?" Connect.
     Adapt—compare and think metaphorically. "What is this like?"
     Modify—change colour, size, shape, ...
     Magnify—add to or make larger.
     Minify—make smaller.
     Put to other uses
     Eliminate—subtract something.
     Reverse or rearrange—backward, upside down, inside out.

Incubation (unconscious) and Illumination (semiconscious)

6. *Rest:* Let the subconscious go to work. Plan idle time. Get away from the whole project.
7. *Insight:* A light goes on; "ah-ha" stage. It's exciting because an idea has popped out.

Evaluation and Action (conscious)

8. *Use judgment:* Preset criteria (time, money, morals, etc.) and visual imagery to decide which solutions are best. Piaget: *"The second goal of education is to form minds which can be critical, can verify, and not accept everything they are offered. The great danger today is of slogans, collective opinions, ready-made trends of thought."* (Piaget in Ginsberg and Opper, 1969)
9. *Put the idea into action:* Try it. Elaborate. Revise.
10. *Share, publish (make public):* Celebrate.

The chart information was mainly culled from the work of Wallas (1926), Czikszentmihalyi (1990), and Dewey (1920).

est. External reinforcers like stamps, stickers, and praise can decrease interest in doing something for its own sake. People are motivated by challenge, but if it is not appropriate, it will lead to frustration or boredom.

Creativity. People are creative and can learn to intentionally use their creative capacities. I believe the arts provide some of the richest arenas for developing creative capacities. Evaluation, certain time restraints, and close surveillance can inhibit creativity. Humour and play are essential to developing creativity capacities.

Teachers. A teacher's own knowledge, strategy repertoire, enthusiasm, humour, creativity, and passion are forces so powerful they can change a child's universe, as well as the future we all share. A teacher's artistry can give hope and vision to tackle personal and world problems.

Post It Page • 1-6

Ways to Jump-start Creative Thinking

- Brainstorm: (1) Go for quantity first. (2) List all ideas. Keep driving and don't brake! (3) Include way-out ideas. (4) Piggyback on each other's ideas. (5) Set a time limit. After finishing, ideas can be grouped and then evaluation begins (Osborne, 1963). Some research supports doing individual before group brainstorming to produce *more* ideas. Giving evaluation criteria before the brainstorming session will reduce the number of ideas, but may increase quality. *Variation: Reverse* brainstorming. Brainstorm non-examples instead of examples.
- Word association (similar to brainstorming): List everything connected to a given word. Use to introduce a lesson (e.g., I've used "courage" as the concept to introduce the book, *Mirette on the High Wire.* Ideas can be written down by the teacher or by students).
- Use question frames as prompts: "How might we . . .," "What if . . .," "What are all the ways . . .," "An idea nobody would think of is. . ." Focus on a problem under study (e.g., What are all the ways we could build a catapult?).
- Stumped or stymied? Stop and do something else. Listen to music or do something physical (e.g., stretches and bends to music).
- Turn mistakes into opportunities. See *The Big Orange Splot* by D. M. Pinkwater.
- Sometimes there just isn't enough of a knowledge or skill base. Stop and read, observe, i.e., data gather.
- Don't take the first idea. The best idea may be the one right after you think you've run out.
- Mind meld. Open an encyclopedia, dictionary, or magazine and pick an idea (noun, verb). Combine this idea with the one you are trying to develop. Don't worry about weird or distorted ideas. Just stretch mentally: "An imagination once stretched will never again have the same dimensions." *Example:* I spotted a pair of scissors by my computer. I can meld the scissors with this chapter: I want to *cut out* drab teaching and can make *points* for why to use arts-based teaching. Scissors and the arts can be used and abused. There are different kinds of scissors (pinking, pruning, etc.), just as there should be a variety of arts-based programs.
- Thinking Hats: Get with four other people and each of you "wear a hat" or take a perspective on a problem: #1 describes what is known, #2 gives feelings about the problem, #3 tells what is not known, #4 thinks of any associations or images, #5 lists ideas not at all related, i.e., non-examples (adapted from deBono, 1991). This is similar to the "cubing" strategy (Neeld, 1986) in which a topic is explored in six ways: describe it and tell its parts, tell how it feels, what do you associate with it, what could you do with it, what is it like, argue for or against it. This can be timed (e.g., spend two minutes on each "side" of the cube, or with young children do one or two sides a day).

Selected Teacher Resources

See the Bibliography of Recommended Reading and Viewing in the appendix for additional resources.

Arts for life (1990). The Getty Center for Education in the Arts. 15 min. (Gives rationale for arts integration and classroom examples.)

Teaching in and through the arts (1995). The Getty Center for Education in the Arts. 25 min. (Classroom examples at the elementary and high school levels are shown.)

The Getty's Art Education web site is: www.artsednet.getty.edu; E-mail: artsedne@getty.edu

Activities:

Why Do We Create?

Think of the artists you've known and your own experiences creating through the arts. Add ideas to this list, give examples from your life, or argue some of the points. *We create to*

- Construct personal meaning and search for "truth"
- Cope and solve problems
- Make beauty or express an idea aesthetically
- Have fun and play! As humour guru Joel Goodman says, to maintain the "elf in self."
- Be with others who are being creative
- Pursue an interest or add something new to a field

Arts Intelligences

Pretend you teach third grade and want to use musical, dance/movement, drama, visual art, and linguistic smarts to help students work on multiplying by fives. Think of an activity for each of the intelligences/arts areas:

For example,

- *Musical:* Sing the American folk song "Weavily Wheat." The chorus contains the five times table.
- *Dance/drama:* Give small groups problems (e.g., 5×5 is 25). Ask them to figure out ways to show this with body shapes and movement patterns.
- *Art:* Use collage to create art with combinations of five. Art focus: use of space.
- *Literature/creative writing:* Pattern poetry in which each line has five beats/syllables and final poem is entitled whatever the number of lines *times* the beats is.

  "Four Times Five Is Twenty"
  I love to do math
  It makes my mom laugh
  When I multiply
  Two times five is ten. HA!

Scaffold for Success

Think of a time someone helped you by scaffolding with cues, encouragement, assistance, etc. Maybe when you were first trying to play an instrument, ride a bike, or learn a dance? When do teachers give too much assistance and cause students to become "learned helpless" or dependent?

Activities:

Your Creative Spirit Profile

Directions: Use 1 = low, 3 = medium, and 5 = high level to self-evaluate. Follow with goal setting.

Personality Characteristics

1. Curious and questioning. Wants to know more and why. Likes to explore. Seeks adventure.
2. Stable, emotionally secure.
3. Risk taking and courageous. Doesn't care what others think. Not inhibited by fear of failure. Uses mistakes to solve problems. Spontaneous, impulsive, and uninhibited. Takes chances, but not reckless.
4. Not time bound. Loses track of time. Doesn't like deadlines set by others. Becomes immersed in projects for personal meaning.
5. Self-confident in own worth and work.
6. Independent and nonconforming. Likes new ideas and has own original ideas. Unlikely to follow the crowd. Skeptical of accepted positions and authority. Likes to set own rules and standards. Does not conform to gender stereotypes. Likes to find out things independently. Resistant to "right answers." Easily bored with routine.
7. Well developed sense of humour. Playful with words and ideas.
8. Critical of self. Not often satisfied, but not easily discouraged either. Uses own standards or criteria to judge.
9. Likes to work alone. May appear aloof and withdrawn. May not fit in or seek out groups.
10. Motivated. Very hardworking and persistent. Not easily frustrated by obstacles. Willing to struggle and suffer. Sustains effort and concentrates.
11. Unusually developed sense of wonder and delight—almost childlike in this respect.
12. Tolerant of ambiguity. Tolerates anxiety. Doesn't need one right answer.
13. Broad interests and hobbies.
14. Empathetic. Feels others' pain.
15. Strong sense of destiny.

Cognitive Characteristics

16. Fluent: Can generate lots of ideas.
17. Flexible: Can shift perspectives easily and change categories quickly.
18. Original: Comes up with ideas that are not ordinary or usual. Likes to transform ideas.
19. Elaborates: Can flesh out ideas with details.
20. Observant: Sensitive to the environment. Notices details about people, places, things that others miss. Five senses more acute.
21. Intelligent: There is a correlation between creativity and intellect. Intellect does not guarantee high amounts of creativity, but is a necessary part of it (i.e., a threshold level is necessary).
22. Uses logical thinking: Details and evidence to support.
23. Imaginative. Can combine ideas in new ways with vivid detail. Resourceful.
24. Uses own hunches. Intuitive. Makes guesses.
25. Seeks possibilities and variety. Likes divergent thinking and novelty. First inclination is to explore possibilities versus do critical thinking or say, "It won't work." Approaches problems playfully. Can become overly excited. Likes openendedness. Is a problem finder.
26. Uses visualization and metaphoric thinking to problem-solve.
27. Likes to create order from chaos; organizer. Prefers complexity and asymmetry.
28. Goal and task oriented.

Barron, 1969; Dacey, 1989; Isaksen and Treffinger, 1985; MacKinnon, 1978; Torrance, 1962; Tardif & Sternberg, 1988.

References

Books, Articles, and Videos

Armstrong, T. (1994). *Multiple intelligences in the classroom.* Alexandria, VA: Association for Supervision and Curriculum Development

Arnheim, R. (1989). *Thoughts on art education.* Los Angeles: Getty Center for Education in the Arts.

Aschbacher, P., & Herman, J. (1991). "The humanities program evaluation" in *The arts and education: Partners in achieving our national education goals* (Jan. 1995). Washington, DC: The National Endowment for the Arts.

The arts and education: Partners in achieving our National Education Goals (Jan. 1995). National Endowment for the Arts, 1100 Pennsylvania Ave., NW, Room 515, Washington, DC 20506.

Barron, F. (1969). *Creative person and creative thinking.* New York: Holt, Rinehart & Winston.

Begley, S. "Your child's brain." *Newsweek,* Feb. 19, 1996.

Bennett, W. (Dec./Jan. 1987–88). "Why the arts are essential." *Educational Leadership,* 4–5.

Blythe, T., & Gardner, H. (April 1990). "A school for all intelligences." *Educational Leadership,* 33–36.

Brownlee, S. "What science says about those tender feelins." *U.S. News and World Report,* Feb. 17, 1997.

Bruer, J.T. (1999). *The myth of the first three years: A new understanding of early brain development and lifelong learning.* New York: The Free Press (Simon & Schuster)

Catterall, J. (1995). *Different ways of knowing.* 1991–94 National Longitudinal Study Final Report.

Chauvet, J., Deschamps, E., & Hilliare, C. (1996). *Dawn of art: The Chauvet Cave: The oldest known paintings in the world.* New York: Harry N. Abrams.

Consortium of National Arts Education Associations (1994). *National Standards for Arts Education: What every young American should know and be able to do in the arts.* Reston, VA: Music Educators National Conference.

Csikszentmihalyi, M. (1990) "The domain of creativity" in M. A. Runco & R. S. Albert (eds.), *Theories of creativity,* 190–212. Newbury Park, CA: Sage.

Dacey, J. S. (1989). *Fundamentals of creative thinking.* Lexington, MA: Lexington Books.

deBono, E. (1991). *Six thinking hats for schools: 3–5 resource book.* Logan, IA: Perfection Learning.

Dewey, J. (1920). *How we think.* Boston: D. C. Heath.

Eberle, R. (1971). *Scamper: Games for imagination development.* Buffalo, NY: DOK.

Edwards, C., Gandini, L., & Forman, G. (1993). *The hundred languages of childhood: The Reggio Emilia approach to early childhood education.* Norwood, NJ: Ablex.

Edwards, K. L. (1994). North American Indian music instruction: Influences upon attitudes, cultural perceptions and achievement (D.M.A. dissertation). Tempe, AZ: Arizona State University.

Eisner, E. (Apr. 1992). "The misunderstood role of the arts in human development." *Kappan,* 591–95.

Ellison, L. (Oct. 1992). "Using multiple intelligence to set goals." *Educational Leadership,* 69–72.

Erikson, E. (1950). *Childhood and society.* New York: W. W. Norton.

Gardner, H. (1983). *Frames of mind.* New York: Basic Books.

Gardner, H. (1993). *Creating minds: An anatomy of creativity seen through the lives of Freud, Einstein, Picasso, Stravinsky, Eliot, Graham & Gandhi.* New York: Basic Books.

Gelman, R. (1979). "Preschool thought." *American Psychologist,* 34, 900–905.

Getzels, J. W., & Jackson, P. W. (1962). *Creativity and intelligence.* New York: Wiley.

Ginsberg, H., & Opper, S. (1969). *Piaget's theory of intellectual development.* Englewood Cliffs, NJ: Prentice Hall.

Goleman, D. (1995). *Emotional intelligence: Why it can matter more than IQ.* New York: Bantam.

Greene, M. "Why ignore forms of art?" *Education Week.* Feb. 19, 1997.

Gregorian, V. "10 things you can do to make our schools better." *Parade Magazine,* Mar. 23, 1997.

Hanna, J. (Apr. 1992) Connections: Arts, academics and productive citizens. *Kappan,* 601–607.

Hubel, D. (1988). *Eye, brain, and vision.* New York: Freeman. 191–217.

Isaksen, S. G., & Treffinger, D. J. (1985). *Creative problem solving: The basic course.* Buffalo, NY: Bearly Limited.

Larson, G. (1997). *American canvas.* Washington, DC: National Endowment for the Arts.

Lowenfeld, V., & Brittain, W. L. (1975). *Creative and mental growth.* New York: Macmillan.

Luftig, R. (1994). *The schooled mind: Do the arts make a difference? An empirical evaluation of the Hamilton Fairfield SPECTRA+ Program, 1992–93.*

MacKinnon, D. W. (1978). *In search of human effectiveness.* Buffalo, NY: Creative Education Foundation.

Maslow, A. (1970). *Motivation and personality.* New York: Harper & Row.

Murfee, E. (1995). *Eloquent evidence: Arts at the core of learning.* The President's Committee on the Arts & the Humanities & the National Assembly of State Arts Agencies with the National Endowment for the Arts.

Nash, J. M. "Fertile minds." *Time,* Feb. 3, 1997, 48–56.

Neeld, E. C. (1986). *Writing,* 2nd ed. Glenview, IL: Scott, Foresman.

Osborne, A. (1963). *Applied imagination,* 3rd ed. New York: Scribner's.

Perkins, D. N. (Dec./Jan. 1987–88). "Art as an occasion of intelligence." *Educational Leadership,* 36–42.

Perrin, S. (Feb. 1994). "Education in the arts is an education for life." *Kappan,* 452–53.

Piaget, J. (1950). *The psychology of intelligence.* New York: Harcourt Brace.

Piaget, J. (1952). *The child's conception of number.* New York: Humanities Press.

Piaget, J. (1954). *The construction of relativity in the child.* New York: Basic Books.

Piaget, J. (1980). *To understand is to invent.* New York: Penguin Books.

Pitman, W. (1998). *Learning the arts in an age of uncertainty.* Toronto: Arts Education Council of Ontario.

The power of the arts to transform education (1993). Los Angeles: J. Paul Getty Trust.

Rauscher, Shaw, et al. (1997). "Music training causes long-term enhancement of preschool children's spatial–temporal reasoning." *Neurological Research,* 19, 208.

Remer, J. (1996). *Beyond enrichment.* New York: American Council for the Arts.

Smithrim, K., Upitis, R. & LeClair, J. (1999). When classroom teachers become musicians and artists. In B. Hanley (Ed.), *Leadership, advocacy, communication: A vision for arts education in Canada.* Victoria, BC: The Canadian Music Educator's Association, pp. 93–106.

Statistics Canada, Focus on Culture , Vol. 8, No. 2 (Summer 1996), p. 6.

Starko, A. (1995). *Creativity in the classroom: Schools of curious delight.* White Plains, NY: Longman.

Sternberg, R.J. (1986). *Practical intelligence: Nature and origins of competence in the everyday world.* New York: Cambridge University Press.

Sternberg, R. J., & Lubar, T. I. (1991). "Creating creative minds." *Kappan,* 72, 608–14.

Tardif, T. Z., with Sternberg, R. J. (1988). "What do we know about creativity?" in R. J. Sternberg (ed.), *The nature of creativity.* New York: Cambridge University Press, 429–40.

Torrance, E. P. (1962). *Guiding creative talent.* Englewood Cliffs, NJ: Prentice Hall.

Torrance, E. P. (1973). Is creativity teachable? Bloomington, IN: Phi Delta Kappa.

The truth about teachers (video, 45 minutes). Santa Monica, CA: Pyramid Film & Video.

Valliant, G. E., & Valliant, C. O. (1981). "Natural history of male psychological health, X: Work as a predictor of positive mental health." *American Journal of Psychiatry,* 138, 1433–1440.

Vygotsky, L. S. (1994). *The Vygotsky reader.* Cambridge, MA: Blackwell.

Wallas, G. (1926). *The art of thought.* New York: Harcourt Brace.

Welch, N. (1995). *Schools, communities, and the arts: A research compendium.* National Endowment for the Arts and The Arizona Board of Regents.

Zamdmer, M. (1994). *Learning to read through the arts: Its emergence in context.* (Report No. E90 2301-022). New York: New York University. (ERIC Document Reproduction Service No. ED 378 103).

Children's Literature

Krull, K. (1995). *Lives of the musicians: Good times, bad times, and what the neighbors thought.* San Diego: Harcourt Brace.

Lionni, L. (1987). *Frederick.* New York: Knopf.

McCully, E. A. (1992). *Mirette on the high wire.* New York: G. P. Putnam's Sons.

Montgomery, L. M. (1908, 1935). *Anne of Green Gables.* Toronto: Seal Books

Paterson, K. (1979). *Bridge to Terabithia.* New York: Harper & Row.

Pinkwater, D. (1993). *The big orange splot.* New York: Scholastic.

White, E. B. (1952, 1980). *Charlotte's Web.* New York: Harper Collins

Wisniewski, D. (1997). *Golem.* New York: Clarion.

Yashima, T. (1965). *Crow boy.* New York: Scholastic.

Integrating the Arts Throughout the Curriculum

2

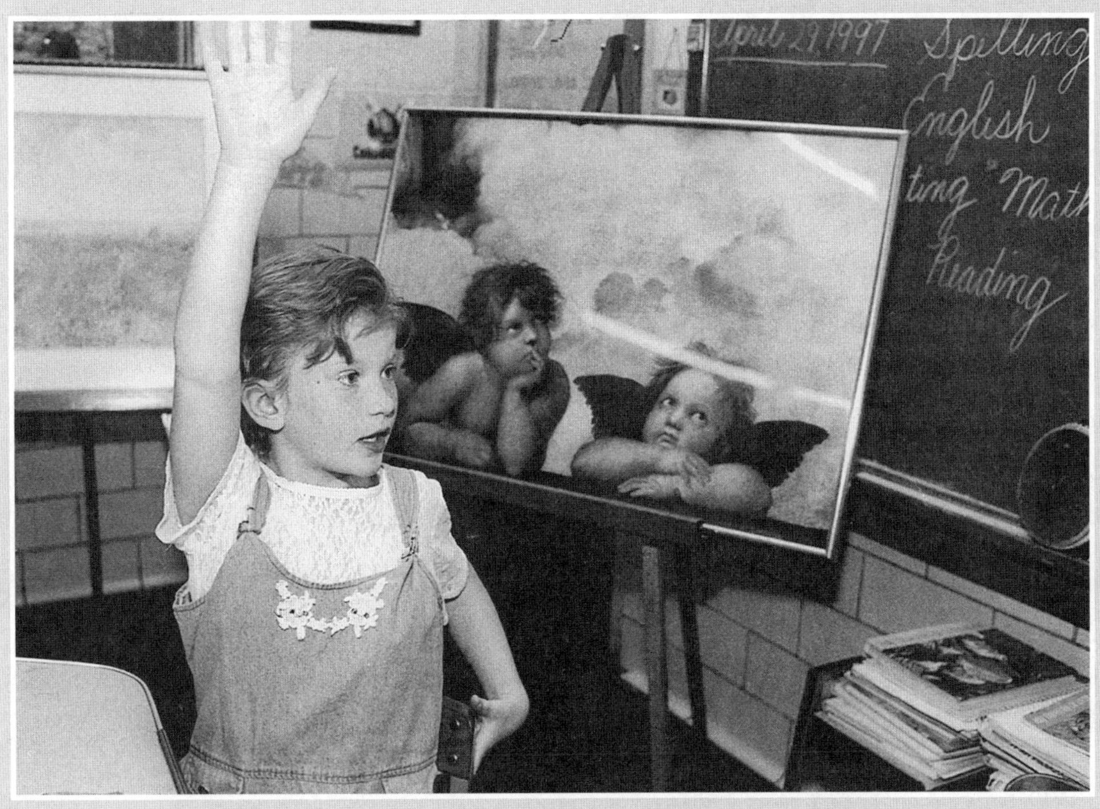

In a world where soul is neglected, beauty is placed last on its list of priorities. In the intellect-oriented curricula of our schools, for instance, science and math are considered important studies, because they allow further advances in technology. If there is a slash in funding, the arts are the first to go, even before athletics. The clear implication is that the arts are dispensable: we can't live without technology, but we can live without beauty.

Thomas Moore, *Care of the Soul* (1992, p. 277)

Classroom Vignette

A Visit to Ms. Lucas's Class: *"The Art of Teaching and Teaching the Arts"*

What a visitor notices first about Ms. Lucas's room is outside the door. On a long wall is a timeline, at children's eye level, of birthdays of artists. Students have added comments about the artists and their work using "speech bubbles." To the left of the door is a large, framed watercolour mural painted by the students, a product of a study of Monet's water lily series. Beside the mural is a reminder to see the class's "Monet's Garden" outside the window.

The school, built in the 1920s, has remnants of the era—a huge closet bears the label Cloak Room. But the room is alive with the arts. Four *substantial* easels display framed prints by Monet, Van Gogh, da Vinci, and Rembrandt. More prints hang at eye level. In one corner there is a learning centre on Van Gogh and baskets of art materials on a work table below a bulletin board of Van Gogh's portraits and landscapes. A stack of student journals with "Arts for Life" on the cover of each is on the bookshelf. A yellow crate holds books about art—some are biographies and informational books like *Painting with Children* and *Crayons.* In another corner of the room the old wood floor has been carpeted with squares secured with doubled-sided tape. A sign proclaims this area to be the Book Nook. Pillows and a bean-bag chair look inviting, couched among the classroom library. A recipe box holds student recommendation cards with comments and a "smiley face" rating for each book. A ficus tree fills a corner, philodendron tentacles crawl across the window sill.

The bell rings and Ms. Lucas hustles to her CD player. The room fills with Vivaldi. Smiling children burst in and one boy yells, "The Four Seasons!" when he hears the music. A debate ensues about which season is playing as the kids hang up their coats and greet Ms. Lucas with *bonjour* and *goedemorgan.* (Ms. Lucas teaches a bit of the language the focus artist spoke. So far they've managed greetings in German, Italian, Russian, French, and presently Dutch, for Van Gogh.) Students scurry to get their journals and sit at their desks or at learning centres around the room's perimeter. Ms. Lucas explains how some choose to do artwork in their journals, so the art centre offers more media options. She shows a blank wallpaper book with "Arts for Life Journal" on the front. Inside the journal there is a note that says, "The arts are what give heart to our lives. Imagine a day without literature, music, art, dance, drama. Write or do a piece of art about how the arts are a part of your life." Looking around the room at the 27 third graders, while Vivaldi plays on, one can't help but feel excited, and relaxed. After about 15 minutes, Ms. Lucas asks the students to "find a place to pause" and morning routines continue. The agenda on the board gives the order of events. The children seem to be well rehearsed to take their turns:

Composer of the day. Marie-Lynne and Jacques give a one-minute biographical report on Vivaldi. They tell what they think was most interesting in his life.

Riddle of the day. Miyoko has written on the board, "What did the artist say when his minibus stopped in the middle of the street?" There are cue blanks below: V__ __ G__ __ __ . Students are reminded to guess letters—not the answer. Soon thumbs are up as letters are guessed. Finally there is a chorus of "Van Gogh!" Miyoko proudly tells the class she made it up herself.

Art docent. Tony takes a seat in a special chair and begins to talk about a piece of art he made. It is a portrait of himself on cloth. It was done on wet cloth with chalk, and he explains how he used Van Gogh's poses, lines, and colours as starter ideas as he attempted this first self-rendering.

Looking closely. Three children unveil a new print on an easel. This one isn't framed. They take turns explaining and questioning the class. *"What do you see? How does that make you feel? Why do you think the artist did that?"* It is obvious the class has been taught to ask "fat questions" and are at ease with giving many interpretations. The students are excited to have a new *White Iris* print by Van Gogh (they guessed the artist during the discussion) and appear touched by the story of the single white iris representing the artist, who felt alone and different.

A poem a day. Two children put up a transparency of Bogart's "Poems can give you" from Booth's *'Til All the Stars Have Fallen.* Sarah points at the "Poetry Alive" poster while Douglas reviews the directions for "echoic" reading. Sarah and Douglas then take turns reading each line of the poem, with the class echoing their volume, rate, tone, pitch, pauses, and stress. The class claps at the end. Ms. Lucas asks if anyone wants to talk about the poem. Several hands go up and a short discussion takes place.

Sing in. Ms. Lucas asks for song nominations, and there is agreement on "Oats, Peas, and Beans" and "The Green Grass Grew All Around." Song posters on a clothesline across the back of the room have the lyrics of these songs written large enough to read from a distance. Julian is given a long-handled pointer and takes charge: *"We'll start with the oats song. Everyone stand up and take a deep breath. Now, ready, 1–2–3–begin!"* When they sing "The Green Grass Grew All Around," another student takes a stack of cards from Ms. Lucas that have the key words of the cumulative song written on them (hole, root, tree, branch, etc.). She places them in the right order in a pocket chart while the class sings the song.

The arts routines take about 15 minutes. Ms. Lucas has organized the rest of the morning around a science unit from the required third grade curriculum. The unit is built around the questions *"How do plants affect people? What causes these effects?"* and *"What affects plants?"* with the central concern being an exploration of causes and effects. Students are involved in working at centres, in learning circles, at independent work, and in direct instruction groups led by Ms. Lucas. She explains how reading, writing, speaking, and listening skills are taught in science and social studies units. For example, in this unit students are reading informational books, like Cruxton's *Discovering the Amazon Rainforest,* and writing observation reports, original poetry, and reader's theatre scripts (from books they are reading). Every unit involves the use of literature, art, drama, dance, and music to introduce and respond to unit content.

Every unit also includes a focus on people (scientists, composers, poets) who have wrestled with the same questions that the unit addresses. Van Gogh is a part of the plant unit because of his expressive paintings of plants. The study of Van Gogh is not limited to his plant paintings, however. The goal is to find a meaningful connection, but to then delve into the connection by exploring why Van Gogh painted the *way* he did and *what* he did (causes). Science becomes the study of people who have discovered relationships among living and nonliving things, rather than just a study of things and isolated processes. Vivaldi's compositions on seasons are an obvious connection to plants and the effects of the seasons on plants and the effects of this music on people. What Vivaldi conveys about the seasons and their effects is very different from what the students glean from reading an expository passage about the cycle of seasons and plant life. Ms. Lucas explains that the goal is to have students know and *feel things* about the ideas they are learning. Much thought has gone into the role of *emotional intelligence* in structuring these integrated units.

Each unit culminates in a *portfolio* of work representing what has been learned. Basically, these are pocket folders. The unit questions are followed by a table of contents in each folder:

I. Music and plants: songs and pieces
II. Art and plants: artists and their artwork
III. Drama and plants: reader's theatre scripts and drama workshops
IV. Dance/movement and plants
V. Literature and plants: fiction and nonfiction
VI. Writing about plants: information and creative writing

Bulges in the pocket folders testify to the use of audio and videotape evidence and Ms. Lucas explains that shoe boxes are also often used to house portfolios, because art projects are sometimes three dimensional. Portfolio highlights are presented at the end of the unit, and each student is allowed to invite guests to an hour performance. Guests can be parents or even friends from other classes.

In the afternoon Ms. Lucas uses similar strategies with a social studies unit. Sometimes the science and social studies units are combined, but combinations are not forced. For the same reason, math is integrated as appropriate. This means students get intensive instruction in math skills or reading and language arts skills as needed, and teacher-directed lessons may be taught separately from the units. Ms. Lucas tries to tie skill-based lessons to units so that students see the relevance of skills; integration is not done just for its own sake, but only when there is a natural connection.

It would be impossible to describe all that happens in Ms. Lucas's class. The first day ends with another set of student-directed routines. They sing and tell about what they liked learning that day and there are "book talks" to advertise "must reads." The grand finale is a narrative pantomime: the whole class become seeds and grow into tall irises. The silent drama is interrupted by the bell of reality, and the day ends with calls of *arrivederci* and *bon soir!*

When asked about her methodology, Ms. Lucas is quick to respond.

"Being an artist is a part of being human. To say you aren't an artist—not a creative being with unique ways to understand and express thoughts and feelings—is to say you're less than human. Teachers *must* be artists. Anything less than an artist–teacher is just not good enough for my children, your children, or anyone's children. Integrating the arts begins with a mind-set: we decide the arts are what make us alive and make life livable. We tell each other and our students that the arts are for life and school is not just getting ready for life—it is life. In my 'living room'—some call it a 'classroom'—every person is an artist. The teacher must proclaim her artist status. To do less is to harm your own potential and the hope we can give children in hopeless circumstances."

Visit Postscript. Ms. Lucas teaches in an inner-city school. Her students face poverty, drugs, violence, parent apathy, and abuse. The school district has struggled financially and been forced to cut elementary arts specialists. Classroom teachers became responsible for implementing the courses of study for art and music. The district provided some staff development, but most K–5 teachers felt unprepared to teach art and music. Teachers were concerned about preparation time and getting materials for art projects and music experiences. Three years later, there seems little likelihood the specialist positions will be restored by voters. The same concerns about quality arts experiences still exist, but many teachers, including Ms. Lucas, have viewed the loss as a chance to try research-based arts infusion strategies used throughout the North America. These programs view the arts as significant, separate disciplines *and* as tools to learn content in science and social studies and skills in math and language arts.

Introduction

In Chapter 1 the idea of integrating the arts was introduced using a levelled concept of teaching *with, about, in,* and *through* the arts. Three main questions that teachers need to answer to teach anything were also presented: *WHAT* do teachers need to know and teach? *WHY* should we integrate the arts? and *HOW* can integration be accomplished? These ideas structure this chapter and other chapters, along with a series of principles for integration.

Why Integrate the Arts Throughout the School Day?

When children create they are making sense of the world.

Robert Alexander

An Arts Integration Movement?

Why would teachers want to join an arts integration movement? On the practical side is the fact that there is just too much to know and not enough time to teach it all. More has been published in the past ten years than in the previous hundred years. Integration allows connections to be made, so instead of continuing to cram in more information, the focus is on bigger issues, questions, and problems. Time is simply used differently in integrated classrooms. Isolated and outdated information is dropped from the curriculum through a process of prioritizing and allocating time to learning deemed most essential in an integrated world.

Which leads to the next reason for arts integration: the arts are integral in the world outside school. For example, adults get much of their entertainment and information from the arts and use arts-based goods to demonstrate status. The 1997 Renoir Portraits exhibition at the National Gallery in Ottawa generated more than $66 million in revenue. Consider the film industry, television and radio, and our clothes, cars, and favourite websites.

Presently, the school day is often organized around isolated skill teaching and fragmented into subjects—life isn't. Structuring school more like life is motivational since success in life is important. People learn better in a context—that's the whole-to-part idea, and integration allows students to bring to bear the world's information and meaning-making tools on interesting problems. Since many current problems are new, solutions must be both creative and built on information from the past. Content and skill teaching are thus combined for a meaningful purpose.

Finally, the track record for integrating the arts to effect academic gain is strong. This isn't surprising, since arts integration involves intentionally developing everything from a larger vocabulary to analytic thinking, historical and cultural perspective, and self-discipline. In addition, studies of successful people demonstrate how persistence pays off; the arts engage students in a manner that causes them to want to persist; often it isn't that students *can't* learn, it's that they *won't*. The "Learning Through the Arts™" program, originally a joint venture of the Royal Conservatory of Music and the Toronto District School Board, has now expanded into six other regions across the country: Vancouver, Calgary, Regina, Windsor, Corner Brook, and Cape Breton. It is an outcome-based program focusing on curricular integration. The arts are not treated as a separate area of learning and appreciation, but are infused directly into the general curriculum. This integration is done in a manner that enhances the child's ability to learn concepts required in disciplines such as math, science, and language arts. The arts motivate and actively engage students in the learning process. At the heart of this innovative program lies the conviction that the disciplines of cooperation, creativity, and self-esteem developed in the arts are essential to life skills.

This degree of integration is only possible as a result of the collaboration of artists and teachers over time. Together they develop strategies and activities that draw on the resources and address the needs of their particular learning and teaching environment. An emphasis has been placed on sequential professional development for teachers and artist educators to develop skills in communication, program design, and meeting curricular outcomes.

In these programs, whole schools become involved, with every child actively engaged in the learning process. This model reflects the commitment of Learning Through the Arts™ to equity and sustainability. Initial anecdotal reports suggest enhanced communication ability, greater participation, increased use of technology, and improved literacy skills for students taking part in the Learning Through the Arts™ program. The following are some examples:

- Teachers report that grade one students involved in Learning Through the Arts™ are comfortable using vocabulary not normally heard until the grade four level. Students who learn arts vocabulary like glockenspiel, jumbo, and marionette through artist visits find it easy to learn and use more sophisticated vocabulary.
- Another teacher wrote, "Learning Through the Arts™ gets children to think and take part. One of my students had not spoken up in class all fall. After three Learning Through the Arts™ sessions, not only is he contributing, he has become one of the class leaders!"
- Grade nine students involved in a study of drums around the world each selected a particular drum and used the Internet to research its country of origin. They then used computers to analyze the drum's acoustical pattern. Teachers described this as one of the most successful technology projects ever!
- After participating in Learning Through the Arts™, students at the grade seven level improved their scores in standardized literacy testing from 10 percent below the Board average to 13 percent above. No controls over variables such as other special programs were in place, so no cause and effect relationship can be claimed. However, the results did demonstrate that involvement in the Learning Through the Arts™ program did not come at the expense of achievement in other academic areas.

What Should Teachers Know About Integration?

Recommendation for elementary schools: "that one hour per week be given over to nature study . . . and that all work be conducted without the aid of a textbook. In addition, every attempt should be made to correlate the science observations with work in language, drawing, and literature" (Committee of Ten, 1892). Integration is not a new notion, though we have a plethora of contemporary labels for it: *interdisciplinary instruction, unit teaching, project approach* and *whole language,* to name but a few. What is integration? It involves combining diverse fragments into harmonious systems, which brings satisfaction. Gestalt psychologists tell us it is only natural for us to want to bring pieces and parts together to make comprehensible wholes. What is a buckle without its belt or a sleeve without a shirt? The part is not usable, nor even understandable, without the whole; in art terms it is figure with its ground, the particular in a context. But learners need a balance of attention to wholes and parts as they develop, and even adults, who are novices at a task, proceed from the gross to the particular, dwelling first on the most obvious, such as larger shapes or intuited feelings. Psychologist Daniel Goleman explains the evolutionary significance of humans reacting first to the holistic experience and then to details by describing a jogger who spies a long slender dark curved *something* coming up along his path. "Snake!" screams the ancient emotional impulses and the jogger stops dead in his tracks. Saved from a poisonous bite by primitive instincts, the jogger now uses his newer (in evolutionary time) powers of logic to discern the details of the *something*. And this time it's just a stick. Think of the consequences if we stopped to analyze all the pieces before responding to the whole.

The arts play an integral role in integrating wholes and parts, and it is how literature, visual art, drama, dance, and music interact with science, social studies, math, and the language arts to support learning about important life skills, concepts, and themes that is the goal. Traditional lines become muddied in integrating the arts. "Is it art or science as a child mixes colours and discovers that blue and yellow make green? The child notices curves and angles in letters and then makes them with his or her own body or draws them in the air; is this language arts or dance?" (Stinson, 1988, p. 95). Literature, art, drama, dance, and music draw on the common concepts of shape, action, motion, pattern, and rhythm and can be tapped for their power to reveal these same aspects in other curricular areas. This way of thinking about teaching and learning, using the arts as meaning makers, begins with viewing the curriculum from the vantage point of an artist. For example, to integrate dance one must think about movement *possibilities* in lessons and units—not just *how* something moves, but how it *might* move under different circumstances, while maintaining a focus on the particular curricular concepts, skills, or themes that are to be learned. What this means is that arts integration is a different vehicle for more students to achieve more academic success and life satisfaction by using ways of knowing available only through the arts.

How Can Classroom Teachers Meaningfully Integrate the Arts?

If you believe in great things, other people will too.

Oliver Wendell Holmes

Teaching *With, About, In,* and *Through* the Arts

It is not beyond the teacher's competence to talk with the children about the bark paintings of the Australian aborigines. Not everywhere, she will explain, do people have paper. On whatever material they can prepare, they tell of their concerns and beliefs . . . they describe what matters most about boating and hunting. . . . The kinship between the simply shaped but impressive and beautiful paintings of a distant race and the children's own artwork is established without effort.

Arnheim, 1989, p. 48

In this book the term *integration* is used to denote a variety of ways and intensities with which classroom teachers include the arts. Integration of the arts can occur along a continuum from a small degree, at a surface level, to total arts infusion throughout the curriculum. The latter idea includes a respect for the arts as unique disciplines that use particular communication vehicles useful in understanding science, social studies, math, and the language arts. For example, learning or expressing ideas about "courage" through poetry is very different from examining this concept through painting, music, or sculpture—think of the ineffable messages about courage possible from Auguste Rodin's sculpture *The Burghers of Calais* or the themes about how fear is necessary for courage in literature like Lunn's *The Hollow Tree*. In a total integrated arts design, teachers present information and skills *from* arts disciplines and use the arts as teaching tools and learning processes. This requires classroom teachers to have basic arts knowledge, but does not necessitate that they become bona fide artists or specialists to teach *with, about, in,* and *through* the arts. However, research shows that when teachers are supported in becoming beginning artists, they experience transformations in both their personal and professional lives (Upitis, Smithrim, & Soren, 1999). Consider the possible combinations of each of the following designs for classroom teachers.

Teaching **WITH:** The goals of teaching *with* the arts are for students to get pleasure from the arts and have chances to work creatively. At this level, the arts are casually used by teachers in isolated lessons and opportunities to explore materials or ideas that are provided with minimal teacher guidance. For example, teachers may include a visual art project, teach a song related to a holiday, or set up a classroom routine (e.g., the singing of "O Canada" every morning or daily expressive reading to children—a book, story, or poem). These activities may not necessarily be linked to curricular expectations.

Teaching **ABOUT** *and* **IN:** When teachers use the *about* and *in* structures, they plan for students to learn *about* the arts and to do work *in* the arts. The goal is to have students enjoy and develop both *creativity* and *artistry*. At this level, learning events are planned that focus on arts *content* and *skills*. The structure of the art form, its elements, history, special vocabulary, artists, techniques, and skills, are taught. Often general classroom teachers work with school arts specialists or guest artists to construct substantive units around an artist or art form, with other curricular areas pulled in to support the focus. For example, a unit on Van Gogh's struggles and triumphs could involve learning about art and artists at the turn of the century, historical events during his life, the use of maps and globes to pinpoint Van Gogh's life journey, reading biographies, and writing informational and creative pieces. At a modest level, teachers may give substance to casual routines, like opening songs, by adding short minilessons about the composer or musical elements. Most importantly, when teaching *about* and *in* the arts, there is a conscious effort to develop students' aesthetic sensibilities through guided experiences. Students are involved in exploration, creation, response, performance, and evaluation, and experiences are tied to the provincial school district's required course of study (i.e., what the school promises to assess, teach, and evaluate).

Teaching **THROUGH** *the arts:* The arts are prominent through *focused* daily arts routines, an aesthetic classroom environment, and as both *content* and *means* of learning in units specified by the curriculum. Usually this model involves using content areas such as science and social studies as the centre of units in which the arts, language arts, and math are used to explore the central topic, problem, or questions. Since the arts are content disciplines, as well as processes, any art can serve as a unit centre or focus, too. Teaching *through* the arts involves creating a classroom in which students actually live and learn through the arts.

Jacobs's *disciplines*-focused integration can be used to think about the teaching *through* the arts concept. She proposes using central concepts and particular disciplinary skills for a unit core and emphasizes student creative problem-solving, active inquiry, and discovery about important issues (Jacobs, 1989). The process entails continuous questioning as integration progresses:

- Does the integrative structure reveal basic "secrets of the universe?" (patterns, truths)
- Does it fascinate, challenge, and interest students? (a sense of mystery or empowerment)
- Is it inclusive enough to pull in many disciplines in meaningful and natural ways?
- Is it worthy of time and attention?
- Is it appropriate at this time for these students? (interests, skill levels, cognitive development)
- Does the structure allow for students to use real methods to investigate? (primary source material, authentic strategies of researching and coming to know)
- Does the structure allow students to view an issue from the viewpoints of the various disciplines? (How would an artist describe this picture? a scientist? a mathematician?)
- Is the integrity of each discipline maintained in integration? (Are the arts trivialized?)

In addition, teaching *through* the arts means developing high aesthetic standards by involving students in significant arts experiences. Arts advocate Jane Remer (1996) warns:

> Producing 25 identical Kachina dolls from a pattern or slopping paint thoughtlessly on brown kraft paper to represent ancient cave drawings does not exemplify high aesthetic standards. Moreover, dancing in geometric patterns will not substitute for learning how to calculate area, perimeter, and volume. Spending a lot of time working on colonial artifacts is only going to be worthwhile if students also understand the meanings and know how these objects symbolize the cultural history and values of a particular time and place. (p. 339)

So, while the emphasis in teaching *through* the arts is the process of meaning making using the arts, the subject matter of each of the arts is still valued and taught. The end goal is to have students construct personal messages using the unique communication forms that the arts provide. In a manner, this can be thought of as *applied* arts because of its practical life goals.

More Than Entertainment

It is desirable and feasible for teachers to move in and out of the phases of teaching *with, about, in,* and *through* the arts during a school year. Each type of integration offers important avenues for arts integration and should be selected to fit student needs, curricular structures, available materials, time constraints, and the teaching personnel. Teachers need to feel comfortable drawing on and developing their backgrounds in the arts, so the type and pace of integration depends on the people involved. In addition, classroom teachers who wish to work with school arts specialists and visiting artists need to learn how to plan with specialists and must have the time to do so. Ineffective integration happens when arts specialists come in for one-shot performances without pre- and post-performance lessons with students. Whether a teacher chooses to integrate several disciplines or just a couple, work alone or with a group of colleagues, use a project approach or thematic units, set up learning centres or simply start ongoing arts routines, work with a school-wide theme or try an integrated day in the classroom, target student interests or focus on essential "big questions," remain at school or emphasize field work, the goal is still the same—to make natural and meaningful arts connections that add depth to learning, not adding more *things* to the already jam-packed school curriculum, and to ensure that the arts are not reduced to only entertainment.

General Principles and Strategies for Integration

What is now proved was once only imagined.

William Blake

While the concept of teaching *with, about, in,* and *through* the arts provides a perspective on integration, teachers need more specific ideas to use. The model suggested in this book to assist in implementing integrated teaching embraces ten principles:

1. Infuse the arts.
2. Teach arts concepts and skills.
3. Develop teacher habits that promote artistry, creativity, and independent meaning making.
4. Use energizers and warm-ups to facilitate the problem-solving process.
5. Support the arts with great children's literature.
6. Establish routines that both structure the school day and promote student independence.
7. Adapt the curriculum for integration.
8. Plan arts-based field trips to extend learning.
9. Exhibit student progress to support the program and student satisfaction.
10. Use specialists as important resources for ideas and support.

Principle One: INFUSE the Arts

Eighteenth-century novelist Henri Beyle, who used the pseudonym Stendhal, observed how beauty had the power to stun people, to stir them emotionally and even physically. The arts can be a form of beauty that can uplift, give energy, or excite a passion for living. But such power is not used enough in Canada's classrooms. Teachers can create classrooms that are more like living rooms—aesthetically pleasing, comfortable, and full of sensory stimulation. The "regular classroom" can be transformed into a place that smells wonderful and is filled with beautiful music and provocative art—all to help children want to come to school, love learning, and see life as filled with possibilities. Here are a few inexpensive ideas to begin.

The Aesthetic Environment. Think of the spaces and places that cause good feelings. Furniture arrangement can suggest a pleasant openness—groups of desks versus rows. Plants, flowers, special things to taste, textures to feel, artwork on easels, dramatic prop boxes, poems and songs on posters, centres with buckets of brushes and sponges for art, and tapes and CDs to listen to, create changes in the feel of the environment. This is what Elliot Eisner means when he says the "subtle is significant." Small changes *can be* significant in a classroom, and an aesthetic awareness can be developed by stimulating the senses.

Art Displays and a Beauty Corner. There are many ways to bring the arts into a classroom. Students can make *beauty boxes* of things that evoke pleasant responses. Art prints, displayed at children's eye level, allow concentration on one piece of art for a day or a week; the use of an art easel conveys the feeling that the work is special. Prints can be accompanied by questions to stimulate close examination and critical creative responses: *"What title would you give to this piece? How many words can you list to describe how this art makes you feel? What catches your eye first? What do you see that you think no one else sees? What are some adjectives you'd use to describe how this feels? How would a mathematician describe this art?"* Teachers may also show a title and then ask for predictions about colour, line, and media before the art is revealed. Alternatively, show a painting and ask for title possibilities. The **Partial Picture Preview** strategy involves showing only part of the picture and asking students to predict the remaining portion. A large magnifying glass is a motivating prop to use with the **I Spy** strategy. The teacher begins by saying, "I spy . . ." and gives a challenge related to art elements (e.g., "four geometric shapes" or "three primary colours"). Students look closely to try to meet the challenge, and volunteers come up and "show they know" with the magnifying glass. The student then takes over the "I spy . . ." and challenges the class. (Fine-art prints are available from art gallery gift shops and poster stores, and calendar art is often available at a discount in January. Invite students to bring in art to display—prints, sculpture, and paintings.)

Background Music. More schools now play music in the halls and the cafeteria to create a civilized school atmosphere. Music can energize, calm, and help to focus students. People tend to be *entrained* to the rhythm and tempo of music, so it's not surprising to feel energetic after hearing Sousa marches. We respond physically to the fast rhythms of the Celtic fiddle and even smile. Rock 'n' roll makes us want to move, and classical music, like that of the Baroque period, can give a sense of grandeur; think of Bach or Vivaldi. Loreena McKennitt's music can trigger dreamy images, and Puccini's operas exude passion. Playing background music sets a tone, and music can be an important learning tool during sustained silent reading and writing times. Why? Gardner's musical intelligence aspect of multiple intelligence theory and implications from brain-based learning provide support for using music in this way; music without lyrics, especially classical pieces like Mozart's, may stimulate brain activity, particularly in the right hemisphere, so there is more brain power for children to access during work. This is evident from imaging devices that now give us pictures of the brain at rest, the brain on words, the brain listening to music, and the brain receiving words and music. These pictures show entirely different active areas of the brain when music is played. Hypothesis? More brain activity may cause more learning.

An Arts-for-Life Centre. A special arts-based learning centre can include inspirational quotes about the arts and artists, or students can be assigned the classroom job of writing Arts for Life quotes in a special corner of the chalkboard. Definitions of art can be included that are found or created by students as they explore the idea of using the arts as learning tools. An arts timeline with birthdays of artists and other significant arts events, like the invention of photography in the 1830s, can be located in the centre, along with a map to pin the homes of artists. Don't forget informational books, biographies, poetry, and fiction about the arts. See the Arts-based Children's Literature bibliography in the appendix for books categorized by individual arts areas.

A Classroom That Celebrates the Arts. Posters of Jean Luc Picard (Star Trek actor) and other art that students bring enrich the classroom, and a part of a morning routine can include students explaining their arts contributions. Once children understand and experience the concept of creating an aesthetically pleasing environment, they can become both creative and adventuresome in the joint effort. Get ready for fresh flowers and unique CDs. If a student brings in a Diana Krall CD, you could extend the interest in jazz by introducing other jazz greats like Oscar Peterson and Wynton Marsalis.

Principle Two: Teach Arts Concepts and Skills

Freedom without tools is really no freedom at all; for example, asking children to discuss picture book art when no basic art elements have been taught can frustrate students and teacher. Just teaching a few words and concepts, such as colour, line, shape, and texture, can free students to tap thinking structures (brain schema) to talk about what they see. While the regular classroom teacher may not have the background to go into *depth* when teaching *about* or *in* each art form, it is feasible to teach basic knowledge for making sense (i.e., key concepts, elements, media, styles, genre, art forms, and artists). Since the arts are integral to functioning and understanding in our world, such basics need to be taught so that students have language to talk about, respond to, and create with the arts. Gardner expressed his concern about this issue when he visited schools and found that

> few teachers had artistic skills, and because those who did were skittish about exposing their works to students, the chief activity was simply giving children opportunities to paint, to pot, or to dance. This ploy was fine during the early years of childhood but made little sense in middle childhood and preadolescence when youngsters crave skills. The resulting works were either derivative from the mass media, or showed a vestige of a good idea but lacked the technical means to express it properly. In my terms, a creative spark, but no basic skills. (1989, p. 141)

Basic background gives students the knowledge to ask questions, strategically pursue interests, make choices, give interpretations, express meaning, and identify worthiness of ideas. All these are higher-order thinking skills that can be developed through the arts and then used in other areas. In addition, using arts content to make meaning is a part of teaching the general process of understanding or comprehension. We generally teach the process of understanding or comprehending well at a literal level. However, students have greater difficulty with implicit messages — making sense, rather than just getting an explicit main idea. They often do not have the knowledge or thinking skills to get beyond the obvious. Teaching arts concepts and skills and using the other principles for integration can help fill this gap.

Teachers also need instructional tools and can use arts concepts to form provocative questions: *"What colours does Ted Harrison use? How would his books feel different if he used more pastels?"* Basic knowledge enables teachers and students to be more creative because concepts can be combined in an infinite number of ways to create more art or diverse interpretations of art.

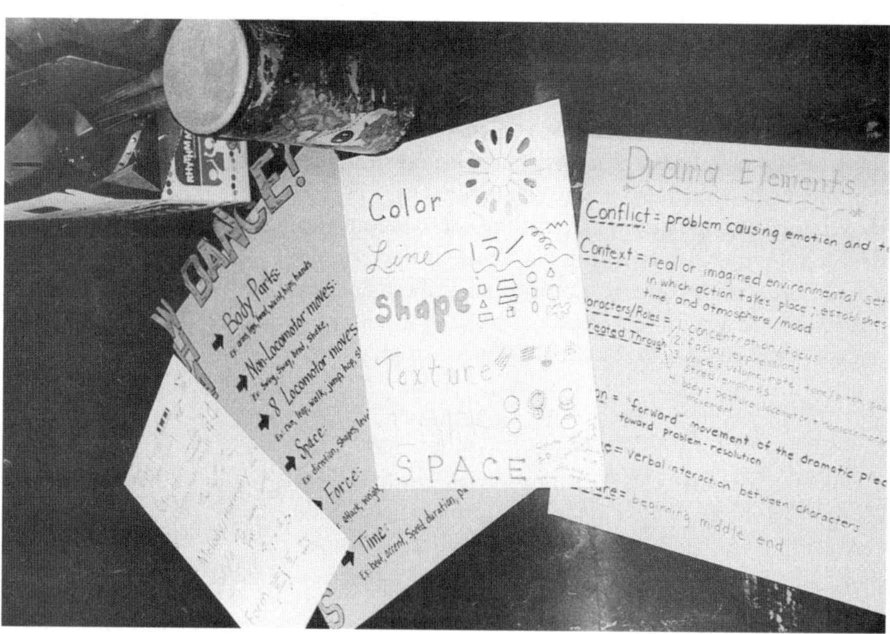

Elements Charts

For example, think about how much harder it is use the *general* idea of "integrating art" than to plan ways to use a specific idea like collage or 3D art in a unit.

Finally, when teachers integrate core arts content they help students understand the adage "you can't break the rules until you've mastered them." Even Picasso and Michelangelo copied the greats and perfected their techniques before striking out on their own. Indeed, knowledge of the components used to create meaning in the arts liberates and empowers children to make meaning from or with all art forms. Here are other guidelines to use when teaching arts content.

Age-stage Appropriateness and Teachable Moments. Suggested basic arts content teachers should know and teach in each of the art forms is presented in the **WHAT** sections in chapters of this book. In addition, teachers can talk with arts specialists in their schools or school boards to coordinate efforts. Implications from the learning and teaching theories presented in Chapter 1 should be applied during the teaching of arts elements and skills. For example, the work of Piaget, Maslow, Vygotsky, and others support Arnheim's (1989) conclusion that

> At no level of development can either children or accomplished artists state, to their own satisfaction, what they want to say unless they have acquired the means of saying it. In the beginning, these means are simple . . . no attempts should be made to foist upon the learner technical tricks that go beyond his or her stage of conception. Nor should the means of visual expression be taught as isolated devices. The need to master them should naturally emerge from the demands of the task, and whenever possible the learner himself ought to be made to discover them by himself rather than have them supplied by the teacher. (p. 42)

Social learning theorists also suggest we keep in mind that students are usually most successful applying or practising new learning in a group situation, before going it alone. To simply say "write a song" or "make a play" or "do art" or "make up a dance" is overwhelming, even for adults.

Teaching Students How Artists Work. Knowing that real artists take time to look and listen and study other artists' use of techniques, before adapting one another's ideas, helps students understand how to begin. From the research on creative individuals and the creative problem-solving process, it is clear we should encourage students to use strategies that have heretofore been considered problematic or even cheating. For example, we *should* suggest that students pursue the same subject time and time again, just as Monet painted and painted his water lilies.

Charts and Visual Aids. We learn what we live with and we remember what we see repeatedly. In each of Chapters 3, 5, 7, 9, and 11 there is a concise set of basic arts concepts, elements, and definitions that can be adapted and posted for students to use as references; for example, in any one day the art in picture books may be discussed, as well as the illustrations in science and social studies texts, using posted chart concepts. Banners and "big books" can also be made and used as visual reference tools. All these references serve the same function as "fix-up" charts that teachers post as reminders of what to do when encountering unknown words while reading or how to edit writing.

Using the Arts to Learn Key Arts Content. Arts concepts can be learned *through* arts strategies, too. For example, lyrics can be created to fit familiar tunes, or other mnemonics can be used to learn visual art elements: ROY G. BIV is a common acronym to remember the spectrum of the rainbow: red–orange–yellow–green–blue–indigo–violet. "Every good boy deserves fun" is a time-tested mnemonic for musical notes on the staff lines for the treble clef, just as do–re–mi–fa–sol–la–ti–do is a tool to sing the scale.

Teaching "Why" Is Important. Students need real-life reasons for what we are teaching to activate the motivation to learn. This is especially important when introducing a new idea like using the arts as learning tools. Teachers need to explain how impossible it is to understand a culture without having access to its music, art, drama and theatre, dance, and literature, since people express what is most important to them through the arts. What's more, to understand the art of a culture, we need conceptual anchors that structure each art, be that the *rhythmic* (music element) differences between African music and Western music, or the concept of collage (media and technique). Teaching basic arts components is also letting students in on a "secret of the universe": language liberates, and each of the arts has a language all its own. Learning the language of the arts increases literacy, not in the narrow sense of just reading words during language arts time, but understanding major concepts about all people and the world we share. When teachers are explicit about such connections, students are more likely to feel there is purpose to learning.

Principle Three: TEACHER HABITS That Promote Artistry, Creativity, and Meaning Making

It seems only logical that encouraging [children to be] explorers and questioners rather than passive acceptors cannot help honing creativity, thinking and learning.

Starko, 1995, p. 114

Integrating the arts isn't a unit to do and be done with. It involves changing what is done on a daily basis. It includes how teachers view and present themselves to students and how they interact and react to classroom events. Here are general teaching habits that can profoundly influence the success of arts integration.

Frameworks for Integrated Lessons. A lesson or series of lessons using the arts as teaching tools begins with planning the arts content to be integrated with another curricular area. This planning respects that important concepts and skills will be taught *about the arts,* as well as from other curricular areas. The goal is to use the arts, not abuse them. So, while there may be several integration *prongs,* there needs to be at least one significant arts focus and one focus in another discipline if integration is to be meaningful. This *pronged focus* should come out of the curriculum. From the pronged focus, student objectives are written that explain what students should know and be able to do by the lesson conclusion. Because student progress will be assessed, it is important to write objectives in *assessable* ways (i.e., be clear and use observable verbs to describe the evidence for student learning).

Just as a good meal or a well-written paper has a beginning, middle, and end, so does an effective lesson. A short *introduction* prepares students for learning and allows teachers to assess students' background. The mood of the lesson is set, and the purposes or focus of the lesson should be made clear so that students feel the lesson is meaningful. Teachers may begin with a titillating question or the introduction of new vocabulary through a riddle or "mystery bag" holding things related to a key lesson concept. The introduction should be brief but, if skipped, students may never tune in and be lost for the remaining lesson segments.

In the *development* the teacher presents or demonstrates. A sense of the whole is developed, perhaps through storytelling, sharing artwork, or listening to a piece of music. A skill or strategy may be presented to use with a problem or question previously introduced. Students explore and discuss, practise, and apply skills, strategies, or media use in this stage.

Finally, there is the lesson *conclusion* in which students are expected to go beyond mere imitation of demonstrated skills and pull together problem solutions, showing they have learned and used personal creativity, artistry, and higher-order thinking skills. The conclusion provides the satisfaction of completion and is an important part of continuing learner motivation.

In general, most lessons proceed in a whole–part–whole manner, giving opportunities to experience art forms and ideas in aesthetic ways before examining the parts and pieces. This allows the arts to work their motivational magic on students and shows respect for the arts. How this is accomplished is part of the art of teaching, but usually involves individual teacher variations on the lesson framework previously described. Post It Page 2–1 is a summary of a framework for integrated planning. Examples of integrated lesson plans are given in each integration chapter.

Teacher Enthusiasm and Passion. The etymology of the word *enthusiasm* is interesting. It originally meant to be "in god" (*theo*) or "in spirit." When students are around teachers who have a creative and artistic spirit, they are drawn to their enthusiasm. We can tell students what we feel passionate about and share personal stories of our own creative and artistic efforts, being sure to include stories of struggle, to dispel the widely circulated misconception that artistic and creative individuals don't have to work hard. We can share personal arts experiences and remember how artists and authors persist: Dr. Seuss persisted in his efforts to publish even after being rejected eighty some times.

Transferring Creative and Artistic Strategies. All *meaningful* learning is essentially creative, since only we can *make or create* meaning for ourselves. What the word *dog* means to your friend is not the meaning you make, because your "dog" experiences are not the same. Reminders to use specific creative and artistic meaning-making strategies in math, science, social studies, reading, and writing are helpful to students, because this assists in establishing why they are learning them. In addition, being explicit about the need for students to *make the effort to create* can cause a transfer of creative thinking skills. Post the *creative problem-solving process* (Post It Page 1–5) and refer students to it as a resource. Better yet, model creative strategies during teaching so that they see you practise what you preach.

The Power of Choice. The power of choice in motivation was made clear in an experiment in a factory where buttons were provided to control noise level. One group had noise-level buttons and another group did not. The group with the buttons were found to like their work more, missed less work, and were more productive than the no-button group. Interestingly, no one in the button group ever *used* their buttons—they just had the choice. However, offering choice does not mean unrestricted options. For example, the choice could be among art media to use in a social studies response or writing a poem in one of the many *poem patterns* (Post It Page 3–4). *No* response should not be a choice, since it is only through active interaction with ideas that we learn.

Can Artistry and Creativity Be Increased by Structure and Restrictions? Consider the difference between (1) "I'll give you time to be creative. Get ready. Go." and (2) "I'll give you one minute to think of all the ways we could use this pencil." The real world does not permit unlimited time and resources. Let's prepare children for the real world by appropriately structuring time and being clear about the necessary restrictions on materials, ideas, and how they are to be used. Criteria can be set in advance for creative work to let students know if a response needs to include specific components (e.g., your dance needs a beginning, middle, and end).

Time and Materials

Individual Projects Students Care About. It isn't difficult to set aside time, at least once a week, for personal interest work or to encourage students to develop personal collections (e.g., rocks, cards, pictures). Whatever students pursue during project time becomes rich material to connect with the arts (e.g., writing poems about work, assuming the role of "expert" to do a class presentation).

Explore and Experiment. Creative ideas don't pop out of nothingness. Students need to know this. Time needs to be spent playing with art media, observing the work of others for ideas to adapt, brainstorming, reading, and listening to songs or music for nuggets of ideas. Exploration time is not "doing nothing," but using specific strategies to get started—to get material to work with and the time needed to explore elements, media, and techniques whenever something new is introduced. Have fun first and then, when students are feeling good, give directions and expectations. Students can also make an "Idea Keeper" folder for sketches, notes, pictures, words—anything to use later in a creative way. Stacks of old magazines can be kept to cut up for picture files to use as resources. Greeting cards, old calendars, clippings, wrapping paper, buttons, and even objects work, too.

Real-world Materials and Methods. Students want to play significant roles in the real world and are more likely to feel worthy when they use materials used outside school to learn. Primary source material like diaries, autobiographies, actual paintings, and music, rather than textbooks or drill sheets, promote authentic learning. In addition, students can use the methodology of researchers, such as surveys and interviews, rather than passively reading *about* the work of others.

Alternative Views and New Perspectives. Delight in and respect for diverse viewpoints are shown verbally and nonverbally with comments like *"I hear what you are saying"* and *"I never thought of that"* and *"What an unusual idea!"* We need to *show* we value the unique and different by forming supportive, honest, and descriptive verbal habits. Saying *"Marla has a new idea"* or *"Joe's idea is so different from anyone else's"* and asking questions like *"What are some other answers? What's another way we could do this?"* conveys potent

Post It Page • 2-1
Integrated Lesson Plan

Pronged Focus: What specific skills and concepts are to be taught? Prongs include what to teach about/in the arts *and* concepts and skills from at least one other area (e.g., science concepts, reading skills).

Student Objectives: What important student behaviours will be developed, assessed, and evaluated at the lesson conclusion? These are tied to the focus prongs.

Teaching Procedure: How will the arts and other strategies be used to help students make meaning? (**I–D–C** organization.)

- **Introduction:**

  Get *attention* by eliminating distractions and using signals (see Post It Page 7–3).

  Interest by using questions, a riddle, or mystery or presenting a problem to solve.

  Mood set with voice, music, use of the lights.

  Set *purposes and reasons* so that students feel the lesson is meaningful. Discuss connections to life outside school.

  Review prior knowledge with prediction and anticipation activities, fat questions, brainstorming or webbing (also yields assessment data).

  Make sure ground *rules and expectations* are clear. Some teachers post these.

  Energizers and warm-ups help students to get mentally and physically ready.

  Basic *elements* or important concepts can be introduced at this time. A visual aid is very important to make these memorable and interesting.

- **Development:** Next the teacher presents or demonstrates. A sense of the whole is given by sharing a story or piece of artwork. A skill or strategy may be presented to use with a problem or question previously introduced. Students explore, discuss, experiment, practise, and apply skills, strategies, or media in this stage. Students may plan and rehearse as the teacher coaches and gives feedback while circulating around the classroom.

- **Conclusion:** This is when the students "show they know." Students are expected to go beyond mere imitation of a demonstrated skill or ideas. They are to pull together a problem solution, apply new knowledge and skills, and show they have learned and used personal creativity and artistry. This could include a performance for peers. Self and peer evaluation, as well as teacher evaluation, should occur through a debriefing activity. End with a calming activity (e.g., fantasy journey, journal entry).

Assessment: Return to the student objectives to gauge student progress. Items may be added to a portfolio and work connected to general goals in the portfolio.

values. Of course, it isn't just what is said, but *how* it is said, so it's a good idea to periodically self-assess *tone* by listening to a tape of a lesson.

The Unusual, Novel, and Curious. If we are serious about promoting creativity, we need to encourage unpredictable answers and products. "Question of the day" and "answer of the day" are examples of routines teachers set up and then encourage students to assume. Begin by posting intriguing questions or answers. Children can even do research based on each others' questions; for example, one student wanted to know how much trash the school threw away, so a group interviewed custodians and cafeteria workers. Surveys were made to find out how much kids left on their plates. The result was colourful graphs and students in the role of "reporters" (drama) to present findings.

Variety of Forms of Expression. Ralph Bell didn't begin painting until he was nearly seventy. He had cerebral palsy, was wheelchair bound, and for most of his life was not able to express himself—he could not talk. One day an art therapist attached a stylus to a head band. A paint brush was attached and Ralph Bell proceeded to paint every day for the rest of his life, producing over 1,000 paintings. Students need to hear these kinds of stories so that they can realize all that is locked inside waiting for a door to open.

Context is Critical. Stanford educator Elliot Eisner explains this point:

> to read a map meaningfully it must be perceived as a configuration, not simply as a collection of discrete units. Where a nation is situated within a continent and where a continent is situated on the globe are as important in understanding geographical space as where a city is located within a nation. The optimal development of mind requires attention not only to intellectual processes but to intuitive ones as well. Children . . . should be encouraged to see the whole, not only the parts . . . a part without a field is without an anchor. (Elliot in Arnheim, 1989, p. 5)

Any of the creative thinking strategies discussed in Chapter 1 could be used as examples, but brainstorming is a good one to illustrate this point. Students need a real problem in science, social studies, or literature to brainstorm about if the process is to be meaningful. Brainstorming as an isolated skill is useless. Attention to the whole and to its components is one of the important lessons the arts can teach. Fragmenting learning into isolated skill or concept lessons does not yield a satisfied feeling and can lead to dissatisfaction with school and learning. Unhappily, too much of the teaching and curricula in our schools has a piecemeal character. To truly understand, students must be helped to perceive pictures, poems, and songs as wholes, while attending to the patterns and pieces that contribute to making the entirety possible.

Open or Fat Questions. Fat questions are open-ended and ask for many responses. Even a bland question like *"Who was the first Prime Minister of Canada?"* can be made interesting when changed to "*What do you know about the first Prime Minister of Canada?* Fat questions call for students to do more integrated thinking because they ask for ideas to be retrieved and synthesized from many areas of the brain. One way to start is to use questions beginning with *What if? Why? How?* Avoid yes–no questions beginning with *who, could, would, should,* and *when.* When fat questions are coupled with a wait time of at least five seconds, more students will have responses and the responses will be of better quality. Post It Page 2–3 on the *art of teacher questioning* includes more pointers on habits to increase student thinking.

Clear Purposes. From early childhood on, people have a strong desire to know the reasons why. Purposes motivate. Students need examples of why strategies like SCAMPER (Post It Page 1–5) should be used in art projects, in drama responses, or to solve problems in math. One study done in a public area with a copy machine demonstrated the power of purpose giving. Researchers approached people and asked to be allowed to "cut in" to copy. People often did allow cutters to do so. But when researchers gave a reason like "I'm in a hurry because my boss is waiting and I'll get in trouble if I'm late!" the allowance percentages increased into the nineties. It is also effective to ask students to *figure out* the purposes, although this generally takes longer.

Grouping for Creative Work. Planning a pantomime is much more fun when done with a partner, in a triad or quad, and there is the potential for piggybacking on each other's creative ideas. This teacher habit is drawn from Vygotsky's ideas about social interaction stimulating thinking. In addition, groups who take risks together feel better about sharing their efforts in public.

Creative Problem-Solving and Thinking Focus. We can encourage students to have a "what if" approach to problems and show them the power of hope and imagination. When they complain about a short recess, ask, *"What if there were no recesses or what if we only* *had recess and no school?"* Ask them to generate as many "what ifs" as they can in one minute. Use strategies like Eberle's SCAMPER (see Post It 1–5) to help students learn to stretch and twist ideas. SCAMPER time can even be scheduled once a week and the verbs posted on a chart. Students can become expert at creative problem-solving if they learn to use the process. Again, it is helpful to post the *creative problem-solving process* (Post It Page 1–5) for students to use as a reference.

Encouraging Risk Taking to Develop Courage. We live in a world full of problems and danger, but hiding in a hole solves nothing. The classroom is an ideal safe setting for students to experiment and make mistakes, to "give it a try and see what happens." We can celebrate risk taking, even when the results don't work: *"I'm glad you tried to write a poem that doesn't rhyme. I hear you saying you don't like the poem. Is there a part you do like? What could you do to make it suit you better?"* Both teachers and students can collect stories about people who take risks and may have appeared foolish to others at the time. The newspaper is a good source. Another idea is to create a class add-on bulletin board to acknowledge risk takers entitled "Risk Taking Takes Courage."

Descriptive Feedback, Praise, and Extrinsic Reinforcers. If our goals are to enable students to think originally and be independent, we need to examine the kinds of feedback that we give them. "Good! Great! Awesome!" are value-laden vague words that students may or may not believe are genuine, especially if overused. People tend to believe specifics. By truthfully commenting on a child's work, a teacher can provide valuable guidance and cause the child to feel important because time, honest thought, and attention were given to her. Consider the difference between *"Good job!"* and *"Rudy, you really used a lot of different facial expressions in your pantomime. That showed you were really into your character."* Imagine how you'd feel if a teacher told you you'd get an A or a certificate on Friday—if you were good all week. You'd want to know exactly what the teacher meant by "good" first of all. Then you could decide whether you wanted to "be good" and whether you wanted to be good just to "be good" or be corrupted by a focus on what you'd *get* for being good. The point is that it is very helpful for teachers to have specific language to give descriptive feedback, in addition to praise, to liberate student thinking. In the arts the basic elements offer such focus to specifically describe what each child is doing or saying. In addition, by using each child's *name* and emphasizing positive progress, the feedback is made more potent in helping reach goals.

Examples, Not Always Models. Albert Schweitzer declared that examples weren't the important things, they're *everything* to understanding. There is a mountain of difference between examples and models, however. Think of a teacher who shows a collage as a model and presents a step-by-step collage-making process. If the model is left up, students are likely to try to copy it. The teacher who decides to use collage as a *meaning maker* may show several examples and describe some of the options for creation. But by *removing* the examples, students are left to create their own meaning. Of course, it's all in the presentation. Teachers who make it clear that copying is not the goal, but encourage gleaning ideas from a variety of sources, give students tools without squashing individual creative capabilities.

Student Independence and Self-discipline. It is time consuming, frustrating, sometimes even painful, to

Take Action • 1

Use Descriptive Feedback

Find a partner and take turns giving each other descriptive feedback. Be honest and focus on the positive; e.g., "I see you are wearing your favourite T-shirt with the geometric shapes all over it." Remember, people like to hear their names used in a positive context. Here are some sentence stems to prime the pump: I see . . . , I feel . . . , I hear . . . , I liked. . . . You can also ask questions: e.g., "Jenny, why did you choose to write a diamante?" Or use a request: "Todd, tell me about your collage." As a challenge, try to make a comment related to LADDM (Literature, Art, Dance, Drama, Music); e.g., "You're sitting in a shape that has lots of angles." (Dance/movement element = shape.) Try to keep going for a set time, e.g., three minutes. Stop and then tell each other how it felt to give and receive descriptive feedback.

watch students struggle to do what we could do *for* them so quickly. It is so much easier to just draw a horse for the child who can't seem to get down an image that pleases him. The question is, what is the goal? If the goal is to end up with a great drawing of a horse, perhaps the teacher should do it. Usually, this is not the goal of arts-based school activities. The goal is to engage students in the process of learning all kinds of concepts and skills, including how pride only comes when you do the work yourself. If someone else does it, maybe you'll be grateful, but you can't be proud of yourself unless you struggle and have some sense of triumphing. Many well-intentioned teachers and parents shield children from the necessary frustrations inherent in achieving independence. The *learned helpless* syndrome is the result. We can tell children about the hard work we've attempted and about both the successful and unsuccessful results. We can share our efforts at creative production, showing that the focus is on effort, not necessarily the product. We also need to dispel the notion that great ideas just pop out—a balloon must be pumped full before it pops. So it is with people and creative problem-solving. We need to input the knowledge and skills relevant to the task and then bright ideas will seem to pop out. Few artists hit the jackpot on the first or even second try, so they serve as pertinent biographical examples of how persistence pays off.

This doesn't mean teachers can't teach students self-help "fix ups" and other strategies to deal with problems. In fact, it is important to post problem-solving steps, arts elements charts, and book response choices. We can also directly teach strategies that students can use independently, such as "set work aside and come back later, stop and get input from another source, use music to relax, examine past work for ideas, make use of mistakes, brainstorm or web." A general classroom expectation is in order for students to "try *something*" before asking for help. Teachers can then attend to help signals (like a red flag stuck in a ball of clay on a desk) by asking, *"What have you tried? What do you know? What could you try? What has worked before when you were having trouble?"* This helps children develop ways of coping rather than waiting for someone else to solve problems.

Process versus Product Focus. There are times when an art product, a piece of creative writing, or an actual dance performance is the expected outcome in a lesson. However, the rule of thumb for regular classroom arts integration is to emphasize the *processes of knowing* that the arts offer by giving time to explore techniques and materials. Students might perform a play for an audience each year, but drama can occur *daily* in a fully arts integrated classroom. Artwork by children can be displayed in a class gallery that changes weekly, but discussing art in picture books and texts needs to happen every day. Using art as a pre-writing or post-writing response or as an alternative way to keep a journal are daily teaching and learning strategies. Creative movement and dance, singing, hearing music—all are a part of the daily life in an integrated classroom. These are ways to make sense and express meaning, not merely to entertain parents or the principal. It is the inner audience that children need to learn to please.

No Dictated Art! Art educator Peggy Jenkins (1986) calls colouring books and other fill-in outlines and patterns "dictated art." She decries this adult habit and summarizes research on its effects: children lose creativity, sensitivity, self-confidence, and independent thinking. In addition, children tend to become conformists and perfectionists and seek stereotypes when focused on dictated art, and it provides little outlet for individual expression and emotional release. Children can become confused and rigid as they struggle to "stay in the lines." Fill-in art is often "doing without thinking" and promotes mindless obedience to authority, rather than creative problem-solving. The sense of achievement and pride that should come from art is lacking in dictated art. Where are the creative decision-making options that art should provide? Where is the thinking to prepare children to live in a democratic country whose citizenry values freedom, choice, and individuality? (pp. 27–28). "But children like it," some say, and "it keeps them quiet and busy." To respond, we must ask about the goals of arts integration. At least, if such material is occasionally used, we need not call it *art* and can make creative modifications. For example, teachers can encourage adding lines, using unconventional colours, tearing off sections, pasting materials on, adding captions or titles, and scrunching the paper to give it texture.

Where to Start

Aesthetic Responses First. It would be easy to drop into using the arts as meaning-making tools, while neglecting their power to stimulate aesthetic sensibilities. One good way to ensure respect for the unique nature of the arts is to get into the habit of starting discussions with a focus on how students *feel*, rather than what they think. Instead of first using the art in picture books to predict problems, events, and characters, ask students to take time to look at the art and share how it makes them feel. Volunteers can try to explain what the artist has done to create that feeling, but often the stimulus is as inexpressible as the feeling itself. The same is true for music, drama, dance, and literature.

The arts have tremendous potential to engage emotions that cause us to be more sensitive and empathetic. As teachers, we can provide the time and the direction for children's emotional intelligence to be activated. *"How does this make you feel? Why?"* are powerful questions that acknowledge infinite individual responses residing in all of us.

Start with the Known. In our cynical, critical world it has become common to dwell on what students don't know and can't do. It's much more pleasant, and likely to encourage more risk taking, if we do the opposite. Arts lessons are natural contexts for practising a habit of introducing lessons with an affirming question or strategy that serves as a model for students as they approach problems: *"What do you know about shapes? colours? Emily Carr? jazz? Beethoven? Charlie Chaplin? pantomime? characters? mysteries?"* By activating the known, we cause students to open schema that can subsequently be used to understand a lesson and finally store new information. If not a question, try small groups or partners to brainstorm or web a key idea. The KWL strategy (Ogle, 1986) is based on this idea. Students begin by listing what they *know* in one column, what they *want to know* in a second column and, finally, after the lesson is finished, what they *learned.*

Look and Listen More Closely. To view meaning making through the prism of the arts is not a fast or particularly efficient way of teaching. The artist in us will not be hurried. As teachers, we need to relax and begin to carefully observe children, ourselves, and special moments. Taking time for students to explore all the shapes they can make with their bodies and translate new-found shapes into messages about science or other cultures takes time. But using movement to *show* understanding of verbs like "hunker down" or "slink" gives students the chance to *do.* During the joy of movement, teachers can take time to watch, listen, and give descriptive feedback, piggyback on students' ideas, and even assess. Integrating the arts requires habits of the heart and mind that help remove the "get it covered" guilt—it's just fine to stop a lesson to examine a spider web glistening with morning dew or listen to the principal whistle as she walks down the hall.

The Teacher's Personal Attributes. Who we are as teachers begins with who we are as persons. Teachers need the uplifting and provocative experiences that the arts provide to keep themselves alive with the energy and examples that all great teachers have in such immense quantity. Go to the museum, join the symphony, go dancing, sing in the choir, take up watercolours, or do cross-stitch. Seek out the arts as a person and as a professional. Pretty soon you'll find you can't turn it off and you'll be taking lesson plan notes in the dark at *Les Miserables.*

No Personal Put-downs. For a teacher to say "I can't sing" or "I'm not good at drawing" writes the arts off. It's as if the person is saying, so what—it's not important anyway. As Ms. Lucas reminded us, no teacher would claim he was poor at reading or math when talking with a class, the principal, or parents. A commitment to weaving the arts throughout the curriculum brings many benefits; it also brings the obligation for teachers to approach the arts with a *can do, will do, want to do attitude.* Sometimes that's scary. But we do it with a belief in what can be accomplished. So, no put-downs, please, especially arts self-deprecation.

Principle Four: ENERGIZERS and Warm-Ups Set the Stage for Creative Thinking

In the same way that runners warm up before setting out on a run, students need to warm up to be prepared and receptive to a class or lesson. Divergent thinking needs to be unlocked, muscles need to warm up, and voices need to be prepared. Energizers don't need to be lengthy, but are essential to activating the creative problem-solving process and giving focus. In each of Chapters 4, 6, 8, 10, and 12 there are activities to warm up for creative and artistic work: see *Energizers and Warm-ups.* Many collections of energizers are also available, such as *Solid Gold for Kids: Musical Energizers!* by Louise Cullen and *Shake, Rattle & Learn: Classroom Tested Ideas That Use Movement for Active Learning* by Janet Grant. See the bibliography in the appendix for more. Here are a few example energizers and warm-ups for creative problem-solving:

Focus Ball. This is a mirroring activity for concentration. A leader puts her hands together, as if holding an invisible ball. Students mirror the leader as the ball is slowly raised, lowered, and so on.

Tongue Twisters and Lip Blisters. In addition to favourites like "Bugs Black Blood" and "Swiss Wrist Watch," there are challenging new ones in books like *Six Sick Sheep.* "Aluminum Linoleum" and "Zip zap zot" get everyone puckered, giggling—relaxed and ready to be creative.

Games. (1) *The Bell Tolls* is a category game that requires fast thinking and movement. You need a half-inch piece of masking tape for each participant. Everyone stands in a circle with an IT in the centre. Each person stands on a piece of tape. IT begins by saying *"The bell tolls for all those who . . ."* and plugs in a category (play an instrument, know Picasso's first name). Anyone who fits the category must move and try to get a new spot while IT tries to get a spot. Whoever doesn't have a tape spot is the new IT. At any point in the game, IT can shout "tornado" and everyone must move to a new spot not right next door. (2) *Name Sock* is an energizer that requires everyone to learn names. Make two balls by winding up old socks; use two per ball to make a big ball. First, stand in a circle and have everyone say his or her name. Next, the leader says her name and the name of another person, to whom she throws a ball. That person says her own name, another person's, and throws to that person, and so on. When things are going well, the leader throws a second sock ball and uses the same rules. *Variation:* Use character names.

Rhythms. The leader creates a rhythm and the group echoes it. Keep going, getting increasingly complicated, with whistles, clicks, claps, slaps, slower and faster. At any point the leader can "pass it on" and another person becomes leader.

Chants, Action Poems, and Songs. These warm up the voice and the body. Many good collections are available, such as Fowke's *Sally Go Round the Sun* and *Ring Around the Moon*, and Booth's *Dr. Knickerbocker.* Teach by asking students to echo line by line. Words can be displayed on a transparency and actions added. For example, with "Dr. Knickerbocker" the chant suggests actions: "Let's put the rhythm in our hands" (clap clap).

Word Play. These are creative thinking and voice warm-ups like *"Uncle Charlie likes . . . but not . . . ,"* which starts with the leader thinking of a category and giving clues. For example, *"Uncle Charlie likes pepper but not salt."* If someone wants to guess, the person responds by saying, *"Uncle Charlie likes . . ."* and gives an example that fits. The leader then says, *"Yes, you can come in,"* meaning they are right or *"No, you can't come in,"* meaning they are wrong. Here's another clue for the example: *"Uncle Charlie likes butter but not bread."* (If you responded *"Uncle Charlie likes hammers but not saws,"* you can come in, because the category is *"words with double consonants!"*

Principle Five: GREAT CHILDREN'S LITERATURE about the Arts

One of the richest and most available resources that classroom teachers have for integrating the arts is our vast store of children's literature. In this book, literature is treated as an art form, and there is a separate chapter on how to integrate literature with skill and content areas. There is also an extensive arts-based bibliography, by art form, in the appendix. A bibliography of award-winning children's books like the winners of the Caldecott Award (for the American Library Association's best picture book of the year) and the Canadian Governor General's Award for Children's Literature is also in the appendix. Here are a few important strategies teachers can use to integrate the arts using children's literature.

Sustained Silent Reading (SSR). Since its conception, this planned time for students and teachers to read choice materials, for pure enjoyment, has proved itself. Research confirms that time spent reading causes students to significantly increase vocabulary and comprehension. A variation of SSR involves giving students a choice *within a topic* (e.g., biographies or books related to music or dance). While it is important to have "free reading" every day, some days can be designated as "Arts Alive" SSR times. Generally, the period is fifteen or twenty minutes, but for young children the time should be less and they won't be *completely* silent. SQUIRT (sustained quiet individual reading time), another popular acronym, may be more appropriate for younger readers.

Expressive Daily Reading. Expressive Daily Reading (EDR) is a daily event in which the teacher reads a piece of literature aloud, focusing on providing an aesthetic experience through student involvement in a story or poem. Like SSR or SQUIRT, EDR can be based on children's literature related to the arts. The important feature of this strategy is that the teacher read *expressively*, using voice to convey mood and character so that the piece comes alive. EDR makes literature a lived-through experience memorable to students, often for the rest of their lives. It is a time to laugh together, experience danger vicariously, share beautiful art in picture books, and make mental images of places real and imaginary. Teachers who read expressively also show students how to use a dramatic vocal skill to share words with others.

Visual Literacy: Reading the Art of Picture Books. We are most fortunate to have fine art readily available to children in school and public libraries in the form of picture books. There are numerous awards for picture books to aid teachers in selecting picture books for art study. The Governor General's Awards for Children's Literature present an annual prize for illustration in an English-language book and a French-language book. Two other Canadian awards for illustration are the Amelia Frances Howard-Gibbon Award and the Elizabeth Mrazik-Cleaver Canadian Picture Book Award.

The recipients of these awards are listed in Appendix B. Picture books are meant to be examined as art, but teachers often feel unprepared to teach children how to enjoy and understand the art. (See Post It Pages 5–5 and 5–12 for questioning strategies and picture book teaching ideas.) Teachers should take heart in that teaching about picture book art can begin with taking time to look closely and discussing the emotional impact of the composition. As mentioned before, using questions to ask about how the art evokes feelings is a good start. Students can later learn to examine elements of colour, line, shape, and texture to understand what the artist has done. Even primary students can see the effect of brush strokes, and how colour can balance a composition, and how a line can lead the eye and make the reader turn a page, and how shapes are repeated to move the eye around and give a sense of rhythm. In addition, by doing a bit of research on picture book artists, teachers can build a repertoire of information about how these special people work.

Literature Centres. Special areas for arts books and related activities can be established and offered as "choice" work, or students can be scheduled into the centres for a time each day or week. Centres can be set up for each arts area or changed to reflect units or projects (e.g., "Life Struggles of Artists, Authors, and Musicians" or "Exploring Space through the Arts"). Chapter 3 provides more guidelines for setting up and managing centres and stations.

Literature-based Units. Just as units can be centred around science, social studies, or arts themes, they can be built around literature. Important structures for integrating the arts into literature include genre studies (a folk tale or mystery unit), author or artist studies (these focus on the person and his or her style, as well as the literature itself), and single or core book studies (an example is a unit on McCully's *Mirette on the High Wire,* which provides an opportunity to study impressionism, turn of the century music and composers, and unusual art forms like tight-rope walking).

Principle Six: ROUTINES Make Learning Predictable and Structured

We all know the best way to diet, exercise, or learn is to set up an ongoing regular schedule. One of the most effective ways to ensure that the arts are a living part of the class is to establish daily arts routines in which students assume the roles of researchers and presenters. Ms. Lucas used this strategy in the opening vignette. Here are some possible choices. Generally, each takes a few minutes and occurs at the beginning of the day, end of the day, or at some other break point, like after lunch. Students can sign up or be selected, just as they would for classroom jobs.

Composer, Artist, Dancer, Actor, Writer, Genre, Style. Students find fascinating facts to share about a person or an artist's way of creating. Information can be presented on an overhead, which gives experience using visuals and makes students more comfortable talking in front of a group. Students may work on these "mini-reports" in pairs. Presentations can become very creative by encouraging students to make them as songs, poems, or with accompanying art.

Docent Talks. The word *docent* simply means teacher and has long been used in the art world: art docents give museum tours to teach about art and artists. When students do docent talks they present a piece of art (original or that of an artist they've researched) and teach about the work. Students can tell about the media used, aspects of the creative process tried, what they learned by experimenting and making mistakes, and so on. Classmates then respond with descriptive feedback about what they see or how the piece makes them feel or they ask the docent questions.

Arts Riddle of the Day. Riddles have potential to trigger higher-order thinking skills, especially creative problem-solving, and contain attractive language for quick lessons on patterns (e.g., spelling–phonic patterns). Since riddles are basically a question and an answer, students can write their own about any topic and show they have learned important content. For example, *What do you call a boy that hangs on the wall?* The answer is Art.

Word of the Day. Word of the Day involves students or the teacher choosing a word (e.g., baroque, scumbling, motif, onomatopoeia) and displaying it. A one-minute lesson on the word is then presented. Effective word teaching involves saying the word, using it in context, explaining or showing examples, giving non-examples, and then asking the class to think of sentences to use it.

Poem a Day. This routine begins with displaying a poem, usually related to a unit, on the overhead or on a chart. The poem is expressively read so that all enjoy the sounds and images. A pointer can be used with primary students to connect the oral reading with the print. If the teacher wants to then engage the class in bringing the poem to life with choral reading, echoic reading, movement, music, and drama, there are about a dozen strategies to choose from in *Poetry Alive* (see Post It Page 4–4).

Pattern Finds. Any material can be used to engage students in finding high-frequency symbol patterns, both graphic–visual and aural–oral. Coming to recognize the importance of redundancy is a learning breakthrough that empowers students; once they realize that artists, authors, musicians, dancers, and actors use many of the same ideas over and over, they feel it's okay for them to do so in their creations. Repeated elements can be found in music (refrains), art (geometric shapes), dance (non-locomotor moves), or drama (facial expressions). Groups of patterns, such as the patterns found in the twelve-bar blues sequence, can become the distinguishing features of genres.

Storytelling Club. Clubs can be scheduled to meet for students to share original stories or ones found and prepared. Children get a sense of belonging in a club that represents their interests. By using puppets, music, and other props, students can develop oral expression dramatic skills so important in life in and outside of school. Booth's *Stories to Read Aloud* is a great resource book for teachers who want to use storytelling in their classrooms. Also see the special section in Chapter 8.

Sing In. During a sing-in routine, poems or songs are displayed on charts or on the overhead. (It is important for students to first *hear* a song all the way through before singing it—to enjoy it for its aesthetic properties—but also so that they get a sense of the whole before attempting the parts.) Like music, songs set mood. Many songs are meant to stimulate movement and actions, and children do love to move. Songs can start and end a day, be sung during cleanup (create lyrics for "I've Been Working on the Railroad": "*We've been working in this classroom, all the live long day. We've been working in this classroom—its a mess now, wouldn't you say? Can't you see the clock a ticking. Soon the bell will ring. Let's clean up this dear old classroom. Clean up as we sing*"). Rhythmic words can be chanted as attention getters: *"Mozart, Beethoven, Manalow, Bach. Get cleaned up and beat the clock."* Even a name or word that has musical powers can be used as the attention getter of the day: "Rimsky-Korsakov." See Post It Page 11–4 and the appendix for more on teaching songs and song book titles.

Arts for Life Journals. By using a journal routine that focuses on the arts, students learn to reflect on how the arts are integral to life. Students can discover how pervasive and important the arts are—economically, spiritually, politically, culturally, and historically.

Principle Seven: ADAPT Curriculum for Integration

Arts integration and the concept of teaching *with, about, in,* and *through* the arts are broad ideas that include several frameworks adjustable for the special needs of a school or classroom. For example, an entire elementary or middle school curriculum can be organized around important integrative themes and problems at the centre of life. The goal is to plan around topics or problems that make a difference. Do a unit on inventions and discoveries resulting from happy accidents or the creative problem-solving process so that students get a sense of relevance from school. *Meaning construction by students* is a core concept in arts integration. Meaning comes from grappling with problems and questions of importance. Grappling is done when we apply ideas and skills to troublesome situations, which assumes we have key concepts, strategies, techniques, skills, and processes in our background and know when and why to use them. What follows are general principles for adapting curriculum and instruction for this kind of integration.

Surveying Interests. Interest has astounding effects on learning and accounts for much of the variance in reading success. While it is delightful to watch the joy of curiosity young children display, it is equally disheartening to witness the lack of interest students as young as third and fourth grade may show. Are students regularly given opportunities to study interests in which the arts and other meaning-making tools could be used? From interviews about memorable school experiences and projects, Starko (1995) found that not a single eighth grade student remembered ever being allowed to select to study a personal interest (p. 136). While teachers may not be ready to make all lessons interest based, certainly we can shift the balance in that direction and still guide students through important traditional academic content. "Texture may be explored in the paintings of Seurat, in wooden masks, in stuffed toys, or in the costumes of 'grunge' musicians. Economic development can be studied through the activities of prospectors as well as pioneers, through the fate of the local mill as well as the growth of economic centers, or even through the potential economy of Tolkien's fantasy world" (Starko, p. 136). However, the quality of choice that teachers give is important, too. "If student selections are limited to Which Greek god will you study? or Which system of the body will you choose for your report? students are unlikely to view the process of selecting and investigating as a powerful, interest-driven experience" (Starko, p. 136).

It is human to return to areas with which we've had positive experiences, and we need not wait for students to just *get* interests; interests can be developed. People develop a taste for chocolate chip cookies because they have eaten them. Teachers who expose students to the arts and teach them about the unique natures of each art form are providing experiences that students can pursue independently at school and at home, given time, materials, and encouragement. Students must be *taught* to care about content, to feel how a question can perplex and provoke, puzzle or intrigue, and to delight in insights discovered through getting involved in interest areas. (There is an example interest inventory in the appendix.) Or try this: ask students to draw a line down the middle of a piece of paper. At the top of one column write *Interests and Talents* and at the top of the second, *Problems and Questions.* Turn the students loose for five minutes to list everything they can. This solves the problem of students not knowing what to write, read, and create and is a strategy that artists and authors use. (Students can keep this in an *Ideas* folder.)

Connections to Life. The brain is a neural network system that works through connections. Learning depends on accessing and forging brain connections, so connections need to be made across grade levels and among disciplines so that students see how the arts fit into the big picture of life from a variety of angles. To begin with we need to connect the arts to symbol systems used in English, math, and science to help students find the common purposes of symbols and learn how the same concepts occur repeatedly in separate areas of life. For example, these concepts express meaning and emotion in many different arenas: *rhythm* is found in music, art, dance, poetry, and science; *composition* is equally important in writing and art; *shape* is critical to math, dance, and literature. Students need to be prodded to find how *mood* is created in stories, paintings, and pieces of music and helped to see that people involved in the arts are multifaceted and cross reference ideas: da Vinci studied plants, designed flying machines, studied anatomy, and painted; Michael Snow, the award-winning visual artist, is also a musician and filmmaker. The richer a person's expe-

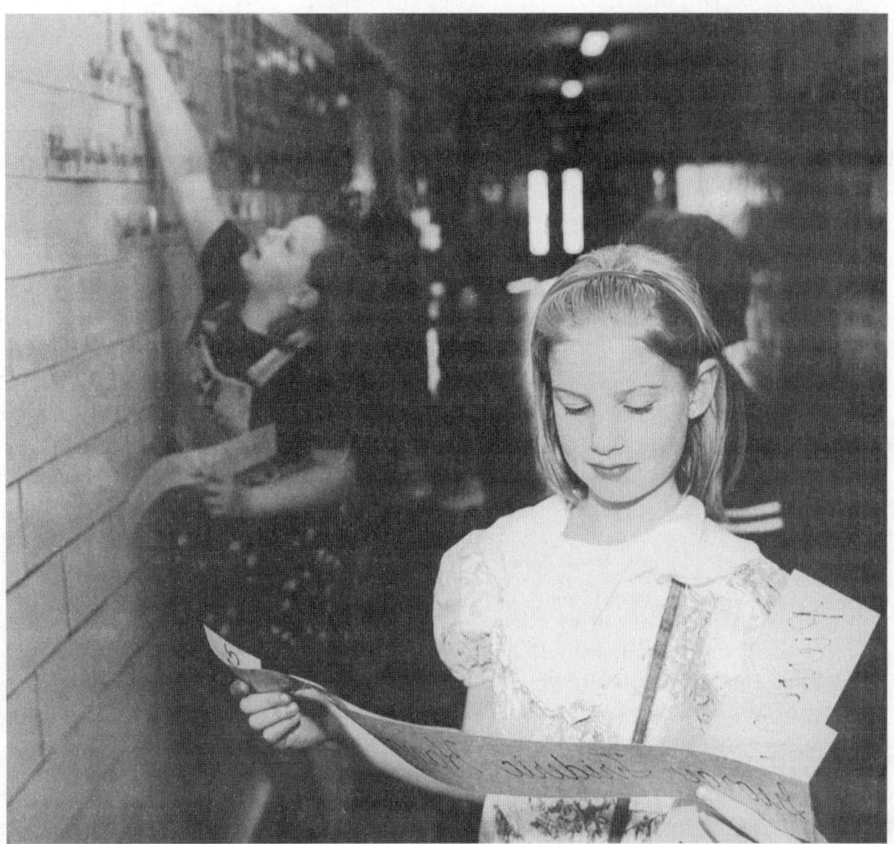

Artist-Composer Timeline

riences, the more connections are possible, and when the arts are interwoven with life, additional dimensions of understanding and expression are made possible. A caveat is in order, however: it is important that natural and meaningful connections be developed; it is a stretch to consider counting the beans Jack bought in the folk tale "Jack and the Beanstalk" as meaningful integration of math and literature.

Depth and Breadth. Broad important ideas and processes, not just a tally of facts, dates, and isolated skills, cause a unit to fly rather than flounder. Every human being wants to know secrets and truths about people and the world, the ways to succeed and be happy. Themes from literature, generalizations in social studies, axioms of science, all offer paths to the secrets. *Charlotte's Web* is not about a pig and a spider, nor is it simply about the topic of friendship. It is about *particular truths* about friendship that we understand as we mature—how good friends stick by each other during tough times, how good friends believe in you and see good in you that you may not have discovered, how friends live on in our hearts and minds because they positively alter our existence. Literature and the arts offer powerful material to explore big ideas about the spirit-honing quality of struggle, how wisdom is achieved and where beauty is found. Teachers can access this power by planning for focus on significant ideas and taking time to explore them in depth. One planning design is given next.

Themes versus Topics. In the past teachers have worked hard to develop units around topics such as plants, quilts, and dinosaurs. These topics often served as content for integrating the arts: large papier-mâché dinosaur sculptures, plant dances, and cooperative quilt making. But are these truly thematic units or simply activities associated with a topic? Edelsky, Altwerger, and Flores (1991) distinguish between thematic units that are topic based and thematic cycles.

> . . . theme cycles are a means for pursuing a line of inquiry. They consist of a chain—one task grows out of questions raised in the preceding tasks all connected to an original theme or initiating questions (e.g., Were there prehistoric people living where we live now? How do supermarkets really work? How can we get rid of drug dealers on the playground? . . . subjects and skills (science, math, reading, etc.) are used for investigating the topic. . . . Since thematic units are skills-driven, they are also full of exercises or strings of "activities" related to one topic. . . . Theme cycles, by contrast, are not loaded with exercises or "activities." Theme cycle centers that pull together resources in one location are not established to rev up lagging interests but to satisfy already heightened curiosity or to answer questions raised. . . . (pp. 64–66)

The concept of the theme should take the topic focus a step further. In literature, a theme is a complete thought: "If you keep trying, you have a good chance of success," "Evil beings usually lose at the end," and "There are patterns and cycles that occur over and over in life." When teachers start with essential questions for students to explore and predict conclusions that students might draw from topics, they can build units to cause students to think more deeply about life issues and options. This does not mean students are to be led to derive only the themes the teacher identifies or that the teacher is the only creator of questions. On the contrary, using the arts and other learning tools to develop particular themes only ensures meaningfulness if students actively participate in searching for "big thoughts." This search assumes that students are asking questions and the teacher is listening. The teacher that intends to cause thinking about principles of living would also teach students that an infinite number of themes can be pulled from any given experience. Individual people make interpretations based on their peculiar prior experiences, and it is a time for celebration when students synthesize their own themes, and they do so, even in primary grades, when teachers ask questions like, *"What did you learn? What was this mostly about? What did this tell you about people or the world?"* and *"What will you remember forever from this book* or *song?"*

Integrated Unit Structures. Units are often structured in the following ways: (1) around life problems, topics or themes, or important questions that form the content of all disciplines, i.e., science, social studies, the arts, math, and language; (2) with an artist, author, or some person at the centre of study; (3) focusing on a genre or form, e.g., poetry, historical fiction, symphonies, plays, sculpture; and (4) using a single or core book, a poem, song, or piece of art (e.g., a particular piece of literature might be studied and used as the integration centre). Books like Elwin and Paulse's *Asha's Mums* offer plentiful opportunities to examine themes like "Families can be structured in a variety of ways" using music, art, drama, dance, poetry, and writing containing such themes or as tools to express thoughts and feelings about these themes.

The arts can be used to develop any unit, and the arts can be integrated with other arts, as happens in life: Beethoven used the poem "Ode to Joy" as inspiration for his Ninth Symphony. See Post It Page 2–2 for the four-body, nine-legged model, which is a variation of the curricular design options Jacobs (1989) recommends. Her model includes the following aspects: (1) *discipline based:* specific skills, concepts, and main ideas or themes of a subject area like science or social studies; (2) *parallel:* two or more teachers plan so that units coincide (e.g., art teacher does masks while classroom teacher does Africa); the students may have to make the disciplinary connections if teachers do not make them explicit; (3) *multidisciplinary:* themes, topics, and concepts are the focus and several disciplines are used to explore the focus; (4) *interdisciplinary:* similar to multidisciplinary, but cuts across disciplines (e.g., the history of music or the art of science); (5) *integrated day:* student interests and problems are used throughout the day; and (6) *field based:* outside of class work (e.g., environmental lab).

School-wide Topics. Discoveries, patterns, cycles, problem-solving, creativity, and dreams are topics to unite a school in a several-month or year-long integrated study. Each grade level or teacher team addresses the topic by developing questions and themes appropriate to the developmental levels of their students. Often these topics are recycled every two or three years.

Centres or Stations Related to Themes. Centres allow students to work independently with self-directed materials. In this book a *station* is a narrowly focused area (e.g., a computer station might have software to explore unit themes or topics). A *centre* is a space that has independent learning options from several sources (e.g., art materials, CDs, props, game boards, and other activities all related to a unit topic, such as "Recurring Patterns and Cycles in Our World").

Multiple Intelligences Lesson Formats. By using a spreadsheet to graph the days of the week along one axis and the seven intelligences along the other, teachers can map out what music, art, dance or movement, drama, and literature (linguistic intelligence) is addressed on which days. This serves as a monitoring device to make sure no area is neglected to the detriment of another.

Arts with Arts Integration. Remember that aspects of each art discipline can serve as the focal point of study, and other arts areas can then be pulled in. A visual art unit on the "nature and effects of colour" would be well served by children's literature that explores colour like Kusugak's *Northern Lights: The Soccer Trails,* the poetry in O'Neill's *Hailstones and Halibut Bones: Adventure in Color,* creative movement in response to colours, and music that stimulates colour imagery or songs about colour. Chapter 13 is a compendium of strategy *seed* ideas for integrating the arts with the arts in ten combinations.

Lesson Introductions, Developments, and Conclusions. These three lesson parts are the workhorses of planning and teaching (see the integrated lesson plan in Post It Page 2–1). The arts are natural motivators, attention getters, and interest generators in the introduction to a lesson: Picasso's painting *Guernica* or Alex Colville's war paintings, such as *Tragic Landscape*, could provoke discussion before a lesson or unit dealing with war; drama activities, like pantomime, put students in a role so that they become part of the learning and might introduce a unit dealing with cycles or patterns by involving students in the mime of everyday activities done in the morning, afternoon, and evening; Lunn's *The Hollow Tree* could be read as a source of feelings and messages before beginning a unit on the United Empire Loyalists. The arts are equally valuable as responses to learning in a lesson conclusion. By writing songs and poems, making art, and performing skits and dances, students show what they know.

Principle Eight: TAKE Arts-based Field Trips

Field trips to an art museum or to hear a concert are not unusual in elementary and middle school. What is unusual is the *meaningful integration* of these trips. Without pre-trip lessons to prepare students and follow-up assessment, field trips can become little more than social time.

Field trips should be directly connected to curriculum goals and objectives. If they are to be meaningful experiences, teachers need to plan teaching strategies for *before* the trip, *during* the trip and *after* the trip. Here are a few trip tips.

Pre-trip. Ask students to generate questions they want answered during the trip and role play how to act on the trip. Concept minilessons that focus on crucial ideas like museum, sculpture, abstract, orchestra, conductor, and song versus musical piece can be presented to prepare students.

- *Behaviour expectations need to be made clear to students.* This includes consequences. This means the teacher must know the expectations of the site being visited. For example, art museums do not allow people to touch works of art and run in the galleries. Teachers need to know these rules and convey them to students.

- *Obtain information from the arts organization about the nature of the visit.* Some museums, orchestras, and arts centres provide activity packets to use to prepare ahead of time.
- *Make a visit to the site prior to the field trip.* Check about coat racks, restrooms, seating, and so on. At this time, try to generate questions or points to focus on in pre-trip lessons, such as,

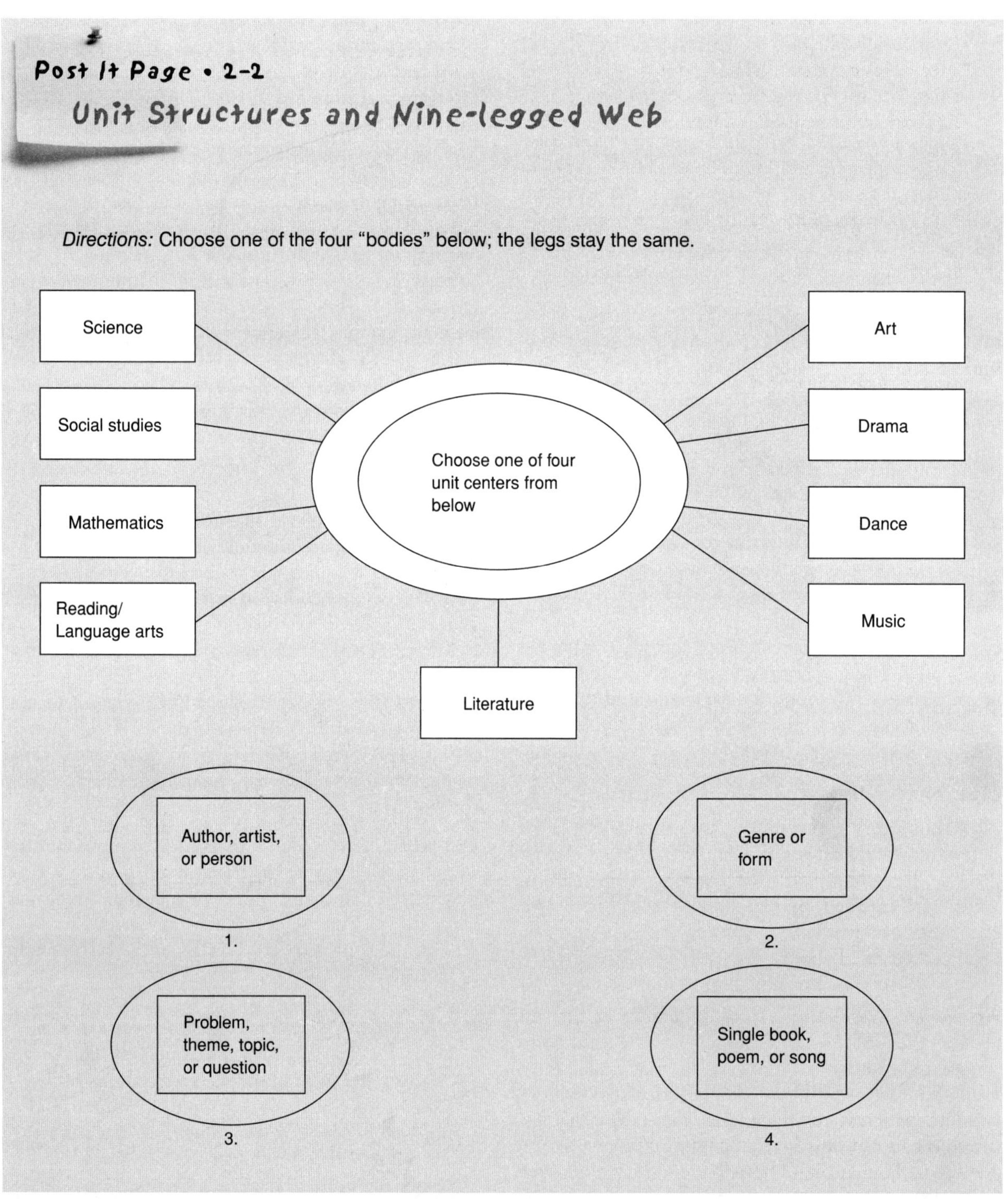

concepts or questions related to special exhibits at an art museum. Pick up printed information at the site to share with students.

- *Students need guidelines about what they are expected to learn from the field trip and should be held accountable.* If students know there is to be an assessment after the trip, they are more focused on the trip's purpose and less on socializing with peers. This can be accomplished by reviewing specific study sheets or general questions before the trip that are to be used upon return from the trip: *What was the most important thing you learned? What is one thing you could follow up on and find out more about? How did the experience make you feel? Why? What did the trip have to do with what we've been studying? Write about the trip and what you learned about. Show what you learned with art materials, drama, music, or dance and movement. Write a poem about the trip. Write a letter to the teacher convincing her that field trips like these are important in school. Write a thank you note to. . . .*

During the Trip. It is important for teachers to participate as learners and as managers of their classes. Teachers should be models of active learning.

Concluding the Trip. Teachers may wish to debrief students before leaving the site and let hosts know some of what students gained. Students need to be made aware that the teacher will do this so that they can prepare during the visit and not embarrass themselves and their teachers with poor responses. Responses to field trips can be in many forms: journal entries, skits, or artwork. Whatever form responses take, they should be selected to reveal the quantity and quality of the meaning making that students did related to the visit.

Take Looking–Listening Walks or Discovery Trips. These can be field trips in and of themselves for students to find colours, textures, sounds, roles in which people are engaged, or ways people and things move. Field trips don't have to mean a bus trip. Students often get so excited about field trips they can't get *serious about learning.* We can take so few field trips. But short, close to school trips can be fun and great practice for larger trips.

Principle Nine: EXHIBITION of Student Progress

Student progress toward curriculum objectives and school goals can only be determined if there is assessment and evaluation—assessment to gather information and evaluation to place a value on the progress in relation to predetermined criteria. (See Chapters 14 and 15 about this topic.) Student progress can be shown in the arts through the following:

School Museums and Displays. "If you build it, they will come!" Class museums and other displays are a visual means for students to show their work. A school museum can just as well be a class museum consisting of a special bulletin board. Mounting or framing student art shows it is valued. Museum information plaques should accompany work and contain the artist's name and birthdate, the title of the work, the media used and surface, and the date the work was completed. Students can also prepare catalogues to go with exhibits for visitors to gain information about the works and the artists.

Designated tables or cases for completed projects are other ideal ways to make students' progress public. By expecting students to have three-dimensional results that others will want to see, we set up a way of thinking and planning for students. Meaningful displays also include titles with works "tagged" so that others understand their significance, much like a museum plaque.

Portfolios. Portfolios of work have long been common in the arts. Students need large pocket folders to hold art (e.g., made from two pieces of poster board and attached ribbon or rope handles; boxes to hold audio and video tapes of drama and dance performances; divided notebooks to keep written materials—creative writing, learning logs, and journals). All work needs to be dated. Students can learn to do self-evaluation with much of the same criteria the teacher will use to evaluate work if they are given the means to do so. See the "Skills Checklist" example in Post It 7–2. While not every piece of work needs to be kept, work that shows something important about the learning going on should be selected. Keeping just the good work doesn't allow students to view their progress over time and return to pieces to celebrate growth or past successes.

Audiences Are Motivational. When students think others will hear their songs and poems or watch their dances and drama responses, they often become more concerned about quality. This doesn't mean arts activities should be done just for audiences. It does mean students can benefit from performing in front of a group, even if it's just the other half of the class. And students benefit from learning how to be an audience—how to be active listeners and show appreciation. Audience etiquette needs to be taught: when to applaud in a concert, when to stand, what an ovation means, what happens if you arrive late to a play. Consider offering a standing invitation to parents to come visit and not wait for the annual school play. Cooperate with teachers in lower grades to allow your students to perform for their classes. Seek out audiences from unconventional sources (e.g., custodians). Think about taking performances on the road to nearby nursing homes or senior citizen centres. The important idea is not to think that the yearly play or concert that students rehearse for weeks and weeks is the only time an audience is in order.

Morning announcements are another way to get an audience. Invitations for other classes to view a new exhibit can be extended or students can share song compositions over the school address system. One local elementary just spent the whole school year playing different genres of music each morning, followed by two-minute genre reports done by students. Its amazing how much can be learned about jazz on the morning announcements on the two-minute-a-day plan.

Teach How to Respond. This relates to audience etiquette, but goes beyond into the area of giving feedback to peers. After drama presentations or art docent talks, students can be given structures to help them learn to articulate their thoughts and feelings. Let students know they can give feedback by simply telling what they saw or heard, i.e., describing honestly—hopefully using new-found arts elements. They can also use sentence stems like these to help express their feelings: I liked . . . , It made me feel. . . . A strategy called **Liked–Wondered–Learned** can be used after a presentation by giving students time to jot down responses in columns with these labels, or the teacher can scribe on the overhead as ideas are generated in each category. Finally, students should learn that asking questions of other students is a form of feedback. Because receiving feedback is hard for some students, it helps to take time to role play giving and receiving feedback. This also helps students realize how rude or thoughtless remarks can make a person feel. Sensitivity and empathy are important factors in giving feedback.

Speaking and Writing About the Creative Process. One way to help students describe growth in their uses of the creative process is to provide questions to guide sharing that will come after creating a poem, drama, dance, or other work of art. Example questions for written or oral sharing include:

- How did you get your idea?
- Why did you do what you did?
- Where did you gather ideas?
- What were you trying to do?
- What did you try that you've never tried before?
- What did you learn most?
- How is this connected to other things you are learning?
- What ideas did you use from learning about the arts? (elements, skills, concepts)

All these questions help students think more deeply and facilitate success in expressing their ideas.

General Assignment Criteria to Guide Work. Rather than squelch the urge to create by using only grades and traditional forms of evaluation, teachers can give basic framework criteria, ahead of time, to facilitate success. For example, "Fill up your space, and use collage materials to create a response with a key idea from the fairy tale unit" leaves plenty of room to use the process of creative production, but puts structure limitations to ensure thoughtful connections to content and growth in the use of arts concepts. Boundaries focus mental energy and increase creative thinking.

Principle Ten: SPECIALISTS Are Important Resources

Specialist arts teachers, professional artists, and community arts organizations are crucial resources. It is part of every classroom teacher's role to seek out these specialists, who can show where connections between the arts and other disciplines exist and how to make them without damaging the integrity of the art form. Arts teachers in schools are often willing to plan with teachers, especially if the teacher expects integration to go both ways: the art or music teacher should be able to expect the classroom teacher to support a unit on a theme or topic in art or music.

Making It Easy for Arts Teachers. At minimum, teachers can give specialists a month by month list of units, concepts, and skills to be presented in science, social studies, reading and language arts, and math and invite arts connections in special classes. But arts specialists should be invited to do the same for classroom teachers. Classroom teachers can solicit ways to follow up on arts classes to extend art, music, dance, and drama. In addition, it is important for classroom teachers to sit in on special classes to learn more about the arts and about students' arts intelligences.

School Arts Directory. Additional specialized help can be located by doing a school and community survey. Circulate a form to adults requesting names and contact information for persons who could be used as arts resources. Encourage people to list themselves. The teacher next door may own every piece of big band music ever written, and the principal just may play the African slit drum. Students can also be surveyed, as well as parent-teacher organization members. Use the Internet to locate home pages of arts organizations in your province and community. See the appendix for starter addresses. Finally, ask the parent-teacher organization to *assemble* the directory!

Arts Organization Collaborations. Teacher workshops conducted by artists and classroom teachers engaged in integrating the arts are becoming more common. Several organizations across the country are helping schools learn ways to integrate the arts. ArtsStarts in Schools in Vancouver can be reached at 604-878-7144 or by e-mail at artstarts@bc.sympatico.ca. Calgary Arts Partners in Education (CAPES) can be contacted at 403-294-6347 or by e-mail at capes@nucleus.com. The Learning Through the Arts™ in Toronto can be reached at 416-408-2824, Ext 800 or by e-mail at angelae@rcmusic.ca. For information on arts education organizations in other parts of the country, contact the Canadian Conference of the Arts at 613-234-2742, or by e-mail at Susan_Annis@mail.culturenet.ca.

Plan for Artist Residencies. Arts specialists may be available through a local arts council or by contacting artists in the community. It is important to realize that artists often have little or no background in teaching or in child development. Before bringing an artist to the school or class, teachers need to meet with them to prepare. Both parties need to agree on and know the following:

- Goals of the visit (e.g., the objectives from your unit and course of study)
- Composition of the class (economic, social, developmental levels)
- Exact time limits
- Physical limitations of the classroom (materials you have and don't have)
- Students with special needs
- Discipline system used and who will handle discipline during the visit
- Basic effective teaching strategies (e.g., use of proximity, questioning, eye contact, hands-on, pace, transitions, use of students' prior knowledge)
- How to prepare students for the visit
- How the classroom teacher can participate
- How to assess and evaluate what the students learn
- How the classroom teacher can follow up after the visit to extend learning

Arts Education for All

Overriding the concept of integration is a perspective that any model or strategy must be adjusted to differentiate for the range of student needs.

Here are general strategies to adapt the curriculum for particular situations or individual students. The strategies are based on the belief that each child needs *particular* accommodations to ensure progress toward independence. Basically, teachers increase the likelihood of student success when they make adjustments for place, amount, rate, target objective, instruction, curriculum materials, utensils, levels of difficulty, assistance, and response. Especially consider how to alter the *structure* of the lesson and classroom, the number and kinds of *practices,* the kind and amount of *feedback,* the amount and kind of *choice* and control given, the teaching *strategies* used, the nature of *examples,* and the *motivational* strategies (e.g., encouragement strategies such as belief statements). Post It Page 2–4 gives adaptations for exceptional populations.

Place. Change the environment. Limit the amount of space. Use carrels and centres. Play music. Use different desk arrangements. Have carpet squares available. Lower or brighten lighting. For example, provide headphones and classical music to listen to during independent work.

Amount. Give more or less time (e.g., to explore materials). Use more repetition and break into smaller steps. Reduce or increase the number of things to be learned. Alter the amount of examples and feedback given. Give additional practices. For example, focus on a few concepts or strategies, such as locomotor moves in dance, to convey interpretation of characters in literature or people in social studies ("Walk like . . ."). Teach one thing well, and make sure it is learned before proceeding.

Rate. This is the "oftenness." Change the pace. Give more breaks. Create more or less time structure for the activity (e.g., intensity of teacher-directed lessons). For example, let students set their own time or give a short time to do a small amount. "As I count to five, make shapes to show *fear.*"

Target Objectives. Make clear goals or outcomes. Set sights on alternative goals or alternative means of reaching goals. Decide what a child can realistically achieve (know and be able to do). Make objectives life centred and connected to student interests. For example, instead of "create a whole new . . .," adapt from a model (e.g., use a poem frame like haiku to create a poem).

Instruction. Use more or less direct instruction (models, demonstration, examples, descriptive feedback, reassurance, scaffolding). Cause students to be mentally and physically active, engaged and involved with fat questions and Every Pupil Response. Organize lessons in whole–part–whole fashion, and use inductive as well as deductive methods. Set up routines and other structures to provide security, but use multiple possibilities within the structure. Consider Gardner's seven intelligences to plan the day and monitor the week. Chart intelligences made available to students. Use a multisensory approach: visual, auditory, kinesthetic, tactile, and humour.

Curriculum Materials. Give easier materials to read or adapt materials (e.g., highlight important parts with pen, tape record, or rewrite). Give more or less choice. Use more hands-on materials like games or art media. Use computer software.

Utensils. Use visual and auditory aids. Teach meaning-making tools and strategies—that is, ways to learn or comprehend, like fix-ups, shortcuts, cue sheets, cue cards, mnemonics (acronyms and acrostics). Focus on patterns and students making the meaning by using utensils. Teach strategies and *when* and *how* to use them. For example, post arts elements so that students can refer to them (e.g., concepts to use when making or discussing visual art). Demonstrate how to do a portrait by examining the subject in sections. Teach how to identify and make basic lines and shapes.

Level of Difficulty. Make the lesson easier or harder to challenge appropriately. Alter complexity. Allow notes or cue cards during tests. Give more or less structure or surveillance.

Assistance (from other people). Scaffold or help with peer tutoring, grouping, structure, changes, and prompts. Focus on the goal of independence attained through pattern finding and mnemonics use. For example, group students to do a drama response (e.g., a tableau to represent an important moment in a piece of literature). Ask students to think of ideas they've used successfully before in their art or writing if they are stymied in a search for a topic.

Response. Allow students to show that they know in many ways (e.g., perform what they know and can do). Connect responses to real life. Use projects that call for a product or piece to perform as a result of problem solving. Distinguish between assessment, evaluation, and grading by thinking of assessment as *getting information to inform instruction,* evaluation as *judgment of progress against criteria after lessons have taken place,* and grading as *a scale applied to responses.* Give exemptions (e.g., from oral reading) or pass options.

Inclusion: Specifics for the Arts

The subject of the arts is the subject of life. The arts provide avenues to understand ourselves, make meaning of the world, express abilities in unique ways, and create empathy for others different from ourselves. Through the arts, children discover common bonds with people. This understanding and awareness are the essence of the arts and can build a feeling of kinship. In a world where quality of life depends on the quality of our relationships with others, the arts can lessen feelings of alienation and be great levellers among students, because no one is considered greater or lesser than another in his or her creative expressions or aesthetic tastes. With this in mind, we can think about how diverse populations of students are more similar than different and stress commonalities, not just differences. We are all human and need to be respected, to belong, to achieve, and to communicate. Suggestions are given on Post It Page 2–4 to stimulate thinking about adaptations for students' particular needs.

Post It Page • 2-3

The Art of Teacher Questioning

- Ask open or fat questions that require students to think divergently and answer with more than a one-word or yes–no answer. Limit use of "Do you . . . ? Could you . . . ? Would you . . . ? Should you . . . ?" Rephrase, instead.
- "What if . . . ?" questions stimulate creative thinking at the *synthesis* level.
- Ask questions that call for students to use both their experiences and text evidence. Ask "What evidence or examples can you give?"
- Follow fat questions with a period of wait time, at least five seconds. This yields longer, better answers and more students will participate.
- Ask for an *every pupil response* (EPR) after questions. "When you have an idea, put your thumb up or turn the card over." More students will *expect* to participate, and you can call on anyone who signals. Give wait time for all, or most, to signal.
- Offer a pass option for students to use when they are called on and go blank. (Some use a "pass" coupon.) Do private conferences with students if they pass too often.
- Consider posting Bloom's taxonomy or another set of thinking categories. Everyone can use the poster to formulate questions and do self-checks to ensure that not all questions are literal or memory level. (Benjamin Bloom's thinking levels are memory, interpretation, application, analysis, synthesis, and evaluation.)
- Not all literal questions are bad. Consider these two memory questions from "Little Red Riding Hood": "What did Red do that started her troubles?" versus "How many items were in Red's basket for Grandma?" All questions should lead toward meaning and, in the case of literature, toward themes.
- Focus on getting students to generate their own questions by posting examples of good questions (fat, related to important ideas, etc.). Do minilessons on good questions. Remember to discuss the importance of asking questions that (1) you can't answer yourself and (2) you really *care* about. Another strategy: ask all students to write down a question or point to discuss on a card before the discussion, or pair students to generate "All the questions they can think of about . . . ?" Questions can be collected and drawn from a hat.
- Instead of taking volunteers, use a random method that ensures that all genders, races, and ability levels are included. (Number students and draw out numbers, or simply monitor by checking off students called on or ask students to keep track.)
- During discussions, devise ways for students to get a turn besides raising their hands. This can be distracting and turn into a competition for attention. Use an "I have the floor" object (scarf, small box). The object can be passed to responders.
- Model and teach students how to paraphrase responses of others, piggyback on others' answers, and ask clarification questions. For example, "What do you mean by . . . ?" Active listening by everyone creates an opportunity for a meaningful exchange of ideas.

Post It Page • 2-4

Working with Exceptional Populations

Children with Developmental Delays

- Give many concrete experiences. Use pictures, props, labels, charts, name tags, and other similar aids to help children understand information and concepts.
- Make extra efforts to plan activities that move from simple to complex. Repeat activities more often and plan more time for exploration and practice.
- For those with less advanced verbal skills, use lots of hands-on art, and activities with rhythm instruments, creative movement, and pantomime.
- Seek the appropriate level of challenge so that students will be successful. Children can surprise us with their insights when working in the arts because they are using a form of communication different from the norm. They may also show more concentration and involvement. Be sure to reinforce things students do well with specific descriptive feedback.
- Students need opportunities to participate in mixed-ability groups to develop their social skills.

Children with Physical Disabilities

- Adapt the space to make it easier for children to manage.
- Use a "buddy system." A partner can quietly explain points that may be confused by children with hearing impairments, help move a wheelchair, or make an area accessible for those with limited mobility. With a sighted partner, space can be explored gradually.
- Focus on movement activities that can be adapted to include each child. For example, facial expressions can be a focus for those whose arms and legs are impaired or gestures can be emphasized if hands and arms are mobile.
- Describe in detail art materials, tools, pictures, and props and tell stories with great detail to create mental images for those with visual impairments.
- Create opportunities for students with visual impairments to explore and learn through all their senses.
- Place children with hearing impairments close to the music source to feel the vibrations.
- Be sure children with hearing impairments can see your face, especially the lips. Don't stand against a window or a shadow will be cast on your face. Take similar care with artificial light sources. Don't exaggerate your speech; in fact, this distorts the sounds children are taught to observe.
- Teach all the children in the class to speak clearly and to face the child with a hearing impairment when speaking.
- Use visual cues, pictures, props, gestures, and directions on cards.

Children with Emotional Needs

- A secure, consistent, and supportive environment is important. These children struggle with self-esteem issues. They need experiences of success to feel good about themselves. Start with a series of short activities, like energizers and warm-ups, so that they feel comfortable. Instructions need to be concise and clear.

- Children with short attention spans need to change frequently from one task to another. Be alert to their responses and need for physical movement. Be ready to cut an activity short and go to another.
- Extending students' length of concentration and developing the ability to focus are desirable. Move in slow increments and select activities to increase attention span. See Energizers and Warm-ups throughout this book.
- Body-movement activities, murals, and other large art activities are particularly useful. Movement activities involving large muscles are often successful.

Children and Cultural Diversity

- Children whose first language is not the language of instruction can participate in dance, art, and drama activities that call for nonverbal communication.
- Infuse connections to special cultural holidays, customs, people, and experiences in arts activities. Invite students to share their rich backgrounds and use this as a basis for artistic creations. Invite parents as guests to share diverse art forms.
- Folk literature is a universal literary form. (Many plot lines, like that of "Cinderella," have been found in hundreds of cultures and written in dozens of languages.) Encourage students to share their own cultural stories and use these for drama, dance, art, and music activities.
- Drama, art, dance, or music based on children's literature can be a good vehicle for learning English vocabulary. Songs are most helpful for learning the rhythmic and prosaic elements of a new language.

Children with Speech and Language Difficulties

- Provide an open, relaxed atmosphere that encourages rather than inhibits children.
- Being able to engage in oral activities that have a "play" feel to them is useful for children with speech impairments. When children are having fun, they tend to forget about speech difficulties, so get them involved *actively* through dance, art, and pantomime experiences.
- Puppetry allows students to speak through a puppet and may give security and develop confidence.
- Provide give opportunities to sing, speak, and hear others use language.
- Rhythmic activities, singing, unison choral speaking, and character role playing can lessen stuttering.

Students Who Are Gifted

- Some students can bypass basics. Allow them to do so.
- Gifted children are usually ahead of their peers in language development. They may excel in dialogue, improvisation, and writing. Give students opportunities to create their own materials by writing Reader's Theatre Scripts and sound effects stories. Show students how to use diverse materials as subject matter for art, dance, and drama.
- Ensure that children who are gifted have many opportunities for creative expression. Encourage them to write plays, create puppet shows, and write and bind their own books. They can assume leadership roles in dance, drama, and music activities.
- Children may be interested in exploring a particular topic in great depth. Find mentors for them.
- Gifted students often pursue interests alone and may have difficulty working in a group. Because dance, drama, and music are often group activities, they are important opportunities for learning social skills. Be alert to the discomfort that group work may cause and ensure that solo activities are an option.

(Thanks to Andrea Martin, Faculty of Education, Queen's University for her contributions to this Post It Page.)

Activities:

Integrated Thinking

Randomly select two or three objects and brainstorm all the ways that they can be both creatively and meaningfully linked together. Do in groups or pairs. Groups can do the same objects. Afterward, compare the length and quality of the lists and the many variations people created.

Use Positive Comments

Do this one with peers or with children. Divide into four or five groups. Each group needs a recorder and a piece of paper. Divide the paper in half and brainstorm "Uplifting Comments" and then "Discouraging Comments" that teachers and others use. ("What a stupid idea" versus "Keep trying. You'll get it!") After a few minutes, bring the whole group together. Each individual can choose one negative comment to say out loud, with lots of expression and facial and body communication. Go around the room. Repeat using the uplifting comments. Discuss how the two kinds of comments felt.

Life-centred Topics

This activity works best in pairs or a small group. Take five minutes to brainstorm problems and issues confronting the world. Then put the list in high, middle, and lower priority by viewing it from the point of view of an elementary or middle school teacher. Take the top item on the high list and brainstorm again. This time list ideas under science, social studies, and math that connect to the problem. Branch off these three areas with LADDM connections. Remember, when brainstorming, go for quantity of ideas first, rather than stopping to judge the quality of the ideas.

Birthday Buddies: Artists, Authors, and Musicians

Here's an integrated idea to weave throughout the school year. The first step is to help students find an artist, author, or musician born on their birthdays. Students can use encyclopedias or references like *Something about the Author* or Krull's *Lives of Musicians* to do research.

1. *Research* his or her life: basic biographical facts, unique artistic style, the time in which he or she lives or lived, the geographic area(s) in which he or she lives or lived, the country or area he or she is from, and the time period of the literary, artistic, or musical work.
2. *Collect* quotes from your birthday buddy, fascinating or funny facts about the person, and pictures or other information available from publishers.
3. *Make a timeline of* the artist, author, or musician's life and works.
4. *Use a map* to locate where the artist, author, or musician lives or lived, the birthplace, the city where she or he worked, and where the person is buried, if deceased.
5. *Write* a newspaper story with headlines about the artist, author, or musician, a letter to the artist, author, and composer with whom you share a birthday, an article for the newspaper as if you are a critic. Write about the artistic, literary, or musical work by your birthday buddy, about your favourite artistic, literary, or musical work created by your birthday buddy, a tribute to your birthmate, a poem (couplet, diamante, haiku, etc.) about

Activities:

your artistic friend, a dialogue between you and your birthmate if you were to meet, a scene about your birthmate visiting your town or school, or a list of questions to ask your birthday buddy.

6. *Create* a birthday card for your birthmate or riddles about your friend. Create a birthday present for your artistic birthday buddy (e.g., a piece of art, song, or poem), a time capsule of items your birthday buddy would want saved for the future, an exhibit of the artist, author, or musician's work, or a hat your birthday buddy would wear.
7. *Orally share* information about your birthmate with the class. Sit in a special birthday chair. Share an original work created by the birthday buddy (e.g., art, poem, or passage from a book). Share by pretending you are your birthmate and use props or costumes, and tell the class about yourself. Expect them to ask you questions.
8. *Watch* a video or listen to a tape about the life of your birthmate.
9. *Have a birthday party* for kids and their birthday buddies. For summer birthdays, pick a special day during the academic year for the celebration. For example, select a special date in the life of the birthday buddy, e.g., first publication or exhibit or concert.

Arts Education Organizations

There are several fine arts education organizations. So far, there is not a national arts education organization in Canada. Most provinces have provincial arts councils, and many of these have arts education branches.

The Arts Education Consortium

The Arts Education Consortium in Ottawa is a partnership of national cultural institutions and teaching institutions. Its mandate is to promote teaching, learning, and inquiry in arts education. The partnership is committed to supporting educational programs for teachers that provide contact with professional artists and arts institutions, and that foster reflection and research on artistic processes and arts education. In conjunction with the University of Ottawa, it offers an intensive two-week summer program. For information, contact Susan Annis at the Canadian Conference of the Arts at 613-234-2742, or e-mail Susan_Annis@mail.culturenet.ca.

The Arts Education Council of Ontario

15 Oakburn Crescent, North York, ON, M2N 2T5

The Arts Education Council of Ontario publishes a quarterly newsletter, *The Artspaper*. Contact *The Artspaper* c/o the Council, by fax at 416-235-3545, or e-mail Artspaper@hotmail.com.

Getty Center for Education in the Arts

1875 Century Park East, No. 2300, Los Angeles, CA 90067, 213-277-9188

Formed in 1982, the Center is dedicated to improving arts education in grades K–12 and focuses on issues at the national, state, and local levels. The Center considers the arts as the principal means of understanding human experiences and transmitting cultural values and believes that the content of the arts must include instruction in four disciplines: art production, art history, art criticism, and aesthetics. This approach is known as DBAE (discipline-based art education). The Center coordinates partnerships between arts agencies and schools and disseminates information about arts education through books, newsletters, and an Internet site, ArtsEdNet, which reviews trends and has lesson plans and curriculum resources, an idea exchange, and seminar information.

Lincoln Center Institute

Lincoln Center for the Performing Arts, Inc., 70 Lincoln Center Plaza, New York, NY 10023-6594, 212-875-5535, Fax 212-875-5539

In 1975, the institute was created to fulfil a commitment to aesthetic education programs for teachers and students. The institute's purpose is to promote aesthetic education as an important part of learning through educational partnerships with schools. The focus is on developing perception through understanding of art forms, of how artists make choices, and how these understandings relate to life. The institute believes that perceiving and understanding aesthetic qualities in art and in life are as basic to enlightened citizenship as are understanding of math or social studies and that this kind of understanding has an important place in student learning. There are seventeen institutes in the United States and Australia. See appendix for member sites.

References

Books and Articles

Arnheim, R. (1989). *Thoughts on art education.* Los Angeles: Getty Center for Education in the Arts.

Booth, D. (1992). *Stories to read aloud.* Markham, ON: Pembroke.

Cullen, L. (1995). *Solid gold for kids: Musical energizers!* Scarborough, ON: Prentice Hall Ginn.

Edelsky, C., Altwerger, A. B., & Flores, B. (1991). *Whole language: What's the difference?* Portsmouth, NH: Heinemann.

Gardner, H. (1989). "Zero-based arts education: an introduction to ARTS PROPEL." *Studies in Art Education,* 71–83.

Grant, J. M. (1995). *Shake, rattle & learn: Classroom tested ideas that use movement for active learning.* Markham, ON: Pembroke.

Jacobs, H. (ed.) (1989). *Interdisciplinary curriculum: Design and implementation* (videorecording). Alexandria, VA: ASCD.

Jenkins, P. (1986). *Art for the fun of it.* New York: Simon and Schuster.

Moore, T. (1992). *Care of the soul: A guide for cultivating depth and sacredness in everyday life.* New York: HarperCollins.

Ogle, D. (1986). "K-W-L: a teaching model that develops active reading of expository text." *Reading Teacher,* 39, 564–70.

Pitman, W. (1998). *Learning the arts in an age of uncertainty.* Toronto: Arts Education Council of Ontario

Remer, J. (1996). *Beyond enrichment.* New York: American Council for the Arts.

Starko, A. (1995). *Creativity in the classroom: Schools of curious delight.* White Plains, NY: Longman.

Stinson, S. (1988). *Dance for young children: Finding the magic in movement.* Reston, VA: American Alliance for Health, Physical Education, Recreation and Dance Education.

Upitis, R., Smithrim, K., & Soren, B. (1999). "When teachers become musicians and artists: Teacher transformation and professional development." *Music Education Research,* 1(19), 23-35.

Children's Literature References

Booth, D. (1989). *'Til all the stars have fallen.* Toronto: Kids Can Press.

Booth, D. (1993). *Dr. Knickerbocker and other rhymes.* New York: Ticknor and Fields.

Cruxton, J. (1998). *Discovering the Amazon rainforest.* Toronto: Oxford University Press Canada.

Elwin, R., & Paulse, M. (1990). *Asha's mums.* Toronto: Women's Press.

Fowke, E. (1969). *Sally go round the sun.* Toronto: McClelland & Stewart.

Fowke, E. (1987). *Ring around the moon.* Toronto: NC Press.

Harrison, T. (1982). *A northern alphabet.* Montreal: Tundra Books.

Kusugak, M. (1993). *Northern lights: The soccer trails.* Toronto: Annick Press.

Lunn, J. (1997). *The hollow tree.* Toronto: Alfred A. Knopf Canada.

McCully, E. A. (1992). *Mirette on the high wire.* New York: G. P. Putnam's Sons.

O'Neill, M. (1989). *Hailstones and halibut bones—adventures in color.* New York: Doubleday.

Integrating Literature Throughout the Curriculum

3

Consultant:
Sylvia Pantaleo

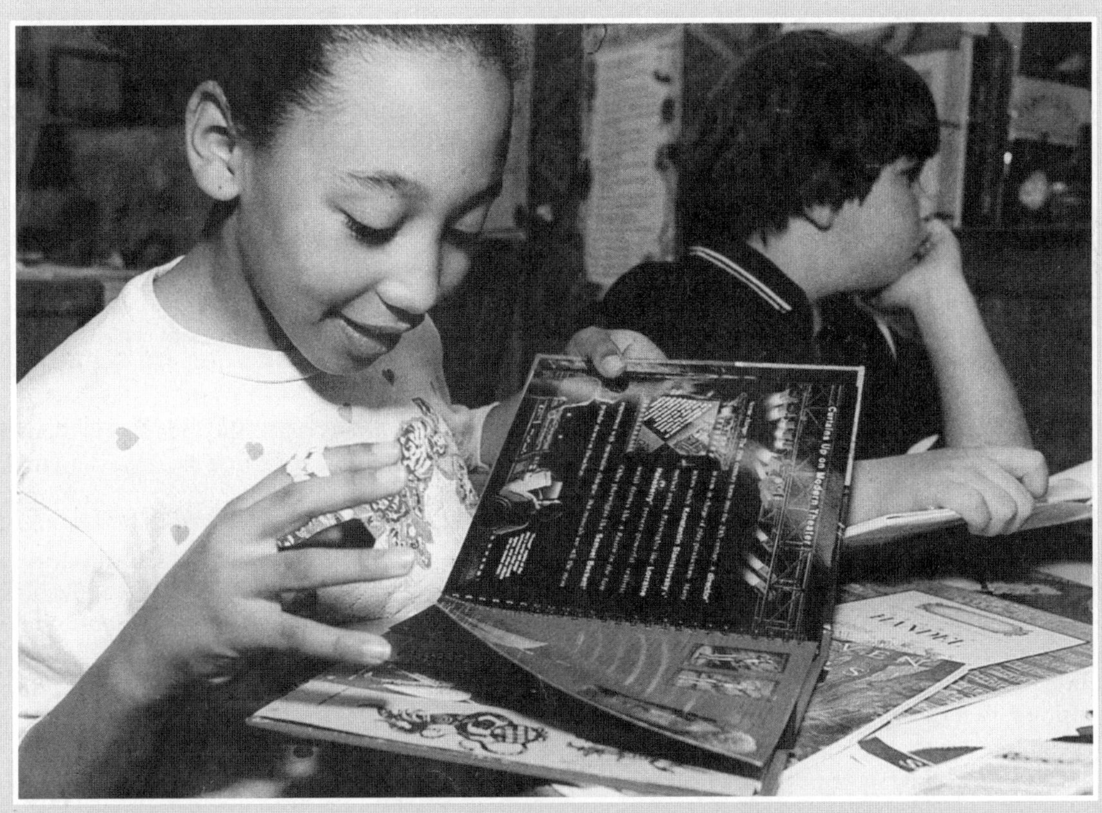

"I now enjoy Tolstoy and Jane Austen and Trollope as well as fairy tales and I call that growth; if I had had to lose the fairy tales in order to acquire the novelists, I would not say that I had grown but only that I had changed. A tree grows because it adds rings; a train doesn't grow by leaving one station behind and puffing on to the next.

C. S. Lewis (1980, p. 11)

Classroom Vignette

Amy Weiss's Lesson

The students in Mrs. Weiss's grade three class are seated on an oriental carpet in the front of the room. Mrs. Weiss writes on the board "Write Right Away." Immediately children raise their hands, eager to describe this type of writing as they have engaged in this activity on previous occasions.

Rich explains, "Write Right Away means you just write whatever you think about for a certain amount of time."

Mrs. Weiss replies, "Exactly. What else do you remember about this writing strategy? Lisa?"

"It gets your brain going. It's just like a quick write," Lisa says. Paul adds, "It helps you think because you start with what you know and then you think about more after you write. We did it when we first started talking about Canada in social studies."

"Right," replies Mrs. Weiss. "Does anyone remember doing Write Right Away another time?"

Julie describes how they utilized the strategy in Health when they were discussing friends.

Mrs. Weiss explains to the students that they will be engaging in a Write Right Away before she reads a Canadian picture book. The class has been involved in a picture book unit that has focused on Canadian authors and illustrators. Mrs. Weiss has gathered multiple copies of various titles and the children have been reading the books individually and then discussing the books in dyads or small groups. Today she is using one of the books in a whole group activity. Mrs. Weiss writes the word "fear" on the board. She directs the children to think about a time when they were afraid. After pausing for several seconds she further explains how the children are to write about anything that has to do with being afraid—the purpose of the writing is to communicate their ideas on paper.

The children are dismissed from the rug in an orderly fashion. On returning to their desks, they take out their literature logs. Mrs. Weiss circulates as the children begin to write and once all are working, she begins to write her own piece about a time when she was afraid. After about five minutes of writing, Mrs. Weiss instructs the class to find a place to stop. She waits and adds, "We'll use the pairs share strategy, today. You can either read what you wrote or pick out ideas to tell."

Pairs form. One boy explains to his partner how afraid he was when he became separated from his parents in a busy mall at Christmas. A girl describes her fear of the first day of school when she moved to a new town.

Mrs. Weiss circulates, listening, questioning, and commenting. After a few minutes, she stops the conversations and instructs the students to leave their literature logs on their desks and to return to the carpet. Once everyone is assembled she asks, "Who heard a story that they would like to share with everyone or who would like to share their own personal experiences?" Hands go up quickly and several students volunteer their partners. One girl recalls that as a small child, she believed there was "something" under her bed. Many children nod in agreement. Another boy recounts the time he became lost on a hike, and a girl talks about her fear of heights. Another student describes her fear when her parents told her they were getting a divorce and a boy explains how frightened he was when his dog became ill and had to be taken to the veterinarian.

Mrs. Weiss encourages the children who share their experiences to describe the accompanying emotional and physical responses, as well as the thoughts associated with the particular incident of fear. After several minutes of whole group sharing, Mrs. Weiss instructs the children to think about what they wrote and to think about what has been shared about "fear." She then shows them the cover of the book, *Very Last First Time* by Jan Andrews. Mrs. Weiss asks the children to make predictions about the story based on the cover of the book and the fact that fear plays a role in the story. The students contribute predictions and Mrs. Weiss records them on the board. Some children ask questions about the picture on the cover, and Mrs. Weiss scaffolds the students' understanding by posing further questions and providing some information. Once Mrs. Weiss locates Ungava Bay, the setting of the story, on the map of Canada on the bulletin board, further predictions are generated.

Mrs. Weiss begins to read the book and stops when Eva Padlyat, the main character, is about to descend under the ice. Mrs. Weiss has the class return to their predictions. Which predictions have been confirmed or realized? Which predictions have been rejected? Why? What further predictions can we make based on what has happened in the story to this point? Additional predictions are recorded on the board. Once finished reading the book, Mrs. Weiss has the students return to the predictions and complete the same process as at the midpoint of the book. She leads the class in a discussion about Eva's experiences of going under the ice to search for mussels. One student comments, "At first I didn't understand how she could go under the ice but then I remembered how it said in the book that the tide was out." Mrs. Weiss provides the students with the opportunity to express personal comments and observations about the book.

Next, Mrs. Weiss explains to the class that they are going to represent Eva's fears through body movements and sounds. The students find a personal space where they have some room to move. Mrs. Weiss instructs the students to imagine that they are Eva under the ice and to move like she would as the story is retold. Mrs. Weiss retells the part of the story from where Eva begins to explore the sea bottom to where she rediscovers the ice-hole. Once completed, the children return to the carpet and discuss the dramatization. Many talk about how they altered their body posture once they were lost. Several children comment about how their peers' facial expressions changed as the dramatization continued. Mrs. Weiss asks the children to articulate the thoughts and feelings they experienced as Eva throughout the drama activity.

After much discussion, Mrs. Weiss explains how the students are now going to make sound effects using musical instruments (e.g., cymbals, triangles, sticks, small drums, kazoos), items in the room, and themselves to depict the noises that Eva heard under the ice from the time she initially descends to the sea bottom and starts collecting mussels to the time she rediscovers the ice-hole. The students are organized into four groups, and once prepared, each group shares their sound effects with the class. Feedback is provided by peers.

The final task requires the students to combine the two previous activities. One person in the group is Eva, one person narrates Eva's experiences, describing Eva's inner thoughts and emotions as well as the story events, and the remainder of the group provides the sound effects they developed earlier. Again, peers provide feedback about each dramatization of Eva's experiences under the ice.

At the end of the activity, the children return to their desks, take out their literature logs, and write about their experiences with the book *Very Last First Time.*

Introduction

When we teach a child to draw, we teach him how to see. When we teach a child to play a musical instrument, we teach her how to listen. When we teach a child how to dance, we teach him how to move through life with grace. When we teach a child to read or write, we teach her how to think. When we nurture imagination, we create a better world, one child at a time.

Jane Alexander, chair for the National Endowment for the Arts (*imagine!*, NEA, 1997)

A powerful and controversial aspect of art is its role as a vehicle for truth. This chapter includes a discussion of how authors are artists who share their truths through the creative art forms of story and poem. In Chapters 1 and 2, research about child development, creativity, multiple intelligences, and differentiating instruction was used to build a philosophy and a model for integrating literature and other arts throughout the curriculum; those theories and principles will be now be applied to literature. Viewing literature as a discipline in its own right, as well as an art form to teach and learn, is a key chapter concept, too, as is the idea of using class time differently by tapping strengths of holistic approaches and explicit parts instruction. The chapter is organized into sections: WHY teachers should integrate literature, WHAT to know to do so, and a HOW section with the principles of integration. Chapter 4 is a compendium of specific *seed* ideas to integrate literature throughout the curriculum. In addition, Chapter 13 has a collection of strategy seed ideas for integrating literature with the other arts.

Why: Rationale for Integrating Literature Throughout the Curriculum

The book that made the greatest difference in my life was The Secret in the Daisy *by Carol Grace, Random House, published in 1955. . . . It took me from a miserable, unhappy wretch to a joyful, glad-to-be-alive human. I fell so in love with the book that I searched out and married the girl who wrote it.*

(Walter Matthau in *Books That Made the Difference* by Gordon and Patricia Sabine, 1983)

1. **Literature combats illiteracy and aliteracy.** Illiteracy renders people incapable of reading newspapers, food labels, and job applications. Many people *can* read, but *don't;* these aliterates never develop a love of stories, poetry, or plays (what David Russell calls "belletristic reading"). These bookless individuals suffer a poverty of mind and spirit. Millions never read literature that can broaden experience, widen perspective, stimulate imagination, and refine aesthetic sensibilities. Educators have looked to reasons *within* learners, as well as *outside* classroom variables, such as reading materials and approaches, to discover why. Findings? In classes where literature is integral to instruction, students did read more, enjoyed it, and performed as well or better on tests than control groups without trade books (see Post It Page 3–1). These studies show good books do more than teach the *skill* of reading. The word and visual artistry of literature gives an aesthetic experience that captures readers, personally. It is this experience that creates bibliophiles.

Students who read a *lot* get better at it, so it's disheartening that less than 1 percent of children read in their spare time and only about 5 percent of the

Post It Page • 3-1

NEWS BULLETINS

Literature Research You Can Use

- Literature approaches, supplemented by short, special "decoding lessons," were favoured over other approaches in a study using 50 classrooms and 1,000 grade two students in Utah. Treatment groups were superior to control groups in achievement gains and attitudes toward reading (Elridge & Butterfield, 1986).
- Sixty-three grade one children in Utah matched with more than 2,000 books yielded impressive results on a state proficiency test: student scored 93 percent by January (13 points higher than the state standard and four months earlier than the normal testing time). Reading scores were in the 99th percentile for the group, and all but four children scored above grade level (Reutzel & Cooter, 1992: Tunnell & Jacobs, 1989).
- Children in literature-based reading programs read as many as one hundred books in a school year, as compared with programs without literature, where students read an average of only seven minutes during reading class and only one or two textbooks during the year (Anderson et al., 1985: Hepler, 1982).
- The use of literature in classrooms has been shown to:
  - develop an interest in reading
  - provide language models for students' own writing
  - foster critical thinking
  - develop vocabulary
  - promote awareness and development of social and cultural understanding
  - motivate children to read
  - promote learning
  - develop literacy
  - spark readers' imagination
  - develop a sense of story (Fuhler, 1990; Galda & Cullinan, 1991; Higgins & Roos, 1990; Smith & Powers, 1989)

population checks out library books. Many readers do buy books and read magazines or newspapers, rather than go to the library, but we cannot assume that by teaching a child *to* read, even with literature, she will automatically *become* a reader and enjoy and use this skill for a lifetime. Good books must be used *wisely,* helping to develop tastes for genres and authors, and treating literature as an art to be savoured. Literature integration can help with illiteracy and aliteracy problems if books are explored for their capacity to stimulate the senses, challenge the intellect, and touch the heart. A childhood spent in vicarious experiences with Pooh, Max, and Stellaluna increases the likelihood that books will be sought out as sources of pleasure.

2. **Literature builds basic skills: reading, speaking, writing, and listening.** Of primary interest is making sure the next generation has the skills to survive and thrive. Tests will continue to be important gauges of student abilities to use English, so it is important to know that standardized vocabulary and comprehension tests show that basic skills are learned well when literature is plentiful and times to write imaginatively are frequent. Gains of as much as four years occur when literature is the core of the reading program, and attitudes toward reading are more positive when trade books replace basals and workbooks (Five, 1988; Reutzel & Cooter, 1992; Tunnell & Jabobs, 1989). For those involved in special education and inclusion, the results of using literature-based approaches with at-risk students is encouraging (see Allen et al., 1991; D'Alessandro, 1990; Roser et al., 1990). Reading literature can also have a dramatic effect on writing. Students who read good books with well-developed literary elements write with higher quality, use more complex sentences, use a greater variety of literary forms (genre), and include a greater range of poetic devices (rhythm, rhyme, repetition, alliteration) (Dressell, 1990). Many artists recall learning by "aping the greats"; when children write they need to believe that they are artists *creating art,* free to employ strategies used by other artists and authors. In the language area of oral expression, a high correlation exists between the amount of experience with literature and linguistic development (Chomsky, 1972). Children who enter school having had hundreds of books read to them (successful readers have been read to some 5,000 hours) know how "book language" is different; people don't normally say things like "he sailed off through night and day and in and out of weeks and almost over a year to where the wild things are" (Sendak, 1963). Reading literature *to* children helps them learn about invisible people whose words speak through print. Jean-Paul Sartre recalled grappling with the notion of "reading."

> Anne Marie sat me down opposite to her, on my little chair. She bent forward, lowered her eyelids, fell asleep. From that statue-like face came a plaster voice. I was bewildered: Who was telling what and to whom? My mother had gone off: not a smile, not a sign of complicity. I was in exile. And besides, I didn't recognize her speech . . . a moment later, I realized: it was a book that was speaking. Frightening sentences emerged from it: they were real centipedes . . . sometimes they disappeared before I was able to understand them; and other times I understood in advance; and they continued to roll nobly to their end without sparing me a single comma.

Sostarich (1974) found good readers usually had been read to from age three, valued reading more, and planned to read throughout life. The rhyme, rhythm, and repetition in good literature like "Mother Goose" lays groundwork for enjoyment and attunes the ear to language sounds. Those rhymes and onsets, vowels and consonant sounds played with in poetry and Dr. Seuss introduce the musical aspect of language that delights and informs us about the feelings of words. In addition, when children are read to they gain general vocabulary and assimilate sentence patterns they hear into speech and writing (Purcell-Gates, 1988). Through enjoyable "lap reading" with parents and hearing teachers read expressively, children also develop the concept of story structure; discoveries about the universal patterns of plot, character, and theme are bedrock for understanding other books and writing original stories. Even young children enjoy discovering motifs—how fairy tales often have "threes" (three pigs or bears or tries), how characters are often all good or bad, and how good triumphs over evil. Understanding the structural elements of fairy tales facilitates children's appreciation for other versions of the story that "play with" and "break" the structural "rules" (e.g. *The True Story of the Three Little Pigs*, Scieszka, 1989; *The Three Little Wolves and the Big Bad Pig*, Trivizas, 1993). Reading to students and providing opportunities for self-selection and times to read independently are means to foster a love of reading. What adults do influences children. The significance of teachers as reading models who demonstrate enthusiasm, enjoyment, and respect for reading cannot be overemphasized.

3. **Literature stimulates interest and gives enjoyment and respite.** Interest is a mighty motivator. People simply read more and better when materials are related to interests; interest accounts for more than twenty-five times the variance in reading comprehension (Anderson et al., 1986). Abundant fictional and nonfictional literature is now available in any area, from sports to fantasy to cooking, and source books like *A to Zoo: A Subject Access to Children's Picture Books* and *The Bookfinder* can help match readers with interests. Teachers can discover students' interests and introduce books that allow students to develop and pursue independent reading (see the sample interest inventory in Appendix D).

4. **Literature provides for the aesthetic need for beauty, pleasure, awe, and joy.** Children's literature should be viewed as an art form, primarily, and a tool for teaching, second. Just like all art forms, books can elicit the Stendhal effect (see Chapter 2 about the power of beauty), and it would be art abuse to think that the instructional possibilities of literature were paramount. Children's literature grew out of an oral tradition of stories that endured because words were made into art, and children seek out literature when they've heard the music of poetry and experienced the thrill of folktale journeys. In our efforts to use the power of literature to boost skills, we may destroy its potential to affect children aesthetically. Rosenblatt's (1985) work on aesthetic reading has made a great contribution in helping teachers think about attuning students to the beauty of books. She believes that when readers adopt an aesthetic stance or approach to a text, they attend and respond to sounds and images associated with words and experience the emotional as well as denotational properties of words. This includes discussion of how a word's sound makes us feel certain things and how words are labels. Children must be given time to experience the potential of books to make us laugh or sob, to stir the imagination with "what if" questions, and to give a new perspective on a problem. In addition, picture books offer a visual art dimension of aesthetic experience through the diverse styles and forms used today.

   We cannot assume that children will automatically gain aesthetic joy from books. Children with reading difficulties may have difficulty suspending belief so that they can use their imaginations (Purcell-Gates, 1991). Experience with being read to may be missing, and the struggling child may see only a troublesome decoding task ahead as she or he confronts a page. A level of fluency is needed to enjoy a story, without having to dwell on word identification, and it may be necessary to use supportive reading strategies like choral reading, taped books, and partner reading so that all can relax and share feelings and thoughts. Even fluent readers benefit from the use of strategies that foster and extend ideas, make connections, help draw conclusions, and evaluate judgments. Chapter 4 has examples like EPC (exciting–puzzling–connecting), Write Right Away, double-entry journals, and student-led discussions.

5. **Literature provokes creative problem solving and higher-order thinking.** Literature is a vehicle that can move us from an egocentric, one-point-of-view perspective into complex abstract thinking (see Chapter 1 on Piaget). At the core of literature and drama is conflict—even in nursery rhymes, albeit introduced and resolved quickly; in three lines Little Miss Muffet encounters a problem—the spider—and solves it by running away. Children must use higher-order thinking skills (HOTS) to analyze and make sense of these problems. It is important for children to be explicitly taught, guided through, and actively involved in creative problem-solving processes as these skills are essential for success outside of school.

   Other thinking skills developed through literature include considering alternative perspectives, evaluating character actions, and deriving personal meanings (themes); for example, when students retell a story from another character's point of view (e.g., Cinderella from the stepmother's point of view), they learn how problems have many sides. In addition, connections to life can be made as students learn how to use *point of view,* a key literary element; for example, after reading Roy Brownridge's *The Moccasin Goalie*, grade three children discussed the issue of exclusion and inclusion in physical activities from the points of view of people with physical disabilities. Kindergartners, too, can abstract generalized themes from literature (Lehr, 1991). The key is that teachers must "model literature as a way of learning about life, participate as learners rather than experts, and offer students choices in how they respond to literature; [then] students are more likely to make strong connections between literature and life" (Tompkins & McGee, 1993, p. 15).

6. **Literature triggers empathy and respect for others.**

Literature is indispensable to the world. . . . The world changes according to the way people see it and if you alter, even by a millimeter, the way a person looks at reality, then you can change it.

James Baldwin

"For decades experienced educators have reported success stories about using children's literature to broaden attitudes toward people from a variety of cultures" (Hansen-Krening, 1992, p. 126). Books can bring us close to characters of every nationality and racial, ethnic, and religious group and lessen the fear of those we don't know. Through literature, readers can meet characters from every imaginable culture, country, and time period. Given the chance to "walk a mile in the moccasins of others" with contrasting beliefs and lifestyles, learners can develop empathy. Beyond sympathy, empathy involves using the senses to perceive and understand another's viewpoint. Empathy includes using emotions and intellect and is much needed in this time when getting along is rated among the highest concerns of business and industry. Combining literature with drama strategies like *empathy roles* allows students to *become* characters from other cultures and share about their lives.

Respect for diversity begins, however, with respect for self and personal background. Through literature, students can discover commonalities among peoples, as well as differences, and in so doing begin to think about positive aspects of their own background. For example, hard work is a value shared among most cultures and is a character trait that pays off in most stories; for example, in the African trickster stories of the lazy spider Anansi. In *Anansi and the Magic Rock*, laziness gets him nowhere and ends up earning him a bad reputation among the other animals.

7. **Literature is part of our cultural heritage.** History has long been passed on through story. The ancient art of storytelling grew out of the need to make sense of human existence and the natural world. Our world treasury of literature is the result of a continuous search for truth and celebration of the uniquely human need to create and consume art. For example, on the surface "Jabberwocky" seems like wonderfully alliterative nonsense, but can be enjoyed for the pure sound of it—wondering at Lewis Carroll's creativity in showing how sense and nonsense collide. His feelings for words are illuminated, his command of his craft revealed, and one is made to think differently about what makes sense and nonsense.

Through literature, children learn the lessons of history. Books allow us to stand on the shoulders of ancestors, the best of whom held fast to strong beliefs about dreams setting the course of life and good conquering evil through the courage of single individuals. Canadian authors William Kaplan and Shelley Tanaka tell the true story of Kaplan's father's and grandparents' escape from the Holocaust in *One More Border: The True Story of One Family's Escape From War-Torn Europe*. The narrative is gripping and the sidebars, archival photographs, and maps assist readers in understanding the geographical and historical context of the story.

8. **Literature addresses big questions and reveals the grandeur of truth in themes.** Good literature deals with universal concerns about how obstacles are surmounted. Sometimes the problems have to do with relationships; other times they grow out of conflict between nature and humans. Literature is appealing because it parallels our interest in discovering the meaning of life, what author Katherine Paterson and psychiatrist Robert Coles have called finding the "secrets of the universe." From the early myths, which explained mysteries through memorable gods and goddesses, to one of the newest genres, science fiction, we have a literary bank to help us consider what we are and imagine what we might become. Through the creative genius of storytellers, we find friends who share private secrets and heroes willing to confront fear and fight evil. We can travel back in time or forward to the future. Books take us places we will never physically go, and yet who has read *Charlotte's Web* and not felt that he has been in the cozy barn, sitting on the stool, watching Charlotte, and listening to the barn sounds E. B. White evokes with artful imagery.

What's more, good literature reveals life truths, often beautifully, and helps satisfy the human need to know. It is through the creative writing form of literature that we are persuaded to think about essential life questions: What is good? right? wrong? What is my place in the world? What contribution can I make? How do I do what I am afraid to do? The themes of literature are the meanings we derive from being engaged with this thoughtful emotional art form. By integrating fine literature into a curriculum, we provide students with a potent tool to pleasurably gain information and learn to apply moral and ethical standards to universal problems that they are likely to confront.

9. **Literature increases self-understanding and knowledge through bibliotherapy.**

> *You think your pain and your heartache are unprecedented in the history of the world, but then you read. It was books that taught me that the things that tormented me most were the very things that connected me with all the people who were alive, or had ever been alive.*
>
> James Baldwin

It is through stories that we are given a palatable way of understanding ourselves—to realize we are not unique nor alone in our suffering. Such insight gives solace. The process of reaching that point has been called *bibliotherapy*, book or story therapy, and involves using books to promote insight or comfort. Stories are thought to "heal the soul" when a person encounters just the right book at the right time (Cornett & Cornett, 1980); readers vicariously experience a character's joys and struggles and actually feel they *are* the characters. While teachers are cautioned not to begin bibliotherapy without careful study, anytime a book is used to give emotional comfort a degree of bibliotherapy is taking place. For example, the Canadian novels *Finders Keepers* (Spalding), *Hey, Chicken Man* (Brown), and *The Daring Game* (Pearson) focus on peer relationships. *Bridge to Terabithia* (Paterson), *Mama's Gonna Buy You A Mockingbird* (Little), *On My Honour* (Bauer), and *A Taste of Blackberries* (Smith) combine the issues of family, peers, and the death of a friend or family member. Teachers interested in the selection of appropriate books and strategies to involve students in the process are encouraged to consult references such as *The Bookfinder.* In the meantime, teachers who select fine literature to meet course of study goals will automatically set up opportunities, especially if they use approaches, such as Rosenblatt's reader response, that call for readers to make personal connections to stories and poems.

10. **Literature stimulates moral thinking about values and issues of right and wrong.** While the teaching of values is a sensitive area, no one denies that children must learn right from wrong and come to understand and behave using common standards for honesty, justice, responsibility, initiative, and so forth. Literature is value laden, and literature integration offers a chance to use personal value systems to think about and respond to conflicts inherent in story. From Aesop's fables to *Goosebumps,* authors write about what they believe is important. They cause characters to act in ways that reveal meaning. Great literature does this subtly and allows many interpretations, while plot-driven mediocre books may leave us entertained, but without increased insight about life issues. The point is that values are important, and we *can* respect the diversity of values of students' families while integrating literature. For example, when students discuss stories with others who bring unique backgrounds to bear on topics, they have a chance to sort out thoughts and feelings and reach conclusions based on broadened perspective. By using a variety of discussion strategies, students learn to question and comment using evidence in the story (text based), connect experiences others may not share, and do creative extrapolations using "what if?" In this chapter and the next, discussion and response strategies are described that target the idea of student-led discussions (see Censorship in Chapter 15 for concerns about objections to particular literature).

11. **Literature gives both meaning and enjoyment.** Like all art, good literature offers both information and entertainment. Think of the best book you've ever read. Did it not *teach* something—facts, main points, concepts? For instance, *Anastasia's Album* (1996), compiled by Hugh Brewster, includes letters written by Grand Duchess Anastasia of Russia and photographs taken by members of the royal family. The photographs and letters provide an intimate look at the last years of the Romanovs. Colour photographs of Russia by Peter Christopher complement the period photographs. The book is beautiful and compelling; readers learn much about the life of Anastasia but are also haunted by the tragic ending to the Romanov family.

12. **Through good books children learn concepts and skills in math, science, social studies, reading and language arts and art, drama, dance, and music.** Can it be by coincidence that in the word *history* there is "story"? History would be a jumble of lifeless facts without its stories, and so would science, math, art, music, theatre, and dance. Integrating literature throughout the curriculum literally means bringing in the stories and poems that give life to numbers and verbs and dates and names. The results can be phenomenal. For example, grade six students who learned history through historical fiction learned more history than those who used the social studies text (Levstik, 1986).

How can stories be integrated into the curriculum? Source books are now available to find picture books on nearly every topic (e.g. *Adventuring with Books: A Book list for Pre-K-Grade 6*, by Sutton, and

Worth a Thousand Words: An Annotated Guide to Picture Books for Older Readers, by Ammon & Sherman). Other aids help teachers find fiction and informational books for social studies and science. There is a math-based literature bibliography in Chapter 4, and the appendix includes an arts-based bibliography divided into art, drama, dance, and music.

What: Teaching With, About, In, and Through the Arts

> *When I was ten, I read fairy tales in secret and would have been ashamed if I had been found doing so. Now that I am fifty I read them openly. When I became a man I put away childish things, including the fear of childishness and the desire to be very grown up.*
>
> C. S. Lewis, 1980, p. 210

Much of what we call civilization and culture is stored in the art created by each generation. Some records of human history are left only on shadowy cave drawings and haunting stone sculptures. We prize these documents for their extraordinary beauty and the insight they offer about who we are and from whence we came. But art and culture have certain ephemeral qualities, and huge quantities of music, dance, and literature have been lost because they were not recorded—literature began as oral art preserved only through the retelling of stories. Early ancestors must have huddled around flickering campfires sharing stories about heroes on noble quests, adventures of clever animals, acts of foolish peasants, and the search for perfect love. Mixed with dance, mime, and song, all literature grew from these tales and became a vast *oral tradition* of fables, rhymes, parables, and proverbs used to both entertain and instruct in primitive societies.

Today *written* literature is taken for granted, and more than 5,000 books published each year in the United States are considered *children's* literature. The Canadian Book Review Annual [CBRA] produces a yearly publication called *Canadian Children's Literature*. This publication provides evaluative guides to the English-language children's books published in Canada each year. The CBRA makes every effort to locate and include all children's and young adult books that were published in Canada in a given year as well as written, illustrated, compiled, and/or translated by Canadians. The 1997 Canadian Children's Literature volume contained 396 entries, and the 1998 volume contained 426 entries. Although Canada's publication of children's literature is much smaller than that of the United States, the number of children and young adult books published in Canada each year has grown substantially over the past twenty years.

How did we come to have such a surfeit of this specialized literature? How did it take shape? All art reflects the milieu in which it was created, and so it is with children's literature. Attitudes toward children and schooling evolved in response to political, social, religious, and economic forces. In between *Aesop's Fables* and *Jumanji* (VanAllsburg) lie centuries of changing beliefs about childhood and children's education, mirrored in stories and poems. Until "childhood" was recognized, there was no literature for children. Another reason has to do with the dual nature of children's literature: *to offer enjoyment and to teach*. During some periods the instructional or didactic purpose has overshadowed the aesthetic; authors and publishers still struggle to maintain balance—after all the audience is children, vulnerable to the power of art to shape thoughts, actions, and feelings. Then there are the children themselves, eavesdropping by ancient hearths to hear tales of journeys plagued with horrific beasts with magical powers, culling out stories with animal characters, fast action, magic, and swift justice. Aesop's fables, now an important part of early literary experience, were not created for children. Only through the evolution of literature, in response to a societal change, did fables became the province of youth. Other books now associated with children, like *Robinson Crusoe* (1719), were also written for the general public. Youth usurped this book, with its captivating characters and adventure; we now think of it as children's literature. When *Treasure Island* was published in the 19th century, children gobbled it up, too, and the story's realism stimulated an appetite for more books in this genre. As new genres now emerge, it is odd to imagine a time when genres like science fiction did not exist.

Definitions: Children's Literature—A Hopeful Idea?

When teachers integrate literature throughout curricular areas, they involve students in *discovering* truths about life from implicit and explicit themes of stories. In many elementary classrooms, students spend significant time discussing, creating, sharing, and performing literature through approaches using daily time blocks to read, write, talk about, and listen to good stories and poems. But what is included in children's literature? Art is difficult to define, and one definition never seems to quite get it all, but two features seem to distinguish *children's literature:* (1) it is intended for a young audience and (2) unlike adult literature, it nearly always holds out a degree of hope. For example, there is hope in *Underground to Canada* (Smucker) that the runaway slaves will reach their destination and be free people. McGinty gives us hope in *Hold on McGinty* (Harty) when he shows his courage to travel across Canada in order to fish again. Most art offers some hope, even if it's just hope born of expanded perspective. Here are three perspectives on what makes children's literature to help you create your own definition.

> [Literature is] an art form, as are painting, sculpture, architecture, and music. (Russell, 1994, p. 212)

> [Literature is] all instances in which language is used imaginatively. . . . Literature speaks of the mysteries of the human condition, although in books for children, treatment of these themes is adjusted according to the age-related interests and capacities of the audience. (Cullinan, 1989, p. 8)

> In both its meaning and in the words and images that convey that meaning, literature encourages a thoughtful, aesthetic response. . . . Literature for children differs from adult literature in degree rather than kind. The same themes or topics may be addressed and the same elements manipulated, but the experiences and understanding of children determine whether a book is "for" them . . . the main characters themselves are often children, and often more emphasis is placed on the actions than on the thoughts of the characters. . . . The book becomes a child's book when children read, enjoy, and understand it. (Glazer, 1997, pp. 5–7)

Basic Goals for Integrating Literature

While there is diversity of opinion about what students should know and be able to do in the art domain of literature, there is also much agreement about (1) studying the historical, social, and cultural role of literature, (2) learning how people communicate through literature by reading, writing, performing, and responding to it, and (3) developing an aesthetic sense by studying the roles of beauty and emotion in words and visual art in literature. To accomplish these goals, classroom teachers who integrate literature throughout the curriculum need to teach the following:

- *The history of children's literature,* including classic books that are part of a common culture.
- *Many good children's books,* found through using selection sources to evaluate and locate books for units (core book, author study, genre study, and topic or problem focused) and books for individual student interests and levels.
- *The basic structure of literature:* literary elements, genre structures, and other types of writing authors use.
- *Actual authors and artists,* including how and why children's authors and artists create literature and art.
- *Many strategies,* to teach students how to understand, create, and respond to literature.

Here is a checklist of titles for folder tabs to organize information for literature integration:

- Literary elements (to think about and write literature)
- Styles, forms, or genres of literature (include bibliographies of each)
- Authors and artists who create children's literature (include biographical information, quotes about and from authors and artists, book lists of their works)
- Significant literature and recommended lists
- Bibliographies of books for each curricular area (e.g., science fiction and science informational books, historical fiction, biography, books about language or parts of speech)
- Bibliotherapy aids (books that can be used to give perspective on problems)
- Approaches to teaching literature (e.g., reader response theory and the critical approach)
- Other possibilities: history of children's literature, science of bookmaking, the math of creating literature (e.g., Edgar Allen Poe's mathematical formulas for "The Raven"), process writing stages, economics (book selling, publishing, advertising)

Instructional Approaches

When determining "what" to teach, it is fundamental for teachers to consider their reasons and goals for integrating literature throughout the curriculum. Teachers must also be cognizant of the influence of their theoretical stances and beliefs. How teachers work with various aspects associated with literary elements and genres will be determined by their underlying theoretical beliefs about literature itself, as well as their personal philosophies regarding the integration of literature throughout the curriculum. There is a continuum of approaches to working with literary elements and genres; some approaches are more analytical in nature and other approaches are more aesthetic, focusing on and extending readers' personal responses to the literature.

Gail Heald-Taylor (1996) describes a framework to assist teachers in identifying the curriculum paradigms they may align with in using literature in the classroom. Heald-Taylor believes that understanding the various curriculum paradigms will help teachers examine their current practices and reflect on ways to enhance the effectiveness of their programs. Heald-Taylor's framework demonstrates how the adoption of each of the three curriculum paradigms, "curriculum as fact," "curriculum as activity," and "curriculum as inquiry," affects the role of teachers, the role of students, the learning materials, the student activities, and the decisions and meaning.

Literary Elements

The elements of plot, theme, character, point of view, and style are the building blocks used to write and understand literature. Authors' decisions create the memorable writings of our literary tradition, as well as forgettable dull works. How can this be so? The elements are but tools in the creative process—it's artistry and imagination that make the magic. By giving students tools, techniques, and materials to work with, we provide them with the chance to read and write creatively. Literary elements assist in understanding the unique attributes of literary genre and subgenre. For these reasons teachers need to understand the elements described below. The teaching of literary elements (i.e. the "how" of instruction) will depend on the teacher's theoretical stances, beliefs, and goals.

Theme *is the unifying truth or universal message in literature.* When we read and write stories and poems, private meanings are constructed as authors reach out to us to make public their messages. These messages are literary themes, value-laden statements that tie a story together. It helps to ask, "What is the story *really* about?" and go beyond just stating the topic. For example, *Charlotte's Web* is about the *topic* of "friendship." To pull a theme together, ask an additional, "What *about* friendship?" One answer is "Good friends stick by you during tough times." This is a clear theme statement. There are two types or ways that themes occur in literature:

Explicit themes are directly stated. These are present as *morals* in fables. In other genres, authors may state themes, but often *imply* them. An explicit theme from *Charlotte's Web* is "Life is always a rich and steady time when you are waiting for something to happen or to hatch" (p. 176).

Implicit themes are not directly stated, but are truth statements inferred by reading between the lines. The theme statement above about the topic of friendship is an implied theme.

Themes can be further drawn out by asking, "What does the author seem to believe?" If he seems to say "We only show courage when we are afraid," then characters, plot, and other elements must unite around this idea. Often, there is more than one theme occurring in a story.

Plot *is the order of events in a story.* The question "What happened?" gets at the plot. Plot is the sequence of events usually set in motion by a *problem* that begins the action or causes conflict. *Conflict* is tension between opposing forces; author Robert Newton Peck calls this the "two dogs and one bone" idea. Conflict motivates characters to act and keeps our interest. Four types of conflict are:

1. Between a character and nature (*Ticket to Curlew* by Lottridge)
2. Between a character and society (*The Hollow Tree* by Lunn)
3. Between the characters (*A Handful of Time* by Pearson)
4. Within a character (*Jasmin* by Truss)

The *climax* is the high point of the plot. Tension breaks, the problem begins to be resolved, and conflict lessens. The *denouement* is the final pulling together or conclusion. All these plot aspects usually come together in patterns. (See plot lines strategy in Chapter 4.) Common plot structure patterns are:

Linear plot pattern: In the beginning section a *problem is introduced.* In the middle section the plot is developed by *rising or increased action,* and there may be several events and consequences. In the conclusion, or end, the action peaks (*climax*), and the *problem is resolved. Cinderella* is an example.

Cumulative plot patterns have repeated phrases, sentences, or events that keep adding up or accumulating, for example, *The Napping House* by Wood.

Episodic plot patterns are like several ministories tied together. For each episode there is a complete linear plot development. An example of this is *Frog and Toad.*

Creative variations in the basic plot patterns can be made using ***cliff-hangers,*** which consist of unresolved suspense, usually at the end of a chapter, and ***flashbacks,*** which create suspense and excite through use of look-backs at previous events or times. This complicates the plot and halts forward progression, because events are out of the chronological time order of the main plot. ***Foreshadowing*** gives a clue or hint about something to come later. It is a way to make the reader feel involved and can add excitement because it heightens anticipation. For example, White foreshadows the conflict with the question "Where's Papa going with that ax?" (*Charlotte's Web*, p. 1).

Character *is a person, animal, or object taking on a role.* Through characters, children can begin to understand the many sides of being human, both the dark and the light. By reaching out imaginatively to characters, a child vicariously lives a slice of another's life and gains perspective on who she is and what she might become. Only with close friends do we share the kinds of secrets that we learn about literary characters. These are the Pooh bears and Cats in the Hat who become dear friends, who make us laugh and weep, who become heroes and heroines and inspire dreams for the future. And then there are horrid characters, like those in folk tales, who show how a character's decision to behave bravely or badly is duly rewarded or punished. A realization that character choices create triumph or failure gives the growing child an important insight—the world is something over which she, as a character in life, has a measure of control. It is through the characters, their motives, actions, and dialogue, that the theme is uncovered. To help children unravel story characters and create their own characters, the following writing categories are helpful:

Characters are shown by: (1) *descriptions,* (2) *actions they take,* (3) *their speech and thoughts,* and (4) *what others think and say.*

- *Protagonist:* the main character (hero or heroine). This is the character who changes the most (e.g., Wilbur in *Charlotte's Web*).
- *Antagonist:* the character who opposes the protagonist by creating obstacles or problems; "between characters" conflict pattern (e.g., Mr. McGregor in Beatrix Potter's *Peter Rabbit*).
- *Round character:* well-developed character. Many traits are revealed, both positive and negative (e.g., Max in *Where the Wild Things Are*).
- *Flat or stock character:* has little or no development, is one sided (all good or all bad); author gives only a few traits (e.g., Prince in *Cinderella*).
- *Dynamic:* character that takes action, makes a substantial change during the story, and causes events to happen (e.g., Peter Rabbit).
- *Static character:* character who does *not* change; may be round or flat (e.g., Charlotte).
- *Foil:* character with traits opposite to the main character. Foils help clarify the protagonist by contrast. Foils are usually flat (e.g., Beauty's sisters in *Beauty and the Beast*).
- *Stereotype:* character who exhibits only *expected* traits of a group. Stereotypes are destructive when they use narrow and negative images.

Setting *is the time and place: when and where.* Setting provides the backdrop or "scenery" for the characters to act out the plot. *When* the story happens may be a past or future time *period* or a certain month or *day. Where* it happens can be vague and unimportant, as in folk tales ("a kingdom far away"), or specific and integral, like the farm on the Canadian prairie in *Dust Bowl* by Booth. In fantasy, setting is especially important because the reader must believe in a whole new world. In realistic stories the setting can function as an antagonist, as in survival stories like *Hatchet* (Paulsen), where a young boy fights the Canadian wilderness. If the title of the story includes the setting, then it is probably more than a mere backdrop; for example, in *At Grandpa's Sugar Bush* (Carney) and *Out on the Ice in the Middle of the Bay* (Cumming), the settings help create mood. The big, homey barn in *Charlotte's Web* creates a different mood than the bustling fair where Wilbur must perform to save himself. The setting can also be a *symbol* of what the story is about; for example, one setting of *Walk Two Moons* (Creech) is a car that, like the main character, is controlled by others and on its way to a mysterious destination. The car with its hard exterior and comfortable interior is a safe place in a time, within a "larger" time that is frightening. The car also foreshadows another important vehicle in the book—a bus.

- *Types of settings:* scenery backdrop or integral.
- *Aspects of setting:* place or location, time or time period, weather.

The ***primary world*** is a realistic world used as a setting for fiction (realism or fantasy). An example is the "real" world of Theo in *Awake and Dreaming* (Pearson). The secondary world is a "created" world used in fantasy. An example is the world Theo finds herself in when she awakens from sleeping on the ferry ride to Victoria to visit her Aunt Sharon. Theo finds herself in a world where she is living in Victoria with the Kaldor family, whom she has watched on the ferry.

Point of view (POV) *is the vantage point from which a story is written.* The angle from which the action is viewed may be through the eyes of one character or many. When one character tells the story and uses "I," the POV is first person and allows the reader to identify with one character; it is used a lot in realistic fiction. Many children's books have an *outside* narrator who sees and hears all, including what's inside characters' minds. This is called the omniscient (all knowing) POV and allows the reader to know many characters; it is as if the author has a godlike power to be in on everything. White takes this POV in *Charlotte's Web* as does Berton in *The Secret World of Og*. An author may combine or alternate first person and a limited version of omniscient POV by using two or three characters.

- *First person point of view:* uses "I" to tell the story; one character's perspective.
- *Omniscient or third person:* an all-knowing point of view using the third person (he, she, it). The narrator tells the story from above the action and can tell about any character's thoughts.
- *Limited omniscient:* same as omniscient, but only a few characters are targeted.
- *Objective:* the third person is used by the narrator to tell the story, but there is no subjective interpretation of what characters feel or of events. The author is like a video camera recording action.

Stylistic or poetic elements *are the creative use of words for artistic effect.* Style is how an author crafts words to express ideas and feelings. In both prose and poetry, carefully selected words determine what we know and feel about character, theme, setting, and plot. When used with skill and artistry, the reader may not notice the poetic devices of rhyme, rhythm, repetition, or figurative language adding impact or beauty or the dialect in which a character speaks, but we feel the effect. An author may choose unemotional language and short sentences to create a controlled seriousness or may use flamboyant words, even nonsense, and defy conventional sentence structure to create humour. To understand style, examine how words are used in special ways:

Figurative language is the use of words to stand for other things:

Imagery appeals to the senses of smell, taste, feel or texture, vision, and hearing. Such language triggers concrete images that engage a reader or listener. For example, "The morning light shone through its ears, turning them pink" (*Charlotte's Web,* p. 4).

Personification: giving of human traits, such as feeling, actions, and the ability to speak, to animals or objects. For example, "The streams and ditches bubbled and chattered with rushing water" (*Charlotte's Web,* p. 176).

Metaphors are comparisons that create mental images because they connect something familiar with something less familiar. By comparing unlike things we see things in novel ways. Simile is a kind of metaphor using an explicit comparison and is set up in the pattern of_____ *is like* _____ or _____ *as* _____ . For example, Charlotte is "about the size of a gumdrop" (p. 37).

Connotation and denotation: denotation is the dictionary definition, while connotation is the use of words in a way that has come to be understood, but nonliterally. For example, saying "the car was a real dog" is using the connotation of the word "dog" to give a feeling.

Motifs are recurring patterns and can be images or events, such as plot patterns. Openings and closings of folk tales are motifs: "Once upon a time" and "They lived happily." Huck et al. (1987) lists six folk tale motifs: (1) a long sleep or enchantment (*Rapunzel*); (2) magical powers (*Cinderella*); (3) magical transformations (*The Frog Prince*); (4) magical objects (*Mollie Whuppie and the Giant* by Muller); (5) wishes (*The Three Wishes*); and (6) trickery (*The Three Little Pigs*). Common *plot* motifs are (1) a cyclical pattern of a young character leaving home, having a dangerous journey, and coming home with new wisdom (*Peter Rabbit*); (2) journeys with obstacles and confrontations with giants or monsters (*Jack and the Beanstalk*); (3) helpless characters (often female) rescued from dire circumstances (*Cinderella*); and (4) miraculous events that help a hero or heroine end up with a happy life (*Cinderella*). These motifs are frequent in traditional literature, but less so in modern genres.

Archetypes relate to motifs, but go beyond being a pattern. They are universally understood symbols, centuries old. Archetypes trigger unconscious and conscious feelings and beliefs through images, situations, events, plot patterns, characters, and themes. Understood the world over, archetypes occur in myths, folk tales, religious ritual, songs, dances, theatre, and visual art forms. Common archetypes are (1) seasons (spring = rebirth and beginning, summer = celebration, autumn = tragedy, and winter = death and despair); (2) plot pattern of the hero on a quest (Odysseus) or the hero rescuing a helpless maiden; (3) colours and shapes (circle = cycles, white = death or purity), (4) settings (forests = danger and the unknown, moving water = journey). Water is used to signal birth, baptism, and transformation. In *Tuck Everlasting* the archetypes of the forest, water, and seasons are all used as symbols, along with the archetype of the cycle of life pattern (see Carl Jung's work on the mandala) (Frye, 1957).

Symbols stand for or represent someone or something else. They are more recent and not as universally understood as archetypes. In *Charlotte's Web,* the web is a symbol of the connectedness of things and how life and death are interwoven. Symbols are difficult to explain since they exist to fill in where words, alone and literally, are inadequate.

Allusions are indirect references to something well known or common knowledge; we allude to "building a house of straw" from *Three Little Pigs* to refer to foolish decisions.

Mood is a feeling created by many literary elements. Style contributes to mood when language signals the emotional state of the story (e.g., humorous or mysterious). Mood is related to the *tone,* which is the feeling infused by using style devices such as sounds of language and imagery.

Irony is deliberately saying the opposite of what is meant. It highlights the discrepancy between what is stated and what is known to be true. By juxtaposing opposite but balanced ideas, a story or poem can be made more interesting. For example, Wilbur says, "I'm less than two months old and I'm tired of living" (*Charlotte's Web,* p. 16).

Humour is the simultaneous juxtaposition of sense and nonsense to produce a surprising result. When Razorhead asks Mike for a Pepsi in Chapter 17 of *It Seemed like a Good Idea at the Time* (Godfrey), Mike replies "We have Coca-Cola Classic. Sorry, no Pepsi. Gives the cat gas you know. The little tabby won't touch it." Razorhead replies incredulously, "Your cat drinks Pepsi?" Mike responds "No, she drinks Coke. Remember, Pepsi gives her gas." Razorhead's insightful commentary is "Wow! What a weird family."

Homophones, homographs, and polysemous words (double meaning) can create puns, riddles, and witty remarks. Poetic language and surprising word use also create humour, like the goose's speech in *Charlotte's Web* ("poking-oking-oking") that makes humour through sound repetition, but make sense, too—if a goose *could* talk, it might sound just so.

Sound and musical features of style include the following:

- *Rhyme:* the repetition of phonograms (sound-spelling patterns that start with a vowel—ack, ick, eet); often at the ends of lines of poetry. (See rhyme patterns under genre of poetry.)
- *Rhythm:* a pattern of sounds. Includes beat and accent.
- *Repetition:* the repeated use of sounds, words, or patterns of words.
- *Alliteration:* the repetition of the same sound in a series (as in the preceding phrase) of words. It refers to beginning sounds.
- *Consonance:* the repetition of consonants any place in a series of words. For example, "slip slop slap" (p) or "little kitten knitting" (t).
- *Assonance:* the repetition of vowel sounds any place in a series of words. For example, the following stanza in Sheree Fitch's poem "The Gnu-Ewe-Cockatoo-Emu All Are Welcome Crew" in *If You Could Wear My Sneakers*:

  Then a gnu asked a cockatoo
  Who asked another two
  Our membership expanded
  How our happy crew grew (p. 6)

- *Onomatopoeia:* use of words that sound like their meanings, such as *whack* or *clap.*

Post It Page 3–3 summarizes the literary elements.

Genre: A Category of Literature That Shares a Set of Similar Traits

In human history, millions of pieces of art and music have been created—millions more stories and poems. To comprehend this vast creative storehouse, we need to separate it into piles, and that's what's been happening for centuries. Several ways to classify children's literature are by age of *intended audience* (baby books), *topic* (humour, travel), *problems* (disease, aging), and *length* (novella, short story). Each has a specific purpose useful in planning lessons and units. Source books, libraries, and bookstores organize by these groupings. Going further, however, we find divisions of a different sort. Poetry and prose represent distinct bodies of writing, with poetry being among the oldest valued writing and clearly a genre all its own with many divisions. Prose also covers a wide range of forms, subject matter, and style; it can be narrative or expository, fiction or nonfiction. Fiction can be subdivided into traditional literature, realistic fiction, fantastic fiction, and historical and contemporary fiction. What is left is nonfiction, which includes informational books from alphabet books to biography. But literature is the creation of human beings who defy classification schemes. Many books fit into many groups and often in more than one genre; for example, picture books are published in every genre from fables to science fiction and are enjoyed by adults as well as children.

Because the goals of integrating literature are to give both meaning and information, as well as an enjoyable aesthetic experiences, knowledge of how literature works is crucial. In addition, teacher genre knowledge helps ensure that students receive breadth of exposure to books and is invaluable to children in understanding books and forms of writing, since the brain operates using categories. A genre is a literary category. Understanding the characteristics of genre improves students' comprehension and provides them with more freedom in writing different genre. This is not to suggest that we subject children to lessons demanding formal, lifeless analysis of genre and elements. If taught effectively, literary knowledge helps us make richer interpretations by finding creative variations on writing patterns that have evolved over time. Once discovered, patterns become tools to adapt present genre and create new genre. Moreover, understanding how *particular* literary elements have significance within a genre helps classify literature and reveal the genre's composition. This knowledge (1) increases appreciation of literature, (2) establishes *generic expectations* to aid comprehension by showing how a story is constructed and why characters act in predictable ways, and (3) helps writing by providing insight into how authors (and artists) use compositional elements to create books.

Each genre has evolved through the imaginative powers of storytellers and scribes and is further divided into subgenres, that is, more detailed classifications; for example, there are several different kinds of realistic fiction. There is a set of genre types in Post It Page 3–2. The discussion that follows includes examples of how literary elements are treated differently in each.

Poetry

Poetry *is a genre of literature with many forms and characteristics that include, but are not limited to, rhythm, rhyme, repetition, and metre.*

Every Friday is Poetree Day in Rebecca Hofmeister's grade five class. Students rehearse during the week and then, on Friday, perform poems they have found or written. They make it sing with their voices, and they dance their poems, too. Using performance techniques such as choral or antiphonal reading, character voices, and sound effects gives life to poetry. After each poem is shared, it is ceremoniously hung on a "poetree" made from a real tree branch set in plaster of Paris. After the weekly performance the class sings a song they wrote together:

Oh Poetree Oh Poetree
How funny are your verses
They make us laugh
They make us grin
They make us feel all good within
Oh Poetree Oh Poetree
Thank you for your verses.

Post It Page • 3-2

Seven Genres and Example Subgenres

Poetry	Couplet, limerick, concrete or shape, diamante, haiku, free verse
Traditional	Folk tales, Mother Goose rhymes, proverbs and parables, fables, myths and legends, tall tales
Fantasy	Animal, toy, and tiny-being tales, modern, folk, and fairy tales, science fiction, high fantasy, time fantasies, supernatural elements, mystery fantasy
Realistic fiction	Contemporary stories about sports, animals, survival, school, and family; also includes mystery; often occur in a series
Informational	Factual writing about art, music, dance, theatre, ecology, psychology, sexuality, technology; also includes alphabet books, counting books, concept books, biography, and autobiography
Historical fiction	Fictionalized memoirs, fictionalized family history, fiction based on research
Picture books	Combines art and text, but can be wordless stories (all art); available in all genre

After a year-long poetry focus, Ms. Hofmeister's class is quick to talk about what they think makes poetry: (1) compact and emotional language, (2) rhythm and rhyme and other sound patterns created by alliteration and repetition, and (3) metaphor and other figurative language. But these aspects of poetry were undoubtedly experienced by these grade five students long before they were conscious of their impact. Through nursery rhymes, Dr. Seuss, and other forms of word play, infants and toddlers learn to enjoy language and hear poetic words that attract attention and give comfort. Poetry is a natural language of childhood that conveys the difficult concept that "to read well one must make music from print." Unfortunately, many children turn away from poetry. What happens to the joyous language play with rhyme, rhythm, and repetition of words and sounds of preschoolers? How can teachers involve children with poetry they do enjoy—usually poems that tell a story or use rhyme, rhythm, and humour—but also provide bridges from light verse to poetry that is more diverse? How can interest in reading and writing a range of poetry be broadened? These are important questions, and answers rest with teachers knowing the basics about this genre and knowing poets and poetry.

Poetry elements are used across genre and are included in the literary element of *style:* imagery, figurative language (personification, metaphors, connotation and denotation, motifs, archetypes, symbols, and allusions), mood and tone, irony, humour, sound, and musical features (rhyme, rhythm, repetition, alliteration, consonance, assonance, onomatopoeia). Then there are the many ***structures*** and forms that poets use to weave their word magic:

- *Verse* is a line of poetry or a stanza, particularly one with a refrain like the verse of a song. ("Verse" is also used to refer to poetry, in general, or light-hearted poetry as opposed to serious.)
- *Stanza* is a grouping of several lines together.
- *Metre* is related to repeated patterns of words, including the beat and accent.
- *Rhyme scheme* is a pattern of rhyming words in a line, stanza, or poem. Letters are used to code lines that rhyme. For example, *abab* is a four-line poem with lines 1 and 3 rhyming and lines 2 and 4 rhyming.
- *Blank verse* is unrhymed iambic pentameter (used a lot by Shakespeare). An iamb is the accent pattern "dah DAH," as in "*Do what?*" Iambic pentameter is five iambs, as in *"I like to eat my peas without a fork."*
- *Free verse* is free of the usual or formal traditional metre or stanza patterns.
- *Lyrical poetry* is flowing, descriptive, and personal, follows no form or pattern, and can be set to music—hence the word *lyric* in both music and poetry.
- *Narrative poetry* tells a story. It usually has no refrain. *The Cremation of Sam McGee* (Service) is an example.
- *Ballads* are narrative poems with short stanzas, with or without music.
- *Sonnets* are fourteen lines long, often in iambic pentameter, and often with the rhyme scheme *abab cdcd efef gg*.

The different forms of poetry have recurring patterns that can serve as scaffolds as children experiment with recording ideas, feelings, and images. Post It Page 3–4 summarizes some of the variety of poem patterns children can find and use for writing. By using creative problem-solving strategies like data gathering and brainstorming, ideas can be generated *before* writing and children can experiment with the feelings and images that words create. Poems can then be written as a whole class, in small groups, or individually. Students do need help learning what they can write poems *about* and the many *ways* in which poetry is written. Without guidance, student interest generally declines as they advance in school (Kutiper, 1985). Without exposure to many types of poems, children, and adults, think poetry must rhyme and be cute. We can broaden the poetry experience for children by sharing the breadth of poetry available so that they come to understand that poetry is about things a poet knows and feels strongly about and is made in many forms, which may or may not include rhyme.

Finding Good Poetry. With the barrage of books published each year, it can be hard to know where to find poetry for a particular unit or a child's interests. Places to start are (1) lists of children's favorite poems and poets, (2) collections of particular poets and anthologies that contain the works of many poets, and (3) poetry awards. Kutiper and Wilson (1993) examined school library circulation records and found the humorous contemporary poetry of Shel Silverstein and Jack Prelutsky dominating children's choices in recent years. Other children's poets that teachers should know include Dennis Lee, Sheree Fitch, Robert Priest, Sean O'Huigin, David Florian, David McCord, Aileen Fisher, Myra C. Livingston, Eve

Merriam, Lilian Moore, Arnold Adoff, Valerie Worth, John Ciardi, Eleanor Farjeon, Ann Hoberman, Langston Hughes, Edward Lear, Ogden Nash, Judith Viorst, Paul Janeczko, and Jane Yolan (Fisher & Natarella, 1979; Kutiper & Wilson, 1993). Post It Page 3–5 lists a *sampling of poets and poetry.* The following poems are common favourites.

Dennis Lee's "Alligator Pie"

Eleanor Farjeon's "Cat"

Ogden Nash's "Adventures of Isabel"

John Ciardi's "Mummy Slept Late and Daddy Fixed Breakfast" and "Why Nobody Pets the Lion at the Zoo"

Ann Hoberman's "A Bookworm of Curious Breed"

Karla Kuskin's "Hughbert and the Glue"

Irene McLeod's "Lone Dog"

Laura E. Richards's "Eletelephony"

Judith Viorst's "Mother Doesn't Want a Dog"

Shel Silverstein's "The Unicorn" and "Sick"

Jane Yolen's "Homework"

Langston Hughes's "Dreams"

Jack Prelutsky's "Willie Ate a Worm Today," "Oh, Teddy Bear," and "The Lurpp Is on the Loose"

Traditional Literature

Folktales . . . resonate with the truths of life across cultures and times.

The names of the creators of most traditional literature have been lost in time, since these anonymous rhymes, folk tales and fairy stories, myths, legends, and tall tales mostly predate the printing press. But this "old stuff" has remained popular, along with modern versions with new twists, like *The True Story of the Three Little Pigs by A. Wolf* (Scieszka, 1991), Jane Yolen's *Sleeping Ugly,* and Munsch's *The Paper Bag Princess.*

***Folk tales** are stories passed down through the oral tradition.* (*Note:* Folk*lore* is the beliefs and customs of a society.) This subgenre includes fairy tales, cumulative stories, talking beasts, and noodlehead and fool stories. Point of view is omniscient and characterization is narrow and static and often includes archetypes: a wicked stepmother, a cunning animal or trickster (Frye, 1957). Settings are vague, with time and place referred to as "long ago in a faraway land" or "in a land before time."

Fairy tales include magical objects, spells, wishes, and magical transformations as key plot events. Characters are either ordinary humans or humanlike animals transformed because of an extraordinary kindness or sacrifice. These are also tales of unfortunate heroines rescued by true love. The characters are often flat and static, and stories contain many stock characters like witches, giants, and fairy godmothers. The themes relate to good overcoming evil or the importance of perseverance and hard work. The style of fairy tales includes the use of conventional openings and closings, repetition, and archetypes: the colours red, black; dark forests; types of water. (See Bettleheim, 1977.)

Cumulative tales have a unique plot structure because characters or objects are added in a chain of events. Animals occur often and sometimes rescue human friends.

Talking beast stories have characters who are anthropomorphized animals. There is usually a lesson at the end, much like a fable. The plot conflict involves a confrontation between two characters who are flat—portrayed as good or bad, stupid or clever.

Trickster tales have a character who outsmarts other characters. The trickster often takes animal form, like B'rer Rabbit in the Uncle Remus stories, or Anansi the Spider in African tales.

Noodlehead or *fool tales* involve characters that are stupid or clever, good or bad. Foolish decisions result in silly consequences, so these tales are full of absurdities that delight and surprise. When characters confront the problem, the story can be like a roller-coaster ride, but by the end everyone is happy. Examples of folk and fairy tales are

Aardema, V. (1975). *Why mosquitoes buzz in people's ears.* Dial.

Climo, S. (1989). *The Egyptian Cinderella.* Crowell.

Huck, C. (1989). *Princess Furball.* Greenwillow.

Louie, A. (1982). *Yeh-Shen: A Cinderella story from China.* Philomel.

Muller, R. (1982, 1995). *Mollie Whuppie and the giant.* Firefly Books.

Paterson, K. (1992). *The King's equal.* HarperCollins.

Trivizas, E. (1993). *The three little wolves and the big bad pig.* Macmillan.

Wallace, I. (1994). *Hansel and Gretel.* Douglas & McIntyre.

Wegman, W. (1993). *Little Red Riding Hood.* Hyperion.

Yolen, J. (1986). *The sleeping beauty.* Knopf.

***Fables** are brief narratives with explicitly stated morals about behaviour.* Main characters are one-dimensional personified animals that are strong or weak, wise or foolish. The plot centres on one event and the setting is a barely sketched backdrop. Conflict is between characters. Theme is stated as a moral at the end. Example collections are

Aird, P. (1997). *Loon laughter: Ecological fables and nature tales.* Carleton University Press.
Lionni, L. (1985). *Frederick's fables.* Pantheon.
Lobel, A. (1980). *Fables.* Harper & Row.
Paxton, T. (1988). *Aesop's fables.* Morrow.
Yolen, J. (1995). *A sip of Aesop.* Scholastic.

***Nursery rhymes** include Mother Goose rhymes and other poetry, light verse, chants, laments, and songs.* They are usually short and full of action and memorable characters—Old King Cole, the crooked man, and pencil-thin Jack Sprat. Some are life stories in a few lines like "Solomon Grundy." Themes have to do with concerns, happenings, and struggles of everyday people, who may be single parents with children to feed or worried about someone not getting home on time. Beautiful lines are contained in the treasure house of Mother Goose such as "Over the hills and far away" and "One misty moisty morning when cloudy was the weather." Like much original traditional literature, they are full of violence and death, from drowning to decapitation. Example collections of nursery rhymes or books based on nursery rhymes are

Ahlberg, J., and Ahlberg, A. (1978). *Each peach pear plum: An I spy story.* Viking.
De Angeli, M. (1954). *Margaret De Angeli's book of Mother Goose and nursery rhymes.* Doubleday.
Denton MacDonald, K. (1998). *A child's treasury of nursery rhymes.* Kids Can Press.
de Paola, Tomie (1985). *Tomie de Paola's Mother Goose.* Putnam.
Little, J. (1991). *Once upon a golden apple.* Viking.
Opie, I., and Opie, P. (1992). *I saw Esau: A schoolchild's pocketbook.* Candlewick.

***Myths** are stories in which gods and heroes have supernatural and magical powers.* Myths explain natural phenomena, such as the origin of the world, human beings, the seasons, and animal features, for example, *pourquoi* (French for why) tales about how the tiger got its tail or the elephant its trunk. Minimal information is given about the setting.

***Legends** are tales usually based in historical fact and originating with a person who did something courageous or made an important contribution to society.* Over time the character becomes regarded as a hero or heroine, and the events related to the deed often become embellished and romanticized. *Epics* are long narratives or poems about legendary figures. The *Iliad* and *The Odyssey* are Greek epics, and *Beowulf* is a Norse epic.

***Tall tales** are based on actual people and some exaggeration of fact is the distinguishing feature.* Tall tales are relative newcomers to the traditional literature genre, with the most well known finding their source in North America. Paul Bunyan, Pecos Bill, Johnny Appleseed, and John Henry are famous characters from this subgenre. Examples of myths, legends, and tall tales are

D'Aulaire, I., & D'Aulaire, E. P. (1967). *D'Aulaires' Norse gods and giants.* Doubleday.
de Paola, T. (1988). *The legend of the Indian paintbrush.* Putnam.
Dixon, A. (1993). *How raven brought light to people.* Macmillan.
Galloway, P. (1995). *Aleta and the Queen: A tale of ancient Greece.* Annick Press.
Galloway, P. (1997). *Daedalus and the minotaur.* Annick Press.
Goble, P. (1968). *Iktomi and the boulder.* Orchard Books.
Hodges, M. (1984). *Saint George and the dragon.* Little, Brown.
Houston, J. (1973). *Kiviok's magic journey: An Eskimo legend.* Atheneum.
Issacs, A. (1994). *Swamp angel.* Dutton.
King, T. (1998). *Coyote sings to the moon.* Groundwood Books.
Lawson, J. (1992). *The dragon's pearl.* Stoddart.
McLellan, J. (1991). *Nanabosho dances.* Pemmican Publications.
Oliviero, J. (1993). *The fish skin.* Hyperion Press.
Steptoe, J. (1984). *The story of jumping mouse.* Mulberry Books.

Fantasy

When I examine myself and my method of thought, I come to the conclusion that the gift of fantasy has meant more to me than my talent for absorbing knowledge.

Albert Einstein

The timeless quality of fantasy has provided us with such diverse classics as *Alice in Wonderland* and *Charlotte's Web.* Perhaps the things most real in life can best be understood through the distant perspective that fantasy offers. How does the creator of fantasy make it so believable? The overlap between traditional literature and fantasy may hold some clues.

In fantasy, reality is abstracted to make special imaginary worlds come to life. The reality-based world helps readers to believe that such worlds exist. For this reason, the setting is integral; time and place significantly affect plot action. For example, in the subgenre of science fiction, a spaceship may house an entire community as in *Star Trek,* where all character actions and thoughts are tied into the *Enterprise.* Themes in fantasy are lofty and have to do with an idealized world of truth and goodness and may evoke strong emotion. Good destroys evil in spite of great odds, but usually with struggle and suspense. Sometimes characters possess supernatural traits, and there are both good and bad characters; a few are round and dynamic, but most are flat and static, firmly on one side or the other of the "dark." Point of view is often omniscient to give readers the necessary background. All this is especially true of *high fantasy* and *science fiction.* The plot is often straightforward, or linear, with few digressions, but with impossible events and magical objects. Often the hero is forced to go on a quest and is pulled into another world that is threatening. There are usually trials to be endured to forge the hero's character, but often there is a protector to help out. When the spirit of the hero is finally honed, he is able to go home. (For more information see Joseph Campbell's *Hero with a Thousand Faces.*)

Key differences in fantasy and realistic fiction are most obvious with characterization, which is more narrow and static in fantasy (and traditional literature). With the exception of a dynamic hero and a small number of round characters, high fantasy is full of flat characters, either good or evil. An idealized "other world," based on what we know to be true, reveals truths through a different dimension. Flat characters allow this abstraction to occur more easily.

The subgenres of fantasy often overlap and include the following:

Animal fantasy has the distinguishing feature of personified animals (e.g., *Charlotte's Web,* in which the magic object is a web and a spider is the protector of the hero pig). Other examples are

Grahame, K. (1961). *The wind in the willows.* Scribner's.
Howe, D., & Howe, J. (1979). *Bunnicula: A rabbit-tale of mystery.* Atheneum.
Oppel, K. (1997). *Silverwing.* HarperCollins.
Oppel, K. (1999). *Sunwing.* HarperCollins.
Selden, G. (1960). *The cricket in Times Square.* Farrar, Strauss & Giroux.

Toy or tiny beings are the peculiarity of one subgenre: *Pinocchio* comes to life to grow a long nose, and inch-high borrowers live under the floor and snatch things in Norton's *The Borrowers.* Other examples are

Hughes, M. (1995). *Castle Tourmandyne.* HarperCollins.
Lewis, N. (1992) *The steadfast tin soldier.* Gulliver.
Lionni, L. (1969). *Alexander and the wind-up mouse.* Knopf.
Van Allsburg, C. (1981). *Jumanji.* Houghton Mifflin.

Modern folk and fairy tales take up the tradition of oral tales in their elements, but are *written* works with identifiable authors. Examples are

Calmenson, S. (1989). *The principal's new clothes.* Scholastic.
Ehrlich, A. (1982). *The snow queen.* Dial.
Thurber, J. (1943). *Many moons.* Harcourt Brace Jovanovich.
Yolen, J. (1972). *The girl who cried flowers.* Crowell.

Fantastic events, situations, or imaginary worlds use exaggeration, the ridiculous, and imagined settings. In Dahl's *James and the Giant Peach,* an unhappy child can travel inside a huge peach, and in Barrie's *Peter Pan,* Never Land is where one never grows up. Example books are

Barrett, J. (1978). *Cloudy with a chance of meatballs.* Macmillan.
Berton, P. (1961). *The secret world of Og.* McClelland & Stewart.
Brittain, B. (1983). *The wish giver.* Harper & Row.
Carroll, L. (1985). *Alice's adventures in Wonderland.* Holt.
Dahl, R. (1982). *The BFG.* Puffin Books.
Juster, N. (1961). *The phantom toll booth.* Random House.
Rowlings, J. (1997). *Harry Potter and the philosopher's stone.* Bloomsbury Publishing Place.
Rowlings, J. (1998). *Harry Potter and the chamber of secrets.* Bloomsbury Publishing Place.
Sendak, M. (1983). *Where the wild things are.* Harper & Row.
Van Allsburg, C. (1985). *The polar express.* Houghton Mifflin.

Time warp fantasy distorts time as we know it, so Tom can enter a special garden that existed in the past in Pearce's *Tom's Midnight Garden.* Other examples are

Babbitt, N. (1975). *Tuck everlasting.* Farrar, Straus & Giroux.
Buffie, M. (1987). *Who is Frances Rain?* Kids Can Press.
Hammond, E. (1998). *Explosion at Dawson Creek.* Ragweed Press.
Haworth-Attard. (1995). *Dark of the moon.* Roussan Publishers.
Laurence, M. (1979-1998). *The olden days coat.* McClelland and Stewart.

Science-fiction fantasy is set in future time and relies on fictional inventions, often extensions of modern technology and scientific fact, for example, L'Engle's *A Wrinkle in Time* and John Christopher's *The White Mountains.* Other examples are

Godfrey, M. (1990). *I spent my summer vacation kidnapped into space.* Scholastic.
Hughes, M. (1980). *The keeper of the Isis light.* Mammoth.
Hughes, M. (1998). *The story box.* HarperCollins.
Lowry, L. (1993). *The giver.* Bantam Doubleday Dell.
O'Brien, R. C. (1971). *Mrs. Frisby and the rats of NIMH.* Atheneum.
Sleator, W. (1984). *Interstellar pig.* Dutton.

High fantasy is a subgenre that has the characteristics of a romance. The forces of good and evil collide in ultimate confrontations. Examples are

Alexander, L. (1968). *The high king.* Henry Holt.
Cooper, S. (1973). *The dark is rising.* Atheneum.
Jacques, B. (1987). *Redwall.* Philomel.
LeGuin, U. (1968). *A wizard of Earthsea.* Parnassus.
L'Engle, M. (1962). *A wrinkle in time.* Farrar, Straus & Giroux.
Lewis, C. S. (1950). *The lion, the witch, and the wardrobe.* Macmillan (Narnia series).
McKinley, R. (1989). *The hero and the crown.* Ace Books.

Supernatural elements and mystery fantasies speak to the human urge to be a little afraid—under safe circumstances. Wright's *The Ghost Comes Calling* is an example, as is the *Goosebumps* series. Other examples are

Bellairs, J. (1989). *The chessmen of doom.* Dial Books.
Bellairs, J. (1995). *The doom of the haunted opera.* Dial Books.
Hahn, A. (1994). *Time for Andrew. A ghost story.* Clarion.
Hancock, P. (1994). *Strange and eerie stories.* Scholastic Canada.
Hughes, M. (1998). *What if...?: Amazing stories.* Tundra Books
Lunn, J. (Ed.) (1994). *The unseen: Scary stories.* Lester Publishing.
Mahy, M. (1982). *The haunting.* Atheneum.

Realistic Fiction

Realistic fiction has had great success among modern children, perhaps because it is closer to life as they know it, a reason that gives pause in light of horrific fantasy being hard on the heels of realism in popularity. The subject matter of realistic fiction includes a child's whole world of relationships with self and others. Some aspects of human life treated in realistic fiction include families (nuclear, extended, alternative), peers, adolescent issues, survival and adventure, persons with disabilities, and cultural diversity. Recently, the content has included a range of alternative lifestyles and views of society, and has addressed sensitive issues like homosexuality, AIDS, and gangs. In most if not all realistic fiction books, authors address more than one of the aforementioned issues. Some popular topics in realistic fiction include sports, mysteries, animals, humour, and formula fiction (i.e. series books). Often there is an overlap of topics in books; for example, Roy MacGregor's Screech Owls series includes elements of sports, mystery, adventure, and humour.

In terms of literary elements, realistic plots are structured using many patterns, but are more given to include flashbacks or other events that stretch out problem resolution. First-person child-narrator point of view is common in young adult realistic novels, probably to give immediacy and facilitate reader identification, but a variety of points of view may be found. Themes are usually related to modern life, and the setting is generalized from reality. Characterization is realistic and fully developed, like ourselves and our friends, showing conflicting emotions and motives. This multidimensionality gives realistic fiction its power to cause reader identification with characters. Examples are

Andrews, J. (1985). *Very last first time.* Douglas and McIntyre.
Bauer, M. D. (1986). *On my honor.* Houghton Mifflin.

Bunting, E. (1991). *Fly away home.* Clarion.
Bunting, E. (1994). *Smoky nights.* Harcourt Brace Jovanovich.
Byars, B. (1977). *The pinballs.* Harper & Row.
Doyle, B. (1997). *Uncle Ronald.* Groundwood Books.
Fox, M. (1988). *Wilfrid Gordon McDonald Partridge.* Kane Miller.
Harty, N. (1997). *Hold on McGinty!* Doubleday Canada Limited.
Hatchet, P. (1987). *Hatchet.* Bradbury Press.
MacGregor, R. (1998). *The Quebec City crisis.* McClelland & Stewart.
McNicoll, S. (1995). *Bringing up beauty.* Maxwell MacMillan.
Paterson, K. (1977). *Bridge to Terabithia.* Crowell.
Spinelli, J. (1990). *Maniac Magee.* Little, Brown.
Viorst, J. (1972). *Alexander and the terrible, horrible, no good, very bad day.* Atheneum.
Wynne-Jones, T. (1992). *The maestro.* Groundwood Books.

Historical Fiction

"Historical fiction is widely viewed as a work of fiction set in a time prior to when it was written" (Temple, Martinez, Yokota and Naylor, 1998, p. 309). Some books deal with recent historical periods, events, and people, while others address distant times. When reading historical fiction, students often need some knowledge of the period and place in which the story is set; in some cases, this knowledge is essential. Well-crafted stories encourage attitudes about caring for and appreciation of others not like the reader and provide rich opportunity to make history memorable. For example, Janet Lunn's *The Hollow Tree*, set during the American Revolution in the Thirteen Colonies, gives both information and emotional connection to real characters and events, but with fictional dialogue. This is the line that separates informational books from realistic ones. The use of historical fiction to teach history should be contingent on (1) the book having an authentic setting and accurate historical details and (2) making clear to students that the book is *fiction*, meaning that aspects of the plot, setting, and characters are invented. The 1998 Newbery Award winner, *Out of the Dust* (Hesse), is a fine piece of historical fiction, as are these:

Avi. (1990). *The true confessions of Charlotte Doyle.* Orchard Books.
Curtis, P. (1995). *The Watsons go to Birmingham-1963.* Delacorte.
Cushmen, K. *The midwife's apprentice.* HarperCollins.
Fleischman, S. (1986). *The whipping boy.* Greenwillow.
Fox, P. (1973). *The slave dancer.* Bradbury Press.
Greene, B. (1973). *Summer of my German soldier.* Dutton.
Lottridge, C. (1992). *Ticket to Curlew.* Groundwood Books.
Lottridge, C. (1997). *Wings to fly.* Groundwood Books.
Lowry, L. (1989). *Number the stars.* Houghton Mifflin.
Naidoo, B. (1986). *Journey to Jo'burg.* HarperCollins.
O'Dell, S. (1970). *Sing down the moon.* Houghton Mifflin.
Pearson, K. (1989). *The sky is falling.* Viking Kestrel.
Smucker, B. (1977). *Underground to Canada.* Clarke, Irwin.
Speare, E. G. (1958). *The witch of Blackbird Pond.* Houghton Mifflin.
Speare, E. G. (1983). *The sign of the beaver.* Houghton Mifflin.

Informational or Nonfiction

These books are fact-based writing about people and natural phenomena, and include biography and autobiography. Informational or nonfiction books include books about all of the sciences (natural, physical, and social), sports, history, biography, drama, art, music, and more. However, children's books are becoming increasingly difficult to classify as fiction or nonfiction because many present information in a story format. Bamford and Kristo (1998) maintain that one helpful way to categorize informational or nonfiction books is to classify them according to the ways in which they are organized or presented. Informational books can be classified into the following categories: narrative nonfiction, biography, photo documentaries, how-to books, activity and experiment books, question and answer format books, survey books, and field guides or identification books.

Narrative nonfiction texts incorporate details and explanations into a story. Successful narrative nonfiction manages to be nondidactic but remain interesting and entertaining as well as informative. *Where the Forest Meets the Sea* (Baker) is a narrative nonfiction picture book that chronicles the reflections of a young boy exploring with his father in the rainforest of northern Queensland, Australia. Baker's illustrations consist of relief collage constructed from a mix of natural materials including lamb's wool, fabric, and leaves. The effect is a rich, three-dimensional perspective on the rainforest which invites the reader to explore the secrets of the rainforest and the majesty of nature. Other examples of narrative nonfiction include

Anno, M. (1979). *Anno's medieval world.* Philomel Books.
Godkin, C. (1989). *Wolf Island.* Fitzhenry & Whiteside.
Godkin, C. (1997). *Sea Otter Inlet.* Fitzhenry & Whiteside.
Kramer, S. (1995). *Theodoric's rainbow.* (Ill. Daniel Mark Duffy). W. H. Freeman & Co.
Tripp, N. (1994). *Thunderstorm!* (Ill. Juan Wijngaard). Dial Books.

Biographies are a form of narrative nonfiction. The information contained in a biography is true, but the style of the telling causes it to be read like fiction. ***Authentic biography*** is a well-documented account of a person's life. Only facts supported by solid research are used, and dialogue or statements by the subject are included only if they are known to have actually been made by the subject. Consequently, there is a heavy reliance on letters, diaries, and the recollections of reliable persons. Even so, it is possible for a biographer to slant even the most solid evidence through highlighting some facts and downplaying others. ***Fictionalized biography*** may be grounded in thorough research, but the author dramatizes certain events and personalizes the subject rather than presenting a straightforward report. Fictionalized biographies are discernible by the amount of dialogue that cannot possibly be historically accurate. ***Biographical fiction*** is different from both authentic and fictionalized biography, in that it consists entirely of imagined conversation and restructured events.

A good biography for children includes supplementary material such as an index, bibliographies of related material, and sources of photographs and other documents. It also avoids sentimentality and oversimplification, just as any other work of nonfiction does. *Anastasia's Album* (Brewster), a book discussed earlier, is a partial and authentic biography based entirely on historical documents found in Moscow and on the recollections and writings of Anastasia's Aunt Olga. The book contains an epilogue that includes information gleaned from Anastasia's Aunt Olga, who had escaped from Russia to Canada during the Russian Civil War. Aunt Olga became a reliable source of information after the deaths of the Romanovs. The book also contains a glossary of terms and a map of Russia as it was during the reign of Nicholas II. There is a detailed list of picture credits, a list of primary works consulted, and acknowledgments of the help provided by individuals from a large number of archives and museums in preparing the book.

This Land Is My Land, an autobiography by George Littlechild, is a picture book more appropriate for readers in grades three and above. Using very simple language, Littlechild tells the story of his ancestry within the Plains Cree Nation. From the birth of his great-great-grandfather in 1858 to the present day, Littlechild relates the story of his people in a moving narrative that attempts to confront bigotry, racism, and poverty, and points to a future in which all people can share the land and its wealth. Like all autobiographies, *This Land Is My Land* represents the opinions and story of one individual.

Photo documentaries first appeared in the late 1970s. A good photo documentary or photo essay must have photographs and text in balance. A heavily illustrated book is not the same as a photo documentary; a photo documentary conveys much of the information through the photographs, and the text is tight and concise. *Journey to the Planets* (Lauber) was one of the best and earliest photo documentaries, along with *Small Worlds Close Up* (Grillone & Genarro) and *The Hospital Book* (Howe).

A wide range of quality photo documentaries are now available, and recent advances in technology have made the photographs and the layout more enticing and more exciting. *A People Apart* (Kenna) was an "Our Choice" award selection (Canadian Children's Book Centre) in 1996. The book reveals the lives of the Old Order Mennonites in Canada, describing their style of clothing, their services at the meeting house, barn raisings, and horsedrawn farm equipment. The book underscores how little life has changed in these communities over the past hundred years. The black-and-white photographs add to the effect of the book.

How-to books are exactly that: how to make a kite, build a boat, play baseball, cook or make paper airplanes. How-to books must be clearly laid out so that readers can follow the directions. One well designed Canadian children's how-to book is *Let's Play* (Gryski). The book contains instructions for playing simple games from leapfrog to sardines and marbles. Two other how-to books are *Hopscotch Around the World* (Lankford) and *The Grandma Poss Cookbook* (Vivas).

Experiment and activity books describe basic science experiments for children to do at home or at school. Generally these books are in a picture book format, designed for interest and enjoyment. Etta Kaner's *Towers and Tunnels* is an introduction to design and technology and is intended to be a resource for children interested in exploring the challenges of engineering. One of the Structures Series by Kids Can Press, this book includes current and historical information about towers and tunnels around the world. Each feat of engineering is accompanied by an activity demonstrating the principles described.

The Science Book for Girls and Other Intelligent Beings (Wyatt) is a collection of activities that explores many aspects of science, and *The Jumbo Book of Nature Science* (Hickman) contains more than a hundred activities and experiments that explore nature indoors and outdoors.

Question and answer books, such as Catherine Ripley's *Do the Doors Open By Magic and Other Supermarket Questions* and *Why do the Stars Twinkle? and Other Nighttime Questions,* are intended for children from preschool to grade two. *You Asked?* (Ferris) contains more than 300 questions and answers about why things happen. The book is divided into chapters on the human body, the technology of everyday life, space, and the natural world. *Funny You Should Ask* (Meekly), winner of the 1999 Ontario Silver Birch award for nonfiction, provides "weird but true answers to 115 1/2 wacky questions" such as "How can chickens run around with their heads cut off?"

The ***survey book*** is defined by Bamford and Kristo as a nonfiction book that provides "an introduction to a topic and includes representative subtopics, but it may not necessarily cover all information" (1998, p. 9). *Cowboy: A Kid's Album* (Granfield) is a fine example of a survey book, as is *A Pioneer Story: The Daily Life of a Canadian Family in 1840* by Barbara Greenwood. Greenwood's book won the Children's Literature Round Tables of Canada Information Book Award in 1995.

The Magic School Bus series by Joanna Cole and the Eyewitness Guides are also survey books. Each book in The Magic School Bus series narrates the adventures of a class of children and their teacher, Ms. Frizzle, on one of Ms. Fizzle's "field trips" (e.g., the solar system, the human body, inside the earth) in the magic school bus. The Eyewitness Guides are available on every topic from the skeleton, trees, insects, fossils, inventions, knights, cowboys, and castles to writing and Ancient Rome.

Field guides, or ***identification books***, are labelling books in their simplest form. A field guide can help a reader identify birds, animals, plants, trees, seashells, tools, houses, and any other area of life that can be categorized and labelled. *The Kids Canadian Tree Book* (Hickman) is an excellent field guide to Canadian trees. The Crabapple Books published by Crabtree Publishing contain a number of field guides for young children (e.g., Horses, Everts & Kalman, 1995).

Canadian Books of Nonfiction for Children

Beatty, O., & Gieger, J. (1992). *Buried in ice: Unlocking the secrets of a doomed arctic voyage.* Random House.

Bondar, B., & Bondar, R. (1993). *On the shuttle: Eight days in space.* Greey de Pencier.

Chase, E. N. (1993). *Waters.* North Winds Press.

Dudley, K. (1997). *Wolves: The untamed world.* Weigi Educational Publishers.

Hedge, D. (1996). *Bears: Polar bears, black bears and grizzly bears.* Toronto: Kids Can Press.

Kalman, B. (1994). *Homes around the world.* Crabtree Publishing.

Love, A., & Drake, J. (1997). *Fishing (Canada at work).* Kids Can Press.

Love, A., & Drake, J. (1998). *The kid's cottage games book.* Kids Can Press.

MacLeod, E. (1994). *Dinosaurs: The fastest, the fiercest, the most amazing.* Kids Can Press.

MacLeod, E. (1996). *Stamp collecting for Canadian kids.* Toronto: Kids Can Press.

Newlands, A. (1996). *Emily Carr: An introduction to her life and art.* Firefly Books.

Raskin, L. & Pearson, D. (1998). *52 days by camel.* Annick Press.

Reeves, N., & Froman, N. (1992). *Into the mummy's tomb: The real life discovery of Tutankhamen's treasures.* Scholastic Canada.

Shell, B. (1997). *Great Canadian scientists.* Polestar Book Publishers.

Springer, J. (1997). *Listen to us: The world's working children.* Groundwood Books.

Suzuki, D. (1994). *If we could see the air.* Stoddart.

Tanaka, S. (1998). *The buried city of Pompeii: What it was like when Vesuvius exploded.* Scholastic Canada.

Thornhill, J. (1991). *A tree in a forest.* Greey de Pencier Books.

Webb, J. (1995). *What's a zoo?* Key Porter Books.

Picture Books

Picture Books use art as well as text to convey meaning, with each playing an important role in telling the story. In some cases, the artwork may tell the whole story (wordless picture books).

Picture books are available in every genre from poetry to information. For today's children, bombarded with myriad visual images, picture books can be an important introduction to *fine* art; we learn visual preferences based on what is seen, so if we expose children to diverse styles, media, and representations of people, children may form more generous and inclusive viewpoints.

Picture books can be used to teach "book parts": *title and half title pages, borders* that may be used to even tell a side story, *gutters* that connect two pages and become important in *double-page spreads* of art over two pages. *Endpapers* are the sheets immediately inside the front and back covers of a book that can be used to set mood with art. Of course, the art styles and media used by the artist are crucial concepts. See the section in Chapter 5 for a discussion and Post It Pages 5–4, 5–7, 5–8 and 5–9 on the visual aspect of picture books. When selecting picture books, it is important to examine the art to see if it dates otherwise timely content and to determine how the media and techniques interface with the mood and tone of a literary work. Ask *to what degree does the art:*

1. *Extend or elaborate* on the setting, plot, characterization, and theme? How do the *art elements* of colour, line, shape, texture, use of space, and perspective do so?
2. *Foreshadow* events *and* show *action?*
3. Show *detail?* Are the details *accurate* (historically, culturally, geographically) and nonstereotypical?
4. *Media* (collage, photography, paint, etc.) contribute to the development of setting, plot, characterization, and theme? How does the media do so?
5. *Style* affect the book? Is the mood created by the art style appropriate to the story?
6. *Interact* with the actual print on the page?
7. Play an *integral* role in the book? Does the art *conflict* in any way? (Adapted from Norton, 1995)

Picture books are available for all ages to enjoy. The most common types of picture books include wordless books, concept books (such as counting and alphabet books), predictable books, easy-to-read books, and picture story books. It is important to remember that there is often overlap among the types of picture books.

Wordless picture books depend on pictures to tell all, and "reading" them requires careful observation and interpretation. Indeed, the "text" is constructed in the mind of the reader. Some excellent wordless picture books include

Anno. M. (1983). *Anno's USA.* Philomel.
Baker, J. (1991). *Window.* Greenwillow Books.
Briggs, R. (1980). *The snowman.* Ramdom House.
Day, A. (1985). *Good dog, Carl.* Green Tiger Press.
de Paola, T. (1983). *Sing, Pierrot, sing.* Harcourt Brace Jovanavich.
Krahn, F. (1983). *The secret in the dungeon.* Clarion Books.
Mayer, M. (1967). *A boy, a dog and a frog.* Dial.
Rohmann, E. (1994). *Time flies.* Crown.
Tafuri, N. (1988). *Junglewalk.* Greenwillow Books.
Turkle, B. (1976). *Deep in the forest.* Dutton (a Goldilocks variation).
Weisner, D. (1988). *Freefall.* Lothrop.
Weisner, D. (1991). *Tuesday.* Clarion.

Concept books attempt to make abstract and concrete ideas more understandable to readers by explaining or exploring an activity such as a given occupation, a concept or idea such as light, or an object such as a boat, rather than focusing on telling a story. Concept books are generally children's first informational books. Some concept books include

Aliki. (1990). *My hands.* Crowell.
Barton, B. (1986). *Trucks.* Crowell.
Hoban, T. (1986). *Shapes, shapes, shapes.* Greenwillow Books.
Hoban, T. 1990). *Exactly the opposite.* Greenwillow Books.
MacDonald, S. (1994). *Sea shapes.* Gulliver.
Nolan, H. (1995). *How much, how many, how far, how heavy, how long, how tall is 1,000?* Kids Can Press.
Oppenheim, J. (1996). *Have you seen bugs?* North Winds Press.

Alphabet books are a type of concept book. Jacobs and Tunnel note that "most alphabet books are not well suited to teaching the ABC's along with their phonic generalizations, and they are not intended to serve such a purpose" (1996, p. 146). Rather, most alphabet books entertain and introduce new vocabulary and concepts. Often the alphabet is used as a categorization scheme or as an organizational structure to present concepts and/or information. *The ABC of Things* (Oxenbury), John Burningham's *ABC*, *A Northern Alphabet* (Harrison) and *A Caribou Alphabet* (Owen) are high-quality alphabet books. Other examples of alphabet books include

Chin-Lee, C. (1997). *A is for Asia.* Orchard Books.
Hepworth, C. (1992). *Antics! An alphabetical anthology.* G. P. Putnam's Sons.
Hunt, J. (1989). *Illuminations.* Aladdin Books.
Pelletier, D. (1996). *The graphic alphabet.* Orchard Books.
Powell, C. (1995). *A bold carnivore: An alphabet of predators.* Roberts Rinehart.
Van Allsburg, C. (1987). *The Z was zapped: A play in twenty-six acts.* Houghton Mifflin Company.
Whatley, B., & Smith, R. (1994). *Whatley's quest: An alphabet adventure.* Angus & Robertson.

Counting books, also a type of concept book, usually assist children in learning basic numbers and provide practice with counting. Most counting books include the printed Arabic number and the accompanying number of like objects on each page. Examples of counting books include

Anno, M. (1977). *Anno's counting book.* Crowell.
Anno, M. (1983). *Anno's counting house.* Crowell.
Geisert, A. (1992). *Pigs from 1 to 10.* Houghton Mifflin Company.
Giganti, P. (1992). *Each orange had 8 slices: A counting book.* Greenwillow Books.
Hutchins, P. (1986). *The doorbell rang.* Greenwillow Books.
Kusugak, M. (1996). *My arctic 1,2,3.* Annick Press.

Easy-to-read books often "use larger print, more space between lines, limited vocabulary, as well as such devices as word patterns, repeated text, rhyming text, and illustration clues" (Tomlinson & Lynch-Brown, 1996, p. 78). The reading level of beginning-to-read books varies as these books may have very few words (e.g., *Rosie's Walk*, Hutchins) or they may include considerable text and be divided into short chapters (e.g., *Frog and Toad are Friends*, Lobel). Other easy-to-read books include

Cohen, M. (1990). *First grade takes a test.* Greenwillow Books.
Fleming, D. (1993). *In the small, small pond.* Henry Holt and Company.
Gelman, R. (1985). *Why can't I fly?* Scholastic-TAB Publications.
Lobel, A. (1981). *Uncle Elephant.* Scholastic Book Services.
Rylant, C. (1990). *Henry and Mudge and the happy cat.* Bradbury Press.
Van Leeuwen, J. (1991). *Amanda Pig on her own.* Puffin Books.
Wood, D., & Wood, A. (1991). *Piggies.* Harcourt Brace & Company.

Picture story books are readily available for children in the elementary grades, and there is a great wealth of high-quality titles. Many picture story books are challenging in both style and content, and are appropriate for older readers. A wide range of topics and themes are represented in picture story books. Some books deal with everyday experiences, and others deal with difficult subjects such as divorce, death, war, and prejudice. The plot structures of picture story books range in complexity from the very simple as in *Who is the Boss?* (Goffin), to the more complex like *Miss Rumphius* (Cooney), to books with parallel plots such as *Black and White* and *Shortcut* (Macaulay). A small sample of outstanding picture story books includes

Andrews, J. (1985). *Very last first time.* Douglas & McIntyre.
Browne, A. (1983). *Gorilla.* Alfred A. Knopf.
Browne, A. (1989). *The tunnel.* Julia MacRae Books.
Burningham, J. (1984). *Grandpa.* Jonathan Cape.
Cannon, J. (1993). *Stellaluna.* Harcourt Brace & Company.
Gay, M. (1998). *Stella star of the sea.* Groundwood Books.
Gilman, P. (1992). *Something from nothing.* North Winds Press.
Henkes, K. (1996). *Lilly's purple plastic purse.* Greenwillow Books.
Innocenti, R. (1985). *Rose Blanche.* Creative Education.
Kusugak, M. (1993). *Northern lights: The soccer trails.* Annick Press.
Lawson, J. (1997). *Emma and the silk train.* Kids Can Press.
Say, A. (1993). *Grandfather's journey.* Houghton Mifflin.
Van Allsburg, C. (1985). *The polar express.* Houghton Mifflin.
Wallace, I. (1999). *Boy of the deeps.* Groundwood Books.

Predictable books contain stories or poems with a repetitive structure. When research showed that children learn to read more easily with stories and poems with a repetitive structure, parents and teachers clamoured for bibliographies of such literature. In addition, these books provide patterns usable as frames or scaffolds to help children write their own books (i.e., make a copycat book). Here are examples classified by unique features:

- ***Repeated phrase, sentence, or refrain.*** These stories often have a musical or poetic quality. In Martin's *Brown Bear, Brown Bear,* a rhythmic question is repeated, "Brown Bear Brown Bear, What do you see?" In Barrett's *Animals Should Definitely Not Wear Clothing,* the title repeats.
- ***Word play and rhyme books*** have predictable word patterns or poetry elements (e.g., couplets or internal rhymes) as in Cameron's *I Can't Said the Ant* and Gwynne's *The King Who Rained* (idiomatic and homophonic expressions with literal art from a child's point of view).
- ***Predictable plots.*** In Charlip's *Fortunately,* a boy has both fortunate and unfortunate events in his life in an alternating pattern.
- ***Cumulative books*** have a series of words and events that repeat and build on one another until a climax is reached. The process is then usually reversed, as in Wood's *The Napping House.*

Multicultural Literature

Multicultural and international or transcultural literature provides a vehicle for promoting the acceptance and understanding of difference. James Banks (1989) defines multiculturalism as an educational reform movement that seeks to affirm equal opportunity for all students to learn regardless of their background, gender, class, race, ethnicity, or culture. The definition by Banks encompasses multiethnic education and global awareness as well as a recognition of racism, prejudice, discrimination, equity, and values. Many educators understand multiculturalism to mean simply an appreciation of ethnic difference, and so they attempt to select literature for use in their classrooms depicting various ethnic and religious groups; books such as *Something From Nothing* (Gilman, 1992), and *Northern Lights: The Soccer Trails* (Kusugak, 1993) meet this requirement. Multiethnic education does indeed refer to the study of the ethnic diversity of society, and the histories, cultures, and experiences of ethnic groups (Finazzo, 1997). Multicultural education is an "integrated teaching process which deals with ethnic groups, religious groups, gender, children's issues, handicaps and special needs, giftedness, ageism, and other important issues that influence and enhance the lives of our citizens" (Finazzo, 1997, p. 101). Multicultural literature is literature that depicts and explores the lives of individuals belonging to a wide range of groups.

Canada proclaims itself to be a multicultural society, and at the present time has the highest rate of population increase in the Western world except for New Zealand (Statistics Canada, 1997). The increase is due to immigration rather than to birthrate, and the phenomenon is strongly reflected in Canadian classrooms, especially those in urban areas. Canada's policy can be described as one of "cultural pluralism," where strength is drawn from the acceptance of different races, ethnicities, languages, and cultures. Nieto describes cultural pluralism as "a model based on the premise that all newcomers have a right to maintain their languages and cultures while combining with others to form a new society reflective of all our differences" (1992, p. 307). Banks (1994) maintains that teachers who apply a multicultural perspective to their teaching honour both the cultural diversity of ethnic groups and the shared national culture.

James Zarrillo (1994) has suggested three categories of multicultural literature. The first category consists of fiction with characters from underrepresented cultural and ethnic groups (for example, Canadians of Japanese descent, Aboriginal peoples, Afro-Canadians, and people belonging to religions other than Christianity). The second category includes fiction that takes the reader to places and cultures outside North America. This is now often termed ***international*** or ***transcultural literature***. The third group consists of information books (including biographies) of underrepresented groups. Some individuals include a fourth category in multicultural literature, consisting of fiction that deals with gender issues and underrepresented social groupings such as gay and lesbian partnerships.

Multicultural books exist in every genre. *Kaleidoscope: A Multicultural booklist for Grades K-8* (Barrera, Thompson & Dressman, 1997) provides annotations of selections of children's and young adult multicultural literature, listed alphabetically and organized topically.

Criteria have not only been developed to test the authenticity of children's literature in general, but also for specific types of literature including multicultural literature (see Finazzo, 1997). Literature can be considered multicultural today when it contains a central character, plot, theme, setting, or style that is culturally or socially diverse in nature. *Very Last First Time* (Andrews), a story about an Inuit girl collecting mussels from under the ice at the edge of the ocean, and *Roses Sing on New Snow* (Yee), a story that takes place in Vancouver's Chinatown, are multicultural in all of these elements. The picture book *The Always Prayer Shawl* (Oberman), a story about the passing on of a prayer shawl through the generations in a Jewish family, is another outstanding example of the successful portrayal of cultural values. Other Canadian multicultural books include

Edmunds, Y. (1993). *Yuit.* Napoleon Publishing. (Traditional Inuit)

Eyvindson, P. (1996). *Red parka Mary.* Pemmican Publications. (Contemporary Aboriginal)

Garrigue, S. (1985). *The eternal spring of Mr. Ito.* Silver Burdett Ginn. (Japanese Canadian internment during World War II)

Gilman, P. (1992). *Something from nothing.* North Winds Press. (Jewish)

Gilmore, R. (1996). *Roses for Gita.* Groundwood Books. (South Asian)

Gilmore, R. (1998). *A gift for Gita.* Groundwood Books. (South Asian)

McGugan, J. (1994). *Josepha.* Red Deer College Press. (Immigrant to Canada, 1900)

Smucker, B. (1977). *Underground to Canada.* Clarke, Irwin. (Black slavery)

Spalding, A. (1995). *Finders keepers.* Beach Holme Publishing. (Aboriginal Canadian)

Takashima, S. (1971). *A child in prison camp.* Tundra Books. (Japanese Canadians in prison camps during World War II)

Truss, J. (1977). *A very small rebellion.* Lebel Enterprises. (Aboriginal Canadian)

Wallace, I. (1984). *Chin Chiang and the dragon's dance.* Groundwood Books. (Chinese Canadian)

Waterton, B. (1978). *A salmon for Simon.* Scholastic-TAB. (Aboriginal Canadian)

Wiseman, E. (1996). *A place not home.* Stoddart. (Refugee child from Hungary)

Yee, P. (1996). *Ghost train.* Groundwood. (Chinese Canadian)

Books by Aboriginal Canadians. There are many Aboriginal-Canadian authors and illustrators publishing material for children. *Harpoon of the Hunter* (Markoosie, 1970) was the first piece of Inuit fiction to be published in English. Since then, many excellent Aboriginal writers and illustrators have published their work in both Canada and the United States. Stories by Aboriginal authors generally embody the values of the individual tribes, and they tend to relate their spirituality in subtle, holistic ways. A common theme among Aboriginal authors is the need for Aboriginal people to learn more about themselves.

Aboriginal Canadian authors and illustrators creating works for children include George Littlechild, Leo Yerxa, C. J. Taylor, Michael Arvaarluk Kusugak, Thomas King, and Jordan Wheeler. Wheeler's short stories for elementary-age children are superbly crafted and highly enjoyable. His work can be found in *Achimoona* (Campbell) and *Adventure on Thunder Island* (King & Wheeler).

The visual elements of culturally diverse books are extremely important, especially in a picture book. The Amelia Frances Howard-Gibbon Award, an award that honours excellence in illustrations from the Canadian Library Association, was awarded to *Ghost Train,* written by Paul Yee and illustrated by Harvey Chan, in 1997, and to *Last Leaf First Snowflake to Fall,* written and illustrated by Leo Yerxa, in 1994. Michael Arvaaluk Kusugak's *Northern Lights: The Soccer Trails,* winner of the 1994 Ruth Schwartz Children's Book Award, is illustrated by Vladyana Krykorka. This book, as with the other books by this writer/illustrator team, embodies the life and spirit of the Inuit people of northern Canada. Other books by Kusugak include *Hide and Sneak, Baseball Bats for Christmas, My Arctic 1, 2, 3,* and *Arctic Stories.* George Littlechild's book *This Land Is My Land* is a particularly stunning introduction to Cree literature, with personal stories about Littlechild's family members and ancestors. The illustrations in the book are unique, and Littlechild's use of colour is spectacular.

Other selections of fiction books by Aboriginal authors and illustrators include

Bouchard, D., & Vickers, R. H. (1990). *The Elders are watching.* Eagle Dancer Enterprises.

Campbell, M. (Ed.). *Achimoona.* Fifth House.

Clutesi, G. (1990). *Stand tall, my son.* Newport Bay Publications.

King, E., & Wheeler, J. (1991). *Adventure on Thunder Island.* James Lorimer.

Loewen, I. (1993). *My kokum called today.* Pemmican Publications.

McLellan, J. (1989). *The birth of Nanabosho.* Pemmican Publications.

Paul-Dene, S. (1992). *I am the eagle free (sky song).* Theytus Books.

Plain, F. (1993). *Amikoonse (Little Beaver).* Pemmican Publications.

Sanderson, E.(1990). *Two pairs of shoes.* Pemmican Publications.

Taylor, C. J. (1994). *Bones in the basket.* Tundra Books.
Waboose, J. (1997). *Morning on the lake.* Kids Can Press.
Weber-Pillwax, C. (1989). *Billy's world.* Reidmore.

International or Transcultural Literature

International or transcultural literature refers to (1) literature that is originally written and published in English in another country and then published in Canada, (2) literature that is written and published in a foreign language in a foreign country and then translated into English and published in Canada, or (3) literature that is written and published in a foreign country for children of that country, and later published or distributed in Canada in the original foreign language. Some individuals include literature set entirely in foreign countries and written and published in Canada in the international literature category as well.

Pratt and Beaty write that "citizenship is extending beyond the traditional boundaries of individual countries" (1999, p. 1). It is important to affirm and celebrate the differences and similarities of the children in Canadian classrooms and throughout the world. It is hoped that through exposure to transcultural or international literature, children will develop a strong awareness of themselves as individuals as well as a sense of the similarities and differences in lifestyles, learning styles, customs, and values of people of varying backgrounds. An underlying goal is to help children develop an awareness of a more inclusive world, and an understanding of how that world relates to those of us living in Canada. Transcultural literature, like multicultural literature, exists in all genres. Pratt and Beaty have proposed guidelines for selecting appropriate transcultural literature for use in classrooms (1999, pp. 13–15).

It is imperative that in transcultural literature, the details of the setting be accurate and authentic. Tololwa Mollel is a Canadian writer and storyteller well known for his retellings of traditional African stories. In *The Orphan Boy*, his first and probably best-known book, the text and the illustrations work together to create the atmosphere and setting of Africa. The book is based on a Maasi legend about the planet Venus, and tells the story of an orphan boy, Kileken, who comes to live with an old man, bringing him good fortune. Other selections of Canadian international or transcultural books include

Bell, W. (1997). *The golden disk.* Doubleday Canada. (China)
Comissiong, K. (1997). *Mind me good now.* Annick Press. (Caribbean)
Matas, C. (1987). *Lisa.* Scholastic. (Jews in Denmark during World War II)
Mollel, T. (1992). *A promise to the sun.* Little, Brown. (African folk tale)
Sacks, M. (1985). *Themba.* Penguin Canada. (South Africa)
Santos, J. (1995). *Jack's new power.* HarperCollins Canada. (Caribbean)
Wolf, G. (1994). *Mala: A women's folktale.* Annick Press. (Indian folktale)
Ye, T. (1997). *Three monks, no water.* Annick Press. (Chinese folktale)
Zhang, S.N. (1995). *The children of China: An arist's journey.* Tundra Books. (Traditional Chinese)

The following is a small selection of high-quality transcultural literature written by foreign authors:

Choi, S. N. (1991). *Year of impossible goodbyes.* Dell Books for Young Readers. (Korea)
Coerr, E. (1993). *Sadako.* Putnam. (Japan)
Dorris, M. (1992). *Morning girl.* Hyperion Books for Children. (Bahamas)
Fox, M. (1987). *Possum magic.* Bradbury Press. (Australia)
Naido, B. (1986). *Journey to Jo'Burg.* New York: Harper Trophy. (South Africa)

How: Integrating Literature Throughout the Curriculum

The study of children's literature is the study of childhood, of human aesthetic development, of human intellectual development, of social development. The purpose of children's literature and its study is to bring the advantages and the joys of reading to all children, for without reading the ideas of the past would be lost forever, and we would be forced naked into the world. The more that we, as adults, know about children's literature, the better equipped will we be to help children discover these advantages and these joys.

David Russell (1994, p. 16)

Guidelines and Principles for Integrating Literature

In Chapter 2 a model for how the arts can be used as teaching tools throughout the curriculum was introduced. The ten principles of meaningful arts integration presented are applied to literature in the next section.

Principle One: INFUSE THE ARTS

A Literary Environment. Visualize a classroom with a carpeted book nook with pillows, a sofa, and a rocker, and stocked with books from every genre and reading level. Some teachers have brought in claw-foot bathtubs and telephone booths, and have built lofts to give comfortable places to read. The chalk tray is a convenient display for "books of the week," with enticing advertising slogans or questions: "*How is maple syrup made? Read* At Grandpa's Sugarbush *to find out.*" Or "*A girl who loved the colour red* - Sarah May and the New Red Dress (Spalding)." Special pages can be tabbed to give readers a quick look, and displays can be connected to units. Poem charts are another way to display literature. Using a wire clothesline, poster-sized charts can be changed regularly. Daily poem sharing is an important routine, so charts make poems ready to go. A poetry wall can be a place to post favourites, and poem pockets can be made from library pockets or manila folders. Students can add art to poem pockets and keep their own anthologies of favourite poems.

Centres and Stations. A centre can be a transportable shoebox of activities or an elaborate bulletin board–table combination. Reading and writing centres may focus on literary genres, such as historical fiction or folk tales, and have activities for students to explore genre characteristics, culminating in original writing in the genre. A block of time each day can be set aside to work at choice stations; time may be allotted for specific work, such as a listening station to hear poetry or stories read by authors that penned them or interviews on tape with authors and artists like Robert Munsch. A listening station can also have music available to listen to during silent reading. A "real-life writing" centre would have examples of common writing forms—invitations, friendly letters, notes of apology, lists, riddles, and job applications (see Post It Page 4–2 for different formats). An alphabetized set of file folders, tabbed with common writing forms, is useful in this type of centre. Stocked with art supplies to mount, frame, bind, or suspend finished writing products, the centre is a "must visit" for students each day. Centre and station visits can be organized with a class chart of names down the left side and a symbol for each centre across the top.

Literature Collections. Invitations for children to share well-loved books, poems, and stories from home, as well as posters and quotes that celebrate books, extend space ownership; we tend to "own" what we help create, so children need to participate in the design of the classroom. When children are encouraged to root out the writers and readers in their families and make public how literature is alive outside of school, everyone benefits. Children are proud to discover uncles and aunts and dads and cousins who write poetry or short stories. Even if the school has a wonderful book collection, the classroom is simply closer than the library. Availability of books is crucial to creating a love of literature. Some schools provide "trade books" for each classroom. Teachers can also begin collecting books in relatively inexpensive ways: send home a letter asking for used book donations, go to garage or tag sales, buy from book clubs like Scholastic (teachers get bonus books), or ask the PTA to conduct an old-fashioned book drive in the community (set limits on what can be contributed). Of particular importance is having multiple copies of books that will be used as core book studies. This means enough copies for small groups to form and read the same book (four to six copies or class sets of books). In addition, teachers need to accumulate *text sets* of literature around unit plans for the year, for example, sets of books, stories, and poems around the topic of weather or text sets of fairy tales for a genre unit.

Principle Two: TEACH Literary Concepts and Elements

Charts of Elements, Banners, and Big Books as Reference Tools. In Chapter 2 the idea of teaching the building blocks of the art forms was introduced. In the area of literature this includes the *literary elements* and the *traits of each genre* so that students have tools to read with more depth and write with greater variety. As mentioned previously, teaching the concepts and elements can be dull and irrelevant if students don't understand how these ideas can be used; this is not information that stands alone in its worth; hence the principle of explaining *why* to learn the elements. In general, the process of teaching elements and other arts content begins with experiencing the art *first*. In literature, this means reading aloud stories and poetry, as well as providing daily time for independent reading. Once students have enjoyed poems, fables, or mysteries in an aesthetic manner, they are ready to discover the inner workings and create their own. This kind of instruction can be summarized by thinking of a teaching sequence that goes *whole–part–whole*. It begins with reading and oral sharing of literature, moves to examining elements and traits, and returns to the whole literature again to generate new works or reread favourite familiar ones with new perspective.

Genre charts, with the traits of a genre down the left side and actual book, poem, or story titles across the top, are tools to help discover examples that support each genre trait. A pocket chart can be used to create a chart by asking students questions such as *"What are the characters like in fables? What do you notice about the action (plot)? How do you know what the fable is really about? Not the topic but the theme?"* As stated earlier, these types of activities are most helpful after students have had opportunities to share and reflect on their aesthetic reading experiences of the books.

Principle Three: TEACHER HABITS to Integrate Literature

Pre–During–Post. A special literature lesson framework divides the teaching and learning sequence into *pre–during–post* stages based on the process that good readers and writers commonly use. Children who are taught about the complementary nature of reading and writing—both are *composing meaning* processes—and how both have three stages become more skilled and motivated, since this knowledge builds independence and fluency. The *pre* or before reading and writing stage is necessary to prepare the brain. This is a getting-ready stage much like the first stage in the creative problem-solving process (see Post It Page 1–5) and includes activating prior knowledge, making predictions, and data gathering. The *during* stage is the doing part, actually reading and writing. This should be a very active stage, with readers asking themselves questions to monitor understanding and using strategies to fix themselves up when they aren't understanding a word or passage. This is a time to *draft* in writing—to just get ideas down without concentrating on spelling or grammar. In both reading and writing, the *during* stage focuses on attending to words—finding, appreciating, and using new ones. Finally comes the *post* stage of reading and writing, which involves pulling ideas together; it entails getting a piece of writing into a final form or responding to a piece of literature through a discussion or an art form that captures themes.

Pre–during–post are parts of an important learning principle about connecting school activities to life through clear *purposes and goals* linked to life, because to reach a goal a person must know it. One strategy to use during the reading or writing processes is **KWL** (Ogle, 1989). In KWL, a chart is divided into three columns. The first is entitled **K** for *What I Know*, the second is labelled **W** for *What I Need to Know*, and the final is labelled **L** for *What I Learned*. The first two columns are used for prereading and prewriting. Students list what they already *know* about a topic. Then they list what they *want* to learn. The class then reads to *learn* more and keeps track of important ideas in the third column. Writing products are then drafted or other arts responses are made based on what was learned.

Encourage Risk Taking and Creativity. If children are to interpret literature aesthetically using genuine personal reactions to beauty and write with passion, it is necessary to form the habit of sharing *examples* of what stories and poems can mean, not giving answers in the attempt to model thinking. Parallel to this habit is being careful to give *examples* of types of writing, to clarify structural conventions, but to emphasize using personal ideas in poems and other writing (See Post It Page 4–2).

Words have the power to give hope and a way to encourage risk taking and creativity: *"That's an original interpretation of the story," "You took the idea of the fable and wrote one never written before"* (flexible thinking), *"You really took a key idea in the book and explained in detail to make us all think more about it"* (elaboration) are comments that teach the creative process, are fun to give, and uplift students. Encourage risking and develop courage by giving *encouraging* messages and feedback.

Creativity is also encouraged by giving choices. Why must everyone write a sequel to a book or a letter to a character? Why should all students read the same stories at the same time all year long? Teachers need a repertoire of choices before they can offer them to students, and throughout this book there are such choices; see Post It Page 4–1, *A Hundred Plus Book Response Options*, options to use *instead of book reports*, and *Things to Write and Say from A to Z* (Post It Page 4–2). Writing literature can also be made more imaginative by using the creative problem-solving process. For example, brainstorming and data gathering work well to get ideas before writing. The process can be used to think about literature, too. For example, data can be gathered, through close examination of picture books, to discover the art media, style, and techniques used.

Structure Group Work. Writers talk with others to get feedback, generate directions, and get angles on ideas. In real life, people pair up to discuss books and join book clubs. At family gatherings, grandparents tell stories that might embarrass grown aunts and uncles, but further bond the family together with laughter and memory. The social nature of literature and writing is a force to put to motivational use. By making it a habit to group students in different ways and allowing choice groups to form based on interests and needs, we can meet the basic need to belong, facilitate exchange of points of view, and develop cooperative skills.

Focus on Process. This habit entails considering the thinking behind students' words, not just whether the words are spelled correctly or all the lines rhyme. What happens *during* the reading of a book or *during* a literature discussion is fundamental to readers' understanding and interpreting that text. It is important to emphasize and model how to be *actively engaged* during reading (make mental pictures in your head, stop and think how the story relates to life, jot down questions to discuss later) and during discussion.

Start with Aesthetic Response and Ask for Evidence. This habit is particularly important for literature discussions or when students are sharing writing. The habit acknowledges literature as an art form, first, and allows students to express feelings and attitudes from the emotional intelligence, which tends to overshadow other intelligences if not permitted expression. Here are example questions to initiate such discussions: *How did the story or poem make you feel? Why? What was the mood of the story? How did the author create the mood? What struck you about how the story was written? How were words and pictures used to create a feeling in the book?*

Look and Listen More Closely. When teachers meaningfully integrate the arts, class time use is changed. Examining art in a picture book to find how text and illustration mesh takes time. Teaching students to engage in significant literature discussions that go beyond plot retellings takes lots of time. There is no doubt that students who are taught to *take time* to look and listen more closely become more interested in books and writing. This is the path to the intrinsic rewards of literature. The poignant moments possible when time is taken to *really* discuss books are remembered and "remember" students—to make them members again—by drawing them into the human family, held together by common beliefs and history, both of which can be known through the vehicle of literature.

Time for a Variety of Individual Projects. When undergraduate teaching students are told *"Book reports are not to be used below ninth grade!"* the class usually cheers. Eighteen-year-olds have fresh memories about book reports and claim that they singlehandedly made many of them not want to read. One of the primary themes of this text is the need to implement multiple intelligences theory and other research on alternative ways of expressing and knowing. A strong implication from this work is using the many real-life writing structures, which form the genres we read, and choice options for literature response. Alternative meaningful options to the book report can be found in Post It Page 4–1, *A Hundred Plus Book Response Options.* Two sources for writing forms are Post It Pages 4–2 and 3–4.

Principle Four: ENERGIZERS and Warm-ups

Just as in other arts areas, we need to help students get ready to read literature and write about it. Chapter 4 includes energizers that have to do with word play and other creative language ideas, and check the energizers and warm-ups from all the arts chapters, since many work for literature and writing.

Principle Five: GREAT CHILDREN'S LITERATURE

What Makes Great Literature? So many books, genre, and literary elements mean many decisions about writing and reading. The goal is to integrate fine literature so that students are immersed in the creative and artistic use of words. This leads to a consideration of what criteria can be used to determine *great* literature. What makes a piece of writing truly excellent? As with all art, this is a sensitive, difficult, and to some extent very personal decision. However, using standards to make wise judgments is crucial for teachers, who must select from thousands of available books. Equally important is for students to learn to present informed opinions derived from anchor ideas about quality. Here are three *anchor concepts* teachers can use.

Creativity. Are the elements used in original ways? Remember from Chapter 1 how a creative idea is not "entirely new," but a twist, stretch, or substitution of others' ideas. The key is whether the author makes a creative leap to mold and shape new characters, context, and plots from the literary clay. Is there energy or a spark to the work that makes it seem alive and leaves us with a sense of rejuvenation and hope? Are the basic and universal themes, motifs, and archetypes varied

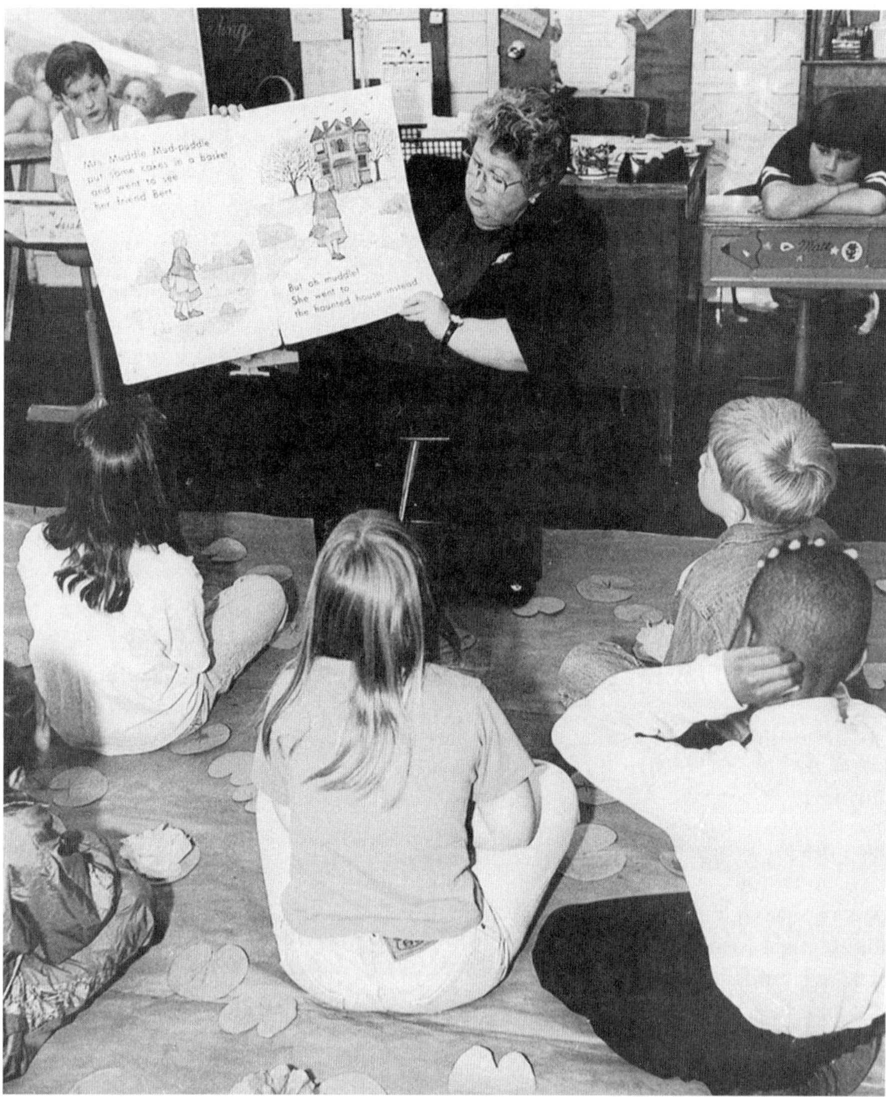

On Monet's Lily Pond

to create a story or poem that seems to be both a new invention and a comfortable friend? Or is the plot tired, the style cliché, and the characters dull?

Unity and Balance. Do the literary elements work in concert to make an integrated whole? Characters may be believable and fascinating, but they need a plot that intrigues the reader and a setting that is appropriate for the story to unfold. Beautiful words that go nowhere soon frustrate even the most poetic soul, and a well-drawn setting without characters to act in it is useless. Finally, as in all good art, we expect good literature to be provocative—a creative invention that will disturb our universe by unveiling enduring truths about people and the world, without ramming them down our throats. We must feel that the story has united the elements in an inviting way and allows readers to make discoveries about themes, rather than be victimized by didacticism.

Taste. A book can be judged high in creativity, unity, and balance (i.e., be a quality piece of literature) and still not be beloved. Judging art always includes personal taste, which has to do with what we like, relate to, feel comfortable with, and just plain suits us at a particular time. Many children's books, such as the series books like Hardy Boys and Nancy Drew, are judged to be mediocre and formulaic by critics, but they are as popular now as they were in the 1950s and are now joined by a host of children's favourites, including The Babysitter's Club and Goosebumps books. Indeed, research has documented a divergence between children's and adults' selection of books (i.e., topics of interest, evaluation criteria). See Activities for a scheme for evaluating children's literature using literary elements.

Awards bibliographies provide another way to find books recommended based on certain criteria. *Children's Books: Awards and Prizes* from the Children's Book Council is a handy book that summarizes most awards. The Canadian Children's Book Centre summarizes Canadian award-winning books on their web site: www3.sympatico.ca/ccb. Also see the literature web site addresses in the appendix. Here are some prominent awards that teachers should know about. The ones with asterisks are listed in the appendix.

- **Newbery Medal Award* (since 1922): Presented by the American Library Association to the American author of the most distinguished contribution to children's literature published during the preceding year. An award winner and runner-up honour books are chosen.
- **Caldecott Medal Award* (since 1936): The American Library Association awards this medal to the artist of the most distinguished picture book published in the United States in the preceding year and recognizes honour books as well. Only U.S. residents or citizens are eligible.
- *Governor General's Literary Awards (Governor-General's Awards for Children's Literature* since 1975*)*: The award was established as the Canada Council Children's Literature Prize. The Canada Council annually awards four prizes are awarded annually by the Canada Council in each of the following categories: text in an English-language book, text in a French-language book, illustrations in an English-language book, and illustrations in a French-language book. Initially, awards were presented for best writing, but in 1977–78 awards were added for illustrations.
- *The Canadian Library Association Book of the Year for Children (*since 1947): Presented by the Canadian Library Association since 1947, the award recognizes the most distinguished children's book published that year by a Canadian citizen. In 1954, an additional award was created for a French-language book.
- *Canadian Library Association Young Adult Book Award* (since 1980): Awarded annually by the Canadian Library Association for the best work of creative literature (novel, play or poetry) for young adults. The author must be a Canadian citizen, and the book must be published in Canada.
- *The Amelia Frances Howard-Gibbon Illustrator's Award* (since 1971): Awarded by the Canadian Library Association, this medal honours excellence in children's illustration in a book published in Canada. The award must go to a citizen or resident of Canada.
- *Elizabeth Mrazik-Cleaver Canadian Picture Book Award* (since 1986): Established by the National Library of Canada and the International Board on Books for Young People in memory of children's book illustrator Elizabeth Mrazik-Cleaver (1932–1985), this award is presented annually, unless no book is judged deserving of the award, to a Canadian children's book illustrator whose work on a new book is deemed both original and worthy.
- *The Geoffrey Bilson Award for Historical Fiction for Young People* (since 1988): Established in memory of respected historian and children's author Geoffrey Bilson, the annual prize of $1,000 has been made possible by the Canadian children's publishing industry. It is awarded to a Canadian author for an outstanding work of historical fiction for young people by the Canadian Children's Book Centre.
- *Mr. Christie's™ Book Award* (since 1980): Sponsored by Christie Brown & Co., a division of Nabisco Brands Ltd., the award was established to encourage the development and publishing of high-quality Canadian children's books and to stimulate children's desire to read. Books must be created by a Canadian author and/or illustrator. Currently, there are three categories in both English and French.
- *Information Book Award* (since 1987): Established by the Children's Literature Roundtables of Canada, this award recognizes an outstanding information book for children ages five to fifteen, written in English by a Canadian citizen, and published in Canada during the previous year.
- *Hans Christian Andersen Award* is an international award, given every two years, and is sponsored by the International Board on Books for Young People. A living author is honoured and, since 1966, a living illustrator whose complete works are an important contribution.

- *Orbis Pictus Award* is sponsored by the National Council for the Teachers of English and is given to an author for excellence in nonfiction for children published in the United States.
- *Children's Choices* are lists of "best books" selected by children. The list is published annually in the October *The Reading Teacher,* a journal of the International Reading Association.

Source books are resources to help teachers and parents find books and information about books and authors. Post It Page 3–6 lists useful sources to find books for integrated arts units.

Classic literature is "news that stays news" (Ezra Pound) and includes books that have endured the test of time; they continue to delight and inform audiences. The significance of the theme, credibility of the characters, reality of the conflict, and a style that engages are why some books remain in circulation. This relates to the discussion about human needs in Chapter 1: we need to know, belong, feel safe, and have beauty in our lives. Horn Book publishes a list of such children's classics, as do organizations like the Children's Literature Association. (See the list of organizations at the end of the chapter.) On nearly every list are Aesop's fables, Andersen's fairy tales, Mother Goose rhymes, Perrault's fairy tales, *Charlotte's Web, Little Women, Winnie the Pooh, The Wizard of Oz,* and *The Adventures of Huckleberry Finn,* among others.

Principle Six: ROUTINES

Effective daily routines to make literature integration a way of life in the classroom include the following:

Expressive Daily Reading. The focus of this kind of teacher oral reading is on giving an aesthetic experience—hearing good literature read interpretively. Through expressive daily reading, teachers engage children in making "mind pictures" from "word music," and they hear book language, very unlike normal talk. When a teacher reads a book like Oppel's *Silverwing* to a third grade, students hear words and think about ideas that may very well be above their *reading* level, but match their *interest* level. In addition, experiencing a book together bonds a group in the way that singing does. Expressive daily reading should be scheduled each day and may include pre–during–post reading arts responses, like those Mrs. Weiss used to prepare for and follow up *Very Last First Time.* In addition, pausing to discuss words and inviting students to chime in with predictions increases involvement.

Independent Reading. There are many names for the classroom routine involving silent reading of choice books each day. SSR stands for "sustained silent reading," SQUIRT is "Super quiet uninterrupted independent reading time," and DEAR is "drop everything and read." Whatever it is called, it is essential for children to read and not just have lessons *about* reading. Crucial to the success of this routine is the full participation of everyone, including the teacher, who acts as a role model. Here are the basic guidelines to ensure success.

- Plan a regular time of ten to twenty minutes (shorter at first and with younger children).
- Everyone needs a book ready and an extra book in case the book is finished during SSR.
- Everyone should be in a comfortable place and stay put. Teachers may allow buddy or partner reading, especially with young children who need to read aloud or have the support of a partner. Books on tape may also be used as a support.
- After reading, time may be planned to record responses in lit logs and discussed in small or whole group. Generic questions can be used: What was the most exciting or interesting part? What were some special words? How did the pictures make you feel and why? What have you figured out about the characters? (See the *generic discussion questions* in Post It Page 3–7.)

Repeated Reading. This routine is especially important for beginning readers who need regular practice with skills to become fluent. Fluency, in turn, increases enjoyment of literature. By reading the same story or poem several times, students become familiar with the text and gain confidence and comprehension. Through repeated readings, beginners realize that words have meaning and can be said many ways to give personal interpretation. Thus vocabulary grows.

Literature Discussions. Begin discussion routines by assuming that they are a rewarding human experience that all will *want* to participate in. Once students learn how to use the process, it holds excitement and unmatched potential to make meaning. It is through talking out thoughts and listening to others that students create a web of meanings, but discussions that promote interconnecting are not made of question and answer turn taking between teacher and students or of dull plot retellings. On the contrary, they are more like "grand conversations" (Eeds & Wells, 1989) among people who have all shared in the same experience (know the plot already) and wish to share. This implies a leadership shift away from the teacher. However, teachers need to provide instruction about how to *prepare for* and *participate in* discussions among equals.

Student-led Discussion. The goal is to eventually have students hold their own small-group discussions in which all come away with new perspectives. This is a learned skill that becomes an art as students are guided through the process. To begin, develop discussion rules.

- Everyone who has read the book can participate. Come prepared with questions or issues to discuss.
- Finding different interpretations is important.
- Opinions should be supported with examples or evidence.
- Differences of opinion are respected and accepted.
- Restate the other person's idea before you present an opposite opinion.
- Think about how the book connects to your own life and to other books you have read.
- Show you are an active listener with "body talk" and by responding to the ideas of others with positive comments.

In addition, students need ways to organize thoughts so that they feel prepared to share. Even adults are reluctant to speak up if they don't feel prepared or feel their point of view will not be respected. There are several discussion strategies in Chapters 4, 5, 6, and 8. Here are a few to get started:

1. ***Discussion cards.*** Each student is given an index card to jot down interesting ideas she or he wants to discuss. The goal is to cause students to become engaged with reading and prepare for a student-led discussion. Some categories to give students to think about are important events, puzzling things, exciting parts, emotional parts, and connections to other texts.
2. ***EPC charts*** (Cornett, 1997). Students are given a frame with the categories of exciting part, puzzling part, and connecting part. (These can be three large circles or three columns.) During reading, students note sections that fit into these categories (*connecting* means parts that relate to your life) and jot down page numbers. Ask students to star the one or two that they want to discuss.
3. ***Read alouds.*** Students choose a part of the story or poem that they want to read aloud as a discussion focus. They should be able to tell why they chose it (e.g., important event, use of language, connected to their lives). Students rehearse the section so that the reading will be pleasant for all. Suggest to students that the section be a certain length and discuss the importance of voice intonation and expression when reading aloud.

Strategies to Organize the Actual Discussion. After students read and prepare, it is time to begin: (1) Take a few minutes and role play the discussion rules. For example, *"Show me you're an active listener." "Use your face and body to make me believe." "Now show me you are not listening actively."* Practise giving each other descriptive feedback, paraphrasing ideas, and asking clarification questions with partners. (2) Sit in a circle so everyone can see. To create comfort when starting discussion routines, the *fishbowl* technique can be used: Volunteers come into an inner circle to discuss while an outer circle listens in. At stop points, members of the outer circle have a chance to follow up on comments made by the volunteers in the middle. Next, the circles exchange positions. This helps all to learn to really listen, as well as speak. (3) Use the Write Right Away strategy with a good question—one that requires students to connect their lives to the text and to extend their thinking in some way.

During the discussion, students can be encouraged to participate by starting with volunteers or calling on students (all should have something prepared). The web of meaning is made stronger when student responses are woven together by questions like *"What do the rest of you think about Shannon's idea?"* and *"Did anyone have the same idea?"* and *"Is this a new idea for anyone?"* or *"Who has another idea that relates to Shannon's"* and *"What in the story supports Shannon's idea?"* Periodically stop and ask students to recap the most important ideas that have been shared so far.

The discussion can be brought to a conclusion by asking students to comment on the ideas shared during the discussion (e.g., most important or new idea, common or conflicting points of view).

Post It Page 3–7 includes recommended *generic questions for discussing literature* to post so that students can choose questions to discuss and become skilled at creating their own questions, with the focus on asking about things that they really *care* or *wonder* about.

Reading and Writing Workshops. These are routines that include other routines like free reading. Blocks of time are set aside to read and write, with a focus on trade books, poetry, and a variety of writing generated in the writing process (prewriting, during, and afterwriting strategies). During workshop times, students may write in Arts for Life journals, lit logs, and Look Back and Laugh Logs (journals on humour in their lives), do SSR, repeat readings, or work at learning centres.

In the case of literature, students write original pieces and then gather around a special chair in which one student sits to read his piece. Listeners are directed to be active nonverbally and think of questions and comments to give the reader. Feedback is given, another student proceeds to read, and so on. This strategy helps children to feel that writing is more than an assignment, because it becomes a way to share feelings, emotions, and ideas. For example, students write a fantasy during a genre unit using the genre characteristics learned. The author's chair is used to share. See Atwell (1998), Bainbridge & Pantaleo (1999), and Tompkins (2000) for information about reading and writing workshops.

Book Ads or Talks. The purpose is to interest others in a book. Weekly or daily times can be set for students to do book ads. Children have seen so many TV and radio ads that they can offer ideas for what makes a good ad, and the teacher can demonstrate how to do a two or three minute ad with an *introduction* (attention getter; tell book title and author, display a few pictures, read chapter titles or book blurb, or share author facts), *development* (read short excerpt; perhaps a section of dialogue), and *conclusion* (ask for predictions about the book and invite the audience to read the book to find out if they are right). Students may choose to make a tape or a video or write a jingle or slogan, too. Ads are more interesting if props, visual aids, and music can be used.

Weekly Reader's Theatre Presentations. Students can do *expressive* oral reading of their original scripts or those of others. The focus is on using just the voice to create a "theatre of the mind" (see Reader's Theatre in Chapter 8).

Principle Seven: ADAPT CURRICULUM

In Chapters 1 and 2, the concept of teaching *with, about, in* and *through* the arts was introduced, and this can be applied to the integration of the art form of literature. The goal is to get beyond casual entertainment *with* books and narrow artificial writing assignments; students need to learn significant information *about* literature and its creators and how to use these ideas *in* writing and reading. Beyond the *about* and *in* is teaching *through* literature by connecting books and writing to science, social studies, math, music, art, drama, and dance so that all curricular areas are enhanced. The curriculum delivery models discussed in Chapter 2 can be adapted for literature integration.

Curriculum Documents. It is important to plan with curriculum documents in hand. Integrated units should focus on life-centred issues and questions, be adapted to accommodate for student diversity, and be structured so that depth of learning happens. In integrated units, discipline-based methods, as well as content (facts, broad trends, and concepts that organize each discipline) are combined into a meaningful whole. How do students learn about justice, power, human rights, or interdependence? Textbooks offer explanations and definitions, but the arts, and in this case, literature, offer the *lives of people.* In Paul Ye's *Ghost Train* (1996), readers travel with Choon-Yi from China to British Columbia to join her father who is working on the railway. However, upon arriving in the new world, she discovers her father has been killed in an accident. Choon-Yi uses her artistic abilities to release the soul of her father as well as those of the many other Chinese men who have been killed building the railway.

Readers meet Charlotte Haines in *Charlotte* (Lunn, 1998), a true story about an eight-year-old girl who was disowned by her father and banished from New York to Canada with many other Loyalists in 1783. Charlotte grew up along the Saint John River, and one of her grandchildren, Sir Samuel Leonard Tilley, became premier of New Brunswick and one of the Fathers of Confederation in 1867.

Four Integrated Unit Structures. Unit structures can be planned for varying lengths of time. Four unit types centre around (1) core or single literary work, (2) genre (focus on traits), (3) person, or (4) problem or topic or theme question. An excellent book, story, or poem can be the core work, any literary genre can be a focus, an author and/or artist of picture books can organize a unit on the person's life and works, or a unit can be designed around real-life issues (see Chapter 2 for examples). The nine-legged unit web is a planning device to integrate curricular areas with one of the four unit centres. An author–artist unit web is included in Post It Page 5–6. Information sources and guidelines for artist–author studies appear in Post It Page 3–6 and in Chapter 5, along with names of authors and artists for this kind of unit.

The Two-Pronged Integrated Lesson Plan. The concept of an integrated arts lesson, with at least a two-pronged focus (an art form and another curricular area) and a teaching sequence with the introduction, development, and conclusion (IDC) pattern, was introduced in Chapter 2. This suggested structure can be used to plan and teach lessons that integrate literature with other curricular areas.

Principle Eight: TAKE FIELD TRIPS

Tips for Trips: Before–During–After Guidelines. Literature-focused trips include visits to art museums to compare with picture book art the styles, media, and art elements used; to public libraries to hear stories or talks about special collections; to the newspaper to understand publishing; or to studios or artists or writers.

Principle Nine: EXHIBIT STUDENT PROGRESS

Create a School Museum with Ongoing Displays. Displays of books that students have made based on the different genres and of literature response projects, are important items to include in a school museum. Many book response projects are arts activities, and the overlap between visual art and literature allows the "minigallery" for art projects to function as a way to share excitement about books. Displays of poetry anthologies that children write or collect are another example of a way to show off growth and make an event out of an assignment completion.

Class Library of Books Children Write. It is not unreasonable to expect all children to write and bind many books in a school year. These can be class collaborative books, co-authored books, and single-author works. The project nature of writing and bookmaking motivates students and is a *concrete progress indicator.* Books can be pocketed and placed in a special class library. Autographing parties can mark the "publication" of each new book.

Portfolios. Portfolios of student writing have become a staple in elementary and middle schools. Besides writing samples, students can show literary growth through logs of books read, charts that show the distribution of reading across genres, and lists of favourites (characters, words, books, authors). Literature log entries and other written responses to literature can be included to document growth toward specific goals and objectives. A way to make portfolios meaningful and manageable progress exhibitions is to organize the collecting with items connected to goals attached to the front of the portfolio.

Individual Conferences. Key assessment information is gathered during times when students "show they know" in a one-on-one setting. It is ideal to have at least a five-minute conference weekly with each student to review the portfolio, discuss progress, and set goals (e.g., plan book responses or review a list of books each child wants to read). Conference time can be used to discuss books and listen to a child orally read to check fluency progress. It is helpful to keep a conference notebook, with a page for each child, to note goals and progress made toward each goal.

Principle Ten: SPECIALISTS Are Important Resources

Many teachers and librarians are specialists who can work collaboratively to enrich literature integration. A good librarian can help find excellent trade books for a social studies unit or a genre study. To find book specialists, use the idea of creating a directory, using computer technology to survey and list interests and talents. There are poets, novelists, authorities on genres, and artists among the faculty and staff of most schools.

Children's Authors and Artists. Writers and illustrators of children's literature travel to schools for residencies and draw admiring audiences at conferences. An author or artist visit is an exciting occasion, but, as with any art event, planning is critical. A package produced by the Canadian Children's Book Centre (CCBC) contains two resources to assist in planning an author or illustrator visit. The package includes *Company's Coming: How to Host a Successful Author or Illustrator Visit* (1999) and the Canadian Children's Book Centre's *1999/2000 Directory of Authors and Illustrators Available for School and Library Visits* (1999). Here are tips for planning to work with children's book writers and artists.

- Plan early, even a year in advance. Most authors and artists make school visits, but not all. Contact the latest publisher to make arrangements with an appearance coordinator.
- Plan a budget to cover the author's honorarium, travel, food, etc.
- Phone interviews aren't usually free. Generally, \$50 to \$75 for a half-hour is expected, and you need a speaker phone for the whole class to benefit.
- Decisions have to be made about the agenda for the day, what you want the author to do, how many presentations, how to handle autographs, and ordering books in advance.
- Request publicity materials from the publisher (e.g., biographies in quantity, black and white pictures, book lists, posters, bookmarks, and jackets).

- Prepare the students: do an author–artist study, read lots of books, see videos and listen to tapes, respond to books, and make lists of questions to ask the author.
- Have definite curricular objectives for the visit to get the most out of it. Expect students to get both enjoyment and information from the visit.
- Follow up visits with "what did you learn" activities and thank-you notes from students.

Conclusion

21st Century: Trends

Social, religious, and economic forces continue to influence human history and the evolution of children's books. The definition of childhood will no doubt change in the next era, with a distinct effect on literature for children. It is already apparent that children are expected to be independent earlier and, some say, are hurried into adolescence. With many overscheduled and overstressed, we must ask questions about the roles literature can play in their lives and how books can be viable in a media-saturated world. How *can* entertainment and enjoyment be balanced with information and instruction as we integrate children's literature throughout the curriculum? Multicultural and feminist concerns about contemporary literature exist, and progress can be monitored on the web sites of book publishers. Teachers will need to increase connections between the interests of youth and books if they are to influence reading habits. Perhaps the nature and concerns of childhood will change so radically that some books will not be relevant. We need to consider this possibility in our integration efforts. We must also take seriously possible abuses of literature, as we implement research on its power to motivate children to read, write, and learn in curricular areas. Literature needs to be regarded for its aesthetic nature, and not simply as a tool to achieve literacy. Finally, children will undoubtedly continue to cull from the book supply the literature that gives them information and enjoyment, just as they have for centuries. Informed adults can share with children both contemporary literature and enduring classics that encourage reflection on what it means to be human.

Post It Page • 3-3
Literary Elements

Theme: *the unifying truth or universal message in literature.*

Key question: What is the story or poem really about? (Go beyond a topic to a complete truth statement.)

Explicit themes: messages directly stated.

Implicit themes: indirectly stated truth statements.

Plot: *the order of events in a story set in motion by a problem or conflict.*

Key question: What happened?

Four types of conflict: between (1) character and nature, (2) character and society, (3) character and another character, (4) within a character.

Types of plot patterns: *Linear three-part:* Introduction–Development–Conclusion (includes *climax* and *denouement*); *Cumulative:* events build on one another; *Episodic:* mini-stories tied together.

Techniques to vary plot patterns: *cliff-hangers, flashbacks, foreshadowing.*

Character: *person, animal, or object taking on a role.*

Key questions: Who is it about? Who wants something? Who is a problem? Who changes the most?

Ways characters revealed: (1) descriptions, (2) their actions, (3) their speech and thoughts, (4) what others think and say.

Types: *protagonist/antagonist, round or flat/stock, dynamic or static, foil, stereotype.*

Setting: *the time and place.*

Key questions: When and where does the story take place?

Types of settings: scenery backdrop or integral.

Aspects of setting: place or location, time or time period, weather.

Primary world: real world.

Secondary world: a created world used in fantasy.

Point of View: *the vantage point from which a story is written.*

Key question: Who is telling the story? How?

First person point of view: uses "I" to tell the story.

Omniscient or third person: all-knowing, using third person (he, she, it).

Limited omniscient: omniscient but only a few characters.

Objective: events reported with no interpretation.

Stylistic or poetic elements: *creative use of words for artistic effect.*

Key question: How are words used in special ways?

Figurative language is the use of words to stand for other things: *imagery, personification, metaphors, connotation and denotation, motifs, archetypes, symbols,* and *allusions.*

Mood is the feeling created. Mood is related to the *tone.*

Irony is deliberately saying or doing the opposite of what is meant.

Humour is the simultaneous juxtaposition of sense and nonsense to produce a surprising result.

Sound and musical features of style include *rhyme, rhythm, repetition, alliteration, consonance, assonance,* and *onomatopoeia.*

Post It Page • 3-4

Poem Patterns

Suggestions: Orally share poetry before showing it. Ask students to examine poems to make discoveries and brainstorm about personal and important ideas, images, and feelings in poems. Encourage varying repetition in lines and words and the use of poetic elements like alliteration, rhyme, onomatopoeia, imagery, and metaphor. See the special section on poetry in Chapter 4.

Repeated lines: Write as many lines as desired using these frames.

I wish . . . *I wish the sky would stay red all day. I wish I could touch a cloud.*

Colour poems *Yellow is . . . Red is . . .* (see *Hailstones and Halibut Bones* as an example).

Is . . . *Thunder is . . . Happiness is . . .*

I used to (think or feel), but now I (think or feel) *I used to think poetry had to rhyme, but now I think I can just write my feelings and have a good time.*

Five sense *Sounds like . . . Looks like . . . Tastes like . . . ,* etc.

If I were . . . *If I were a light bulb / I would glow hot and bright / So people could read in bed*

Five-line poem: Each line has a focus: (1) a thing, (2) a person, (3) special place, (4) a feeling, (5) a sound.

Riddle poems: Give three clue lines with the first most general and the third most specific.

Easy to carry. Full of words inside. Rhymes with cook. _ _ _ _

Lie poems: Each line is something not true (do collaboratively).

Preposition poem: *Within the drawer / In a desk / Inside the metal tray / Like a row of teeth* (staples in a stapler).

Concrete or shape: Words of a poem are placed on the page to look like the poem's topic (e.g., a swing, tree, ocean, a kiss shape for a love poem).

Couplet: Two lines that end in rhyming words. *What if trees / Had knobby knees?*

Triplet: Three lines that rhyme.

Quartet: Four lines with a variety of rhyme patterns: *aabb, abab, abcb, abca.*

Clerihew or bio poem: Quartet about a person: *Pat Benne / Did marry Kenny / But they are poor / And want money more.*

Limerick: Humorous five-lined rhymed verse with an *aabba* pattern. The rhythm pattern is important:

There once was a cat on a porch
He sat in the sun 'til he scorched
Both his paws and backside
Were both nearly fried
So his friends starting calling him "Torch."

Syllable and word count poems

Haiku: Japanese lyric verse consisting of three unrhymed lines. The subject is nature and there are seventeen syllables in the entire poem distributed by line as 5–7–5.

Tanka: Five lines with these syllables per line: 5–7–5–7–7.

Cinquain: Five-line poem that does not rhyme. Number of words per line: *2–4–6–8–2* (subject, adjectives, action, feeling or observation, adjective/synonym).

Diamante: Seven-line poem, shaped like a diamond. Pattern for each line: one noun, two adjectives, three ing words, four word phrases or four nouns, three ing words, two adjectives, one antonym. *Note:* The poem topic can be reversed in the middle to relate to the antonym. For example,

Halloween
Spooky Fun
Running Screaming Eating
Costumes Candy Bunny Baskets
Hunting Coloring Singing
Happy Pastel
Easter

Found poems: Random phrases are cut from magazines, newspapers, or greeting cards. Phrases are arranged until any form of poem is created (need not rhyme).

Other pattern possibilities: Tongue-twisters, jump-rope rhymes, and advertising jingles.

Post It Page • 3-5

Poets and Poetry: A Sampling

Collections of Single Poets

Adoff, A. (1979). *Eats.* Lothrop, Lee & Shepard.

Chertle, A. (1994). *How now, brown cow?* Browndeer.

Fitch, S. (1987). *Toes in my nose and other poems.* Doubleday.

Fleischman, P. (1988). *Joyful noise: Poems for two voices.* Harper & Row.

Florian, D. (1994). *Beast feast.* Harcourt Brace Jovanovich.

Greenfield, E. (1988). *Under the Sunday tree.* Harper & Row.

Grimes, N. (1994). *Meet Denitra Brown.* Lothrop.

Hughes, L. (1994). *Sweet and sour animal book.* Oxford University Press.

Lee, D. (1977). *Garbage delight.* Macmillan Canada.

Livingston, M. C. (1986). *Earth songs.* New York: Holiday House (see also *Sea songs* and *Space songs*).

Lobel, A. (1983). *The book of piggericks.* Harper & Row (limericks).

Moss, Jeff. (1989). *The butterfly jar.* New York: Bantam.

Pomerantz, C. (1982). *If I had a paka: Poems in 11 languages.* Greenwillow.

Prelutsky, J. (1976). *Nightmares: Poems to trouble your sleep.* Greenwillow.

Prelutsky, J. (1984). *The new kid on the block.* Greenwillow.

Silverstein, S. (1974). *Where the sidewalk ends.* Harper & Row (also *A light in the attic* and *Falling up*).

Yolen, J. (1990). *Bird watch: A book of poetry.* Philomel.

Anthologies (many poets under one cover)

Bryan, A. (1997). *Ashley Bryan's ABC of African American poetry: A Jean Karl book.* Atheneum.

de Paola, T. (1988). *Tomie de Paola's book of poems.* Putnam.

de Regniers, B. S., Moore, E., White, M. M., & Carr, J. (1988). *Sing a song of popcorn: Every child's book of poems.* Scholastic.

Dunning, S., Leuders, E., & Smith, H. (1967). *Reflections on a gift of watermelon pickle, and other modern verse.* Lothrop, Lee & Shepard.

Kennedy, X. J., & Kennedy, D. M. (1982). *Knock at a star: A child's introduction to poetry.* Little, Brown.

Nye, N. (1992). *This same sky: A collection of poems from around the world.* Four Winds.

Prelutsky, J. (1999). *The 20th century children's poetry treasure.* Alfred A. Knopf.

Worth, V. (1994). *All the small poems and fourteen more.* Farrar, Straus, & Giroux.

In Picture Book Form

Baylor, B. (1977). *Guess who my favorite person is.* New York: Scribner's

Blake, W. (1993). *The tiger.* Harcourt Brace Jovanovich.

Fitch, S. (1992). (Ill.by M. Mongeau). *There were monkeys in my kitchen.* Doubleday.

Fitch, S. (1995). (Ill.by M. Kovalski). *Mapel Murple.* Doubleday.

Frost, R. (1988) (Ill. by E. Young). *Birches.* Henry Holt.

Granfield, L. (1995). (Ill.by J. Wilson). *In Flanders Fields: The story of the poem by John McCrae.* Lester Publishing

Hopkins, L. (1993). *Poems of Halloween night: Ragged shadows.* Little, Brown.

Johnson, J. (1993). *Lift every voice and sing.* Walker.

Lesser, C. (1997). *Storm on the desert.* Harcourt Brace.

Lobel, A. (1984). *A rose in my garden.* Greenwillow.

Longfellow, H. W. (1990) (Ill. by T. Rand). *Paul Revere's ride.* Dutton.

Noyes, A. (1981) (Ill. by C. Keeping). *The highwayman.* Oxford University Press.

Pomerantz, C. (1974). *Piggy in the puddle.* New York: Aladdin.

Thayer, E. L. (1988) (Ill. by P. Polacco). *Casey at the bat: A ballad of the Republic, sung in the year 1888.* Putnam.

Westcott, N. B. (1988). *The lady with the alligator purse.* Little, Brown.

Award-winning Poets

Book of the Year for Children (Canadian Library Association) was awarded to *Alligator Pie* (Lee, 1974) and *Garbage Delight* (Lee, 1978).

Information Book Award in Canada awarded to *In Flanders Fields: The Story of the Poem by John McCrae.* (Granfield, 1995).

Excellence in Poetry for Children Award (given by the National Council of Teachers of English) since 1977 for a body work). ***Recipients:*** David McCord, Aileen Fisher, Karla Kuskin, Myra Cohn Livingston, Eve Merriam, John Ciardi, Lilian Moore, Arnold Adoff, Valerie Worth, Barbara Juster Esbensen.

The Newbery Medal has gone to two poetry books: *A Visit to William Blake's Inn* (Willard, 1981) and *Joyful noise: Poems for two voices* (Fleischman, 1988).

Horn Book Magazine and the *Bulletin of the Center for Children's Books* regularly review poetry.

Post It Page • 3-6

Locating and Selecting Literature

Use the resources to find books for genre studies, problem or topic studies, author and artists units, read alouds, bibliotherapy, and particular age groups. Also see Teacher Resources at the end of the chapter.

A to zoo: Subject access to children's picture books, 4th ed. (1993). Bowker.

Adventuring with books: A book list for pre-K and grade 6 (1997). National Council of Teachers of English.

Accept me as I am: Best books of juvenile nonfiction on impairments and disabilities (1985). Bowker.

Children's books: Awards and prizes. Children's Book Council (revised periodically).

Award-winning books for children and young adults. Scarecrow (annual publication).

Best books for children: Preschool through grade 6, 4th ed. (1990). Bowker.

Books kids will sit still for: The complete read-aloud guide, 2nd ed. (1990). Bowker.

Books to help children cope with separation and loss, 2nd ed. Bowker.

Canadian children's literature. Canadian Book Review Annual. University of Toronto Press (annual publication).

Children's books in print. Bowker (annual edition).

Choosing books for children, rev. ed. (1990). Delacorte.

The elementary school library collection: A guide to books and other media (1992). Brodart.

Hear no evil, see no evil, speak no evil: An annotated bibliography for the handicapped (1990). Libraries Unlimited.

Horn Book guide to children's and young adult books. Vol. 7, No. 2 (1996). Horn Books.

The literature of delight: A critical guide to humorous books for children (1991). Bowker.

Our choice. The Canadian Children's Book Centre (annual publication).

Pass the poetry please (1987). HarperCollins.

Science and technology in fact and fiction: A guide to children's books (1989). Bowker.

Author–Artist Studies

Contemporary authors: A biographical guide to current writers in fiction, general non-fiction, poetry, and journalism, drama, motion pictures, television, and other fields (122 volumes). Gale Research.

Something about the author: Facts and pictures about contemporary authors and illustrators of books for young people (1971+) (Vols. 1–50). Gale Research.

A state-by-state guide to children's and young adult authors and illustrators (1991). Libraries Unlimited.

An author a month (for pennies) (1991). Libraries Unlimited.

Bookpeople: A first album (1991). Libraries Unlimited.

Bookpeople: A second album (1991). Libraries Unlimited.

An author a month (for nickels) (1990). Libraries Unlimited.

Behind the covers: Interviews with authors and illustrators of books for children and young adults (1990) (Vol. 2). Libraries Unlimited.

Something about the author autobiography series (1986–1987) (Vols. 1–4). Gale Research.

Sixth book of junior authors and illustrators (1989). Wilson.

The storymakers: Illustrating children's books (1999). Pembroke.

The storymakers: Writing children's books (1999). Canadian Children's Book Centre.

Twentieth century children's authors, 4th ed. (1995). St. James.

Post It Page • 3-7

Generic Questions for Discussing Literature

Guidelines: Choose *one* or *two* questions in each discussion segment to go into in depth. Have students stop and write down ideas related to a question before talking about responses so that there is reflection *before* and focus *during* the discussion. Remember that the keys to comprehension are connecting text to students' lives and causing them to respond to literature cognitively and aesthetically. To increase aesthetic response, read the story *first for pleasure,* and reread using questions like those that follow to guide thought.

Look at the title and a few pictures; then ask:

Who do you think this is about? When and where? (characters/setting)
What might this story be about? (theme/plot/characters)

Read a bit; then ask:

What kind of person do you think this character is? How do you know?
What do you think the character should do? Why? (critical thinking)
In your opinion, what are the important things that have happened? Why are they important? (plot)
Whose story is this? (point of view)
What do you notice in the pictures? (colour, texture, shape, line, perspective) How does this affect the story?
What do you think will happen? Why? What would you like to find out?

Read more; then repeat from above or ask:

What do you now know that you didn't know before?
Did any questions get answered? (confirm/reject predictions)
What events are important? How do you know? (critical thinking)
Do any words or language stand out? Why? (style)
What does this story make you feel? Why? (illustrations, mood)
Does the dialogue tell you anything about the main character?

After the entire reading ask:

What did you like? What were your favourite parts? Why? (critical thinking)
What was this story about? (themes/key concepts)
Was there anything in this story like something in your life? (connections)
Do you think it was right that . . . ? Why or why not? (critical thinking)
Was . . . a believable (seem real) character? Why? (evaluation)
Was there anything special or important about . . . ? (inference)
What will you remember about this story next week? next year?
Is this story like any others you've read? (connections)
Was there anything special or unusual about the illustrations?
How did the author make the story interesting? (style)
Does the story tell you anything about people and behaviour?
Did the story end the way you thought it would? Why or why not?
Did the characters change in the story? If so, how and why? (characterization)
Why do you think the author wrote this story?

Teacher Resources for Integrating Literature

Also see Bibliography of Recommended Reading and Viewing in the appendix.

CHILDREN'S LITERATURE WEB SITES

Below is a small sample of the approximately 600,000 web sites that focus on some aspect of children's literature. Not only do sites "come and go," but sites regularly update their information and revise their offerings. It is important to remember that once a site is accessed, one can easily link to other sites that provide additional information and references.

1. **Starting Points.** The following are excellent starting points for surfing the web for children's literature sites. Each leads to more specific information.

The Children's Literature Web Guide
www.acs.ucalgary.ca/~dkbrown/
This is the most comprehensive Internet site on children's literature. This site includes resources for teachers, parents, storytellers, writers, and illustrators. D. K. Brown's site is very popular, and many other children's literature sites link back to this one. The following are some of the subsites located in the Children's Literature Web Guide.

Web-Traveller's Toolkit: Essential Kid Lit Websites
Conferences Bulletin Board
Children's Literature Organizations on the Internet
Lots of Lists: Recommended Books
The "Lots of Lists" site includes lists of best books, banned books, subject bibliographies, and award-winning books.

Carol Hurst's Children's Literature Site
www.carolhurst.com/

This site contains a collection of reviews of excellent children's books. The books are rated on a three-star system: recommended, highly recommended, and outstanding. Hurst's past articles and sections from her professional books offer ideas about themes, curriculum, and other books and services.

Kay Vandergrift's Special Interest Page
www.scils.rutgers.edu/special/kay/kayhp2a.html

This special interest page allows visitors to link to many other sites generated by Dr. Vandergrift. Some of these links include Censorship, the Internet, Intellectual Freedom, and Youth; Materials for Children; Gender and Culture in Picture Books; Materials for Young Adults; Linking Literature with Learning; History of Children's Literature; and more.

How Novel!: Canadian Young Adult Literature
strobe.lights.com/novel/welcome.html

This online resource is produced by the Saskatoon Public Library. The site features information on Canadian fiction written for readers aged 12 to 18 and focuses on materials written from 1985 to present.

Fairossa Cyber Library: Children's Literature
www.users.interport.net/~fairrosa/door.html

This site allows visitors to access several other links including articles about children's literature, book lists, book reviews, information about authors and illustrators, and other children's literature web sites.

2. **Resource, Reference and Bibliographic Materials.**

Internet Sources for Children's Literature
www.unisa.edu.au/library/internet/pathfind/childlit.htm

This guide is designed to assist visitors in finding electronic resources in various disciplines. It contains useful starters such as "AskERIC", Children's Bookwatch, Fairrosa's Cyberlibrary, and Canadian Children's Literature Service Collection Electronic Products. It also provides connections to discussion lists such as KidLit and Childlit and newsgroups, and links to electronic journals such as the Canadian Review of Materials.

Children's Literature Reference
mahogany.lib.utexas.edu/Libs/PCL/child/

An electronic bibliography of children's references to guide visitors to basic resources in the area of children's literature. Topics include awards and honours; classics; authors and illustrators; genres; teacher resources; suggested web sites; reviews and criticisms; and electronic journals.

Canadian Children's Literature Service: National Library of Canada
www.nlc-bnc.ca/services/eelec.htm

Information is available about Canadian children's award-winning books, Canadian authors and illustrators, and Internet sites that pertain primarily to Canadian children's literature. This site also identifies suitable books for children and young adults written in both English and French. Books date from the nineteenth century to present day.

Children's Literature: A Library Timesaver—SFU Libraries
www.lib.sfu.ca/kiosk/finlayso/childlit.htm

This site lists useful children's literature reference books. It also explicates the research steps for accessing children's literature resources by discussing a number of frequently asked questions on the topic. Found in the table of contents are the online catalogue, and links to journal articles, reading lists by age and genre, book reviews, and electronic information.

The IPL Youth Division: Reading Zone
www.ipl.org/youth/lapage.html

The International Public Library site focuses on the following: Ask the Author, Story Hour, and a Writing Contest. The link "World of Reading" contains book recommendations written by children.

The Canadian Children's Book Centre
www3.sympatico.ca/ccbc/

This organization was formed to promote and encourage the reading, writing, and illustrating of Canadian children's books. The web site contains information about the CCBC, Our Choice (book recommendations), reviews, recommended links, and details of a writing contest.

CM: Canadian Review of Materials
www.umanitoba.ca/cm/

This is an electronic journal that reviews Canadian materials for pre-kindergarten to young adults. It provides descriptions of books as well as author and illustrator profiles.

3. Links to Other Sites

Children's Literature: Suggested Web Sites Worth Visiting
www.lib.utexas.edu/Libs/PCL/child/sites.html

This site provides links to children's literature under the following categories: Associations and Discussion Lists; Children's Literature Information Sites; Electronic Books and Serials on the Web; Indexes, Abstracts, and Internet Searching Aids; Libraries; and Sites Especially for Kids.

Around the Net
www.macabees.ab.ca/net.html

The creators of this site claim to have identified the best sites that feature information about Canada, Canadian authors, and Canadian literature. The following are some of the recommended sites:

The Canadian Children's Book Centre
Children's Literature Web Guide
CCL: Canadian Children's Literature (periodical)
The National Library of Canada: Forthcoming Books

4. Specific Topics. The following sites deal with specific issues or special topics in children's literature.

NICHCY A Guide to Children's Literature and Disability
www.kidsource.com/NICHCY/literature.html

This site is intended to assist parents/guardians, teachers, and other professionals in identifying books that are written about or include characters who have a disability. Books are categorized by age group or grade level appropriateness. This site also includes a guide to other children's literature selections about particular disabilities.

Multicultural Book Review Homepage
www.isomedia.com/homes/jmele/homepage.html

This home page allows visitors to link to reviews of multicultural books and to other multicultural web sites.

Dealing With Sensitive Issues Using Children's Literature
www.scils.rutgers.edu/special/kay/issues.html

This site lists books that identify sensitive issues in regards to inclusion, multiculturalism, and gender. It also provides guidelines and resources to refer to when dealing with sensitive issues in children's literature.

Mathematics Is Elementary: Suggested Children's Literature
206.106.95.11/groups/mathematics/booklist.htm

This web page identifies children's books that focus on various mathematical concepts.

Classics in Children's Literature

www.scils.rutgers.edu/special/kay/classics.html

This site encourages the visitor to read or reread books that have achieved classic status in children's literature. Some books are completely reproduced online. Visitors are invited to consider whether these works appeal to and are of interest to today's young people, or whether these books should be retained as historical artifacts.

Audio Visual Sources for Children's Literature and Authors

Booklist (published by the American Library Association) reviews AVs in each issue.

Elementary School Library Collection: A Guide to Books and Other Media, Bodart.

American School Publishers, Box 408, Highstown, NJ 08520

Pied Piper, P.O. Box 320, Verdugo City, CA 91046

Houghton Mifflin, 2 Park Street, Boston, MA 02108

Weston Woods, Weston, CT 06883

Journals (Research, Articles, Reviews of Books)

Bookbird (International Board on Books for Young People)

Booklist (American Library Association)

Books Links (American Library Association)

Bulletin of the Center for Children's Books (University of Illinois Press)

Children's Book Review Index (Gale Research)

Children's Literature in Education (APS Publications)

Horn Book Magazine (Horn Book, Inc.)

Journal of Children's Literature (National Council of the Teachers of English)

Language Arts (National Council of the Teachers of English)

The New Advocate (Christopher–Gordon Publishers)

Reading Teacher (International Reading Association)

School Library Journal (Bowker)

Activities:

Reasons to Integrate Literature

Take a few minutes to make a reference list of important reasons to integrate literature that you might use as you discuss this topic with parents, school administrators, and community members.

Evaluating Children's Literature Using Literary Elements

Directions: Try your hand at evaluating a piece of children's literature. If an element is very evident, circle 1; not evident, circle 5. Indicate 2, 3, or 4 for ratings in between. Circle NA for not applicable.

Plot

1. Has sense of momentum based on the conflict.	1	2	3	4	5	NA
2. Conflict is clear and believable.	1	2	3	4	5	NA
3. Does not depend on coincidence.	1	2	3	4	5	NA
4. Original, not *dully* predictable.	1	2	3	4	5	NA
5. Suspense created by not allowing obstacles to be resolved easily or choices easily made.	1	2	3	4	5	NA
6. Includes subplots and/or flashbacks that enhance without overly complicating.	1	2	3	4	5	NA
7. Contains a climax of action or hints that the conflict will be resolved.	1	2	3	4	5	NA

Theme

1. Universal truths or meaning that can be understood on more than one level.	1	2	3	4	5	NA
2. Contains one or more subthemes to support main theme.	1	2	3	4	5	NA
3. Provokes reader to confront a problem or see life as it might be.	1	2	3	4	5	NA
4. Avoids imposing values, prejudices, and opinions.	1	2	3	4	5	NA

Characters

1. Revealed through:						
a. Physical description	1	2	3	4	5	NA
b. Actions	1	2	3	4	5	NA
c. Speech and thoughts	1	2	3	4	5	NA
d. Others' thoughts and words	1	2	3	4	5	NA
2. Mostly developed through action rather than description.	1	2	3	4	5	NA
3. Believable, original, convincing, and consistent (i.e., age, background, ethnicity).	1	2	3	4	5	NA
4. Protagonist is a character who changes or grows.	1	2	3	4	5	NA
5. Foils and flat characters are used novelly.	1	2	3	4	5	NA
6. Avoids stereotypes.	1	2	3	4	5	NA

Setting

1. Sets the stage for coming action with details and background.	1	2	3	4	5	NA
2. Time and place developed or implied by references to well-known site or language use.	1	2	3	4	5	NA
3. Details are appropriate to the time and place.	1	2	3	4	5	NA

Point of View

1. Strongly influences how the characters are revealed.	1	2	3	4	5	NA
2. Contains an amount of objectivity appropriate to the reader's maturity level.	1	2	3	4	5	NA

Style

1. Language appropriate to the characters and intended reader's age.	1	2	3	4	5	NA
2. Language used in artistic and creative ways, but without drawing attention to itself.	1	2	3	4	5	NA
3. Used effectively to create mood.	1	2	3	4	5	NA

Conclusion

How well written is this piece of children's literature?	1	2	3	4	5	NA

(1 = well written to 5 = poorly written)

References

Books and Articles

Alexander, J. (1997). *imagine!* Washington, DC: National Endowment for the Arts.

Allen, J., et al. (1991). I'm really worried about Joseph: reducing the risks of literacy learning. *The Reading Teacher,* 44, 458–472.

Ammon, B., & Sherman, G. (1996). *Worth a thousand words: An annotated guide to picture books for older readers.* Englewood, CO: Libraries Unlimited.

Anderson, R. C., et al. (1985). *Becoming a nation of readers: The report of the Commission on Reading.* Washington, DC: National Institute of Education.

Anderson, R. C., et al (1986). Interestingness of children's reading materials. In R. Snow & M. Farr (eds.), *Aptitude, learning and instruction.* Hillsdale, NJ: Erlbaum.

Atwell, N. (1998). *In the middle: New understandings about writing, reading, and learning (2nd ed.).* Concord, ON: Irwin Publishing.

Bainbridge, J., & Pantaleo, S. (1999). *Learning with literature in the Canadian classroom.* Edmonton, AB: The University of Alberta Press/Duval House Publishing.

Bamford, R., & Kristo, J. (1998). *Making facts come alive: Choosing quality nonfiction literature K–8.* Norwood, MA: Christopher-Gordon Publishers.

Banks, J. (1989). Integrating the curriculum with ethnic content: Approaches and guidelines. In J. A. Banks (Ed.). *Multicultural education: Issues and perspectives* (pp. 189–207). Boston: Allyn & Bacon.

Banks, J. (1994). *Multiethnic education: Theory and practice.* Boston: Allyn & Bacon.

Barone, D., & Lovell, J. (1990). Michael and the show-and-tell magician: A journey through literature to self. *Language Arts,* 67, 134–43.

Barr, R., Kamil, M. (eds.), & Mosenthal, P. (1996). *Handbook of reading research.* Vol. 2. Mahwah, NJ: Lawrence Erlbaum.

Barrera, R., Thompson, V., & Dressman, M. (Eds.). (1997). *Kaleidoscope: A multicultural booklist for grades K–8 (2nd ed.).* Urbana, IL: National Council of Teachers of English.

Berthoff, A. (1981). *The making of meaning.* Upper Montclair, NJ: Boynton/Cook.

Bettleheim, B. (1977). *The uses of enchantment.* New York: Vintage Books.

Chomsky, C. (1972). Stages in language development and reading exposure. *Harvard Educational Review,* 42, 1–33.

Cohen, D. (1968). The effect of literature on vocabulary and reading achievement. *Elementary English,* 45, 209–13, 217.

Cornett, C. (March 1997). Beyond plot retelling. *The Reading Teacher,* pp. 527–528.

Cornett, C. (1986). *Learning through laughter: Humor in the classroom.* Bloomington, IN: Phi Delta Kappa.

Cornett, C., & Cornett, C. (1980). *Bibliotherapy: The right book at the right time.* Bloomington, IN: Phi Delta Kappa.

Cullinan, B. (1989). *Literature and the child,* 2nd ed. New York: Harcourt Brace Jovanovich.

D'Alessandro, M. (1990). Accommodating emotionally handicapped children through a literature-based reading program. *The Reading Teacher,* 44, 288–93.

Dressel, J. H. (1990). The effects of listening to and discussing different qualities of children's literature on the narrative writing of fifth graders. *Research in the teaching of English,* 24, 397–414.

Eeds, M., & Wells, D. (1989). Grand conversations: An exploration of meaning construction in literature study groups. *Research in the teaching of English,* 23, 4–29.

Eldredge, J. L., & Butterfield, D. (1986). Alternatives to traditional reading instruction. *The Reading Teacher,* 40, 32–37.

Fader, D., et al. (1976). *The new hooked on books.* New York: Berkley.

Finazzo, D. (1997). *All for the children: Multicultural essentials of literature.* Albany, NY: Delmar Publishing (ITP).

Fisher, C. J., & Natarella, M. A. (1979). *Poetry preferences of primary, first, second, and third graders: Studies in lan-*

guage education. Unpublished doctoral dissertation, University of Georgia, Athens.

Five, C. (1988). Fifth graders respond to a changed reading program. *Harvard Educational Review,* 56, 395–405.

Frye, N. (1957). Theory of symbol. In *Anatomy of criticism.* Princeton, NJ: Princeton University Press.

Fuhler, C. (1990). Let's move toward literature-based reading instruction. *The Reading Teacher,* 43 (4), 312–315.

Galda, L., & Cullinan, B. (1991). Literature for literacy: What research says about the benefits of using trade books in the classroom. In J. Flood, J. Jensen, D. Lapp, & J. Squire (Eds.). *Handbook of research on teaching the English language arts* (pp. 529–535). New York: Macmillan Publishing.

Glazer, J. (1997). *Introduction to children's literature,* 2nd ed. Upper Saddle River, NJ: Prentice Hall.

Heald-Taylor, G. (1996). *Three paradigms for literature instruction in grades 3 to 6.* The Reading Teacher, 49 (6), 456–466.

Hepler, S. (1982). *Patterns of response to literature: A one-year study of a fifth and sixth grade classroom.* Unpublished doctoral dissertation, The Ohio State University, Columbus.

Huck, C. (1996). *Children's literature in the elementary school,* 6th ed. William C. Brown.

Huck, C., Hepler, S., & Hickman, J. (1987). *Children's literature in the elementary school,* 4th ed. New York: Holt, Rinehart & Winston.

Huggins, L. J., & Roos, M. C. (1990). *The shared book experience: An alternative to the basal reading approach.* Louisiana, U.S.A. (ERIC Document Reproduction Service No. 319 018).

Jacobs, J., & Tunnell, M. (1996). *Children's literature, briefly.* Englewood Cliffs, NJ: Prentice-Hall.

Johnson, T., & Louis, D. (1987). *Literacy through literature.* Portsmouth, NH: Heinemann.

Kutiper, K. S. (1985). *A survey of the adolescent poetry preferences of seventh, eighth, and ninth graders.* Unpublished doctoral dissertation, University of Houston, Houston, TX.

Kutiper, K., & Wilson, P. (1993). Updating poetry preferences: A look at the poetry children really like. *The Reading Teacher,* 47(1), 28–35.

Lehr, S. S. (1991). *The child's developing sense of theme: Responses to literature.* New York: Teachers College Press.

Levi-Strauss, C. (1967). *Structural anthropology.* Garden City, NY: Doubleday.

Levstik, L. (1986). The relationship between historical response and narrative in a sixth-grade classroom. *Theory and Research in Social Education,* 14, 1–15.

Lewis, C. S. (1980). On three ways of writing for children. In S. Eghoff et al. (eds.), *Only connect.* New York: Oxford University Press.

Macon, J. (1991). *Responses to literature.* Newark, DE: International Reading Association.

Nieto, S. (1992). *Affirming diversity.* New York: Longman.

Norton, D. (1995). *Through the eyes of a child: An introduction to children's literature,* 4th ed. Englewood Cliffs, NJ: Prentice Hall.

Ogle, D. (1989). The know, want to know, learn strategy. In K. Muth (ed.), *Children's comprehension of text: Research into practice.* Newark, DE: International Reading Association.

Ohlhausen, M. M., & Jepsen, M. (1992). Lessons from Goldilocks: Somebody's been choosing my books but I can make my own choices now! *The New Advocate,* 5, 31–46.

Pratt, L., & Beaty, J. J. (1999). *Transcultural children's literature.* Columbus, OH: Merrill (Prentice Hall).

Purcell-Gates, V. (1988). Lexical and syntactic knowledge of written narrative held by well-read-to kindergartners and second graders. *Research in the Teaching of English,* 22, 128–60.

Purcell-Gates, V. (1991). On the outside looking in: A study of remedial readers' meaning-making while reading literature, *Journal of Reading Behavior,* 23, 235–53.

Reutzel, D., & Cooter, R. (1992). *Teaching children to read: From basals to books.* Englewood Cliffs, NJ: Merrill/ Prentice Hall.

Rosenblatt, L. (1985). Viewpoints: transaction versus interaction—a terminological rescue operation. *Research in the Teaching of English,* 19, 98–107.

Roser, N. L., Hofman, J. V., & Farest, C. (1990). Language, literature, and at-risk children. *The Reading Teacher,* 43, 554–59.

Russell, D. (1994). *Literature for children: A short introduction, (2nd ed.)* New York: Longman.

Schmidt, B. (1991). Story map. In J. Macon, *Responses to Literature.* Newark, DE: International Reading Association.

Smith, J., & Bowers, P. (1989). Approaches to using literature for teaching reading. *Reading Improvement,* 26 (4), 345–348.

Sostarich, J. (1974). *A study of the reading behavior of sixth graders: Comparisons of active and other readers.* Unpublished doctoral dissertation, The Ohio State University, Columbus.

Spiegel, D. (1998). Reader response approaches and the growth of readers. *Language Arts,* 76 (1), 41–48.

Starko, A. (1995). *Creativity in the classroom: Schools of curious delight.* White Plains, NY: Longman.

Stauffer, R. (1969). *Directing reading maturity as a cognitive process.* New York: Harper & Row.

Sutherland, Z., Arbuthnot, M. (1986). *Children and books.* Glenview, IL: Scott Foresman.

Sutton, W. (Ed.). (1997). *Adventuring with books: A booklist for pre-k-grade 6* (1997 ed.). Urbana, IL: National Council of Teachers of English.

Terry, C. A. (1972). *A national study of children's poetry preferences in the fourth, fifth, and sixth grades.* Unpublished doctoral dissertation, Ohio State University, Columbus.

Tomlinson, C., & Lynch-Brown, C. (1996). *Essentials of*

children's literature (2nd ed.). Needham Heights, MA: Allyn & Bacon.

Tompkins, G., & McGee, L. (1993). *Teaching reading with literature: Case studies to action plans.* New York: Merrill.

Tompkins, G. (2000). *Writing: Teaching balancing process and product (3rd ed.).* Upper Saddle River, NJ: Prentice-Hall.

Tunnell, M. O., & Jacobs, J. S. (1989). Using "real" books: Research findings on literature-based reading instruction. *The Reading Teacher,* 42, 470–77.

Zarrillo, J. (1994). *Multicultural literature, multicultural teaching: Units for the elementary grades.* New York: Harcourt Brace College Publishers.

Children's Literature

Andrews, J (1985). *Very last first time.* Vancouver, BC: Douglas & McIntyre.

Babbitt, N. (1986). *Tuck everlasting.* New York: Farrar, Strauss & Giroux.

Baker, J. (1987). *Where the forest meets the sea.* New York: Greenwillow Books.

Barretts, J. (1977). *Animals should definitely not wear clothing.* New York: Atheneum.

Bauer, M. D. (1986). *On my honor.* New York: Bantam Doubleday Dell Publishing Group.

Berton, P. (1961). *The secret world of Og.* Toronto: McClelland & Stewart.

Booth, D. (1996). *The dust bowl.* (illus. Karen Reczuch). Toronto: Kids Can Press.

Brewster, H. (1996). *Anastasia's album.* Toronto: Penguin Books Canada.

Brown, S. (1978). *Hey, chicken man.* Toronto, ON: Scholastic-TAB Publications.

Brownridge, W. (1995). *The moccasin goalie.* Victoria, BC: Orca Books.

Burningham, J. (1967). *John Burningham's ABC.* New York: Bobbs-Merrill.

Cameron, P. (1961). *I can't said the ant.* New York: Putnam.

Campbell, M. (Ed.) (1985). *Achimoona.* Saskatoon, SK: Fifth House.

Carney, M. (1997). *At grandpa's sugar bush.* (illus. Janet Wilson). Toronto: Kids Can Press.

Charlip, R. (1984). *Fortunately.* New York: Simon & Schuster.

Christopher, J. (1967). *The white mountains.* New York: Simon & Schuster.

Cooney, B. (1982). *Miss Rumphius.* New York: Viking Penguin Inc.

Creech, S. (1994). *Walk two moons.* New York: Harper Collins.

Cumming, P. (1993). *Out on the ice in the middle of the bay.* Toronto: Annick Press.

Dahl, R. (1983). *James and the giant peach.* New York: Puffin.

Farris, K. (1996). *You asked?* Toronto: Greey de Pencier Books.

Fitch, S. (1987). *Toes in my nose and other poems.* (illus. Molly Lamb). Toronto: Doubleday.

Fitch, S. (1997). *If you could wear my sneakers!* (illus. Darcia Labrosse). Toronto: Doubleday.

Gilman, P. (1992). *Something from nothing.* Richmond Hill, ON: North Winds Press.

Godfrey, M. (1987). *It seemed like a good idea at the time.* Edmonton, AB: Tree Frog Press.

Goffin, J. (1992). *Who is the boss?* New York: Clarion Books.

Granfield, L. (1995). *In Flanders Fields: The story of the poem by John McCrae.* (illus. Janet Wilson). Toronto: Lester Publishing.

Granfield, L. (1993). *Cowboy: A kid's album.* Toronto: Groundwood Books.

Greenwood, B. (1994). *A pioneer story.* Toronto: Kids Can Press.

Grillone, L., & Gennaro, J. (1978). *Small worlds close up.* New York: Crown Publishers.

Gryski, C. (1995). *Let's play.* Toronto: Kids Can Press.

Gwynne, F. (1970). *The king who rained.* New York: Trumpet Club.

Harrison, T. (1982). *A northern alphabet.* Montreal: Tundra Books.

Harty, N. (1997). *Hold on, McGinty.* Toronto: Doubleday Canada.

Hesse, K. (1997). *Out of the dust.* New York: Scholastic.

Hickman, P. (1995). *The kids Canadian tree book.* Toronto: Kids Can Press.

Hickman, P. (1996). *The jumbo book of nature science.* Toronto: Kids Can Press.

Howe, J. (1981). *The hospital book.* New York: Crown Publishers.

Kaner, E. (1995). *Towers and tunnels.* Toronto: Kids Can Press.

Kaplan, W., & Tanaka, S. (1998). *One more border: The true story of one family's escape from war-torn Europe.* (illus. Stephen Taylor). Toronto: Groundwood Books/Douglas & McIntyre.

Kenna, K. (1995). *A people apart.* Toronto: Somerville House.

King, E., & Wheeler, J. (1991). *Adventure on Thunder Island.* Toronto: James Lorimer & Co.

Kusugak, M. (1990). *Baseball bats for Christmas.* Toronto: Annick Press.

Kusugak, M. (1992). *Hide and sneak.* Toronto: Annick Press.

Kusugak, M. (1993). *Northern lights: The soccer trails.* Toronto: Annick Press.

Kusugak, M. (1996). *My Arctic 1,2,3.* Toronto: Annick Press.

Kusugak, M. (1998). *Arctic Stories.* Toronto: Annick Press.

Lankford, M. (1992). *Hopscotch around the world.* New York: Morrow.

Lauber, P. (1982). *Journey to the planets.* New York: Crown Publishers.

L'Engle, M. (1962). *A wrinkle in time.* New York: Farrar, Strauss & Giroux.

Little, J. (1984). *Mama's going to buy you a mockingbird.* New York: Viking Kestrel.

Little, J. (1986). *Different dragons.* Toronto: Penguin Books Canada.

Littlechild, G. (1993). *This land is my land.* Emeryville, CA: Children's Book Press.

Lobel, A. (1970). *Frog and Toad are friends.* New York: Harper & Row.

Lobel, A. (1979). *Frog and Toad together.* New York: Harper & Row.

Lottridge, C. B. (1992). *Ticket to Curlew.* Toronto: Groundwood Books.

Lowry, L. (1989). *Number the stars.* New York: Houghton Mifflin.

Lunn, J. (1997). *The hollow tree.* Toronto: Alfred A. Knopf Canada.

Lunn, J. (1998). *Charlotte.* Toronto: Tundra Books.

Macaulay, D. (1995). *Shortcut.* Boston, MA: Houghton Mifflin Company.

Macaulay, D. (1990). *Black and white.* New York: Houghton Mifflin.

Markoosie. (1970). *Harpoon of the hunter.* Montreal: McGill-Queen's University Press.

Martin, B. (1992). *Brown bear, brown bear, what do you see?* New York. Henry Holt.

Meikle, M. (1998). *Funny you should ask.* Markham, ON: Scholastic Canada.

Mollel, T. (1990). *The orphan boy.* Toronto: Oxford University Press.

Muller, R. (1982, 1995). *Mollie Whuppie and the giant.* Vancouver: Firefly Books.

Munsch, R. (1980). *The paper bag princess.* Toronto: Annick Press.

Norton, M. (1953). *The borrowers.* New York: Harcourt Brace.

Oberman, S. (1994). *The always prayer shawl.* Honesdale, PA: Boyds Mills Press.

Owen, M.B. (1990). *A caribou alphabet.* New York: Farrar, Straus & Giroux.

Oxenbury, H. (1983). *The ABC of things.* New York: Delacorte.

Paterson, K. (1977). *Bridge to Terabithia.* New York: HarperCollins.

Paulsen, G. (1987). *Hatchet.* New York: Bradbury Press.

Pearce, P. (1958). *Tom's midnight garden.* London: Oxford University Press.

Pearson, K. (1986). *The daring game.* Markham, ON: Puffin Books.

Pearson, K. (1987). *A handful of time.* Markham, ON: Viking Kestrel.

Pearson, K. (1996). *Awake and dreaming.* Toronto: Viking.

Ripley, C. (1995). *Do the doors open by magic and other supermarket questions.* Toronto: Owl Books.

Ripley, C. 1996). *Why do stars twinkle at night? and other nighttime questions.* Toronto: Owl Books.

Scieszka, J. (1991). *The true story of the 3 little pigs.* New York: Viking.

Sendak, M. (1963). *Where the wild things are.* New York: Harper & Row.

Service, R. W. (1987). *The cremation of Sam McGee.* (illus. Ted Harrison). New York: Greenwillow.

Smith, D. B. (1973). *A taste of blackberries.* New York: Scholastic Inc.

Smucker, B. (1977). *Underground to Canada.* Toronto: Clarke, Irwin.

Spalding, A. (1995). *Finders keepers.* Victoria, BC: Beach Holme Publishing.

Spalding, A. (1998). *Sarah May and the new red dress.* Victoria, BC: Orca Book Publishers.

Trivizas, E. (1993). *The three little wolves and the big bad pig.* London: William Heinemann.

Truss, J. (1982). *Jasmin.* Vancouver, BC: Douglas (Groundwood Books).

Van Allsburg, C. (1981). *Jumanji.* New York: Houghton Mifflin.

Verne, J. (1997). *20,000 Leagues under the sea.* New York: Random House.

Vivas, J. (1985). *The Grandma Poss cookbook.* Adelaide, Australia: Omnibus Books.

White, E.B. (19152). *Charlotte's Web.* New York: Harper Trophy.

Wisniewski, D. (1997). *Golem.* New York: Clarion.

Wood, A. (1984). *The napping house.* New York: Harcourt Brace.

Wright, B. R. (1994). *The ghost comes calling.* New York: Scholastic Trade.

Wyatt, V. (1993). *The science book for girls and other intelligent beings.* Toronto: Kids Can Press.

Yee, P. (1991). *Roses sing on new snow.* Toronto: Groundwood Books.

Yee, P. (1996). *Ghost train.* Toronto: Groundwood Books.

Yerxa, L. (1993). *Last leaf first snowflake to fall.* Toronto: Groundwood Books.

Yolen, J. (1997). *Sleeping ugly.* New York: Coward, McCann & Geoghegan.

Sylvia Pantaleo acknowledges the contributions of Judy Bainbridge to this chapter. Some sections of Chapter 3 appear in similar form in Bainbridge, J., & Pantaleo, S. (1999). *Learning with literature in the Canadian classroom.* Edmonton, AB: The University of Alberta Press/Duval House Publishing.

Literature Seed Strategies

Consultant: Sylvia Pantaleo

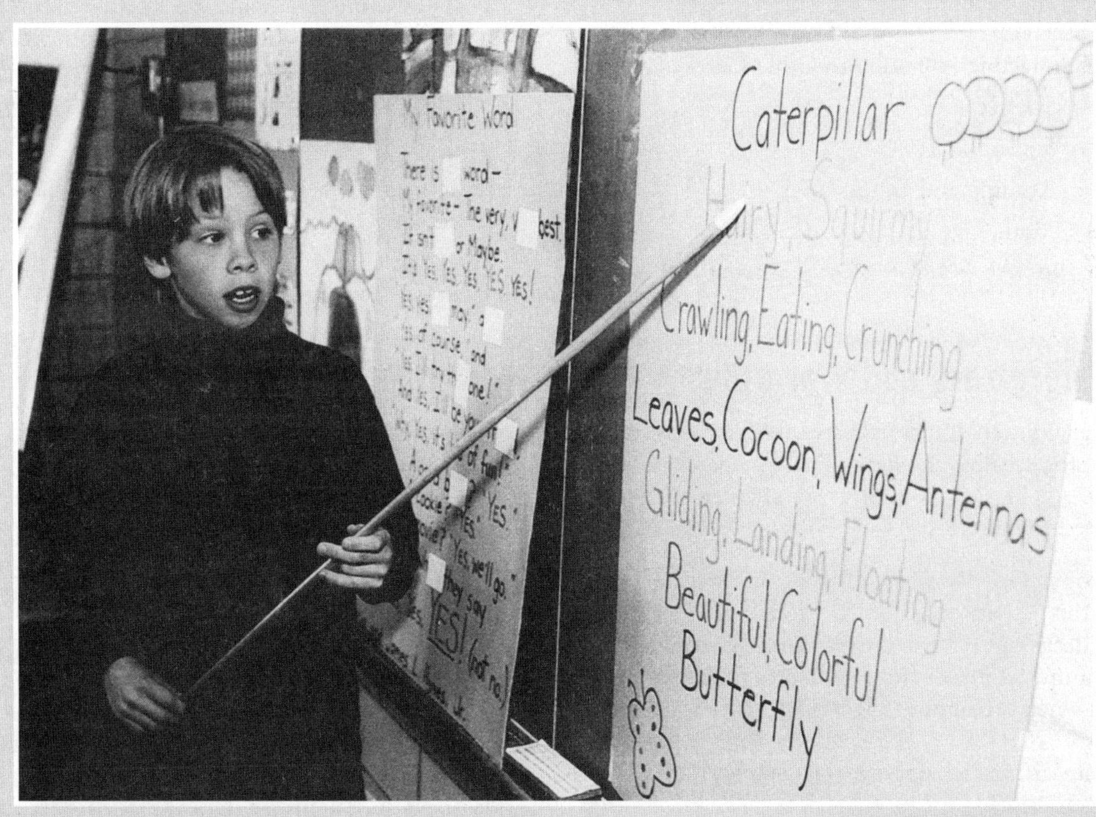

This chapter includes specific ways to integrate literature throughout the curriculum. The strategies are in seed or kernel form, and most are adaptable for elementary and middle levels. They are intended to prompt thinking, not lay out recipes. The ideas should be considered flexible, and adaptations are encouraged as teachers use literature to reach curricular goals and do unit planning. The strategy seeds are organized into the following sections, but many relate to more than one section. The sections on *energizers* and *elements and genre traits* do *not* represent an integrated focus, but are provided to ready students for creative problem-solving and teaching tools so students can participate in integrated lessons. It is important to keep in mind that *meaningful* integration of the arts, with each other and other curricular areas, does not happen unless the lessons have at least one focus on an art form and one in another curricular area. For ideas on integrating the art of literature with the four other arts areas, see Chapter 13.

I. Energizers and Warm-ups
II. Teaching Literary Elements and Genre Traits
III. Connecting Literature to Other Curricular Areas:
- Science
- Social Studies
- Reading and Language Arts
- Math

IV. SPECIAL FOCUS: Poetry Sharing and Writing

I. Energizers and Warm-ups

Energizers and warm-ups are used to get students ready for creative thinking. There are *energizers and warm-ups* in each seed strategy chapter that can be adapted to literature.

Analogy Go Round (Based on Starko, 1995). Base this activity on a book or story students all know. The idea is to stretch and twist thinking, even if it turns out funny. Sit in a circle and set up a *frame* for each to fill in when it comes to them. Oral frames to use are:

- ***Opposites:*** Pick opposite characters and force together: "*Jacob Two-Two is like the Hooded Fang because* _____ ." This can be done with any literary element: "*Jacob Two-Two's real world is like his fantasy world because* _____ ."
- ***Random combinations:*** Combine a random idea with a literary element: *The Hooded Fang is like a pencil because* _____ . Plug in different ideas in the first blank and students give reasons in the second.
- ***Personal analogies:*** "*I am like Jacob Two-Two because* _____ ." (Students fill in a character and the blank or all use the same character.)

Prereading and Writing. Here are two *before* reading or writing energizers:

- ***Webbing*** is brainstorming on paper. Put a topic in the centre and think of ideas connected to it. Draw out legs from the centre and write ideas on them. Try to fill up the paper. Next, group ideas together by circling or coding like ideas with a symbol (diamond, heart, etc.). For example, to get ready to read *Jack in the Beanstalk,* web the word "greed." *Variations:* Any literary element, genre, topic, person, etc., can be webbed.
- ***Cubing*** (Neeld, 1986) is based on the idea that a cube has six sides and is a way to explore a topic from six angles. For example, Cube "greed": (1) describe it, (2) analyze it (what are its parts), (3) associate feelings with it, (4) apply it (what can it be used for), (5) argue for it (pro), (6) argue against it (con). *Variation:* Give a time limit (e.g., one minute on each side).

Prediction Teachers guide student predictions during and after reading. The basic steps are:

1. Show the book cover, read aloud the title, and show a few pictures (if illustrated).
2. Ask students to predict in three areas: (1) Who will it be about? (2) When and where? (3) What problems might be in the story?
3. Record predictions on a chart or overhead, or in individual journals.
4. Students read or teacher reads to students.
5. Build in think stops for students to discuss predictions. Confirm or reject and tell why. Celebrate rejections as much as confirmations.

Mystery Bag. Students try to figure a connection as the teacher reveals one object at a time from a sack or box. For example, for *Little Red Riding Hood:* a stick (forest), red handkerchief, a Lone Ranger-type half-mask, and a basket. Take out the easiest last, to draw out suspense. To ensure that all students are involved, have them write down their guesses as each object is revealed. *Variation:* Students can make collections and present a mystery bag as a book response.

Story or Book Riddles. Show students how to write and share riddles about characters. Simple ones just give three clues, from broad to specific, but even grade one students can learn to do a bit of punning.

Write Right Away (Quickwrites). Students write freely for a few minutes on a topic to either activate prior knowledge or pull together information (e.g., after a discussion). Often a time limit is set of about five minutes.

CAP Prediction. This is a prereading warm-up. List words from an upcoming book that relate to *characters, actions,* and *problems.* Have students sort the words into these categories by predicting how they would connect with C, A, or P. Students can then make predictions about the book or story based on the words.

Word Pairs. This can be used for prereading or as an energizer for creative thinking for writing. Select an even number of important words from an upcoming book or poem. Ask students to pair the words any way that makes sense, as long as they have a good reason. Students can then share their reasons for pairing words.

II. Teaching about Literature: Elements and Genre Characteristics

Venn Diagrams. Venn diagrams are used to compare and contrast different aspects of two books or stories: literary or art elements; genre traits; versions of the same story; or books by the same author. Two overlapping circles are drawn. Each separate circle is for the individual characteristics of the two things being compared. The overlap area is for commonalities.

Character: Web and Wheel.

- *Web.* A character's name is written in the centre. Draw legs on the web to represent aspects of the character and label them: how the character talks, thoughts of the character, actions, appearance, what others think or say about the character. (Other categories: the character's feelings, worries, hobbies, talents, skills, personality, etc.). *Adaptations:* For biographies, change the web legs to include fitting categories: obstacles faced, significant achievements, special life events.
- *Sociowheel.* Put the name of a character in the centre or hub of a wheel drawn on paper. Write the names of three or four other characters around the rim. Draw a spoke to connect the hub character to each of the rim characters. On each spoke, write how the hub character is connected or related to each rim character to show the relationships. *Suggestion:* Do on the overhead as a whole class or on a large chart. *Variation:* Students need two circles: make one about as big as a coffee can lid and the other an inch in diameter bigger. Fasten the circles in the centre with a brad. Students then write the names of important story characters around the edges of both circles. When wheels are ready, students can line up character names and discuss the ways the characters relate. Turn the wheel and a new character pair lines up and discussion proceeds.

Character Inventories. Students fill out a personality inventory on a character. Possible items: Favourite foods? Likes? Dislikes? Favourite books? Films? Hobbies? Encourage students to think beyond literal information in the book to conjecture logically.

Character Poems. Use any of the *Poem Patterns* in Post It Page 3–4 to write poems about characters.

Somebody–Wanted–But–So (character, motive, problem, plot) (Macon, 1991). Make a chart with the four words across the top. Students draw or write about the main character (*somebody*) in the first section, what the character *wanted* (second section), character's roadblocks or conflict *(but),* and the story resolution in the *(so).*

Plot Lines (Tomlinson, 1996). The linear mountainlike, cumulative, and episodic patterns of events in a story can be shown by *drawing the plot line* and writing events along it. Roadblocks or obstacles are indicated by bumps in the line. For example,

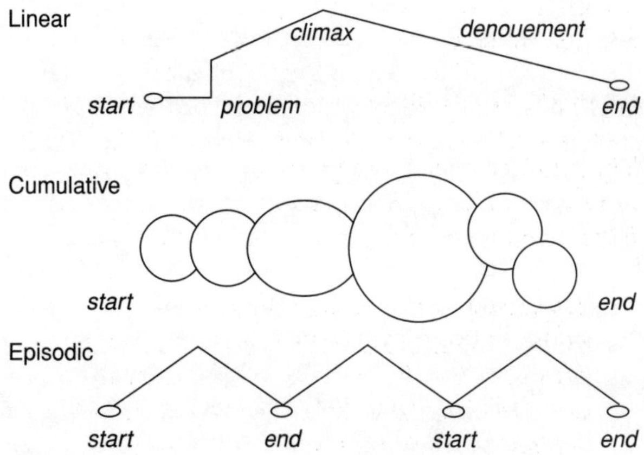

Episode Plot Cards. Key events are brainstormed and each written individually on cards. Cards are then placed in order. *Variation:* Use a pocket chart or clothesline to order the ideas or create timelines, as a group.

Home–Adventure–Home Map. This plot structure is also called the BME: Beginning–Middle–End (Tompkins & McGee, 1993) and the I–D–C (introduction, development, conclusion). It involves categorizing a story's plot into three main parts. This can be used as an *after* reading strategy or *during* reading to help structure comprehension. The objective is to learn how a *problem* sets the plot in motion in the beginning, the middle section is a series of events (the "adventure") that deals with the problem, and in the end events happen to resolve the problem. Students can map out original stories by dividing their papers into home–adventure–home parts and planning the events that will happen in each section they write. This can be used as a planning device for drama responses and to prepare for student-led discussions by asking students to star items they wish to talk about on their maps.

Circle or Pie Story Maps. Diagram story events or the plot of the home–adventure–home pattern (stories begin and end in the same location) on a large circle divided into pie-shaped sections. At the top of the circle, a house can be drawn to show how stories often begin in a safe, homey place. Then characters have an adventure and return home again. The events of the story are written or drawn, one at a time, while moving clockwise around the circle. The pie slice below the house is where students begin to put down important events. When the circle is complete, the story ends in the same place it began. *Adaptations:* Make a large circle pie map on the board or on chart paper and do this together as a class. Use the completed maps to do retelling of stories.

Setting Sense Web. The setting of a story is put in the centre. Five legs extend with the labels see, taste, smell, hear, and touch. Students record what can be known about the setting using each of these senses. For example, *What would you see, hear, taste, smell, touch in the setting of Peter Rabbit?*

Genre Traits.

- *Chart:* Write several story titles, from the same genre, in boxes across the top of a page. The characteristics of the genre are then written along the left-hand side. Examples from each book are then sought to go with each trait.
- *Web:* The title of a story is written in the centre. Each of the legs extending from this centre contains one of the traits of the genre to which the story belongs. For example, for a folk tale (1) opening or closing language convention, like "Once upon a time," (2) setting vague—could be anywhere, (3) plot is a simple order of chronological events, (4) flat or one-dimensional characters (good or evil, foolish or genius), (5) problem revolves around a journey from home to perform tasks and confrontation with obstacles, (6) miraculous events, happy ending. *Variation:* Do as a whole class.

Bio Webs (for biographies). A person's name is placed in the centre and legs are drawn to important events in that person's life. Legs can be webbed off the main events to go into more detail. *Extension:* Students can use the webs to write biographical summaries or poems.

III. Connecting Literature to Other Curricular Areas

Book Report Alternatives

To begin this section, Post It Page 4–1 lists book report alternatives.

Science Focus

- Natural world, systems of the body, seasons, weather, plants, animals, the environment, machines, electricity, magnets, space, gravity, and states of matter
- Finding out how and why things happen in the world through careful observation, hypothesis making, and prediction

Informational or Nonfictional Books. Informational books allow students to make discoveries about the world and become involved in the scientific method. See Post It Page 3–6 for source books that list books by topic. Here are examples of books to integrate into science units:

Aliki. (1985). *Dinosaurs are different.* Harper & Row.

Bateman, R., & Archbold, R. (1998). *Safari.* Penguin Books Canada.

Cole, J. (1989). *The magic school bus inside the human body.* Scholastic.

Cruxton, J. (1998). *Discovering the Amazon rainforest.* Oxford University Press Canada.
Curnie, P., & Mastin, C. (1998). *The newest and coolest dinosaurs.* Grasshopper Books.
Gallant, R. (1989). *Before the sun dies: The story of evolution.* Macmillan.
George, J. C. (1995). *Animals who have won our heart.* HarperCollins.
Gibbons, G. (1987). *Weather forecasting.* Four Winds Press.
Hartman, G. (1991). *As the crow flies: A first book of maps.* Bradbury Press.
Hickman, P. (1998). *Animal senses: How animals see, hear, smell and feel.* Kids Can Press.
Lauber, P. (1990). *Seeing the earth from space.* Orchard.
Lowry, L. (1991). *Earth day.* Carolrhoda.
Mastin, C. (1997). *Canadian wild flowers and emblems.* Grasshopper Books.
Oppenheim, J. (1996). *Have you seen bugs?* Scholastic Canada.
Pringle, L. (1997). *An extraordinary life: The story of a Monarch butterfly.* Orchard Books.
Simon, S. (1991). *Earthquakes.* Morrow.
Simon, S. (1995). *Sharks.* Harper Collins
Swanson, D. (1998). *Welcome to the world of bats.* Whitecap Books.

Reading Engagement: Informational Books. To increase engagement, provide students with generic prompts for noting ideas as they read an informational book. Brozo (1998) lists these types of questions: *What is:*

1. The most interesting or exciting word, phrase, sentence, or picture?
2. An idea, detail, issue, or concept you feel strongly about?
3. A feeling about this idea, detail, issue, or concept? Why ?
4. A connection between your own experiences and the ideas, details, issues, and concepts?
5. A place in the book that made you think of something you have experienced, seen, or know about? Why?

Things to Write and Say. See Post It Page 4–2. Any of the writing forms can be used in science. For example, write a *letter* to a character about what you are learning in science.

Poem Patterns. See Post It Page 3–4. These patterns can be used to write about science topics or processes. For example, write a five-sense poem about the circulatory system.

Five W's and H Webs. After reading an informational book or story, students web who, what, when, where, how, and why to summarize learning. Add details to answer the five Ws and H questions.

Social Studies Focus

- Relationships among human beings, occupations, transportation, communities, governments, customs, cultures, holidays, and use of natural resources
- History, geography (use of maps), civics (citizenship and government) or political science, economics, anthropology, and sociology
- Investigations into cultural diversity and global understanding
- Special questions: How did it used to be and why? Why is it like it is today? What can I do about it? Thinking processes: cause and effect, sequence, gather data, discover relationships, make judgments, draw conclusions, and problem-solve about community issues, e.g., economic issues like school funding or values conflicts related to free speech
- Use of primary source material like newspapers, art, music, diaries, letters, journals, books, and artifacts, rather than use of textbooks, and gathering data through interviews, surveys and other investigatory strategies that historians and other social scientists use

Informational Books for Social Studies

There are now excellent informational books available on many topics in the social studies. Each volume in the *Discover Canada* series by Grolier and the *Hello Canada* series by Fitzhenry & Whiteside provide an informative overview of a province or territory. Other appropriate titles for social studies are:

Berton, P. (1995). *Attack on Montreal.* McClelland & Stewart.
Comber, J., & Evans, R. (1997). *Women changing Canada.* Oxford University Press Canada.
Cruxton, J., & Wilson, W. (1998). *Discovering castle days.* Oxford University Press.
Delainey, G., & Jamieson, M. (1996). *So, this is Canada!* Oz New Media.

Granfield, L. (1995). *In Flanders Fields: The story of the poem by John McCrae.* Lester Publishing.

Greenwood, B. (1994). *A pioneer story: The daily life of a Canadian family in 1840.* Kids Can Press.

Greenwood, B. (1997). *The kids book of Canada.* Kids Can Press.

Greenwood, B. (1998) *The last safe house: A story of the underground railroad.* Kids Can Press.

Hancock, P. (1998). *The kids book of Canadian Prime Ministers.* Kids Can Press.

Jamieson, M. (1996). *Beginnings: From the First Nations to the great migration.* Reidmore Books.

Kalman, B. (1998). *Pioneer life from A–Z.* Crabtree Publishing.

Kenna, K. (1995). *A people apart.* Somerville House Publishing.

Lunn, J., & Moore, C. (1996). *The story of Canada* (Rev. Ed.). Lester Publishing.

Massey, D., & Shields, P. (1995). *Canada: Its land and people* (2nd Ed.). Reidmore Books.

McTeer, M. (1995). *Parliament: Canada's democracy and how it works.* Random House of Canada.

Morton, D. (1996). *Shaping a nation: A history of Canada's constitution.* Umbrella Press.

Owens, A., & Yealland, J. (1996). *Forts of Canada.* Kids Can Press.

Yee, P. (1996). *Struggle and hope: The story of Chinese Canadians.* Umbrella Press.

Genre Studies in Social Studies. While any genre has potential connection to social studies, general informational books, biography, and historical fiction have particular value because each can elaborate on a unit from a different angle. With historical fiction, students can use informational books and their texts to verify what details are accurate and which are fictionalized. In addition, poetry can be found on unit topics and paired with informational books.

Culture Unit Maps and Webs. One way to structure a culture unit is to "map" findings as students read a variety of literature. Here are important category legs to map or web: (1) ***language:*** dialect or actual words used in a book; (2) ***values:*** contrast with mainstream Canada; (3) ***art, music, drama, or dance in the book*** and what they reveal; (4) ***historical information;*** (5) ***customs and traditions;*** (6) ***contributions the culture has made;*** and (7) ***events and issues*** associated with the culture.

Mystery Person. After reading a piece of historical fiction or a biography, students choose a book character and find three objects that represent him or her. Objects are then revealed to the class one at a time, with the least obvious one (in its connection to the character) coming last. Students try to guess who the person is by connecting the three items.

Biography Boxes. Students fill boxes with objects, pictures, and poems that may have been important to a person's life. Boxes can then be shared. Students learn that things used or seen each day are also things famous individuals might use.

Book Mapmaking (Johnson & Louis, 1987). A biography or piece of historical fiction is used. The setting or a portion of it is drawn to show where and what story events take place. It is important initially to demonstrate mapmaking with students. When reading aloud a story with simple events and setting, teachers can keep track of characters on a setting drawing. Teachers can continue to guide students in mapmaking by reading aloud another story with simple events and settings. Students track where the characters are and the events of the story. Each decides what he or she would like to include in the map and how.

Time Lines. Time lines are visual representations of historical events and can be used to summarize an informational book or historical fiction. Use a horizontal line and make hash marks vertically to write chronologically important dates and events.

Lifelines (Tompkins, 1990). The goal is to record important events in a person's life by doing careful rereading to choose important and specific information. Long shelf paper or a piece of large paper is cut. A line is drawn down the middle. Dates of important events are put chronologically on the line, marked by a hash mark. Beside, above, or under each date a title, description, and/or picture of that event are shown. Photocopied pictures can be used or students may create their own illustrations and descriptions.

Reading and Language Arts Focus

- Reading, listening, viewing, representing, speaking, written composition (including handwriting and spelling, grammar, usage, capitalization, and punctuation), since reading and language arts are processes they must be connected to a subject to have meaning (i.e., something to read and write about)

- Goal: *Create* meaning and enjoyment using print through thinking, at every level from memory to critical thinking or evaluation
- The printed word and its components (letters, syllables, spelling patterns), how words combine to make phrases and sentences and sentences combine to make paragraphs and other forms of discourse from tongue twisters to novels

Lit Logs. Literature logs (wallpaper books, composition books, or a section in a notebook) can be used along with free reading. Students make dated entries, note the stories they are reading (titles and pages), and write reactions or questions about the story. They may also make predictions, write a poem about what they have read, or free write about feelings, criticisms, or opinions related to the text. *Variation:* Logs may be exchanged to share written reactions, or the teacher may collect logs and write comments. If students write in each other's logs, they should be taught how to respond positively. This can be modelled using an example log entry on the overhead.

Prequels and Sequels. After reading a story, students write about what may have happened *before* the book was written or after the end. Students attend to details and literary elements to use the same style, characters, and a fitting plot. Emphasize consistency with characters and style, as well as probability in the plot.

Class Newspaper. News articles, weather forecasts, advertisements, articles, interviews, police reports, classifieds, comics, and obituaries can be written by students about literature they are reading. For example, a newspaper could be constructed around Rowling's *Harry Potter and the Philosopher's Stone* so that students learn about the parts of a newspaper, the five Ws and H structure of news articles, etc. The newspaper could be a culmination of a core book unit or developed chapter by chapter (e.g., do cartoons for one chapter, classifieds for another, and obituaries at the end).

Real-Life Writing. Post It Page 4–2 shows many of the forms that people write in. Students can use these forms to write about any topic or book they have read.

It is fundamental for teachers to provide instruction about various types of writing before students are assigned particular writing tasks.

Word Sorts. Students list interesting words they find as they read a book, story, or poem (use index cards). Afterward, students pair up and categorize the words. *Adaptation:* Present a list of words from the story or poem *before* the students read it. Students group the words as a prediction exercise. This can be done as a whole group on the overhead or in small groups.

Partner Writing. Students read a story and then write to a friend about it. Possible written entries are a letter, a note about what they liked or didn't like and why, or a mini book review (appropriate for intermediate students who've read book reviews; consult *Book Review Digest* in a library or get reviews from journals like *Horn Book* or *School Library Journal* to use as examples). For example,

> *Dear Jenny,*
>
> *I want to recommend* Walk Two Moons *to you. The book really makes you think because there are lots of flashbacks. It is sort of like a mystery because you only get clues to what is going on and then you find out the truth at the very end.*
>
> *I think you would want to read this book because the author makes you love the characters—especially the grandparents. It is a book that made me cry, but I felt like it all made sense at the end. This book made me treasure my parents and grandparents.*
>
> *Your buddy, Lou*

Double Entry Journals A line is drawn down the middle of a page. The left-hand side is used to write down words, phrases, sentences, or passages students find interesting or important as they read a book. On the right-hand side, students connect the ideas from the left column to their own experiences. *Variation:* Use to help students prepare for discussion by asking them to write questions, as well as connections, in the right column. These can then be prioritized by starring the ones that are most important to raise. Follow discussions with time for students to write about how the discussion changed their ideas about things noted.

Anticipation Guides (Tierney & Readence, 2000). This is a prereading strategy. Students are given several statements related to a book they will read. They indicate or rate their degree of agreement or disagreement. Time can be taken for students to discuss reasons for ratings. They then read and decide whether each rating was confirmed or should be rejected. *Adaptation:* Do as a follow-up reaction rating and use to stimulate discussion of the book (for example, based on *The Sky is Falling* by Pearson).

Directions: Rate your agreement from 1 to 5 with 1 = Strongly Agree and 5 = Strongly Disagree.

1. Change is good for people.

2. It is important for people to feel they are needed by other people.
3. Courage can be displayed in many ways.
4. If two people talk together about something, they will understand each other.

Variation: Use an alternative rating system: True, Sometimes True, False, Sometimes False, or Agree or Disagree, with an explanation to support the rating.

Sentence Frames. Sentence frames are prompts to help students respond verbally to a book or topic. The structure gets them started, which is the hardest part for many children. They can be used after any book or lesson and for writing, as well. These are mostly taken from children's books. Repeat the frame as many times as desired (e.g., three fortunately–unfortunately statements).

1. *Fortunately . . . Unfortunately . . .*
2. *Someday . . .*
3. *Why . . .? Because . . .*
4. *. . . is the hardest when . . . and is the easiest when . . .*
5. *I used to (think or feel) . . . But now I (think or feel) . . .*
6. *When I . . . I look or feel like . . . Because . . .*
7. *I seem to be . . . But really I am . . .*
8. *The important thing about . . . is that . . . It's . . ., It's . . ., And it's . . . But the most important thing about . . . is that it . . .*
9. *I am . . . I saw . . . I heard . . . I smelled . . . I tasted . . . I felt . . .*

Letters (Tierney, Soter, O'Flahavan, & McGinley, 1989). (1) Use Beverly Cleary's *Dear Mr. Henshaw* as an introduction to writing letters to an author or book artist. In the letter include questions about how particular characters were created, ideas or feelings about books, and why the artist chose to use a specific art medium or style. (Explain that they may not receive a personal reply from the artist.) (2) Letter to the editor: Present an issue to the class that will appear in an upcoming book. Students take a stance on the issue and think of ways to defend it. They then write a letter to the editor, share letters, and defend opinions with evidence. Next, they read the book. *Note:* A fascinating book in which actual letters are delivered to fairy tale characters is *The Jolly Postman or Other People's Letters* (Ahlberg, 1986). The letters can form the basis of drama or many writing possibilities (e.g., writing letters to other characters).

Writing Take-offs or Copycatting. Take-off or copycat writing is adapting a book pattern to make a new story. The degree of adaptation depends on the writer. Predictable books like Williams' *I Went Walking* provide a framework to write in. For example, Zolotow's *Someday* is a series of episodes that all begin with the word "someday." Books can then be illustrated and bound using options in the art chapter.

Math Focus

- Daily living situations involving counting, measuring, probability, statistics, geometry, logic, patterns, functions, and numbers
- Problem solving through the use of skills (raising questions and answering them, finding relationships and patterns)
- Concepts about numbers, operations, and concepts like bigger, longer, greater than, less, three, four, even and odd
- Problem-solving in other ways, focus on explaining and thinking, rather than just correctness, and using a hands-on approach.

Teachers often feel that math is harder to integrate with literature and writing than other areas. But there really are many delightful pieces of literature that are math-based, such as:

Anno, M. (1983). *Anno's mysterious multiplying jar.* Philomel. (estimation, multiplication and division, number relationships)

Capie, K. (1985). *The biggest nose.* Houghton Mifflin. (length, capacity, area and volume)

Kasugak, M. (1997). *My Arctic, 1, 2, 3.* Annick (counting)

Myler, R. (1962). *How big is a foot?* Atheneum. (length, capacity, area and volume)

Nolan, H. (1995). *How much, how many, how far, how heavy, how long, how tall is 1000?* Kids Can Press. (many concepts)

Ross, C. (1994). *Squares.* Kids Can Press. (shapes)

Ross, C. (1994). *Triangles: Shapes in math, science, and nature.* Kids Can Press. (shapes)

Schwartz, D. (1989). *If you made a million.* Lothrop, Lee & Shepard. (money, numbers)

Scieszka, Jon, and Lane Smith (1995). *Math curse.* New York. Viking. (many aspects of math)

Tompert, A. (1990). *Grandfather Tang's story.* Crown. (geometry, shapes, tangrams)

Post It Page 4–3 is a bibliography of math-based literature from all genres to make it easier to introduce or reinforce math concepts. A recommended source book, published by the National Council of Teachers of Mathematics, is *The Wonderful World of Mathematics: A Critically Annotated List of Children's Books in Mathematics* (Thiessen & Matthias, 1992).

Math Shape or Concept Books. Students choose a geometric shape or a concept (addition, fractions, etc.). They write stories in which their shapes or concepts are characters or create an information book with pages that describe facts about the math concept. Books can be illustrated and bound. *Variation:* Show the video *"Dot and the Line,"* a romance between these two shapes (also art elements).

Math Copycat Books. Use math-based children's books as frames for students to write a copycat book of their own. For example, McMillan's *Counting Wildflowers,* Carle's *The Very Hungry Caterpillar* and MacDonald's *Sea Shapes* can all be used as frames.

IV: Special Focus: Poetry Sharing and Writing

Poetry is sound and sense and singing words.

This is a brief overview of how to make poetry a *daily* part of arts integration. Why? Poetry has particular importance in reading and language arts because it is through poetry that children are usually introduced to the music of print (Mother Goose rhymes, Dr. Seuss). Fortunately, there is poetry about science, social studies, and math that can be shared using the *poetry alive* strategies in Post It Page 4–4, and children can use poetry writing strategies to transform subject matter. Poetry and the other arts of art, drama, dance, and music can also be connected using strategies like poem prints (art strategy) and setting poetry to music. See Chapter 13 on integrating the arts with the arts for ideas and consult Post it Pages 3–4 and 3–5 on recommended poets and poems. The WHAT? Literary Elements section of Chapter 3 includes a discussion of *poetic elements.*

General Principles for Poetry Integration

As with any arts area, the emphasis in poetry integration is on the process of sharing and creating poetry, not perfect performance or product. Here are other general principles:

Poetry is sound. Nothing is as important as sharing poems *orally,* using a variety of strategies to make it live.

Poetry is sense. Share poetry *first* and discuss afterward. No one knows what a poem really means, so encourage many types of student response and go light on interpreting *for* students.

Creating and sharing poems give children a sense of control over language. This confidence leads directly to both reading and writing growth.

Encourage children to take risks. The strange, the silly, or the far-fetched can be freely explored when reading and writing poetry. Poetry plays with and breaks many of the "rules" of conventions and mechanics of language (e.g. punctuation, capitalization).

Help students discover what makes poetry. For example, it usually is *compact, emotionally intense,* and *full of sound patterns* (rhythm and rhyme, onomatopoeia, alliteration) and *figurative language* (metaphor, imagery).

Teach about the musical qualities of poetry. Rhyme, rhythm, repetition, onomatopoeia, and alliteration are what make poetry often seem like songs. Knowing this helps students understand the difference between prose and poetry.

Set Up Ongoing Poetry Routines

- **Sharing Poetry.** There are numerous ways to share poetry (see Poetry Alive Strategies, Post It Page 4–4). The use of poem charts and enlargements of poems on posters ensures that all students can see the poem.
- ***Poetry anthologies.*** Students create their own collections of favourite poetry by writing their own, trading, and copying poems from source books. Personal anthologies can be made into books or organized in recipe boxes under common categories like animals, humour, weather, people, places, holidays, and feelings.

Pointers for Poetry Sharing

- Warm up the face and voice. See *energizers and warm-ups* in Chapters 8 and 10.
- Repeated sharing of the same poems increases enjoyment and attunes the ear to the special uses of words in poems.
- Vary volume, pitch, tempo, juncture, etc., when reading poetry selections and discuss the effects of changing these phonological elements.
- Choral reading allows the power and support of the group to be used, especially when you first

start doing poetry. Teach choral reading through lessons on musical dynamics: sing together; do rounds; group the class into twos, threes, or fours and give each a musical phrase, ostinato, or refrain.

- Use signals for *start, stop, slow, fast, loud,* and *soft.* Conduct poems like an orchestra conductor (see Chapter 12).
- Teach students to use rhythm and beat by encouraging clapping, snapping, and tapping of feet, or divide the class in half, with one group chanting a phrase or refrain while the other claps out the beat. Challenge by giving the second group a different, syncopated refrain to the same simple beat.
- Focus on thinking about the images in the poem, add simple gestures and movements, try the poem in different voices, try reading louder and slower.
- Asks students to give each other feedback on what worked.
- Students should be able to choose their own poems to memorize, and there should be many options for recitations: partners; tape recordings; use of visual aids, props, or puppets.

Composing Poetry: Written and Oral

- Start with oral sharing of poetry. See Post It Page 4–4.
- Coach children to write about concrete things, use specific details (especially the five senses).
- Sharpen the powers of observation:

Ask students to describe an object in the room, then one not in the room; go for details.

Ask students to describe an object in the room using only three words.

Offer a series of nouns, such as *cat, tree,* and *sky.* Ask students to list possible varieties using adjectives. Coach to go beyond the obvious.

Provide a line. Challenge students to expand using details. For example, *The man walked down the street.* (Expand and elaborate by inserting words and adding phrases.)

- Teach about imagery:

Use categories, such as places, feelings, animals, colours, flowers, noises, smells, vehicles, weather, etc., and develop lists to keep in an idea book for writing.

- Teach metaphor:

Ask students to look at a familiar object or out the window at the sky. Ask what it looks like. What it *is* like. What it reminds them of. Use cubing (see Energizers).

Make two lists of nouns and compare something from one list to something on another.

Offer a choice of several objects; then ask students to write an accurate, detailed, objective description of it. Then have students write a poem made up of one-line comparisons to something. For example, A _____ is like a _____ because_____ .

- Use selections from literature as examples of good description and imagery.
- Use *poem patterns* (Post It Page 3–4) to give structures to adapt. For example, for the "I wish . . ." pattern, have each child write a line that includes a colour. The class shares the poem using line-a-child. Another example: select an object or person. Each child says one line about it. Students can be encouraged to use the five senses (e.g., I see, I hear, It feels . . .).
- Teach the concepts of line, syllable, and counting syllables:

Cut up a poem into lines. Have students reassemble it. Discuss the effects of assembling the poem in different ways.

Put separate lines in a pocket chart or have students each hold a sentence strip with a line as the class reads or it is read by the teacher.

Count lines in a poem.

- Teach about rhyme:

Read a poem, leaving out the rhyme words. Pause for students to provide (cloze strategy).

Challenge: write a silly poem using as many rhyming words as possible.

Pick a word and ask for three to five rhymes. Write a poem using those as end words. Repeat with three pairs of different rhymes.

Orally compose a poem in rhymed couplets. Give the first line, and the students supply the second, back and forth.

Write quatrains in different patterns: *aabb, abab, abcb, abca.*

- Teach rhythm and beat:

Start with songs, keeping time with hands, feet or rhythm instruments.

Overemphasize the beat in choral recitations.

Replace the words with numbers or scat phrases like "doo-wop."

Post It Page • 4-1

A Hundred Plus Literature Response Options

Overview: Students decide on projects to show understanding of a book and further investigate interests in a book. The options vary in time commitment, instructional presentation, and the degree of capturing and extending aesthetic reading experiences.

Poetry

Poem match: Find a poem that complements the book. Place a copy in the book.
Poem patterns: Write a cinquain, diamante, or clerihew about the story, a main point, or a character.
Poetry alive: Share a poem using a *poetry alive* strategy (Post It Page 4–4): choral, antiphonal, cumulative.
Write a poem: Create a poem in the style or form of the poetry in a book.

Writing and Speaking

Author study: Research the author and give a report about him or her and why he or she writes.
Biography: Write a biography of one of the characters.
Book dedications: Dedicate a book to a character. Tell why the character should read the book.
Book improvement: The author writes to you and wants to know how the book could be improved.
Book reviews: Read example book reviews and then write your own about the book and its art.
Call an author: Plan the questions and use a conference call setup.
Cliffhanger: Read aloud a part and stop at a suspenseful point. Ask for predictions from others.
Connecting: Write or tell about how the book connected to you or your life.
Copycat story: Write your own story using the same title, theme, or pattern of the book.
Decision making: At midpoint in a story, stop and speculate on what would have happened if a character had made a different decision.
Demonstration: Show something you learned and tell about why it is important.
Diary: Write a few entries from a diary as if you were one of the characters.
Episode cards: Put all the plot events on individual cards and arrange them in order to tell the story.
Episode or sequel: What happened next after the story ended?
Exciting happening: Write or tell about the most exciting event.
Facts: Make a list of facts you learned from reading a nonfiction book.
Fan mail: Write a letter of appreciation to an author. Ask questions and share thoughts.
Favourite parts: Write or tell about your favourite parts. Explain why these parts were your favourites.
Friendship: Choose a character. Tell why you would or would not like to have him or her as a friend.
Humorous event: Write or tell about the funniest part.
Important part: Write or tell about the most important part of the book. Use a sentence frame.
Interview: Write an interview between a character and the author or between you and the author.
Letter: Write a letter about the book to a friend.
Library recommendation: Write a recommendation to the librarian to buy a book you have read.
Lifeline: Put all the events in a character's life along a line.

Literature logs: Use a spiral notebook to make notes as you read: special words, ideas, feelings.

Movie: Write or tell why a book could (or could not) become a movie.

Newspaper: Write news stories, advertisements based on characters and episodes from the book.

Object talk: Give an oral summary of the story. Use a box of objects props.

Oral Book Reviews: Present oral reviews to a younger class to "sell" the book.

Past to present: Bring a book character from past to present. How would the character act today?

Puzzling: Write or tell about the most confusing or puzzling event in the story. Explain why the part was puzzling.

Research a topic: Pick an interesting idea in the book. Present the information in a report.

Scrapbook about the book. Collect items and create a scrapbook. Write a short description of the items.

Summarization: Get the plot down to one paragraph.

Time line: Make a time line of the events in the book.

Venn diagram: Compare this book to another. Diagram common literary or art elements.

Write: Write a letter to a favourite character or to a classmate, friend, or pen pal.

Music and Dance

Dance moves: List movements in the story. Show them with different body parts: head, hand, fingers.

Dancing characters: List the kinds of dances characters might like to learn and why.

Favourites list: Make a list of songs and music that the main character would like. Explain your reason for selection.

Make a mix: Collect music that goes with aspects of the book (special scenes, overall mood or theme).

Music mesh: List ways music connects to the book: songs, music, rhythm, melody, instruments, etc.

Rap: Write one about the book or read aloud a favourite part to a rap beat.

Songwriting: Write a song with lyrics that represents the book, its characters, or the setting.

Tape recording: Tape part of the story for the class with appropriate musical background.

Three-part dance: Choreograph a shape–moves–shape dance about feelings or main ideas in the story.

Art

Book jacket: Create a book jacket for the book or story to advertise it. Place it on the book.

Bulletin board: Make a bulletin board about the book.

Cartoon characters: Draw cartoons of the characters in important scenes.

Cartoon strips: Sequence the main points of the book with cartoons.

Clay model: Use clay to model a character, setting, or special object in the book.

Clothesline props: Make props and picture cards to pin up as you retell the story.

Collage: Use found objects, torn paper, and wallpaper to assemble a collage about the theme.

Cooking: Prepare and serve a related food from the book.

Diorama: Create a diorama that illustrates the setting of the book.

Flannel board pieces: Cut pieces and glue on sandpaper backs. Use to retell the story.

Literary cartoons: Collect cartoons that use literary allusions found in books you have read. Explain your choices.

Map: Make a map of the country or imaginary land in the book.

Map or relief map: Create a map of the setting using a dough recipe.

Media and style: Experiment with the techniques in the book.

Mobile: Make a mobile from drawings of people or objects in the book. Organize by literary elements.

Model: Make a model of something in the story: house, log cabin, rocket, etc.

Movie time: Make a hand-rolled movie of your book using shelf paper.

Mural: Create a mural about the book. Use charcoals, crayons, cut paper, watercolours.

Photography: Photograph people, settings, events, etc., that illustrate your book.

Photography: Take pictures related to the themes or places that could be settings in the book.

Postcard: Create a postcard that describes your book.

Poster ad: Create a poster that sells the book. Try cutting block letters or using calligraphy.

Puppets: See ten types of puppets to make in Chapter 6.

Routes: Make a map showing routes taken in the story.

Scrapbook: Prepare a scrapbook illustrating the book.

Scroll: Create a scroll to unroll and show important things about the book.

Sculpture, diagram, or model: Make 3D art about an important idea in the book.

Seed, button, cut paper mosaic: Make a mosaic to illustrate a setting or event. Explain your mosaic to the class.

Stage: Use a box to design a miniature stage setting for a portion of the story.

Story map: Draw a map that illustrates the main events of the story.

Travelogue: Create a travelogue using pictures, postcards, magazine clips to show the development of the story.

Wordless book: Make a book about the story and use no words. Use any media or techniques.

Drama

Author: Become the author and tell why you wrote this story. Use a prop.

Author's prerogative: Tell how you would change the story if you were the author.

Be the book: Pretend to be a book and tell what you hold within your pages. Advertise yourself.

Be the character: Imagine you are a character. Tell what you think of the author, and how the author has depicted you.

Chalk talk: Give a chalk talk by drawing on the board as you tell the main story events.

Character interview: Write an interview between two characters in the book. Role play the interview.

Commercial: Do a one-minute advertisement for a book.

Dress up: Create a character costume from the book and answer questions in character.

Flannel board: Prepare flannel board characters and use to tell the story (or part of it).

Minor character: Place yourself in the role of a minor character and tell the story from your point of view.

Movie version: Compare the movie or television version with the book. You could use a Venn diagram.

Panel discussion: Organize a pro and con panel and debate an issue. One person can be the author.

Persuasive speech: Persuade the audience why they should (or should not) read the book.

Pretend and write: Be a character and write to another character or keep a journal.

Puppets: Make a puppet or puppets of the characters. Set up dialogue or retell the story.

Radio announcements: Broadcast an advertisement for the book. Use the morning announcements.

Readers' theatre: Write a script and present the book.

Reporter: Be a TV reporter and report on the book. Choose an exciting part for "Live on the scene . . . ."

Sales talk: Make a sales talk. Pretend your audience is bookstore clerks. You want to push the book.

Skit: Pantomime or use dialogue in a skit about an important event.

Television show: Create one based on the book, e.g., game show, news show.

Unpopular position: Choose a character and defend why his or her role in a story should be made different.

Literature

Character web: Web what the main character looks like, acts like, feels like, and says.

Comparison chart: Compare with another version or with the film version.

Critical reading: Evaluate the book using literary elements.

Fairy tales: Read several fairy tales and list the common elements of the stories.

Fairy tales: Read several fairy tales and create your own tale using the common elements.

Folk tales: Mix the characters of several familiar folk tales and write the story that results.

Genre change: Make a case for how a certain book could be used in another genre. Write it.

Historical fiction: Find music that was popular during the same period as the book. Share the music and provide some key points of information about the historical period.

Mystery: Put an object from the story inside a box. Give clues to guess the book.

Point of view: Rewrite the story from the perspective of a different character.

Read another book: Same author, same illustrator, same theme, same genre, or with same character. Share your thoughts by comparing the two books in some way.

Post It Page • 4-2

Things to Write and Say from A to Z

Directions: Use this list of forms as a reference for responding to any work of art by using visual, representative, or written or oral language activities.

Acceptance speech
Advertisement
Advice column (Dear Abby)
Announcement
Apology
Award presentation
Brief biography
Campaign speech
Certificate
Chant
Cheer
Cinquain
Commercial
Complaint
Compliment
Contract
Definitions (of unusual words, e.g., *tuffet*)
Diamante
Editorial
Epilogue

Excuse
Fable
Greeting card
Haiku
Headline
Horoscopes
Introduction
Invitation
Irony
Jingle
Journal, log, or diary
Jump-rope rhyme
Letter (business or friendly)
Lie
Limerick
List (to-do, grocery, wishes, etc.)
Love note
Marquee notice
Menu
Mixed metaphor
Nominating speech
Note
Obituary
Ode
Paradox
Poem (see Post It Page 3–4)
Postcard
Poster
Propaganda (e.g., card stacking, glittering generalities, etc.)
Remedy
Report
Résumé
Slogan
Telegram
Thank-you note
Tom Swifty
Tongue twister
Tribute
Triplet or tercet
Understatement
Wanted poster
Will
Wish

Post It Page • 4-3

Math-based Children's Literature

Addition and subtraction	Galdone, P. (1986). *Over in the meadow.* Prentice Hall.
	Hoban, T. (1985). *Is it larger? Is it smaller?* Greenwillow.
Attributes	Hoban, T. (1978). *Is it red? Is it yellow? Is it blue?* Greenwillow.
Attributes and measurement	Horenstein, H. (1993). *How are sneakers made?* Simon & Schuster.
Estimation	Clement, Rod. (1991). *Counting on Frank.* Gareth Stevens.
	Heller, R. (1987). *A cache of jewels.* Grosset & Dunlap.
Fractions	Shotwell, L. (1963). *Roosevelt Grady.* World Publishing.
Geometry, shapes, sequence, pattern	Bang, M. (1985). *The paper crane.* Greenwillow.
	Flournoy, V. (1993). *The patchwork quilt.* Lee & Low.
	Hopkins, D. (1993). *Sweet Clara and the Freedom Quilt.* Knopf.
	Hoban, T. (1986). *Shapes, shapes, shapes.* Greenwillow.
	Jonas, A. (1983). *Round Trip.* Greenwillow.
	Mac Donald, S. (1994). *Sea Shapes.* Gulliver.
	Wildsmith, B. (1982). *Red is best.* Annick Press.

Large numbers	Estes, E. (1971). *The hundred dresses.* Harcourt Brace Jovanovich.
	Gag, W. (1988). *Millions of cats.* Random House.
	McKissack, P. (1992). *A million fish, more or less.* Knopf.
	Petie, H. (1975). *Billions of bugs.* Prentice Hall.
	Schwartz, D. (1985). *How much is a million?* Lothrop, Lee & Shepard.
Logic	Anno, M. (1985). *Anno's hat tricks.* Philomel.
	Guarino, D. (1989). *Is your mama a llama?* Scholastic.
Measurement and size	Briggs, R. (1970). *Jim and the beanstalk.* Hamilton.
	Carle, E. (1987). *The tiny seed.* Picture Book Studio.
	Kellogg, S. (1992). *Much Bigger than Martin*. Dial Books for Young Readers.
	Krauss, R. (1973). *The carrot seed.* HarperCollins.
Money	Axelrod, Amy. (1994). *Pigs will be pigs.* Simon & Schuster.
	Mathis, S. B. (1975). *The hundred penny box.* Viking.
	Viorst, Judith. (1978). *Alexander, who used to be rich last Sunday.* Atheneum.
Multiplication and division	Dubanevich, A. (1983). *Pigs in hiding.* Four Winds Press.
	Mahy, M. (1987). *17 Kings and 42 elephants.* Dent.
Numbers, counting, sequence, patterns	Anno, M. (1992). *Anno's counting book.* HarperCollins.
Numbers and counting	Archambault, J. (1989). *Counting sheep.* Henry Holt.
	Crews, D. (1986). *Ten black dots.* Greenwillow.
	Dee, R. (1988). *Two ways to count to ten.* Henry Holt.
	Haskins, J. (1989). *Count your way through Africa.* Carolrhoda.
	Martin, B. (1987). *Knots on a counting rope.* Henry Holt.
Number relationships	Hulme, S. (1991). *Sea Squares*. Hyperion.
	Larrick, N. (1988). *Cats are cats.* Philomel.
	Lottridge, C. (1986). *One watermelon seed.* Oxford University Press.
	Ormerod, J. (1983). *101 Things to do with a baby.* Lothrop, Lee & Shepard.
Probability	Lobel, A. (1972). *Mouse tales.* HarperCollins.
Problem-solving	Hutchins, P. (1967). *Rosie's walk.* Macmillan.
	Jonas, Ann. (1987). *Reflections.* Greenwillow Books.
	Thurber, J. (1990). *Many moons.* Harcourt Brace Jovanovich.
Sequence and pattern	de Paola, T. (1978). *Pancakes for breakfast.* Harcourt Brace Jovanovich.
	Friedman, A. (1994). *A cloak for the dreamer.* Scholastic Day.
Sorting and classifying	Hoberman, M. A. (1988). *A house is a house for me.* Viking Penguin.
Sorting, classifying, and graphing	Freeman, D. (1978). *Corduroy.* Puffin.
Spatial relations	Berenstain, S. (1968). *Inside outside upside down.* Random House.
	Maestro, B. (1976). *Where is my friend?* Crown.
Time	Anno, M. (1986). *All in a day.* Philomel.
	Carle, E. (1977). *The very grouchy ladybug.* Crowell.
	Lionni, L. (1967). *Frederick.* Pantheon.
Miscellaneous math	Anno, M. (1987). *Anno's math games.* Philomel.

Post It Page • 4-4

Poetry Alive Strategies

Directions: Here are ways to orally share poetry throughout the curriculum.

Choral or unison. Do all together.

Cumulative. One or two start and gradually more voices come in; all together on last line.

Antiphonal. Two opposing groups, e.g., high and low, loud and soft.

Line-a-child. One line per person.

Refrain with groups. Repeated lines are done by a chorus.

Character voices. Assume a character and use dialect or idiolect, e.g., southern.

Narrative pantomime. Do actions that poem suggests as narrator reads or recites.

Sign language. Use finger spelling or American Sign Language to perform.

Background music or art. Play or show as poem is read, e.g., transparencies, CDs.

Cloze. Use post-its and cover predictable words; students then orally guess them.

Reader–responder. Reader reads one line and responder orally improvs. For example, *Mary had a little lamb.* Responder: *I bet her husband was surprised.*

Reader's theatre. Set up poem like a script with names and parts to be read.

Use props. Add musical instruments, puppets, objects.

Sound effects. Assign sounds to be made when certain words are read.

Question and answer. Find poems that are set up in question and answer form. For example, Q = Who has seen the wind? A = Neither I nor you (Christina Rossetti). Everyone gets a Q or A and reads when it makes sense. *Note:* Students can then write their own Q + A poems.

Actions. Children do an action for certain words or phrases, i.e., dance or mime.

Memorize and recite. Add volume, pitch, tone, rate, pause, stress, and emphasis to give special oral interpretation. Use Q–U (cue you) cards: you read the line on your cue card after you hear your cue. For example,

Q = Mary had a little lamb.

U = Its fleece was white as snow.

Q = Its fleece was white as snow.

U = And everywhere that Mary went. . . .

Call and response (echoic). Students echo leader's oral interpretation line by line.

Canon or round. Read like a round in which different groups start at different times.

Ostinatoes. Repeat a word or phrase that is important, e.g., Who has seen the wind? (Repeat *Wind–Wind* or chant throughout poetry reading.)

References

See Appendix: Recommended Reading and Viewing for additional resources.

Books and Articles

Brozo, W. (1998). *Readers, teachers and learners: Expanding literacy across the content areas.* Columbus, OH: Merrill.

Johnson, T., & Louis, D. (1987). *Literacy through literature.* Portsmouth, NH: Heinemann.

Macon, J. (1991). *Responses to literature.* Newark, DE: International Reading Association.

Neeld, E. C. (1986). *Writing.* Glenview, IL: Scott, Foresman.

Starko, A. (1995). *Creativity in the classroom schools of curious delight.* White Plains, NY: Longman.

Thiessen, D., & Matthias, M. (1993). *The wonderful world of mathematics: A critically annotated list of children's books in mathematics.* Reston, VA: National Council of Teachers of Mathematics.

Tierney, R., et al., (1989). The effects of reading and writing upon thinking critically. *Reading Research Quarterly,* 24, 134–73.

Tierney , R. &Readence, J. (2000). *Reading strategies and practices: A compendium (2nd. ed.).* Needham Heights, MA: Allyn & Bacon.

Tomlinson, C., & Brown, C. (1996). *Essentials of children's literature,* 2nd ed. Boston: Allyn and Bacon.

Tompkins, G. (1990). *Teaching writing: Balancing process and product.* Columbus, OH: Merrill.

Tompkins, G., & McGee, L. (1993). *Teaching reading with literature: Case studies to action plans.* New York: Merrill.

Children's Literature

Ahlberg, J. (1986). *The jolly postman's or other people's letters.* Boston: Little, Brown.

Carle, E. (1984). *The very hungry caterpillar.* New York: Putnam.

Cleary, B. (1996). *Dear Mr. Henshaw.* New York: Avon.

MacDonald, S. (1994). *Sea shapes.* New York: Gulliver.

McMillan, B. (1986). *Counting wildflowers.* New York: William Morrow & Co.

Pearson, K. (1989). *The sky is falling.* Markham, ON: Viking Kestrel.

Rowling, J. (1997). *Harry Potter and the philosopher's stone.* London, UK: Bloomsbury Publishing Place.

Williams, S. (1990). *I went walking.* New York: Harcourt.

Zolotow, C. (1989). *Someday.* New York: HarperTrophy.

Integrating Visual Art Throughout the Curriculum

5

Consultants:
Jeri Harmsen, Angela Solar

Every genuine work of art has as much reason for being as the earth and the sun.

Ralph Waldo Emerson

CLASSROOM VIGNETTE

Mr. Novak's Multiage Class: Fantasy Unit with Chagall's *I and the Village*

Every child is an artist. The problem is how to remain an artist once he grows up.

Pablo Picasso

The artist easel at the front of the room is draped with a black cloth. Mr. Novak is sitting on a low chair in front of his class of fourth and fifth graders. This is the language arts block scheduled each morning around a *reading–writing workshop* approach designed to let students read a variety of genres and do many kinds of real-life writing during the two hours.

"What is this?" Mr. Novak begins.

"It's your mystery bag," the class chorally responds.

"Right. You know the routine. First item." Mr. Novak pulls a yellow rubber duck from the bag. He places it on the table next to him. Students giggle.

"Look closely. Think about what it is, the colours, what it means, how it makes you feel." He pauses. "Next item." He reaches into the brown sack and slowly reveals a yellow plastic ball.

"Oh, oh," one boy raises his hand, "I know."

"Keep looking. We have two more items. Charles, glad you are making connections. Next item." Mr. Novak theatrically struggles to reveal a furry, floppy teddy bear. Charles looks puzzled.

"Last item. Think about how all these items are related." Mr. Novak pulls out a well-worn child's tutu and places it on the table. There are giggles, but students now put their thumbs up.

"I see several thumbs up. I'll give everyone a few more seconds. Look closely. Make associations. Okay, Michael, don't tell us the category—just give us a clue."

Michael pauses, "I think they're all things from our past."

"Great clue. Why do you say that?"

"Because, they are kids' stuff. They are all soft, too, though—and man made."

"Yes. You're right. Who else? Sonya?"

"I think they are all happy things. They remind me of playing and just having fun when I didn't have to go to school so much." The class laughs and so does Mr. Novak.

"What do you think of Sonya's idea about how these things make you feel? Clarence?"

"I agree about how they make you feel happy and I agree with Michael about the past. I think it can all go together. Soft toys in our past remind us of good pleasant memories." Several children shake their heads to agree with Clarence.

"Charles, you had an idea early on. What were you thinking?"

"I thought you were just doing 'yellow' or 'plastic.' Then you brought out the teddy bear. But at least the yellow part fits because yellow is such an uplifting colour in its feeling."

The discussion continues for a few more minutes. Mr. Novak then ceremoniously unveils the bottom half of the shrouded art reproduction.

"Cool," one boy says.

"What is it?" someone else says.

"Look closely. What do you see?" asks Mr. Novak.

"Really weird stuff. Is that a tree?"

"I see two people and one is green with white lips."

"Look, a cross. He has on a ring, too."

"The nuts or flowers are exploding or something. See the splattered paint!"

"Wow, those are strange shapes, like a moon eclipse or something. But it's red. Look there's a ring with an apple on it. Maybe this artist didn't have a lot of toys and had to play with this stuff."

"It's not a person on the right. Look. It's more the shape of a snout or something. Maybe he played with a pig!" The class laughs again.

"You are really noticing colours, shapes, and images. What else? How does this make you feel?"

"It has bright yellow so it's happy. There is the cross. Maybe he's really religious."

"But the guy is green. Of course, when you're a kid, colours don't matter so much. Maybe a kid painted this?" Kristen asks.

The class continues a few more minutes with many more discoveries until Mr. Novak asks them to get ready to see the rest of the work. The whole class gets still and many lean forward.

Slowly Mr. Novak pulls the black cloth up. Little by little the reproduction is revealed. The kids gasp.

"Make some connections," Mr. Novak urges them.

"This is crazy. Look the people and houses are upside down and the woman is milking a cow in the head of a horse!"

"But the colours are really interesting. It's like a dream or something. You know, things can be anything in your dreams," a red-haired girl who hasn't spoken before is quite passionate.

The class discussion becomes animated, with students finding more and more things in the reproduction. Comments seem to converge on ideas about dreams, toys, happy memories, and childhood. One child actually uses the term "abstract" and another mentions "collage."

About fifteen minutes into the lesson, Mr. Novak finally tells them the painting was made by a Russian artist named Marc Chagall in 1911. He takes about five minutes to explain how Chagall was inspired to paint pleasant childhood memories—his experiences and things from folk tales he had been told. He then spends a few minutes asking them about their memories of stories from childhood, and they share lots of fairy tale titles and Disney films.

The lesson introduction ends and Mr. Novak moves into the development by asking what makes fantasy, and as students call out characteristics, like "something not real," "dream-like places and events," he writes them on the overhead. He then explains they are starting a genre unit on fantasy and asks them why they think Chagall might have painted fantastic images like those in *I and the Village*. The students return to the "good feelings and freedom" ideas generated earlier. He then asks them about the book *Charlotte's Web* and how it might relate to the discussion. Students comment on the elements of fantasy in the story (e.g., animals talking) and also how it was a book most of them heard a teacher read aloud in second grade; it was a good memory from their childhood.

The lesson is brought to a conclusion when Mr. Novak asks them why people might write or read or paint fantasy, and there are many responses: for entertainment, relaxation, to make money, to be creative, to get ideas out, to feel good. He then shows them five fantasy books (Rowling's *Harry Potter and the Philosopher's Stone*, Berton's *The Secret World of Og*, Hughes' *Castle Tourmandyne*, Howe and Howe's *Bunnicula*, and Bellairs' *The Doom of the Haunted Opera)*, from which they'll be able to choose as they study fantasy and try to find out more of its characteristics. He tells them he'll put them on the chalk tray for browsing and ask them to rate their choices by the end of the day. Five book circles will then form to read together. He also explains that the unit will involve them in the creation of fantasy because they'll be doing their own fantasy art responses.

Postscript: Mr. Novak spent a month on the fantasy unit, and students met daily to discuss their books. He displayed and held "What do you see?" discussions of other fantasy paintings, Henri Rousseau's *The Dream* and Marcel Duchamp's *Nude Descending a Staircase,* and students explored the artists' motives and means for creating these works. The unit culminated in a fantasy museum display of student paintings. All the paintings were framed, in some sense. One special day students acted as docent guides for small groups of students and adults who came to tour the museum (a converted area of the hall) and find out about the paintings and the painters. The unit had indeed integrated art with the language arts of reading, writing, speaking, and listening.

Introduction

The arts—literature, visual art, music, drama, and dance—are our culture's most powerful means for making life in its particulars vivid. In this way the arts escalate consciousness.

Elliot Eisner

Stop to See Details

Mr. Novak is like many teachers who use art to cause students to notice details and patterns, remember past experiences, and come to realize how the world is a complex and intriguing place. But, according to art educator Rudolf Arnheim, school learning too often emphasizes commonality, generalization, and classification, rather than *individuation,* or concentration on one special thing. Of course, both uniqueness and commonality are important and can be treated simultaneously in a lesson, as Mr. Novak did. The point is that in art meaning comes more from details and specifics, in the kind of way we know a person by particular features. Art study involves examining how a work is made by an artist's slightly different use of light or line, like the line that creates Mona Lisa's smile. How different the impact would be if da Vinci had painted her with a mouthful of teeth. Elliot Eisner (in Arnheim, 1989) believes it is crucial to tune in on such details. "Unless such perceptivity is developed students are not likely to have much that is interesting to write about, and unless they learn to hear the music of language, what they write is unlikely to be a pleasure to read. Attention to the sensibilities and to the distinctive is not attention to educational ornamentation, but attention to the core of education" (p. 7).

Post It Page • 5-1

News Bulletins

Art Research You Can Use

Since integrating art into the curriculum in 1983, test scores for average grade three students in Eliot Elementary, a racially mixed school, have increased to the 99th percentile. *Needham, Massachusetts.*

Writing skills showed significant improvement when drawing and drama strategies were used in the primary grades (Moore and Caldwell, 1993). *Rocky Mountains.*

CBS This Morning, February 28, 1997: Teacher Mrs. Fodero said her students with learning disabilities gained one to two years in developmental levels after eight weeks of special drawing instruction that focuses on attending to five elements of shapes: circles, dots, straight lines, curved, and angle lines. The program has been found to increase reading, writing, math, and language skills up to 20 percent in other schools.

Art Literacy

In this chapter the concept of art and visual literacy will be examined as related to general student goals for the development of higher-order thinking skills and creative problem-solving. This is not a new idea. Visual art has long been associated with literacy. For example, historically, religious frescoes and paintings in churches throughout the world were intended to not just adorn, but to educate illiterate people about powerful events. What is new is our reawakening to these abandoned learning tools. Moreover, there is a growing respect for how creating art involves more than simple use of the hands; it is much more than mindless sensation. Indeed, the use of the senses in art is "a cognitive event . . . the eye is part of the mind" (Eisner, in Arnheim, 1989, p. 4). Consider how a piece of art is a reflection of an artist's experiences in a particular time and culture; each work is a "dramatic puzzle cast in a beautiful form." Students who learn to "read" art become literate in profound ways, since they learn to decode the symbol systems to interpret or make meaning from visual images. By peeling away layers and unwinding bits of the message, people develop the aesthetic sense to make judgments, like a subject of psychologist Abraham Maslow's (1968), who observed "a first-rate soup is more creative than a second-rate painting" (p. 136).

Through art making and art discussions, children experience the joy of discovery and learn how much of life is ineffable—the search for meaning does not always end in the finding, but in a satisfying journey. Students learn to go beyond the literal and gain new forms of making meaning. For example, students can be shown how cubism is an artist's effort to say, without words, something strongly felt. Art can be seen as a tool to create for myriad reasons and in many ways. Unfortunately, art is unduly viewed as a way to amuse. We have cultural bias in favour of words, particularly in school, where verbal learning is stressed, despite the intensely visual nature of our world (television, billboards). This preference for the verbal over the visual–spatial leads to less attention to visual or pictorial *details* during teaching, even by teachers who may include picture books in the reading or literature program. The scarcity of instruction in visual literacy is evident in children's stereotyped use of symbols, when they are capable of more mature perceptions. For example, middle school students often depict the sun as a mandala or birds as joined commas; they are capable of seeing and representing the details of both if given the time and ways to look closely.

Why Should Teachers Integrate Art?

A painter takes the sun and makes it into a yellow spot.
An artist takes a yellow spot and makes it into a sun.

Pablo Picasso

What's so special about learning through art? Examine research on integrating art in Post It Page 5–1 before reading further about reasons to integrate visual art throughout the curriculum.

Contributions Art Makes to Learning and Motivation

1. **Art activates the emotional intelligence and motivates.**

   We enter the twenty-first century with a new respect for the centrality of intuition in thinking and understanding. The author of *Emotional Intelligence,* Daniel Goleman, claims that "a view of human nature that ignores the power of emotions is sadly shortsighted . . . intelligence can come to nothing when the emotions hold sway" (1995, p. 4). The roots of the words *emotion* and *motivate* have to do with motion or movement. Emotions and motivation cause us to take action that can result in positive or negative consequences. While art involves the intellect, it also activates *affective* ways of knowing. It is an outlet for ideas and feelings—a release, a safety valve—and can give an emotional catharsis. Jenkins (1986) calls this "externalizing" what we feel and know (p. 15). Both *viewing* and *making* art can give emotional release or response. This is evident in art therapy sessions when clients report feelings of relaxation or a joyous high. There is delight in making a line that curves in a special way and pleasure in seeing an artist's new view on a subject.

2. **Art is a way of communicating through visual and spatial symbols.**

   The most fundamental fact to be understood about art is that whatever it shows is presented as a symbol. A human figure carved in wood is never just a human figure, a painted apple is never just an apple. Images point to the nature of the human condition.

   (Arnheim, 1989, p. 26)

   Imagery and metaphor are keys to thinking and learning used from early childhood. A child sees a "fingernail" in the night sky by comparing a known image with something inexplicable, the new moon. There is little teaching and learning in any discipline that doesn't include use of concrete images. Think of drawings in the dictionary, photographs in history textbooks, plastic models in science class. Often these images are not realistic; a map is an abstraction, as are charts, diagrams, and other visuals, because, as Arnheim points out, "images produced for practical purposes have more sophisticated functions than that of supplying faithful duplicates . . . what an illustration needs to show is not an object as such but some of its *significant properties*" (emphasis added, p. 30).

   When we teach the understanding and use of visual symbols, we involve children in thinking about and expressing what is often beyond *linguistic* capabilities. This can be as simple as asking students to look closely and observe repeated elements that make patterns in fabrics or plant leaves. Since children are attuned to metaphoric thinking, this taps into a strength and stimulates the use of *multiple* schemata—understanding from logical analysis *and* affective response to forms that create beauty. A strategy used to develop imaging is *guided visualization trips:* Students are asked to relax and make pictures in their heads as a story is read or told about an imaginary journey; for example, before a plant unit, students might visualize a trip through a plant and hear vocabulary used that will be seen later. Vivid and accurate adjectives activate the brain to make individual pictures or meanings. This strategy can be a powerful motivator to read and learn more.

3. **Art is a means of thinking through our senses.**

   It is more than likely that if men [sic] *were ever to lose the appetite for meaning, which we call thinking, they would lose the ability to produce those thought-things we call works of art.*

   Hannah Arendt

   Arnheim (1989) thinks that "at the root of knowledge is a sensible world, something we can experience" (p. 7). Art is hands-on and tangible. We touch materials to make art and manipulate colour, line, and shape to create it. When we *view* a piece of art, kinesthetic and tactile senses are activated by the artist's brushstrokes that go up or down or are heavy or light. Visual perception is a cognitive event because interpretation and meaning are indivisible parts of seeing. What we see is a function of intellect; for example, a painting can evoke the sounds and smells of a summer boat ride or a raucous party. As the senses are stimulated, we experience a union of mind, body, and emotions. So the symbols used in art are also thinking tools. These sensory-rich symbols form a special language that beckons us to consider a new perspective and use prior knowledge to interpret, apply, analyze, synthesize, and evaluate what we are creating or viewing.

4. **Art develops aesthetic sensitivity and satisfies the basic need for beauty.**

For the soul, beauty is not defined as pleasantness of form but rather as the quality in things that invites absorption and contemplation . . . beauty is a source of imagination . . . that never dries up. A thing so attractive and absorbing may not be pretty or pleasant. It could be ugly, in fact, and yet seize the soul as beautiful in this special sense. James Hillman defines beauty for the soul as things displaying themselves in their individuality. . . . Some pieces of art are not pleasing to look at, and yet their content and form are arresting and lure the heart into profound imagination.

(Thomas Moore, Care of the Soul, 1992, p. 278)

It is puzzling that aesthetic awareness does not attract more attention from educators. According to Broudy (1979), aesthetic sensitivity is the "primary source of experience," and he believes aesthetic experiences are vital to every child's education (p. 636). Aesthetic responses lie at the heart of many daily events. Aromas, sounds, colours, tastes, and textures fill our environment and contribute to aesthetic response. Perhaps we shy away from drawing instructional implications because *aesthetics* and *beauty* are hard concepts to get a purchase on. We are aware that in aesthetic response there is a sharpening of the senses—an awareness or appreciation of pleasant experiences (Feeney & Moravcik, 1987). Lowenfeld and Brittain (1975) explain aesthetic sensitivity as an active perceptual process, "an interaction between a person and an object (natural or man made) that gives a stimulating and harmonious experience." While children may not have language to express aesthetic awareness, they do have a much higher level of aesthetic appreciation than previously thought. Think of their open sensory responses to things of beauty—gasps and sighs that show heightened sensory responses. Eventually, this sensitivity can grow into an ability to critically evaluate works of art using the criteria defined by each culture. Michael Parson's research on the *stages of aesthetic development* is summarized in Post It Page 5–2 and is presented to show the progression of development and give teachers a basis for making appropriate instructional decisions.

5. **Art develops higher-order thinking, creativity, and creative problem-solving capabilities.**

Artistic and creative problem-solving begins early. As children draw people and trees, they show they are shrewdly analyzing and translating observations into basic shape patterns. This is not a mechanical imitation of reality, but an expression of the *essence* of things. For example, young children usually make the head the largest part of a person; it is the most relevant feature. When given materials and tools to create art, children experiment and use imagination. When taught skills to use the materials and tools, they work with greater satisfaction. We can show possibilities for painting using different strokes, amounts of paint, and effects of splattering and dripping and follow with exploration time with tools and media—to create a product or just explore, period. In addition, when teachers expect students to think for themselves, to generate rather than imitate, more personal involvement in learning occurs. In contrast, teachers distort art when they give black-line pages to colour in or oral directions that mimic painting by number. It's no wonder the result is a series of look-alike products; students are not engaged in higher-order thinking or using creative problem-solving capabilities. Aesthetic development is nurtured by personal confrontation with words and images; artists and authors give us cues to arrive at our own conclusions, feelings, or products. While pedagogy abandoned copying at the turn of the century, there are art specialists and classroom teachers who still either ignore or do not understand problems made by dictated art. Teaching can both advance and thwart development. In no area is this more obvious than when teachers damage students' concepts about what art is and how it comes to be. If taught art must always be representational, children can lose faith in their abilities to use art; some refuse to even try for fear that their art will not look like a "real" artist's or the teacher's. Arnheim reminds us that realism may be needed for *technical* purposes, but is *not* even appropriate under some circumstances; for example, representing Pharoahs *realistically* conveys a kind of humanity incongruous with some religious views; no Pharaoh believed himself or herself to be a mere mortal.

One way to nurture thinking during art creation or response is to use Benjamin Bloom's taxonomy of thinking to create questions. Bloom (1956) divided cognition into levels:

- ***Memory:*** just the facts, literal thinking. Example: *What are the primary colors?*
- ***Interpretation:*** reading between the lines, adding your own experiences to make an inference. Example: *How could you explain in your own words how to create shades and tints?*

- ***Application:*** putting a skill you've learned to use. Example: *Use what we've been learning about mixing colours to make different skin tones.*
- ***Analysis:*** examining the parts or pieces to come to understanding. Example: *Look closely to discover all the repeated elements in this piece of art.*
- ***Synthesis:*** putting parts or pieces together to make a creative whole; requires invention and imagination. Example: *What can you create with these collage materials that shows what you have learned about the environment?*
- ***Evaluation:*** making a judgment based on the goodness or badness, rightness or wrongness of something using some criteria. Example: *What do you think about this piece of art and why do you think what you do?*

Teachers and students can use Bloom's model to generate questions and respond to work in any art form. The goal is to make sure students think above the memory or literal level much of the time so that they use higher-order thinking skills.

Ways to nurture the creative problem-solving process were presented in Chapter 1. Take time to review the creative thinking process and strategies like SCAMPER on Post It Page 1–5.

6. Art strengthens self-understanding and can give confidence about being unique.

Art is an extension of a person, an expression of who I am and what I am.

Sabe and Harrison

Through the inventive and imaginative processes of art, students are empowered to make discoveries and generate principles. Promoting personal investigation should be central to teaching, and children are often more willing to try new things in the art arena where creativity is more openly valued. When

Post It Page • 5-2

Stages of Aesthetic Development

Stage 1: **Favourites.** Children delight in virtually all paintings, especially the colours. They like to pick favourites and talk about personal connections.

Stage 2: **Subject matter.** Focus on representational art; it's better if it is more realistic. The artist's skill is admired.

Stage 3: **Emotions.** Concern is for emotional stimulation, the more intense the better. Now the person has more than a personal preference and has developed an appreciation for how an artist causes the viewer to respond with emotion.

Stage 4: **Style and form.** The viewer now understands that art is socially and culturally influenced and is important because of its meaning-making capabilities. Art is viewed as an important communication vehicle, with its power to give meaning being primary. Colour, texture, space, form are analyzed as the person judges the competence of the artist to create new perspectives.

Stage 5: **Autonomy.** Judgments are made on a personal and social basis. Art is viewed now as an important means of helping humans consider the human condition and life itself through the questions it raises and the ideas and feelings it evokes. The work is used to seek truth and shared meaning with others in a kind of "conversation about life."

Adapted from Parsons, Michael, J. (1987). Talk about a Painting: A Cognitive Developmental Analysis. *Journal of Aesthetic Education,* 21 (1), 37–55.

Red Parrots

art is coupled with other areas of study (science, social studies, math), students can associate positive feelings and powerful thinking processes from art within these areas. Art also offers ways to control emotions, images, and even the environment, which yields a sense of delight. There is a Jewish folk tale about a tailor who continually makes "something from nothing" and brings joy to himself and his family in the doing. (See Gilman's picture book version, *Something from Nothing*.) Self-expression is a primary goal of integrating art. Even when students explore interpretations of a work of art, it is their *different* perspectives, not coming to one answer, that is the goal. This noncompetitive nature of art allows students to vie only with their own internal standards.

7. **Art creates respect and sensitivity for diversity.**

If you walk around the world with black and white film in your camera, you are not especially inclined to look for colour on your travels.

Elliot Eisner in Arnheim, 1989, p. 7

To see the world from an artist's viewpoint is to look for what is special and different. There is a book called *God Is in the Particular,* and the title reminds me how often a small difference provokes thought and interest. Since art reflects culture, it is an ideal medium to learn about the unique values, habitats, habits, dress, food, and work of peoples and how similar problems are addressed in diverse, but equally effective, ways. A cultural print or artifact can be an effective lesson introduction, because different ideas and novel objects grab attention. Students can be motivated to find out more when shown portraits, landscapes, still lifes, sculptures, or architecture that illuminates the past, especially if asked what each shows about the people who created it.

In a classroom infused with the visual arts, students also have the opportunity to learn to respect the variety of products fellow classmates create. As students share work during times like art docent talks, all come to realize how no one's work is the same and that differences are exciting.

8. Art develops responsibility, focus, concentration, and self-discipline.

For those parents and teachers that decry the inability of children to stay on task and complete work with pride, art offers a viable means of developing important social and character habits. Students soon learn that nothing can be created without learning to use materials and tools and sticking with work to completion. As peers admire the work of those who are self-disciplined, all gain insight into what it takes to be successful, and students see that those who handle materials responsibly are given privileges not available to those who do not.

9. Art reflects life, so it naturally integrates all curricular areas.

Art is to society as dreams are to a person.

Laliberte and Kehl

Art more than reflects life—it is life. Look around and find the art of life. Think of types of chairs; from the regal throne to the bean bag chair. We devise ways of sitting that signal relationships, scientific advances, and economic situations. Art demonstrates how we create to survive and thrive. This life-centredness invites students to transfer meaning-making processes of art to other curricular areas. Consider how the writing composition process can be studied by first struggling with composition through painting or sculpture. The lessons of art have to do with exploring, experimenting, and learning to use tools and materials—the same thinking necessary to produce good writing. Essential properties of a writing topic may even best be captured through art making first, rather than words.

Multiple perspectives enlarge previous viewpoints, so we need to encourage looking at topics throughout the curriculum from an aesthetic perspective, one that questions and explores. In addition to reading expository material in science or social studies texts, students can examine art about plants, animals, historical events, and people. Information gathered in such investigations can change frames of understanding, much as a piece of art is changed by its frame. The aesthetic *feeling* frame of reference liberates beauty and richness embedded in the subject matter of any discipline. Students who learn to savour learning, by taking time to reflect, explore, and respond emotionally, develop new perspectives and sensitivities. Broudy (1979) contends this form of aesthetic interaction is a "primary form of experience on which all cognition, judgment, and action depend. It is the fundamental and distinctive power of image making by the imagination. It furnishes the raw material for concepts and ideals" (p. 63). Art can also link curricular areas to life, in which cognitive, affective, and psychomotor (physical–mental coordination) aspects are always linked. Art is an alternative way of knowing that promotes learning in and across domains. For example, how can one ever think of an iris in the same way after seeing Georgia O'Keefe's paintings? Could the horror of war ever be explained more poignantly than through Picasso's magnificent *Guernica*? Heart, head, and hands are used in creating, evaluating, understanding, and responding to art. It is dreary to imagine studying a discipline without art—books without photos, illustrations, diagrams, or maps; science, social studies, and math without models to show the human body, the atom, or the world. Students need to be alerted to this use of art that assists us by making the invisible visible.

10. Art is a way to get inside students' heads, to understand and to assess.

Art is a private feeling made into a public form.

Judith Rubin

A child's art gives a peek inside a private world of thoughts and feelings. While teachers must be cautious in inferring meanings from a child's art—excessive use of black may occur because the black crayon was nearby—it is possible to examine work for conceptual and motor development. For example, the strokes necessary for handwriting success (circle, vertical, horizontal, diagonal lines) should appear in children's art before introducing them in formal handwriting instruction. In addition, just as student writing gives clues to thinking and learning, so can artwork provide evidence of cognitive development. In fact, children who aren't verbally fluent may be able to express ideas with paint or clay or may have their words released through art. Stories told through art are often passionate tales of events that capture children's imaginations. Here is six-year-old Liza's story based on a drawing she did of an erupting volcano.

> All the town was afraid. They could hear the insides making growling sounds. Then it happened. The lava broke out and ran all over the people. It was blood red because it was hot rock. Hot hot rock. So hot it burned up the people. But see here. This is a people bird. The people were burned to ashes but the ashes molded into lava birds that could fly so high no volcano could ever touch them again. The end.

Canadian Visual Arts Guidelines

The Canadian Society for Education through Art has produced a national policy and supporting perspectives for practice guidelines. The document suggests that art programs are to:

1. Include international, national, regional, and local interests. In a multicultural country such as Canada, care must be taken to examine national concerns that have a particular relevance for specific groups or communities.
2. Include making art, studying art history, and engaging in critical dialogue about art.
3. Support continuity within and between grade levels. Students should encounter and apply a similar range of experiences and materials at various grade levels, at increasingly sophisticated and complex levels, which cater to the cumulative experience of the learner.
4. Make use of community resources, such as galleries and museums.
5. Be included in college and university programs for all elementary preservice teachers to promote a positive attitude toward art through an understanding of the basic principles of art.

For a full description of these Policies and Supporting Perspectives for Practice Guidelines, see the Canadian Society for Education through Art's publication, *The CSEA National Policy and Supporting Perspectives for Practice Guidelines*, edited by Rita L. Irwin (1997).

What Do Teachers Need to Know and Teach to Integrate Art?

Every artist dips his brush into his own soul.

Henry Ward Beecher

The integration process occurs when two or more ideas are combined and all parts of the process have worth. This implies that teachers must know *about* art to teach through it. In elementary and middle school, these aspects of art are considered basic content and skills: the historical, social, and cultural role of each art in our lives; communication through art forms by *creating* art and *responding* to art; and valuing art and developing aesthetic sensitivity (helping students understand the roles of beauty and emotion in life). Art study includes ideas related to art elements, artists, pieces of art, art forms, styles, history of art, artistic tastes, art making through a variety of media, art in our lives, the art of other cultures, and museums. Here is a checklist of titles for file folder tabs to collect resources for visual art integration:

- Basic art elements and concepts used to create and think about art
- Artist information (biographies, styles, and techniques used)
- Styles of art, such as impressionism, expressionism, and cubism
- Forms, types of art, and media like collage, sculpture, painting
- Subject matter (portrait, landscape, abstract, still life)
- Actual pieces of art (calendar art, prints, art postcards, sculpture)
- Cultural artifacts like masks and pots
- Other possibilities: art history, science of art (pigment making), math of art (perspective), sociology of art, economics (museum shows, selling art), psychology (art therapy).

Art's Connections to Cognitive, Affective, and Psychomotor Development

Children who are encouraged to draw and scribble stories at an early age will later learn to compose more easily, more effectively, and with greater confidence than children who do not have this encouragement.

What Works: Research about Teaching and Learning (1986), U.S. Department of Education, Washington, DC, p. 14

Thanks to researchers like Rhonda Kellogg, Victor Lowenfeld, and Howard Gardner, we now look on children's early drawings as evidence of brain growth and development, rather than poor attempts at art making. Drawing is a natural form of human communication that develops the world over, and children's drawings give evidence about how they think (cognition), their emotional state (affective domain), and fine and gross motor development. By observing efforts to control drawing tools and examining what drawings say about thoughts and feelings, much can be learned.

What Scribbles Really Mean. Symbolic drawing development occurs in stages, similar to growth in verbal communication, from small steps to giant leaps, from general to particular. Beginning with the basic element of *line*, art development can be seen in toddlers who soon discover how art tools extend fingers to make marks, everywhere, much to the chagrin of fastidious parents. Kellogg (1969) broke ground in recording children's art development. She spent twenty years collecting over a million samples of children's drawings that showed that the artistic journey from scribbling to enclosed shapes to use of graphic symbols is universal. Analysis of research samples reveals patterns of growth she grouped into stages beginning with twenty basic scribbles. Her developmental sequence describes children moving from random scribbles to more controlled scribbling and then to formation of enclosed shapes that indicate increased understanding of spatial relationships. Shapes evolve into symbols, like mandalas and suns, used to create people shapes. Lowenfeld and Brittain (1987) took this line of research through the adolescent years and theorized that children made advances naturally, without being taught to draw. By age nine, base lines and skylines appear, and "x-ray drawings" show under-

Post It Page • 5-3

Basic Scribbles and Evolution of Pictures from Scribbling

Note: Children's drawings reflect growth in thinking (cognition) and in physical control (gross and fine motor) over materials and art tools.

Ages	Benchmarks
1–2 years	*Random scribbling.* Exploration of tools and materials, showing increasing fine and gross motor control. Single and multiple dots and lines (vertical, horizontal, diagonal, and wavy) produce some twenty basic scribbles that eventually include loops, spirals, and circles. Examples:

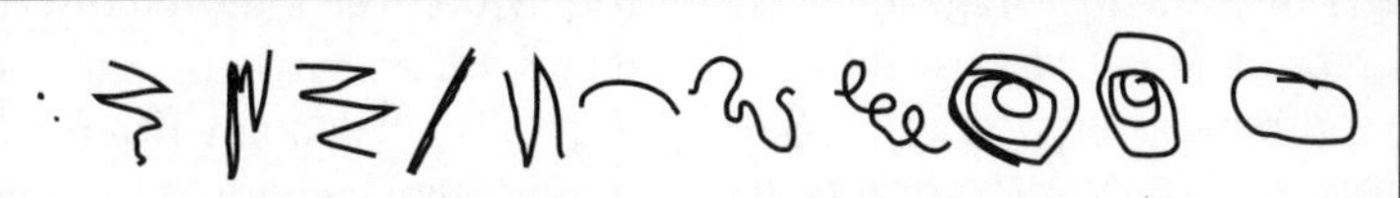

Ages	Benchmarks
2–7 years	*Shape making.* Scribbles begin to be intentionally used to make basic shapes or diagrams. Children combine shapes and use overlapping. Eventually, the shapes form aggregates (three or more diagrams together). Examples:

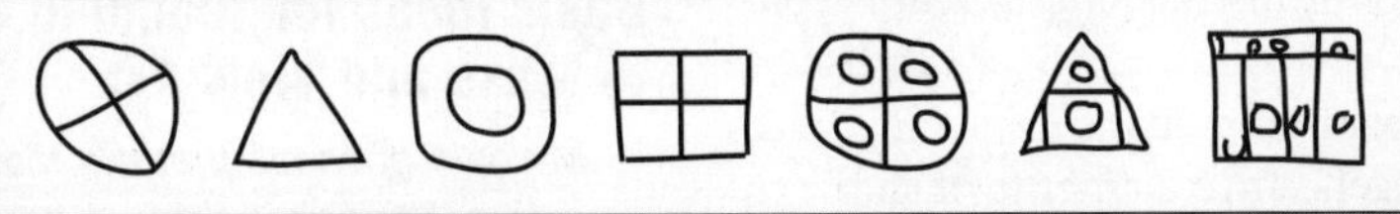

Ages	Benchmarks
3–5 years	*Symbol making.* Lopsided geometric shapes are made. Mandalas and suns are drawn and evolve into human figures. At first, arms and legs stretch from the head. Eventually, torsos emerge and human figures are drawn with more and more completeness. Examples:

Based on Kellogg (1969) and Lowenfeld and Brittain (1987).

standings developed about the unseen. Unfortunately, by age twelve many were observed to abandon spontaneous drawing.

Art educator Mona Brookes (1996) offers an explanation for why children often stop drawing. She thinks *symbolic* and *realistic* drawing are two different types of drawing and should not be compared. Symbolic drawing is natural drawing that children produce that develops in a predictable progression like all human communication. It is *nonverbal* communication used for self-expression. Children create symbols for animals, people, houses, and trees and even talk to themselves as they draw, often telling a story. For example, "Here is my dad shaving. He has lots of cream on his face. It makes him funny." Symbolic drawing usually culminates in abstract stick-figure images. About age eight or nine, children give up symbolic drawing and want to draw realistically, to record an image artistically so that it is recognizable by others (p. 15). But Brookes argues that this skill doesn't usually happen without instruction, just as children need instruction to learn to spell or use handwriting to represent language in conventional ways. (Spelling development begins with scribbles and "pretend writing" and proceeds from gross approximations of beginning and ending sounds to representing all the sounds in a word to conventional spelling. Educators recognize the importance of giving instruction to facilitate the move to correct spelling.) Realistic drawing demands attention to detail, a degree and kind of focus and concentration that Brookes thinks can be taught. She gives examples of drawings done from prompts to "draw a person," which produced simple stick-figure images, and drawings done after *one* lesson on analyzing elements of shape and attending to detail. The two sets of drawing show dramatic differences caused by explicit instruction and demonstrate children are capable of sophisticated *realistic* drawing. Brookes uses a *drawing alphabet* to provide the "basis for seeing with an educated eye" and teaches five elements of shape to "analyze and break down what is seen" (1996). While Brookes shows that children can be taught to do realistic work, she emphasizes that they should be encouraged to do free symbolic drawing (1996, pictures throughout). Post It Page 5–3 shows basic scribbling stages through which children progress.

Waves of Development. Gardner's research on art development led him to postulate growth in *waves,* rather than stages (1990). His theory depicts waves of knowledge rising higher and higher in a specific intelligence area and then spilling over into another intelligence. For example, children begin to draw animals and make the sounds of the animals as they draw, which he thought showed that they pull from their musical intelligences into the visual–spatial. By age five, children begin *digital mapping,* which entails careful representation of numbers of fingers, legs, and arms in drawings. By seven, children begin to invent original notation systems to catalogue belongings and experiences.

To summarize, artistic growth proceeds from the gross to the particular, from uncontrolled to controlled, from exploration of media and tools to skilled use of lines to represent ideas. As more and more detail emerges, we can infer the child has keenly observed lines, shapes, colours, and textures in the world. Each piece of art is tangible evidence of connections forged in the child's brain. While art development begins with drawing, drawing is much more than entertainment for children. By examining samples of children's art and writing over time, it is possible to track developmental patterns that parallel the process that early human ancestors used to move from pictograph (early written human language) to alphabetic code to written language. Children's drawings contain symbols to represent objects and actions important in their lives, and show how drawing is a communication tool closely linked to linguistic growth. Artistic growth signals the cognitive and physical growth necessary to write, so teachers should view drawing tools as writing tools, too. Moreover, children can return to artwork to revise it and use art as a source for new ideas, the same thinking skills needed in written composition. Finally, when we encourage children to draw and engage them in dialogues about their work, we acknowledge that marks have meaning. Thus, children's art can record experiences, ideas, and feelings related to curricular studies.

Basic Ideas for Teaching Students to Make and View Art

My own guess is that the fear of being disturbed by external direction occurs in individuals in whom the intuitive impulse and control are weak or hampered by some other influences and who therefore, in fact, cannot afford any distraction . . . it should serve as a warning to us educators. The growth of the young mind is at best a delicate process, easily disturbed by the wrong input at the wrong time. In the arts as well as elsewhere in education the best teacher is not the one who deals out all he knows or who withholds all he could give, but the one, with the wisdom of a good gardener, who watches, judges, and helps out when the help is needed.

Arnheim, 1989, p. 37

While Arnheim and others acknowledge how young artists may be distracted, at first, by raising to a conscious level what they have been doing unconsciously, this is necessary to help move them to higher levels of artistry. Arnheim calls the discomfort an "intermediate phase of frustration." Students who know the language and tools of art have conceptual anchors and skills to create, discuss, understand, and make judgments in the visual domain. But some remain dubious about giving children explicit art instruction, fearing it may conflict with "natural" art development. Mona Brookes, founder of the teaching philosophy *Monart,* counters that because symbolic art development and the ability to create representational art are two *different* entities, direct instruction in realistic drawing will not hinder symbolic natural expression. Without direct instruction, she believes most children will not automatically discover the artistry of making realistic drawings and will abandon drawing in the teen years. (See more discussion about Monart in Chapter 6.) It seems clear teachers need to know and teach basic art concepts to *meaningfully* integrate art, since students need to be taught to successfully use art to make meaning throughout life. Such focus ensures that art not simply become an amusement added to curricular areas. What's more, it appears instruction in art basics may counter the tendency most children have to abandon art as a form of expression. Essential information that teachers need is summarized in Post It Pages 5–4, 5–7, 5–8, and 5–9.

However, as with other arts, visual art needs to be experienced as a *whole* before it is broken down into component parts, which means children need to view and make art first, so that a desire to want to know more is developed. Elements can be introduced formally and informally, using labels *as natural opportunities arise.* For example, teachers can point out lines, shapes, textures, and colours in picture book art, in illustrations of texts, and in examples in the natural world. Posters and charts of visual elements are useful references to do so. See Chapter 6 for ideas to teach art elements.

Post It Page • 5-4

Visual Art Elements and Design Concepts

Colour: primary and secondary hues, tints, and shades created by light and pigments

Line: a horizontal, vertical, angled, or curved mark made by a tool across a surface

Shape: the two dimensions of height and width arranged geometrically (e.g., circles, triangles), organically (natural shapes), symbolically (e.g. letters)

Texture: the way something feels or looks like it would feel

Form: three-dimensional quality (height, width, and depth), e.g., sphere, pyramid, cube

Pattern: something that is repeated, e.g., shapes, lines

Space: the areas objects take up (positive space) and that surround shapes and forms (negative space)

Contrast: created by lighter colours next to darker ones

Light: illusion created with lighter colours like white

Composition: arrangement of the masses and spaces

Perspective: illusion of distance and point of view created by techniques such as size, overlapping, atmosphere, sharpness or blurriness, and angles

Foreground, middle, and background: the areas in a piece of art that appear closest to the viewer, next closest, and farthest away

Other concepts: **balance, symmetry, asymmetry.**

Women and wolf

Art Materials and Techniques

Teachers with a repertoire of strategies beyond "draw a picture" can offer students media and techniques that enliven learning throughout the curriculum. Media use changes the content or message—the same idea presented in a cartoon comes across differently in a collage—and students simply have a broader range of tools to use to communicate when they have a knowledgeable skilled teacher. Flexible use of many media and tools helps students know in different ways, and it is more interesting to have choices. Post It Pages 5–7 and 5–8 summarize possibilities.

Subject Matter: What Art Is About

> *The source of art is not visual reality, but the dreams, hopes, and aspirations which lie deep in every human.*
>
> Arthur Zaidenberg

The basic art subject matter groupings can help students understand art and give more options for original art making. For example, a response to a piece of literature focused on characterization might be a portrait. Here are the most common classifications:

Portrait: person(s)

Cityscape: city view

Landscape: outdoor scene

Seascape: a view of a body of water

Interior: inside view of a room or building

Still life: arrangement of nonliving objects

Abstract: colour, shape, line, texture is the focus

Narrative: a moment in a story

The People of Art: Artists and Their Styles

Another important area that offers classroom possibilities for integration is the study of the people of art and the unique styles they have created. Children find the childhoods of famous artists interesting, and studying artists is a natural connection to the literary genre of biography. Timelines about artists' lives emerge in classrooms where teachers provoke students' interests about the period of history when the person lived. Maps and globes become important tools to locate places where men and women created the world's art treasury. Since styles of art reflect the society in which they are created, students discuss economic and social circumstances under which new styles were born. For example, the chaotic turn of the century was the context for the birth of abstract art, cubism, Dada, and other forms. Higher-order thinking skills are honed when students analyze and evaluate style attributes as they learn to discriminate and appreciate art styles. Finally, students learn about the personal struggles of artists and the many styles that represent the courage to take risks. This gives robust models and a source of ideas for experimenting with ways to express ideas. Even learning how artists often copy styles of artists who have gone before them helps children understand that being creative doesn't mean starting with nothing. Picasso copied styles of African masks, Michelangelo copied other artists for years to train himself, and Degas worked from photographs; each adapted, twisted, combined, reshaped, stretched, or expanded others' work and in so doing made creative contributions to self and society. Post It Page 5–9 lists art styles to help teach students to understand art and as a resource for their art making. *Note:* The bibliography of arts-based literature in the appendix has books about artists and styles. There are also video and software resources. For example, see the book of interviews with children's book illustrators entitled *Talking with Artists* by Pat Cummings (1992).

Special Arts Integration Projects

Learning Through the Arts™ (LTTA™). Learning Through the Arts™ is an intensive, three-year program that transforms the environment for learning within public schools and equips all children with the learning skills, social intelligence, and creativity to succeed in our global society. The Learning Through the Arts™ program presently includes seventy schools in Vancouver, Calgary, Regina, Windsor, Toronto, Cape Breton, and Corner Brook in settings ranging from inner-city to rural sites.

LTTA™ was initially inspired by research indicating that the arts—conceived in the broadest sense as tools for learning—could help children grasp foundation concepts and skills in math, science, history, social studies, and language. LTTA™ establishes long-term partnerships between teachers and specially trained artist-educators who serve as change agents within the school, promoting collaboration, risk taking, and continuous learning by teachers and students alike. (For more information, visit www.rcmusic.ca)

ArtsSmarts. Partners across Canada have joined The J.W. McConnell Family Foundation in its national ArtsSmarts initiative to promote the active participation of young people in the arts. Through local school-based and community-based projects, the arts are integrated throughout the curriculum; dancers help teach math and sculptors help teach geography. ArtsSmarts puts artists and the arts into schools and communities. Through ArtsSmarts, the power of the arts is being used to release the creative potential of young people to positively shape their intellectual and emotional development. For more information, see the ArtsSmarts web site: www.nlac.nf.ca/html/asmarts.htm.

The National Arts Education Institute. The National Arts Education Institute is a partnership of national cultural institutions and teaching institutions. Members include the Canada Council for the Arts, Canadian Conference of the Arts, Canadian Museum of Civilization, Canadian Music Centre, National Arts Centre, National Gallery of Canada, National Library of Canada, The School of Dance (in Ottawa), and the University of Ottawa. Its mandate is to promote teaching, learning, and inquiry in arts education. The partnership is committed to supporting educational programs for teachers that provide contact with professional artists and arts institutions, and that foster reflection and research on artistic processes and arts education. The National Arts Education Institute (NAEI) delivers two Masters Credit courses granted by the University of Ottawa, consisting of the two summer courses and related thesis papers to be completed over the following year. One of the courses addresses curriculum needs directly (Learning and Teaching in the Arts), and the other is about experiencing the arts through direct contact with artists and arts institutions. These credits will be transferable to universities across the country. For further information, contact the Canadian Conference on the Arts at 613-234-2742, by e-mail at Susan_Annis@mail.culturenet.ca, by fax at 613-234-7556, or write to the Canadian Conference of the Arts, 804–130 Albert Street, Ottawa, ON, K1P 5G4.

Getty's Discipline-Based Art Education (DBAE) In the 1980s, the John Paul Getty Center for Education in the Arts created a curricular model for art education that recommended decreased emphasis on art making and increased focus on teaching art history, aesthetics, and art criticism. The model retained hands-on art as a focus, but stressed discussion of art as a discipline of inquiry. The rationale was grounded in the belief that an art program, based entirely on creating art, does not give a sense of the place of art in life and the world, and art making does not prepare children to respond to the work of others or to develop a visual aesthetic sense important in our highly visual world. The Getty curriculum proposal raised questions about how children were being educated as whole persons in schools that treated art as hands-on construction only. The curriculum developers expressed concern about the lack of visual and artistic literacy among students who could complete thirteen years of education and have little opportunity to reflect on the vast treasury of art that is their cultural heritage. On the other hand, *discipline-based art education* (DBAE) has been criticized, especially by early childhood educators, who believe art making should be the focus. For the most part, it has come to be accepted that a balanced program of art experiences is needed. While children's cognitive growth (e.g., language and conceptual development) is greatly facilitated by exploration through drawing and other artwork, even young children benefit from opportunities to examine and discuss their art and that of others. Classroom teachers interested in DBAE can visit the Getty web site www.artsednet.getty.edu (Eisner, 1983; Gardner, 1990; McWinnie, 1992; Winner et al., 1983).

Lincoln Center. There are numerous initiatives across the United States concerned with meaningful art integration and balanced art instruction. The Lincoln Center project in New York City is one example of a program focused on classroom teacher development.

Curriculum Goals and Expectations

Teachers should use the goals and expectations for the arts as outlined in their provincial or district curriculum and the National Guidelines of the Canadian Society for Education through Art to plan lessons and units that are directed toward learning about art and using art as a teaching and learning tool.

How Can Classroom Teachers Use Art to Enhance Other Curricular Areas?

> *Good teaching makes for good learning in more or less the same way in all fields of study. . . . Good work in biology or mathematics is done when the student's natural curiosity is awakened, when the desire to solve problems and to explain mysterious facts is enlisted, when the imagination is challenged to come up with new possibilities. In this sense, scientific work or the probing of history or the handling of a language is every bit as "artistic" as drawing and painting.*
>
> Rudolf Arnheim (1989, p. 33)

General Principles

In Chapter 2 a framework for achieving arts integration was described for teaching *with, about, in,* and *through* the arts. The principles of integration are grounded in this framework and are ways to achieve curricular goals, while maintaining the integrity of each art form. In examining the following ten integration principles, keep in mind the balance between using art as a teaching and learning tool and respecting art as a special discipline itself.

Principle One: INFUSE THE VISUAL ARTS

> *Though we travel the world over to find the beautiful, we must carry it with us or we find it not.*
>
> Ralph Waldo Emerson

The Aesthetic Classroom Environment. We create our home environments to satisfy individual taste and comfort needs; the same consideration needs to be given to the design of a classroom. Children feel and behave better in environments that please the senses. Broken blinds, dirty floors, mismatched furniture, and peeling paint indicate apathy and imply a low priority for aesthetics. What makes a pleasing classroom? Cleanliness is basic, and it is important for colour schemes to complement one another and light to be soft, not glare white, to relax and make learning pleasant. Storage areas are needed to organize tools and materials. Framed art, plants, music, good smells, fresh air, and art displays all contribute to a heightened sensory awareness. Such an environment inspires positive attitudes and uplifts spirits. While there is no one *best* aesthetic environment, consider these questions when planning or evaluating a classroom (Koster, 1997):

- Is there plenty of soft, natural light?
- Are there carpeted and uncarpeted areas that are visually pleasing, inviting, and functional?
- Are there designated learning station nooks and centres balanced with open areas?
- Are walls and furniture neutral in colour so that they give the illusion of space and wear well over time? Note that bold primary colours may inhibit the learning of some children.
- Are walls a neutral backdrop for displayed art?
- Does there seem to be planning in the displays or do they look like a chaotic hodge-podge?
- Are there easels on which art prints are displayed? Are they changed regularly?

- Are displays at students' eye levels?
- Are bulletin boards teacher-made, using commercial art cutouts that limit aesthetic development and reinforce stereotypes?
- Are holiday decorations stereotypical? Is cultural art trivialized by displaying it only for particular holidays?
- Are there focused displays of artifacts, a few select items at a time?
- Is there a sense of organization and order for supplies and books?

Children grow to like what is comfortable and familiar and may shrink from the strange. If they are to become accepting of differing forms of beauty, they need immersion in all its variations. For example, a classroom should contain art of many styles showing people of different ages, ethnic backgrounds, sexes, and skin colours. It is important for students to see art from different places and time periods—images of people going about life in ways that may be foreign to children, and yet show how basic needs for food, clothing, shelter, knowledge, love, and beauty are universal. Respect for diverse peoples can be encouraged by displaying works in which individuals are portrayed in dignified contemporary situations, not just historical garb. Avoid commercial cutouts, cute cardboard pin-ups, colouring books, patterns of ethnic groups and races *only* in historical traditional clothing, which suggests they are less advanced and still live this way (think how silly it would be to show Canadians in Victorian dress as a "typical" Canadian image). Original art and a variety of types of art show children there are many possibilities. Sculpture, fine art prints, postcard prints, and art books are ways to show authentic cultural images. Most schools and public libraries have children's literature containing art in every style and media, and students can be invited to bring artifacts from home (pottery, quilts, photographs) that may be stunning sources of aesthetic stimulation and family heritage. We can cultivate the aesthetic by planning quiet times to pass around objects for close examination or taking time to stop and listen to nature sounds or patterns of sound created as people and machines go about their work. We can encourage children to find beautiful objects to bring in to a "beauty centre" (shells, leaves, rocks) and discuss the special "magic" feelings possible from seeing a field of sunflowers or touching an infant's velvety hand. All in all, there is no dearth of available resources (Koster, 1997).

Balancing Creation and Appreciation Activities. Integrating art experiences means balancing *impression* and *expression, viewing* and *doing art.* Balance can be achieved through:

1. *Discovery or studio situations* during which materials and tools are provided for children to explore. Even adults begin new experiences by gravitating to the stage of "messing around" with materials to try possibilities. (Think of the first-time use of drawing tools on a computer; often adults revert to scribbling with the drawing tool before trying to create a shape.) Once students gain confidence in using tools and materials, they want to do actual art making during studio times.
2. *Discipline-based study* where children's art is discussed, artists and their work are introduced, art is placed in historical and social contexts, and there is opportunity to reflect and refine aesthetic criteria. Copying adult art is *not* the goal, but children need time to examine art for ideas and learn artistic terms to describe aesthetic qualities (e.g., colour, texture). The teacher's role is to scaffold or support children's efforts to acquire language and concepts. Art integration involves looking and understanding, as well as making.
3. *Art-enriched contexts* in which students are surrounded by art and invited to examine artworks and use materials. This is what was previously discussed as the aesthetic classroom environment, but can include areas beyond the classroom, such as a classroom garden, since the outdoors possesses rich opportunities to investigate colour, texture, line, and shape.
4. *Meaningful art integration* with other arts and curricular areas. Meaningful integration suggests the use of, at least, two-pronged lessons when integrating art: art focus and math focus, art focus and language arts focus, art focus and dance, and so on (see examples of two-pronged lessons in Post It Pages 5–13, 7–7, 9–5 and 11–11). Integration should maintain the integrity of each area being integrated. Suggesting that children just draw pictures after reading something, when time has never been spent teaching anything about possible materials or drawing tools, does not do justice to art as a discipline in its own right. A critical question when doing integration is "What did my students *learn* about all the areas being integrated?" *not* "What areas were *used* in the lesson?" This does not mean the classroom teacher must be able

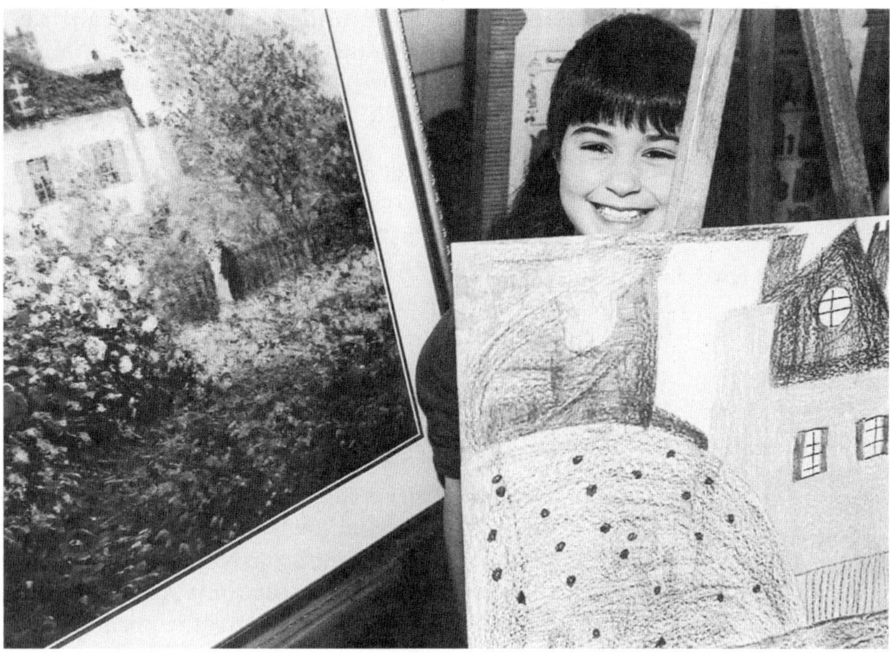

Aping the greats!

to draw well; it does mean the teacher needs a basic knowledge and skill level to use language and present examples of possibilities to students. This also does not mean students shouldn't have free time to make art without instruction (see item 1); children also need free reading time, but we acknowledge the need to teach them *to* read.

Basic Materials. Architect Frank Lloyd Wright said that he "could feel in the palms of his hands the Froebel blocks." He recalled that it was in early childhood when these shapes "had become instinctive to him, giving him his first strong perception of the meanings of volume and form" (Bill, 1988, p. 29). No teacher's words or any book can ever substitute for giving students the actual tools and materials of art. Kinesthetic–tactile intelligence is activated in these encounters and may indeed trigger the beginnings of a magnificent life devotion. What is considered *basic* for a regular classroom? At minimum, each classroom needs:

- An assortment of brushes, chalk, pencils, water-based markers, crayons, and paints (including tempera, watercolours, and paint crayons)
- Different kinds, sizes, and colours of paper, including everything from brown kraft paper to sketch pads to construction paper
- Clays and doughs to use for sculpting and modelling
- Glues and pastes, especially white glue
- Scissors
- Collage materials like shells, buttons, pebbles, lace, ribbon, and fabric
- All shapes and sizes of boxes and tubes for construction and for papier mâché bases
- Cleanup supplies
- Work space (e.g., painting easels and tables that can be covered with old sheets or shower curtains for messy work)

In addition, art reproductions, children's literature about art and artists, quotes, cartoons, facts about artists, songs, photographs, and artifacts are important components of an environment for an integrated arts program. Begin a collection of basic materials by surveying what you have and then think of ways to get what you need without undue time and money. Give friends, other teachers, the school staff, and parents a list of materials to save that would normally be thrown out (e.g., paper towel tubes). Stores that sell wallpaper may give away old wallpaper books that make perfect quick book binders for children's stories. Paper, printing, framing, and photography companies often give paper products. Ask the principal about purchases, but don't despair if the budget is small and don't feel everything must be had the first day of school.

One invaluable freebie is a **picture file.** Collect pictures from magazines and calendars, save postcards, greeting cards, old photographs, and even restaurant placemats to use as sources for art study. For example, besides examining pictures to determine subject matter (landscape, portrait, etc.), media, style, artist, and art elements, children can use pictures as prompts for creating art compositions. Picture files can also become actual art-making materials (e.g., for collage) and be used for drama, storytelling, discussions, and writing prompts. Start by collecting many pictures and include interesting words and phrases that provoke images; headlines and advertisements are good sources. *Sort them into categories:* words and phrases, art styles, art subject matter, other cultures, people, holidays, emotions, places, toys, dance and movement. Mount pictures and words or use plastic sleeves so that they are ready to use. Attach to each file drama or oral expression ideas and writing uses: see Post It Page 4–2 and the discussion questions for the art in Post It Page 2–3, and art discussions in Post It Page 5–5. Tab category sections and make a table of contents.

Another resource is collections of poems, quotes, and cartoons about art and artists to use in routines and bulletin boards, or as inspiration for students to make poem or quote books. Once the scavenging begins, you and your students will find something about art everyday.

Principle Two: Teaching Art Concepts and Skills

Arnheim (1989) denounced the Western notion that the "arts cannot be taught" and that reasoning about them endangers creative invention: "the acquisition of appropriate techniques and the insistence on acceptable results are as necessary in the arts as they are in the other areas of study" (p. 57). He justifies teaching the tools because "At no level of development can either children or accomplished artists state, to their own satisfaction, what they want to say unless they have acquired the means of saying it" (p. 57). The intention is not to foist technical tricks on children that go beyond their ability to use or understand them, nor is the goal to teach visual expression as a set of isolated skills. Instead, tools and technique should naturally emerge from the task demands, when possible. Ideally, students ought to *discover* as much as possible, rather than depend on the teacher; if taught at the wrong time, concepts and skills are meaningless to children. Forced learning can even engender "disturbance and arouse resistance" (p. 33).

Teach What Art Is. We can develop a concept for art by having students discover aspects of what makes something art. For example, ask students to picture an item they believe is art and then share reasons why. We can also explicitly teach about the elements, forms, styles, and media used to make art by displaying elements charts and using art concepts as categories for games and questions. (Post It Pages 5–4, 5–7, 5–8, and 5–9 summarize elements, forms, and media.) In Chapter 6 there are ideas to teach colour, line, shape, texture, etc., including sorts, games, and questioning strategies.

Principle Three: TEACHER HABITS for Integrating Visual Art

Dictated art is not art but a contradiction of it.

Blanche Jefferson

Think Artistically. You need not be able to draw or sculpt *well* to help children do so. Artistic teachers are ones that know how to set up an *aesthetic* classroom, ask good questions, respond with descriptive comments, and show children how to listen, look, and feel the beauty of the world. Here are four examples of developing students' aesthetic senses.

Look Closely. Walt Whitman knew little about the brain, compared to what we know today, and yet, when he wrote about a child that went forth each day and became the object he looked upon, he poetically expressed what research now confirms: the images that enter the brain become the basis for the images we create and the people we become. We need to see to it that children have beautiful images to look on. We can begin by showing how to make discoveries about everyday things, taking time to see details. Offer paper towel tubes or magnifying glasses to look at fabrics and prints to make discoveries. Coloured overhead transparencies and cardboard transparency frames make interesting "windows" to examine the known to find the new. Books like Hoban's *Look Again* can be inspirations to examine the visual world by looking at parts of plants, animals, and clothes. Hoban overlays shape frames over her photos to cause the viewer to focus on a tiny piece of a whole, before seeing the whole. A similar effect can be achieved by masking with note cards or post-its a part of a picture or object (e.g., half of a reproduction could be masked for a guessing game to predict images, colours, shapes). Teacher can use descriptive language like *"I see rounded shapes or a muddy brown colour"* and ask students to describe using the *"I see . . . and . . . structure."*

Aesthetic Aromas. The perfume industry knows well the power of smell to affects behaviour. We avoid nasty smells and seek out wonderful aromas. A class with flowers, potpourri, and fresh air provides for aesthetic sensing and creating. It is, however, becoming increasingly important to be aware of sensitivities and allergies to various substances (e.g. chemicals, perfumes, and mould). Encourage students to share discoveries about good smells through discussions, journals, and charts. Give descriptive feedback to stretch language and encourage use of descriptive words, for example, *"You like the lemony clean smell of this soap!"*

Aesthetic Sounds. Students can make rhythm instruments to explore the differences in sounds. Tape record environmental sounds and create art to go with the sounds. At times, play music as students create. Discuss an art reproduction or other art in terms of the sounds associated with it (e.g., a seascape or landscape). Write sound poems about art, like the *onomatopoeia poem* made using sounds of a place or a period of time. Here is a "schoolday" example: *Ring/ ha ha ha/ patter patter/ slam/ creak/ ring ring/ achoo/ gobble crunch slurp/ scribble/ sigh/ whew/ ring/ trip-trap, trip-trap/ honk toot roar.*

Texture and Touch Aesthetics. To develop tactile modes of perceiving so that students can express texture in artwork, (1) orally describe and ask for students to describe the feelings as they finger paint, use collage materials, or experiment with different pressure of chalk and crayon. For example, *"When I press hard the line is darker and thicker."* (2) Make feely bags of textured items. Put them at a station to explore or use in circle times; students reach in to feel an object and either describe its nature or use it in an add-on storytelling. For example; *There was once a thin, soft bendy creature (stick of gum) who lived in a cave. One day he inched out to look for food and met a long, thin, soft creature with a rough, stringy tongue (tapered candle).* (3) Ask students to bring items for a topical display: rough, soft, silky, cold, hard. (4) Go on texture walks to find items in categories (thin, thick, heavy). The items can be used for nature or "found things" collages or table displays. (5) Involve students in making texture books (e.g., fabrics, foils, papers) by gluing items to card stock and fastening with brads or make big books with text dictated or written by students.

Guide or Director. Classroom teachers often lack confidence about their own art abilities and may have limited personal experiences. Lack of confidence manifests itself in rigidity: using precut assembling activities, painting by number, colouring in the lines, cutting out black line masters, and tracing activities that are no more than following direction exercises. The purpose of art integration is not to have students always arrive at recognizable products. This book should provide enough basic philosophy, research, and knowledge for readers to reject destructive notions that focus on convenience, tradition, and just entertaining children with the arts. Activities that squelch the development of creativity, risk taking, and independent thinking cannot give students substantial experiences for them to grow into capable contributing adults. We lay the foundation in the elementary school. That foundation must be strong. Here are signs that the foundation is not grounded in what we know of child development, nor respectful of children's experience.

- Models and step-by-step directions to copy rather than create
- Commercial bulletin board materials that are cute and convenient (e.g., bunnies and kittens)
- Stencils to trace or punch out letters for displays
- Teacher-made bulletin boards, rather than students planning and creating them
- Colouring-book-type activities in which staying in the lines and stereotyped use of colour is stressed (colour the sky blue and the grass green).
- Students saying, "I can't do it" or "I can't draw" when art activities are introduced or exhibiting frustration and little confidence in their own creativity
- Teachers intervening to do parts of art projects *for* students or having "artistic" students do work for other students
- Students knowing few ways to express themselves through art—only drawing
- Students saying that they hate certain styles of art without ever studying them (e.g., abstract)

Creative Problem-Solving and Authentic Art. Teachers who are committed to arts integration approach most teaching learning opportunities with a "what if . . ." perspective that invites students to experiment, investigate, gather ideas, pose potential solutions, speculate, reflect, evaluate, and feel the joy of discovery. (Now would be a good time to review the creative problem-solving process presented in Post It Page 1–5.) But pressing students to deal with the dissonance created during creative problem-solving can be exasperating for teachers and even for master artists. Georgia O'Keefe spent her early years teaching in Amarillo, Texas, and started teaching college in Canyon, Texas, about 1916. There is a story about how frustrated she became one day when trying to get her students to think for themselves. She went to the board and wrote, *"Would all the fools in this class please leave!"* One student immediately asked, *"Then who will teach us?"* To her credit, Miss O'Keefe had a good laugh at her own expense. We cannot back away from posing creative problem-solving situations to students, even if we expect them to struggle. We can teach *how* to massage the process so that ideas are more likely to be forthcoming. As children's author Katherine Paterson wrote in *Sign of the Chrysanthemum,* "it is only through fire that the spirit is forged."

Guidelines for Teaching Students about *Making* Art. Here are key ideas to help students "do" art successfully:

- Teach *how* to use a variety of media, tools, and techniques: printing, collage, watercolour, chalk, tempera, original stencilling, mobiles, sculpting, rubbings, papier mâché, and use different surfaces (e.g., fabric, wood). Students will not discover these things on their own. See the Chapter 6 strategy seed ideas for ideas on each of these.
- Provide several examples, not models, and then remove them so that students can't copy.
- Use an *explore–practice–express* lesson sequence. Demonstrate ways to use materials and tools and give time to explore and experiment. Students need to repeat use of good materials and media, and sometimes materials and tools can be put out without an introduction for students to discover possibilities—we want doers, not just viewers. Keep in mind the focus on involving students in actual use and practice with materials so that they learn how to *use them to communicate.* Exploration often causes students to want to learn more about how to use a tool or material, too. Give time to try, first, so that they develop a *need to know,* which builds readiness for direct instruction. Consider a teaching sequence of (1) time to explore, (2) time for practice with teacher feedback, as needed, and (3) actual use of materials.
- Limit direction giving. Even adults get impatient with long explanations.
- Give more descriptive feedback than praise as students work. Describe what a student is doing and use an *artistic vocabulary* to teach words and concepts. Focus on what is being learned. "Good job!" and "Great!" are too vague and really teach nothing. *Note:* Don't interrupt students who are actively engaged with comments. They are intrinsically motivated and that's enough.
- Do not ask, "What is it?" since this may insult a student. Instead, offer comments or ask about art elements, the process (*"How did you do this? I see you are trying to put the wash over the candle drawing"*), artistic decisions (*"Why did you do it this way?"*), or predictions (*"What do you think will happen if. . .?* or *How could you. . .?"*).
- Create an atmosphere and expectation for appropriate behaviour. Art making should be a time for focus and concentration. Play music, without lyrics, or make a rule about quiet. Brookes (1996) believes children must be taught the pleasures of silence because they so rarely experience it. She has found it takes a while for children to be comfortable with quiet, but stresses that it is necessary for most people to truly concentrate. She offers strategies to teach the value of silence in her book.
- After students finish, invite them to do docent talks about their work to explain their creative problem-solving process.
- Invite students to write or tell stories about their art, find music that goes with the art, and even create original musical compositions for the art.
- Instead of taking dictation on student art—it is common to ask children to give a sentence about the art or a title and the teacher writes it—have students write for themselves, even if it is in developmental spelling. This builds independence. Instead of anyone writing on a child's art, it is better to write on a separate piece of paper; artists usually don't write anything except their signatures on their art.
- Connect art to the students lives—a part without a whole is a "field without an anchor" (Eisner in Arnheim, 1989, p. 5). Instead of isolated art activities or art used only as a reward for finishing work, integrate art by using the *with, about, in,* and *through* model, discussed in Chapter 2, that includes meaning making through art in routines and units.
- Refrain from using paint by numbers, colouring books, and dittos that are not art at all. This teaches conformity and discourages creativity and problem-solving.

Stations and Centres for Art Investigations. Centres and stations provide opportunities for independent work that extend a lesson or a personal interest. A centre does not have to be elaborate. Here are important *continuous* centres or stations (a station is a place with a single focused activity while a centre has many activities around a topic):

- *Book-making station* with wallpaper, fabric, and other materials to bind student-made books
- *Puppet-making station* with examples of different types of puppets and materials to make them (see the types in Post It Page 6–4)
- Books about art and artists in a *book nook centre* with shelves or areas with children's literature related to other arts areas, too
- *Art-making centre* with collage materials (feathers, buttons, variety of papers), watercolours, pastels, markers, watercolour crayons, different papers, and a posted list of ideas to try in an art response to a book or unit under study. See art response possibilities in Post It Page 5–7. A few books that show how artists use different media and styles are important resources for data gathering to have at this centre.
- *Multicultural arts centre* with many examples of different kinds of art and actual artifacts. This is the place to include a picture file of art to examine for different styles or media use.

Evaluative Judgments. Students don't automatically know how to make good judgments, especially when looking at art. Without instruction, they tend to want to stop at loving or hating a work. These kinds of reactions halt thinking. Children need to be taught to take time and just describe what they see and the feelings a picture or object evokes. Then they can be guided to give reasons *why* they like or dislike a piece or think it is good or bad. This can be done by "thinking aloud" to model responses and by forming the habit of asking students for evidence for opinions they express. This creates an expectation for reflection to be done. A respect for considered thinking can develop, and breezy conclusions are soon seen as just that. Another strategy is to rate judgments of "goodness," or how much a work is liked, using a 1 to 5 scale. Ratings can then be discussed. Ultimately, students need to grasp the concept that to *appreciate* art means to understand it—not that you have to like it.

Teach How to Decode Art. Students who know the basic art elements and concepts that artists use will be more able to talk intelligently about art and this increases understanding and enjoyment. *"What do you see?"* and *"Take time and look closely"* discussion strategies help students learn to concentrate, take time (most people average less than ten seconds looking at individual works in museums), and move from merely identifying and describing to becoming storytellers about art. Use of open questions and directed viewing (e.g., *"Notice the use of overlapping"*) causes students to think at higher levels and do creative problem-solving. Eventually, students see how artwork, done by others, gives perspective on important issues. Group discussions move into meaningful areas, connected to life concerns children have, but may not express without a safe structured opportunity that is interesting and grounded in topics of substance. Post It Page 5–5 can help implement these kinds of discussions.

A Few Other Pointers about Art Discussions. Because detail is so important in art, it is helpful to have a large magnifying glass to examine brush strokes and other aspects of art. Children are intrigued by details that emerge when magnified that were insignificant or invisible before. A flashlight can also be used to highlight areas during discussions. Progress from asking students to describe art to asking for interpretations (e.g., *"What does this mean? Why do you think the artist did that?"*) and into getting them to create stories about the art, as soon as feasible. These levels of discussion are more engaging than ones that focus on identification or description. Another effective strategy is to cover half of a painting or ask groups to choose a section on which to focus (e.g., foreground, background). Small groups can then serve as "experts" on their sections and report back. Finally, try asking students to imagine what happened one minute *before* or *after* an art piece was finished. Students come up with very creative ideas and this can evolve into a drama activity or spark a series of related art works.

Principle Four: ENERGIZERS and Warm-ups

Energizers and warm-ups prepare students to make meaning through art by attuning them to thinking like an artist and activating the senses. These and other examples are described in Chapter 6:

- Listening and looking walks
- Collections
- Displays
- Mystery bag
- Brainstorming

Post It Page • 5-5

Art Discussions: Questioning and Other Strategies

Directions: Use these strategies to teach students to decode artwork and engage them in personal connections and storytelling.

- **Children's thinking develops from concrete to abstract.** Young children have difficulty with questions like *"Why might the artist have painted this?"* (motives or intentions) and understanding visual symbols like colours or objects to represent seasons. Primary students can interpret art, however, so try these types of questions and, if they have trouble, back up to more concrete ones. *Note:* Young children need chances to examine abstract art and often prefer it to detailed realism.
- **Plan questions ahead of time** that form a *line of questioning* that leads to a point. Help students see something they would not have seen otherwise. Go for the "Ahhh" response.
- **Ask open or fat questions:** *"What do you see? What's this about? What does this tell us about people? What story does this tell?"* These require higher-order thinking skills. Assure children there is no single interpretation of a work of art, and honest responses are welcome.
- **Give sufficient time to LOOK before questioning.** Encourage curiosity and commitment by guiding children to "look closely and take time." Set an amount of time for all to look and not talk.
- **Speak to children at their level, but don't paternalize.** Relate to their experiences and try to include each child, at least with eye contact. Vary voice and smile to sustain interest.
- **Use wait time and every pupil response signals.** More students will respond with longer and more meaningful answers if you ask, wait three to five seconds, and then ask for a response signal like "thumbs up." Wait for everyone to think of a response for certain questions so that all feel "expected" to be active. Then call on selected students as time permits.
- **If your question doesn't work, rephrase it.**
- **Be sensitive to interests** and take advantage of unexpected teachable moments to follow through on an expressed curiosity.
- **Listen and be responsive to children's answers.** Don't rush. Give time to think and speak.
- **Compliment and praise honest or appropriate answers.**
- **If a wrong or inaccurate response is given,** don't embarrass the student, but respond *"That's an interesting idea. Who has a different idea?"* Use "dignifying" techniques: Ask the student to explain why he thinks this is right; ask for the ideas of others about the question; attempt to direct students toward accurate answers, but allow responders to save face. *Note:* This only is necessary in obvious situations (e.g., the student says the painting is by van Gogh when it is actually by Rembrant). Try to find ways to dignify any honest response. In this case you might say, *"This was done by a Dutch artist but not van Gogh. Do you know another Dutch artist that might be the artist for this?"*
- **When an answer is partly correct,** rephrase the question, using the correct information to create another question. *"Yes it is true that . . . but let's look again and see if we can find. . . ."*
- **Follow through on student responses:** Ask for evidence for their ideas. An example sequence is: *Question:* "What season of the year is it?" *Answer:* "Winter." *Follow-up:* "How does the artist show this?" *Question:* "How does this painting make you feel?" *Answer:* "Sad." *Follow-up:* "Why? What makes you feel that way?"

or "Why do you think that?" Ask them to "tell more" about their thinking. Paraphrase or repeat responses and ask if you've done so accurately. Ask other students to respond or piggyback on a student's idea (e.g., *"What do the rest of you think about Joan's point?"*).

- **Encourage student questions** with requests like *"What questions do you have?"* or invite students to all write out questions. Put them in a hat and draw out to help students feel safe.
- **Plan small-group discussion.** Start with pairs or trios with immature students and work up to groups of four to six. Give a few minutes to discuss a question among themselves (e.g., *"Find a partner and talk about what choices this artist had to make to create this work (materials), how it was arranged."* This allows shy students to participate and is a way to prepare for a larger-group discussion.
- **End the discussion.** Ask students to tell something they learned, what someone said that made sense, something that was surprising, or just repeat an idea they heard that was interesting.

- Twenty questions
- Sense stations
- Browsing picture file and books
- Exploring and messing around

Principle Five: GREAT Children's Literature about Visual Art and Artists

We are fortunate to have technology to make exquisite literature containing visual art. In addition to the genre of picture books, there are hundreds of books whose themes make powerful statements about art's central place in life. In the appendix there is a bibliography of award-winning art-based children's literature, including winners of the Governor General's Awards and the Caldecott Award. The Caldecott Award is presented yearly for excellence in picture books—books that contain pictures that are more than illustrations, pictures that make aesthetic statements. Post It Page 5–10 has a few annotated books that show the variety of art topics in books, making them an important teaching resource. Included are notes about media, art elements and concepts, and culture.

Author–Artist Studies. One of the basic types of units used in integrated teaching is the author–artist study. The purpose of this unit is to learn about the creators of books. Students learn biographical information, the process of creation, and the artist's style, and other arts, skills, and subject areas are used to explore the person being studied. *Source books* for information on artist–authors appear in Post It Page 3–6. Post It Page 5–6 depicts a web for a study. Here are guidelines to plan an artist–author unit, and Post It Page 5–11 has a list of author–artists to focus of this type of unit.

Artist–Author Study Unit Guidelines and Ideas

- Start by collecting material about authors and artists in a file. Use source books, filmstrips, and audio and video tapes to find biographical information, quotes, and interesting facts. (See Post It Pages 3–6 and 5–11.) Organize information on an author–artist "map" with these categories: name and vital statistics, books written and/or illustrated, awards, information about the books (genre, problems, themes, style), childhood, hobbies, interests and favourites, how and why the person writes or creates, idiosyncracies about the person, special quotes about or from the person.
- Read a biography or autobiography of the author or artist.
- Locate where the person lives on a map.
- Collect and read all the works by the author or artist.
- Experiment with art media and styles of an artist. Invite a local artist to demonstrate or visit an artist's studio.
- Find other art and trade books in the same media and style. Read *If You Were a Writer* (Nixon, 1988) to learn how a writer works.
- Arrange a conference telephone call with the author or artist (check with the publisher).
- Write a letter to the author or artist.
- Do a presentation about the person and his or her work (biographical information, style; share examples by showing art and reading aloud sections). Do a drama presentation in which you become the author or artist.

- Make a bulletin board, display, posters, booklet, or brochure on the person and his or her work.
- Write and bind a book about the author or artist.
- Interview a local author about the writing process.
- Create author and artist blurbs to include in books in the classroom so that future readers have this information.
- Visit a local publishing company or newspaper to see the publishing process.

Finding Art-based Literature. Locate information about authors and artists in source books. Post It Page 3–6 can also help you find materials for units.

Picture Books Related to Curricular Areas. Picture books are now available on nearly every curricular topic and are fine additions to science, social studies, and math. For example, during a Canadian Arctic unit, the pictures in Houston's *Tikta' Liktak* can be enjoyed while providing significant factual information. The illustrations by Paul Morin in *The Orphan Boy* (Tolowa) describe an East African folktale and the life of a Masai boy. Ron Lightburn's pictures in *Waiting for the Whales* (McFarlane) can enlighten a unit on mammals. Seymour Simon's books contain wonderful examples of photography and science. Any fine picture book can serve as material to develop language arts and visual literacy skills by asking students to tell what they see (see Post It Page 5–5). Art strategies for picture book art exploration are given in Post It Page 5–12.

Principle Six: ROUTINES

Daily Art Routines and Rituals. Two examples of short routines to integrate arts are (1) have an "artist of the day" or daily "art concept" (an art form, element, or style) and (2) do art book ads to promote art-based literature. Invite students to become "experts" to present routines, as a means of developing speaking and listening. For shy students, use a puppet (named "Art" with a smock and beret?) to speak in front of the group. Daily riddles, poems, and songs about art and artists that you find or are written by the students are other possible routines. (Barbara Streisand's song "Putting It Together" is about making art.) Also see Chapter 6 for seed ideas.

Masterpiece Corner. Art reproductions from large format to postcard size are easy to obtain and often inexpensive (see sources at the end of the chapter). Calendars in every art style are available at huge savings in January and February. (Explain that reproductions are photographs of original art so that students understand the real thing may be much larger and look different. Students are interested in the dimensions of original art and locations where they might travel to see it in a gallery.) Display reproductions at children's eye level on easels, which adds a feeling of importance because they are special furniture, just for art. They can be found at flea markets for as little as a dollar. Provoke thought about the art by displaying the title and asking students to predict colours, mood, and so on, before showing a reproduction; asking students to compose a title, after viewing the reproduction and taking time to discuss it; or displaying a question with a reproduction as a journal stimulus. For example, *"Why do you think the artist chose to paint this?"* or *"What do you see in this reproduction that you don't think anyone else will see?"* Postcards, matching the large reproduction, can be used to make comparisons or to set up as a matching station. Another idea is to buy two copies of the same print and cut one up so that students can attend to art details by matching pieces with the whole. Students also enjoy playing "I spy" with reproductions with a large magnifying glass. The teacher begins by saying *"I spy . . .* (a cat, triangle, the colour puce, etc.), and the first student or team to see it signals and is given the magnifying glass to prove the find. Provide students with information about artists and share books about artists when displaying a work of art. Krull's *Lives of Artists* is a source, and others are given in the appendix under Arts-based Children's Literature.

Principle Seven: ADAPT CURRICULUM MODELS to Integrate Art and Meet Student Needs

Units and Projects for Art Integration. Of course, art can be the body of a unit or one of the legs. Any of the four unit types presented in Chapter 2 can be used to integrate visual art. When planning any unit, remember to web ideas, align activities with the course of study and provincial or district curriculum goals and expectations, plan initiating or starting events, a sequence of lessons to develop the unit, and a culminating event to wrap it up. An example author–artist unit web appears in Post It Page 5–6.

Similar, and often overlapping with unit study, are projects. Projects are usually interest based and often done in small groups. They involve students in discovery learning and creative problem-solving. Projects begin with exploration of an idea followed by planning. Students are encouraged to take on decision making, as appropriate for their age and stage. Schools like Reggio Emilia in Italy (Edwards, Gandini, & Forman, 1993)

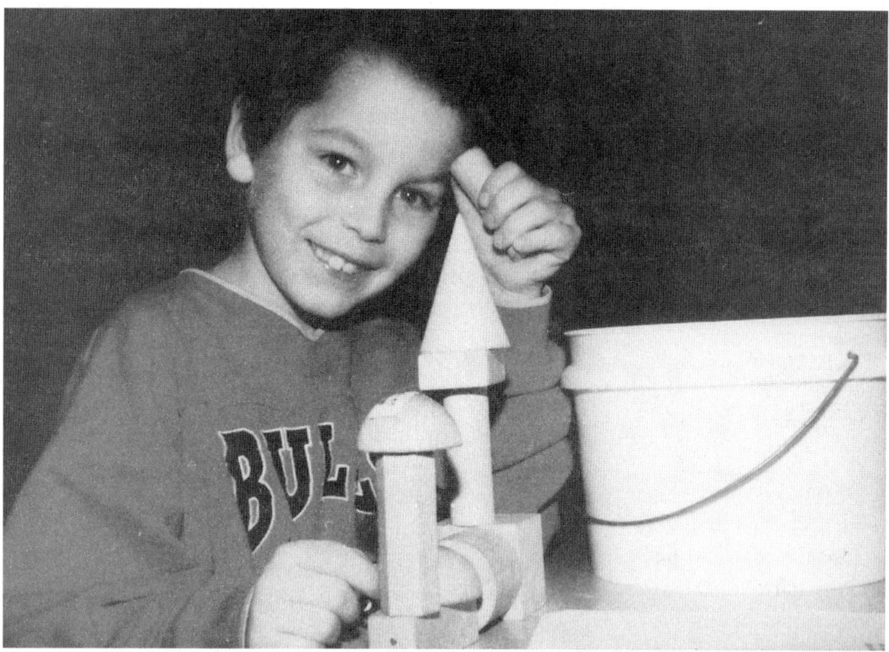

Shape and form

have formed the entire curriculum based on hands-on projects that result in student products to be shared or displayed. A project could involve the construction of a mural in science or social studies or the making of papier mâché sculptures of characters in a core book unit.

General Connections to Math, Science, Social Studies, and Language Arts

Art is the lie that enables us to realize the truth.

Pablo Picasso

What does art have to do with science or social studies or math? How does art show what we know about people or places? Consider these connections:

- ***Social studies*** can centre around the lives of particular artists, artworks, styles, societal influences, cultures, and careers in art.
- ***Science*** can be learned by examining pigments, how colour is made, the chemistry of art materials, the physics of art forms like sculpture and mobiles, the creation of optical illusions, and the photographic process.
- ***The language arts*** of listening, speaking, reading, and writing are developed when students learn the special vocabulary associated with visual art and learn to write about art in both creative forms (stories, poems) or using art criticism.
- ***Literature and art*** are naturally connected through picture books, but pre- and post-reading art strategies enrich both art forms by stimulating imaging and imagery (e.g., authors like Natalie Babbitt use a lot of verbal imagery that can be transformed into a visual form).
- ***Math and art*** are integrally related. For example, linear perspective is math based, and both art and math include a focus on geometric shapes. Post It Page 5–13 is an example of a math and art integrated lesson using the plan format from Chapter 2.
- ***Music and art*** share many of the same elements, for example, rhythm and pattern. Think of looking at art and imagining what you hear. Music can inspire art, and vice versa.
- ***Theatre*** includes art in the sets and costumes of the actors.
- ***Dance and art*** share elements like lines that move and shapes that create a composition. Dancers have been an inspiration for art making (e.g., Degas's ballerinas).

Post It Page • 5-6

Unit Web: Author-Artist Study

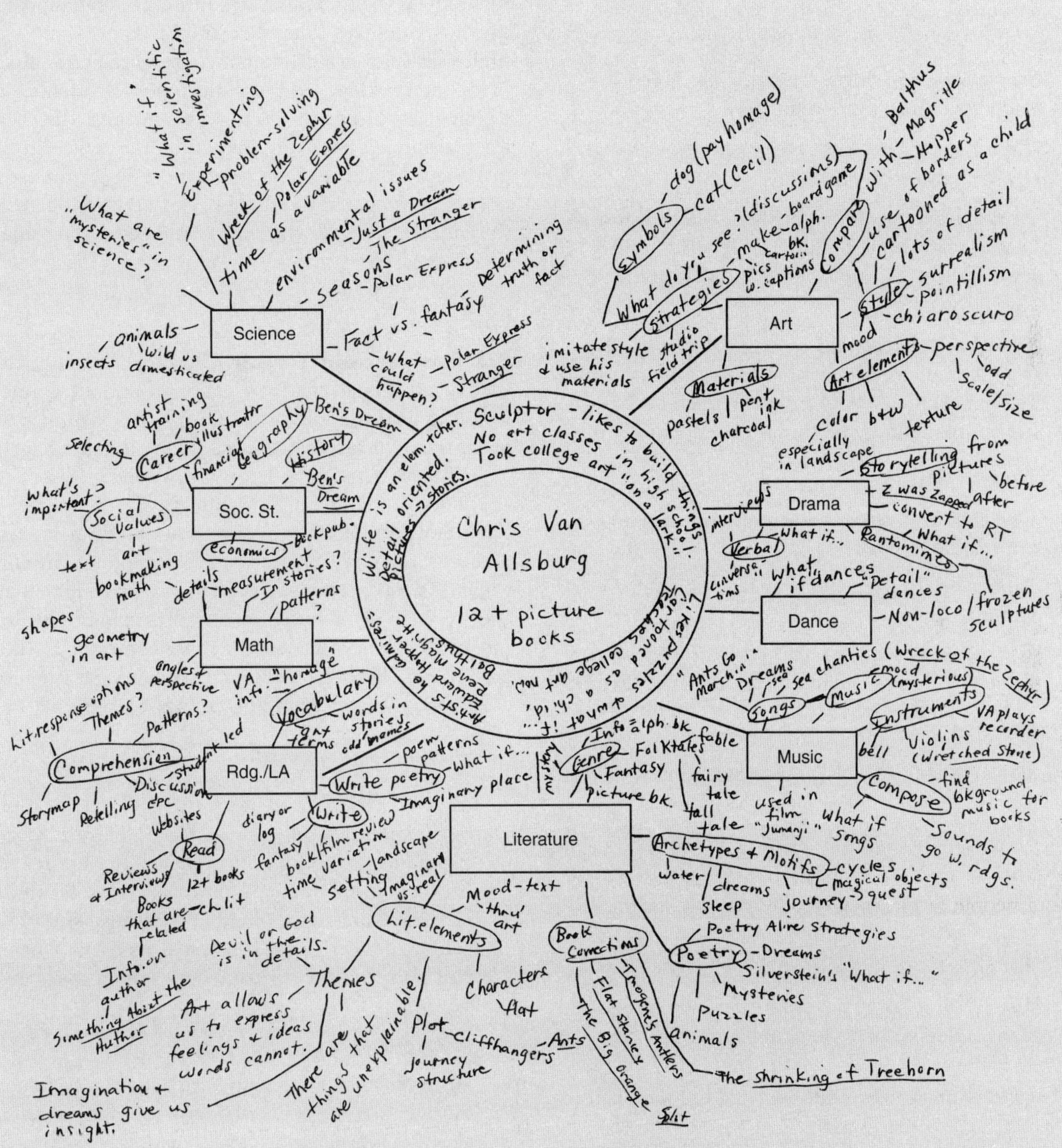

Differentiating Instruction. In Chapter 2, a set of strategies to differentiate instruction was presented. Here are some ways to individualize instruction using those strategies:

Place: Set up work areas where children who are distractible have few distractions.

Amount: Use projects that require just a few simple steps for children who need success.

Rate: Go more slowly when giving directions and allow more time to finish.

Target objectives: Make the goals clearer by showing more examples.

Instruction: Give more explicit instruction with clear art language; build more repetition into lessons through questioning and asking for choral responses.

Curriculum materials: Use more visual aids (e.g., colour wheel, elements chart with symbols, and personal elements charts for each desk to help remember all the things to try).

Utensils

- Use a children's rotary cutter for those who cannot handle scissors.
- Tape paper to the table so that it won't move around.
- Use scented paint and markers for those who are colour blind or have limited sight. Scents can be added (vanilla, lemon, etc.). Be aware of students' allergies and sensitivities.
- Attach drawing and painting tools to headgear or tape to a hand to improve control.
- Thicken paint and use shorter and larger brushes.
- Use collage materials that can be arranged and rearranged. Start with larger pieces or objects that are easy to grasp.
- Wrap crayons and markers with masking tape or foam curlers to provide better grips.

Level of difficulty: Build in more time to explore materials so that students feel more in control.

Assistance: Use the "guided hand technique" to help students get the feel of drawing or painting (put your hand over theirs or theirs over yours); allow students to work with a partner.

Response: Consider different ways students can respond besides the project selected. For example, give materials choices, rather than all make a paper bag puppet from collage materials.

In general, consider ages, stages, and interests when designing art-making or art-looking lessons. Remember, young children are more concrete and less product oriented. They like bright colours and may prefer abstract art or simplified representational art. With intermediate and middle school students, use frequent small-group discussions and give direction; for example, discuss why they think the artist did this piece and how; tell them you expect all group members to be prepared to report back to the whole group so that everyone will be actively engaged during small-group times.

Principle Eight: TAKE FIELD TRIPS

See Tips for Field Trips in Chapter 2. Opportunities for art-related field trips abound and art connections can be made to most field trips; for example, connect art like Picasso's "Paul as Harlequin" or Chagall's "The Blue Circus" to a circus visit. Walking trips to examine local architecture of churches, monuments, or cemeteries are chances to build art vocabulary, data gather for an art project, and develop community pride. Just a trip around the block can provide rich images to categorize by colours, lines, shapes, and textures. Museum visits are the most common art field trip, so guidelines to make sure students get the most out of the trip appear in Post it Page 5–14.

Plan art gallery visits:

- *Before the visit:* Check with the gallery education department for self-tour materials, current school programs, exhibition information, teacher resources, and guidelines for group visits. Study art elements, practise looking at paintings, study artists and forms you'll see, make a list of what you want to find out together.
- *During the visit:* Give students specific things to look for and do.
- *After the visit:* Follow up with activities to find out what students learned. Ask them to write about favourite paintings, do art response projects (media, styles, forms, etc.).

See the books in the arts-based bibliography in the appendix about museum and art gallery visits (e.g.,

Lionni's *Matthew's Dream* and Brown and Brown's *Visiting the Art Museum*). Post It Page 5–14 has strategies for museum visits.

Principle Nine: EXHIBIT STUDENT PROGRESS

Task Completion. It is difficult to judge results unless work is completed. The satisfaction of success is withheld if effort is not made to reach closure, and we cannot improve without opportunity to understand failures. Self-discipline is developed by working through problems and frustrations with the support of others. Therefore, it is valuable to insist an art project, once undertaken, be carried as far as possible, provided it is self-chosen. Such a discipline is not an unwarranted imposition. Anybody who has watched children "spend long periods of time on some challenging piece of construction or deconstruction knows that there is no end to patience, once the goal is sufficiently attractive. . . . The discipline needed for the completion of the tasks of life must be trained from the beginning" (Arnheim, 1989, p. 34).

Student Portfolios. Student growth, both artistic and cognitive, can be documented by setting up portfolios that are organized around a few basic goals attached to the front of the container (folder, box). Goals may include using many types of media, experimenting with styles of different artists, using art to respond to science, social studies, and math, writing stories and poems about art, learning about art in another culture, and finding out about specific artists and their work. Large art portfolios can be made using packing tape to bind together two large pieces of cardboard and connecting strings to tie it shut. Items placed in the collection should be dated and titled; include a note about the media and the assignment and how it is connected to one or more of the goals.

Principle Ten: SPECIALISTS ARE IMPORTANT RESOURCES

Collaboration between classroom teachers, art teachers, guest artists, and artists in residence is only fruitful if all participants feel they have an important role. While the classroom teacher will know the students better, the specialist knows more about doing art or a particular artist, which brings expertise and depth to art integration efforts. A successful collaboration begins with planning together. Questions that need to be asked and discussed include:

1. What are specific things students should know and do by the end of the lesson or unit?
2. How is art to be *meaningfully* integrated? What is to be the art content of the lesson and to what is it to be connected?
3. What are the children like? (interests, developmental levels, amount of structure needed)
4. Are there allergy or safety issues? Specialists, outside schools, may not be aware of safety concerns related to toxicity of materials and fumes from markers and sprays. This needs to be discussed.
5. How should the space be arranged? What materials are needed? What about time?
6. Should the specialist work with the whole group or should small groups be rotated?
7. Specialists may not have a wide range of teaching strategies and need to understand that children need active involvement through questions, visual aids, and demonstrations, rather than a lecture. Discuss a lesson introduction that begins with questions or a demonstration.
8. What is the discipline and management system in the classroom? How should problems be handled if they arise and who will handle them?

A number of community-based programs are available that offer trained volunteers to teach lessons about artists and subject matter or to do art projects. An example is *Agnes Goes To School* at the Agnes Etherington Art Centre in Kingston, Ontario (www.queensu.ca/ageth/html/1_education.html). Contact your local public art gallery and inquire about possibilities for in-gallery or in-class collaborative programming with one of the education curators.

Conclusion

Life is a great big canvas and you should throw all the paint you can on it!

Danny Kaye

This chapter presents an introduction to visual art integration throughout the curriculum for the general classroom teacher. Of particular importance are the rationale for integrating art (WHY), basic information teachers need to know and teach to accomplish art integration meaningfully (WHAT), and general principles for doing art integration (HOW). The next chapter is a categorized collection of strategy starter ideas that extend the focus of HOW to a more specific level in an effort to help teachers plan units and lessons with a strong visual art component.

Post It Page • 5-7

Media Techniques to Use Throughout the Curriculum

Directions: Use these ideas to integrate art making throughout the curriculum, including art responses to any topic.

Bookmaking: pop up, accordion, big books, mini-books, sewn books, etc.

Calligraphy and block lettering: embellished lettering or letters simply cut from standard-sized blocks, e.g., construction paper

Collage: design made by pasting or gluing assembled materials on a surface

Craft: handcrafted item like pottery, weaving, quilt square, or whole quilt

Diorama: shadow box, often made with shoe box to create a scene

Display or bulletin board: arrangements around a concept or theme

Drawing: linear art made with pencil, charcoal, marker, pen and ink, or crayon

Enlargement: use of overhead projector to make images larger

Fibre art: fabrics, yarn, string, etc., used to create art

Fresco: paint on wet plaster

Intaglio: process of engraving used in the production of early picture books

Lithography: printing method in which an image is drawn with oil-based material on a prepared stone or plate. The surface is dampened with water and a greasy ink applied. The ink adheres to the image, not the wet surface. The stone is placed in a press and the image printed on paper.

Mask: paper bag, tag board, balloon with papier mâché

Mixed media: paper, wire, paint, fabric etc. used in one artwork

Mobile: three-dimensional art that moves, usually suspended in space

Montage: combination of several distinct pictures to make a composite picture

Mural: large wall art

Painting: tempera (pigments in egg base), acrylic (made from polymer), watercolour, oil (pigments in oil base)

Pastel: chalk art

Poster: an advertisement or announcement using text and art

Print: process of transferring an original image from a surface onto paper (e.g. woodcut, engraving, silkscreen, lithograph, monoprint)

Puppet: bag, hand, stick

Rubbing: paper is placed on objects and crayon, marker, etc., are used to bring up images

Scratchboard: black crayon or ink is placed over another colour, e.g., silver or multiple colours; sharp tool is used to scratch surface and reveal colour

Sculpture: three-dimensional art made from wood, clay, metal, found objects, plaster, papier mâché

Wash: translucent watercolour used over another medium

Post It Page • 5-8

Art Media Used in Children's Literature

Directions: Use these books to show examples of artwork in a medium or to teach about a medium.

Cartoons and Caricature

Baker, K. (1992). (Ill. by H. W. Zimmermann). *Finster frets*. Oxford University Press.
Fraser, S. (1998). (Ill. by E. Fernandes). *Tom and Francine: A love story*. Key Porter Books.
Harrison, T. (1997). (Ill. by G. Clement). *Don't dig so deep, Nicholas!* Owl Books.
Rae, J. (1998). (Ill. by R. Cowles). *Dog tales*. Whitecap Books.

Collage

Baker, J. (1987). *Where the forest meets the sea.* Greenwillow Books.
Borden, D. (1983). (Ill. by L. Smith). *Yeah, I'm a little kid*. Annick Press.
Creighton, J. (1995). (Ill. by P. Pariseau). *8 o'clock*. Scholastic Canada.
Downie, M. A. (1975) (Ill. by E. Cleaver). *The Witch of the North*. Oberon Press.
Ehlert, L. (1991). *Red leaf yellow leaf.* Harcourt Brace.
Gilman, P. (1992). *Something from nothing.* Scholastic.
Hughes, L. (1995). *The block.* Metropolitan Museum of Art.
Lionni, L. (1959). *Little blue and little yellow.* Mulberry Books.
Toye, W. (1977) (Ill. by E. Cleaver). *The Loon's necklace*. Oxford University Press.
Yerxa, L. (1993). *Last leaf first snowflake to fall*. Douglas and McIntyre.

Crayons and Coloured Pencils

Coffey, M. (1998). (Ill. by E. Fernandes). *A cat in a kayak*. Annick Press.
Cumming, P. (1993). (Ill. by A. Priestley). *Out on the ice in the middle of the bay*. Annick Press.
Gregory, N. (1995). (Ill. by R. Lightburn). *How Smudge came*. Red Deer College Press.
Jam, T. (1991). (Ill. by J. Fitzgerald). *Doctor Kiss says yes*. Douglas and McIntyre.
Lionni, L. (1970). *Fish is fish.* Knopf.
Van Allsburg, C. (1986). *The stranger.* Houghton Mifflin.
Zeman, L. (1999). *Sindbad: From the tales of the Thousand and One Nights*. Tundra Books.

Drawing

Barrett, P., and Barrett, S. (1972). *The line Sophie drew.* Schroll Press.
Blanchet, M. W. (1983). (Ill. by J. M. Mathews). *A whale named Henry*. Harbour.
Charlstrom, N. W. (1992). *Northern lullaby.* Philomel.
dePaola, T. (1989). *The art lesson.* Trumpet Club.
Houston, J. (1965). *Tikta' Liktak*. Longmans.

Johnson, C. (1955). *Harold and the purple crayon.* Harper & Row.
McCloskey, R. (1942). *Make way for ducklings.* Viking.
Munsch, R. (1992). *Purple, green and yellow.* Annick Press.
Schinck, E. (1987). *Art lessons.* Greenwillow.
Wynne-Jones, T. (1992). (Ill. by E. Beddows). *Zoom upstream*. Groundwood Books.

Fiber Art

Hall, D. (1980). *The ox-cart man.* Viking.
Kroll, V. (1992). *Wood-Hoopoe Willie.* Charles Bridge.
Roessel, M. (1995). *Songs from the loom.* Lerner Publications.

Mixed Media

Burningham, J. (1989). *Hey! Get off our train.* Crown.
Cleaver, E. (1980). *Petrouchka*. Macmillan.
Lunn, J. (1988) (Ill. by K. La Fave). *Amos's sweater.* Douglas and McIntyre.
Tololwa, M. (1995) (Ill. by P. Morin). *The Orphan boy*. Stoddart.
Wildsmith, B. (1963). *The lion and the rat.* Oxford University Press.
Young, E. (1989). *Lon po po. A Red Riding Hood story from China.* Philomel.

Mural

Gerstein, M. (1984). *The room.* Harper & Row.
Winters, J. (1991). *Diego.* Random House.

Painting

Agee, J. (1988). *The incredible painting of Felix Clousseau.* Farrar, Straus & Giroux.
Bouchard, D. (1997). (Ill. by Z.-Y. Huang). *The great race*. Millbrook Press.
Butler, G. (1995). *The killick: A Newfoundland story*. Tundra Books.
Collins, P. L. (1992). *I am an artist.* Millbrook Press.
Cooney, B. (1982). *Miss Rumphius.* Viking. (acrylics)
Crook, C. B. (1997). (Ill. by S. Cameron). *Maple moon*. Stoddart Kids.
Demi, T. (1980). *Liang and the magic paintbrush.* Henry Holt.
de Paola, T. (1988). *The legend of the Indian paintbrush.* G. P. Putnam's.
Harrison, T. (1992). *O Canada*. Kids Can Press.
Kurelek, W. (1973). *A Prairie boy's winter.* Tundra Books.
Lawson, J. (1997). (Ill. by P. Mombourquette). *Emma and the silk train*. Kids Can Press.
McGugan, J. (1994) (Ill. by M. Kimber). *Josepha: A Prairie boy's story*. Red Deer College Press.
Mollel, T. M. (1997). *Kitoto the mighty*. Stoddart.
Nichol, B. (1992) (Ill. by S. Cameron*). Beethoven lives upstairs.* Lester.
Perrault, C. (1990) (Ill. by F. Marcellino). *Puss in boots.* Farrar, Straus & Giroux. (oil paints)
Price, L. (1990) (Ill. by L. & D. Dillon). *Aida.* Harcourt Brace Jovanovich. (acrylics)
Taylor, C. J. (1992). *Little Water and the gift of the animals: A Seneca legend.* Tundra Books.
Wood, A. (1984). *The napping house.* Harcourt Brace Jovanovich. (oil paints)
Yee, P. (1996) (Ill. by H. Chan). *Ghost train.* Douglas and McIntyre.

Pastels (Chalk)

Dewey, A. (1995). *The sky.* Green Tiger Press.

Howe, J. (1987) (Ill. by E. Young). *I wish I were a butterfly.* Harcourt Brace Jovanovich.

Jukes, M. (1984) (Ill. by L. Bloom). *Like Jake and me.* Knopf.

Van Allsburg, C. (1985). *The polar express.* Houghton Mifflin.

Pen and Pencil/Ink

Downie, M. A., & Rawlyk. G. (1980) (Ill. by R. Berg). *A Proper Acadian*. Kids Can Press.

Downie. M. A. (1991). (Ill. by J. Huffman). *Honor Bound*. Quarry Press.

Gag, W. (1956). *Millions of cats.* Coward, McCean & Geoghegan.

Lionni, L. (1961). *On my beach there are many pebbles.* Mulberry Books.

Macaulay, D. (1977). *Castle.* Houghton Mifflin.

Mayer, M. (1974). *Frog goes to dinner.* Dial.

Van Allsburg, C. (1981). *Jumanji.* Houghton Mifflin.

Viorst, J. (1972) (Ill. by R. Cruz). *Alexander and the terrible, horrible, no good, very bad day.* Atheneum.

Photography

Angelou, M. (1994). *My painted house, my friendly chicken.* Clarkson-Potter.

Brown, L. K., and Brown, M. (1996). *Visiting the art museum.* E. P. Dutton.

Freedman, R. (1987). *Lincoln. A photobiography.* Clarion.

Hoban, T. (1990). *Shadows and reflections.* Greenwillow.

Kissinger, K. (1994). *All the colors we are.* Redleaf Press.

Lauber, P. (1990). *Seeing earth from space.* Orchard.

Patterson, F. (1985) (Ill. by R. H. Cohn). *Koko's kitten.* Scholastic.

Roalf, P. (1993). *Looking at painting. Children.* Hyperion.

Walter, M. P. (1995). *Darkness.* Simon & Schuster.

Plasticine

Burton, K. (1995). *One grey mouse*. Kids Can Press.

Fernandes, K. (1991). *Zebo and the dirty planet*. Annick Press.

Reid, B. (1997). *The party*. North Winds Press.

Reid, B. (1999). *Acorn to oak tree*. HarperCollins.

Printmaking

Bouchard, D. (1990). (Ill. by R. H. Vickers). *The elders are watching*. Eagle Dancer Enterprises.

Brown, M. (1961). *Once a mouse.* Aladdin Books.

Carl, E. (1987). *The tiny seed.* Picture Book Studio.

Downie, M. A. (1975) (Ill. by E. Cleaver). *The witch of the north*. Oberon Press.

Downie, M. A., & Robertson, B. (1969) (Ill. by E. Cleaver). *The Wind has wings.* London: Oxford University Press.

Emberley, E., & Emberley, B. (1967). *Drummer Hoff.* Prentice-Hall.

Haley, G. E. (1970). *A story, a story.* Atheneum.

Lionni, L. (1963). *Swimmy.* Random House.

Tajima. (1987). *Owl lake.* Philomel.

Toye, W. (1977) (Ill. by E. Cleaver). *The Loon's necklace.* Oxford University Press.

Waber, B. (1996). *"You look ridiculous," said the rhinoceros to the hippopotamus.* Houghton-Mifflin.

Sculpture (three-dimensional art)

de Paola, T. (1982). *Giorgio's village.* Putnam. (paper sculpture)
Feelings, M. (1974). *Jambo means hello: Swahili alphabet book.* Dial.
Haskins, J. (1989). *Count your way through Mexico.* Carolrhoda Book. (papier mâché)
Hawkinson, J. (1974). *A ball of clay.* Albert Whitman. (firing clay)
Hoyt-Goldsmith, D. (1990). *Totem pole.* Scholastic. (wood carving)
James, B. (1994) (Ill. by P. Morin). *The Mud family.* Oxford University Press.
Miller, J. (1983). *The human body.* Viking. (paper sculpture)
Price, C. (1975). *Dancing masks of Africa.* Charles Scribners Sons. (masks)
Prokofiev, S. (1985) (Ill. by B. Cooney). *Peter and the wolf.* Viking. (paper sculpture)
Reid, B. (1997). *The Party*. Scholastic Canada.

Watercolour

Asch, F. (1995). *Water.* Harcourt Brace.
Bunting, E. (1990) (Ill. by R. Himler). *The wall.* Clarion.
Jennings, S. (1993)(Ill. by M. Levert). *Sleep tight Mrs. Ming*. Annick Press
Lawson, J. (1992). (Ill. by S. Lott). *A morning to polish and keep*. Red Deer College Press.
Lawson, J. (1995). (Ill. by K. Naylor). *Blown away.* Red Deer College Press.
Le Ford, B. (1995). *A blue butterfly. A story about Claude Monet.* Doubleday.
Potter, B. (1902). *The tale of Peter Rabbit.* Warne.
Say, A. (1990). *El chino.* Houghton Mifflin.
Waterton, B. (1978) (Ill. by A. Blades). *A Salmon for Simon*. Douglas and McIntyre.
Yolen, J. (1987) (Ill. by J. Schoenherr). *Owl moon.* Philomel.

Weaving

Allen, C. (1991). *The rug makers.* Steck-Vaughn.
Castaneda, O. S. (1993). *Abuela's weave.* Lee & Low.
Miles, M. (1971). *Annie and the Old One.* Boston: Little, Brown.

Post It Page • 5-9

Some Artistic Styles: Children's Literature Examples

Cartoon Style: Simple lines and use of primary colours

Cole, J. (1989) (Ill. by B. Degen). *The magic school bus inside the human body.* Scholastic.
Schwartz, D. M. (1985) (Ill. by S. Kellogg). *How much is a million?* Scholastic.
Seuss, Dr. (1957). *Cat in the hat.* Random House.

Spier, P. (1980). *People.* Doubleday.

Westcott, N. B. (1984). *The emperor's new clothes.* Little, Brown.

Expressionism: Leans toward abstract style, focuses on showing emotions

Bemelmans, Ludwig. (1939). *Madeline.* Viking

Carle, E. (1984). *The very busy spider.* Philomel.

Ehlert, L. (1989). *Color zoo.* Lippincott.

Livingston, M. C. (1985) (Ill. by L. E. Fisher). *A circle of seasons.* Holiday House.

Martin, B., Jr., & Archambault, J. (1989) (Ill. by L. Ehlert). *Chick chicka boom.* Simon & Schuster.

Williams, V. B. (1982). *A chair for my mother.* Mulberry.

Folk Art: Various media used by artists without formal training

Aardema, V. (1975) (Ill. by L. Dillon & D. Dillon). *Why mosquitoes buzz in people's ears.* Dial.

Hall, D. (1979) (Ill. by B. Cooney). *The ox-cart man.* Viking.

Lindbergh, R. (1990). *Johnny Appleseed.* Little, Brown.

O'Kelley, M. L. (1986). *Circus!* Little, Brown.

Polacco, P. (1988). *Rechenska's eggs.* New York: Philomel.

Xiong, B. (1989) (Ill. by N. Hom). *Nine-in-one. Grr! Grr!* Children's Book Press.

Impressionism: Dream-like quality, relies on play of light

Baker, O. (1981) (Ill. by S. Gammell). *Where the buffaloes begin.* Warne.

Bjork, C. (1985) (Ill. by L. Anderson). *Linnea in Monet's garden.* R&S Books.

Howe, J. (1987) (Ill. by E. Young). *I wish I were a butterfly.* Harcourt Brace Jovanovich.

Wildsmith, B. (1966). *The hare and the tortoise.* Oxford University Press.

Zolotow, C. (1962) (Ill. by M. Sendak). *Mr. Rabbit and the lovely present.* Harper & Row.

Realism: Represents reality in shape, colour, proportion

Holling, H. C. (1969). *Paddle-to-the-sea.* Houghton Mifflin.

McCloskey, R. (1969). *Make way for ducklings.* Viking.

Turkle, B. (1976). *Deep in the forest.* Dutton.

Viorst, J. (1972) (Ill. by R. Cruz). *Alexander and the terrible, horrible, no good, very bad day.* Atheneum.

Ziefert, H. (1986) (Ill. by A. Lobel). *A new coat for Anna.* Knopf.

Surrealism: Distorts and plays with images; fantastic quality

Bang, M. (1980). *The grey lady and the strawberry snatcher.* Four Winds Press.

Burningham, J. (1977). *Come away from the water, Shirley.* Harper & Row.

Sciezka, J. (1989) (Ill. by L. Smith). *The true story of the three little pigs.* Viking.

Van Allsberg, C. (1981). *Jumanji.* Houghton Mifflin.

Winter, J. (1988). *Follow the drinking gourd.* Knopf.

Post It Page • 5-10

Children's Literature and Art Concepts

Adoff, A. (1973). *Black is brown is tan.* HarperCollins. (Art elements = colour. Describes the skin colours in an interracial family.)

Allington, R. (1979). *Colors.* Raintree Press. (Art elements = colour. Twelve base colours and how to mix them.)

Blizzard, G. S. (1992). *Come look with me: Exploring landscape art with children.* Thomason-Grant. (Art concept = landscape. Twelve landscape paintings are shown, with information on the artists. Part of a series: *World of Play, Animals in Art, and Enjoying Art with Children.*)

Brown, M. (1979). *Listen to a shape.* F. Watts. (Art elements = shape. Basic shapes of square, circle, and more are introduced using poetry and nature.)

Cheltenham Elementary School, Kindergarten (1994). *We are all alike . . . We are all different.* Scholastic. (Art concepts = portraits. Also in big book.)

Crews, D. (1995). *Sail away.* Greenwillow. (Art elements = colour, pattern, shape. Airbrushed shapes provide a way to show the concept of pattern through repeated images of objects.)

Crosbie, M. J. & Rosenthal, S. (1993). *Architecture COLORS.* Preservation Press. (Art concept = architecture. Art elements = colour, form. Each colour is illustrated with a photograph of an architectural feature opposite the word for the colour. Series by the National Trust for Historic Preservation includes *Architecture SHAPES* and *Architecture COUNTS.*)

Ehlert, L. (1994). *Color zoo.* HarperCollins. (Art concept = using your senses. Art elements = space. Wordless book. Layered holes form abstract animals that change shape.)

Enrico, J. (1984). (Ill. by Gitsgah). *The man who became an eagle*. Pacific Education Press, University of British Columbia. (Northwest Coast art and culture.)

Everett, G. (1991). *Li'l sis and Uncle Willie.* Hyperion. (Culture = African-American. African-American artist William H. Johnson's art is used to create this story of his life.)

Heller, R. (1995). *Color! Color! Color!* Grosset & Dunlap. (Art elements = colour. Art concepts = mixing colours. With rhythmic language, Ruth Heller presents concepts about colour with colour acetates that overlap to show mixing.)

Jonas, A. (1989). *Color dance.* Greenwillow. (Art elements = colour. Children dance with transparent cloth that overlaps to create new colours.)

Lepschy, I. (1992). *Pablo Picasso.* Barron's Education Series. [Art as a career. This biography of Picasso as a child focuses on his difficulties. Recommended for teachers. Part of a series called *Children of Genius.* Also in the series is *Leonardo da Vinci* (1984).]

Lewis, S. (1991). *African American art for young people.* Davis. [Culture = African-American. Twelve African-American artists are the topic of the book. Example artwork is reproduced: Powers (quilting), Barthe and Lewis (sculpture), Tanner, Hunter, Hayden, Johnson, Jones, Bearden, Lawrence, and Catlett (painting), and Butler (found art constructions) are presented.]

Lionni, L. (1991). *Matthew's dream.* Knopf. (Art as a career. Art concepts = museums. A young mouse is inspired to become a painter.)

Locker, T. (1994). *Miranda's smile.* Dial. (Art concepts = portrait. Art as a career. Media = painting. An artist tries to paint his daughter's portrait.)

McDermott, G. (1993). *Raven: A trickster tale from the Pacific Northwest.* Harcourt Brace. (Art elements = shape, pattern. Culture = Native American. Pictures are based on the traditional art forms and patterns of the Northwest coastal tribes.)

McGovern, A. (1969). *Black is beautiful.* Scholastic. (Art elements = colour. Celebrates the colour black.)

McLerran, A. (1991). *Roxaboxen.* Lothrop, Lee & Shepard. (Art concept = architecture. Media = construction. Children build "houses" from stones, old pottery, and crates.)

Micklethwait, L. (1994). *I spy a lion: Animals in art.* Greenwillow. (Find animals and details in famous artworks.)

Muller, R. (1989). *The magic paintbrush*. Doubleday Canada. (A folktale about a young artist.)

Paul, A. W. (1991). *Eight hands round.* HarperCollins. (Art elements = pattern. Media = quilting. Traditional American quilt patterns are shown along with explanations for their origins.)

Pfister, M. (1992). *The rainbow fish.* North-South Books. (Art element = colour. The most beautiful fish in the ocean discovers how to find happiness. The scales are made with real reflective foil.)

Pinkwater, D. M. (1977). *The big orange splat.* Scholastic. (Art element = colour. Story about a creative man who paints his house his own unique way.)

Polacco, P. (1988). *Rechenko's eggs.* Philomel. (Art elements = pattern. Culture = Ukrainian. Patterns are everywhere in this story of a magic goose and beautiful Pysanky eggs.)

Polacco P. (1990). *Thunder cake.* Putnam. (Art elements = pattern. Clothing and quilts are full of patterns. Story of a grandmother who teaches her granddaughter about bravery.)

Ringgold, F. (1991). *Tar beach.* Random House. (Culture = African-American. Media = quilting. Autobiography about growing up in Harlem. Painted and quilted fabrics.)

Rodari, F. (1991). *A weekend with Picasso.* Rizzoli. (Uses facts from Picasso's life to create a fictional weekend spent with the artist. Illustrated with photographs and Picasso's artwork.)

Sendak, M. (1964). *Where the wild things are.* Harper & Row. (Art elements = line. A little boy does not want to eat supper. Sendak uses expressive lines to add detail to his drawings.)

Shalom, V. (1995). *The color of things.* Rizzoli International. (Art elements = colour. Colours are drained from a town and children paint them back again. Helps children see how important colour is.)

Shaw, C. G. (1988). *It looked like spilt milk.* Harper Trophy. (Art element = shape. Free-form shapes turn into ordinary objects. Also in big book.)

Turner, R. M. (1993). *Faith Ringgold.* Little, Brown. (Media = quiltmaking. Biography of African-American quilt maker Faith Ringgold. Provides background for Ringgold's *Tar Beach.*)

Venezia, M. (1991). *Paul Klee.* Children's Book Press. [Biography of Klee starting in childhood. Illustrated with reproductions of his artwork. One of a series called *Getting to Know the World's Greatest Artists.* Other books include *Rembrandt* (1988), *Monet* (1989), *Cassatt* (1990), *Michelangelo* (1991), *Botticelli* (1992), *Bruegel* (1992), *Pollock* (1992), *Goya* (1993), and *O'Keefe* (1993).]

Wilson, F. (1969, 1988). *What it feels like to be a building.* The Preservation Press. (Art concept = architecture. People shapes illustrate an analogy of how buildings are constructed. Beside each architectural feature, such as a column or arch, the illustrations show how the stress and strains would feel if the structure were built out of people.)

Wistow, D. & McKinley, K. (1999). *Meet the Group of Seven.* Toronto: Kids Can Press. (Looking at Canadian painting. Art gallery visit.)

Yenawine, P., and the Museum of Modern Art (1991). *Colors.* Delacorte. (Art elements 5 Artwork from MOMA illustrates this art concept book. Series includes *Lines, Shapes,* and *Stories.*)

Yolen, J. (1988). *Owl moon.* Philomel. (Art elements = colour/white. Art concept = perspective. Media = painting. A boy and his father go for a walk on a snowy moonlit night.)

Young. E. (1991). *Seven blind mice.* Philomel. (Based on the tale of the blind men and the elephant, seven blind mice use their senses to investigate an elephant. Available as a big book.)

---

†Governor General's Award

Post It Page • 5-11

Artist-Author Study Information Examples

Andersen, Hans Christian

"Meet the author: Hans Christian Andersen," American School Publishers (SF or V).

Greene, C. (1991). *Hans Christian Andersen: Prince of Storytellers.* Children's Press.

Brown, Marcia

Brown, M. (1983). Caldecott Medal Acceptance. *Horn Book Magazine,* 59, 414–422.

Carle, Eric

"Eric Carle, Picturewriter," Searchlight Film (V).

Dahl, Roald

"The author's eye: Roald Dahl," American School Publishers (V).

de Paola, Tomie

de Paola, T. (1989). *The art lesson.* Putnam.

"Tomie de Paola," (1986). Authors on Tape. Trumpet (audiotape).

Dillon, Leo, and Diane

Preiss, B. (1981). *The art of Leo and Diane Dillon.* New York: Ballantine.

Dr. Seuss

"Who's Dr. Seuss?: Meet Ted Geisel," American School Publishers (SF).

Roth, R. (1989). On beyond zebra with Dr. Seuss. *New Advocate,* 2, 213–226.

Fox, Mem

Manning, M., & Manning, G. (March 1990). Mem Fox: Mem's the word in down under? *Teaching PreK–8,* 20, 29–31.

Hamilton, Virginia

"First Choice: Authors and Books—Virginia Hamilton," Pied Piper (SF).

"Meet the Newbery Author: Virginia Hamilton," American School Publishers (SF).

Highwater, Jamake

"Meet the Newbery Author: Jamake Highwater," American School Publishers (SF).

Keats, Ezra Jack

"Ezra Jack Keats," Weston Woods (film).

Lanes, S. G. (1984). Ezra Jack Keats: In memoriam. *Horn Book Magazine,* 60, 551–558.

Pope, M. (1990). Ezra Jack Keats: A childhood revisited. *New Advocate,* 3, 13–24.

Kellogg, Steven

"How a Picture Book Is Made," Weston Woods (V).

Konigsburg, E. L.

"First choice: Authors and books—E. L. Konigsburg," Pied Piper (SF).

Jones, L. T. (1986). Profile: Elaine Konigsburg. *Language Arts,* 63, 177–184.

L'Engle, Madeline

"Meet the Newbery Author: Madeline L'Engle," American School Publishers (SF).

Raymond, A. (1991). Madeline L'Engle: Getting the last laugh. *Teaching PreK–8,* 21, 34–36.

Livingston, Myra Cohn

"First choice: Poets and poetry—Myra Cohn Livingston," Pied Piper (SF).

Porter, E. J. (1980). Profile: Myra Cohn Livingston. *Language Arts,* 57, 901–905.

Lobel, Arnold

"Meet the Newbery Author: Arnold Lobel," American School Publishers (SF).

Lobel, A. (1981). Caldecott Medal acceptance. *Horn Book Magazine,* 57, 400–404.

Lobel, A. (1981). Arnold at home. *Horn Book Magazine,* 57, 405–410.

Macaulay, David

"David Macaulay in his studio," Houghton Mifflin (V).

Ammon, R. (1982). Profile: David Macaulay. *Language Arts,* 59, 374–378.

MacLachlan, Patricia

Babbitt, N. (1986). Patricia MacLachlan: The biography. *Horn Book Magazine,* 62, 414–416.

Langu Courtney, A. (1985). Profile: Patricia MacLachlan. *Language Arts,* 62, 783–787.

MacLachlan, P. (1986). A Newbery Medal acceptance. *Horn Book Magazine,* 62, 407–413.

Raymond, A. (May 1989). Patricia MacLachlan: An advocate of 'bare boning.' *Teaching PreK–8,* 19, 46–48.

McDermott, Gerald

"Evolution of a Graphic Concept: The Stonecutter," Weston Woods (SF).

McDermott, G. (1988). Sky Father, Earth Mother: An artist interprets myth. *New Advocate,* 1, 1–7.

Merriam, Eve

"First choice: Poets and poetry—Eve Merriam," Pied Piper (SF).

Cox, S. T. (1989). A word or two with Eve Merriam: Talking about poetry. *New Advocate,* 2, 139–150.

Sloan, G. (1981). Profile: Eve Merriam. *Language Arts,* 58, 957–964.

Milne, A. A

"Meet the Author: A. A. Milne (and Pooh)," American School Publishers (SF or V).

O'Dell, Scott

"Meet the Newbery Author: Scott O'Dell," American School Publishers (SF).

"A Visit with Scott O'Dell," Houghton Mifflin (V).

Roop, P. (1984). Profile: Scott O'Dell. *Language Arts,* 61, 750–752.

Paterson, Katherine

"The author's eye: Katherine Paterson," American School Publishers (V).

"Meet the Newbery Author: Katherine Paterson," American School Publishers (SF).

Jones, L. T. (1981). Profile: Katherine Paterson. *Language Arts,* 58, 189–196.

Namovic, G. I. (1981). Katherine Paterson. *Horn Book Magazine,* 57, 394–399.

Peet, Bill

"Bill Peet in his studio," Houghton Mifflin (V).

Peet, B. (1989). *Bill Peet: An autobiography.* Houghton Mifflin.

Polacco, Patricia

Babushka's Doll (1995). Scholastic (audiotape).

Patricia Polacco: Dream keeper (1996). Philomel (V).

Vandergrift, Kay E. (1995). "Patricia Polacco," *Twentieth-Century Children's Writers,* ed. by Laura Berger, 4th ed. St. James, 759–760.

Potter, Beatrix

"Beatrix Potter had a pet named Peter." American School Publishers (SF or V).

Aldis, D. (1969). *Nothing is impossible: The story of Beatrix Potter.* Atheneum.

Collins, D. R. (1989). *The country artist: A story about Beatrix Potter.* Carolrhoda.

Prelutsky, Jack

Raymond, A. (Nov./Dec. 1986). Jack Prelutsky . . . Man of many talents. *Teaching PreK–8,* 17, 38–42.

Vardell, S. (1991). An interview with Jack Prelutsky. *New Advocate,* 4, 101–112.

Rylant, Cynthia

"Meet the Newbery Author: Cynthia Rylant." American School Publishers (SF or V).

"Meet the Picture Book Author: Cynthia Rylant." American School Publishers (V).

Silvey, A. (1987). An interview with Cynthia Rylant. *Horn Book Magazine,* 63, 695–702.

Sendak, Maurice

"Max Made Mischief: An Approach to Literature" (1977). Pennsylvania State University (V).

"Sendak," Weston Woods (F).

Sendak, M. (1983). Laura Ingalls Wilder Award acceptance. *Horn Book Magazine,* 59, 474–477.

Van Allsburg, Chris

Keifer, B. (1987). Profile: Chris Van Allsburg in three dimensions. *Language Arts,* 64, 664–671.

McKee, B. (1986). Van Allsburg: From a different perspective. *Horn Book Magazine,* 62, 566–571.

Van Allsburg, C. (1986). Caldecott Medal acceptance. *Horn Book Magazine,* 62, 420–424.

White, E. B

"Meet the Newbery Author: E. B. White," American School Publishers (SF).

Newmeyer, P. F. (1987). E. B. White: Aspects of style. *Horn Book Magazine,* 63, 586–591.

Yolen, Jane

White, D. E. (1983). Profile: Jane Yolen. *Language Arts,* 60, 652–660.

Yolen, J. (1989). On silent wings: The making of Owl Moon. *New Advocate,* 2, 199–212.

Yolen, J. (1991). The route to story. *New Advocate,* 4, 143–149.

Also see Post It Page 3–6. V = video; SF = sound filmstrip; F = film.

Post It Page • 5-12

Art Strategies and Picture Books

1. **Ape the greats.** Explore picture book styles and media using Post It Page 5–8. Invite experimentation with an artist's media and styles, and encourage adapting ideas using SCAMPER (Post It Page 1–5).
2. **Predict from art.** Activate thinking before reading a picture book by showing one or two pictures and giving time to look closely. Ask for predictions about (1) Who? *characters,* (2) When and Where? *setting/time,* and (3) What might be the problems? from pictures. Challenge students to support predictions with evidence from the art. Record ideas on a chart divided into three columns so that the class can return to predictions to confirm or reject them during and after the book.
3. **Clothesline art prediction.** You need two copies of the same book. One is taken apart and the text is cut off. Display the pictures, before reading the book, and invite students to arrange them in the order they think they will occur. Students have to listen to one another and come to an agreement about the most probable order. Use a clothesline to hang them up in order or a pocket chart. Next, read the book and check picture order. Rearrange as necessary. *Variation:* Ask students to write stories to go with the pictures before reading the book.

4. **Experts.** Each child or group selects a picture from a book on which they will become experts. The goal is to notice everything they can by looking closely. Small magnifying glasses or toilet paper tubes make this more fun. Prepare cue sheets that give categories to observe: elements, media, style, decisions the artist made, composition (arrangement). Experts report back to entire group.
5. **Blow up art.** Many picture books are available in big book format. This size enables a group to see the art more easily. Use the *art discussion strategies* in Post It Page 5–5 with any picture. Another option is to make colour transparencies of selected pages to examine. Stewig's series called *Reading Pictures* (1988) has lesson plans and poster-sized art from picture books that work well, too.
6. **Partial picture preview.** This is a strategy based on the idea that insight is gained and attention focused if we view objects from different perspectives. Cover a portion of the picture and ask students to examine the remaining part. Use *"What do you see?"* and other open questions. Ask students to predict what is in the covered portion. *Variation:* Look at pictures in a mirror (reverse image), upside down, or from far away to discover colours and shapes not previously noticed. Composition can be studied by squinting to see the "masses," instead of the details, and students can hypothesize why the artist did what she did.
7. **Prints style match.** Find other art done in the same style as the book: impressionistic, folk art (see Post It Page 5–9). Compare, for example, the work of Monet and Emily McCully's art in *Mirette on the High Wire* to find how each treated light, colour, shapes, and edges.
8. **Scavenger hunts.** Media, style, borders, perspective (within and among books). Students enjoy searching picture books to find specific items. Set up in a format, like a bingo board, and play in groups or individually. Make sure students have access to many books and that they know the meanings of the elements they are looking for. This can last a day or a week or turn into an ongoing routine.
9. **Wordless books.** Language experience approach is a classic strategy to teach reading and writing. Use it with wordless books by asking students to dictate a story that goes with the pictures or write their own in groups or individually. Finished stories can then become the material for reading lessons (e.g., play "I Spy" to locate high-frequency spelling or phonic patterns, parts of speech, etc.) or for important daily free reading. *Suggestion:* To build independence, ask students to do the spelling when taking dictation from them. This also helps keeps attention. At least ask students to give beginning and ending sounds.
10. **Book parts.** Teach students about the parts of books. Endpapers set the mood of the book. Look for gutters that break up pictures that run across double-page spreads to find out how well this has been accomplished. Examine the effects of borders on pages. Teach about title page, half-title page, credits, etc., to help them become visually literate.
11. **Compare–contrast two books by different artists.** Use a Venn diagram to record likenesses and differences between the same story written and illustrated by two different picture book artists. This provides an opportunity to work on the higher-order thinking skills of analysis.
12. **Create characters.** Use body, head, and legs from different characters in picture books and combine these to make new characters. Either cut up tattered picture books or use the art as an inspiration for drawing (not copying). Write a story to go with the new creatures.
13. **Make a picture book.** Students should have opportunities to write and illustrate their own picture books based on inspirations from a variety of genres: alphabet books, concepts books, pattern or predictable books, fairy tales, etc. Encourage the use of a variety of media and styles.
14. **Frame favourite pictures.** Use pictures from calendars, posters or art reproductions, or use publishers' catalogue pictures to create framed art. Create a gallery of favourites.
15. **Play concentration or memory with the artists' photographs and book art.** Use publishers' catalogues to find pictures of the artists and book covers or interiors. Write to publishers for photos and examples of book art. To play concentration, make six to ten pairs (e.g., a card with the artist's photo and one example of his or her art). Paste all on same-sized cards and turn upside down to play. The goal is to remember the location so that pairs can be picked up.
16. **Set the scene.** Recreate a scene in a book using tableau (see drama). Students may want to use props, costumes, etc. *Example:* Make whole classroom into a water scene from Lionni's *Swimmy.*

17. **Puzzles.** Cut up pictures and give each child a piece. Each person is to study the piece to try to tell as much as possible about it. Then assemble to see the whole picture. Can be done in groups, with each group getting a different or the same picture. Do before or after reading a book.
18. **Special days.** Everyone brings a certain kind of picture book (e.g., pop up, alphabet, one with special endpapers, borders). Each child should have studied the book so that she or he can present the focus in a minute or less.
19. **Storytelling.** Read a story without showing the pictures. Ask students to draw or paint one moment in the story that they thought was important. Then show what moments the artist chose to illustrate. Alternatively, ask students to story-map their own stories.
20. **Collages.** Use calendars, newspapers and magazines as source material for picture collages—e.g., by media (cartoons, watercolour), subject matter (portraits, landscape), or topics (plants, animals).

Post It Page • 5-13
Example Integrated Art-Math Lesson

Two-pronged Focus: Art elements of shape, pattern and repetition, abstract, and asymetrical. Math concepts of pattern and geometric shapes.

Objectives: By the end of the lesson students will be able to:

1. Use five elements of shape and repetition to create a pattern.
2. Orally label geometric shapes (rectangle, circle, triangle, square).
3. Write examples of how shapes are a part of life and why pattern is important.

Teaching Procedure: The teacher will . . .

Introduction (AIM-PREE)

Post ground rules (for discussions, about looking closely, use of art materials, etc.).

Tell students we'll do two activities and they are to figure out how they are related. (1) Mystery bag: draw out fabrics in three different patterns (dots, plaid, stripes) and ask them to look closely to think what these have in common. (2) Without talking, put five cards in pocket chart that have five elements of shape (Brookes, 1996): circle, dot, straight line, curved line, and angled line.

Gesture for students to draw these. Repeat with eight cards that have a series of elements of shape to make a pattern (dot, dot, horizontal line, horizontal line, curved down line, curved up line, triangle, triangle).

Development

Ask: How were the mystery bag and the drawing activities related? If necessary, scaffold by holding fabric up to cards. What did both have?

Tell students the goal is to learn the five elements and to create an abstract work of art.

Show two art reproductions: for instance, Jack Bush's *Spot on Red* (collection of the Agnes Etherington Art Centre, Kingston) and Alex Colville's *Horse and Train* (collection of the Art Gallery of Hamilton). See end of chapter for sources. Explain the difference between a fine art reproduction and an original work of art.

Ask: How are these two artworks alike and different? Probe for five elements. When they are named, write them on the board.

Tell students that Colville's work is called *realistic* because we recognize what it is right away and Bush's work is called *abstract* because the focus is on colour and elements of shape, not on representing things in a real way—the feel is more important. Clip cards with "abstract" and "realistic" on each work.

Divide into small groups and give a task to find examples of elements of shape, geometric shapes, and patterns (repeated elements). Give each group a clipboard to record. Allow ten minutes.

Assemble group and take reports by randomly calling on a student.

Ask: Why did you find so many examples? Where are there shapes outside of school? Why are patterns made? Used? How do patterns affect people?

Tell about making abstract art and how it is important to experiment, fill up the space with elements, shapes, patterns. Give paper, markers, and about ten minutes to explore. Play tranquil New Age background music.

Reassemble group and ask students to tell one thing they discovered about materials, elements, patterns. Ask if these drawings are realistic or abstract, and why.

Do *directed abstract* activity: (1) draw two lines that go to the edges of the paper, (2) draw three dots, (3) draw four curved lines (4) draw a circle that touches another line. Fill in all the spaces with colours or collage materials.

- **Conclusion:** Circulate and give descriptive feedback about elements and concepts as students work. Do art docent talks in fishbowl arrangement, with docents telling elements, shapes, pattern, how they got ideas. Audience members each need to ask one question or comment. Use a frame to wrap up: The five elements of shape are _____ and five geometric shapes are _____. When elements are repeated they form _____. Patterns in my life are (1) _____ and (2) _____. Frame art and put up in class gallery.

Post It Page • 5-14

Art Gallery Scavenger Hunt and General Strategies

Directions: Use this information *before* the trip and to prepare guides for *during* the visit.

Ask students to find examples of . . .

- Striking use of colours (e.g., complementary)
- Art where use of line is important
- How artists create texture
- Art where light is important (use of white?)
- Art with different moods
- Shapes and masses in art (e.g., geometric, organic)
- Subject matter: still life, landscape, portrait, abstract, seascape, cityscape, interior, narrative storytelling
- Examples of perspective: atmospheric, linear, overlapping, etc.

- Paintings with lots of detail and ones without
- How unity is achieved
- Patterns or motifs or repeated elements
- Different arrangements or compositions
- Media examples: sculpture (materials), watercolour, acrylic, oil, tempera, collage, fabric art
- Different time periods
- Art that tells a story (narrative art)

Things to look for . . .

- What's in the background?
- Eyes: where do they look? do they follow you?
- Hands: details? where, why, and how placed? folded?
- Brushstrokes, e.g., scumbling (dry brush painting)
- Edges: lost and found, contours and shadows

Questions and Directives: Things to say and do.

- "Take a few minutes to look around and I'll meet you in the next gallery."
- "Look up close, middle, and far away . . . find the magic viewing spot."
- "Look closely, study for twenty seconds, go beyond the obvious, look at details."
- "What is going on in the art?"
- "What is the mood? How does it make you feel?"
- "What do you see? Colours? Shapes? Images?"
- "Where does artist want you to enter the work? What is the focal point?"
- "Where does your eye go first? Why? Next?"
- "Decode or read the painting. Squint. See the shapes, colours, what stands out/pops out?"
- "Use your senses: see? feel? smell? hear? music? taste?"
- "What do you notice about the brushstrokes? Why did the artist do this?"
- "What story did the artist want to tell?"
- "What is the subject matter: landscape, seascape?"
- Portraits: "What about the background? effect? essence of the person? hair? hands? eyes?"
- "What adjectives or nouns can be connected to the art?"
- "What is the time of day? Describe the weather."
- Nudity: "Why is it used?" (shows timelessness, e.g., no clothes to date the work; symbol of superiority or shows person has nothing to hide; beauty of human curves)
- "What about edges? hard? lost?"
- "What did the artist choose to do? arrangement? what purposes?"
- "What does the title have to do with the work?"
- "How does the artist use colour to move your eyes around?"
- "What did the artist want you to think or feel?"
- "How are . . . and . . . alike and different?"
- "What if . . . changed?" (size, colour, materials)

Teacher Resources and Art Supply Sources

An excellent Canadian resource is Irene Naested's 1998 book *Art in the Elementary Classroom: An Integrated Approach to Teaching Art in Canadian Elementary and Middle Schools.* Toronto: Harcourt Brace.

Videos

The National Film Board of Canada (NFB) has videos on Canadian artists and art movements. Catalogue available. www.nfb.ca

Atlantic Canada 1-800-561-7104

Quebec 1-800-363-0328

Ontario 1-800-267-7710

Western and Northern Canada 1-800-661-9867

Some examples:

Art of the Inuit. NFB. (artists Kenojuak and Pitseolok).

Alex Colville: The Splendour of Order. NFB. (his life and art).

Group of Seven. NFB. (a series on the artists).

Jack Bush. NFB. (abstract expressionist works).

The Little Men of Chromagnon. NFB. (simple colour mixing).

Modern and Abstract Painting in Canada. NFB. (includes artists discussing their works).

Paul Kane Goes West. NFB. (the artist's journey across Canada in the 1800s).

The View From Here: A Canadian Picture Show in 9 Acts. NFB. (a tour of the National Gallery, Ottawa).

What's This? Understanding Contemporary Art. NFB. (contemporary Canadian art).

TV Ontario (www. tvo.org) also has a video catalogue, which includes videos on Canadian art and artists.

A recommended American video is

What Do You See? Art Institute of Chicago (how to discuss art with children).

World Wide Web

Visit museums around the world through the Internet and see examples from current exhibits. Download the material in advance to save class time to receive graphic images. Here are examples of places to visit. See the appendix for more addresses.

Canadian sites:

Agnes Etherington Art Centre, Kingston www.queensu.ca.ageth/

Art Gallery of Ontario, Toronto www.ago.net

Royal Ontario Museum, Toronto www.rom.on.ca

McMichael Canadian Art Collection, Kleinburg www.mcmichael.ca

Musée des Beaux-Arts, Montreal www.mbam.qc.ca

National Gallery of Canada, Ottawa www.national.gallery.ca

Canadian Museum of Civilization www.civilization.ca

Vancouver Art Gallery www.vanartgallery.bc.ca

Royal British Columbia Museum rbcm1.rbcm.gov.bc.ca

Hamilton Art Gallery www.culturnet.ca/agh

Winnipeg Art Gallery www.wag.mb.ca

Art Gallery of Nova Scotia www.agns.ednet.ns.ca

Kids Space Art Gallery www.kids-space.org/gallery

TV Ontario www.tvo.org

Canadian Museums Association www.museums.ca

Canadian Heritage Information Network www.chin.gc.ca

Reading The Museum program (literacy and museums/galleries). See Canadian Museums Association site.

National Film Board www.nfb.ca

Canada's School Net schoolnet2.carleton.ca

The Children's Literature Web Guide www.acs.ucalgary.ca/~dkbrown/

American and international sites:

Virtual Museums www.icom.org/vlmp

Smithsonian ftp://photo1.si.edu

The Louvre, Paris

The Exploratorium, San Francisco

The Museum of Modern Art (MOMA), New York City

Multicultural Art Sources: Artifacts

Museum and art gallery gift shops, including:

Museum of Civilization Shop, Hull, Quebec (www.civilization.ca)

Giraffe, Ottawa (African sculpture, musical instruments, textiles, etc.). 615-562-0284

SELECTIONS from Canadian Museums (a CMA catalogue). 615-233-5438

Art Institute of Chicago (yarn painting, beadwork, weaving) (800-621-9337)

Museum of Modern Art (Chinese brush paintings) (800-447-6662)

Oxfam Canada (handmade items from India, Africa, Indonesia, South and Central America) (800-466-9326)

Sources of Fine Art Reproductions and Posters

Most Canadian public art gallery shops stock reproductions and posters of works from their permanent collections and as well as from those of other galleries. See World Wide Web listings above. Framing shops often have fine art reproductions in stock or can order from catalogues.

Art and Computer Supplies

Pottery House, Oakville 1-800-465-8544 (source for clay)

Gwartzman's, Toronto 416-922-5429

Woolfit's, Toronto 416-536-7878

Opus, Vancouver 1-800-663-6953

Software Examples:

Art Explorer by Adobe

ClarisDraw by Claris: MAC Plus or better

Color Me by SVE: APL/IBM

Crayola Art Studio 2, Micrografx: 800-326-3576

Dabbler by Fractal Design: MAC/Power MAC/PowerMAC/WIN

Delta Drawing Today by Power Industries: APL

Flying Colors by Davidson: 800-545-7677

Incredible Coloring Kit: 800-653-8298

Kid-Pix 2 by Broderbund

Kids Riffs; IBM: 800-426-7235

Kindercomp Draw by Spinnaker

MacPaint by Claris: MAC

CD-ROM

Electronic Library of Art (Sony)

Exploring Modern Art: Tate Gallery (Microsoft)

History and Cultures of Africa (Queue)

History through Art Series (available through Quality Computers, 1(800)777-3642)

Le Louvre, The Palace and Its Paintings (Montparnasses Multimedia)

Look What I See! (Metropolitan Museum of Art)

Microsoft Art Gallery (Microsoft)

With Open Eyes: Art Works from the Chicago Institute of Art (Chicago Institute)

Activities:

Opening Vignette: Why? What? How?

Discuss *why* Mr. Novak integrated visual art, *what* he taught about art, and *how.*

Why Do We Create?

Discuss how and why humans create things. Make a list of reasons to bring up with students.

Guided Visualization

Pick a topic studied in elementary science or social studies. (Check courses of study or textbooks.) Write a one-page guided imagination trip with a "you are there" feel to it. Use the pronoun "you" to direct the listener to feel a part of the trip. Try it out on students and ask for responses (what they saw, felt, questions they have). Invite them to do a piece of art or writing after the trip.

What Is Art?

Take an ordinary object (eraser, paper, safety pin) and discuss the steps and thought process an artist uses to create, produce, and market a project. Discuss whether such an object is art or not.

Subject Matter

Start a collection of fine art reproductions (from postcards, calendars, magazines) that represent subject matter areas. Books are other resources to teach subject matter. If possible, teach a lesson and involve students in sorting examples by categories. With older students, use an "open sort" to find out what they already know: tell them to group them in any way that makes sense. Give them a set number (e.g., seven groups) if you have examples from each of the above. Do in small groups.

References

Books and Articles

Arnheim, R. (1989). *Thoughts on art education.* Santa Monica, CA: Getty Center for Education in the Arts.

Bill, B. (1988). *Many manys: A life of Frank Lloyd Wright.* London, Heinemann.

Bloom, B. (1956). *Taxonomy of educational objectives.* New York: Longman.

Brookes, M. (1996). *Drawing with children.* New York: Putnam.

Broudy, H. S. (1979). How basic is aesthetic education? or is it the fourth *r*? *Language Arts,* 54, 631–37.

Carpenter, J. (1986). *Creating the world: Poetry, art, and children.* Seattle: University of Washington Press.

Eberle, R. (1971). *Scamper: Games for imagination development.* Buffalo, NY: DOK.

Edwards, C., Gandini, L., & Forman, G. (1993). *The hundred languages of childhood: The Reggio Emilia approach to early childhood education.* Norwood, NJ: Ablex.

Eisner, E. (1983). *Beyond creating.* Los Angeles: Getty Center for Education in Art.

Feeney, S., & Moravcik, E. (1987). A thing of beauty: aesthetic development in young children. *Young Children,* 42(6), 7–15.

Gardner, H. (1990). *Art education and human development.* Los Angeles: Getty Center for Education in the Arts.

Goleman, D. (1995). *Emotional intelligence: Why it can matter more than IQ.* New York: Bantam.

Jenkins, P. (1986). *Art for the fun of it.* New York: Simon & Schuster.

Kellogg, R. (1969). *Analyzing children's art.* Palo Alto, CA: Mayfield Publishing.

Koster, J. (1997). Albany, NY: *Growing artists.* Delmar.

Lowenfeld, V., & Brittain, W. L. (1987). *Creative and mental growth.* New York: Macmillan.

Maslow, A. (1968). *Toward a psychology of being.* Princeton, NJ: Van Nostrand.

McWinnie, H. J. (1992). Art in early childhood education, in C. Seefeldt (ed.), *The early childhood curriculum.* New York: Teachers College Press.

Parsons, M. (1987). *How we understand art.* Cambridge University Press.

Winner, E., et al. (1983). Children's sensitivity to aesthetic properties in line drawings, in D. R. Rogers & J. A. Sloboda (eds.), *The Acquisition of Symbolic Skills.* London: Plenum.

Children's Literature References

Bellairs, J. (1995). *The Doom of the Haunted Opera.* Dial Books.

Berton, P. (1961). *The secret world of Og.* Toronto: McClelland and Stewart Limited.

Brown, L. K., & Brown, M. (1992). *Visiting the art museum.* New York: E. P. Dutton.

Cummings, P. (1992). *Talking with artists.* New York: Bradbury.

Gilman, P. (1992). *Something from nothing.* New York: Scholastic.

Heller, R. (1995). *Color! Color! Color!* New York: Grosset & Dunlap.

Hoban, T. (1971) *Look Again,* New York: Macmillan.

Houston, J. (1965). *Tikta' Liktak.* Longmans Canada.

Howe, D. (1979). *Bunnicula.* New York: Atheneum.

Hughes, M. (1995). *Castle Tourmandyne.* Harper Collins.

Krull, K. (1995). *Lives of the artist: Masterpieces, messes and what the neighbors thought.* San Diego: Harcourt Brace.

Lionni, L. (1963). *Swimmy.* New York: Pantheon.

Lionni, L. (1995). *Matthew's dream.* New York: Knopf.

McCully, E. A. (1992). *Mirette on the high wire.* New York: G. P. Putnam's Sons.

McFarlane, S. (1992). (Ill. by R. Lightburn). *Waiting for the whales.* Orca Book Publishers.

Nixon, J., & Degen, B. 1988. *If you were a writer.* New York: Four Winds.

Pateson, K. (1973). *The Sign of the Chrysanthemum.* London: Thomas Y. Crowell.

Rowling, J. (1997). *Harry Potter and the philosopher's stone.* London, UK: Bloomsbury Publishing Place.

Tolowa, M. (1990). (Ill. by P.Morin). *The orphan boy.* Oxford University Press.

Art Seed Strategies

Consultants:
Jeri Harmsen,
Angela Solar

6

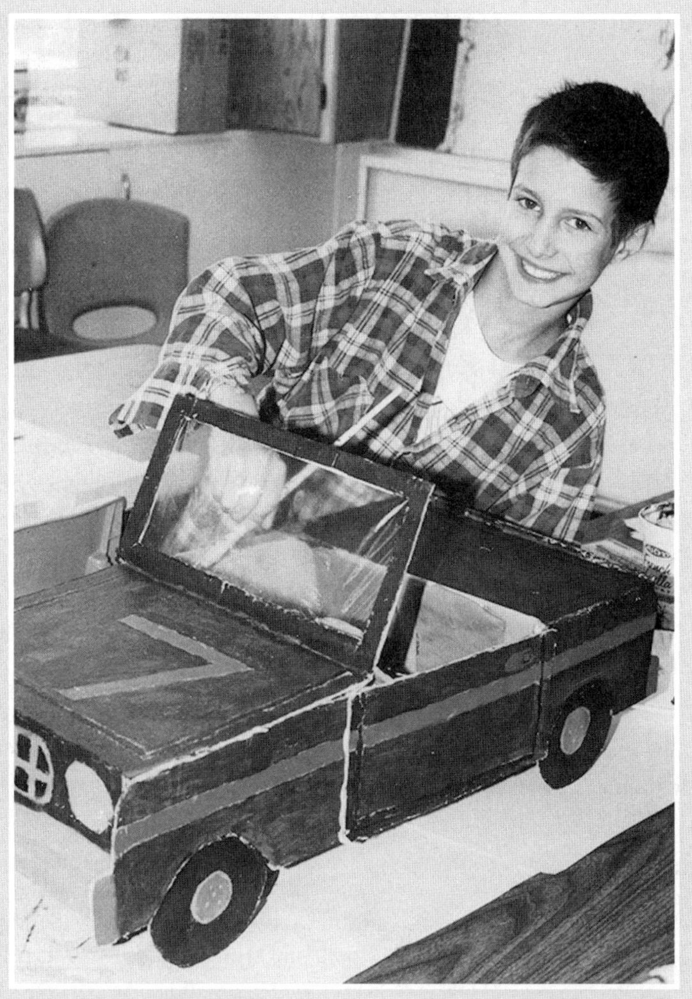

Pyramids, cathedrals and rockets exist not because of geometry, theories of structures or thermodynamics, but because they were first a picture—literally a vision—in the minds of those who built them.

Eugene Ferguson (historian)

This chapter includes specific seed or kernel ideas to help create lessons and units that integrate visual art throughout the curriculum. The seed strategies are generic in that they are not geared to particular ages or stages—most can be adapted for students in grades K–8 and for students with special needs. The strategies are organized into sections, but many fit in more than one section. The separate sections on *energizers* and *elements and concepts* do *not* represent integration, but are provided to help teach these concepts so that students can meaningfully participate in integration of the arts throughout curricular areas.

I. Energizers and Warm-ups
II. Teaching Art Concepts and Elements
III. Using Different Media
IV. Connecting Art to Other Curricular Areas
- Science focus
- Social Studies focus
- Reading and Language Arts focus
- Math focus

I. Energizers and Warm-ups

Creation begins with a vision.

Henry Matisse

Brainstorm. Stretch students' thinking before starting an art project. Brainstorm how to substitute, combine, adapt (change), modify (minify or magnify), put to other uses, eliminate, or rearrange or reverse any idea. For example, if the art theme is fish, explore through discussion the many ways an artist could express the idea of fish: made of paper and painted (flat or stuffed), many tiny fish or one enormous fish painted on paper, a mural of collaged fish prints, fish mobile, clay fish container, fish approaching or retreating, fantasy fish made of "found" materials, a dying fish on a hook, big fish swallowing little fish, part of a fish entering the picture, a fish composed of geometric shapes, a fish in a marine (or kitchen) still life. The process becomes an exciting game of visual ideas. Ask if anyone has a pet fish or a fishing story. Review some features of a fish. Ask what colours fish could be. Remind them that Picasso made a bull's head from a bicycle seat and handlebars.

Walks. Go on walks to find art and beauty in nature. Return to the same spots to find differences during a year. Note colours, textures, shapes, lines, shadows, light and dark, smells, and sounds. Use blindfolds on a listening walk. During walks, collect natural items to use in displays or collages. After walks, draw or paint the experience.

Eye Relaxation. Students warm hands by rubbing them together and then place them lightly over their eyes. *Variation:* Students close eyes and imagine colours and shapes as they are mentioned by the teacher.

Scribble and Doodle. Tell students to make lines, dots, and circles of all shapes and sizes to fill up their paper. Encourage overlapping and working both rapidly and freely.

Talking Lines. Extend the above by asking students to draw a line and then make it: lazy, nervous, confused, loud, quiet, tumble, rainy, tangled, seasick, geometric, joyous, musical, sad. This collection of line interpretations can be used in future projects.

Elements of Shape. Give teams one minute to find all the circles, dots, straight lines, angled lines, and curved lines they can find in the room. *Variation:* Just do one element of shape for one minute.

Mirror Image. Give students a line drawing and ask them to draw the mirror image. The drawing can be an abstract scribble (e.g., a curved line or a jagged line).

Matching Shapes. Prepare a set of cards each with a bold outline drawing of a shape found in the classroom (include the basic geometric shapes as well as freeform). Have each student pick a card and find the shape. Once the shape is found, the student can pick another card, and so on. Prepare another set for a large reproduction of a painting to have students discover the element of shape in art.

Collections. Start scrapbooks, photo wallets, and albums or use clear shoe bags to help students save and organize items that grab their aesthetic attention. Even beans, sand, or pebbles can be layered in jars to study the effects of pattern on our eyes. Collections can be shared and written about to involve students in meaningful talk and writing about things they know about.

Displays. Students can learn about organizing ideas and composing from arranging flowers, furniture, or collected nature items. Labelling of displays involves students in the use of the language arts.

Art Songs and Chants. Compose songs together to familiar tunes. For example, *"There was an artist* *had some paints—red and yellow and blue. And with the paints he made his art—red and yellow and blue. Here a red, there a blue, now its purple—what a hue!"*

Art Poems. Look at and talk about a large reproduction of a painting and have students write a short poem (e.g. a cinquain) about it.

Art Riddles. Find or create riddles about art, artists, styles, particular works, etc. It's easy to write your own. Start with an *answer* like "Picasso." Take each syllable in the word and think of other sound alikes. Make up a question: *"What pig artist liked to make abstract paintings?"* Answer: Pigasso. Or *"What did the art loving horse say?"* Answer = mon neigh!

Make a Mess. Give children time to play with new materials and techniques before asking them to create a product. During play they'll make discoveries and gain confidence and control that will yield success.

Brain Squeeze. Before doing a piece of art or individual art interpretation, take time to squeeze out all the ideas from the group. For example, *"What are all the things we can look for in art?"* Ideas can be recorded in web form or on a list.

Mystery Bag Collection. Introduce a piece of art or an art project by finding three to five objects that connect to it in some way. Pull each out of a bag and ask students to connect the objects to solve the mystery. This is the strategy Mr. Novak used in the case at the beginning of Chapter 5.

Five Senses Stations. Stimulate the senses before doing or viewing art by setting up centres for students to:

Taste: Close eyes and taste salt, sugar, lemon. Use popsicle sticks for individual dips.

Touch: Feely boxes with sandpaper, silk, foil.

Sight: Magnifying glasses, tubes, kaleidoscopes.

Smell: Perfumes, potpourri, oils, candles.

Hear: Tapes with environment sounds, boxes and bags to shake, conch shells to listen to.

Look Back. When students have trouble coming up with ideas, suggest they look through past art for ideas, something to redo in a different way. A part of a past piece can become a whole piece; a tree or shape in the background can be the full subject of a new work. If students have a picture file, or the teacher does, browsing through it can spark ideas (see Chapter 5 for picture file categories).

Picture Book Starters. Picture books are rich sources for ideas about how to use different media, styles, and subject matter. For instance, Paul Marin's illustrations for *The Mud Family* (James) are an inspiration for clay modelling, and Elizabeth Cleaver's work shows collage and printmaking. Many of Eric Carle's books are collages made from "painted papers" he paints and cuts up.

II. Teaching Art Concepts and Elements

Questions. Use open or fat questions to stimulate thinking about art: *What is special about. . . ? What is happening? What does this make you think about? How did the artist make this? How do you think the artist felt when she created this? Why?*

Compare and Contrast. Use a Venn diagram to find likenesses and differences between two paintings or reproductions. For example, compare the treatment of elements (line, shape, colour, texture, space), media, and subject (portrait, landscape, still life, narrative, abstract) in portraits by Van Gogh and da Vinci.

Art Postcards.

Card Sorts. Students hone observational skills by categorizing art postcards according to classifications. For example, sort by colour, style, artist, type of art, or subject matter. Students can work in groups to place cards in the categories designated (a closed sort), or students can be given a stack of postcards and asked to create their own categories (an open sort). Art postcards also make wonderful cards to remember children's special days or as note cards to send home to parents. If the teacher is enthusiastic about collecting the cards, children often catch the spirit and want to collect them, just as kids collect baseball cards. Students can make art postcards using index cards and original art, or pictures of fine art from magazines like *Canadian Art* or from gallery brochures and announcements.

Art Element Drawings. Give a grid (paper divided into eight to ten sections). Label each box with an art element: colour, line, shape, texture. Students then do a drawing that serves as a mnemonic for each element and its aspects.

One-minute Element Find. Call an art element category and give groups of students one minute to find as many examples as they can (e.g., kinds of lines in the classroom).

Post It Page • 6-1

Questions and Activities for Art Elements

Line What kinds of lines do you see? Straight, curved, etc.? How do the lines make you feel? Tired, busy, angry, relaxed, peaceful? Which are repeated? Why, do you think? Which lines are strong? Which are faster? *Activities:* Ask students to pick a line and follow its movement with their hand or draw in the air the predominant line in the painting or sculpture. Use a flashlight to "trace" a line or kids can make light lines on the wall or floor to get the feel of all sorts of lines. Use lines as a stimulus for dance or movement: shape your body in angles, move in a zigzag pattern, make curves with different body parts (e.g., arms, fingers). Draw lines while listening to a short piece of music with quiet and lively parts.

Shape What kind of shapes do you see in the painting? How do the shapes create a pattern? Which are organic? geometric? *Activities:* Students make a particular shape with their arms, fingers, or bodies. Ask them to look for a shape around the room. Then find that same shape in a painting or a sculpture. Go on a shape walk around the school to find all the shapes within shapes (e.g., windows, roofs, cars).

Texture If you were able to touch the objects in the painting, how would they feel? How has the artist made the textures appear real? *Activities:* Ask the children to touch the floor, face, hands, a bench and describe how each feels. Have them cup their hands and use them as telescopes or cameras to isolate an area of a painting and ask them what kinds of brushstrokes the artist used.

Colour How has the artist used colour? How does it make you feel? Why? How would the painting be different if . . . was changed to. . . ? Name all the colours. What colours are used the most? What are some unusual uses of colour? What happens when white is used? What happens when colours are put next to each other, e.g., red and green? *Activities:* Close your eyes and think of a colour in the painting. Imagine yourself turning that colour. How do you feel? Find complementary colours, primary colours, and examples of hues, tints, and shades. Get paint chips from paint stores to show hues and enjoy naming colours similar to those companies use.

Space and Composition Why and how has the artist established foreground, middle ground, and background? (Introduce perspective.) How is the space broken up? Where do you think the artist was standing? Why? Where does your eye go next in the painting? Why? Squint and look at a picture. What masses stand out? Why are some things smaller, blurrier, overlapping? How did the artist do that? *Activities:* Choose a small part of a picture and use paint or markers to enlarge it, i.e., magnify. Children create a tableau (frozen picture) of a painting, placing themselves in the proper perspective. Have the children become different things in the painting: a tree, pond, hills, etc.

Light and Shadow What is the light source? From what direction is it coming? How has the artist created volume (modelling—gradations of light and dark)? *Activities:* Have the children imagine the painting in a different kind of light. Ask how their response to the painting would change. Use a flashlight and shine it in different directions on a person or object and ask what the children notice.

Perspective How does the artist show that some things are close and others are farther away? Talk about how this is done (overlapping, size, placement in foreground, middle ground and background; making distant things look out of focus; arranging shapes along diagonal paths that meet at a distant point; foreshortening; modelling with light and dark areas; areas you can "see through"). *Activities:* Draw a jug, an apple, and a box using the "trick" of overlapping. Draw three trees of equal size but each progressively farther away from the other. Look at reproductions of landscape and still life painting and point out the way the artist used perspective. Look at and draw a selected object from different angles, including above and below.

Emotion and Senses How does the painting make you feel? Why (use of colour, expressions)? How do you think the artist felt about his or her subject? *Activities:* Look at a painting or reproduction of a landscape and pretend to walk into the picture. What do you hear? Smell? Describe the weather.

Big Book or Poster Elements. Books or posters of art elements and concepts are useful references during art viewing and doing. Class or individual big books or posters with titles like *The Facts about Colour* or *What to Know about Shape* can be made as a class. Poster board can be used for the front and back covers of big books; bulletin board paper can be folded and stapled with a long-arm stapler for pages.

Word Charts. The goal is to find unusual and descriptive words to expand the concepts of each of the elements and add words to charts, for example, for the category of *textures.* Student then chart words like rough, smooth, silky, bumpy. For *pattern,* these might be used: checked, striped, borders, dotted. Use sympathetic materials to make the letters (e.g. sandpaper for rough).

Elements Exploration with Paint. Start with lots of newsprint and one colour of paint. Invite students to bring in brushes from home (e.g., sponge, baster, dishwashing sponge, bottle washer). Give a series of directed explorations: *Paint different lines: straight, angled, curved, lying down, angry, happy, calm, excited, thick, thin. Create different shapes: dots, circles, squares, triangles, uneven, loose, happy, sad. Take one shape and paint it different sizes. Group the same shapes together. Group shapes that are the same size. Change colours and colour code "same" shapes or same sizes. Outline shapes in a lighter colour. Try outlining in a darker colour. Try painting very slowly. Try using very little paint to dab. Smear a lot of paint on.* Give feedback as students work. Afterward, ask students what they discovered about the elements and use of paint with different tools. *Adaptation:* Ask students for ideas to try.

Slide Show. Have students use fine, indelible, nontoxic marker pens to draw an abstract composition using line, shape, and colour on a blank slide transparency. Slide mounts and transparency sheets are available in camera shops. Project the results on a screen. Comment on these huge abstract works in terms of the use of art elements to create an abstract work of art.

Texture Rubbings. Place a light, flexible paper over a variety of textured surfaces (crinkled foil, bark, brick, burlap, netting, leaves, basketry). Use the rubbings in a collage project.

Art and Feelings. Hang or prop a varied collection of art reproductions around the classroom. With thick marker, print "feeling" words (e.g. sad, happy, scary, warm, cold, etc.) on individual cards. Distribute cards and ask students to place their card at the picture that matches it in their view. Gather to look at each picture with its cards and question how the artist made people have each feeling. This can be done in a public art gallery (with permission) by placing cards on the floor below paintings.

Subject Matter: Questions and Activities. Post It Page 6–2 lists ways to involve students with the art concept of subject matter.

Parent Tips. Parents often don't know how to respond to children's art and don't know why and how to encourage art making. Here are suggestions to share with them:

Art Minipage for Parents

- Tell what you see in your child's art (e.g., colours, shapes, lines).
- Explain how the art makes you feel or what it makes you think of.
- Ask your child to "tell about the art."
- Don't ask "what is it?" because that's insulting.
- Ask how the art was made. Emphasize the process and the effort.
- Make art projects with your child. Avoid "follow-the-step" projects.
- Keep a folder of your child's art and date the pieces.
- Set up a special place or table to do art.
- Visit museums and other special art displays and stop to talk about what you see and feel.

- Share what you think is beautiful and tell why.

Art Bags. Use large zip lock bags to send home a piece of art, a book related to it, and a related artifact or object. Invite students to check these out and share with their families. For example, prints or postcards of Monet's garden art, the book *Linnea in Monet's Garden,* (Bjork) and a packet of flower seeds to be planted at home in the spring is a popular take-home bag.

III. Using Different Media

Mixing Colours

To remember the primary colours and the secondary colours made from them, post a triangle with the three points being *red* (top point), *yellow* (next point moving clockwise), and *blue.* Draw an upside-down triangle over the first triangle to create a star shape. Label these three points (moving clockwise from top right) *orange, green,* and *purple* (the last is also called indigo violet). Note that by combining two adjacent points on the first star you get the colour in between them (e.g., red and yellow make orange). Students can make their own colour triangles to keep on their desks as cues.

Other Mixing Hints. (1) White paint tints or makes lighter. It makes colours pastel. Because it is used so much, purchase extra or double the amount of white paint. When creating tints, start with white and add the colour a bit at a time. (Always start with the lighter colour and add the darker when mixing.) (2) Black shades or makes darker or duller. Add a small amount of black to a colour (e.g., black to white makes gray and black to red makes brown). Remember to add to the lighter colour. (3) Skin colours can be made with black, brown, yellow, red, and white. Start with lighter and add darker colours to create desired shades; for example, blend white chalk with orange crayon to create a skin tone. (4) Use a clear pie pan on the overhead projector to drop in food colouring and show changes from mixing colours. (Turn out the lights and let the colours fill the room.) (5) Overlap primary colour acetate sheets on the overhead projector. (6) Show how to mix colours on a colour wheel. (These can be purchased at any art supply store.) (7) See children's literature in the annotated bibliography in Post It Page 5–10 for books about mixing colours (e.g., Heller, R. (1995), *Color! Color! Color!* and Felix, M. (1993), *Colors*).

Drawing and Rubbing

To draw you must close your eyes and sing.

Pablo Picasso

Human beings seem to be born to draw. Think of the joy children get from scribbling, especially on forbidden surfaces. *Drawing* is linear art made with any tool that can make a mark; it is also a precursor to writing. *Rubbings* are made by placing paper over objects like coins, shells, wire, or any texture and then using crayon, marker, and so on, to bring up the lines from the objects or textured surfaces underneath. *Scratch art* or *etching* is scraping away a surface to reveal a lighter colour. *Resist* consists of using a wash of paint over something that resists it (e.g., crayon.)

Tools and Media. Fingers, sticks, toothpicks, and straws can be used, along with pencil, charcoal, marker, pen and ink, crayon, pastels or chalk, or shaving cream. Children can draw *on* a blank surface or *in* paint or a medium, like glass wax sprayed on windows. (Colour glass wax with tempera paint or add food colouring to hand lotion or toothpaste as a drawing medium. *Note:* Food colour stains.)

Surfaces. Experiment with a variety of papers, cloth, sandpaper, bags, towels, wrapping paper, paper doilies, graph paper, or chalk board. T-shirts can be drawn on with fabric markers or crayons (cover with a paper bag and iron on warm to fix crayon). Scratch board (light colour goes under and dark colour is over it; the latter is usually black) can be purchased or made by using light crayons first and then covering entire surface with heavy black or dark crayon. Scratch board can also be purchased with silver on top and black underneath. Use a nail or sticks to etch drawings.

Drawing Ideas.

Lifelike images are still popular. It is a preference commonly found together with a materialistic interest in tangible things.

Arnheim, 1989, p. 180

Buy or make sketchbooks for students to capture ideas. Encourage "looking closely" and sectioning off an area (e.g., if it's a portrait, try thinking of the face in fourths). A squiggle on a paper, traced hands, and feet and thumb prints can be starters to create animals, objects, people, or abstract art. Try drawing to music or drawing something without looking down as a "model" is studied. Some artists have success drawing upside down.

Crosshatching is a technique in which artists draw fine black lines parallel to one another and then cross them. Crosshatching can be light or heavy and is used to add depth and texture.

Brookes (1996) suggests these "five elements of shape" (p. 59) be taught directly and used to analyze any image and assembled to produce a realistic drawing of most anything:

1. Dots in different shapes (oval, round, elliptical and kidney)
2. Circles in different shapes (oval, round, elliptical, and kidney) and that are "empty" rather than "coloured in" like dots.
3. Straight lines
4. Curved lines
5. Angled lines

Take a Break. Short drawing breaks interspersed within the daily class schedule build confidence in using lines. Make them "seeing" exercises (e.g. sketch your shoe, a crushed pop can, or the back of someone's head).

Drawing Figures. Start with a focal point: eye, hole, centre, and so on. Look closely and analyze. Notice dots, circles, straight lines, angled lines and curved lines. For overlapping, draw things in the front, first, and then draw things farther away. If a mistake happens, make something out of it by repeating it, adding to it, or transforming it. Break people down into circles and tube shapes—the head is an egg shape and the neck is a tube. Grid off faces to position eyes, nose, and so on.

Crayon Ideas. Peel and break crayons, use them on their sides, or even tape several together. Encourage mixing of colours and creation of hues of one colour by using different amounts of pressure. Blend white chalk with orange crayon to create a skin tone, and rub crayon drawings with a cloth to give them a gloss. For crayon resist, try painting over crayon drawings with tempera, watercolour, or food colour. Try using black construction paper for the background and painting over crayon drawing with white paint; or use a white crayon or candle to draw on white paper and then wash over with paint to reveal the image. The kids will think it's magic!

Chalk Ideas. It's cleaner to use chalk if tape is put on one end. Encourage children to break the chalk, try using it on its side, or dipping it in water (once dipped it is ruined for regular chalk use, however). Try wetting the paper with a little sugar water and then using chalk. Of course, the chalkboard and sidewalks are surfaces not to be missed because of their size and texture.

Painting and Painting Tools

You paint what you are.

Andrew Wyeth

Types of Paint. Acrylic, oils, tempera (comes in liquid, powder, and blocks), watercolours, watercolour crayons, and even melted crayons can be used to paint. (Turpentine melts crayons. Check about safety issues before using this with children. Always ventilate.) Refillable paint markers with felt tips can be an alternative way to use tempera. Paints can also be created by combining food colour and egg or adding food colour to shaving cream, liquid starch, hair gel, or even Vaseline. Explore stains and other paints made from tea, mustard, berries, bleach, shoe polish, or just water.

Tools. Use a variety of brushes: toothbrushes, hair brushes, combs and brush curlers. Fingers, feet, hands, feathers, rags, old deodorant rollers, sponges, squeeze bottles, sticks, Q-tips, cotton balls, and straws can be used as paint tools. Newspaper can be rolled into tubes and used as a throwaway brush. Chalk can be dipped into tempera to create interesting effects.

Painting Surfaces. Paint can be applied to wood, paper, canvas, fabric, paper plates, windows, doilies, transparencies, plastic sheets, cookie sheets, or wallpaper. (Many stores are glad to donate old wallpaper books to schools.) Rocks can be painted on, too; just add liquid white glue to the paint to help it stick. Frescoes are created by using paint on wet plaster.

Techniques. Have a brush for each colour, but encourage experimentation with mixing colours (e.g., add white to tint and black to shade, and use the colour wheel to mix secondary and tertiary colours from the primary colours of red, yellow, and blue). Introduce *scumbling* by showing how to use thicknesses of paint over dried paint (i.e., dry brush). Explore dabbing, spatter painting (use a ruler to flip paint from a brush), blot painting (place blob on paper and fold paper), and straw painting (blow blobs of paint by using a straw to direct the air and move the paint). Add salt, Epsom salts, flour, oatmeal, sand, sawdust, or soap flakes to paint to give it texture or make it thicker. (Salt gives a bubbly effect.) Liquid starch, corn syrup, or detergent can be added to change how paint spreads. Soap helps tempera adhere to glossy surfaces. Make a class Paint Techniques display board and label the examples.

Hand painting can include pounding, dabbing with the fingers, fist, or side of hand, etc. When *sponge painting*, it helps to clip a clothespin to the sponge as a handle. Bleach can be applied to construction paper or bright cotton fabric. To tie dye, fold cloth or knot and then dip in bleach or dye. For *marbling*, mix linseed oil and tempera powder (children should not breathe this) to a thick cream. Put a half-inch of water on a cookie sheet and drop the mixture on to it. Carefully lay a sheet of paper on top and lift up. Dry. Flatten with warm iron.

Tips. Watercolours can stain clothing. Keep a bucket of soapy water and paper towels handy for kids to clean up. Never have children mix dry tempera powder because it is easily inhaled.

Print Making

Prints are made with techniques which produce many copies (e.g., woodcut, linocut, silk screen). *Monoprints* produce only one print. Prints can be pulled from a surface (e.g., a table on which students have fingerpainted) or stamped with found objects: vegetables like carrots or potatoes, woodcuts, linoleum cuts, or any form that is raised and will make a printing tool. Real flowers can even be pounded into paper to make a monoprint.

Tools. Collect objects to use for printing: pieces of carpet, wire, mesh, bubble wrap, corrugated cardboard, fingers (use watercolours), feet, hands, sponges, erasers, corks, wood block, checkers, nature (leaf prints), and other gadgets. Cut print shapes from clean Styrofoam meat trays, rubber-tire inner tubes, or shoe insoles and glue to blocks for a handle to hold when printing. Vegetables and fruits can also be used, but take care that kids don't confuse food and art materials.

Surfaces. Use paper, fabric, wood, clay, or even paper towels to print on.

Techniques. It is a good idea to place folded newspaper under your printing surface to give it a cushion. Put paint in shallow tray (e.g., cookie sheet or paper plates) and have a separate container for each colour. Use a brayer (roller) to roll paint onto the item you will print with. If there is too much paint, the image will smear. Make repeated patterns: vertical or horizontal prints, and overlap, twirl, and swirl to create designs. A print can also be made by outlining an image in white glue. Let it dry and the raised glue can be rolled with paint and used to print images. By gluing raised items or yarn on paper towel tubes and then coating the items with paint, you can *roll print*. Any carved item (see 3D art) can be used for printmaking.

Children can make their own gift wrap, greeting cards, T-shirts, and stationery by printing or stencilling. *Stencils* can be cut from plastic or paper (e.g., fold paper in half, cut out a shape, open and use as a paint stencil—not much paint is needed). When stencilling, use a sponge or round brush to dab on paint. Use a variety of thicknesses to create a more interesting image.

Collage

The word *collage* derives from the French word *coller*, which simply means to paste on. Pablo Picasso and George Braque invented collage and used it in their abstract cubist works in the early 1900s. Collage consists of assembling materials and ordering this often chaotic assemblage. Children enjoy the tactile nature of collage, and this medium invites an experimental attitude because realism is not the goal. A collage can be stimulated by any topic or theme (e.g., winter, plants, nature, humour, school, etc.). Encourage the use of a variety of shapes and sizes, both torn and cut. Cover desks with newspaper or old magazines to protect them.

Materials. Just about anything can be used, from stones, sticks, and other found objects in nature to every sort of string, yarn, ribbon or button to make a collage. There are thousands of types of paper, and collage can be made from sandpaper, foil, construction paper, cardboard, newspaper, tissue paper, wallpaper, greeting cards, and magazines. Wetting crepe paper and coloured paper can produce interesting effects, but the bleeding may stain clothes. Children's own old paintings can be torn and cut up into collage material. Paper doilies offer wonderful possibilities for adding texture. Broken and shaved crayon pieces can be used to create a mosaic effect, as can small squares of other construction paper shapes. Sprinkle shavings on paper, fabric, T-shirts, or old sheets; then cover with newsprint and press with a warm iron. Look in reference books for examples of mosaics before beginning. Bits of fabric can be used, as well as pasta. For coloured pasta, just combine food colour and ¼ cup alcohol. Put in a covered container and shake (don't have children do this!). Coloured rice, sawdust, or sand can be made by using tempera paint; don't let students use dry paint because it is too easily inhaled. The teacher should do the mixing. Collages can be sprinkled with sugar or salt to increase the texture and sparkle. Make sure you sprinkle over wet glue!

Backgrounds. Use roof shingles, cardboard, poster board, plastic lids, Styrofoam, and sandpaper as surfaces on which to arrange and glue. Leaves, crayons and coloured tissue paper can be pressed between wax paper using a warm iron (cover with newsprint so you don't get a sticky iron). For a thicker base and more texture, a collage dough can be made by combining half salt and half flour and adding water to make a thick dough. Objects can then be pressed into the dough and coated with thinned white glue. Use a shoe box lid, egg carton lid, or Styrofoam tray to hold the pressed out dough. Plaster of Paris can also be used. Just mix according to the directions on the package and press objects like shells or buttons into it. Food colouring can also be added to the plaster. It does set fast—about fifteen minutes.

Collage Glue. White glue is usually best. It can be thinned with water when working with coloured tissue paper or used as an overall coating for a finished work, as in découpage. Paste can be made from flour and water. Add oil of peppermint or wintergreen to keep it from spoiling. Have popsicle sticks or Q-tips available for students who don't want to use their fingers. Have a wet sponge or wet paper towels available to wipe off glue.

Enlarge, Simplify, Crop

Many artists make small things very large or simplify a subject down to basic geometric forms (e.g., triangle or circle). Georgia O'Keefe is an example. She also *crops* pictures (cuts them off so only a part of a flower is showing. Show examples of these techniques and allow students to experiment with enlarging, simplifying, or cropping objects, plants, flowers, animals, and so on. To enlarge, make a transparency of anything and enlarge it with the overhead projector. Pull the projector back to make the image bigger. For example, basic fairy tale character shapes can be traced by taping large paper to the wall and projecting the transparency for students to use. Outlines can then be painted or used in original ways—don't turn this into a big colouring book activity! Students can trace around each other's bodies to get basic outlines for large-people paintings.

Display or Bulletin Board

Students can create displays or bulletin boards about artists and their work. Interactive displays can be made by adding question cards or flip cards to lift for answers. Calligraphy and block lettering are ways students can label. See the appendix for books on calligraphy. An easy form of block lettering is based on the idea that any letter can be made from a block of paper by cutting straight lines. Begin by cutting as many blocks as letters needed; blocks can be as large or as small as you wish. Then imagine the letter and the cutting begins. Don't worry about "hole" letters like B and R. Just cut through the joining areas because they'll be glued or stapled down.

To frame or finish off a bulletin board, make a creative border with ribbons or leaves or by cutting a border the old-fashioned way that strips of paper dolls were cut: first, pull off about three feet of large paper from a roll (bulletin board paper works). Roll into a tube and cut slices about two to three inches thick using a paper cutter. Creatively cut a pattern along one of the longer edges (zigzag or scallops). Open the strip and staple onto the bulletin board. Make as many strips as needed.

Posters and signs can be made to advertise artists, the style, or a piece of artwork. Students should take time to examine ads for ideas they can adapt through creative problem-solving like that used in SCAMPER (see Post It Page 1–5).

Murals

Murals are large wall paintings, but in schools murals can be any large composition and are usually created by groups. They can be made from a variety of media, from crayons to collage. Murals help children learn to cooperate and take pride in group work, because group planning and sharing are essential aspects of mural making. The easiest murals are ones in which students each add an item (e.g., a nature collage mural or a print of a foot or hand). Students can learn how to develop full scenes relevant for science, social studies, or literature.

Mixed Media

Use paper, wire, paint, fabric, and any other materials in one artwork. Banners, murals, and even portraits, landscapes, or abstracts can be made with any imaginable combinations. See children's books like Bunting's *Smoky Night* and Ringgold's *Tar Beach* for examples.

Fibre Art. Cloths and yarns are great for creating art with texture and pattern. Fabric art connects well with social studies: clothing of cultures and time periods and careers (knitter, weaver, quilter, tailor, seamstress). There are wonderful pieces of children's literature that deal with the fibre arts, for example, weaving in *Annie and the Old One* (Miles). For a science connection, explore the use of natural dyes, such as, carrot tops for a green-yellow, onion skins for an orange dye, and tea for brown or orange; coloured drink mixes can serve as dyes. An ordinary crock pot can be used to heat. Be sure to use rubber gloves and rinse with cold water to set the dye.

Crafts. Crafts include handcrafted traditional art like pottery, weaving, and quiltmaking.

Colour Window Quilt or Banner. Give each child a zip lock bag and coloured tissue paper and cellophane. Children cut, tear, and arrange their pieces and then the bags are taped together with clear, wide tape. Make into window banners or quilts.

Class Quilt. Each child uses origami paper and other media to create a piece of art that represents him. Everyone making a quilt piece should use the same size piece. Focus on how to communicate important things about yourself through this piece of art. Experiment with printing, lettering, collage, etc. Encourage students to not do the obvious. (This need not be representational art; it can be abstract.) Glue all quilt pieces on a large piece of black bulletin board roll paper. Put a border on the quilt by cutting rolled bulletin board paper into three to four inch slices and then cutting designs into each rolled slice, like cutting out a string of paper dolls. Glue the border strips to the quilt. Students can make "speech bubbles" telling about their creation process to post with the finished quilt. Quilts are particularly adaptable as art responses for units. For example, students can each make a square about a favourite book to create a book quilt or a square about any unit topic. In math, quilts are used to explore geometric shapes (squares, triangles) and for counting.

Self-portrait Banner. *Materials:* white paper, white fabric (twelve by twelve inches), pencil, chalk, water, mirror, permanent black marker, masking tape. *Directions:* (1) Look in a mirror and examine your face closely. Sketch each half, really thinking of shapes and line. Outline in black marker. Add whatever you want to represent you (e.g., hat or symbols). (2) Put fabric over paper and tape down. Trace black outline with marker. Wet fabric, do not soak. (3) Use chalk to put in colour. When dry, spray with hair spray. (4) Sew all portraits into banners or a quilt.

Photography

Creation begins with vision.

Matisse

Now that disposable cameras are readily available, classroom photography is doable. Students can learn some important aspects of composition by trying a series of tasks (Cecil & Lauritzen, 1994) and then discussing their results: (1) Take the same person or object close up and far away. (2) Take a person or object with a lot of light and then with shadows or less light. (3) Take pictures of different subject matters: people, places (land, water, interiors of houses), animals, and action shots. (4) Create a still-life arrangement and photograph it. (5) Photograph the same person or object in the centre of the picture and then off centre (more to the left, right, top, or bottom). Have students sort pictures into groups depending on what they believe worked best. Display their "best efforts" with captions created by students on poster board. *Variation:* Students can take a series of pictures of people, places, and events and then write a story that pulls all the photographs together. The story and the pictures can then be made into a book.

Three-dimensional Art

Three-dimensional (3D) art can be made from many materials including found objects, papier mâché, paraffin and soap through add or subtract methods. Three-dimensional art projects gives tactile stimulation and provide an emotional outlet through touch because of the versatility of the materials.

Materials. Clays and doughs (see recipes) and firing clay (from earth used for pottery) can be used. See Baylor's *When Clay Sings* for clay examples. Wood, paraffin, and soap can be used for carving, as well as materials from recipes (Post It Page 6–3). Papier mâché is also inexpensive and versatile (see Post It Page 6–3). See the instructions that follow.

Tools. Fingers, spoons, nails, sticks, cutouts (not cookie cutters), rolling pins, and things to press in to give textures (e.g., potato masher) are all possibilities.

Techniques. Use each of these methods to sculpt: add, subtract, punch, slap, pound, pinch, and stack. Children will naturally use clays and doughs to make cylinders and then balls and then pancake shapes. Modelling and plasticine clays hold their shape well, but need to be warmed to make them pliable. Let children know they must knead the clay to warm it, which provides exercise to develop finger strength.

Papier Mâché. This is a molding and sculpting material that is inexpensive and yields delightful shapes that can be painted or collaged. Simply cut or tear up newspaper into two-inch-long strips. Use thinned white glue or wheat (wallpaper) plaster and dip strips in paste. Run strips between fingers to remove excess. Let dry. A base like a Styrofoam tray, box, or tube is needed. Start by using boxes as bases and move to more difficult curved and rounded shapes like balloons and cardboard tubes. It is easier to have one small group at a time work on papier mâché because of the mess. Begin with a project in mind, rather than explore as you would in other media. Be sure to do cleanup immediately because the mix becomes hard and is very slippery on floors. An old shower curtain is useful to cover work surfaces. Puppet heads can be made by starting with a base as simple as a wad of newspaper on top of a toilet paper tube reinforced with masking tape. Spaghetti or candy boxes can be covered with papier mâché, painted, and used for puppets (make sure children can get fingers or hands inside).

Mobiles. These are 3D art that moves. Use sticks, hangers, old picture frames, and so on, to suspend items from wire, yarn, cord, or ribbon. Mobiles can be made from found objects or by attaching any created items. Students need to experiment with balancing the weights of objects.

Other Sculptures. *Stick sculptures* can be made by using a clay ball as a base and pushing in toothpicks, buttons, shells, and the like.

Sand molds can be made by pressing objects into damp sand (lids, pencils, buttons, shells). Pour a thin mix of plaster of Paris (the thickness of salad dressing) about ½ inch deep into the depression. Put a pop-can tab or paper clip in the mixture to make a hanger.

To make *soap clay* for carving, mix ¾ cup soap powder and a tablespoon of water. Whip until stiff. This can be used to coat projects to create a snow effect or molded (with wet hands). It dries hard and can be painted.

Crepe paper sculptures can be made by tearing up the paper, soaking one to two hours, pouring off the water, and adding wheat paste. It dries hard and can be sanded. *Yarn sculptures* can be made by soaking yarn in white glue and then wrapping it around a balloon, as sparsely or densely as desired. When dry, break the balloon.

Vermiculite carvings can be made by combining vermiculite (get at a plant store) and plaster. Add water and stir until thick. Pour into a mold or small box. Tear the box away when dry and carve with a table knife, nail, or blunt scissors.

Diorama or shadow boxes are scenes made by using a shoe box or other container to create a stagelike setting with 3D objects that are made or found.

Architecture. Teach basic shapes such as the cube, arch, sphere, cone cylinder, pyramid, rectangular solid, and triangular solid. Then take a neighbourhood walk to find examples in buildings. Arches can be made with boxes and blocks, and cardboard tubes make a base to construct columns that can become Corinthian, Doric, or Ionic with some papier mâché, glue, and paint. This is a particularly relevant art connection to studies of countries (e.g., Greece or even students' own community). There's probably a post office or government building with columns in nearly every Canadian city. Terms that relate to architecture like arch, beam, column, post, and lintel can be taught to give students conceptual anchors.

Recipes. Post It Page 6–3 contains common easy recipes for clays, doughs and pastes.

Puppets and Masks. Post It Page 6–4 describes ways to make puppets and masks with readily available materials.

Bookmaking

Pop-up, accordion, big books, minibooks, sewn books, and shape books can be made to bind up the writing and art of students. There are many books available on easy binding (staple on a wallpaper cover or "sew" with yarn through hole punches). See, for example, Irvine, J., & Reid, B., (1987), *How to make pop-ups* (New York: William Morrow).

Big Books. Big books are enlarged copies of favourite books, poems, or chants about the size of posterboard. To construct a big book as a response to a book, poem, lesson or unit of study:

1. *Paper:* 18 by 30 inch white chart paper and 12 by 18 inch white construction paper will be needed, plus two pieces of poster board at least 18 by 30 inches, and clips, metal rings, or cord to secure the cover.
2. *Art materials:* Glue, markers, crayons, wallpaper sample, and other collage materials.
3. *Type of book:* Replica or new version? To make this decision, select a predictable story or poem with obvious patterns or rhyme (see example list of predictable books in Chapter 3 under "Genre"). Reading the book or poem several times invites children to chime in. Prepare for writing by brainstorming and webbing ideas. Students then dictate a rough draft, which the teacher writes on a large chart or older students write independently. Then the story or poem is reread and revised.
4. *Text:* Words are printed on white construction paper and glued on the larger sheets of paper.

The text should be divided evenly across the pages of the book so that there is plenty of room left for artwork.

5. *Illustrations:* Students can use a variety of materials, styles, and techniques. They may want to experiment with the style of a particular artist.
6. *Title page with the copyright year and the names of authors and artists:* Design a title page and, if the book is a replica, a statement such as "Retold and illustrated by Mr. Walker's class" should be added. If the big book is an adapted version, a statement such as "Based on Kurelek's book *A Prairie Boy's Winter*" can be added. A dedication page can be made for the beginning of the book, and a page about the authors and even a reader comment page can be added at the back.
7. *Cover:* Students design a front and back cover and it is glued to the poster board.
8. *Page sequence:* Have students order the pages, and put book together with front cover, title page, copyright page, dedication page, story, page about the authors, comment page, and back cover. Use rings, cord, or metal clips to bind the book.

Cleanup and Organization Tips

Before doing art projects, be sure to prepare for contingencies and think about these tips:

1. Make student cleanup a routine part of any art project. Make this clear in advance.
2. If the teacher has to do too much preparation, it is probably not an appropriate art activity for kids. Students should do most of the work to learn (e.g., cutting out of shapes by the teacher is often inappropriate).
3. Collect egg cartons or ice cube trays and use half for different paint colours and the other half for mixing. *Alternative:* Use washed juice cans, cut them in half, and set in student milk cartons for stability. *Note:* Don't try to give students all possible colours. They need to explore mixing their own.
4. Q-tips are paint tools that can be used to make "dot art" similar to Seurat's style. Students can also paint with rolled newspaper "brushes" if tools are in short supply.
5. A ball of clay the size of a baseball can be used to store markers: poke holes so that it looks like a multiholed bowling ball with the markers and let clay harden.
6. Use clear plastic shoe boxes and clear shoe bags to store materials.
7. String a clothesline and use clothespins to hang art. Hang up straw beach mats and use drapery hooks to hang anything on them that you can punch a hole in and put over the hook. Use plastic drying racks that have clothespins on each arm as a way to display or as mobiles.
8. Old shirts can be used to cover clothes. Cut off long sleeves and button them on children backward. Garbage bags can also be used: slit and then cut arm holes and neck holes. Be careful about young children putting bags over their heads.
9. Trim brushes with scissors to keep them fresh.
10. A warm iron flattens curled art.
11. Mount or frame children's art to give it a finished look. Use transparency frames for quick framing. Save the tabs off soda cans to tape on the back of pictures for picture hangers.

IV. Connecting Art to Other Curricular Areas

Science Focus

- Natural world, systems of the body, seasons, weather, plants, animals, the environment, ecosystems, machines, electricity, magnets, space, gravity, states of matter, light, sound, air, energy, heat, structures, and mechanisms.
- Finding out how and why things happen in the world through careful observation, hypothesis making, and prediction.

Art and Reality. Borrow a caged pet rabbit (or mouse) for a day. Before presenting the animal, ask the class to suggest how they should behave to ensure it is comfortable with so many people (calm, quiet, standing a bit back). Have students observe the animal and make sketches and written notes on its features (nose, eyes, fur, body shape, legs, tail). Have students draw the animal from different points of view. Show how other artists have interpreted this animal (Durer's rabbit, Bateman's sketches of mice, cartoon rabbits). Does an artist have to make an object look "real" for us to recognize it? Early scientists used drawings and paintings as well as written descriptions to give us information about things, and thus were concerned with "real." Artists can capture the "spirit" of things, which is often expressed using exaggeration or by leaving details out. *Note:* This can also be done with a flowering plant.

Bird Art. Look at owls by Inuit printmakers (e.g. Kenojuak). Find out about snowy owls in the Arctic: their environment, where they nest, what they eat, survival features (eyes, beak, claws, feathers, shape). Look up the snowy owl in a bird book. Look at Cape Dorset (where Kenojuak lives) on the globe. Make small clay or paper bag owls. Make an owl stencil and print from it. Investigate the raven in West Coast Aboriginal art and in the work of Emily Carr. Learn about the legends surrounding these birds.

Food Mural. Students work in teams to research a food's origin step by step. Use paint and collage materials to construct a mural to show how it ends up on the dinner table. For example, show how wheat is planted, harvested, processed, baked, wrapped, and delivered to grocery stores; or follow a salmon from egg to table.

Habitat 3D. Use boxes to create dioramas of an animal's habitat (land or water). Add clay sculptures, tempera paint, found objects, and papier mâché in construction. Emphasize the importance of showing how the habitat would enable the animal to survive (food, shelter, etc.).

Museum Scavenger Hunt. Give student pairs or teams a scavenger hunt form on which to record "finds" in these categories: animals, plants, and other images related to space and land forms during a museum visit. Make spaces to note title, artist, date, and media for each piece of art.

Pound Flowers. Do this in the spring. Collect a variety of fresh flowers and discuss their names and how they are similar and different. Students then place the flowers on construction paper and cover them with clear plastic wrap. Pound each flower with a hammer until the colour is embedded in the paper. Frame and display.

Clouds. Use types of clouds (stratus, cumulus, etc.) to inspire soft sculptures, paintings, and drawings.

Science of Colour. Recreate Newton's famous light experiment, which showed that white light is composed of colours. Turn out the lights. Hold a prism in the light beam of a slide projector. See rainbow colours dancing on the walls, ceiling, and floors. Note the colour pattern ROYGBIV. Use paint or crayons to record. Discuss how rainbows are formed in nature. Paint a picture with a rainbow. Can all creatures see colour?

Nature Collections and Displays. Students can create collages and displays from "found" nature, for example, a fall collage using leaves, twigs, stones, and dried flowers.

Catch a Spider Web. Slide a piece of black construction paper behind a web and bring it forward so that the web clings to the paper. Dust with flour or dusting powder. Spray with fixative or nonaerosol hair spray. Carefully observe and draw the pattern of lines. Research how a spider makes a web and how the web is used.

Step into the Painting. Tell students to think like scientists and tell or write their observations as they look at a piece of art (e.g., a landscape). Focus on how the painting might have been made and the content.

Grow a Head. Use pantyhose feet to make living heads. Fill hose with a teaspoon of grass seed and then a mixture of soil and sawdust. Tie snugly with a string. Paint on face with fabric paint. Put head in a shallow dish and pour water over it. Place in a sunny area and watch the grass "hair" grow. Discuss the conditions seeds need to germinate and grow (soil, light, water, air). What would happen if the light were left out?

Garbage Art. Have students collect recycled and discarded items to use in collages that promote looking at throwaways in a different way. Emphasize experimenting with how to group items on cardboard and the use of patterns. Encourage tearing, scrunching, and even using pieces of plastic and glass for mosaic effects (take care about sharp edges). Discuss recycling and the environment.

Artist/Scientist. Discuss the similarities between artists and scientists (creative thinkers, imaginative, technically skilled, observers, curious, communicate ideas). What are the differences in the way they work and how they communicate ideas? Copy and distribute drawings from a book on Leonardo Da Vinci that show his work on human anatomy and machines. Have each student imagine a machine and then draw his or her idea. Display the results.

Social Studies Focus

- Relationships among human beings, occupations, transportation, communities, governments, customs, cultures, holidays, and use of natural resources.
- History, geography (use of maps), civics (citizenship and government) or political science, economics, anthropology, and sociology.

- Investigations into cultural diversity and global understanding.
- Special questions: How did it used to be and why? Why is it like it is today? What can I do about it? Thinking processes: cause and effect, sequence, gather data, discover relationships, make judgments, draw conclusions, and problem-solve about community issues, for example, economic issues like school funding or values conflicts related to free speech.
- Use of primary source material like newspapers, art, music, diaries, letters, journals, books, and artifacts, rather than use of textbooks and gathering data through interviews, surveys, and other investigatory strategies that historians and other social scientists use.

Make Me a World. Papier mâché used over a balloon provides a base to create personal globes or planets that can accompany individual research projects that will be presented to the class.

Signature Art. Part of social studies involves coming to respect individual differences. A signature is a line on paper like a drawing. To show how unique in style each person's signature is, put up a big sheet of paper and have students write their signatures with a thick, black felt pen. No two are alike. Ask how the uniqueness of signatures is used in society. Discuss other means of authentication: wax seals, fingerprints, DNA.

Group Composition. Since learning cooperative behaviour is a key goal of social studies, any art project on which students have individual responsibilities and come together to create a whole work is appropriate, for example, murals, class quilts on a topic (transportation, province, city, etc.), group sculptures such as totem poles, or constructing with cardboard boxes, tubes, or papier mâché around a topic such as inventions. Emphasize that the art need not be representational.

Multicultural Art. Any country or culture can be studied through its art forms. Assemble prints, pictures, and artifacts and then discuss the details and patterns. Ask about what the figures are doing and why. Students can research the background of pieces of art (media, techniques) and then experiment with these. Emphasize the values that are portrayed in each art form by asking, "What does this show about the people?" *Variation:* Each child begins a personal collection of art from different cultures and ethnic groups using magazines, advertisements, and postcards.

Artifacts. Artifacts are another type of art students can learn about and, in doing so, come to new understandings about different cultures. These handmade art forms are usually three-dimensional and are related to the everyday life of a people. Baskets, carvings, quilts, pots, and jewellery give us hints about the artist's values and needs. Invite students to bring in artifacts and create displays with written "museum tags" about each piece. Artifacts can be coordinated with social studies units and used for writing and discussion. For example, write or tell about a family artifact.

Holidays. There are many complaints today about the "holiday curriculum" overtaking the curriculum. The problem lies in the superficial ways in which holidays are studied and the lack of connections to courses of study. Stereotypical and dictated art abound and need to be avoided. Instead of tracing and colouring turkeys at Thanksgiving, it is more substantial to engage students in using a variety of art media to express ideas and feelings about major themes. For example, (1) meals are rituals used to celebrate events in many cultures, (2) people offer food as a gift to show appreciation and love, and (3) there are many ways to give thanks.

Mandalas. The mandala is a circular shape that has been used in all cultures for eons. First, get students to search out examples of circles or compositions arranged in circular patterns in the art of a variety of cultures and in contemporary art. Brainstorm all the circular things in nature, like the sun and moon or the cycle of seasons. Students can then make their own mandalas by creating a piece of art that has the concept of the circle. This is a broad idea that can be interpreted any way students like, from round abstract artworks to poster-sized realistic works containing many circular-shaped images. Any material may be used, and young children especially enjoy collage mandalas.

Class Flag. Examine the flags and symbols of countries. Discuss how and why they use the colours, shapes, designs, materials, and lines that they do. Divide into groups to create a class flag to represent what's important about the class. Make fabric, paper, paint, and collage materials available for design.

Read an Old Picture. Show a reproduction of the historical painting *The Woolsey Family, 1809* by William Berczy (large and postcard sizes available from the National Gallery of Canada). What clues has the artist given to show the interests of family members? How has the artist connected the figures? Describe the features of the room. Describe how the children are dressed. Is this an average Quebec house and family in 1809? How do you know?

Read what the art historian Russell Harper had to say about the picture in his book *Painting in Canada.* Find another picture that Berczy painted (e.g. *Portrait of Joseph Brant*, Chief of the Mohawks). *Activities:* Collect and/or make the things associated with (or worn by) members of the Woolsey family (hoop, doll, cap, basket, collars, etc.). Have a group of students recreate the picture using these things and then ask the others to refer to the reproduction to "correct" the composition. Create current (contemporary) group pictures by making paper cutouts and pasting them on a painted background. Discuss the role of artists as recorders of our history. How is today's society being visually recorded? Another old painting with historical information is Krieghoff's *Playtime, Village School* (1856). Reproductions are available from the National Gallery of Canada.

Medieval Art. Show students reproductions of pages from medieval manuscripts. Observe the script and the decoration of first letters as well as margins. Talk about how books were made in that period of history. Who made them? What did they write on? How many people had books? Have students design a large black marker outline drawing of a gothic letter (an initial) on a square of parchment-type paper and "illuminate" it with medieval colour (red, green, blue, purple, brown, gold) felt pens.

Reading and Language Arts Focus

- Reading, listening, speaking, written composition (including handwriting, spelling, grammar, usage, capitalization, and punctuation). Since reading and language arts are processes, they must be connected to a subject to have meaning, i.e., something to read and write about.
- Goal: *Create* meaning and enjoyment using print through thinking at every level from memory to critical thinking or evaluation.
- The printed word and its components (letters, syllables, spelling patterns), how words combine to make phrases and sentences and sentences combine to make paragraphs and other forms of discourse from tongue twisters to novels.

Tactile letters

- Types of words: antonyms and synonyms, parts of speech, and figurative language (metaphor, idiomatic expressions).

Storytelling Art. Show the class a reproduction of a narrative painting; for instance, *Running the Toll Gate (1861)* by Cornelius Krieghoff. (Check the AGO or NGC for a reproduction). Discuss the picture in terms of what is happening, why, and what might have happened before and afterwards. Have each student write a short story about the picture.

Talking Art. Each child writes something a person in the print might be saying on a speech bubble. Bubbles are displayed around the art.

Cinco Strategy. Look closely at a piece of fine art. Number your paper 1 to 5. Beside 1, put all the nouns you see; by 2, verbs and actions; by 3, what it is a kind of or adjectives; by 4, adverbs; by 5, a sentence using the words you've generated. *Note:* Abstract art works well with this. Prepare and copy a set of cinquain poem format sheets (include the word category for each line) and have each student fill in the poem to describe his or her feelings about the picture using the word list.

Learn–Wonder–Like. Students pretend they are going to meet the artist of the work and generate a list of comments and questions about what they learned, wondered and liked about the work.

Word Squeeze. Look closely at a piece of fine art to find all the colours, shapes, places, textures, lines, feelings, actions, things, etc. Make columns on a piece of paper and try to get as many words as you can in each. Tell the students to squeeze it like you would a sponge and try to find things no one else sees. *Variation:* Use a magnifying glass or cardboard tube to focus on or examine picture in halves.

Describe a Colour. Make a list of all the colour names the students know. Divide into groups to find words to describe the colours (e.g. cherry red, poison green, sunflower yellow). Follow with doing a piece of art to experiment with making new colours through mixing.

Walk into the Painting. Students pretend to actually enter a landscape, seascape, or cityscape, and then write or tell how they feel and what they see. Use all five senses.

Art Ads. Use propaganda devices to sell a painting, for example, bandwagon, glittering generalities, celebrity endorsement, common folks, everybody's doing it. Break students into groups to create a one-minute ad to sell a piece of art using the techniques. These can be in writing for newspaper, web site, or radio, or presented orally as a script for television. Videotape a presentation complete with set and cue cards.

Artist Interview. Set up partners to take turns interviewing each other about a piece of their own art. Have each student edit his or her interview notes to one page of script. Display the art with the interviews.

Poetry Art. Students examine a piece of art to note how it feels, the mood, use of media, style, and art elements. Give students examples of types of poetry patterns (diamante, cinquain, haiku, limerick, quatrain, triplet; see Post It Page 3–4 for a list and examples). Write some collaborative pattern poems together and then try writing individual ones based on art. *Alternative:* Students write poems and then create art to go with them, for example, print over the poem, collages, watercolours. Print the words in a design to reflect the theme of the poem (concrete poetry).

People Texture. Connect texture with descriptions of personality. What does it mean when someone "bristles," is "soft" or "hard," is "rough," or is "an old smoothie"?

I Spy (visual discrimination). Set this up as a game as in the *Where's Waldo* books. Say *"I spy . . ."* and start the game; ask students to find things that are special to finish the phrase. Encourage students to *look closely* for big shapes, little shapes, curvy lines, light, and dark and to try to find action and details. Use with abstract art to stretch thinking. See the *I Spy* art series for children in which focus is on finding something in masterpieces, for example, letters, animals, toys.

Theatre Arts. Show the animated video *The Owl and the Lemming* (NFB). Turn the story into a short, simple play. Work out the title and dialogue orally as a group, then record the results. Discuss what the set should look like. Talk about the costumes and props. Give jobs to groups (acting, set backdrop, props, costumes, music, choreography, publicity, script). Run through. Adjust. Present!

Memory Game. Tell the students to study a piece of art carefully for a specified period of time and then cover it up. Ask them to then list everything they remember. They could do this individually or in groups, orally or in writing. Uncover the painting and check for the accuracy of their observations.

Word Walls and Webs: Vocabulary Development. Designate a space to put up categories of art words (colour, shape, media, and style). Put each category in the centre of a large piece of paper. Students add to the webs by finding examples of each in artwork, writing on the wall or web, and drawing a line and putting their initials beneath their idea. For example, the line web could have connections such as zagged, straight, curved, pointed, or thin.

Read about Artists. Here is a list of possible things to read and find out about an artist:

- Life of the artist: biographical information such as birth, death, marriage, children, friends
- Who and what most influenced the artist
- Time period in which the artist lived
- Country or countries where the artist lived
- Style in which the artist worked or school of art to which the artist belonged
- Influence the artist had on the world of art (what the artist is known for)
- Other artists of that period
- Medium(s) the artist used
- A particular work of art the artist did, e.g., the most famous or controversial
- Art criticism about the artist and his or her work

Write about Art and Artists. Here is a list of possible writing and art and artist connections:

- Letter to the artist or someone in the picture
- Letter to the curator of a museum to request information about a work of art
- Biographical sketch of the artist
- Story in a modern setting that includes a great artwork
- Description of a piece of art or a criticism
- Possible menu that might have been served during the time the piece was created
- Report on the customs of the time of the artist
- Report on the clothing styles of the time of the artist
- Story about how the work of art came to be
- Report about the period of art
- Paragraph hypothesizing what the artist would do if he or she were alive today
- Play about the artist's life
- Comparison of the work of two artists
- Time line of the artist's work
- Book for children about an artist, medium, or style

Artist Expert. Students pick an artist and do any number of the following activities to become an expert on the person and his or her work. Any of these can culminate in class oral presentations.

- *Collection:* find and save reproductions of works by the artist (art calendars, postcards, art ads).
- *Ape the greats:* use the colours, mood, style, and techniques of the artist to create adapted works of art
- *Vary it:* do another version of the art (e.g. van Gogh's *Starry Night*—do Sunny Day, Rainy Day, Stormy Night, Foggy Night, or Snowy Night).
- *Guests and experts:* invite a local artist, museum curator, or college professor to speak about the artist or interview them
- *Art gallery:* visit an art gallery and see the real thing
- *Artist's studio:* visit the place where an artist works; ask to shadow the person for a day
- *Video:* watch a video of the artist's life (e.g., National Film Board's *Eskimo Artist: Kenojuak; Kurelek, Alex Colville, Riopelle, Lismer)*
- *Mini art display:* in the hall, classroom or a special place in the school; include labelled (artist, dates, title, media, where the original resides) reproductions of works by famous artists. Include students' work "in the spirit of" the masters.
- *Painting of the week:* students select a favourite from among several works of art and display it, with "speech bubbles" around it telling things they know or what they think or feel about it

Story Moment. Everyone who reads imagines pictures in their mind. Read a story with lots of potential for imagining pictures. Have students make a picture of one moment in the story and choose a direct quote to go under (or in) the picture. Display the results in the sequence of the story. Think of reasons why different people would chose different moments.

Arts and Letters. Collect a big box of bold letters and sayings (computer generated and from magazines). Encourage students to use them in their art (posters, collage, mixed media).

Journals and Logs. These could be done individually, as dialogues between two students, or as team journals. Topics to write about: What do you think about the painting? How does it make you feel? What does it make you think about? What mood do you think the artist was in when he or she created this work of art? Why did the artist entitle the work of art as he or she did?

Compare and Contrast. Different messages are conveyed through the use of different media (e.g., sculpture, poetry, dance). Compare and contrast two pieces of art that evoke similar feelings and messages. How does each artist create the response? What do both artists do that it similar? For example, look at art about courage, love, family, war, suffering, or nature.

Math Focus

- Daily living situations involving counting, measuring, probability, statistics, geometry, logic, patterns, functions, and numbers.
- Problem-solving through the use of skills (raising questions and answering them, finding relationships and patterns).
- Concepts about numbers, operations, and ideas like bigger, longer, greater than, less, three, four, even and odd.
- The National Council of the Teachers of Mathematics (U.S.A. and Canada) and the Provincial Math Educators Associations encourage teachers to have children solve problems in many ways, to focussing on explaining and thinking, rather than just correctness, and to use a hands-on approach.

Quilts. Create class geometric quilts using traditional patterns found in folk art collections or by observing patterns in the environment that could be used on pieces (dots, checkerboard, and stripes). Each student uses a square of paper (about 10 by 10 inches) to plan a pattern. Patterns can be painted or made from cut paper, fabric, newspaper, or thin plastic. Squares

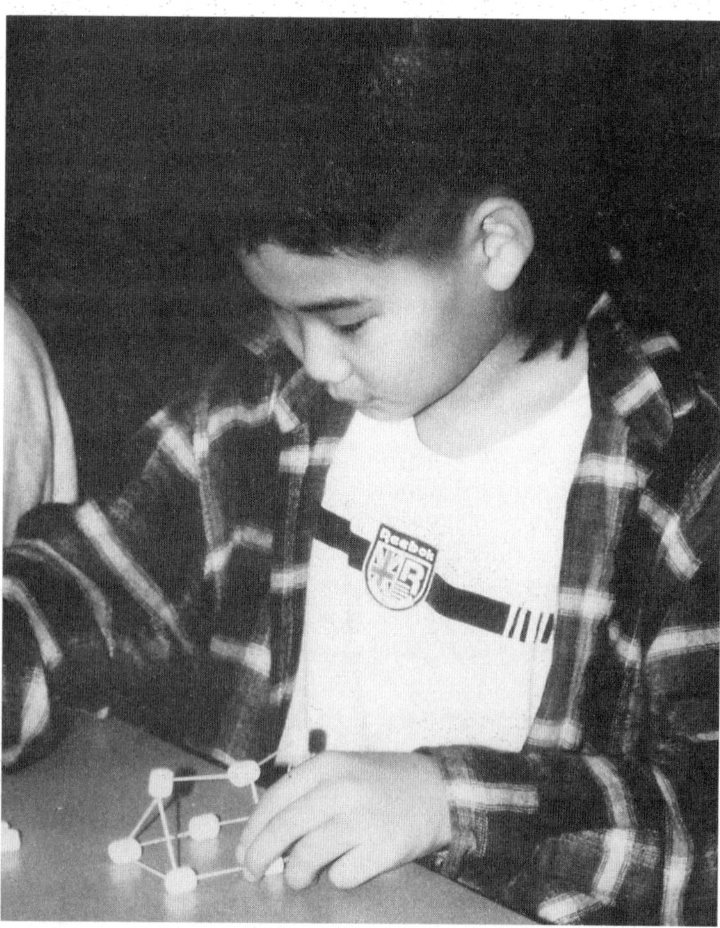

Toothpick Geometry

are completed and then glued on to a large piece of bulletin roll paper (black makes an excellent background). A border can then be added. *Note*: Fitting shapes together to fill a space is called "tessellation" in math. *Variations:* Students can be limited to just one shape so that they can experiment with variations on it (e.g., triangle combinations).

Origami Art. Japanese paper folding art involves the study of shape, line, symmetry, and angle. Special origami paper in a variety of colours works best and is available from any art supply store. There are many resource books on simple origami shapes, such as bird shapes. The children's book *Sadako and the Thousand Paper Cranes* (Coerr) would be a wonderful story addition to this art–math project.

Colour Recipes (measurement). Each pair of students needs an eyedropper and three small cups of tempera (red, yellow, and blue; use ice cube trays broken in half). Students experiment to create colours. They record the number of drops to create each colour. Ask pairs to name their new colour creations and to work out the mathematical ratio of colour to colour. *Variation:* Give students one primary colour and a cup of white and black. Experiment with recipes for shapes and tints (numbers of drops).

SCAMPER. Students are given a shape to manipulate using Eberle's steps: substitute, combine, adapt, minify or magnify, put to other uses, eliminate, and reverse or rearrange. They create a piece of art to show all the things they did with a triangle, square, circle, and so on, using SCAMPER. Use any media.

Count Me In. Groups are given a piece of art to examine for numbers of things. Give a time limit and then share as a group (e.g., eleven curved lines, eight right angles, fourteen red flowers).

I Spy. Find all the math in any piece of art (print, collage, sculpture) or picture book. List geometric shapes, patterns (anything that is repeated), types of lines, use of symmetry. Discuss any parts that give a feeling of infinity and how it is accomplished. Use a large magnifying glass.

Symmetry. Each student gets one-half of a picture from a magazine or print. By carefully studying the half, the student tries to duplicate it on the opposite side.

Making Math Art. Use art that is very geometric, like Mondrian's and Molinari's (see *Contemporary Canadian Art*), and ask students to discuss how the artist might have made it and why. Have students try their own geometric math art by repeating shape patterns.

Math "Eyes." Be mathematicians and tell or write all your observations based on your math point of view. Comment on how the painting might have been made and the content of the work.

Creative Mathematics (Upitis and Higginson, 1997) is an excellent resource for integration of mathematics and the arts.

Post It Page • 6-2

Learning to Read Art Subject Matter: Questions and Activities

Take time to stop and look carefully before asking any questions. Adapt for different ages and stages. Meaningful art experience depends on learning to look longer, notice details, respond personally, ask questions, and think about the meanings of what is seen. Remember, all art is a reflection of the time period and culture that produced it. Art of the twentieth century reflects values about originality and the importance of individuality in a world of mass production and imitation.

Landscapes *are about the land.*

- What is the mood? Season? How do you know? If you were here, how would you feel?
- Where do you enter the work of art? Why did the artist create this position for you?
- Do you feel a part of the scene? If so, what did the artist do to include you? —OR—

- Do you feel like an onlooker? If so, what did the artist do to keep you at a distance?
- Look closely to see if there are any people. If so, how are they related to the landscape?
- Does the landscape seem real or imaginary? Why? Does it describe or capture the real look of a place or does it give more of the feeling of a place (expressive)? Why?
- What title would you give this work? Why?
- Walk into the painting. What do you see, hear, feel? What can you do there?
- Think of a special place you have been? What made it memorable? If you could artistically recreate this setting, what medium would you use (oil paint, watercolour, pastels, charcoal, pencil, collage)? What would you emphasize? Why?

Portraits *are of people but show more than what a person looks like. Artists use a "visual vocabulary" to communicate this. Consider this special artistic vocabulary as you look at a portrait.*

- What does the artist tell you about this person? How does this person feel?
- *Clothing:* What clues does the person's dress give about the person?
- *Facial expression, posture, and gestures:* What does the person's body language say about attitude and personality? What do the eyes, eyebrows, mouth, throat, forehead, and angle of head seem to tell? Where is the person looking? How does this affect you? How is the person positioned? Why? What is he or she doing with his or her hands? Take the position yourself. How do you feel? Would you want to meet the person in this portrait? Why or why not?
- *Background and accessories:* Where is the person? What clues does the environment provide about the person? What might the specific objects in the setting mean?
- *Size and medium:* Is the portrait life size or is it smaller? How does the size of the portrait change how you feel? What media and materials do you think the artist used? What if the materials were different? For example, how would marble give a different feeling than paint?
- Look closely. Start at the head and slowly observe everything. Pretend you are the person and walk, sit, and stand in role. Be the person and say one thing.
- Look at real people through a tube or frame to see shapes of eyes, lips, and head. Observe groups of people: How close are they? How are they grouped (line, circle, random)?

Still lifes *are pictures of single or groups of inanimate objects (e.g., fruit, flowers, bottles).*

- What attracts your eye? What do you discover that you didn't notice at first glance?
- What is the most important part of the painting?
- Where are examples of how the artist makes it seem like there is light on surfaces?
- What kind of lifestyle do these objects represent? Why might the artist have chosen these objects? What might the objects represent (symbols)?
- What objects could you use to make a still life (e.g., toys, fruit, school items)? Why? How would you arrange them? What would you want to say through a still life?

Abstract art *goes beyond showing the visible world to allow expression through colour, line, and shape.*

- What is your first reaction to the work? What did the artist do to cause you to react like this?
- What are you curious about? Why might the artist have chosen to create an abstract work?
- How does the work's abstractness change how it makes you feel?
- How would you describe the personality of the art? What contributes to it? How does it cause you to stop and think?
- What meaning, if any, do you think the artist intended? What does it mean to you?

Post It Page • 6-3

Recipes: Clays, Doughs, and Pastes

Clays and Doughs

Soft Dough (Stays soft for a long time if stored in a plastic bag or closed container.)

1 cup water
1/4 cup salt
1 tablespoon vegetable oil
1 tablespoon alum
1 cup flour (non-rising)
food colouring (optional)

Bring water to a boil. Add salt and food colouring. Remove from heat and add the oil, alum, and flour. While it is still hot, mix and knead for five minutes. *Note:* If you choose to add food colouring, it is best to do so at the beginning or add to dough after mixing by using a few drops at a time and folding dough over colour to mix. Food colouring will stain skin and clothing. To change the texture, add cornmeal, sawdust, coffee grounds, sand, or other grainy items.

Goop: Mix one part cornstarch and one part cold water.

Baker's Clay (makes one cup) Often used to make ornaments or jewellery.

4 cups flour
1 cup salt
1/2 cup warm water
food colouring (optional)

Mix all ingredients and then knead until smooth (about five minutes). Add more flour as needed. *Note:* If you choose to add food colouring, do so a few drops at a time and fold dough over colouring to mix. Food colouring will stain skin and clothing. This dough should be used the day it is made. Add one teaspoon alum and put in plastic bag to keep it longer. The dough can be baked at 300°F until hard, approximately twenty to sixty minutes depending on the thickness of the pieces. For Christmas ornaments, make holes for hanging before baking. This clay can be painted with felt tips or use half tempera and half white glue. Spray with fixative when done.

Soda–Starch Clay (Makes one cup)

1 cup baking soda
1/2 cup corn starch
2/3 cup warm water
food colouring or tempera paint (optional)

Mix ingredients in pan until thickness of mashed potatoes. Stir to boiling. Pour on a cool surface and knead when cool. Add colouring during kneading. Store in plastic bag until ready to use. Shape beads by using a drinking straw to make holes. To speed dry, bake ten minutes at lowest oven setting or thirty seconds on medium in a microwave. *Note:* Make a day or two ahead of time. Make batches in different colours. You can use crayons, paint, or marker to paint this clay. Set with clear nail polish or shellac.

Salt–Starch Clay

1 cup cornstarch
1/2 cup salt
1/2 cup water

Mix and cook over low heat until it hardens. Salad oil delays drying.

Sawdust Clay

2 cups fine sawdust
1 cup wheat paste (wallpaper)
1/2 to 1 cup water
1 teaspoon alum to keep from spoiling

Mix to bread dough consistency. Needs to dry slowly. Keeps in plastic bag or refrigerator. *Note:* Good for making puppet heads and relief maps. Can be painted with tempera.

Pastes
Corn Starch Paste (Makes 1/2 pint)

1/4 cup corn starch
3/4 cup water
2 tablespoons sugar
1 tablespoon vinegar

Mix corn starch and cold water in a saucepan. Add sugar and vinegar. Stir constantly and slowly heat the mixture until it clears and thickens. Cool before using. Paste can be stored in the refrigerator several weeks if kept in a tightly sealed container. *Notes:* Corn starch paste has a pleasant smell and texture. It is not too sticky and is a safe, almost colourless paste—it dries clear. It forms a stronger bond than flour paste and can be used for lightweight items such as fabric, yarn, ribbon, rice, and thin cardboard. This is one of the stronger homemade pastes, but it must be cooked ahead of time. It is also hard to remove from surfaces when dry; it requires soaking and scrubbing.

Flour Paste
Add water to flour until it is thick but spreadable. *Notes:* Children can make this for themselves. This works well on most kinds of paper, and it is safe and does not stain clothes. The texture is different from school paste, so it makes an interesting change for the children. It wrinkles thinner papers and makes a relatively weak bond, so it is not recommended for collage. It washes off easily when wet, but requires soaking and scrubbing if allowed to dry. It cannot be stored and should be used when it is first made. Add oil of wintergreen or peppermint to help resist spoiling.

Post It Page • 6-4

Puppet- and Mask-making Ideas

Finger puppets: Cut off fingers of cheap work gloves to make individual puppets students can develop by gluing on materials or using fabric paints. *Alternatives:* Use small candy boxes as the base on which to create the puppet. Students can also create their own figures from paper or cardboard and attach "finger rings" to slip the puppets on.

Glove puppets: Each child needs one glove. Each finger becomes one character to be created from a story. Five characters are possible and some fingers can be objects in the story.

Stick puppets: Attach a popsicle stick, tongue depressor, ruler, or wooden dowel to a character made of paper, papier mâché, cloth, and so on. *Variation:* Find sticks from trees that can be used as a base to make a puppet.

Shadow puppets: Cut character body parts from construction paper and hinge arms, legs, etc., together with brads. Lay on overhead projector and move body parts to tell story.

Paper bag puppets and masks: Use small paper bags to create a character's face or body using paint, collage, markers, etc. The puppet's mouth can be placed at the fold of the paper bag so that it will look as if the character is talking. Yarn, grass, and twigs can be added for hair and paper or cloth used for clothes. Grocery bags can be used to make puppet masks that students wear on their heads with eyes, mouth, and nose holes.

Sock puppets: Students sew or glue scraps of fabric, yarn, and pipe cleaners on socks. The sock can also be cut at the toe to create a mouth or held so that a mouth is created by a fold.

Paper plate puppets: Paper plates can be used for puppets as well as for masks. Students add materials to create a character and then tape sticks or rulers to the back of the plates for handles. *Variation:* Use plastic coffee can lids instead of paper plates.

Papier mâché puppet heads and masks: Use the recipe for papier mâché and apply to a ball of newspaper with an attached toilet paper tube (secure with masking tape). When dry, paint and attach other materials to create a character. A fabric body can be glued or sewn using a generic body pattern made from two pieces of cloth or paper. To make a mask, papier mâché over a large balloon. When dry, paint and cut holes for eyes, nose, and mouth. Mask can be a full head cover or just cover the face.

Object puppets: Find and adapt objects that relate to a story and lay on top a box (used as a stage) or table as the story is told, e.g., a covered thread spool (tuffet), a plastic spider, a tiny doll (Miss Muffet), a toy spoon. Check craft stores and departments for a variety of these tiny objects, often in packages with multiples. *Variation:* Painted rock puppets: collect rocks and paint to represent characters and display and manipulate as story is told.

Clothespin puppets : Use old-fashioned clothespins as the base to create characters. Clip to a ruler to give extra height.

Envelope puppets: Use large or small envelopes as the character base. Combine several envelopes for a different effect.

Pipe cleaner puppets: Bend, cut, and combine pipe cleaners to form puppets. Create a handle from one pipe cleaner.

Paper cup puppets: Use Styrofoam or paper cups as the creation base. Use cups of different sizes and combine cups for creative effects, e.g., create taller puppets with several cups.

Card puppets: Use index cards as bases. Cards can be attached to sticks or used on a flannel board if coarse sand paper or felt is glued to the back. Card puppets can be placed in a pocket chart as a story is told.

Tagboard masks: Cut tagboard into ovals big enough to cover a face. Make four one-inch slits, one on each "corner" so that the mask can be given contour. Use masking tape to secure. Draw ovals for the eyes and a space to cut out a mouth. Paint and use collage materials to decorate according to a variety of cultures (display books with pictures of masks for data gathering).

Plaster gauze masks: The face is covered with Vaseline and then gauze, soaked in plaster, is applied and allowed to set up. (Keep nose, mouth, and eye areas clear.) Mask is removed and painted with acrylics or tempera.

References

Books

Bateman, R. (1982). *The art of Robert Bateman.* Toronto: Penguin Books Canada.

Brookes, M. (1996). *Drawing with children.* New York: G. P. Putnam's Sons.

Burnett, D. & Schiff, M. (1983). *Contemporary Canadian art.* Edmonton: Hurtig.

Cecil, N., & Lauritzen, P. (1994). *Literature and the arts for the integrated classroom.* White Plains, NY: Longman.

Harper, J. R. (1977). *Painting in Canada.* Toronto: University of Toronto Press.

Murray, J. (1984). *The best of the Group of Seven.* Edmonton: Hurtig.

Silberstein-Storfer, M. (1997). *Doing art together.* New York: Harry Abrams.

National Film Board of Canada (NFB) Catalogue available. www.nfb.ca

Upitis, R., Phillips, E., & Higginson, W. (1997). *Creative mathematics.* New York: Routledge.

Children's Literature

Bjork, C. (1987). *Linnea in Monet's garden.* New York: R&S Books.

Bunting, E. (1994). *Smoky night.* San Diego: Harcourt Brace.

Coerr, E. (1977). *Sadako and the thousand paper cranes.* G. P. Putnam.

Felix, M. (1993). *The colors.* Creative Education.

Heller, R. (1995). *Color! Color! Color!* New York: Grosset & Dunlap.

James, B. (1994). (Ill. by P. Morin). *The Mud family.* Oxford University Press.

Kurelek, W. (1973). *A prairie boy's winter.* Montreal: Tundra Books.

Lamarsh, H. (1985). *Maurice for children.* Montreal: Museum of Fine Arts.

Lamarsh, H. (1985). *Picasso for children.* Montreal: Museum of Fine Arts.

Lamarsh, H. (1987). *Leonardo for children.* Montreal: Museum of Fine Arts.

Lamarsh, H. (1988). *Borduas for children.* Montreal: Museum of Fine Arts.

Lamarsh, H. (1988). *Chagall for children.* Montreal: Museum of Fine Arts.

McLerran, A. (1992). *Roxaboxen.* New York: Puffin.

Miles, M. (1971). *Annie and the Old One.* Boston: Little, Brown.

Ringgold, F. (1991). *Tar Beach.* New York: Crown Publishers.

Toye, W. (1977). (Ill. by E. Cleaver). *The loon's necklace.* Oxford University Press.

Wistow, D. & McKinley, K. (1999). *Meet the Group of Seven.* Toronto: Kids Can Press.

Integrating Drama Throughout the Curriculum

7

Consultant:
Aynne Johnston

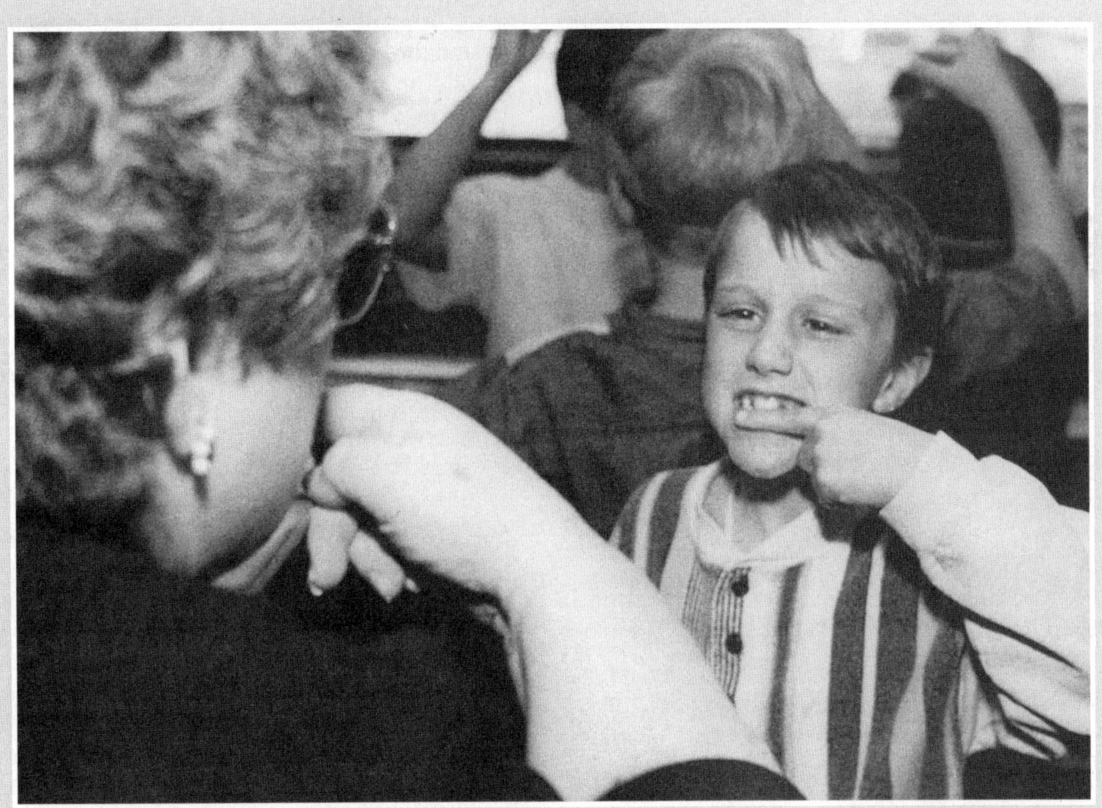

Drama is life with the dull bits cut out.

Alfred Hitchcock

CLASSROOM VIGNETTE

Ms. Tran's Sixth Grade Social Studies Class.

I think that an art gives shape and stability to the valued materials of life, in order that they may be stressed, attended to and preserved.

Josephine Miles

Ms. Tran has been teaching sixth grade for five years. She became interested in integrating drama during a special staff development project on arts integration two years ago. She is a young, vivacious teacher with a contagious sense of humour, and she seems very comfortable using drama on a daily basis. Today's lesson takes place during social studies time, and the students are in the middle of an environmental issues unit focusing on the question of how humans have changed the environment. They have been reading about the problems with the fishery in their province of Newfoundland.

Ms. Tran holds up a cod jig. "I'm going to pass this around and you can each say a one liner about it. Remember, you can pass and we'll come back to you, if you wish."

The students are seated in learning circle groups, and she starts with a student in a group to her left. The boy takes it and grins as he explores the surface.

"I'm a collecter's item now," he says and passes it to a boy next to him.

"They're killing all cod fishery with the processing factory ships," the next boy says and passes the coral on.

A small girl with large, dark eyes takes the jig and says, "I pass." She passes it on to the last person in the first group.

"Probably as many of these in living rooms in Alberta now as shacks in Newfoundland, so many young guys gone to make big bucks in Alberta," the last boy in the group says.

It takes about ten minutes to go around the room. When everyone has had a chance to speak, Ms. Tran nods to the girl who has passed earlier and the girl reaches for the jig.

"Without the fishery, life in the bay can be some sad," she says softly.

"It was really interesting how you took on so many different roles," Ms. Tran remarks. "Shana, I could tell you were a very concerned citizen by the sadness in your voice and how sincere you looked. What did some of the rest of you notice?"

Several hands go up and Ms. Tran calls on students.

"Some people spoke as if they were the jig. That was really cool. I'd never have thought of doing that," a girl in the far right group says.

Other students make comments about how their classmates made clear who they were and how they felt with their words and even how the jig was held.

Ms. Tran then moves further into her planned lesson and summarizes the main topics they've been studying: the Newfoundland economy, lifestyle, and so on, and its relationship to the fishery. She asks the students what she has left out, and several children add comments about the destruction of the fishery.

"Today we're going to go into more depth based on what you read in your assignment and what we've been studying. We want to really go into detail about the interaction between people and the environment. We'll be continuing our work on learning through being different characters and using your voice and body to make us all believe in your ideas. Let's get started."

Ms. Tran picks up a yellow Mr. Mike from the table. "Imagine you are someone who has a specific interest in the fishery—think of all the points of view you read about. We are just getting ready to have a live telecast to inform everyone in the province about the issues."

"Half of you can be the audience and half of you can be the panel. All of you will have a chance to speak. Let's set up. Just five minutes to show time. Panel members take these chairs. Audience, arrange yourselves in two rows."

It seems like chaos for a few minutes, but students decide and soon all but two chairs on the ten-seat panel are taken.

"Great work. Okay. Only two minutes to show time. I'll be asking the panel members to introduce themselves and make a short statement about their position. Audience members, you'll be able to respond to the panel with remarks and questions."

Ms. Tran moves to a CD player and pushes a button. She flips the lights out and stands ready. Jazz music begins and she flips the lights on and holds up the mike.

"Welcome to *Newfoundland Today.* I'm Tina Tran and I'd like to welcome our panel of guests and audience members who are here today to discuss the issues surrounding the fishery. We'll begin with our panel members. Please introduce yourselves and tell us why you have come."

Ms. Tran hands the mike to the panel member nearest her. The panel proves to be a diverse group ranging from fishermen to a politician. Some are vehemently opposed to government interference and others are passionate about the future of the fishery.

After the opening remarks, Ms. Tran opens the discussion up to the audience.

"Please stand and give your name and why you have come," she tells them. The audience offers comments to specific panelists and asks questions. All but two students participate.

After about fifteen minutes, Ms. Tran sums up remarks made during the show and ends with, "I'd like to thank all our guests for coming today and remind you to watch every day at this time to learn more about current issues on *Newfoundland Today.*"

She starts the music again and flips out the lights. She lets the music play a bit and then stops it and turns on the lights.

"Okay, let's talk about what just happened," she tells the class. They seem reticent.

After a full half-minute, Ms. Tran backs up. "I think you all are still processing all this. Let's do a Write Right Away to debrief. Just use the next page in your journal and let's go for two minutes."

Students hustle to their desks for pencils and journals. Ms. Tran moves to an overhead projector and begins to jot down her observations in full view of the students. At first a few students just watch her. She jots down sentence fragments and key words. Gradually, all students begin to write. She actually gives them nearly five minutes and then asks them to find a place to stop (almost everyone is still writing).

"Please form groups of three or four people with the people nearest to you and take a few minutes to share what you wrote. You can read it if you like or just tell it."

Students turn to form groups and Ms. Tran waits until everyone is in a group. When the stragglers have finally joined a group, Ms. Tran circulates as students share.

"You think that you made the politician too stereotyped? Why do you say that?" she asks a boy who has critiqued his own performance.

As she moves from group to group, she comments and asks clarification questions like "What do you mean by . . . ?" and "Are you saying that . . . ?"

The room is full of discussion. After about ten minutes, Ms. Tran brings them back together.

"I could really tell you understood the importance of using details and examples to create believable characters. It sounds like many of you are planning to find out even more specifics before I spring another drama session on you!"

The students laugh and it is apparent they like Ms. Tran's enthusiasm.

"We're going to do some more group work to extend your thinking about the issues and what just happened on the TV program. I'm going to ask you to break into small groups of family, friends, or neighbours that viewed the telecast. I want you to assume a role in this group and discuss the show. I think we'll count off in fives for this one."

After they count off, Ms. Tran directs each number to a certain area of the room. Because the room is carpeted, many choose to sit on the floor. There is a general commotion.

Ms. Tran rings a push bell and announces, "When I ring the bell again, I want you to begin to visit in your group. Ready," she dings the bell.

Another ten minutes pass before Ms. Tran rings the bell and says,"Freeze."
She then goes over to a group and knocks on a desk nearby. She is back in role, this time as a "newcomer."

"Hi everybody. Sorry I'm late. What are you doing?"

A boy in the group tells her what they were just talking about, and he summarizes the gist of their discussion so far. It turns out they are a group of fishermen sitting on a wharf. Ms. Tran becomes a fisherman, too, and they commiserate about the hardships that have been placed on them. A girl in the group brings up the long-term survival of the fishery.

This takes about five minutes. Then Ms. Tran steps out of role and compliments the groups on the diversity of roles they have chosen. She concludes the lesson by making an assignment, due at the end of the week. Students are to do a piece of writing, in a role, to show different perspectives on the fishery issue. It can be a letter, newspaper article, editorial, or even a diary entry or a song.

The students seem excited about the writing and ask questions about whether they will get to share what they write, for example, if it is a song. Ms. Tran seems genuinely delighted with the prospect.

Introduction

Theatre and drama have had a long history of being related to human behaviour and education. Aristotle thought theatre provided audiences with a cathartive effect to release emotions, medieval priests used theatre as an educational vehicle to explain Christianity to the masses, and primitive societies used pantomime and dance in rituals to cast out demons. *Creative drama,* however, had its beginnings in the early twentieth century. In the 1920s the Progressive Education movement emphasized having students *do,* rather than read about or memorize. Progressive educators looked to the arts as possible learning tools and drama was a natural find. During this period Winifred Ward, the mother of creative drama, started a program in dramatics in the Evanston Illinois Public Schools based on the belief that children's literature should be the main stimulus for drama. By 1930, the field of creative dramatics was officially formed.

During the next decades, creative drama in North America was significantly shaped by world leaders in the field from Great Britain, Canada, and the United States. Here is a brief look at ideas from people who have had an impact on the field.

Winifred Ward: Her goals were individual and social development. She used movement, pantomime, characterization activities, dialogue, and story dramas, moving from simple to complex. She believed *performance* was a vital aspect of drama and that a teacher–leader should guide students in their efforts.

Brian Way: His focus was on the process, not product nor performance. He used personal experiences to lead students to self-discovery. He encouraged teachers to "sneak" drama into the classroom, even for five minutes each day. His approach opposes teacher demonstration because he believes acting skills are unnecessary for participation in drama. Life events are used as the drama stimulus, with few student performances and little focus on evaluation.

Dorothy Heathcote: Emphasizes using life experiences to reflect, analyze, and test out conclusions. Students are thrust into a sink-or-swim situation, with the teacher–leader being a significant participant. Heathcote sees four faces of dramatic activity: (1) making plays for audiences, (2) knowing the craft, history, and place of theatre in our lives, (3) learning through making plays, and (4) using "as if it were" drama to motivate study.

Viola Spolin: Her approach emphasizes getting participants to *see* and *do,* not imagine or feel. The goals are to have students lose all inhibition and learn intuitively. Her books of theatre games, originally used in actor training, have been tremendously popular and are used in a workshop format. Performance is a major objective.

David Booth: He makes a strong connection between drama and language arts and has had a significant influence on educators through his work in story drama.

Among these approaches there is much diversity in the goals, role of the teacher, stimulus for drama, and the activities in which students are engaged. In this book, ideas from all the approaches have been culled for their appropriateness to the general classroom.

Teachers often start small, grabbing only a few minutes a day for drama. Eventually, it is possible to integrate drama in science, social studies, language arts, and math and do justice to both drama (as an art) and the basic content and skills in these other core curricular areas. Some have the luxury of being able to teach drama lessons for a full hour or longer, while others prefer to do themed drama over several days time, spending twenty or thirty minutes each day. In any case, it is important to design lesson outlines that are more than just a series of isolated activities.

Why Should Teachers Integrate Creative Drama?

I am concerned, in my teaching, with the difference in reality between the real world where we seem to "really exist" and the "as if" world where we can exist at will. Brecht calls this "visiting another room." . . . actions in the two rooms are to do with: 1. The freedom to experiment without the burden of future repercussions. 2. The absence of the "chance elements" of real life. If we needed a reasonable reason for including the arts in schools, surely it is here in these two rooms.

Dorothy Heathcote (in Robinson, 1990, p. 8)

Teachers who have incorporated drama into the life of school learning report increased enjoyment and substantial effects on skill and content achievement in science, social studies, math, and language arts. Take a moment to become familiar with results of drama integration by reading Post It Page 7–1.

1. **Drama is part of real life and prepares students to deal with life's problems.**

The best drama uses as much truth as possible.

Dorothy Heathcote

Drama can give insight into the world by allowing students to rehearse roles in which they will make myriad life decisions—son, friend, boss, teacher. This rehearsal for life deals with universal questions based on the powerful themes that comprise great literature: *What happens when someone is greedy and causes many others to suffer? How do true friends respond when times are tough? How do humans respond when they are given success, rather than earning it? What is the nature of real happiness? How should evil be dealt with in our world?* During dramatics, children examine different perspectives and try them on for size. In a safe and accepting atmosphere, they are free to sort out beliefs and values. In this way, drama helps give form or shape to ideas and feelings students are naturally experiencing and thus helps children make sense out of issues in their lives.

The teacher who integrates drama is capitalizing on a learning tool well loved by children who naturally pretend and take on roles in their play. Through drama, the number of roles students are able to assume is expanded, as is their perspectives in taking these roles. For example, in science, students may do research and assume the role of experts in debates about real-life problems, like the growing resistance of certain bacteria to antibiotics, or can pantomime various aspects of careers they have investigated during a career education unit. During these drama activities, the seeds are sown for students to grow into people who look at problems from alternative viewpoints, respect diverse thinking, and realize there are many solutions for any one problem.

2. **Drama engages students in creative problem-solving and decision making.**

You can't depend on your judgment when your imagination is out of focus.

Mark Twain

Conflict is the basis for all drama. Consider the difference between pantomiming a squirrel gathering nuts versus miming a squirrel gathering nuts with something sticky all over its paws. It is not surprising that students who have rich drama experiences increase their problem-solving skills. When drama is integrated in the classroom, school is changed from a place where students are told what to think into an experience in thinking. For example, Karioth (1967) found that drama boosted creative thinking in disadvantaged fourth graders, and kindergarten students involved in drama scored significantly higher than a control group on verbal and visual creativity tests (Schmidt, Goforth, & Drew, 1975). Why? During drama, students are exhorted to use their imaginations, make hypotheses, test out solutions, evaluate ideas, and redefine problems. *What are all the ways to show how Jack felt as he climbed the beanstalk each time? How can we show the meanings of words like love, hate, disconcerted, or contrite with bodies, faces, and one spoken word or line? What if Cinderella didn't want to marry the prince and fell in love with the doorman instead?*

3. **Drama develops verbal and nonverbal communication.** When students are asked to become a character and talk about ways to solve a story problem, verbal creative problem-solving skills are engaged. For example, *What should Phoebe do when she finds the note in the tree in Lunn's The Hollow Tree?* is a question with no one answer, that can be discussed using a moral problem-solving process and then played out in a scene (see *moral dilemmas* under social studies strategies in Chapter 8). When students are involved in drama activities, they develop fluency in language and nonverbal communication skills—use of the body, face, and voice to communicate. It is essential for students to learn how to match words and actions as they move through life, as in the old adage, "I hear what you say but I believe what you do." Through drama, students learn the importance of a look, a gesture, and posture and even how a walk can communicate hesitancy, excitement, or fear. We become skilled at what we practise. Drama is a pleasurable and powerful practice for self-expression through speaking and listening.

4. **Drama can enhance students' psychological well-being.**

Improvisation is a way of achieving identity.

Alfred Nieman

Drama allows students to express feelings and emotions under the protection of being in another role. This safety permits them to experience the therapeutic effects of release of emotions and tension. In addition, personal development occurs as students learn to control body and words to best express ideas and feelings. Self-confidence and positive self-image emerge from repeated successes in problem-solving situations.

Through drama, students learn that people feel a range of emotions that need not be suppressed and should be expressed *appropriately*. It is liberating for a child to realize she is not the first person to dislike another and that negative feelings can be worked out in positive ways. For example, drama can develop tolerance and acceptance, rather than feeling a need to confront and destroy those who behave, think, or feel differently.

5. **Drama develops empathy and new perspectives.** Taking on a role involves using the senses of smell, taste, touch, vision, hearing, movement, and even humour to understand. During a study of Louis Riel, students who became comfortable with "I statements" from different people's perspectives showed they were really involved.

Empathy goes beyond sympathy. Empathy means being inside another—feeling what another feels, thinking what another thinks. This is a lived-through experience that gives perspective in a way that facts or logic cannot because emotional intelligence is activated.

6. **Drama builds cooperation and develops other social skills.** As students work in groups to plan and engage in drama, they are developing the ability to give and take. Teachers may say, "But my students can't work in groups!" Yet we never say, "My students can't read so I can't teach them to read." Students learn cooperation and active listening by being involved in group work—there is no other way. Cooperation cannot be taught through a lecture or simply tested with a paper and pencil assessment. To learn to live together, we must work together. Drama allows children to find appropriate roles and develop social awareness through its ensemble focus—drama is a group art. In addition, awareness of social problems grows as children become informed about issues of violence, hunger, poverty, and homelessness as they research dramatic resolutions to

Post It Page • 7-1

News Bulletins Drama Research You Can Use

An Arts Alternatives program involving drama activities, including role playing, improvisation, and writing stories, enabled elementary students to achieve significant gains in vocabulary and reading comprehension. Students also reported significantly improved attitudes relating to self-expression, trust, self-acceptance and acceptance of others (Gourgey et al., 1985).

Sixteen studies of students in grades K–12 showed that drama positively affects the ability of students to take on the roles or perspectives of others, i.e., increases empathy (Kardash & Wright, 1987).

Fifth grade remedial readers who were taught to use drama as a learning strategy consistently scored higher on the Metropolitan Reading Comprehension Test and outperformed a control group who did vocabulary lessons and discussed the stories (Dupont, 1992).

Use of creative drama activities positively affected elementary student achievement in a variety of areas, such as reading, oral and written communication, and interpersonal and drama skills (Kardash and Wright, 1987).

Positive relationships were found between oral language growth (speaking) and use of creative drama in fourth, fifth, and seventh graders (Stewig & Young, 1978; Stewig & McKee, 1980).

When drama was used as a rehearsal for writing, letter writing and narrative writing were significantly improved for second, third, fourth, and eighth graders (Wagner, 1988; Moore & Caldwell, 1993).

ESL (English as a second language) students who were involved in drama exhibited significantly greater verbal improvement than a control group not involved in drama (Vitz, 1983).

Drama was found to serve as a tool to increase interaction among students with and without mental handicaps in a study comparing fifth graders who were involved in either drama or noncompetitive games (Miller, Rynders, & Schleien, 1993).

problems. Finally, as audience members for theatre productions, students can gain social awareness as heart and mind are engaged by the actors.

7. **Drama increases concentration and comprehension through engagement.** Because drama involves all the senses, stimulates emotions, and focuses on the use of creative problem-solving, it should not be surprising that it helps students to attend. When children are actively involved and concentrating on a task, it is more likely they will understand the subject or the material being read. This has been borne out in studies that show when children dramatize stories their reading comprehension scores are greater than for those who only read the story (DuPont, 1992; Henderson & Shanker, 1978). Textbooks are given life when teachers involve students in dramatizing important concepts and main ideas. Students who dislike reading gain a purpose for reading that can change attitude about putting forth effort. For example, if students understand they will be pantomiming significant actions of the main character after reading a story from the basal, this gives them a point of concentration: they are reading so they will be able to *do*.

   In sum, drama fills a basic need for activity or engagement. When used to introduce or preview a lesson, it causes students to think at higher levels, tap into feelings, and develop a goal to want to learn more. A problem from an upcoming lesson can be explored through pantomime or verbal drama, causing interest to develop in the lesson and prediction thinking to be activated.

8. **Drama helps students consider moral issues and develop values.** A lesson is rarely *valueless*, nor can a teacher teach without revealing his values, but it is important that educators not *impose* religious points of view on children. This does not mean that religious issues or religion cannot be a topic of study—they can and should be; how could we ever understand any culture without studying its religion? What drama contributes is a means of allowing students to know the values they have and form additional values as they work through curricular and social problems presented as drama content. In this way, drama helps bring some closure through self-discovery.

   Because conflict is at the core of drama, values and attitudes emerge as students become increasingly involved. Values are the end products of struggles and problem resolutions; beliefs arise from experiences. During drama, values should not be imposed by the teacher, but are discussed as students confront issues about rightness, wrongness, goodness, and badness in literature, math, science, and social studies. This does not mean a teacher need be value neutral; on the contrary, all teachers must make clear their support of universal values such as honesty, truth, hard work, courage, integrity, and respect for others.

9. **Drama is an alternative way to assess by observing, i.e., externalization.** Concepts and facts, like the structure of a cell or the movement of electrons, are abstract and can be better understood when made concrete. Through dramatics, students grapple with making abstract ideas and feelings concrete when they use words and their bodies to express what they know. Therefore, drama can be used to preview or review a lesson, and teachers can assess what students already know or have learned by watching their performances.

   Our current desire to make assessment more authentic can draw on drama's ability to make learning observable. Material learned in any subject area can be demonstrated through mime or verbal activities. Once externalized, the teacher and students can assess growth, given criteria developed based on curricular goals. For example, students can be asked to write to a friend, in the role of a medical doctor, to explain her work in Zaire with Doctors Without Borders. Such a verbal drama gives students an opportunity for achieving depth of understanding through personal involvement and yields documents that show the degree of knowledge developed about scientific concepts.

10. **Drama is entertaining.** While many educators feel uncomfortable justifying inclusion of anything in a curriculum just because it is fun, we can never forget that fun is *fun*damental to happiness. One goal of education has to be to help students be happy. Fun and entertainment can help us forget, enable us to cope by giving respite from problems, and provide enjoyment—a state of elation, upliftedness, or joy that makes us feel full of energy and hope. It is worthwhile to not simply dismiss the importance of fun. Think about things that are fun; they generally involve solving problems, doing interesting things, learning new skills, working with people, meeting challenges, moving around, and making discoveries. Compare these aspects of *fun* with what we want to happen each day at school. Is there much difference between *good* education and fun? What's more, drama includes the above activities.

11. **Drama contributes to esthetic development.**

Reason can answer questions but imagination has to ask them.

Albert Einstein

Drama integrates all the arts (music, art, dance, and literature), so it draws on the beauty-making power of each. Through drama, students learn about dramatic structure involving conflict and characters, deepen sensory awareness, and learn to express themselves through the artistic use of pantomime, dialogue, and improvisation.

12. **Drama offers a learning avenue that enhances other areas of the curriculum.** Drama helps students get at why we need to know about the bones of the body or the circulatory system and who needs to know about these things and under what circumstances. Students can begin to explore characters and their relationships to one another and to problems associated with issues in health, science, and social studies. From language arts to science, drama can be used as a teaching and learning tool to help students make meaning from a sea of skills and facts and ideas. It is a learning tool grounded in exploration and discovery that draws on our innate abilities and desires to assume roles and pretend. We associate actors and acting with drama and theatre, and it is the action of drama that makes it a captivating way to learn. Children want to *do*. We should be glad. We do *not* need a nation of passive citizens. Nor do we want our children to grow up taking action without information and reflection. Drama gives students a chance to act, but with a safety net to catch them when their decisions are not wise. This safety net is the conscientious planful teacher who is knowledgeable about many strategies and how to adapt them for her class.

What Do Teachers Need to Know and Teach about Drama to Use It as a Teaching Tool?

I believe that every child I meet understands deep, basic matters worthy of exploration but they may as yet have no language for them. One of the languages they may develop is through dramatic work.

Dorothy Heathcote (in Robinson, 1990, p. 8)

Successful arts integration with any other discipline depends on teacher knowledge and skill base in each area integrated. In addition, teachers need a repertoire of strategies to teach students how to interact with each other and respond. The knowledge base for drama includes elements or components of drama, kinds of drama, and the skills used to make drama (use of voice and body). Drama and theatre study also includes learning about actors and acting, plays, playwriting, theatre history, drama, and theatre in our lives and in other cultures.

Here is a checklist of folder tab titles to organize a resource collection for drama integration:

- Drama elements, skills, and concepts used to create and think about drama and theatre
- Biographical and style information about actors, playwrights, directors, critics
- Styles, forms, and genres of drama and theatre, e.g., one acts, musical theatre
- Particular examples, e.g., plays like *Les Miserables* and reader's theatre scripts
- Specific approaches or teaching strategies and ideas
- Other possibilities: career information, history of theatre and drama, science and math of theatre (stage construction, makeup, etc.), writing plays, sociology of theatre and drama, economics and theatre and drama, psychology of dance (e.g, drama therapy)

Creative Drama Defined

There is a difference between putting on rehearsed plays a few times a year and the *daily* use of drama. In fact, teachers who use drama as a teaching tool rarely use memorized scripts. This chapter is about a particular kind of drama classroom teachers can use throughout the curriculum called *creative drama*. According to drama educator Ruth Heinig (1993), creative drama is the term most widely used in the United States to describe the idea of drama integration. This kind of drama is more structured than the dramatic play in which children naturally engage during play. Other terms like *improvisation, role playing, informal drama, drama in education (DIE), process drama,* and *educational drama* are used in England and other countries, some of which identify frameworks that have a particular emphasis. For example, Drama in Education strategies focus on causing students to project themselves into a moment in time, and they go on to learn more about a topic after first exploring it through their drama (p. 4).

Creative drama and *educational drama* are the terms commonly used in Canada. In contrast, *theatre* is focused on product because the emphasis is on a spectacle for the audience to see. Drama and theatre share the same basic structures but "the process of drama is in sharp opposition to the theater product . . . theater is concerned with communication between actors and audience; drama is concerned with the experience of the participants, irrespective of the audience" (Brian Way in Rosenberg, 1987, p. 31). Way even contends that young children should not be encouraged to view formal theatre because "such theater attendance can only undermine creativity."

So, creative drama is participant and process centred, with a teacher or leader guiding children though explorations of personal experiences, social issues, or pieces of literature. In creative drama, children improvise action and dialogue and use drama elements to structure the process. They creatively use voice, body, and space to make others believe in a mood, idea, or message and take on "pretend" roles to generate creative problem solutions. Unlike role playing for therapeutic reasons, creative drama's purposes are artistic, emotional, and academic.

Basic Elements to Make Drama

Imagination is more important than knowledge.

Albert Einstein

People create drama using both their outsides and insides. What is shown during drama with one's body, face, gestures, and words reflects the thoughts and feelings perceived through the senses. To create drama, a person must concentrate, sense, perceive, imagine, think, and use the physical body and speech to communicate all these inner processes.

Life is a constant struggle to get basic needs met and deal with conflict. Drama is a slice of life in the shape of characters who encounter problems in a specific setting and who take action to resolve the problems. Actors become or take the roles of characters who become real as they try to convince, convert, coax, sell, feud, and bargain to get their needs met. This structure or organization with specific components is the same for both drama and literature: there must be a conflict or problem that motivates distinct characters to make decisions and face the consequences of their actions (plot); all this occurs in a particular time and place (setting). See Post It Page 7–2.

During creative drama the teacher's role is to guide students to define problems, improvise solutions, try out ideas, reflect, and evaluate. While creative drama is not created for an audience, teachers can justifiably have student groups perform for the class or for each other or other audiences. Creative drama can be simple or complex; Spolin's theatre games and simple pantomimes are accepted as valuable drama work, as is Ward's story drama and Heathcote's in-depth explorations to gain personal meaning and perspective.

Dramatic Elements. Drama and literature share much of the same structural components. These are the elements that create drama.

Plot is the sequence of events set in motion by a problem or conflict. The simplest plot structure is just beginning, middle, and end.

Conflict is the driving force of plot. Conflict sets plot in motion and should create suspension and tension. There are four different types of conflict: (1) between a character and nature (e.g., weather in *The Hollow Tree* by Janet Lunn), (2) between a character and societal rules or institutions (e.g., farm rule that runt pigs are slaughtered in *Charlotte's Web*), (3) between a character and another character (e.g., Anne and Gilbert in *Anne of Green Gables*), and (4) within a character or internal conflict with self (e.g., Ramona constantly struggles against her proclivity for misunderstanding situations). A fifth type of conflict may also occur, especially in science fiction, between a character and technology as in *The Wretched Stone,* a tale about problems created by a mesmerizing rock with a blue glow, like a TV screen.

Characters initiate and carry out the plot (action). The main character must be believable and care about what happens. The main character is the hero or protagonist who must face life, make decisions, and accept consequences. In drama, characters are created through their actions, words, and what others say or how they react. When characters talk with each other, they use *dialogue. Mime* is free, creative, and mindful movement, that is, movement to express specific ideas and feelings. It includes actions with the face and body to show shape, size, emotions, and so on. There is no talking during mime.

Setting consists of a time and place that provide a context for action.

Mood is created by the setting (time, lighting, music, description of the place), pace, and characters' use of word and body. This is the *feel* of the piece.

Dramatic Skills. Students need to learn particular skills to become adept at creating drama. Remember from Chapter 1 how important it is to present a structure for creative and artistic work that includes (1) freedom with limits and (2) empowering students by teaching them the tools and elements of each art form. By teaching the following skills, students are given the means to make meaning in drama.

Use of body: ability to coordinate and control body, use of appropriate energy, display of sensory awareness and expression, use of gestures and facial expressions, communication through pantomime, interpretation of nonverbal communication of others.

Verbal expression: speaking clearly and using appropriate variety in volume, rate, tone and pitch,

Post It Page • 7-2

Drama Elements and Skills

Elements

Conflict: Sets the plot in motion and should create suspension and tension. There are five types:

1. Between a character and nature
2. Between a character and societal rules or institutions
3. Between a character and another character
4. Within a character (internal conflict with self)
5. Between a character and technology

Characters initiate and carry out the plot (action). They must be believable and care about what happens. The main character is the hero or protagonist, who must face life, make decisions, and accept consequences. *Created through* actions, words, and what others say or how they react. When characters talk with each other they use ***dialogue. Mime*** is free, creative, and mindful movement to express specific ideas and feelings with the face and body. There is no talking during mime.

Plot is the sequence of events set in motion by a problem or conflict. The simplest plot structure is beginning, middle, and end.

Setting consists of a time and place or context for action.

Mood is created by the setting (time, lighting, music, description of the place), pace, characters use of word and body, etc. This is the *feel* of the piece.

Dramatic Skills

Use of body: ability to coordinate and control body, use of appropriate energy, display of sensory awareness and expression, use of gestures and facial expressions, communication through mime, interpretation of nonverbal communication of others.

Verbal expression: speaking clearly and using appropriate variety in volume, rate, tone and pitch, pause, stress and emphasis, inflection, fluency, and ability to improvise dialogue.

Focus: concentration and staying involved, making others believe in the realness of the character, following directions.

Imagination: flexible creative thinking, contribution of unique ideas and elaboration on ideas, spontaneity.

Evaluation: giving constructive feedback, using suggestions of others, self-evaluation and adaptation of own behaviour.

Social skills: working cooperatively with groups, listening and responding to others.

Audience etiquette: attending, listening, and responding appropriately to others.

pause, stress and emphasis, inflection, fluency, and ability to improvise dialogue.

Focus: concentration and staying involved, making others believe in the realness of the character, following directions.

Imagination: flexible creative thinking, contribution of unique ideas and elaboration on ideas, spontaneity.

Evaluation: giving constructive feedback, using suggestions of others, self-evaluation and adaptation of own behaviour.

Social skills: working cooperatively with groups, listening and responding to others.

Audience etiquette: attending, listening, and responding appropriately to others.

Curriculum Guidelines

Standards, goals, objectives, and outcomes in curriculum frameworks and courses of study help teachers know *what* to teach, but do not explain *how* to teach. When a teacher signs a contract in a school district she or he is agreeing to teach the adopted course of study and is expected to arrive with methodology to do so: assessment and teaching strategies, ideas about materials, and disciplinary and classroom management tools. All teachers are expected to structure teaching so that students will achieve what the school district has set as performance goals, so teachers need to know the goals and write lesson plans that specify connections between lesson activities and the goals. In addition, it is just good teaching to make sure *students* know the goals, and it is wise to communicate the goals and their source to parents.

How Can a Classroom Teacher Use Drama as an Effective Teaching Tool for Integration?

Good teaching is one-fourth preparation and three-fourths theatre.

Gail Godwin, 1937 *(The Old Woman)*

General Principles

Here are the principles for integration as they apply to drama.

Cast off chairs transformed for a production of a Midsummer Night's Dream.

Principle One: INFUSE the Art of Drama

In a classroom where the teacher has created a climate for risk taking and a value for creative thinking, students will most likely feel comfortable being involved in drama. The aesthetic environment discussed in Chapter 2 lays a foundation for dramatic work to emerge from music, art, literature, and dance.

Principle Two: TEACHING Drama Concepts and Skills

Austrian writer Gustav Meyrink's fable *The Curse of the Toad* is about a millipede who loved to dance. It challenges us to consider the effect of bringing to a conscious level what we do unconsciously. An old toad, who hates the millipede, tests this effect by asking the millipede,

> Tell me then, oh most honorable one, when you walk, how do you know which foot to lift first: which is the second, and the third, which comes next as fourth, fifth, sixth—whether the next is the tenth or the hundredth; what meanwhile the second is doing, and the seventh: is it standing, or moving; when you get to the 917th, whether you should lift the 700th, put down the 39th, bend the 1000th or stretch the fourth? . . . But the millipede was glued to the ground, paralyzed, unable to move one single joint. He had forgotten which leg to lift first, and the more he thought about it the less he could work it out (1994, p. 54).

Children engage in "let's pretend" so readily that it may concern teachers that the joy will be disturbed by instructing students in specific elements and tools of drama. Might we not paralyze them as the toad did the millipede by imposing cognition on intuition? Indeed, most of us are awkward when learning a new skill and may initially resist the learning that is necessary to become more adept. Think of the clumsy attempts children make when first learning to walk or ride a bike. Parents intuitively help toddlers along when they show the desire to stand and step. We demonstrate, encourage, coach, and even add labels: "That's one step. Now step again. Look Joey took three steps by himself!"

Children enter school already showing a love of role playing and pretend, so we can build on these innate propensities by teaching them how to use drama to learn academic material. This involves both explicit or direct instruction (in what drama is and what we can use to make drama) and providing time for discovery learning. Explicit instruction includes demonstration, coaching, giving feedback, and teaching the vocabulary of theatre and drama. In addition, an important part of helping students key in on what is dramatic in a piece of literature, a song or painting, or in life, is to use strategies that cause them to identify the conflict or tension. For example, ask students to think about what decisions must be made to solve a problem to get at the heart of the drama. This is the nitty gritty that gives children tools to use drama as a way to making meaning.

This is a good point to note that, whereas most children understand the difference between pretend and reality, it is useful to periodically tell or ask students about the difference. It just doesn't hurt to ground students in the concept of drama as "pretend" that helps us practise skills for real life.

Principle Three: TEACHER HABITS for Integrating Drama

Creative Problem-Solving. Since drama relies so heavily on creative problem-solving, it is important for teachers to understand the process and influences on this kind of thinking. Use these resources in Chapter 1 to apply creativity principles to drama: Post It Pages 1–5 and 1–6.

Teacher Characteristics.

> *[S]ome of the best work with children is done by experienced teachers who really understand what they are doing and yet, strangely enough, have very little knowledge of drama.*
>
> McCaslin, 1990, p. 443

What is most important to drama integration are the attributes of any good teacher: a sense of humour, high standards, good discipline, sympathetic leadership, imagination, respect for the ideas of others, sensitivity to individuals, ability to guide rather than direct, and a focus on sharing rather than showing. Of course, in the end the imaginative teacher will create his or her own methods. In addition, classroom teachers who have a background in music and dance will be able to integrate these art forms with drama more readily (pp. 441–2).

Teacher Participation in Drama. It is helpful for teachers to show drama elements with voice, faces, and body and to model enthusiasm and commitment. Teachers can take a role for students to respond to—become a bystander in the scene and ask for clarification about what's happening or be the next-door neighbour or a town official. Heinig (1993) explains that when the teacher assumes a role it can extend belief, stimulate thinking, provoke discussion, direct the problem-solving, and break divisions between teacher and students (pp. 265–280). When teachers engage students while "in role," the goal is to be low-key and not overplaying or stereotyping a role. Teachers can assume roles such as: "I don't know and need help" (helpless character), an authority (boss, expert, chief), second in command (someone sent to give orders for someone else or a messenger only), just one of the group, devil's advocate (challenger), or antagonist (p. 277). A variety of props can be used, if desired.

When the teacher takes a role, it allows him or her to control the drama by managing the time and direction. The teacher can go into more depth by questioning students and also build relationships because he or she is a part of the drama. A sense of mystery or urgency, belief, and commitment can be engendered by the teacher's attitude and involvement. (Be sure to tell students when you take a role so that young children, who have particular difficulty differentiating between fantasy and reality, will not become confused.)

Signals to Manage Drama. A teacher who has a habit of using signals is providing students with important structural cues that help them organize their work. For example, use "places," "curtain," "stop–go," "home," or use lights, sounds, music, drum, bell, or tambourine to start and stop dramatic activity. Every Pupil Response (EPR) signals after questions and directions are other important ways to help students learn to control their own actions, as well as learn to direct others. Post It Page 7–3 has a list of attention getters used by teachers as signals for drama and other activities.

Management Strategies and Planning.

> *Inexperienced leaders are often not sure they should plan, direct, or even incorporate discipline attitudes into creative drama lessons for fear of stifling their own and the children's imagination. But groups need organization, people need limits, and creativity needs discipline structure.*
>
> Heinig, 1993, pp. 25–26

Getting attention, giving directions, dealing with disruptions, handling rule breakers, rearranging desks, and keeping order and control all require planning ahead. Here are some basic pointers. (Also see Classroom Management Strategies in the appendix and Management Strategies in Chapter 9, especially the discussion on personal space, time limits, and touching restrictions.)

Set ground rules and expectations. We all need to know the rules and limits in our homes, workplaces, and even in the stores where we shop. When a rule is broken, an effective strategy is to acknowledge the student's feelings (to help the child save face) and then restate the rule. Next, implement a logical consequence, not an unrelated punishment. Consequences should be made clear at the outset, along with the ground rules.

Control the amount of space, time, group size, and speed. For example, *"Stay at your desk or in your personal spot, walk in place, I'll count to five, do this in slow motion."* Larger groups and larger spaces require more planning and controls.

Give clear directions without cute sugar coating. Give expectations in straightforward language. Drama is interesting in and of itself, so students do not need to be cajoled into participating.

Remove distractions from desktops or the area where the drama will happen *before* beginning.

Make transitions by designating groups or rows or by some creative division: eye colour, patterns of clothes, birthdays.

Ignore some complaints and behaviours. Not everyone can be made happy by all circumstances. Usually children who whine will stop if ignored. Every small infraction isn't worth the teacher's attention, and some behaviours are actually done to get attention. Watch for signs of this need, and give attention to those students for *positive* behaviours on a frequent basis.

When mistakes happen, acknowledge feelings and failures. Be honest. This helps model for children how to handle problems. It is not a problem to start over with a revised procedure. Let students know drama is an experiment and is not predictable—that's what makes it fun.

Proximity and eye contact are often enough to get students back on task. Circulate as students work and look children directly in the eye.

When a problem occurs, follow through with the consequences you have previously discussed. Don't threaten, don't hesitate. Stop the activity to get the attention of the group. Don't keep going if only part of the class is involved.

Repeat offenders or very difficult children should be dealt with privately as soon after the lesson as possible. Don't use public humiliation—it is unethical. If offenders must be removed, return them to the activity ASAP. Often a two-minute time out is as effective as removing the child for a whole lesson. Admission back into the group should be contingent on the child agreeing to follow the rules.

Use drama to teach rules. Ask students to create improvised scenes (see the seed ideas in Chapter 8) that show cooperation, active listening, compromise, respect for alternative opinions, and other desirable

Post It Page • 7-3

Attention Getters and Signals

This is a composite list generated by classroom teachers.

1. Whisper directions.
2. Flick lights.
3. Play a favourite tape or CD.
4. Use chimes, piano chord, or some pleasant sound like a rhythm instrument.
5. Have children repeat what you say. *Examples:* "Jambo Jambo" ("Hello Hello" in Swahili) or use a tongue twister (aluminum linoleum).
6. Ask children to mimic or echo a rhythm pattern, sign, or movement.
7. Start a chain reaction: say to one student "Would you tell the person next to you to. . . ."
8. Say, "I'm looking for someone who is . . . (fill in a behaviour like 'in a curved shape')."
9. Write a message in large letters on the chalkboard.
10. Write directions on large cards. *Example:* "Look at me and smile."
11. Say, "Let's listen . . . to hear grass grow, clock tick, or snow fall."
12. Say, "I'd like to see . . . the colour of everyone's eyes or everyone smile."
13. Have a secret code word. *Examples:* foreign language, special vocabulary, or interesting phrases like "chicka boom chicka rucka."
14. Tell students to close their eyes.
15. Say, "Think what is stopping you from listening right now."
16. Count aloud backward from 10 (invite students to join in).
17. Agree on a class signal to get everyone's attention if . . . the ceiling was about to fall in; there was a fire in the wastebasket; etc.
18. Tell a joke or riddle. Knock knocks work.
19. Call students' names who are looking at you and quiet.
20. Have a nonverbal signal. *Examples:* touch pocket or ear, hold up two fingers, thumb up.
21. Give a direction with universal appeal. *Example:* "Sit down if you ever wanted a two-hour recess," or "Freeze if you like money," or "Raise your hand if you'd like some ice cream."
22. Give points to students who are listening. Use a clipboard, board, or overhead.
23. Write on the board the names of the first five students who are ready.
24. Sit in a particular place or use a particular stance to signal.
25. Be creative! Do something different. Attire can attract attention, e.g., "Did you notice that _____ is wearing _____ ?"
26. Say, "If you can hear my voice, _____ (behaviour)."
27. Call and response sequences: T = Good Morning/S = Rice Krispies; T = Guaca Guaca/S = Agua Agua. (T = teacher and S = student.)
28. Use a group reinforcer. *Example:* Use cloze blanks on the chalkboard and say, "I need to see people ready to earn another letter in '_ _ _ _ _ _ _ _ _ _ _' (letters spell out a goal like 'extra recess')."
29. Make up a class chant: "We're ready, we're ready as ready can be. In just five seconds, chicka rucka chicka bees."
30. Use actual sign language for directions like sit down and line up. See *Joy of Signing* (Riekehof, 1987).
31. Ask students to close their eyes and imagine the sun setting, the ripples moving out from a stone in a pond, etc.

behaviours. Direct them to make sure their scenes have a beginning, middle, and end. Scenes can be set up by first identifying characters, a setting, and a problem situation. Challenge them to think about "what if . . . " situations: What if students read each others' private journals, or what if there was a group project and some people didn't do their share of the work? Encourage students to generate lists of ways to settle arguments and encourage everyone to participate and cooperate. Make this into a verbal activity in which students create a pledge based on the Golden Rule. Use a frame to help structure thinking: "Because I like to_____ , I will _____ . Because I don't like _____ , I will _____ . Because I want _____ , I will _____ ." Here is a sixth grade example: *We, the sixth grade class, want to have our opinions heard, so we promise to listen to the opinions of others. We like to be treated with respect, so we will not disrespect each other in this class. We do not like to be touched in unfriendly ways, so we will not touch anyone with fighting on our minds. We want to work in groups with our friends, so we will cooperate and get work done while in groups. We hereby so promise all the above on this day in September, 2000.*

The Goal Is Involvement of All Students. One way to reach this goal is to use the *unison* strategy. Unison means simultaneous "all-at-once" participation. Time is used effectively and no one is waiting for a turn (waiting creates boredom and mischief making). When all the class participates at the same time, students feel the comfort created by safety in numbers. Maximum participation and involvement can also be achieved through double casting (have two or more children perform the same role). For example, have three wolves in "The Three Little Pigs."

Focus on *involvement* and *concentration* directly and honestly by asking students what helps them to concentrate and what distracts them. Practise how to *show* involvement with words and body. Children can reach the state of creative flow in which they are totally involved. (Signs of flow include feeling time goes quickly, children spontaneously adding details to the drama and asking to repeat activities. For example, a class of third graders so enjoyed a narrative pantomime of *The Wretched Stone* they asked to do it again instead of having recess.) When students ham it up or show off, this shows they are not genuinely involved. Let them know this in a kind way before it happens. There are several activities in the **energizers and warm-ups** strategies section of Chapter 8 and in Chapter 10 to help with concentration and focus.

Establish the Role of the Audience. When children are proud of their work, they will want to share what they have planned and rehearsed with the whole class. This is a learning opportunity for all, because students see how groups treat the same drama problems differently. A good strategy is to divide the class in half. One half then performs while the other half views, interprets, and responds. Then reverse. With small groups, take turns presenting. For example, two groups can present their work at the same time while the rest of the class is the audience.

When students perform, the audience needs to be clear about its role, so discuss with students how it is polite to listen attentively, not talk during the performance, be respectful and responsive, and applaud at the end. Additional audience engagement happens when the teachers let the audience know they'll be expected to give feedback to the actors. Put a list of questions they can choose from to respond at the end. For example, What worked? What made the characters believable? (Be sure to keep the feedback focused on the positive.)

To firm up the role of the audience, it is a good idea to take a few minutes and have everyone role play the audience. For example, narrate as students mime: *"You take your seats. You show that you are excited to see the performance. The curtain opens and you examine the scene to see what you can. The scene is a sad one. Then a character does something that is meant to be funny. A character does something wonderful and you applaud. The scene ends and you applaud. The scene has been particularly good, so you stand and applaud. Now you take your seat and think about several things you'd like to tell the actors about their fine performance."*

Using Volunteers and Small Groups. When first introducing drama, it is best to invite volunteers to participate and not force students. Forcing participation can increase reluctance and be contagious. We usually want to know what we are volunteering for, so tell students what they're getting into. For example, *"I need three people who know how to walk in place."* While there is not as much control when students work in pairs and small groups, this is a crucial part of dramatic development. Learning to cooperate in group work is also essential in society, and we only learn to work in groups by working in groups. Create pairs, trios, and quads by counting off or allowing choice based on interests or ability to work together. Instead of *"Find a partner,"* say *"Find a partner that is your same height or find two people you can cooperate with."* Students need to learn to distinguish between those who are friends and those with whom they work.

Avoid cliques by rotating groups. If learning circles are used, these can be the basis for group work. Another option is to give each child a colour or symbol (circle, heart, square, star) and group by having all of the same symbol work together. Group decision making is encouraged and developed by asking students for their ideas and suggestions. Once they understand the variety of choices in drama, ask them to set time limits and space limits and suggest the amount of rehearsal needed and whether to present to an audience or not.

Discussions and Questioning Strategies. In nearly all the chapters, there are Post It Pages on questioning, with example questions and general guidelines for discussions. These ideas are relevant to discussions before and after drama in a lesson. Discussions may take place to clarify key concepts or special language or words, or to stretch thinking. While yes–no, "closed," or "skinny" questions have a place, it is generally preferable to ask open or fat questions that require more thought and more than a one-word answer. Questions that get at universal themes are most likely to engage students in significant ways. For example, *"What causes people to resent those who are different like Frederick?" "Why do characters disobey their parents as in Peter Rabbit or Little Red Riding Hood?"* Frames can be used to extend thinking as well. For example, ask students to complete these sentence stems related to the subject matter under study: "I wonder . . . " or "What if. . . ."

Whole-Group Before Individual and Small-Group Assignments. To make sure students understand what is to be done in a small group or individually, it is important to practise an example or two with the whole group. This goes for any teaching, not just drama.

Using Examples Instead of Models. Just as in art or dance, students need to understand that there are many ways to express feelings and ideas through drama. For example, *Think of all the ways to use pantomime to show a feeling like greed or shyness. What are all the body parts that could be used and in what ways (use the BEST dance elements to help stretch and twist thinking)? What are all the facial expressions that could be used? How could these feelings be shown in pairs or trios?* Teachers can form a habit of asking for examples, rather than giving them, and help students do their own thinking.

Descriptive Feedback Stretches Thinking. It is especially important to note unique and different ideas that students devise. Do so by infusing "I statements" and other general teacher habits (see Teacher Habits in Chapters 2 and 5), but refrain from giving blanket praise. Another idea is to ask students to isolate a part of a drama, such as just one movement in a pantomime, and discuss it. For example, ask a student to repeat just the part where she was grasping the beanstalk before beginning to climb it and then ask other students what they see. This habit of *doing* (showing with hands, face, posture) and then asking for student observations is a discovery or inductive method that promotes reflective thinking about work.

Coaching: The Power of Suggestion. Teachers can remind students about directions and goals, talk them through an activity, maintain general control, help the audience understand what a group is doing, and fill in awkward silences by using coaching. Coaching does *not* mean giving lots of directions, but involves offering suggestions and questions to scaffold a drama. It is a way to stretch or challenge students to use their bodies and voices in new ways. (See BEST in Post It Page 9–2 for movement possibilities.) It is also a supportive measure to ensure success and satisfaction. For example, ask students questions during the drama like: *What could you do to show the character's age or how the character feels?* When coaching, ask "What if . . ." questions to stretch and direct. For example, *What if the weather changed? What if someone got sick? What if things got out of control and you couldn't stop the process? What if the world stopped rotating? What if dinosaurs still lived?*

When coaching to help prepare scenes, ask:

- What does your character want? How can you show this?
- Tell me more about . . . (explore the emotion or thinking of the character).
- What does the place have to do with how the character feels or acts?
- What else might you try?
- How could this problem be solved?
- What do you want the audience to see and feel?
- How could props, lighting, or music be used?

Taking extra time to cue carefully and coach as students work will contribute immensely to their development of skill and confidence.

Teach Students How to Structure. Once students have explored the elements of drama, they are ready to use a beginning–middle–end format to make activities into wholes. This entails telling students to construct scenes that have these same three parts that all literature has. Another structure for planning is the five "ws": who, what, where, when, why? A planning sheet with beginning–middle–end or the questions just listed can be provided to focus student work.

Starting Lessons with Sound Introductions. By being familiar with curricular material and drama components and preparing discussion questions ahead, teachers make student success more likely. The introduction to a lesson is critical to student motivation and readiness for learning. These strategies are often used in introductions:

- Remove visual or auditory distractions and get attention. See Post It Page 7–3.
- Use strategies to establish mood and set a climate for creative exploration (see Chapter l for ideas for stimulating a creative attitude).
- Build on what students know, what they have studied and experienced.
- Direct students to concentrate and focus, to make us believe, and not be a ham.
- Stimulate interest. Interest has been found to account for much of the variance in understanding. Web, ask questions, and do warm-ups to build interest.
- Make sure students are well prepared in the content. If they are to do a drama about pollution, they need to have background gained from a variety of experiences; they need knowledge to inform the drama.
- Make sure students understand that drama is an enjoyable art form used for serious learning purposes. At first they may not see why social studies time is used for drama, because they may not connect the arts with content. Through discussions and actually reaching the point in drama where they experience empathy and insight, students begin to value this art form. For example, students who had not used drama to learn were silly when first miming a First Nations legend. In time, with coaching and teaching, students were able to internalize and then embody the feelings of the characters.

Principle Four: ENERGIZERS and WARM-UPS

Energizers and warm-ups relax students so that they will be more likely to use the creative thinking so important in drama. These short activities contribute to classroom climate, focus students, facilitate concentration, imagination, and cooperation, and develop self-control. Start with simple warm-ups for the body: make circle or jerky movements that slowly travel head to toe or walk across the room in different ways, at different levels or in a variety of "as if . . ." situations. Ask students to pretend they are balloons blowing up and then collapsing (add sound effects, if you like). See the **energizers and warms-ups** in Chapter 8 and in all strategy seed chapters.

Principle Five: GREAT CHILDREN'S LITERATURE

Since both drama and literature share a focus on tension or conflict to propel the story forward there is a natural compatibility. Every genre of children's literature offers potential material for drama, but biography can be particularly useful because the characters are real people in conflict filled real-life situations like the dilemmas of life and death. In the appendix there is a bibliography of books about drama and theatre, as well as children's literature, recommended for drama activities. An annotated sampling appears in Post It Page 7–6.

Principle Six: ROUTINES and Rituals

Routines and rituals establish habits of mind and body. Here are ways to get students in the habit of thinking using drama:

- Use energizers and warm-ups to start the day and/or lessons.
- Use humour strategies to relax students so that they feel comfortable taking risks to be creative.
- Make special times to discuss drama and theatre in student lives. Ask, *What have you noticed?* (roles people play, actors on TV and why they were effective?).
- Announcements of special films or plays.
- Sharing of your own theatre experiences.
- Do morning charades to review yesterday's learning.
- Action songs and poems to start the day.
- Use signals for drama time: lights, desk arrangement routine.

Principle Seven: ADAPT Curriculum and Instruction Models to Meet Diverse Needs

> *Drama . . . can be a mirror, a magnifying glass, a microscope or a searchlight.*
>
> Cecily O'Neill (McCaslin, 1990, p. 294)

> The controversy regarding drama as a means or end is not settled and perhaps never will be. Compelling arguments on both sides press for a curriculum in which there is a place for each. Leading educators have declared drama and speech to be central to a language curriculum. They believe that drama can motivate writing and improve oral skills; they believe that it stimulates reading. Some insist it can be used to teach any subject effectively. (McCaslin, 1990, p. 301)

Since the beginning of the Progressive Education movement, integration of music, art, drama, dance, literature, and creative writing with other curricular areas has been popular. Even in schools that consider themselves traditional, projects and units of an integrative nature have been deemed effective for teaching and learning. While drama and theatre are disciplines worthy of study in their own right, they can be used as learning media. One of the best known advocates of using drama as a learning tool throughout the curriculum is Britain's Dorothy Heathcote.

Real-life Issues at the Centre of Drama. In lieu of putting on plays or memorizing lines, Heathcote has led a movement to use drama to help children make sense of their world, especially through reflection on life issues and experiences. There is no area of the curriculum in which Heathcote has not demonstrated how learning can be given depth and breadth through drama integration (see Heathcote & Bolton's *Drama for Learning: Dorothy Heathcote's Mantle of the Expert Approach to Learning*). At the core of her approach is identifying a point of great interest, tension, or conflict in any unit under study. To get this point, Heathcote begins with discussions to elicit students' ideas, believing this yields a lesson focus. She then usually takes the role of a character herself, and engages students in roles; frequently she steps out of role to speak with children for clarification purposes. Current events, moral and ethical problems, universal themes and questions, and both cognitive and affective domains become grist for the mill as she crafts her drama-based lessons.

"Drama lessons that rely on games and exercises to the neglect of the creation of dramatic roles and context are lacking what is, for me, the essential activity of drama. . . . We create a fictional world not to escape from the real world, but to reflect on it. . . . We are trying to release students into finding their own questions" (O'Neill in McCaslin, 1990, pp. 293–4). See the appendix and references at the end of this chapter for further reading.

Courses of Study. When planning lessons and units, a beginning step is to examine local and provincial documents, such as local curriculum guides or courses of study. These are sources for drama content and can guide teachers in deciding drama skills that can be taught during integrated lessons. A teacher may choose to plan integrated lessons and units, using one or more of the traditional subject areas as the unit body or centre. For example, a literature-based unit study of an author and illustrator like Bryd Baylor can use drama and the other arts, as well as math, science, social studies, and reading and language arts as "legs" to support the centre—the focus on Bryd Baylor. Drama would be used as a learning tool in such a unit, just as any other leg. An adaptation of this more common perspective is to envision a unit with drama as the body with the focus on (1) a person (actor, playwright, director, author, artist), (2) a particular genre or form (improvisation, reader's theatre, comedy), (3) a problem, theme, topic, or question (e.g., how has drama or theatre been used to educate people about the effects of war), or (4) a particular book, poem, song, or play (e.g., *Amazing Grace*), with major concepts and skills in math, science, social studies, reading and language arts, and the other art forms used as support legs. Of course, in any integrated lesson or unit, all bodies and legs should be correlated with courses of study and standards to ensure substantive and focused study. See Post It Page 5–13 for an example of a unit web.

Adjustment for Diverse Needs. In addition to considering information about developmental stages from Chapter 1, teachers can use the basic principles for individualizing or differentiating instruction for at-risk and special needs students presented in Chapter 2. Post It Pages 2–4 and 7–4 give specific strategies. Drawing on students' abilities, rather than focusing just on disabilities, is a key idea when considering adaptations.

Drama is unique in its emphasis on partner or group work and can be particularly enjoyable for special needs students. Reluctant or shy children see they will not be forced to participate in uncomfortable ways and will want to be involved as they see peers having fun. Puppets or props are other ways children are helped to feel safe. In general, it is easier for younger children to do nonverbal (mime) before verbal activities and use solo or individual drama strategies before group work. It works well to start with common ways we all use mime in our lives as nonverbal communication (e.g., to show how something is too hot or cold, to greet others, to show excitement). Space needs to be managed, as appropriate to student needs, too, by beginning with limiting students to small areas like their desks and then moving to large arenas as they show readiness to handle more. Consider that large areas like cafeterias, gyms, or playgrounds may have echoes, signal a recess attitude, and cause chaos if students have not been properly prepared to engage in drama in such large areas.

When planning for students to do creative problem-solving, it is productive to use whole-group teacher-directed strategies before breaking students into groups to work in an open-ended manner or before asking for independent thinking. When planning units and lessons that are success oriented, the rule of thumb is to order activities from easy to more difficult and from low content to more content dense (e.g., move from personal interests to subject area concepts and ideas application). Humour used at the start of a lesson relaxes students and excites creative thinking for serious work (lots of tension and conflict in drama) later in the lesson. Finally, students often see adaptations that teachers don't, so it is important to invite their ideas.

Structuring Lessons. The integrated arts lesson framework introduced in Chapter 2 is a predictable structure that can be used creatively to help students gain skills and learn concepts related to drama and other curricular areas. As discussed previously, integrated arts lessons need to include at least one arts concept—drama, in this case—to ensure that the integrity of the art form is not lost when drama is integrated with another curricular area. By choosing to teach a few concepts, students will be able to go into some depth and become comfortable with the possibilities of each skill or element (e.g., mime). Direct or explicit instruction using the introduction, development, and conclusion structure is used in the example plan that follows in Post It Page 7–7. *Note:* After doing a drama, take time to comment on things you saw or heard during the lesson. No names are necessary, since the focus of drama is on the group working together. The conclusion should be a time for evaluation: What worked? didn't work? why? what you liked? what did you learn? new ideas? do differently? Teachers may also wish to invite students to repeat activities with a novel twist, even two or three times, if interest in this kind of exploration is shown during the concluding discussion.

Principle Eight: TAKE FIELD TRIPS

I am certain that human dignity has its roots in the quality of young people's experience.

Dr. Lee Salk

Theatre Going. Attending plays is an experience with countless values, not the least of which is the opportunity for children to be introduced to a form of entertainment that can last a lifetime. Without school trips to see live performances, many children have only the in-house assemblies as exposure to theatre. Field trips to see children's theatre have the potential to develop children's aesthetic sensibilities, promote educational aims, and offer chances for social awareness and skill development. Just as with other field trips, theatre experiences should be carefully selected to align with curricular goals and become an integral part of a unit through lessons that *prepare for* the trip and *follow up* the play. See Take Field Trips in Chapter 2 for a review of key information to prepare for and follow up on trips. With regards to theatre and drama, students need to understand:

- How live performances are different from video or television dramas, largely because the audience shares in the event and there is a feeling of spontaneity. The more the audience gives to the actors, the more the actors can give back to the audience.
- General aspects of the theatre experience (e.g., expected audience etiquette so that everyone can enjoy the performance and the actors are respected).
- The topics and themes the play will deal with, as well as special language.
- The setup of the theatre and the style of the production.
- The use of cue sheets or "look fors" that help them experience a sense of discovery about the set, costumes, characters, etc.

After the play, it is helpful to have a discussion, and just as in good literature discussions, it is important to encourage a variety of points of view. Some useful questions include *What did you see? How did it make you feel? What in the play made you feel that way? What was important in the play? What was it really about? What was missing? What was the playwright trying to say?*

Simulated or "Mind Trips." Students can use the power of pretending to create vivid field trip-like experiences in their minds. Just as radio and storytelling are able to trigger mental images of places, characters, and events, so can the teacher's voice. These fantasy journeys allow students to visit other countries, ecosystems, and even different time periods. Students' imaginations and creative thinking are stretched as they conjure up mental pictures. Simulated field trips can be used to in-

Post It Page • 7-4

Strategies to Adapt Drama Lessons For All Learners

Place: Limit and define the space for doing drama (e.g., desk area).

Amount: Do fewer activities or shorter ones.

Rate: Go slower or faster to meet student needs.

Target Objectives: Change the goals or make them clearer to students.

Instruction: Use more teacher direction. For example, use narrative mime to start off in drama and consider taking a role, yourself, in the drama.

Curriculum Materials: Use familiar stories or student experiences for drama activities.

Utensils: Use visual aids like name tags or headbands to help students understand the roles.

Levels of Difficulty: Generally, mime is easier than verbal improvisation, and individual drama activities directed by the teacher are easier than group work. Perhaps the material is too conceptually difficult and needs to be altered. If students act silly, it may be they don't know what to do or feel they can't do what is expected. Humour is often used to cover embarrassment. Consider adapting the level of difficulty.

Assistance: For example, children with hearing impairments need to see your face and mouth as you speak. Ask students what to do to help themselves. Don't force shy children to participate because this may increase reluctance. If students don't seem to be able to end the drama, tell them to plan an ending before presenting, ask the audience for ideas, or you take a role and end it.

Response: Alter what you expect in the conclusion. For example, you may have planned for students to present small-group work to the whole group, but group work has been satisfying enough.

troduce a unit or lesson or as a follow up. Here are guidelines to construct simulated field trips.

- Write, tell, or choose trip stories that provoke rich sensory imagery. Use science, social studies, or literature that is a part of your curriculum to obtain ideas for suitable topics.
- Have students clear away distractions from their desks, close their eyes, and be comfortable.
- Use your voice to calm students; speak slowly and softly and use pauses. Read or speak at a steady pace.
- Give students time to create the images in their heads using their senses of sight, hearing, smell, taste, touch or feel, and movement.
- Keep the trip to about ten to fifteen minutes.
- After the trip, have students mentally review the high points. Ask students to share what they experienced in small groups or have them do a five-minute Write Right Away response or even an art response.
- Come together as a whole group to synthesize what was learned (e.g., in social studies, science, or literature) from the trip.

Principle Nine: EXHIBIT STUDENT PROGRESS

Student progress in using drama as a learning medium can be demonstrated and celebrated using portfolios, audio and video taping, displays, and morning announcements and by sharing with audiences, as described in the Exhibit Student Progress section of Chapter 2 and in Chapter 14. What's most important is often hard to evaluate. Goals may be difficult to pinpoint despite curriculum guidelines and courses of study. Measurement is hard because teachable moments and goals emerge *during* drama. One of the best forms of assessment and evaluation is often specific teacher observations of what students *show they*

Post It Page • 7-5

All-Purpose Fat Questions

Directions: Post these examples so that students can learn to use these kinds of questions as they discuss their work. Teachers can model the use of such open or fat questions and show how they provoke more discussion than skinny, closed ones. All these questions help students think more deeply and facilitate success in expressing ideas.

- What worked?
- What did you enjoy?
- What would you change?
- How was the ending? What was the best moment? Why?
- How did you work with others?
- How did you show involvement?
- How did you get your idea? Where did you gather ideas?
- Why did you do what you did?
- What were you trying to do?
- What did you try that you've never tried before?
- What did you learn most?
- How is this connected to other things you are learning?
- What ideas did you use from what we've been learning about drama (elements, skills, concepts)? All these questions help students begin to think more deeply and facilitate success in expressing their ideas.
- What did you learn? What was this mostly about? What did this tell you about people or the world? What will you remember forever from this book or picture or song?

know in lessons. In addition, students can be meaningfully involved in self-evaluation and giving peer feedback as a means of gauging progress.

Rather than squelch the urge to create with grades or traditional forms of evaluation, we can give general assignment criteria before work is done, which gives students guidance as they work. A simple evaluation checklist that teachers and students can use to consider progress in drama follows:

Teach How to Respond. Response relates to audience etiquette, but goes beyond into the area of giving feedback to peers. After drama presentations, students can use structures to help them articulate thoughts and feelings. For example, students can give feedback by simply telling what they saw or heard (i.e., describing honestly, hopefully using new-found vocabulary for arts elements). They can also use sentence stems to express their thoughts and feelings: *I liked seeing . . . , I liked hearing . . . , I liked thinking about . . . , I felt . . . when . . .* The liked–wonder–learned strategy described in Chapter 2 can be used after a drama to record responses in three columns. Students also need to learn that asking questions of others is a form of feedback. Because receiving feedback is hard for some, it helps to role play giving and receiving feedback. This also shows students how rude or thoughtless remarks can make a person feel; sensitivity and empathy are important factors in giving feedback.

To help teach students how to speak and write about their creative drama work, Post It Page 7–5 has questions for students to use as guides.

Drama Skills Progress Checklist

Name ______________________________ Date ______________

Directions: Evaluate using 1,2,3, with 1 = no evidence and 3 = very evident. Add notes and discuss.

Use of body: ability to coordinate and control body, use of appropriate energy, display of sensory awareness and expression, use of gestures and facial expressions, communication through pantomime, interpretation of nonverbal communication of others

Verbal expression: speaking clearly and using appropriate variety in volume, rate, tone and pitch, pause, stress, emphasis and inflection, fluency, and ability to improvise dialogue

Focus: concentration and staying involved, making others believe in the realness of the character, following directions

Imagination: flexible creative thinking, contribution of unique ideas and elaboration on ideas, spontaneity

Evaluation: giving constructive feedback, using suggestions of others, self-evaluation and adaptation of own behaviour

Social skills: working cooperatively with groups, listening and responding to others

Audience etiquette: attending, listening, and responding appropriately to others' performances

Principle Ten: SPECIALISTS Are Important Resources

Drama teachers, professional actors, playwrights, and community theatre organizations are valuable resources for the classroom teacher. It is part of every classroom teacher's role to seek out specialists in theatre and drama. Specialists can help show where connections between drama and other disciplines exist and how to make them without damaging the integrity of the art form.

It is the lucky classroom teacher who has a drama specialist in the school. Specialists usually welcome invitations to plan with teachers, especially if integration is viewed as going both ways; at times the drama teacher should be able to ask for support for his or her unit focus on a theme or topic. Classroom teachers can make it easy for a specialist to assist in integration by providing a month-by-month listing of units and lessons in science, social studies, reading and language arts, and math so they may make suggestions as appropriate. In addition, teachers can invite specialists to do the same for them with a list of topics they plan to develop, and teachers can ask for ways to follow up on drama classes or extend drama work. Most important is to ask to sit in on drama classes to learn more about drama and about students' ability to make meaning using drama.

When There Is No Drama Specialist in the School. By creating a school directory of persons who have drama skills, teachers can find drama expertise when a specialist is not otherwise available. Circulate a form to all adults in the school requesting names and contact information for people who could be used as drama or theatre resources. Encourage people to list themselves. The teacher next door may have had many courses in children's drama, or the principal may write plays. Students, parents, and community groups can also be tapped for potential skills. Use the Internet to locate home pages of drama and theatre organizations at the local, provincial, and national levels. Selected Internet web sites are listed in the appendix for starters. Don't forget to contact the theatre and education departments in nearby universities to find out about student internships or other ways university students might serve as drama resources.

Arts Agency Collaborations. Collaborations among a variety of arts organizations are helping schools in communities across the country learn ways to integrate drama and other arts. These organizations provide workshops for teachers on a low or no-charge basis. Contact local art galleries or arts councils to see if they are involved in such projects or interested in getting started. Use the appendix to contact organizations by mail, phone, e-mail, or fax. Workshops conducted by artists and classroom teachers engaged in integrating the arts are becoming more common.

Artist Residencies with Specialists. Drama and theatre specialists may be available through a local arts council or by contacting artists in your community. Not only are there children's theatre groups that may be willing to be involved in your classroom, but Drama in Education projects are another dimension worth investigating. It is important to realize that artists often have little or no background in teaching or child development. Before bringing an artist into a school or class, it is important to meet ahead of time to prepare. Everyone needs to agree on and know:

- Goals of the visit, including the objectives from the unit and course of study related to the residency
- Composition of the class: economic, social, and developmental levels
- Exact time limits
- Physical limitations of your classroom (materials you have and don't have)
- Special needs students
- Disciplinary system in use and who will handle discipline during the visit
- Basic effective teaching strategies related to use of proximity, questioning, eye contact, hands on, pace, transitions, use of students' prior knowledge
- How to prepare students for the visit
- How the classroom teacher will participate
- How to assess and evaluate what the students learn
- How to follow up after the visit to extend learning

Conclusion

In this chapter the reasons *why* drama should be integrated, *what* a classroom teacher needs to know and be able to do to integrate drama, and the basic principles for *how* to use drama were discussed. The next chapter consists of specific strategy seed ideas that teachers can use to get students ready for creative problem-solving using drama, teaching students the elements and skills to use drama as a learning tool, and examples of ways to use drama throughout curricular areas.

Post It Page • 7-6

Children's Literature for Drama

Literature for Mime Activities

Andrews, J. (1985). *Very last first time*. Douglas & McIntyre. (Inuit girl travels out under the sea ice)

Baker, J. (1987). *Where the forest meets the sea*. Greenwillow Books. (boy's visit to the rainforest in North Queensland, Australia)

Carle, E. (1969). *The very hungry caterpillar.* Philomel/Putnam. (caterpillar becomes a butterfly; challenge to use a variety of actions to eat the foods; good for flannel board or puppet)

Carney, M. (1997). *At grandpa's sugar bush.* (illus. Janet Wilson). Kids Can Press. (spring break visit to a grandfather's sugar bush)

Carroll, L. (1989). *Jabberwocky.* Abrams. (good for imagining ways to move, e.g., gyre)

Cole, J. (1987). *The magic school bus inside the earth.* Scholastic. (field trips in a microscopic bus. See other books in *The magic school bus* series)

Cumming, P. (1993). *Out on the ice in the middle of the bay*. Annick Press. (young child meets a polar bear on the arctic ice)

Emberley, B. (1967). *Drummer Hoff.* Prentice Hall. (cumulative story of a cannon being fired off; good for mechanical movements)

Gilman, P. (1992). *Something from nothing*. North Winds Press. (folk tale of Jewish family life)

Keats, E. J. (1962). *The snowy day.* Viking. (boy explores things to do on a snowy day)

Kuskin, K. (1982). *The philharmonic gets dressed.* Harper & Row. (members of an orchestra are shown getting ready; follow with a symphonic piece and let students conduct)

Kusugak, M. (1990). *Baseball bats for Christmas*. Annick Press. (a shipment of unwanted Christmas trees arrives in an arctic community from the south and the trees are made into baseball bats)

Lobel, A. (1970). *Frog and toad are friends*. Harper & Row. (tale of friendship)

Lunn, J. (1998). *Charlotte*. Tundra Books. (the war of independence in 1783 divides a family)

McCully, Emily (1992). *Mirette on the high wire.* Putnam. (girl learns to walk the highwire)

McDermott, G. (1975). *The stonecutter.* Viking Penguin. (Japanese folktale; no dialogue)

Oberman, S. (1994). *The always prayer shawl*. Boyds Mills Press. (a boy's tale of the Russian revolution)

Parish, P. (1963). *Amelia Bedelia.* Harper & Row. (a maid takes instructions literally; many sequels about misunderstanding idiomatic expressions)

Rossetti, C. (1991) "Who has seen the wind?" In K. Sky-Pock (ed.) *Who has seen the wind?* Rizzoli. (this poem offers pantomime opportunities through the leaf movements of blowing, trembling, and hanging)

Tolstoy, A. (1968). *The great big enormous turnip.* Franklin Watts. (cumulative tale about characters trying to pull up a huge vegetable)

Van Allsburg, C. (1988). *Two bad ants.* Houghton Mifflin. (two ants have adventures)

Literature for Verbal Activities

Bemelmens, L. (1939). *Madeline.*Viking Penguin. (Madeline lives in a Paris convent)

Bennett, J. (ed.). (1987). *Noisy poems.* Oxford University Press. (many sounds)

Brown, M. (1947). *Stone soup.* Scribner's. (three soldiers teach some villagers how to make soup out of stones; follow with actual cooking)

Day, A. (1985). *Good dog, Carl.* Green Tiger Press. (a humorous story of an intelligent dog who babysits a squirmy small child; almost wordless; several sequels)

Gag, W. (1928). *Millions of cats.* Coward-McCann. (old man goes to find a pet for his wife and gets more than he bargained for; there is repeated chant)

Galdone, P. (1968). *The Bremen town musicians.* McGraw-Hill. (four animals encounter a band of robbers and gain wealth to keep them happy)

Granfield, L. (1995). *In Flanders Fields: The story of the poem by John McCrae.* (illus. Janet Wilson). Lester Publishing. (provides context for the poem and the writer)

Haley, G. (1970). *A story—A story.* Atheneum. (African tale about Anansi, who must capture and give to the sky god a leopard, hornets, and a dancing fairy in order to own all the stories)

Harrison, T. *The northern alphabet.* Montreal: Tundra Books. (alphabet book)

Lee, D. (1974). *Alligator pie*. Macmillan Canada. (rich in rhythm and imagery)

Little, J. (1984). *Mama's going to buy you a mockingbird*. Viking Kestrel. (story of a boy whose father dies)

Little, J. (1986). *Different dragons*. Penguin Books Canada. (a boy who overcomes many fears)

Littlechild, G. (1993). *This land is my land*. Children's Book Press. (Cree literature—short narratives)

Marshall, J. (1972). *George and Martha.* Houghton Mifflin. (delightful stories work well for QU readings and interviews; several sequels)

McDermott, B. (1976). *The Golem: A Jewish legend.* Lippincott. (a rabbi in Prague creates a clay figure to stop an uprising; good for debates and interviews)

McGovern, A. (1967). *Too much noise.* Houghton Mifflin. (an old man tries to find the solution to too much noise in his house; use for expert panels)

Munsch, R. (1980). *The paper bag princess.* Annick Press. (a princess rescues a prince but decides not to marry him; use for interviews)

Prelutsky, J. (1999). *The 20th century children's poetry treasury*. Alfred A. Knopf. (superb collection)

Scieszka, J. (1989). *The true story of the 3 little pigs by A. Wolf.* Viking. (wolf tells the story from his point of view; use to stimulate point of view storytelling of other tales)

Service, R. W. (1987). *The cremation of Sam McGee*. (illus. Ted Harrison). Greenwillow Books. (rich internal rhyme and vivid imagery)

Tresslet, A. (1964). *The mitten.* Lothrop, Lee & Shepard. (a lost mitten is a haven for animals)

Turkle, B. (1976). *Deep in the forest.* E. P. Dutton. (a three bears story with a twist)

Van Allsburg, C. (1984). *The mysteries of Harris Burdick.* Houghton Mifflin. (black-and-white surrealistic pictures, each with its own caption; great material for storytelling)

Van Allsburg, C. (1986). *The stranger.* Houghton Mifflin. (a stranger is injured in an accident, suffers from amnesia, and stays with a family until he realizes his identity)

Viorst, J. (1972). *Alexander and the terrible, horrible, no good, very bad day.* Atheneum. (a boy details everything that goes wrong for him in one day; repeated lines)

Wiesner, D. (1991). *Tuesday.* Clarion. (almost wordless picture book about flying frogs)

Young, E. (1989). *Lon Po Po: A Red-Riding Hood story from China.* Philomel. (sisters outwit a wolf)

Post It Page • 7-7

Example Integrated Drama and Science Lesson Plan (2nd Grade)

Narrative pantomime is the core in this lesson during a unit on habitats that began a week ago.

Two-pronged Focus: Drama elements and skills: *pantomime* with focus on control, display of sensory awareness, use of gestures and face, and responding to nonverbal communications of others; focus and concentration; following directions. Science concepts: components of habitat and effects on animals.

Student Objectives: Student will be able to:

1. Use body and face to show specific components of habitats (food, water, shelter, and space).
2. Concentrate and focus to control body and respond to others; follow oral directions (cues).
3. Predict responses of animals who are missing basic habitat components.

Teaching Procedure: The teacher will:

Introduction

1. Use the focus ball strategy to help students focus and concentrate for the lesson.
2. Ask students to list names of animals and places they live—from previous lessons. Record their ideas on a chart (language experience strategy and ask them to spell chorally to help with phonics development). Ask what *habitat* means and clarify, as needed.
3. Tell them today's lesson is about parts of habitats and what happens when a part is missing. Explain we'll be using a special kind of drama called narrative pantomime to show animals in their habitats. Ask what makes drama. (Students can use drama elements chart up in room.) Ask about which kind of drama uses no words (pantomime).
4. Do a series of "Show Me" pantomimes with focus on use of face: happy, thinking, worried, hungry, angry. Repeat with whole body (at desk area). Divide class in half for demos and give time for each half to give the other half feedback on what they did that showed concentration and focus.

Development

5. Explain that narrative pantomime is when someone tells a story while others use their faces and bodies to show the story. Review rules about following start and stop signals. Tell everyone to find a personal space in the centre of the room.

6. Give each a card with an animal name on it. No one knows it but there are duplicates. Say *"When I say 'start' everyone is to explore ways to show their animal in a variety of ways* (e.g., shape, moves, size). *Stay in your personal spot. At the 'freeze' signal everyone should stop. Start."* Give feedback on focus, concentration, unusual ideas. Repeat in *slow motion.*
7. Use start and stop signals for the *narrative pantomime* (read slowly and give time):

   You are hungry. You begin to look for **food** in your habitat. You find the kind of food you eat. Slowly you eat your meal. After a while you start to get full and begin to slow down. In an area nearby you hear a sound and you become afraid. Your body shows you are scared. You look for **shelter** and move there. You watch carefully and you wait, being very still, until you know you are safe. The coast seems to be clear. You are feeling good because you are safe and full of food. You move around your habitat **space** showing you are satisfied. Because you ate so much you are thirsty. You see **water** nearby and move there and begin to drink. The water is very cold. After a long cool drink, you begin to feel lonely and you look for another animal like you. You move around noticing how other animals move to see if you can find another of your species. You greet your fellow animal when you find him or her. It has been a long day and you are getting tired. You move slowly to a place of shelter. You begin to get ready to rest. Slowly you drift off to sleep.
8. Ask students what they thought about, what worked? what problems? How did they find another same animal? Collect cards and repeat with new animals.

- Conclusion

9. Brainstorm what might happen if a habitat part is limited—like space. Ask what information students need to show the parts of habitat and animal behaviour better. List ideas on the chart.
10. Let students choose an animal to read more about habitat needs (library books on display). Tell them we'll do a drama Tuesday using what they find; this time the animals will have inadequate habitat components, so there will be problems (conflict).

Activities:

Opening Vignette: Why? What? How?

Think about Ms. Tran's lesson. What did she teach about both social studies and drama? Why did she do what she did ? How did she cause the students to become engaged in the lesson?

Why Integrate Drama?

If a principal or parent asked you for three good reasons to use drama as a learning tool, what reasons would you select? Why do you believe these are the most important reasons?

Teacher in Role

Try your hand at planning a drama in which you would take a role. Practice on something short, like a fable or Mother Goose piece. Consider the following:

1. Examine the story for problems and themes. What is this really about? What is the conflict? Who has the problem? (Jack in the Beanstalk *is about how goods are not equally distributed and how people are never satisfied with what they have.*)
2. List groups or individuals that might be affected by the problem. (*The giant's family who now has no income; Jack's mother, wife, and friends, who see a changed Jack; neighbours who don't like having a thief around.*)
3. Under what circumstances might these individuals come together (e.g., some kind of meeting)? (*Counselling session for Jack's materialistic addictions.*)
4. Choose a role and plan a short introduction speech about who you are and why you are there (*counsellor*).
5. Plan the roles that the children can become. (*Children choose to be any of the characters affected by Jack's greed.*)

Teacher Resources

See the appendix for drama integration resources. Here is a sampling of what's available:

Theatrebooks in Toronto (416-922-7175, E-mail: action@theatrebooks.com) is an excellent mail-order source of drama education materials for teachers.

Barton, R. & Booth, D. (1990). *Stories in the classroom: Storytelling, reading aloud and role playing with children.* Markham: Pembroke.

Barton, R. & Moore, B. (1999). *Off the page: Reading poetry out loud, choral speaking and drama.* Hamilton: Tree House.

Booth, D. (1994). *Story drama: Reading, writing, and role playing across the curriculum.* Markham: Pembroke.

Creative dramatics: The first steps [video, 29 min.]. Northwestern Film Library, 614 Davis St., Evanston, Il 60201. (drama in a fourth grade)

Dorothy Heathcote talks to teachers—part I and part II [videos, about 30 minutes]. Northwestern University Film Library, 1735 Benson Ave, Evanston, Il. 60201.

Dunn, S. (1999). *All together now: 200 of Sonja Dunn's best chants.* Markham: Pembroke.

Heathcote, D. & Bolton, G. (1995). *Drama for learning: Dorothy Heathcote's mantle of the expert approach to learning.* Portsmouth, NH: Heinemann

Heinig, R. B. (1992). *Improvisation with favorite fairy tales.* Portsmouth, NH: Heinemann.

Heinig, R. B. (1987). *Creative drama resource book for grades 4 through 6.* Englewood Cliffs, NJ: Prentice Hall. (kindergarten through third book also available)

Kemp, D. (1990). *A different drummer: An ideas book for drama.* Toronto: McClelland & Stewart.

Kemp, D. & Danby, M. (1982). *Drama through storytelling: A practical approach for the teacher of elementary grades.* Toronto: Simon & Pierre

Merrion, M. (1996). *Creative drama and music methods: Introductory activities for children.* North Haven, CT: Linnet Professional.

Schafer, L. (1994). *Plays around the year: More than 20 thematic plays for the classroom.* New York: Scholastic Professional Books.

Swartz, L. (1995). *Dramathemes.* Markham: Pembroke

Walker, L. (1996). *Readers theater strategies development through Readers Theater, storytelling, writing and dramatizing!* Colorado Springs, CO: Meriwether.

References

Books and Articles

Barton, R. & Booth, D. (1990). *Stories in the classroom: Storytelling, reading aloud and role playing with children.* Markham: Pembroke.

Booth, D. (1994). *Story drama: reading, writing, and role playing across the curriculum.* Markham: Pembroke.

Dupont, S. (1992). "The effectiveness of creative drama as an instructional strategy to enhance reading comprehension skill of fifth-grade remedial readers." *Reading Research and Instruction,* 31(3), 41–52.

Gourgey, A., Bousseau, J., & Delgado, J. (1985). "The impact of an improvisational dramatics program on student attitudes and achievement." *Children's Theater Review,* 34(3), 9–14.

Heathcote, D. & Bolton, G. (1995). *Drama for learning: Dorothy Heathcote's mantle of the expert approach to learning.* Portsmouth, NH: Heinemann

Heinig, R. B. (1993). *Creative drama for the classroom teacher.* Englewood Cliffs, NJ: Prentice Hall.

Henderson, L. C., & Shanker, L. C. (1978). "The use of interpretive dramatics versus basal reader workbooks." *Reading World,* 17, 239–243.

Kardash, C., & Wright, L. (Winter 1987). "Does creative drama benefit elementary school students: a meta-analysis." *Youth Theater Journal,* 11–18.

Karioth, E. (1967). "Creative dramatics as an aid to developing creative thinking abilities." Unpublished doctoral dissertation, University of Minnesota.

McCaslin, N. (1990). *Creative drama in the classroom,* 5th ed. New York: Longman.

Meyrink, G. (1994). "The curse of the toad" in *The opal and other stories.* Riverside, CA: Ariadne Press.

Miller, H., Rynders, J., & Schleien, S. (1993). "Drama: A medium to enhance social interaction between students with and without mental retardation." *Mental Retardation,* 31(4), 228–33.

Moore, B., & Caldwell, H. (1993). "Drama and drawing for narrative writing in primary grades." *Journal of Educational Research,* 8(2), 100–110.

Riekehof, L. (1987). *Joy of Signing.* Springfield, MO: Gospel Publishing House.

Robinson, K. (ed.) (1990). *Exploring theater and education.* London: Heinemann.

Rosenberg, H. (1987). *Creative drama and imagination: Transforming ideas into action.* New York: Holt, Rinehart & Winston.

Schmidt, T., Goforth, E., & Drew, K. (1975). "Creative dramatics and creativity: an experimental study." *Educational Theater Journal.* March 27, 1975, 111–114.

Stewig, J., & McKee, J. (1980). "Drama and language growth: a replication study." *Children's Theater Review,* 29(3), 1.

Stewig, J., & Young, L. (1978). "An exploration of the relations between creative drama and language growth." *Children's Theater Review,* 27(2), 10–12.

Vitz, K. (1983). "A review of empirical research in drama and language." *Children's Theater Review,* 32(4), 17–25.

Wagner, B. J. (1988). "A review of empirical research in drama and language." *Language Arts,* v.65 n.1, 46–55.

Children's Literature References

Hoffman, M. (1991). *Amazing grace.* New York: Dial.

Lunn, J. (1997). *The hollow tree.* Toronto: Alfred A. Knopf Canada.

Montgomery, L. M. (1908, 1935). *Anne of Green Gables.* Toronto: Seal Books.

Van Allsburg, C. (1991). *The wretched stone.* Boston: Houghton Mifflin.

White, E. B. (1952). *Charlotte's web.* New York: HarperTrophy.

Drama Seed Strategies

Consultant:
Aynne Johnston

8

This chapter includes starter ideas to integrate drama throughout the curriculum. The ideas are seed or kernel strategies to develop for lessons tailored to student needs and curricular goals. The strategies are brief prompts to help teachers think creatively, and most are adaptable for students in primary and intermediate schools. It is important to select, adapt, and expand, as appropriate to particular classrooms. The strategy seeds are organized into the following sections, but many could be placed in more than one section. The sections on energizers, mime, and verbal strategies do *not* represent integration, by themselves, but are provided to teach these drama forms so that students can then use drama to make meaning throughout curricular areas.

I. Energizers and Warm-ups
II. Mime Strategies
III. Verbal Strategies
IV. Connecting Drama to Other Curricular Areas
- Science
- Social Studies
- Reading and Language Arts
- Math

V. Storytelling's Special Relationship with Drama

I. Energizers and Warm-ups

Energizers and warm-ups are used to relax students, give focus, and get them ready for creative thinking. Also see energizers from other chapters, especially for dance, for concentration activities.

Line Up Different Ways. Tell students to line up alphabetically, by birthday, by height, and so on. Once in line, they then interview those around them to find out three things not known before.

Tongue Twisters and Tanglers. Use as vocal warm-ups. Say them as a group and then practise in pairs or go around a circle (make into a game where play begins over if a person mispronounces). Examples are: *A hot cup of coffee from a proper copper coffee pot. Aluminum linoleum. Bugs black blood. Six sick sheep. Rubber baby buggy bumpers. Toy boat. Unique New York.* One collection is *Six Sick Sheep* by Joanna Cole. Follow up: Ask students to collect and create twisters. Put up a Twister Master chart for students to keep track of ones they learn to say three times without error. Many students will want to memorize longer twisters like "Peter Piper" (see Schwartz's *A Twister of Twists: A Tangler of Tongues* for history of this one).

Finger Plays. Traditional finger plays like "The Itsy Bitsy Spider" can be taught, and there are special collections that include other favourites. Here is an untraditional one to calm and focus. Seat everyone on the floor and say:

> *I relax and focus* (point to self with thumb and lay hands in lap)
> *I gather in the good* (gather with hands brought in)
> *I push out the bad* (push outward with both hands)
> *I celebrate the joy all around me* (raise hands, spread fingers, and do silent cheer)

Sound and Action Stories. "Going on a Bear Hunt" is an example of this kind of energizer in which a narrator tells a story while children echo lines and do actions. Narration is accompanied by a steady walking rhythm. Between sections of the story, give time to mime the motions. When the bear is seen, actions are reversed—double time.

Scavenger Hunts. Give groups items to find and a time limit. For example, *"In five minutes try to find a silky item, a book with an r-controlled word in the title, something that moves, and something that can be used to create." Variation:* Use the five senses to organize searches: "Find something that . . . looks like . . . , sounds like . . . , feels like . . . , and so on."

Concentration. Make a tray of items. Students study them and then the tray is covered. Students try to list all they remember. *Variation:* Students close their eyes and an item is removed. They try to figure out the missing item. Try with a group using wipe-off boards so that all can write missing item and then simultaneously show boards.

Word Change. This is a creative-thinking verbal exercise. Sit in a circle. First person gives a sentence (e.g., Mary had a little lamb). Next person repeats the sentence, but changes one word: Mary had a little goat. Keep going all the way around. *Challenge:* Repeat and return the sentence to its original form.

Partner Search. Make sets of cards with sounds or song titles and pass them out. The goal is to have groups form by finding those who are singing the same song or making the same sound (e.g., animal sound), for example, five different song titles on five sets of cards for twenty-five students to break into groups of five.

Three Truths and a Lie. Students write down a list of facts about themselves. One item should be false. Students read aloud items including the false one. The audience applauds to show which one they believe is the lie. *Note:* It is important to discuss how to use creative ideas without being obvious.

Animal–Car–Flower. This creative-thinking activity helps students get to know one another. Students write down the three categories and an example that applies to them. For example, *My name is . . . and I identify with a cat because . . . , a Jeep because . . . , and roses because. . . .*

Reverse Web. This is a creative-thinking team builder. Students get into groups of four or five. Use large paper and have everyone write, or use 8½ by 11 paper with one recorder. A circle is drawn in the centre. A leg is drawn coming out of the circle for each person (five students equals five lines radiating out). Names are written on the legs. In the center, students put things the group has in common—the more unusual the better (e.g., all are left handed or all have traveled to Newfoundland).

Pass and Pretend. Sit in a circle and pass around an ordinary object (pencil or scarf). Students then use it in a creative way by imagining what it can become. For example, a scarf could be rocked like a baby. Encourage focus on details of action. (See **Invisible Object** mime suggestions.) *Variation:* Do this without a prop and ask students to imagine an object and pantomime using it and passing it to the next person, who must use the same object and transform it into something else. To increase difficulty, do with several objects. *Variation:* Use a verbal frame: Pass straw and say, *"This is not a straw, it's a . . ."* and then demonstrate what it has transformed into.

Voice Change. This activity helps students use volume, rate, tone, pitch, pause, stress, and emphasis to convey a character or person. Make a set of character or person cards. Then make a list of random sentences: *"Hi, how are you?" "Can you tell me how to get to the nearest hospital?" "We've really been having bad weather lately." "I'm so tired."* Students each draw a card and say one of the sentences, in character. Others tell what they heard (message, feelings) and who they think it is. For example, Santa might "ho-ho-ho" in between his words or phrases.

Laugh Contest. A panel of students must try to resist laughing as one classmate has a crack at making them laugh by telling jokes, making faces, etc. Discuss school-appropriate humour before doing this!

Nonsense. Use words, phrases, or letters and numbers to create scenes. Practise saying them changing volume, rate, tone, pitch, pause, stress, and emphasis. The expression and intonation carry the meaning of the scene. For example, A can only say "seventeen," B can only say "four," and C can only say "zero" as verbal expressions.

Juggling. An old circus trick, juggling is fun and teaches concentration and hand-eye coordination. If students can juggle and recite a memorized passage at the same time, they will cope well with on-stage situations.

Noiseless Sounds. This is a great classroom management tool. Ask students to think of ways to mime sounds without making any noise: laugh, applause, choke, sneeze. *Variation:* Ask students to divide the sound into three consecutive mime actions (e.g., steps in a sneeze). Groups can practise and present to the whole class.

What's Different? (for concentration). Students partner with one being A and the other B. A studies B concentrating on details of appearance. Leader signals and they turn back to back. B makes a change. Pairs turn around and A gets three guesses to figure out "what's different." Then it's B's turn.

Hot Sock. See Chapter 6 for this game, which develops verbal fluency and categorization.

Voice Stunts. Form groups of four. Give groups a phrase. For example, *"To be or not to be," "Zig-zag-zog,"* or *"Slip-slap-slop."* Each person only says one word in the phrase and play goes around a circle, or IT can pass by eye contact or pointing.

Stunts and Magic Tricks. (builds pride and confidence). Students can learn stunts and tricks to perform, for example, rub stomach and pat head at same time, balance balloon or pencil on the end of your nose, stand with left shoulder and side of left foot snug against a wall and try to raise right leg. See Goodman's *Magic and the Educated Rabbit* and Randi's *The Magic World of the Amazing Randi* for more ideas.

II. Mime Strategies

Mime or pantomime is acting without words and often shows something in the process of "becoming," for example, a seed becoming a plant or a character becoming frustrated as he tries to whistle. It is helpful for shy students or those with limited oral expression skills, because it is the kind of communication used before a child learns to speak. Movement and facial expression are used to show shape, size, weight, texture, and temperature—the things experienced through the senses. Through mime, students can imagine and experience places, events, and things beyond firsthand experiences (e.g., walking on the moon), and in so doing engage thinking, emotions, and body in learning. Mime can be as simple as showing the difference between water and ice, using only the body, or it can be as complex as a performance of John Cabot's travails on his voyage to the New World.

The teacher's role is to set up mimes that focus on action related to children's lives and curricular areas, plus structure the drama for success. For example, a teacher might use narrative mime and comment and coach children as they mime by saying *"I see . . ."* or asking *"What do you see?"* to encourage students to develop skills at observing details. Teachers learn to deal with common problems that frequently arise by anticipating difficulties, such as children wanting to make all mimes into guessing games. (This can be handled by limiting guesses, focusing attention on details that *show,* or asking for evidence to support guesses.) This section includes types of mimes adaptable for use throughout curricular areas. It begins with Post It Page 8–1 to stimulate thinking about how *actions* can be connected to concepts in science, social studies, or math, thereby making learning through mime possible.

Invisible Objects. Use a mystery bag or basket. Each student pretends to pull out an item and *shows* its shape, size, weight, texture, and temperature and how it can be used. Guessers put thumbs up and IT calls on selected peers. To become IT, a student must tell the items and the details the mime used to make the idea clear. To make an object look real, coach students to take time to:

- Slowly study it (size, shape, texture, temperature)
- Reach out as if to touch it (move toward it to show how you will take hold)
- Take hold (imagine your hands on it, then feel its weight)
- Use it like you would if it were really there
- Stop and slowly replace it
- Let go slowly and move away

Afterward, tell students to isolate a part they did the best and demonstrate to the group, or ask them to give each other feedback on which steps looked most real and why. Variation: Objects could come from any curricular area of study (e.g., a butter churn from colonial times).

Number Freeze. Students number off in fives. Give them a setting (e.g., a circus). Teacher calls a number and these students mime an action done in the designated setting. The next number is then called and this group mimes while the others observe.

Quick Change. Give a series of *"Show me with your face and body"* directions. For example, *Show me . . . mad, upset because you dropped your ice cream cone, happy because you got an A on your test. Variation:* use examples from science, social studies, or literature.

Mirrors (to build concentration). Partners face each other. A pretends to look into a mirror and B becomes the mirror. The goal is to align actions so that an observer can't tell the "real" from the "reflection." Start in slow motion. Playing music during mirror activities allows movements to flow and prevents rushed movement. The state of concentration and relaxation is also effective for facilitating music appreciation. *Variation:* Do in small groups and give a context like a beauty salon. One person is the stylist and the rest are mirrors. Do in two facing lines. Children may also do this activity in rows, mirroring the upper torso and arm movements of the person sitting in front of them. This stylized movement lends itself to integration in ritual or dance. *Suggestion:* keep movement slow and evenly paced.

Mime Solo (Heinig, 1993). In mime solos, children work individually but can mime in unison, each in her or his personal space. For example, *You are Little Miss Muffet looking for a place to sit and eat. Remember, you've been frightened by a spider in this garden before.* Give signals to start and end, such as flick lights or use drum, tambourine, or bell. Counting can also signal the playing: *"5–4–3–2–1."* If students are to do multiple mimes, say *"Think of three things Goldilocks might have done while going through the woods and number them, one, two, and three in your mind. As I say one of the numbers, you mime your idea."* This kind of cuing keeps all on task and working together.

Pair Mime. Brainstorm actions requiring two people (e.g., teeter totter, dance, lift a long table, play checkers). Partner students. At a count, or with a time limit, students mime as many as they can. *Example connection to literature:* Prince putting the slipper on Cinderella or Cinderella and the Prince dancing. *Variations:* Do one action in slow, regular, and then in quick time. Add conflict (e.g., Cin-

Post It Page • 8-1

A to Z Mime Possibilities

Directions: Brainstorm with students things that can be mimed about a topic. Use this list to give examples and to create original mimes in any curricular area. For example, mime verbs (action words) in language arts to have students *show* meanings.

Actions: clean, travel, construct, eat, drink, ignore, cough, nudge, videotape

Animals: moving, eating, sleeping; different categories (e.g., insect, bird, mammal)

Chapters: actions in each chapter of a book

Book Characters: spider writing in web, Jack climbing beanstalk

Dessert: ice cream cone, jello, cake, cookies, pudding

Emotions or feelings: happy, sad, angry, disgusted, surprised, sick, embarrassed

Foods: being prepared, eaten (e.g. apples, oranges, bananas)

Getting ready: to go to school, to go to the beach, to play ball

Hobbies and vacation activities: juggling, jumping rope, playing tennis

Holidays and festivals: dances, decorating, gifts, rituals

Incline: climbing up stairs, onto a table, on top of a snow pile, up a ladder

Jobs, occupations, careers

Kitchen: stirring, frying, washing, drying, sweeping

Lipstick: putting on face or clown make-up, write with it, wipe it off your face

Machines: computers, mixers, vacuum, lawn mower

Musical instruments: being played, carried, cleaned

NASA: walk in outer space, bounce in slow motion, climb into rocket ship

Objects: a shoe being made, types of Greek columns, holding and placing objects (fruit, animals, food)

Pairs: folding a sheet, playing tennis, tug of war, Ping-Pong

People: famous celebrities, inventors, politicians

Pets: caring for, behaving like

Places: beach, cave, closet, rooftop, edge of cliff, bodies of water, mountains, beach, city, farm

Plants: changing, growing, blooming, dying

Processes: nesting, cooking, building, manufacturing

Queen: walk with crown on head, wave at people, cut a ribbon, read a speech

Rituals and customs: greetings, farewells, weddings

Sports: how to dress for, actually playing, waiting for your turn, cheering

Things you: like to do; don't like to do

Tools: use of, cleaning, carrying

Toys: using, storing

Umbrella: put it up, walk in wind, walk in rain, use as cane, twirl like a parasol

Vehicles: scooter, inline skates, tricycle

Walking: under different circumstances, in different moods, to different locations, at different levels, taking different pathways, as different characters

Weather: response to different weather conditions or pretending to be a kind of weather

Xtra!: sell newspapers, buy one, read with disbelief

Yell: to be heard, from fear, for joy, cheer for a team

Zoo: walk by cages with lions, monkeys, dolphins

derella's feet smell). Famous pairs can also be mimed (e.g., Wright brothers), and this mime can be adapted to focus on group effort by brainstorming actions it takes a group to do (e.g., carry a bathtub). Groups form and mime. Add conflict in repeat playing (e.g., your hands get sweaty).

Break It Down (analysis and sequencing). Students think of a series of movements associated with an event or a place (e.g., washing a pet, picking fruit). Break each into three to five parts to mime in order. For example, empty hamper. Carry basket down stairs. Sort clothes. Put clothes in washer. Set knobs. Close lid. Start washer. *Variation:* Add conflict (e.g., can't get all the clothes in the washer).

Emotion Pantomimes. Give students a situation with an emotion. For example, *You are alone at home and you hear strange noises in different parts of the house.* Give start signal and feedback about ways students use details to show action. Split the class into presenters and audience to share. Reverse so that all have a chance to observe and discuss what works. *Variation:* Ask students to list emotions and give situations in which each might be felt. Add a problem or conflict to increase interest and mime.

Obstacle Mimes. Students brainstorm actions (e.g., walking to school, driving a car). Do a group unison mime of the ideas. Next, divide into small groups and ask groups to add a problem, obstacle, or conflict to one action. Small groups then mime (e.g., dancing, but with a broken toe).

Kalamazoo (adapted from Heinig, 1993). Divide students into two groups to decide on a mime category (e.g., jobs, animals, toys). Then have them line up facing each other. Group 1 says *"Here we come,"* and group 2 responds, *"Where are you from?"* Group 1, *"Kalamazoo."* Group 2, *"What do you do?"* Group 1, *"Here's a clue."* Group 1 then pantomimes while group 2 guesses. A time limit can be set.

Chain Mime. One person starts a mime and others become involved as they guess (guessers can whisper answers to the teacher or mime), for example, a giraffe walking and eating. Correct guessers can become additional giraffes and can interact with one another.

Categories Mime. Brainstorm words in categories (e.g., B words, rhyming words, silent *e* words). Group students and give a list of numbered items. Half mimes while the other half numbers their papers and writes what they think is mimed, in order. Use a new list for the second half to mime.

Mime Category Ideas

Image: Things that move or are:	Examples
vertical	elevator
horizontal	dust a table
high	clouds
low	caterpillar
fast	electric fan
slow	melting ice
circle	merry-go-round
twisted	pretzel

Five Senses Mimes. Brainstorm things to do in the sense categories: smell, see, taste, touch, and hear. Students mime. *Variation:* Add a problem. For example, you are eating a chicken sandwich, but you bite into something hard, or you are zipping up your jacket, but it gets stuck.

Fights. Drama is made from conflict, and most literature useful for drama involves conflict, so it is a good idea to practise miming fights. Ask students to practise showing different moves in personal spaces *without touching anyone* (e.g., punch, stab, claw, slap). Do in slow motion or to a count. Get into pairs. In slow motion, practise with one person responding. Emphasize *no touching or falling down* (unless you also teach falling). Use start and stop signals. Schools and school boards have policies on violence and the representation of violence. Check these and construct parameters in your class activities that respect and uphold these guidelines.

Action Mime. Brainstorm ways to move or actions. (See BEST dance elements in Post It Page 9–2 and Locomotor and Non-Locomotor Action Bingo in Chapter 10.) Put action words in a basket. Each person picks one and "becomes the move," while others guess its name. This can be done in partners (e.g., all A people "twist" while B's observe and switch).

Charades. This is an old favourite mime guessing game. Form two teams. Each takes a turn. Traditional mime categories are book, song, television show, film, and famous person, but any category can be used: one-, two-, or three-syllable words, rhyme pairs (hink pinks like "sad dad"), synonyms, antonyms, words beginning with a letter or sound, homophones (sum–some, red–read), quotes, proverbs, famous pairs (e.g., peanut butter and jelly), provinces, countries, and so on. Students enjoy creating cues to start the game: sounds like (pull ear), short word (show size with fingers), long word (show with two hands moving apart), syllable numbers (show with fingers), movie (pretend to roll film), book (use hands to show open book).

Imaginary Place (Heinig, 1993). The goal is to create a setting or place by stocking it with appropriate items. Mark off space with masking tape. Students pantomime bringing in items and placing them. Pairs work together for big items. Audience can guess what is mimed. Challenge students to use items they add, plus a previous item, in some way, to fix visual images. For example, two students bring a stove into a restaurant, so the next player brings in a refrigerator. After placing the fridge, the student may check the oven temperature before exiting. Periodically, review all items and their placement. *Variations:* Use settings and places from history and literature.

Count–Freeze. Give students a category to mime (see Post It Page 8–1). Tell students you will count to ten as they mime. They are to freeze on ten. *Variation:* Do in pairs or trios, and count at different speeds. Examples are things you do at school or things you do in threes or twos. Here is a literature example from "The Mouse at the Seashore" fable: things the mouse might have done on his journey in the morning, afternoon, evening (teacher says each time of day and then students mime).

Time Mime (focus on self-control). Students mime at different speeds from slow to fast. For example, slow = move as if you are under water or walking in thick mud. Play slow mood music or a piece like "Clair de Lune." Fast motion mime = move like a fast motion movie. Play Scott Joplin songs or a fast piece like the "Spinning Song." Use this idea to vary any mime, replaying at different speeds.

Transformations. Brainstorm characters or things that change (e.g., young to old, seed to plant). Ask students to break down phases and do in slow motion. Add music. For example, *Become a fairy tale character and change, on a slow count of ten, into another character* (e.g., beast into a prince).

Tableau (frozen picture). Pairs or small groups are given a scene to depict and asked to freeze in appropriate positions (e.g., a tension-filled moment in a story). Students can then be "tapped" to speak aloud and give a one-liner of their thoughts. Audience may be asked to *describe* what they see, what it means, and what makes them believe in the picture. They may also wish to *ask questions* of members of the tableau, especially ones about their feelings and motives. Children may select their own scenes from science or social studies to portray and be guessed by peers as a unit review. *Variation:* Ask students to create three different tableaux to a count. For example, *Remain as the same character but move into three different positions as I count 5–4–3–2–1.* Ask students to freeze, then move, and then freeze on cue to set the tableau to life for a few seconds. Give audience members a role to respond (e.g., if the scene was Wilbur winning the blue ribbon, ask the audience to tell what they see as if they are farmers, Templeton, Charlotte, or the owner of the local slaughterhouse. This increases thinking from a variety of perspectives). *Variation:* Frozen scenes may be performed as shadow pictures or silhouettes by using a light behind a taut sheet. Stand close to the sheet to present a clear image and turn lights off. Coloured gels on the light create interesting effects.

Tableau Captions. Use book titles, newspaper headlines, current events, advertisement slogans, quotes from famous people, or phrases from units as prompts for frozen picture tableaux. For example, *"Why does she always get to sit up front?"* or *"Mars Lander Hits Hard."* *Variation:* Create three different frames.

Creative Mimes. Technically, all mime should be creative, but creative mime offers greater room for improvisation. Instead of interpreting actions, these mimes involve thinking more about "what if." For example, stop reading a story at a poignant point and ask students to review and mime certain activities integral to the story. For example, Cinderella sews gowns for her stepsisters, Cinderella watches everyone leave for the ball. Then have students mime predictions of what might happen next. Emphasize *"what are all the possibilities of what might happen."* For example, *Let's see three things Cinderella might do after she gets home after the first night at the ball. I'll count to signal. Let's begin. One. Variation:* Do half of an experiment or stop partway through a video and ask students to make predictions by miming an event they anticipate.

Improvised Mime Scene. Pick a scene from a story with two or more characters to mime, or dialogue can be added. Simple plot outlines may be suggested. For example, *Let's see the scene when Miss Muffet gets together all the things she needs to eat and then finally sits down on her tuffet."* Use coaching as needed (e.g., *"And then she had to find something to carry it all in"*). Remind students to use start and stop signals for scenes. *Variation:* Give groups a scene to plan. Each group presents a different scene from the beginning, middle, or end of a story. Provide rehearsal time.

Narrative Mime. In narrative mime, someone reads or tells a story with lots of action as others mime. Narrative mime gives security to students because it is teacher directed and usually based on familiar material. Narrative mime can also introduce basic story structure (beginning, middle, end) and literary elements (plot, setting, characters, conflict, resolution).

Many children's stories can be used for narrative mime with slight modification. Just by casting the story in the second person, "you," children feel more like the character. Select stories with much action, a clear climax, and quiet ending. Stories of journeys, trips, or cycles of events (e.g., caterpillar turning into a butterfly or "day in the life of . . ." structures) work well. Lawson's *Emma and the Silk Train*, Gilman's *Something from Nothing*, Van Allsburg's *The Z Was Zapped* and Keat's *A Snowy Day* are stories that need only minor changes to be used for narrative mime. Post It Page 7–6 provides an annotated bibliography of children's literature for narrative mime, and there are more in the bibliography in the appendix.

Edit stories for mime by eliminating dialogue and extraneous description. Action can be added by expanding a line of description (e.g., instead of reading *"It was a hot hazy day"* change to *"You wipe your brow and squint as you look across the hazy horizon"*). In some stories there is a repeated sound, word, or a refrain that is hard to resist, so verbal activity can be added. For example, in Robert Munsch's *Thomas' Snowsuit* there is plenty of action, plus the repetition of the word, "No!" A pause for students to add the word in unison adds

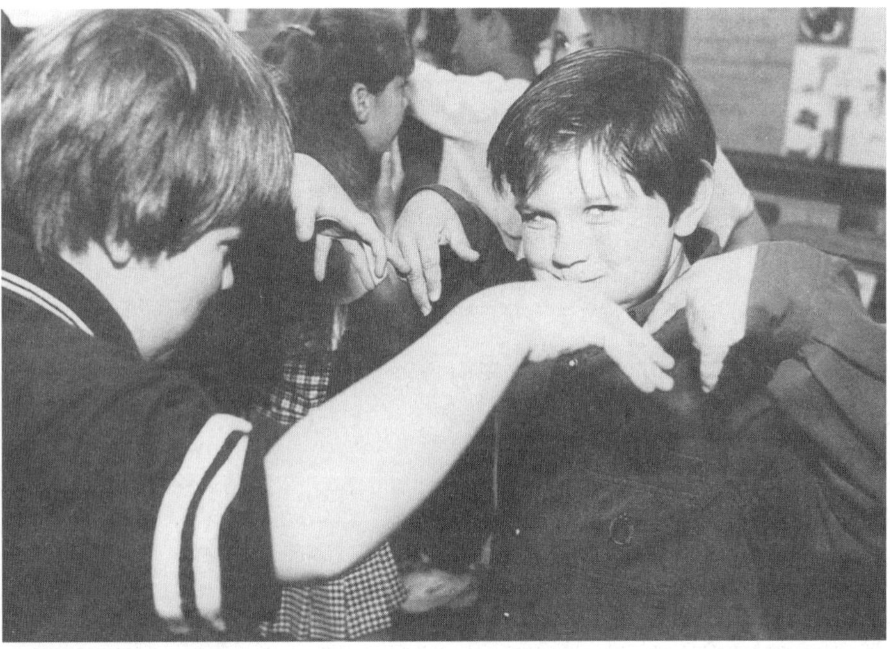

Pantomime Pairs.

spice to this book, which can be converted to a solo narrative mime all do in unison. For chapter books or long stories, isolate one event to mime. For example, do a chapter in *Junie B. Jones and the Stupid Smelly Bus* (Park, 1992) and convert it to "you" while reading, rather than use the first person.

Narrative mimes can be written by the teacher or students. Good stories have a beginning, middle, end structure and conflict or tension that increases interest. Just as with literature selection, beware of too much description and literary devices like flashback. Be sure to keep events in order because it is difficult to mime a nonsequential narrative like *"You wake up. You get up and brush your teeth. First you turn on the water and then you put paste on your toothbrush."* Use the BEST (body, energy, space, time) dance elements in Chapter 9 to put variety into the actions of a story.

When introducing a story for narrative mime, read the story through first, asking students to listen for actions, as well as to enjoy the story. During the mime, the reader needs to read expressively and give the class time to mime. If time is short, students can mime a story they haven't heard, but make sure to anticipate problems.

Props, costumes, and scenery are not necessary, which is an advantage for teachers concerned about time. Imagination can supply all that is needed, along with music, if students are excited about developing the mimes further. In addition, teachers and students can make creative additions of characters or actions for group narrative mimes through imagining others who might enter the story. There is an example of a narrative mime written by a teacher in the lesson plan in Post It Page 7–7. Components of habitat were taught in a previous lesson.

Group Stories. Wallace's *Chin Chiang and the Dragon's Dance, Strega Nona* (dePaola, 1989), *Clown of God* (dePaola, 1986), and *Lentil* (McCloskey, 1978) are examples of children's literature with crowd or group scenes. These stories can be used for narrative mime and for easing students into dialogue by freezing scenes and asking members to give a one-liner about who they are or what they are feeling at the moment. From there students can move into writing dialogue for groups.

III. Verbal Strategies

Improvisation involves creating ideas spontaneously by "thinking on your feet." It can be done using mime or, as discussed in this section, using words. Verbal improvisation can be used to review any lesson, to make predictions at a stop point in a lesson, and to encourage in-depth analysis of material. The following strategies are organized from easy to more difficult.

Sound Effects Stories. Students can add simple sound effects with their voices or music (e.g., rhythm instruments) as the teacher reads or tells a story such as Baylor's *The Way to Start a Day, Too Much Noise* (McGovern, 1966), or *Night Noises* (Fox, 1989). Read the story once and ask students what sounds they heard. Plan how and who will make the sounds. Specific groups can be responsible for certain parts with the whole group involved at other points. *Suggestion:* Use an imaginary volume-control knob and practise controlling loudness before doing the story.

Sound Stories (Henig, 1993). Find or write a story or poem that contains repeated words (e.g. character names). Each time the repeated word is read aloud, students do actions or sounds. To prepare for the reading, have students practise the sounds or actions that go with each cue word. For example, Jack = "oops" and sad face, Jill = giggle and play with curl. Many stories and poems are set up to use sounds, e.g., "Laughing Time" in William Jay's book by the same title, has animal names to elicit a variety of laughs like hee-hee, ho-ho, hee-haw. McGovern's book, *Too Much Noise,* and Murphy's *Peace at Last* are other good ones. *Variation*: Select stories with refrains or repeated lines that students can contribute (e.g., Viorst's *Alexander and the Terrible, Horrible, No Good, Very Bad Day,* Gilman's *Something from Nothing,* Barclay's How *Cold Was It?* and Munsch's *Mortimer*. There is an example sound story in Post It Page 8–2.

Volume Control. Group brainstorm sound categories (e.g., short vowels, city sounds, kitchen sounds). IT stands in front and calls a sound category for the group to make, and can "turn up" the volume by moving closer or "turn it down" by backing up. *Closer* can be designated as the area "downstage." As students back up, the sound decreases as they move "upstage." This can be done in pairs.

Don't Laugh at the Cop. Form groups of six. One is the cop, who points at someone and asks a question. Person *to the right of person questioned* must answer. Everyone tries not to laugh. Go fast. *Variation*: Use stage directions. The child standing *"stage right"* or *"stage left"* of the person indicated must answer the question.

Post It Page • 8-2

Sound Story Example

"Stolen Tarts"

Directions: Rehearse the sounds and actions the audience is to contribute before beginning. Pause after underlined words to give students time to respond.

Heart = thump thump on chest with fist

Queen = "Oh me!" and throw up hands

King = "Find him!" and point finger

Knave = "Tee hee!" while smiling and shaking head

Tarts = "Yum" and rub tummy

Long ago in the Land of Hearts there was a terrible theft. It was on St. Valentine's Day that the Queen of Hearts baked some tarts to celebrate their national holiday. She had baked raspberry, lemon, and custard tarts as a gift for the man to whom she had given her heart—the King of Hearts. The Queen placed her tarts on the window sill to cool. While the Queen straightened up the royal kitchen, the Knave of Hearts sneaked up to the window. The Knave grabbed all the raspberry tarts. When the Queen saw the tarts were gone, she cried, "What heartless fellow has taken my tarts?"

The Queen of Hearts went to the King of Hearts for help. Quickly he dispatched his soldiers to find the thief and the missing tarts, saying, "Find him!"

It wasn't anytime before the soldiers returned with the Knave and what was left of the raspberry tarts. The King ordered that the Knave have no tarts to eat for a whole year. The Knave of Hearts knelt before the Queen, asked for forgiveness, and crossed his heart in promise he would never steal her tarts again. It was a heartwarming ending.

Pair Sound Effects. Partners choose to be A or B. A makes sounds and B must try to coordinate actions with A's sounds. *Variation:* A's sounds could be coordinated with B's actions.

One Liners (with props and pictures). Students use their voices (volume, rate, tone, pitch, pause, stress, and emphasis) to become a character and respond to a picture or object. If a picture is used, students may choose to become characters or objects in it. If an object is used, students choose to be a person who would use the object. Each student says a related one-liner. Others guess their identity and tell how the actor let the audience know who she or he was. For example, pass around a red cape after reading *Little Red Riding Hood* and each uses the cape and says a line to reveal who she or he is. *Variation:* Conflicting messages: say a one liner differently from what the words seem to convey (e.g., "I am happy" said with great sadness). *Note:* Collect interesting pictures and unusual props for one liners. See Chapter 4 for art integration for picture file categories.

Say It Your Way Sentences. Students say a sentence as a character, in a role or in a mood. Others try to guess their identity. Students can be given roles by drawing from a set of prepared character cards and should rehearse reading the sentence many ways (e.g., in a role, or a mood, angry, sad). Different words can be emphasized to change meanings: *Who* is my friend? Who *is* my friend? Who is *my* friend? Who is my *friend?* Here are examples sentences:

I don't like his attitude.
I will pay the bill if you take a cheque.
We had a good time at the party.
Can I have another helping of dessert?
Everyone just left.
How much money have you got?
She has an awful headache.
We only have five left.
Remember to check each answer.
He's one person I won't do business with.
Where do you think you are going?
Who did you meet?
Where are you going?
Close the door.

Conflicting Motives. Ask for two volunteers. One leaves the room and the remaining one is given a motive (e.g., to have partner sit down). Other partner is secretly told a conflicting motive (e.g., to not sit down but to get partner to do so). Both partners are brought back and they improvise a scene. Neither partner can verbally give away his or her motive. *Suggestion:* Brainstorm a list of possible motives (e.g., to sell, heal, forgive, eat, make money to give, get, or win, grow, surprise).

Dialogue Cards. Collect words, phrases, sentences, and headlines from magazines, newspapers, or even greeting cards. Ads are a good source. Paste each on a card. Give each student a card face down. Pair students and tell them to choose to be A or B. Turn over cards and A begins the dialogue using his card. B must respond and incorporate his or her card. *Variations:* Do a chain activity. Everyone lines up and (1) just reads card expressively or (2) goes in order but improvises verbal response that connects to previous person by using what is on your card. Variation 2: Separate question and answer cards (make sure there is an equal number of each). Distribute randomly. Number questioners, who then read in numerical order. Whoever believes they can answer using their card has a go at it.

Emotion Conversation. Two people or characters start a conversation. Add freeze point and have audience tell the emotions of the characters. Then continue the conversation. One character may be given the emotion and the other respond as they choose. Or, each character (A, B) may be given contrasting emotions to play in the same situation (i.e., child is remorseful for losing mittens; parent is angry). *Variation:* Freeze, and audience suggests a new emotion that characters must assume when they start again (e.g., angry, surprised, elated).

Character Monologues. A dramatic monologue is a sustained speech made by one character to a silent audience of one or more characters. The speech reveals the thoughts and emotions of characters and usually occurs at a significant moment when a character must make a decision, or realizes something about his/her circumstances. Students assume a character and make an announcement, a wish, etc. See Post It Page 4–2.

Car Wash. Also known as "corridor of voices." Make two facing lines. Two end people walk between the lines. As they pass, people say positive things to them. Then the next two go, and so on. *Variation:* Everyone prepares a one-liner about a topic or in a role and shares in the same manner. For example, everyone thinks of good things about the dog in *Officer Buckles and Gloria.* Stop at the point where Officer Buckles feels like a fool. Walkers become Officer Buckles and pass through the car wash hearing the "voices" about his friend.

Television Shows. Adapt past and current game and talk shows for classroom use: *"I've Got a Secret," "Jeopardy," "Wheel of Fortune," "Concentration," "Password," "Oprah," "Phil Donahue."* The show adaptations work best after a unit of study (e.g., the Oprah format on endangered species).

Discussions. A discussion becomes a dramatic encounter when students take on roles during the discussion (e.g., characters, famous persons, objects). Students can also brainstorm in the role. See Chapter 1 for guidelines.

Empathy Roles. Each student takes the role of a character in a story or book everyone knows. The teacher begins a discussion or interview with an open question concerning a key moment, problem, or question about a theme. It works best if the discussion is focused on an important question (e.g., moral dilemma). Each child enters the discussion in character and remains in character throughout the discussion. If some don't participate, the teacher can specifically call on them for their ideas.

Journalling in Role. Students write who they are, what they want, and how they act and feel. Situations or topics may be given (e.g., "arriving in Montreal," "storm on the Atlantic while you are travelling to Canada," "making candles"). These writing tasks help prepare students for crafting character both on the page and on the stage.

The Chair. This is an improvisation in which a volunteer sits in a chair. Another volunteer assumes a role and begins a conversation with the person in the chair. The seated person must figure out who the other character is and respond accordingly. For example, volunteer is a mother and the one in chair must figure out that she is the daughter. This is easily adaptable for literature, social studies, and science.

Back to Back Improvisation. Pairs each decide on who they are (take the role of a book character, an occupation, or family role). On signal, they face each other and the first to talk sets the situation. The second person must figure out who his partner is and respond in an appropriate role.

Traffic Jam. Students are in small groups. The place is a traffic jam in which all movement has stopped. They are to think about who they are, what problems they are having, and how they feel. Each person can then be spotlighted to do a monologue or one-liner that will reveal their characters. *Variation:* Do the same with waiting in a grocery store line or any public waiting place. Students can be book characters, persons from paintings, scientists, historical figures, and so on.

Interviews. Teacher assumes the role of interviewer and students take a character role. Students are questioned, in talk show style, and use voice and body to convey who they are. This can be done in pairs with one being the interviewer. For example, the teacher is a radio talk show host interviewing (1) characters in *Charlotte's Web* right after the first word appears in the web, or (2) Harry Potter after his first broom ride. If a panel is used, they can be questioned by the class, who can also be in a role (e.g., mother mouse, news reporter). *Note:* It's a good idea for interviewers to introduce themselves (e.g., *"I am . . . and I want to know. . ."*). The teacher can coach students or play a role. *Variations:* Audience can interview tableau members. Touch each with a magic wand to come alive to speak. (See tableau mime strategy.) Use microphone prop.

Show Time. This is a review drama for after a unit of study. Groups write and present commercials, news updates, songs, and so on, to present important information from a unit. Limit time to three to five minutes. For example:

> ***Newsbreak.*** *We interrupt this program to let you know that animals have now been found to have four components in their habitats. Without water, shelter, food, and adequate space, animals cannot survive. We learned today that habitats are shrinking and our world may soon lose valued animal populations. More on this breaking story on* The National.
>
> ***Commercial Break.*** *High cholesterol? Stressed? Negative attitude? Lethargic? You need the Laughter Prescription! With only fifteen laughs a day you can get your minimum daily requirement and be on the road to an energetic happy life. No more insurmountable problems when you learn to laugh your way through life. Call 1-800-JOKE.* Variation: An item can be advertised (e.g., cotton gin for social studies or a graphing calculator in math). Remind students to include important points and not empty glitz. This provides a good opportunity to teach propaganda devices: bandwagon, glittering generalities, etc.

Have students time words and "budget" the text. For example "Snowed in at Pokeweed Public School" takes up 12 seconds to say three times in a 60-second commercial slot, leaving only 48 seconds for the message.

Book Ads. Individuals, pairs, or small groups set up a scene with a problem from a book they are advertising to the class. The scene is to end before the problem is solved. It is fun to end each commercial with *"If you want to know what happened, you have to get this book." Variations:* Students can create book commercials with music, slogans, props, and the like, to sell books. Limit time to one minute—TV time is expensive!

Debate. Divide class in half and assign each a side in an argument. Give time to plan. At signal, begin debate with a person from each side giving a reason. Alternate back and forth until all reasons have been heard. Rebuttal time can then be given to each side. Teacher can (1) moderate and assume a role (e.g., become a policeman who was called to the scene of the crime in *Little Red Riding Hood*) and (2) comment, question each side, and open it up for audience questions. This drama strategy can be done in pairs, too. For example, one side says Little Red should be taken away from her parents because of negligence, and then the other side takes the opposing position. *Variation:* Do as expert panels (e.g., experts on wolf behaviour).

Improvised Scenes. Begin by giving students short scenes to play. Tell students to plan a beginning, middle, and end and signals to start and stop the scene. Emphasize the need to build in tension or conflict through a problem that is resolved by the end. Examples are (1) stepsisters and stepmother in the coach, going to the ball on the second night, worried about mysterious girl who seems to have charmed the prince; (2) animals who saw the transformations of other animals are talking after Cinderella leaves for the ball. They want to get transformed, too. Eventually, students should begin to think of their own creative scenes. Direct them to focus on the most important moments or emotions in the story. In the case of science or social studies, consider significant events (e.g., when Philo Farnsworth gets the first television picture).

Sources for improvised scenes include children's literature, wordless picture books, and famous last words; use ideas like events, processes, and procedures from science, social studies, and math. Focus on "let's suppose" and "what if" (e.g., switch characters, settings, or circumstances of any story or historical event). Create separate card sets for settings, characters, problems, and props for an infinite number of combinations or *characters, problems,* and *place cards.* For example:

1. Flying frogs. Hungry and lost. In the CN Tower.
2. Hurried shoppers. Grocery. A robbery happens.
3. Family on vacation. West Edmonton Mall. Stuck in elevator.
4. Hungry mosquitoes. On the afternoon when the Fathers of Confederation meet.
5. Five young children. On the porch on a hot summer day. Dad brings out two double popsicles.

Start with discussion questions to develop characters, the setting, plan of action concerning the problem or conflict, and resolution. In other words, students need to be clear about who, where, what problems, what to do or actions, solutions, and resolutions. Eventually, students should be able to discuss in small groups.

Structure scenes with a beginning, middle, and end. Remember, conflict is essential, as is resolution. Make students feel the importance and the tension by giving time limits or telling them to have their characters persuade, argue, obstruct, bargain, and so on. What the characters *want* needs to be emphasized. Use signals to add clear structure (e.g., to begin and end the scene) and music to create mood. Remind students of types of conflict. While drama externalizes conflict, representation and resolution do not need to be physical or violent. Encourage students to create dramas that are physically and psychologically safe for all participants.

Coach during drama. See coaching ideas under **Teacher Habits.**

Follow up with a discussion and replay with a twist (e.g., teacher may take a role or students may be engaged in a writing response such as a five-minute Quickwrite).

Role Play. Role playing involves considering a situation from the viewpoint of another. Because of the added perspective that role playing provides, it can greatly enhance understanding of any subject. In general, teachers use role playing to put students in problem situations so that feelings, values, and viewpoints can be explored. A particular kind of role playing, called sociodrama, focuses on real-world problems of the present and future.

To create a role play:

- Choose problems or topics students know something about
- Define the specific situation that requires the characters to take some action (e.g., factory owner whose factory is polluting a river and a government agent who must enforce the regulations about river pollution are brought together at city council)
- Give the audience a role (e.g., they can become questioners at a break point or evaluators of the different positions taken)
- Plan an introduction to set up the scene
- Play several times with different groups to get a variety of versions
- Discuss the drama aspects, as well as the content of the scenes

IV. Connecting Drama to Other Curricular Areas

In this section there are examples of mime and verbal activities that have been further adapted to show how drama can be used as a teaching tool to enhance academic learning.

Science Focus

- Natural world, systems of the body, seasons, weather, plants, animals, the environment, machines, electricity, magnets, space, gravity, and states of matter
- Finding out how and why things happen in the world through careful observation, hypothesis making, and prediction

Project Wild. *Project Wild* has hands-on, activity-oriented lesson plans for science. In addition to drama, there are music, art, and literature and creative writing

Post It Page • 8-3

Improvised Scene Source Material

Create a resource idea bank for scenes.

Characters: lizard, baker, potter, wise woman, fortune teller, grocer

Places: island, beach, cave, treehouse, barn, boarding house, jungle, elevator, hay wagon

Character conflict ideas: argue, convince, persuade, defend, plot, debate, tease, deny, confess, accuse, beg, forgive, gossip, lie, disagree, demand, complain

Rituals: graduation, inauguration, parade, eulogy, pledge, dinner, award, recognition, wedding, ship christening, ribbon-cutting dedication, nomination, greetings, farewells

Actions: eat, clean, drink, work, bathe, run, cook, swim, dance, drive, throw

Conditions or problems: illness, dark, nervous, hot, cold, embarrassed, odour, anger, stress, excited, hate, pressured, hungry, tired, wet, lost, lonely, noisy, sunburned

activities related to science. *Project Wild* in Canada is sponsored by the Canadian Wildlife Federation, 2740 Queensview Drive, Ottawa, Ontario, K2B 1A2. Tel: 613-721-2286.

Animal Sounds. IT makes the sound of an animal and the group must make shapes and moves related to the animal. *Variation:* IT makes sounds from everyday world (e.g., clock ticking or phone ringing) and group must become the sound.

Nature One Liners. Use pictures of natural forms: mountain, tree, stream. Each student says a sentence, in role as the object, to show specific known facts. For example, for tree: *"My branches hurt under the weight of ice," "My fingers touch the first snowflakes of winter,"* and *"My summer wardrobe was green and in autumn I wore gold and rust and red and now it is November and I stand naked in the cold."*

Whales Debate. Divide students into two teams to research a side to an environmental issue. For example, *"Should whales be hunted?"* Each side presents an opening statement and then gives pros or cons in a time limit. After each side presents, give time for rebuttal and a summary statement.

Famous Science Scenes. Break into groups to do tableaux (frozen scenes) of special moments in science, like Alexander G. Bell's first telephone call, the Wright's flight at Kitty Hawk, or Armstrong's stepping on the moon.

Animal Charades. Students brainstorm (after or before a unit) ways to classify animals (wild, domesticated, herbivores, carnivores, insects, mammals, aquatic, land based). Small groups list animals in each category. (Record on a large chart for younger children.) Each student then picks an animal to mime. Coach to think of how the animal sleeps, moves, eats, where it lives. Set up mimes to be presented in this order: start frozen, move, and then freeze. Teams write animal or category guess on a wipe-off board and display on a signal. The mime confirms correct guesses. Emphasize science content by asking *why* the animal belongs in a category. To emphasize the drama aspect, ask students to give feedback on what the mime did to make them believe in the animal. *Variation:* Limit categories to two for less mature learners. Do with other categories in science: land forms, states of water. Mimes can be planned and presented in small groups, too.

Special Props. Challenge students to use simple props to really feel as animals do. For example, try to actually eat rice with your mouth as birds do or try to drink like a cat or dog from a tub of water. What could students use to get the feel of snakes shedding their skins or birds in a nest?

Social Studies Focus

- Relationships among human beings, occupations, transportation, communities, governments, customs, cultures, holidays, and use of natural resources
- History, geography (use of maps), civics (citizenship and government) or political science, economics, anthropology, and sociology
- Investigations into cultural diversity and global understanding
- Special questions: How did it used to be and why? Why is it like it is today? What can I do about it? Thinking processes: cause and effect, sequence, gather data, discover relationships, make judgments, draw conclusions, and problem-solve about community issues, e.g., economic issues like school funding or value conflicts related to free speech
- Use of primary source material like newspapers, art, music, diaries, letters, journals, books, and artifacts, rather than use of textbooks, and gathering data through interviews, surveys, and other investigatory strategies that historians and other social scientists use

Moral Dilemmas (use with historical fiction or biography). Everyone stops reading at a point where a character has to make a decision. Groups talk about the dilemma and use the information from the story to make decisions in the role of the character. Groups reassemble to tell or dramatize what was decided. *Note:* The dilemma should *not* have a clear right answer so that students are forced to take a stand. For example, Lunn's *The Hollow Tree* has many points where a stop would be appropriate.

Stop when the problem has been found in the story. Then:

1. Figure out the problem:
   - What is it?
   - Who has the problem?
   - What are the general circumstances of the problem?
   - What is the goal for solving the problem?
2. Brainstorm problem solutions:
   - What possibilities are there that would be legal and safe for all?
   - What is the best solution (considering cost, safety, length of time, legal, moral, and practical issues)?
3. Try out the solution:
   - Role play . . . did the problem get solved?
   - What does this say to you for the future?
4. Read the rest of the story and compare your solution with the one in the book (based on the work of Lawrence Kohlberg and adapted from Johnson & Louis, 1987).

Portrait Conversations. Pair students and have them create a conversation between two portraits of famous historical figures that might hang side by side in a gallery. Look closely to examine the works for clues about time period, values, cultural aspects, message, and the like, that would give ideas for dialogue. These can be written or oral.

What's My Line? Based on the television show from the 1950s, this game focuses on finding out the occupations or careers of panel members. Panel members can all be the same occupation or have the same role. The audience can only ask yes or no questions and is given a time limit or a limit to number of questions (e.g., five minutes or twenty questions). The teacher acts as moderator and allows audience members to take turns questioning. To deal with monopolizers, use the rule that if the panel answers *no* someone else takes a turn to question.

Reading and Language Arts Focus

- Reading, listening, speaking, written composition (including handwriting and spelling, grammar, usage, capitalization, and punctuation); since reading and language arts are processes, they must be connected to a subject to have meaning, i.e., something to read and write about
- Goal: *Create* meaning and enjoyment using print through thinking at every level, from memory to critical thinking or evaluation.
- The printed word and its components (letters, syllables, spelling, patterns), how words combine to make phrases and sentences and sentences combine to make paragraphs and other forms of discourse, from tongue twisters to novels
- Types of words: antonyms and synonyms, parts of speech and figurative language (metaphor, idiomatic expressions)

Most drama involves the language arts of listening, speaking, reading, or writing, and nearly all mime and verbal strategies can be adapted for language-based lessons.

Pretend and Write: Journals. Students assume the role of a character and keep a daily journal. The point is not to write about what really happened in the character's life, but about what could have happened, as well as about feelings. In the case of historical fiction or biography, students can extend the journal's authenticity by doing research on characters. *Variation:* For chapter books, students make entries after each chapter to document how a character's thoughts and emotions change through experiences. Students can pair up and read each other's journals to get different perspectives.

Pretend and Write: Letters. This strategy focuses on using conventional letter-writing form, the writing process, grammar, and spelling. Students take a role of a character and write a friendly or business letter and choose to write to another character or real person, so the contents and purposes vary.

Point of View Roles. Students are given a role of a character in a story. They then read the story and answer questions in the role in writing or orally, for example, *Mirette on the High Wire* (McCully, 1972).

Imagine that you are a touring artist staying at the rooming house. Answer these questions (before the high wire act at the end):

1. What have you noticed about the man? How does he make you feel?
2. What do you think about his friendship with Mirette?
3. Why do you think he stays to himself so much?

Reader's Theatre. Reader's Theatre is "theatre of the mind" and is like a radio play. Readers sit or stand while doing oral interpretive reading from a script and try to create the illusion of dramatic action in the minds of the audience. The focus is on using the voice; props are usually not employed. Reader's Theatre is particularly suitable for intermediate students, but can be adapted for younger children by choosing shorter scripts and reading to them as they follow along on the first go-through. Poems can also be used. For example, see Wolf's *It's Show Time! Poetry from the Page to the Stage* (poem scripts).

Reader's Theatre is an appropriate use of oral reading because it is audience oriented and students practise for the presentation, versus cold, round-robin reading, which is deemed detrimental to children. Other values of Reader's Theatre are that (1) it integrates listening, speaking, and reading and can include writing by involving students in creating their own scripts. They can begin by adapting pieces of literature and move on to writing original pieces. Biographical information like letters, diaries, or speeches can also be adapted to script form; (2) because of the ensemble or group project nature of Reader's Theatre, cooperation and other social skills are developed; (3) when readers assume roles of characters they have a chance to empathize and identify with a variety of feelings and viewpoints, which can yield valuable insights about people and the world; (4) self-confidence is increased as students share exciting stories with the support of a script—no lines are memorized. *To use Reader's Theatre:*

- ***Find or create scripts*** appropriate to students' interests and abilities. Several companies publish scripts, and basal readers often contain stories converted to script form. See the bibliography. The Institute for Readers Theatre in California also has a script service. See the bookstore list of more than forty titles at this web site: www.amazon.com (everything from holiday scripts to fractured folk tale scripts).
- ***The script can be read to students*** for the first reading, read silently by students, or orally read by students in small groups.
- ***Groups are formed*** according to the characters outlined in the scripts. Groups can prepare different scripts or perform the same script and then discuss their different interpretations.
- ***Students need time to rehearse their parts.*** Emphasize the need to use volume, rate, tone, pitch, pause, stress, and emphasis to convey meaning. Students can highlight their parts and mark words to stress. Nonverbal communication with the face, some gestures, and even body posture can be added—the focus still remains on oral interpretation, however.
- ***When students do their presentations,*** they need to have their scripts in folders or binders so that they can hold them without distracting the audience with page turning. Students may sit on high stools or stand. By using stools of varying heights, character relationships can be suggested.
- ***When setting up the staging,*** it can be effective to have readers start with their backs to the audience and then turn around as each part is introduced. Characters with major roles might stand to the far left and right, if they don't need to interact with one another. Characters with similar ideas might be grouped together. With younger students it may help the audience to use hatbands or name tags on the characters. Lights can be used to signal scenes.

- *The point of Reader's Theatre is not to create a "spectacle,"* but students may shift position on stage (e.g., to indicate joining a group). Readers may stand when they speak and then sit, or spotlights might be used. Props should be used, only if essential, because it is awkward to handle a script and a prop. Sound effects and music can also be added. Be open to students' creative ideas.
- ***It is desirable for the narrator to make eye contact with the audience.*** Other characters may look up when not reading or when they can during reading.
- ***Make sure the audience is aware of its important role*** in being active listeners. Review appropriate audience responses before the presentations. After the presentations, invite readers and audience members to discuss what worked, what they learned, what they noticed about the use of voice to establish character, what the most important parts were, etc.
- ***Follow up presentations*** with invitations for students to write different script endings, trade scripts with other groups, videotape or even perform for other groups (e.g., a touring troupe to visit other classes) (Georges and Cornett, 1986).

There is an example Reader's Theatre script, converted from an old tale, in Post It Page 8–4.

Antonym Pantomimes. Make a set of cards with two antonyms on each card. A student draws a card and mimes one word. The audience must guess the opposite. This can be done in small groups with a set of cards for each group. *Suggestion:* Instead of students calling out guesses, all should wait until the mime is done, write out a guess, and, on signal, hold it up. *Variation:* Do with synonyms, homonyms, and homophones.

Daffynitions. Teams of four to five students find or are given unusual vocabulary. Each team member writes a definition for the word, but only *one* member writes the correct definition. (Students can use the dictionary.) Each team stands and orally reads their definitions, trying to convince the audience that each of them has the correct one. Audience applauds to vote on which they believe is correct. *Variation:* Use objects instead of words.

Rhyme Change. Nursery rhymes and other chants and poems are adaptable to word play activities that serve as verbal warm-ups and stimulate creative thinking. Here is an example: "Hickory Dickory Dock, A mouse ran up my . . ." (students supply rhyme). You can do all the vowel sounds for phonemic awareness development: Hickory Dickory Dack, Hickory Dickory Deck, and so on.

Math Focus

- Daily living situations involving counting, measuring, probability, statistics, geometry, logic, patterns, functions, and numbers
- Problem-solving through the use of skills (raising questions and answering them, finding relationships and patterns)
- Concepts about numbers, operations, and concepts like bigger, longer, greater than, less, three, four, even, and odd
- The National Council of the Teachers of Mathematics (Canada and USA) and the Provincial Math Educators Associations encourage teachers to have children solve problems in many ways, focusing on explaining and thinking, rather than just correctness, and using a hands-on approach

Fraction Mime. After introducing fractions, use an open space to have the whole group practise dividing themselves up to solve problems that are given: divide in half, fourths, thirds. When numbers are uneven, ask how this can be shown.

Infinity. Students create dramatic presentations about mathematical concepts: infinity, symmetry, Fibonacci series, the Golden Mean.

Math Commercials. Students prepare ads to sell particular math concepts and skills: fractions, time, division. The goal is to convince the audience they need this math item.

Math Improvisation. Make a set of cards with math-related situations. Give each group three cards. They plan a scene using ideas on all three cards. Scenes should have a beginning, middle, and end. Example cards are (1) three men, (2) a quart of milk, and (3) a ten-story building on fire.

V. Storytelling's Special Relationship with Drama

You are the vessel for the tale.

Heather Forrest, storyteller

There once was a rabbi who was a gifted storyteller. Everyone who heard his stories felt the rabbi gave the story just to him. So special were the stories one man

Post It Page • 8-4

Example Reader's Theater Script*

Cast: Narrator, Girl, Old Man

Narrator: A girl once went to the fair to hire herself out as a servant. A funny-looking old gentleman finally agreed to engage her and took her home to his house. When she got there, he said he had some things to teach her, for in his house he had his own names for things.

Old Man: What will you call me?

Girl: Why master, or mister, or whatever else you please, sir.

Old Man: No, you must call me "master of all masters." And what would you call this?

Narrator: The old man pointed to his bed.

Girl: Why bed or couch, or whatever you please, sir.

Old Man: No, that's my "barnacle." And what do you call those?

Narrator: He pointed to his pantaloons.

Girl: By breeches, or trousers, or whatever else you please, sir.

Old Man: No, you must call them "squibs and crackers." And what do you call her?

Narrator: The old man pointed at his cat.

Girl: Cat or kit, or whatever you please, sir.

Old Man: No, you must call her "white-faced simminy." And now this, what would you call this?

Girl: Fire or flame, or whatever you please, sir.

Old Man: No, no. You must call it "hot cockalorum." And what is this?

Narrator: He went on, pointing to the water.

Girl: Water or wet, or whatever you please, sir.

Old Man: No, "pondalorum" is its name. And what do you call this?

Narrator: Asked the man as he pointed to his house.

Girl: House or cottage, or whatever you please, sir.

Old Man: You must call it "high topper mountain."

Narrator: That very night the servant girl woke her master up in a fright.

Girl: Master of all masters, get out of your barnacle and put on your squibs and crackers. For white-faced simminy has got a spark of hot cockalorum on her tail, and unless you get some pondalorum, high topper mountain will be all on hot cockalorum!

*Adapted from the English folk tale "Master of All Masters."

finally asked the rabbi, "How is it we all hear the same story but you touch each of our individual hearts?"

In response, the rabbi told a story of a girl who shot arrows. Wherever an arrow stuck, she pulled it out and painted a bright bull's eye around it. "It is you that paints the target around these stories," the rabbi said, "inviting them into your heart." (story told by Rives Collins at Jackson Storyfest, Jackson, MI, 1994)

The first written accounts of storytelling are thousands of years old. The sons of the Great Pyramid builder, Cheops, told stories to him that were preserved on papyri. This 4000-year-old collection, *Tales of the Magicians,* can be checked out of the local library. Storyteller Rives Collins believes human beings are the "storytelling animals" and that storytelling is a natural and common human activity. Across cultures, people love to tell and listen to stories. The griots of Africa tell stories, as do the Irish shanachies and the Navajo shaman. The bards of medieval Europe, norse skalds, German minnesingers, and French troubadours, all are storytellers who preserve our history and educate, enlighten, and enliven our lives. We tell stories to ourselves and each other. *"How was your day?" "What did you do at school?" "What do you think will happen?"* We tell stories to prepare and reassure ourselves. We invent fantasy stories to amuse others, to make sense of the world, and to build relationships.

Drama and storytelling share many of the same characteristics. Perhaps, most importantly, they both rely on conflict to develop characters and plot and reveal themes. To be a storyteller is to take on a role, to use your voice, face, and body to communicate. In essence, storytelling is a dramatic vehicle. It was Winifred Ward's course in storytelling in the 1920s that led to the evolution of creative drama. Storytelling was at the centre of her work in which she created drama opportunities for children based on stories. "[S]torytelling [is] at the roots of drama/theatre education . . ." (Collins, 1997, p. 6).

Why Storytelling?

> *If teachers should succeed in developing the state of mind that would cause the pupils to go to the printed page as they would go to the feet of one who has a story to tell, we should be willing to ask nothing else of them as a results of all their teaching.*
>
> S. H. Clark,
> *How to Teach Reading in the Public Schools,* 1899

We put much store in the power of stories. From biblical parables, to creation myths and tall tales, stories engage us as no other words can. For example, someone commenting, "We learn from our mistakes" has a very different impact than hearing this story with a similar theme:

> A young man who wished to be wise went to a sage high on the mountain.
> "How can I become wise?" the young man asked respectfully.
> The old man looked thoughtful and replied, "Have wisdom."
> "But how do I get wisdom?" asked the young man.
> "Develop good judgment," the sage answered.
> "But how can I get good judgment?" the young man cried .
> "Experience," said the sage wisely.
> "And how do I get experience?" said the young man in frustration.
> "Bad judgment," said the sage.

Storytelling:

- Brings us together. It introduces listeners to an array of cultures, including relevant symbols and traditions.
- Exposes listeners to fine literature. Many tales are too difficult for children to read independently, but are appropriate for their interest and cognitive levels.
- Whets the appetite for further literary experiences because it creates an interest in reading and writing.
- Gives listeners characters with whom they can identify.
- Creates a special bond between listeners and tellers. Reading aloud and storytelling are very different experiences mainly because storytelling seems much more intimate.
- Develops listening and speaking vocabularies by sensitizing children to language from diverse sources.
- Improves listening comprehension, which is the foundation for reading comprehension.
- Stimulates interest in creative writing and other creative activities.
- Helps the listener learn in a way that doesn't feel like a "taught" lesson. Everyone loves to learn, but we resist didactic teaching.
- Helps the listener to better understand life, to try to make sense of conflict and see that there are patterns, e.g., the relationship between good and evil.
- Provides information, opinions, new perspectives, and knowledge.
- Increases oral communication skills, especially when listeners become tellers.
- Is a holistic activity involving both thinking and feeling.
- Encourages higher-order thinking skills like prediction, analysis, synthesis, and evaluation.
- Stimulates creative problem-solving and decision making.

- Stimulates the use of the imagination and imagery.
- Is powerful entertainment.

Where can you get good stories to tell? There are plenty available, and there are even stories about stories, like this African Anansi tale: "After playing many tricks on them, the trickster, Anansi, got the box of stories from the sky people. He threw open the lid and the stories flew out. Some of them he grabbed and put in his pocket. The others flew to the four corners of the earth."

See the Post It Pages on *Pointers for Storytellers* and an *Example Story Plot Skeleton* (Post It Pages 8–5 and 8–6) to help find stories, learn to tell them, and involve students in storytelling.

Opening Rituals. Collect and create opening rituals from stories. For example:

Call and response: (T = teller and A = audience)

T = Knock knock.
A = Who's there?
T = A story.
A = A story who?
T = A story for you.

African ritual:

T = A story. A story.
A = Let it come, let it go.

From the Sudan:

T = This story is the truth.
A = Right.
T = This story is a lie.
A = Right.
T = This story is both truth and lie.
A = Right.

Candle lighting: "By the flame of the story candle we are freed to travel in our minds to other time and places."

Beginnings: A long time ago back before yesterday and use-to-bes.

Adding Audience Participation. Storytelling is always participatory, as the audience is part of the cocreation of the story through their imaginations. Audience involvement can be extended with some of the following:

- Stop and ask the audience for ideas, e.g., "What kind of fabric might the tailor use?"
- Increase curiosity and "what if . . ." thinking using the *pause* (e.g., "Nothing I'm going to tell you is true (pause) all the time").
- Use a cloze-pause during which the audience supplies refrain, phrase, or word (e.g., and the witch sang, "Bubble bubble pasta pot, boil me some pasta nice and hot," from Tomie dePaola's *Strega Nona*). Or *"Once upon a time there were three bears who got up one morning and made some . . . ."*
- Sound effects: audience supplies these creatively or "as rehearsed" before telling.
- Add sign language to stories that audience can mimic. *Joy of Signing* (Riekehof, 1978) is a clear reference.
- Cumulative stories: ones like *This Is the House That Jack Built* that involve lists that repeat and build. The audience joins in.
- Story stops: audience is invited to simultaneously mime or improvise dialogue with a partner. For example (from *Little Red Riding Hood*), stop at point where Red first meets wolf and ask audience to show how she felt with face and body. Stop and pair a wolf and a Red and ask to have a conversation. Stop and ask audience to give Red advice about what she should do after meeting the wolf. Stop and interview the audience as if they are story characters.
- Questioning: Stop and ask the audience, "What do you know so far?" after the conflict in the story has been introduced. After the story, ask, "What images do you have in your head from the story?" (less judgmental than "What did you like best?").
- Whisper a line to one person, who passes it on until it circulates around the room. This works for special surprises (e.g., "And when he woke up on the end of his nose was a . . ." (huge piece of bologna).

Voices. Brainstorm with students all the different ways they can use their voices as they tell stories, for example, talk slowly, very fast, high pitch, scared, giggly, use regional accents, dialects. Choose a paragraph or sentence out of the newspaper or a book. Have each student read or say it aloud using three different voices.

Talk with Your Body. Practise ways to talk with your body. Ask students to show each of the following: *I'm* *tired. I'm bored. I'm afraid. Go away. It's freezing in here.* Then ask students to think of sentences and pantomime for others to guess. Do as partners to get maximum participation. *Variation:* Try to show emotions without using the face (cover with a neutral mask).

Follow the Leader. This activity encourages students to think about using their bodies to communicate. This can be done in a circle. IT is the leader who mimes going on a walk (in place) and encountering a variety of obstacles (e.g., a crack in the sidewalk, a short wall, a fence with a gate, a puddle). The rest of the class imitates all actions. Limit the obstacles to five or less, and then everyone can guess what they were and a new IT can be chosen. *Variation:* Give students a variety of actions to mime (e.g., opening, reading, and closing a book, throwing many different types of balls, peeling and eating a banana). Invite students to find actions in stories to mime.

Painting Word Pictures. This helps students to learn to use interesting details in storytelling. Sit in a circle. Give students a simple sentence. Go around the circle, with each person repeating the sentence, but with added description. For example, *The woman walked down the road. The bent old woman walked down the narrow road. The spry old woman walked frantically down the long hot road.*

Riddle Stories. Riddles are a comfortable way for students to break into storytelling because they are short. There are hundreds of joke and riddle books available on nearly every topic from computers to insects. Here's a favourite:

> *Two legs was sitting on three legs with one leg in his lap.*
> *In comes four legs and snatches one leg.*
> *Up jumps two legs and picks up three legs and throws it at four legs and gets one leg back.*
> *Note: Ask audience for guesses and then repeat more slowly so they "get it."* (Answer: 1 = chicken leg, 2 = man, 3 = stool, 4 = dog)

Food Stories. Food and stories go together. Each person or group learns a story with a food connection. Stories are told and then everyone feasts. This works well with ethnic stories and folktales.

Circle Stories. Sit in circle and use an opener, e.g., "Once upon a time. . . ." Each person adds just one word or how ever many you want. The goal is to introduce a problem and resolve it after a designated number of rounds. *Variation:* Use to review a subject under study. For example, "In science we've been studying about Mars and. . . ."

Story Challenge. Give three words, phrases, objects, or pictures that must be used (could be a circle story, partner, individual, etc.). Example phrases are a thorny rose, lightning strikes, one lost sneaker. Remind students that stories have a beginning, middle, and end and involve a problem to solve. *Variation:* Open a phone book and point to names for characters, spin a globe to find a setting, and draw from a "problem box" (collection of problems that children generate).

Jigsaw Stories. Cut up a story into parts so that each person has a section. Individuals learn parts and then the group assembles to tell the whole story. Number the sections the first time you try this.

Partner Retelling. Students pair off and tell a favourite story. Partners must remember each other's stories. At a signal, all change partners and tell the story they just heard. This is excellent for increasing listening skills. *Variation:* All students hear the same story and then partner to tell it to each other. Partner A begins and, at a signal, stops and B must pick up the story line.

Personal Story Prompts. Have students choose or draw randomly a stem to use as a starter (e.g., "The funniest thing that ever happened to me was . . ." or "The most embarrassing moment I've ever had was the time . . ." or "The most memorable person in my family . . .").

Story Responses. After a story has been told, invite students to rerun the story in their heads. They may then do an art, music, drama, dance, or creative writing response. Students can also do a partner retelling (described previously).

Round-robin Retelling. This is a kind of circle story. Students can retell picture books, fairy tales, etc., by having one person start and pass the story line on. A ball of yarn with knots about every yard can be passed and used as a cue. *Variation:* Students retell from a different point of view than original story, e.g., *Little Red Riding Hood* from Grandmother's viewpoint. Use in science or social studies to retell events.

Prop Stories. Many stories have an object that can be used as a puppet or visual aid as the story is told. Young children especially love this, and older children are more comfortable telling stories if they can use a prop to focus the audience's attention. Here are examples: the shawl in Oberman's *The Always Prayer Shawl*, the boots in Morick's *Tiger's New Cowboy Boots,* and the rock in Baylor's *Everybody Needs a Rock.*

Storytelling Sources and Resources

Western culture emphasizes happy endings, and folktales have often been sanitized to take out violence or darkness. Many scholars feel this lessens the impact of the story and denies the need to cope with the "shadow" (see, for example, Bruno Bettleheim's classic book, *The Uses of Enchantment*). It is nearly impossible to explore multiculturality without controversy (e.g., many cultures use devils and witchcraft as a part of a belief system).

Printed versions of multicultural folktales and fables can be found in the 398.2 section of the public library. Check both the children's and adult areas. Simplified versions are an excellent source from which students can explore improvisation with storytelling.

Here are some places to start to find stories to tell:

Children's literature, especially picture books

Fables (Aesop, Lobel, Thurber)

Folktales

Your own ethnic traditions

Family stories

Retellings of stories you've heard others tell

Bible stories

Historical events

Contemporary news

Stories from childhood.

Anthology examples:

Barton, B. & Booth, D. (1990). *Stories in the classroom: Storytelling, reading aloud and role-playing with children.* Pembroke.

Chase, R. (1948). *Grandfather tales.* Houghton Mifflin.

Chase, R. (1943). *The Jack tales.* Houghton Mifflin.

Gross, L., & Barnes, M. (1989). *Talk that talk: An anthology of African-American stories.* Simon and Schuster.

Hamilton, V. (1985). *The people could fly: American Black folktales.* Knopf.

Rosen, B. (1988). *And none of it was nonsense: The power of storytelling in the classroom.* Scholastic-TAB.

San souci, R. (1987). *Short and shivery: Thirty chilling tales.* Doubleday.

Schram, P. (1987). *Jewish stories one generation tells another.* Aronson.

Schwartz, A. (1984). *More scary stories to tell in the dark.* Harper & Row.

Yashinsky, D. (1994). *Next teller: A book of Canadian storytelling.* Ragweed Press.

Yolen, J. (1986). *Favorite folktales from around the world.* Pantheon.

NAPPS, the National Association for the Preservation and Perpetuation of Storytelling, Box 309, Jonesboro, Tennessee 37659 (615-753-2171), has workshops, periodicals, and a directory of storytellers.

Post It Page • 8-5

Pointers for Storytellers

Like love, knowledge and fairy dust, stories are best when shared.

Choose stories:

- You like, ones you care about and are important to you—ones you feel compelled to tell—we are the stories we tell.
- That appeal to the better part of our natures, e.g., ones about courage, love, laughter—ones that stimulate our emotions and leave the audience enriched.

- That reveal an aspect of the human condition.
- That evoke emotions.
- That fit your personality.
- That have the force of language—words that evoke images, are beautiful, and specific.
- That are fair to the cultures they came from.
- That are appropriate for the audience that will hear them. Consider your audience—age, stage, time, place, occasion, interests.
- That have a strong beginning and a satisfying ending. Try to end with a "punch."
- That are short; work up to longer ones.

Note: Plan to read ten to find one that suits you.

Know the story.

- Be prepared. Visualize each event and character in relation to the story climax. Rerun the story in your mind's eye like it is a movie.
- Learn using a whole-to-part process in which you read or listen to the whole story several times before beginning to learn the parts.
- Learn the plot first. Focus on getting a clear sequence of images and events, i.e., the story line. Don't memorize the story. Stories have a general structure that answers the questions who? what? where? why? and how? Organize events into beginning, middle, and end to help your thinking. Some tellers make a plot skeleton using a map, chart, notecards for events, or an outline. Storyteller Heather Forrest uses a series of connected circles she calls "steppingstones." Another option is to make a series of stick cartoon drawings of plot events as a rehearsal device. See Post It Page 8–6.
- Memorize your opening and your ending to give yourself a frame to work in. Also memorize any special phrases or refrains. The rest of the story should be rehearsed but not memorized. Just as we use improvisation to give directions, engage in conversation, or give excuses, storytelling relies on improvisation. This gives each telling a spontaneity.
- Practise telling the story out loud. Use a tape recorder. Listen to yourself. Tell to the mirror. Videotape. Practise telling to a friend and then to a group. A story becomes your own the more times you tell it to others.
- Try exaggerating gestures and the use of voice during practice to extend yourself. For example, open your mouth and increase volume, show the "back row" your gestures, go into great detail, count to five during a pause, say some parts very fast. Later you can tone down and select what you want to keep.
- Focus on developing the characters. Imagine what they would wear, what their hands would look like, their posture, voices. Create interesting characters with detail (verbal and nonverbal).
- Select a powerful first sentence to capture your audience.
- Select words to paint pictures and describe feelings, elaborate on details, add sound effects where appropriate.
- If you are going to use puppets or props, plan how you will keep them out of sight until they are needed.

Telling the story.

Dress appropriately for the telling. Choose a location without distractions. Sit in a circle to establish an intimate warm climate.

Introduction ideas

- Use poetry, rhymes, games, sayings, riddles, and tongue twisters to get attention.
- Empower the audience to imagine, to participate, to be together in a mind space.
- Relax the audience with a smile or humour, e.g. knock-knocks.
- Make the introduction short.
- Establish mood with your demeanour.
- Use a ritual, e.g., light a candle, close your eyes, touch fingers of both hands together as if you are holding a ball and bow your head, use an opener, e.g., a call and response like "When I say HI you say HO. HI (you) HO (audience)" or "When I say CRICK you say CRACK." (The latter is opening ritual from the West Indies.)
- Pass around an object or picture and probe with questions, e.g., what does this make you think of or feel?
- Use eye contact with audience members in different locations so that all feel you are telling to them.
- Be as physically close to your audience as possible.
- Look for opportunities to personalize the story to the people and place.
- Motivate the audience to listen, use a hook, make them eager.

Throughout

- Show enthusiasm with your voice, eyes, body, gestures, and tempo.
- Share the power with your audience by involving them; e.g., *pause* to let them image and predict, to savour a moment. "The pause is like the big space that makes the beauty in Japanese paintings" (Heather Forrest). Pause is waiting with a purpose.
- See the story in your own head so that you can make it live for your audience.
- Remember, there is elegance in simplicity. Use only what you need.
- Give the audience a sense of the place and the mood with your voice, body, and actual descriptive words.
- Give each telling a sense of the spontaneous.
- Imagine being your own audience and think about your telling from this perspective.
- Create vivid images by using language that evokes all five senses. Help the audience savour language by using words that are special for the story. Make word pictures for them. For example, when telling *"The Baker's Scent,"* storyteller Heather Forrest says, "The smell rose up like a hand and went down the street collecting noses." (Jackson, MI, "Storyfest," 1994)
- Use your voice to enrich the telling: vary volume, rate, tone and pitch, pause, stress and emphasis. Use pauses and change tempo: whisper, yell, change voices for characters.
- Articulate and enunciate clearly.
- Refrain from using fillers like "uh" and "um."
- Ignore interruptions.
- Use gestures, facial expressions, and movement to help define the characters, create the setting, and set the mood.
- Build suspense.

Conclusion: The last sentence should have a finality to it so that listeners feel satisfied and understand the tale is completed. You may want to use a closing ritual, e.g., "Snip, Snap, Snout, This tale is told out."

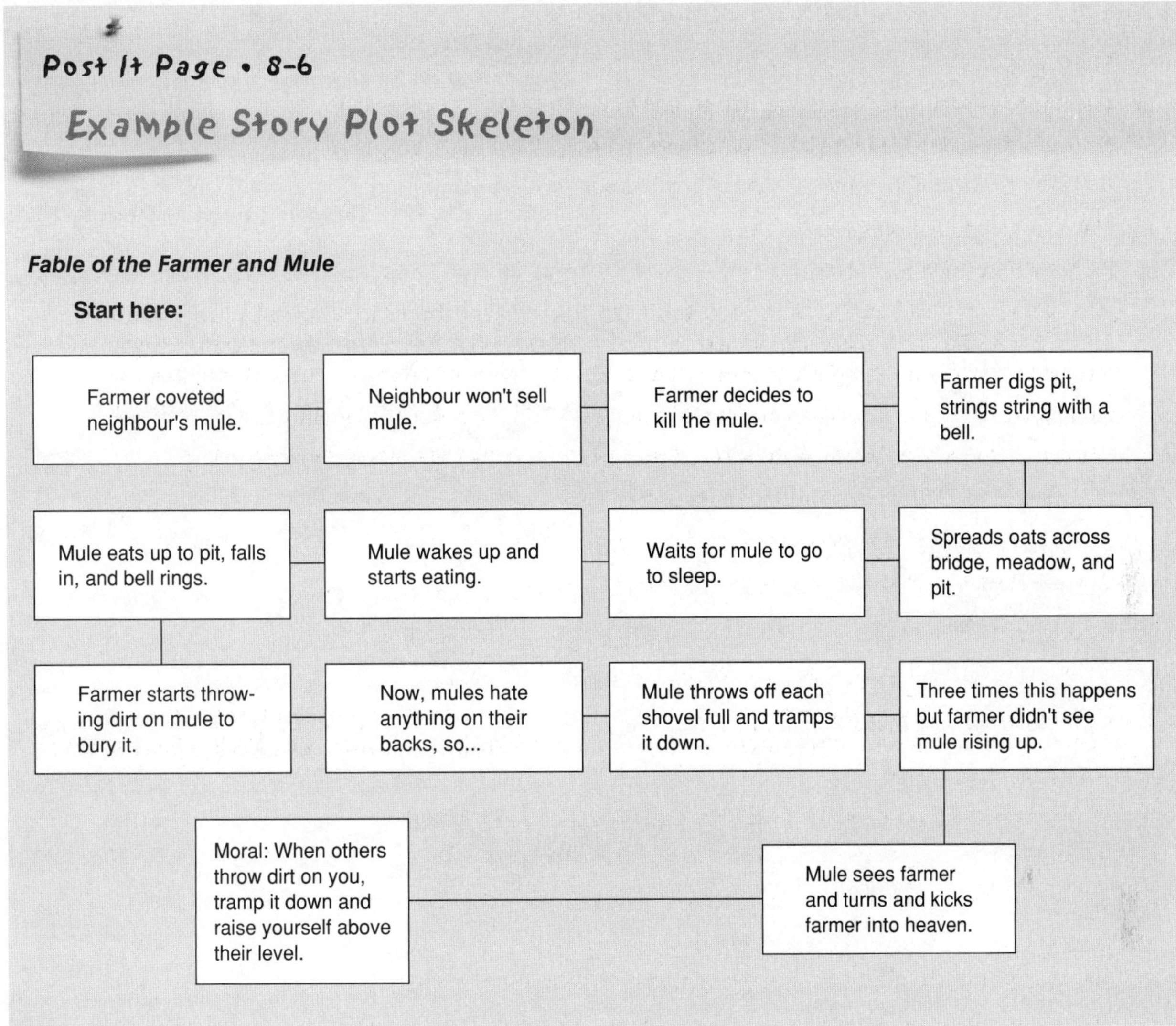
Post It Page • 8-6
Example Story Plot Skeleton
Fable of the Farmer and Mule
Start here:
Farmer coveted neighbour's mule.
Neighbour won't sell mule.
Farmer decides to kill the mule.
Farmer digs pit, strings string with a bell.
Spreads oats across bridge, meadow, and pit.
Waits for mule to go to sleep.
Mule wakes up and starts eating.
Mule eats up to pit, falls in, and bell rings.
Farmer starts throwing dirt on mule to bury it.
Now, mules hate anything on their backs, so...
Mule throws off each shovel full and tramps it down.
Three times this happens but farmer didn't see mule rising up.
Mule sees farmer and turns and kicks farmer into heaven.
Moral: When others throw dirt on you, tramp it down and raise yourself above their level.

References

Books and Articles

Bettleheim, B. (1977). *The uses of enchantment.* New York: Vintage Books.

Collins, R. (1997). "Storytelling: Water from another time." *Drama Theatre Teacher,* 5(2), 6.

Georges, C. and Cornett, C. (1986). *Reader's theater.* Aurora, NY: D.O.K.

Haley, G. (1970). *A story -A story.* New York: Atheneum.

Heinig, R. (1993). *Creative drama for the classroom teacher.* Englewood Cliffs, NJ: Prentice Hall.

Johnson, T., & Louis, D. (1987). *Literacy through literature.* Portsmouth, NH: Heinemann.

Riekehof, L. (1987). *Joy of Signing.* Springfield, MO: Gospel Publishing House.

Children's Literature

Barclay, J. (1999). *How Cold Was It?* Montreal, QC: Lobster Press.

Baylor, B. (1974). *Everybody needs a rock.* New York: Scribner.

Baylor, B. (1978). *The way to start the day.* New York: Scribner.

Bianchi, J. (1991). *Snowed in at Pokeweed Public School.* Newburgh, ON: Bungalow Books.

Carle, E. (1984). *The very hungry caterpillar.* New York: Putnam.

Cole, J. (1993). *Six sick sheep: 101 tongue twists.* New York: Beech Tree Books.

dePaola, T. (1986). *The clown of God.* New York: Harcourt Brace.

dePaola, T. (1989). *Strega Nona.* New York: Harcourt Brace.

Forrest, H. (1990). *The woman who flummoxed the fairies.* San Diego: Harcourt Brace, Jovanovich.

Fox, M. (1989). *Night noises.* San Diego: Harcourt Brace, Jovanovich.

Gilman, P. (1992). *Something from nothing.* Richmond Hill, ON: North Winds Press.

Goodman, J. (1981). *Magic and the educated rabbit.* Paoli, PA: Instructo/McGraw-Hill.

Granfield, L. (1995). (Ill. by J. Wilson). *In Flanders Fields: The story of the poem by John McCrae.* Toronto: Lester Publishing.

Hutchins, P. (1978). *Don't forget the bacon.* New York: Puffin.

Jay, W. (1990). *Laughing time.* New York: Farrar, Straus Giroux.

Keats, E. J. (1962). *A snowy day.* New York: Viking.

Lamorisse, A. (1967). *The red balloon.* New York: Doubleday

Lawson, J. (1997). *Emma and the silk train.* Toronto: Kids Can Press.

Lobel. A. (1980). *Fables.* New York: Harper & Row

Lunn, J. (1997). *The hollow tree.* Toronto: Alfred A. Knopf Canada.

McCloskey, R. (1978). *Lentil.* New York: Viking.

McCully, E. (1972). *Mirette on the high wire.* New York: G. P. Putnam's Sons.

McGovern, A. (1966). *Too much noise.* Boston: Houghton Mifflin.

Morick, I. (1996). *Tiger's new cowboy boots.* Red Deer, AB: Red Deer Press.

Munsch, R. (1985). *Mortimer.* Toronto: Annick Press.

Munsch, R. (1988). *Thomas' snowsuit.* Toronto, Canada: Annick.

Murphy, J. (1992). *Peace at last.* New York: Dial.

Oberman, S. (1994). *The always prayer shawl.* Toronto: Puffin Books.

Park, B. (1992). *Junie B. Jones and the stupid smelly bus.* New York: Random Library.

Randi, J. (1989). *The magic world of the Amazing Randi.* Holbrook, MA: Adams.

Rathmann, P. (1995). *Officer Buckles and Gloria.* New York: Scholastic.

Rowling, J. (1997). *Harry Potter and the philosopher's stone.* London, UK: Bloomsbury Publishing Place.

Schwartz, A. (1974). *A twister of twists, a tangler of tongues.* London: Deutsch.

Van Allsburg, C. (1987). *The z was zapped.* Boston: Houghton Mifflin.

Viorst, J. (1972). *Alexander and the terrible, horrible, no good, very bad day.* New York: Atheneum.

Wallace, I. (1984). *Chin Chiang and the dragon's dance.* Toronto: Groundwood Books.

White, E. B. (1952, 1980). *Charlotte's Web.* New York: Harper Collins.

Wolf, A. (1993). *It's show time!: Poetry from the page to the stage.* Asheville, NC: Poetry Alive!

Integrating Dance Throughout the Curriculum

9

Consultant:
Mary-Elizabeth Manley

If I could tell you what I mean, there would be no point in dancing.

Isadora Duncan

CLASSROOM VIGNETTE

Mr. Moore Uses Dance to Teach Fourth Grade Science

Nothing is more revealing than movement.

Anonymous

The desks are pushed back and twenty-seven students are standing in "personal spaces."

"Okay, everyone. Stretch out your arms to make sure you have enough room and won't be touching anyone during the warm-up."

Mr. Moore is a balding man in his forties who told me he'd been teaching eighteen years. He has a reputation for always being in a good humour, but being a "hard teacher."

In the background soft music is playing. It is a CD with sounds of water rushing and waves crashing on the beach. Nature sounds. No obvious rhythm. Mr. Moore's voice is easily heard as he begins his warm-up.

"Stretches. Reach your arms over your head. Now one arm higher and alternate back and forth. Let's go for eight counts: 1–2–3–4–5–6–7–8. Both arms up and drop to your sides. Relax. Reach up with both arms, now out in front of you. Let your hips tilt so your back and arms are flat and parallel to the floor. Now relax your back and curve it so you can dangle your head and hands toward the floor. Let's slowly roll up with your head coming up last. I'll count down from 8–7–6–5–4–3–2–1."

Students sigh in unison, and there are smiles across the room. Next, Mr. Moore takes the class through warm-ups especially for specific body parts, working from top to bottom: head, neck, torso (shoulders, hips, back, abdomen), arms and elbows, hands, fingers, and wrists, legs and knees, and feet and ankles.

"Ready, shake out! Right arm. Left arm. Shake your whole body out. Take a deep breath now and slowly let it out. Take another. Hold it. Very slowly release it without letting your body slump. I see straight bodies out there. Good concentration. Now, sit in your space, eyes up here."

The warm-ups take about five minutes.

Mr. Moore introduces the content portion of the lesson with a question, "Put your thumb up if you can tell me something about the water cycle we've been studying in science."

Almost everyone responds. The students are anxious to tell about where water is found on Earth, how much water there is, pollution problems, and what makes water. When someone tells the forms of water (ice, liquid, and steam), Mr. Moore asks the class the causes of the various states. There seems to be some uncertainty about this.

"It's fine if you're not sure about what causes water to be solid, liquid, or in a vapour or gas form because that's our lesson focus today. Let's start with what you know. In your space, when I say "three," show me a body shape that feels like water in its solid form. Ready 1–2–3. Yes! I see lots of stiff bodies and straight lines. Without losing your shape, try to look around. What do you notice?"

"People look hard."

"Everyone is compact."

"I see angles."

"Sarah, what do you mean by angles?"

"Like James has his arms and legs bent in straight. I think forty-five degree angles, aren't they?"

"Good observation!"

"I'll count again. This time, every time I say "three" change your solid shape in some way. Try a different level or direction. Look at the Elements Chart. Okay, ready? 1–2–3. 1–2–3. 1–2–3. Wow! You really thought of lots of hard shapes. What made you do what you did?"

Lots of thumbs go up.

"I wanted to do what you said and be different, so I tried to feel really solid, but change to a high level and use different body parts."

"I tried to really think about how it feels inside a piece of ice. I used more energy this time to try to hold my molecules together."

"Hey, I'm getting cold. B-R-R-R." The class laughs.

"But why is ice cold?" Mr. Moore asks.

The class discusses what they know about temperature and its effects on states of water. He then takes the student comment about molecules and asks students about what they think the distance is among the molecules in ice. They concur that they "felt" close together.

Mr. Moore takes the students through similar explorations of liquid water and finally water vapour. He increasingly focuses his questions and descriptive comments on the molecular structure of the three states and how each feels as they make their individual shapes.

After about ten minutes, he tells the students to get into their small groups. Students seem to have been previously assigned and know where their group space is.

"Your group assignment is to create a dance using movements related to all three forms of water. Remember, you're not pretending to *be* the water, but trying to communicate about the states by showing all the possible movements. What do you remember the dance must have?"

"A beginning, middle, and end."

"A starting shape, then our movements, and an ending shape frozen."

"Creative ideas!"

"Thanks for reminding us Liza! Yes, the idea is to think differently about these water states. In your groups, begin by brainstorming ways water gets from one form to another and movements related to these changes. I'll come around as you work."

The students huddle up in groups of about four. Mr. Moore waits as students get started. After a few minutes, he begins to circulate and listen in.

"Let's see. Ice melts when it gets warmer—above thirty-two degrees. We could show melting by starting high and slowly getting lower and spreading out."

"Yeah. We could all be part of a rigid ice sculpture with lots of angles. We need to be really close together." Everyone giggles.

"What about when we melt and spread out. We'd be liquid, then. Somehow we need to show getting hotter so we can evaporate."

"We could be being cooked to boiling. Wow. You'd really have to move fast and jump around. Look at my fingers boiling!" Liza demonstrates with fast wild finger movements and the others join in.

"Look, my foot is boiling!"

Mr. Moore moves to another group that is discussing cloud movements and how to show water moving from a gas to precipitation (liquid). He pauses to ask what the difference is between precipitation and condensation, and they spend a few minutes discussing the terms.

Another group is working on water appearing as frost and is experimenting with "quick-freeze" movements.

After about ten minutes, Mr. Moore announces they have five minutes to decide their starting shapes, how to include movements related to the three states of water, and their ending shapes. He coaches them to think about how to use the space in the room. He tells them to sit in their groups when they are ready.

The students finish planning, and he then has each of the four groups perform their dances as the rest of the class takes the part of the audience. Each performance takes about three or four minutes. After each performance Mr. Moore asks the audience to "tell what they saw," and he compliments students who give really specific observations about shapes, movements, and connections to the states of water.

The lesson ends with a debriefing in which Mr. Moore asks them what they learned about the states of water. Finally, students rearrange their desks and take out "Science Learning Logs" and write for about five minutes on the states of matter lesson. There is a reading assignment on the board about the water cycle in their science book, and students begin to read as they finish their logs. Mr. Moore explains that there is little in the reading that hasn't already come up in the lesson. He is sure many students need the visual or print reinforcement, and he claims he's too traditional to do away with the textbook, completely.

Introduction

Relax! You Need Not Be a Dancer Yourself

Our bodies and how we move them intentionally and unintentionally say so much about us. So much, in fact, that we often recognize and label certain personality characteristics or emotional states by the way people present themselves in movement. Slumped shoulders and a slow walk may indicate that the person is feeling discouraged; a quick, direct walk might mean that the person is anxious to arrive at a destination, while a slow, meandering walk often suggests a relaxed and reflective state. Movement is a powerful communicator that can fascinate or repel, delight, or disgust us. And yet, unlike the use of words, movement is not a communication form considered to be part of the basics in most schools. Perhaps it is so basic we simply take for granted that we all know how to use it effectively. But we don't. Dance is frequently the art form teachers are most unprepared to integrate into their classrooms. In North America, how your body looks is very important; beautiful, intimidating body images bombard us daily through the media. We have become very sensitive about our bodies. It is not surprising that teachers are sometimes uncomfortable using creative movement, especially if they're not sure exactly what that means. No one wants to appear awkward or have their bodies examined for possible ridicule. Teachers who feel uncomfortable need to know that students, especially after the primary grades, often feel the same way. This reticence about dance is interesting, since our society is often riveted on one particular area of movement—sports.

Rather than spend time wringing our hands about the lack of value for artistic movement, we can simply acknowledge the ways dance is important in our lives and move on to strategies for using kinesthetic ways of knowing in creative and artistic ways. Most important is to start with some foundational truths—we all love to move. It feels good to walk, run, stretch, wiggle, and shake. It is also true that we remember what we *do* more easily than what we read about or what we are told to do.

While it is important for teachers to be actively engaged in their own lessons, it is not necessary for teachers to demonstrate specific dances to use creative dance throughout the curriculum. The intent of this chapter is to present strategies teachers can use to cause students to problem-solve creatively through dance. When and if teachers decide to include structured dances (e.g., folk dancing in social studies), they can choose to demonstrate such dances or invite guests in to do the demonstrations (e.g., the physical education teacher or music teacher may serve as a collaborator). If the school has created an arts resource directory, like the one described in Chapter 2, persons can be located who are willing to teach specific dances.

Why Should a Classroom Teacher Use Dance to Teach Curricular Content and Skills?

To dance is to challenge the body, which is also the self. To generate an action which has a force of its own and allow the movement to penetrate the inner sensibilities — this is difficult —

Katherine Litz (dancer)

Eleven Good Reasons to Dance

1. **Dance can increase sensitivity, respect, and cooperation.** When a class is engaged in group or partner problem-solving through creative dance, they can begin to realize how everyone has a different way of viewing a situation. There are numerous ways to express thoughts and feelings about the cycle of life and death through dance; no one body shape or locomotor movement is right or wrong. The emphasis is on finding original ways to think and feel about what is being learned. Students soon see that other students think of things they wouldn't have come to know working alone—two heads are better than one. Students begin to delight in the artistry of fellow classmates as they witness the inventiveness of peers; a graceful slide or a humorous foot dab executed at the right moment can provide a moment of insight—oohs and ahs, laughter, and even awe. Partner and circle dances require students to help each other in an enjoyable context. Students feel the intrinsic motivation to learn under these circumstances.

2. **Dance gives joy.**

The place of the dance is within the heart.

Tom Robbins

Think about people dancing. Eyes sparkle. They smile and laugh. People constantly surprise themselves with all the ways bodies can be made to move—to a musical beat or an internal rhythm. We simply cannot be still. Dance is entertaining to both do and view. Nothing is more interesting, for many of us, than people-watching. What is it that attracts attention? The way people walk, their posture, how they get from one point to the next, the ways they move to music—all these images captivate us as we imagine ourselves moving. Perhaps that's part of why generations have been influenced by Elvis Presley's pelvis and leg moves and Michael Jackson's moon walking. Elizabeth Wall, a Richmond, Virginia, school principal, recalled how students responded when dance was integrated at her school.

> The teachers also seemed to feel that as children use their bodies they become different and that no other previous programs had accomplished this . . . [children expressed] a sense of humor and as attitudes and values changed, self-control developed. . . . They looked forward to school. (Fleming, 1990, p. 32)

3. **Dance improves concentration, responsibility, and self-discipline.** Students involved in exploring the concepts of dance must focus on making their bodies work in the ways that provide solutions to creative dance problems. Teachers using creative dance stress concentration and focus by structuring dances with beginning, middle, and end segments, giving descriptive feedback to students who are showing they are involved and helping students come to appreciate the pleasant feelings possible when we are quiet and still, feeling the sensations of inner peace and pride in controlling the body. Self-discipline develops as students learn how to control their movements, gradually at first and then for in-

Post It Page • 9-1

News Bulletins Dance Research You Can Use

My heart lifted my feet, and I danced.

Nathan of Nemirov

Young children and seniors in rural British Columbia participated in a thirty-minute dance, exercise, and physical education or intergenerational dance intervention twice a week for twelve weeks. The child participants improved motor skills, maintained high affective scores, showed enhanced social skills (cooperation, communication, group membership, and awareness of others), and encouraged emotional expression. For the adults, creative dance improved flexibility and smoothness of movement, decreased mean depression scores from "mid-moderate" to "normal" range, and more adults reported feeling "relaxed." It was concluded that creative dance enhances physical, social, and emotional growth and that an intergenerational creative dance venue helps foster caring, tolerance, respect, and unconditional acceptance between generations. (Rossberg-Gempton, 1998)

Students with physical disabilities who participated in a twelve-week dance program showed significantly higher scores for creativity (fluency, originality, and imagination) than those participating in an adaptive physical education program (Jay, 1991).

Third grade science scores on tests about the water cycle were raised to 97 percent when dance was used as the meaning maker. Previous year's students scored below average on the test ("Scientific Thought in Motion" conference presentation by Randy Barron, the Kennedy Center, February 1997).

creasing lengths of time, and to do more and more original work. Students develop responsibility when they are a part of a group in which their ideas and cooperation are *needed* and when they are taught how to be responsive—that is, how to respond in a group or individually.

Students who are involved in *formal* dance study soon learn the rigour required to develop skills for ballet, tap, and jazz. Any dance demands concentration on the body, energy, space, and time elements. Students who choose to be involved in such study must commit to a regimen of regular practice, and they quickly learn they must struggle and work hard to master a new idea. Why do they choose this? There certainly is a self-pride that comes from conquering obstacles and reinforcement from significant others who come to be your audience.

4. Dance is part of real life, so it should be part of school life.

Today we started a new dance called "A day in the life of . . . ." Its all about us! What happens and how we feel at school, what we do on the way home, what we do in front of the mirror etc. I think its going to be really funny because we can't stop laughing when we make it up . . . . When she said it would be done to classical music I just freaked . . . but it makes it even funnier.

a student
(Garrett, 1994, p.139)

John Dewey's idea that school should not be a preparation for life, but just like life, fits here. Dance is an important part of the rituals and ceremonies of our lives—weddings, inaugurations, proms, and holidays. It has been fascinating to watch the response of audiences to entertainment phenomena like "Lord of the Dance" and "Riverdance." Just as athletic games draw huge crowds, dance can attract entertainment dollars. Certainly, part of the attraction of sports is the movement aspect. We enjoy watching the strong rhythm and seamless flow of Jean-Luc Brassard's skiing or the swift and accurate passing action of Wayne Gretzky. While sports is not the same as dance, there is that movement connection. There are those who would argue that certain individuals make their sport into an art form when they take their movements to a level of beauty that awes and inspires.

5. **Dance develops self-expression, self-concept, confidence, and leadership.**

There is a vitality, a life force, an energy, a quickening, that is translated through you into action, and because there is only one of you in all time, this expression is unique. And if you block it, it will never exist through any other medium and will be lost.

Martha Graham

Through dance, students learn to control the body. Endurance and strength develop, enabling them to be more poised. Satisfaction with one's body and self-confidence increase as students attain mastery of their bodies. We all want to feel good about our bodies, and dance can develop self-assurance when students have successful experiences in solving problems by thinking creatively through dance. Students involved in dance integration also learn ways the body can be used as a language. To reinforce the importance of movement in communicating self-image, take a moment and think of someone whom you respect as a leader. How does the person carry himself? How does she walk? What is the posture of the person? How does this body language affect others?

6. **Dance unites the physical, mental, and spiritual.**

I see the dance being used as a means of communication between soul and soul—to express what is too deep, too fine for words.

Ruth St. Denis

Student journal comments such as "Dance uses all of me," "You have to remember so much it makes my brain hurt," "It's good to get out and be physical for a change," "I don't feel dumb in dance because it's not just my brain that is working," "I feel like I know everyone in the class now," and "I didn't realize I could be creative" suggest that the value of dance as a tool to enhance self-esteem may lie in its holistic nature as a physical, social, creative and cognitive activity. (Garrett, 1994, p. 136–137)

Dance is intellectual and physical activity, possible because there is a mind–body connection. It involves the whole person in its construction. Through dance we communicate what we think, feel, and value, and when students dance ideas from science, social studies or math, they gain a different view on the subject. Because the physical body is engaged during dance, students activate kinesthetic intelligence, which is different from the kind of movement associated with the physical education program. In fact, there are significant differences between dance and physical education, even though both have a movement base. Most importantly, dance has the added dimension of the aesthetic, a potential for creative and inner self-expression, which is crucial for children to be happy and satisfied. "Dance provides a primary medium for expression involving the total self (not just a part, like the voice) or totally separated from the physical self (like painting or sculpture)" (Fleming, 1990, p. 5). Teachers interested in helping children become "whole" people will find the idea of dance integration consistent with holistic learning.

7. **Dance helps us be healthy.** A 1992 ad from the American Heart Association displays a silhouetted child in front of a TV. The boldface caption reads, "Caution: Children Not At Play." Obesity levels of children have risen dramatically as children have developed passive television viewing habits. On the average, children now spend about four hours a day viewing versus doing. And how about during the school day? How much learning time is spent using the body in active physical ways? How much of the ballooning statistics about "hyperactive" kids has to do with children's bodies rejecting the passive lifestyles we've created for them? Dance is exercise, and exercise makes us healthy because it increases blood circulation and muscle tone. Dance also burns up calories. This kind of exercise triggers the brain to produce endorphins that are natural pain killers and catecholamine, an alertness hormone. No wonder children enjoy dance; they are out of pain and full of energy. Dancing can actually give a person a feeling of being "high" or uplifted, just as any creative activity can. So, dance can be a kind of therapy or emotional release to help with stress. Dance used before, during, or after a lesson in reading or math can increase physical readiness for cognitive learning.

8. **Dance gives opportunities for experimentation, creative problem-solving, and imagination.**

How does he learn when he should choose a symmetric rather than an asymmetric movement? Does a skip express better than a jump the idea of what he wants to say? The children in our dance classes are not only making these choices, but learning to perfect the movements and parallel with that, form concepts that will enable them to develop images of their movement patterns and dances. No wonder they are so busy! (Hill, 1978, p.68)

How many ways can you walk across the room? What are all the body parts you can use to make circles? What are all the ways cats move? leaves? water? How can you show the idea of "addition" using dance? What are all the words that describe movements? When teachers ask open or fat questions, such as these, they set up opportunities for creative problem-solving. If the classroom environment is one in which students feel they can risk and are given the time to explore ways to use movement to think and feel, they will use the unlimited powers of the imagination to think about the problems in the subject matter under study.

Remember the creative problem-solving process from Chapter 1? It begins with finding problems and then gathering information to solve the problems. Every dance activity is centred around this idea of experimenting with movement to unleash creative and artistic thinking. In the regular classroom, this means having students come to understand key concepts and acquire basic communication skills through the use of kinesthetic ways of knowing.

9. **Dance is an alternative form of communication.** Dance is a means of *showing* what we know. It enables children to express thoughts and feelings that otherwise may be inexpressible. The kinesthetic mode is the one through which our earliest learning happens, and communication through movement is the most universal form of language. Think about the meanings of an upraised shaking fist or arms stretched high toward the sky or palms open and arms extended. Did you recognize *anger*, *triumph*, and *invitation* in these gestures? The study of dance is not devoid of words, however. Dance is a way to promote learning throughout the curriculum by developing dance vocabulary and forging conceptual anchors related to movement that can be used across disciplines. As students learn the dance elements of body, energy, space, and time, they also learn how to analyze and categorize their thinking. Many concepts, like rhythm, space, and shape, are used in music, drama, and the visual arts, as well. Other dance concepts such as balance can be extended to areas like physics.

10. **Dance satisfies our need for beauty.**

Mine is a proud village, such as it is,
We are at our best when dancing.

Makah Nation Song

There is hardly a sight more beautiful than a graceful human being. When students have opportunities to view dances and participate in dance creation, they can increase their aesthetic sensitivity. In creative dance the expressive and imaginative potential of children is what is emphasized, so dance can also help children get their basic need for beauty met. Beauty uplifts us and makes us feel hopeful. It creates a sense that life is worth living. Captivating dances from other cultures can stretch children's concepts of beauty and offer diverse perspectives on cultural and ethnic groups, extending their understanding of the aesthetic of Western forms of dance. "The process of creativity, of making the connections, and 'tasting the interconnections,' is an excellent road to understanding the connections and interdependence of the global society" (Hunt, 1997, p. 147).

11. **Dance is an important means of understanding and expressing culture.**

Sometimes dancing and music can describe a true image of the customs of a country better than words in a newspaper.

Gene Kelly

All art forms are vehicles for conveying the ideas and values of their creators; they are means of coming to understand other cultures. Dance is no exception. Social studies units are particularly appropriate contexts for using dance to help students feel sensations created by particular dance forms (e.g., hip-hop, tap, jazz, ballroom, country line, jitterbug, mazurka). Students can also view dances and then analyze them for the messages they give about what is important to the dancers and the culture represented. Through dance investigations, historical events can be understood from an entirely different point of view. For example, the First Nations of the west coast of British Columbia traditionally celebrated *potlatch*. At these events the clans gathered together to share details of births, deaths, marriages, transference of property, and culture in story, song, and dance. In 1921, fearing serious hardships due to the generous gift giving at the potlatches, the Canadian government outlawed these festivals. Unique masks and costumes were confiscated and often destroyed. No longer were the people able to dance the business and ancient ceremonies of their lives. While some dances were lost, in 1951, when the ban was dropped, the potlatch ceremonies began again. The strength of their oral culture and the kinesthetic memories of the dances allowed the First Nations to rekindle the ceremony of the potlatch. The film *A Strict Law Bids Us Dance* chronicles this history.

What Does a Classroom Teacher Need to Know and Teach to Use Dance as a Teaching Tool?

Dance is the poetry of movement.

Moira Morningstar

> I believe it can only be done if teachers themselves have had experiences in their professional training (and hopefully before that) which parallel and supplement the expressive, imaginative uses of movement that dance can offer. . . . There is danger that teachers who have had no creative dance in their training and who have been taught only to look and work for efficient, functional movement, will not encourage or even be receptive to a different kind of movement response. [We need teachers who know] children's literature, poetry, music, songs and how to use props for creative movement. More importantly, [we need teachers who have a] sensitivity to children's spontaneous expressiveness, the recognition of imaginative rather than imitative uses of movement. . . . (Fleming, 1990, p. 77)

What Should Be Included in the Study of Dance?

In elementary and middle school, these aspects of the arts are studied: the historical, social, and cultural role of each art form in our lives; communication through art forms by expressing, performing, and responding; and valuing the arts and developing an aesthetic sense. Topics include basic elements of each art form, media, genre, artists, and products (paintings, plays). Of major importance is the role of beauty and emotion in these forms of human communication. Dance study and integration include ideas related to dance elements, creation and composition, presentation and performance, dance history, and dance and society, as well as study of a variety of dance genres or forms. Any of these can be integrated into any other discipline or can be the body or centre of a unit or lesson. Remember the four bodies and nine-legged model from Chapter 2? (See Post It Page 2–2.) For example, clog dancing, a particular dance "topic," could be integrated into a history unit on pioneer life in Acadia.

Teachers who begin to build a repertoire of information about particular dance forms like ballet and jazz, about dances of different time periods and cultures, and about important dancers and choreographers can create a rich resource for interesting study, as well as have invaluable material to integrate throughout the curriculum. This can begin as simply as creating a file folder on dancers into which tidbits of information are saved from magazine articles. There are many biographies of dancers (e.g., *This Passion: For the Love of Dance* by C. Anderson (ed.), 1998) and informational books about various dance forms. Involving students in research on dancers and dance genres enables them to connect literature, social studies, and other art forms as they search for the whys and hows that motivated the creation of dance throughout human history.

Here is a checklist of titles for folder tabs so that you can start collecting information for dance integration:

- Basic elements and concepts used to communicate through dance
- Dance artists: dancers, choreographers
- Styles, forms, and genres of dance
- Actual dances (e.g., the "Electric Slide" is a dance in the genre of country line dances)
- Other possibilities: history of dance, science of dance, math of dance, writing dance (notation systems), sociology of dance, economics and dance, psychology of dance (e.g., dance therapy), dance and performance

Definitions: Creative Dance versus Movement

As I type this sentence, I am moving. This is not dance. And yet I can take my hands from the keys and begin to play with the "typing movement" to experience the feel of it on an abstract level. I can even use other body parts to sense the lightness of touch and the irregular rhythms of this movement, using toes, torso, and hips. The movement is no longer done to get a job done, but to explore how kinesthetics is a way of knowing and feeling.

This chapter has little to do with teachers directing students to mimic, step by step, until a dance is learned. The classroom teacher's purposes are best served by a focus on problem-solving, which includes guided, free exploration and discovery. In this open-ended approach there is a variety of acceptable solutions. "The key to joy in movement lies in such self discovery" (Murray, 1975, p. 7). Dance can include a variety of creative movement explorations or become a holistic entity. "A creative dance is one in which you create and communicate your own movements; it has form, variety, and expressiveness. You often work around a theme, and as your dance evolves you may wish to repeat and modify it giving it a beginning, a middle, and an end, perfecting it as you go. A creative dance may be a group project . . . It is very difficult to say where discovery and repetition of movement end and where creative dance begins, but it depends on the ability to hold onto a nucleus of thought and to create a pattern. It also requires a growing artistic sense of movement" (Morningstar, 1986, p. 1). But for movement to become dance there must be "expressive interest beyond that of its mere physicality since it belongs in the category of art . . . a sequence of learned gymnastic movements, even though they are performed to music, do not make a dance. There must be something present that pertains to the spirit of the performer, and the movement must communicate that spirit" (Murray, 1975, p. 18).

Don't be surprised to find yourself smiling as you change common movements into dance. So do students. Humour is the natural response to discovering something that makes sense, like a new perspective on an idea. Students can also begin to realize that it not only feels great to find new ways a body can be used, but dance enables us to express thoughts and feelings we can communicate no other way. Dance often goes beyond words to reveal truths about people and the world; and dance is a primary vehicle to help us in the universal human search for beauty (Maslow's hierarchy of needs, Post It Page 1–4).

While integrating dance can include teaching students structured folk or fad dances, like the macarena, the mainstay of a classroom teacher's repertoire of dance strategies will not be demonstrating and asking students to learn combinations of memorized steps. If dance is to be a useful and joyful meaning maker, the classroom focus needs to be on teaching the use of the *symbol system* of dance in creative ways to express thoughts and feelings about important life issues. This symbol system, like those of all communication forms such as language, math, art, and music, consists of basic teachable elements—tools for meaning making.

Creative Movement and Dance

Creative movement had its heyday during the middle part of the twentieth century. Based on natural movement, rather than a specific dance genre like ballet, creative movement was especially popular in physical education. Remember, movement becomes dance when the kinesthetic senses are used in original and intentional ways to solve problems and express ideas. This involves becoming conscious of the movement, as when you close your eyes and focus on your body from your head to your toes. In the political fervour over low test scores during the 1980s, many programs were left on the shelves to collect dust. The baby was thrown out with the bath water as schools were frightened into getting students to test well. Often, this happened without carefully considering what *was* working. Gardner's *Frames of the Mind* (1983) brought many educators back to the future as he and others showed how *bodily kinesthetic* intelligence is essential to learning.

Mime versus Creative Dance

Mime is a drama strategy in which people pretend to be something or someone. While it is a very valuable strategy in arts integration, it can be limiting in creative dance. The focus of dance needs to be on the movement itself, not on pretending to move as an animal, plant, or character. Mime can lead to imitation, rather than actual creative movement problem-solving (e.g., "move like a cat" elicits stereotyped paw and claw movements, while "show me the shape of a cat's body, how it walks, how its muscles move, how it would walk backward or on a low level" directs students to explore all the kinesthetic potentials of the concept). Another way of saying this is to think about involving students in the *movement possibilities* of an idea, rather than in the idea itself. This is particularly important when teaching new concepts in fields like science or social studies—the goal is an extended perspective.

While this may seem to be a minor concern, grasping the difference between mime and creative dance can extend students' thinking tremendously. This comes up frequently when teachers use dance related to children's literature. Miming Max during the wild rumpus in *Where the Wild Things Are* is a worthy way to cause students to become part of the story and think about characterization. Creative dance offers another dimension of meaning. For example, children can be helped to work on ways to express anger with the body. In the latter example, movement possibilities are explored, and learning about a concept important to the book's theme is developed. The teacher needs to decide if the goal is to "become" or "be" the character, and move or probe the movement extensions of important ideas and feelings in a lesson.

Imagery and Dance

One very important way people think and learn is through the use of images—visual connections, sound associations, and so on. But imagery is limited to what's in the brain, so it can restrict thinking, too. One way to avoid the downside of imagery in dance, an example of which is literal-level mime, is to explore dance elements related to a topic, first, and then invite students to "become" through drama. This helps stretch and expand the initial imagery associated with the idea. In other words, when imagery is evoked *after* direct exploration and investigation of movement, there is the chance creative thinking will be extended. Similes and metaphors can be powerful helpers to stretch imaginations for movement (e.g., *"Show me you are as solid as igneous rock"* or *"Let me see you shrink as small as you imagine an electron to be"*). You can also ask for images that lead to movement (e.g., *"Make your body stretch as if it is being pulled by magnets on either side of you. Use as many body parts as you can"*), or comment on images that spring from movement (e.g., *"You're in a round shape, what else do you know that is round in our environment?"*). This use of imagery helps extend concepts through movements, rather than trigger stereotyped behaviour. Finally, images can be used as a basis for movement:

Post It Page • 9-2

BEST: Basic Dance Elements with Examples of Each

Body

Actions of body parts: head, neck, torso (hips, abdomen, shoulders, back), arms and elbows, hands and wrists, fingers, legs, knees, and feet (ankles and toes)

Actions of whole body:

Nonlocomotor: stretch, bend, twist, rise, fall, circle, shake, suspend, sway, swing, collapse, turn, stop, rock, wiggle, push, pull

Locomotor: (using feet for support) walk, run, jog, leap, hop, jump, gallop, skip, slide; (using other body parts) roll, creep, crawl, slither

Body shapes: straight, curved, twisted, angular

Effort/Dynamics

Space: direct or indirect
Timing: sudden or sustained
Force/Energy: heavy or light
Flow: bound or free (tight or loose and relaxed)

Space

Personal space
General space
Levels: low, medium, high
Direction: forward, backward, sideways, up, down
Size/range: large and small
Pathways: patterns we make with the body on the floor and in the air (e.g., circular or zigzag)
Place or destination: points at either end of the pathways
Focus: where you look

Time

Rhythm: pulse, beat
Speed: time or tempo
Accent: light or strong emphasis
Duration: length
Phrases: dance sentences, patterns and combinations (e.g., twist, twist, twirl, and freeze)

"What kind of movements might a starfish do?" instead of *"Pretend you are a starfish and move around."* It is a subtle but significant difference in thinking.

Teachers Need to Know the Vocabulary: Basic Dance Elements

There are a number of systems for categorizing the dance tools for meaning making. These concepts develop a conscious awareness of how we move, where, when, and to what effect. The following is a simple system of remembering dance elements that is useful for classroom teachers and students. (Thanks to Randy Baron, dance educator affiliated with the John F. Kennedy Center for the Performing Arts, for this idea.) It is easy to remember because it is organized around the acronym, BEST: body, effort/dynamics, space, and time. Post It Page 9–2 is a summary of BEST.

Body Parts, Actions, Shapes. We use all body parts to communicate, those both outside and inside. Think of the ways to move just your little finger or the effect on the body when you tighten inner muscles. Body shape includes ways to form body parts to create everything from pleasant round and curved shapes to sharp angry angles and pointed shapes. Then there are all the ways to move in place or through a space. Stationary actions are called *nonlocomotor* and include stretch, bend, twist, rise, fall, circle, shake, suspend, sway, swing, collapse, turn, stop, rock, wiggle, push, pull. Movement through space is called *locomotor* movement and includes actions like walk, run, jog, leap, hop, jump, gallop, skip, slide (using feet for support); and roll, creep, crawl, slither (using other body parts).

Effort or dynamics represents how the energy of a movement is distributed in space in relation to the factors of time, force, and flow. It often shares the colour or mood of a dance. It includes the dancer's attack (sudden or sustained), force/weight (heavy or light), flow (bound or free), and the pathway that the movement takes (direct or indirect).

Space is the personal or general area in which the body is used. Space is filled up by changing levels (low, medium, high), directions, size, pathways (how to get to a destination—directly or indirectly), and place or destination. Focus or concentration, or where a person is looking, is also included here.

Time is the last element used during movement. It includes rhythm (pulse, beat), speed or tempo, accent or emphasis (light or strong), duration (length), and phrases (dance "sentences," or patterns and combinations of all different kinds of movements) (e.g., "three different middle-level slow, wringing shapes" is a phrase that may create a message about discomfort or struggle).

Curriculum Guidelines for *Dance*

Dance is not about something. Dance is something.

Mary Joyce, 1994, p. 19

Canada has yet to set national educational standards for dance. The provinces currently formulate their own curriculum guidelines, most often starting from a very general rationale. For example, the aim of dance education is to provide all students with opportunities to experience, understand, and value the language and art of dance (British Columbia's Provincial Curriculum Outcomes). Using provincial guidelines as a framework, individual boards or even schools create their local courses of study. But standards, goals, objectives, and outcomes in curriculum frameworks and courses of study only help teachers know *what* to teach. They do not explain *how* to teach. When a teacher signs a contract in a school district she is making a legal promise to teach the adopted course of study and is expected to arrive with the know-how to do so: teaching strategies, ideas about materials, disciplinary and classroom management tools. What this means is teachers need to structure lessons and units around the school district's performance goals so that students have a better chance of reaching the goals. Therefore, teachers need to know the goals and specify connections between lesson activities and specific goals. In addition, it is just good teaching to discuss with students the goals of the lesson, and it is wise to communicate goals, and the source of the goals, to parents. Curriculum guidelines for dance can be found at individual web sites (see Web Sites under References at the end of the chapter). A summary of the Seven *National Standards* for Dance, a portion of *National Standards for the Arts* used as guidelines in the United States, also appears in Appendix G.

How Should Classroom Teachers Use Dance as a Teaching Tool?

Within integration projects in the earlier grades, dance can be employed in ways that encourage creativity and problem solving over mastery of specific technical skills.

(Fisher-Stitt and Warner, 1997, p. 386)

General Principles

The general principles for effective arts integration described in Chapter 2 apply to all arts areas. Recall how teachers can choose to teach *with, about, in,* and *through* the arts, and use the ten principles for integration.

Principle One: INFUSE the Art of Dance

Set up your classroom so that there is space for dance. Think about setting up your lesson plans with a checklist to remind yourself to plan in kinesthetic ways to introduce, develop, and conclude lessons many times each week.

Principle Two: TEACH Elements and Concepts

> *Child's definition of dance: "It's talking. Telling something with your body. Not using words, just using your body to talk."*
>
> Fleming, 1990, p. 33

Unfortunately, many students think dance is memorizing steps and using bump and grind motions their parents might find objectionable. In the absence of a clear idea of what creative dance includes, kids tend to focus on learning steps or, when asked to move, they try to recall steps they've seen—often very sexualized. Many boys have developed the notion that dance is a girl thing and not masculine.

By doing lessons on the definitions of dance, students can be helped to draw on past experiences and form a clear and comfortable idea of the goals of using the *kinesthetic* intelligence to make meaning. Instead of *giving* the students a definition of dance, help them construct their own. Here are some strategies to do so:

- Web what students already know about dance, dancers, choreographers, and the ways people move as they dance.
- Do a Venn diagram comparing movement, in general, and in dance (e.g., compare and contrast sports moves with dance to consider what makes something "art" and what is "aesthetic" or "beautiful"). Use the children's book *Max* by Rachael Isadora, about a boy who discovers the dance–sports connection.
- Ask students to find a variety of definitions of dance by doing interviews with people and using reference books. They can then synthesize a working definition that makes sense.

Time spent teaching reasons why dance is important in real life (e.g., careers, cultural rituals, entertainment) is time well spent, because motivation is grounded in the perception of relevance. Justification for dance can be developed through discussions that explore how various forms of dance have been a part of each child's life. Better yet, get the kids moving. Ask them to think about the movement of walking. Then brainstorm different ways to walk: angrily, happily, proudly, triumphantly. Invite students to try different walks and report how each feels. Discuss the difference between *daily* walking and the walking exploration they just did to develop the concept of dance as an intentional way to communicate thoughts and feelings.

Of course, students need to be taught the basic dance elements so that they have them to construct meaning through movement. As mentioned previously, these lessons are more successful when visual aids, like posters of dance elements (BEST), are used to reinforce the concepts. These lessons can be organized in an inductive format so that students are led to discover ideas after actually exploring through dance or after reflecting on movement from a real-life context. Inductive or discovery teaching takes a bit more time, but the students will remember and enjoy the lessons more because they were involved emotionally and physically.

It is also useful to address the gender stereotype issue when introducing dance as a learning medium. In schools where dance has been successfully integrated, there has been no doubt that boys love to dance. The key to success seems not to be the actual dance activities, but how dance is approached. It does help to have male role models, but all teachers can discuss the history of dance to show how dance is a masculine activity in many cultures; in fact, there are times when only the males dance (e.g., the *Russian troika*, an extremely strenuous dance). Also consider observations from the experience of others. For example, "Boys like percussive rhythms, architectural structures built with bodies, vigorous locomotor patterns (leaps, jumps), and ethnic dance experiences" (Fleming, 1990, p. 49). If this is a special concern, read Chapter 5 in Fleming's book *Children's Dance.* The chapter ends with this observation: "When boys are no longer given dance activities . . . , not only is their cultural, physical, emotional, and aesthetic growth stunted, but also a great disservice is done to dance as an art form. There is something very incomplete about a whole room full of girls dancing. Yet isn't that what a great deal of the dancing is in our culture?" (p. 49).

Principle Three: TEACHER HABITS for Integrating Dance

Process versus Product. Most of all, students need to understand that the purpose of creative dance is the doing of it—the process not the product. To convey to students how important kinesthetic learning is, do a bit of action research. Give half the class a set of numbers to learn (e.g., 8–3–9–6–11–23–87–92). Send them out of the room to study for ten minutes. With the remaining group, tell them to study kinesthetically by creating dance movements to remember the number sequence (e.g., a movement to go with each number). Have them practise the number movements in order, saying the numbers with the movements for ten minutes. Bring the whole class back together and give them a test in which they take out a piece of paper and write the sequence. Ask students to grade their own papers and then compare the scores of the two groups. Regardless of the scores, ask students to tell *how* they learned and how it *felt*. (Usually the dance group does better and enjoyed the studying more, but results are not guaranteed.)

While there is a place for structured dances in the regular classroom (e.g., when studying Ireland a guest might teach the Irish jig), this will not occur daily or even weekly. If dance is to be used as an important learning tool, the emphasis needs to be on the process strategies teachers can use to help students make meaning kinesthetically, creatively, and artistically.

Descriptive Feedback, Assessment, and Evaluation. Here are a few pointers to follow up on the points presented in Chapters 1 and 2 about developing the important habit of giving feedback to facilitate student growth:

- Give clear and focused descriptive feedback (not just praise) throughout lessons. Describe what students do, and coach them to stretch their imaginations by using questions. Use each child's name in a positive way as feedback is given.
- Watch and listen. Use powers of observation to see if students are learning the focus of the lesson. Jot down notes about specific student behaviours on cards or sticky notes that can be added to student progress folders. This is an effective kind of assessment.
- Self-evaluate after lesson. Ask how fully the concept was explored through movement. How were students challenged? What choices did students have? What did students try that they didn't try before?
- Ask students what they learned, and write their responses on the board to give them value.
- Give concrete progress indicators (e.g., charts; checklists of elements; positive post-its, sticky papers on which you write feedback to give directly to students after a lesson).

- Tell students about their progress. Use charts, checklists, etc., to show them what they have learned.

Free versus Guided Lessons. Undirected versus teacher-guided lessons are an issue throughout education today. In dance integration there are particular concerns about preparing students for success by using guided teaching. Here's the problem. If dance integration is started by playing music and telling students to do any dance they wish, many students will be embarrassed about moving at all, and others will engage in stereotyped rigid movements they've seen others do (MTV). For this reason, free dance should be made available *after teaching dance elements* and after time has been given to explore ways to communicate through the language of the body. This sequence assures student success and builds self-confidence, because students focus what their bodies can do and how it can be done in a cognitive as well as physical way. Art grows from experimentation with knowledge and skill born of control and use of basic elements. "Move any way you want to the music" assumes that students have learned many ways to move when they may, in fact, have very limited experiences, especially on a conscious level. The goal of integrating creative dance is to help students expand communication options. Once students have learned the many possibilities for using their bodies to respond to music, or any other stimulus, teachers can then give time for free creative dance without students feeling awkward. Sequence and balance are the secrets here.

Show versus Tell. Teacher habits, like asking students to "show" an idea instead of telling it, can be woven throughout lessons and in doing so more effectively use the power of learning through dance. Students who may not be able to verbally define "obnoxious" may be able to use hands, head, and body posture to do so—the rest of the class will never forget this definition! When students are asked to both show and then describe and relate (e.g., connect dance to their lives—sports is a natural connection), they begin to form meaningful links between the arts, learning, and life.

Freedom with Structure. Creativity is often enhanced by limitations. Creative dance is no exception. Freedom alone does not promote creativity. Freedom with structure does. Students need to be taught the necessary restrictions on space, time, touching others, following directions, obeying signals, and the use of props that make creative dance work. When rules are clear and consistently applied, students learn self-discipline and are helped to think divergently about the specific context in which they are working. None of us can move "any way we want, any time we want." Purposeful movement done with concentration on a specific problem is the goal; even in free time dance, there needs to be guidelines about space and other issues.

Teacher Questioning. Open or fat questions are a mainstay teacher habit in integrating creative dance: *How many ways? What's another way? What if. . . ? What is the shape of? . . . How might . . . move?* all direct students to think divergently. Alert students to these kinds of questions so that they can also begin to ask these questions of one another, as well as respond to teacher questions.

We Get What We Expect. The hundreds of studies that have examined the influence of teacher expectation make clear how important it is to get in the habit of demanding variety from students. A demonstrated belief in students' creative potential makes it much more likely they will rise to the occasion. Teachers need not limit meaningful dance integration to the common three-part sequence of (1) beginning frozen shape, (2) movements, and a (3) frozen ending shape, even though this is a solid structure to begin with as students learn to create dance phrases or compositions to express thoughts about concepts in science or math. Students soon reach the stage where they can construct their own dances, with an infinite number and kind of organizational structures. Even by asking for dance movements to be done at different speeds and at different levels stretches students' thinking, and teacher descriptive feedback can be used to show delight in the original ideas produced with minimal prompting.

Use of Student Ideas. Once students get comfortable with the general principles of integrating creative dance in science, social studies, math, language arts, and other arts disciplines, teachers can be alert to teachable moments with movement possibilities. There are obvious occasions. When it starts to snow, BEST elements can be explored to develop the concepts of blizzard, snowflake, and sleet. Movements can be abstracted and explored from current events students bring up (e.g., space events like the recent storms on the sun that resulted in magnetic "belches," or the passing of the Hale–Bopp comet).

Choosing Music for Dance. Some dance educators feel recorded music is incidental to the lesson and should mostly be used for warm-ups and creative dance exploration or free dance (Joyce, 1994). When music is used, it needs to be carefully selected. Choose music for dance that promotes creative, not stereotypical, movement and is rhythmic, but not too complicated. Shorter selections of simple classical music (Brahm's Fourth Symphony, Debussy's "Clouds," Wagner's "Forest Murmurs" and Saint-Saëns' "Fossils") work well, as do children's songs that suggest movement like those by Ella Jenkins and Kim and Jerry Brody. Begin with listening to the music and then invite students to respond by clapping or tapping feet and then using the whole body. From there, children can move into using more space. Go through your personal collections of tapes and CDs and look for music that:

- Makes you feel like dancing, that goes somewhere and makes you feel like moving.
- Has a clear quality (could be an inviting marching or delicate movement).
- Has no lyrics, instrumentals (no words), or words that aren't important to the quality (e.g., Enya).
- Has different tempos and moods.
- Has a variety of instruments (saxophone, piano, violins, drum, etc.).
- Contains folk music from different countries or ethnic groups or time periods.
- Is classical, especially soloists and chamber ensembles (symphonies can overwhelm).

Possible artists to use for either exploration or composition include classical composers such as Saint-Saëns, Debussy, Rimsky-Korsakov, Telemann, Schumann, Vivaldi, Bach, and Mozart. Often contemporary musicians and groups have a few selections that can support the dance experience. Try Paul Winter, Windham Hill, Loreena McKennitt, the Robert Minden Ensemble, or Peter Kater and R. Carlos Nakai. Those who specialize in children's music—Sharon, Lois, and Bram; Raffi; and Kim and Jerry Brody—often have one or two pieces that are "danceable." Both soundtrack Performance Group and Ravenna Ventures, Inc. have created music specifically for dance exploration and composition. See categories of music especially helpful for classroom teachers in Chapter 11. Here are some useful addresses for resources:

Soundtrack Performance Group
P.O. Box 22005 Glenridge Plaza
224 Glenridge Ave.
St. Catharines, ON L2T 2C1
Tel: (905) 682-8593
Fax: (905) 688-1900
e-mail: spgroup@vaxxine.com

Ravenna Ventures, Inc.
4756 University Village Place, NE #117
Seattle, WA 9810 USA
email — ravenna@accessone.com
tel: 206-528-7556
fax: 206-729-0377

Can. Ed. Media Inc.
43 Moccasin Trail
Toronto, Ontario M3C 1Y5
416-445-3900
416-445-9976

Classroom Management. Student self-control during creative dance comes from teaching students the discipline of dance, that is, how to control their bodies as they move. There is no magic trick or perfect set of techniques to make a class behave perfectly. A lot of management has to do with a kind of presence the teacher exudes—a demeanour that says "I'm in charge but we can work together and enjoy learning." In Appendix E there is a Post-It Page of time-tested techniques and habits used by teachers for classroom management. Here are a few basics that are particularly important for dance.

Show enthusiasm about teaching. The mood of the day is often set by how the teacher greets the class in the morning. Why not try a bit of sign language or other kinesthetic ways to say "Hello, glad to see you." The book *The Joy of Signing* (Riekehof, 1978) is excellent. Compliment students with descriptive feedback, and ask other students to give each other descriptive feedback to create a positive community feeling. Remember, many students initially feel uncomfortable about dance.

Dance cannot be integrated without movement and noise! Start with this expectation and make it clear to the principal and other teachers, who may not understand what you are doing. Consider holding lessons out of doors, but let students know dance used to make meaning is not free play or recess.

Structure lessons so that students know what to expect. Chaos derives from loss of clarity about goals and how to achieve them. Don't think this means a rigid structure, but a general organizational scheme is needed. An enormous variety of strategies and activities can then be selected within the structure. For example, think of all the ways to *introduce* a lesson—pictures, questions, objects, song, or a dance challenge.

Teach basic rituals for getting attention, start and stop signals, warm-ups, transitions and dividing into groups. All this can be done creatively with a personal flair: For random small groups, ask students to find others whose names begin with the same letter or who are wearing a particular pattern (stripes, circles). Readjust initial groups to even out numbers, if necessary. This causes students to think in categories and take time to examine details. A drum is a good investment because it can be used to get attention and for start and stop signals. Starting the class with students echoing a rhythm is an old favourite strategy for attention getting, and students can feel different rhythms usable in dance exploration. Patterns can be clapped or drummed: 1–2–3, 1–2–3–4, or 1–2–3–4–5–6–7–8. By changing the stress, students can feel and think about the effect of energy in dance or any form of communication. Don't forget to set signals for silence and for "noise," and practise each several times until they are automatic. (See *Joy of Signing* for ideas.)

Teach basic ground rules by explaining, posting them, role playing, and games. One idea is to draw a huge hand on a poster and call it your "Rules of Thumb" or "High Five" rules. Note rules on the hand and use a raised hand as a signal to think about the rules. Here are common rules teachers use: (1) follow directions (e.g., obey cues and signals), (2) respect others (e.g., personal space), (3) be responsible, (4) participate actively (enthusiasm), and (5) concentrate on paying attention (no talking during dance). Take time to have students role play following each rule. Role play non-examples, or the opposite, so that there is no misunderstanding. It's easy to practise rules in a game format. For example, play "home base" by telling students the goal is to not be the last one to get in their personal spot when the signal "home base" is given. Directions can be given in the form of a challenge to create interest (e.g., *"Before I count to eight, see if you can get into a perfect circle"*). Another helpful habit is to invite students to participate, rather than order them to do so (e.g., *"I'd like to invite all of you to try to make a shape on a low level that you think no one else will think of"*).

Teach students how and why to concentrate and focus. The current teacher concern about the perceived decline of student ability to attend may stem from expecting children to do things they have never been taught. Concentration and focus can be directly taught using games: "Frozen shape" challenges students to make a shape on their spot and hold it for so many counts. Students enjoy trying to increase the hold time each day and graph their efforts, and this can be a chance to compliment original shapes, especially stable ones that have a base and are balanced. Concentration is also helped by removing distractions and limiting the space for dancing (e.g., with masking tape or imaginary lines).

Rules are not worth much without consequences. A hierarchy of consequences, appropriate to the transgressions, should be made clear to students. Students are confused by teachers who are inconsistent, and perceive them as unfair. A consequence hierarchy can be as simple as (1) a warning (verbal or nonverbal), (2) a one-minute time out, (3) a five-minute time out and conference with the teacher after the lesson, and (4) loss of a chance to participate in the lesson that day and a phone call to parents. A teacher must be as good as his or her word and follow through, immediately, when a problem occurs; students will not believe or respect the teacher who continually threatens or warns without taking the promised action. Of course, hitting another child or disrespect for the teacher would call for a high-level consequence right away (number four!) and probably would involve the principal. There is no substitute for good teacher judgment and common sense. Finally, post general consequences, with the understanding among all that a teacher must do what is necessary to ensure the class is learning, and discuss them directly during the same time the ground rules are introduced (usually the first week of school).

Teacher habits for using dance are summarized in Post It Page 9–3.

Principle Four: ENERGIZERS AND ROUTINES

Use a Prop for Signals and Accompaniment. Simple props, like a drum or bell, are important tools for teachers to use routinely as start and stop signals and to help children work within a rhythm and tempo structure. Students also enjoy learning to use rhythm instruments to beat out rhythms for dance. Whistles are not the best musical instrument because they tend to demand and alarm, like a scream, rather than create an aesthetic mood. Don't forget that the human voice is a perfect vehicle for accompanying or signalling. If it is comfortable, sing a rhythm for students (left and right and left and right and stop), or use a special word or phrase to signal for attention or as a start–stop. For example, try famous dancers names as signals: "Isadora Duncan" rolls off the tongue and kids enjoy echoing it.

Energizers and Warm-ups. By using creative dance to start each day, students can be put in a better frame of mind and body for learning. Begin with easy movement warm-ups like the ones in Chapter 10. There are also recommended books of dance strategies and activities in the bibliography. For example, Gilbert's *Creative Dance for All Ages* is full of activities useful to energize and warm-up.

Principle Five: GREAT CHILDREN'S LITERATURE Related to Dance

See the appendix for dance-based children's literature that includes informational books, as well as fiction and poetry. For example, *Sometimes I Dance Mountains* (Baylor, 1973) is a lovely book with a poetic text that can stimulate many movement explorations before, during, or after the book is read. (Rhythm instruments can be added for background effects.) Isadora's *Max* can be used to relate dance and sports. Carl Sandburg's "Lines Written for Gene Kelly to Dance To" is a poem that asks the famous dancer to dance such ideas as the alphabet and the wind. The entire poem offers wonderful possibilities. Try it with a musical background, such as Leroy Anderson's "Sandpaper Ballet." (Say a line, turn up the volume, fade down, say the next line, and so on.) There is an annotated sampling of dance-based children's literature in Post It Page 9–4.

Any piece of literature can be examined for potential creative dance ideas. Invite students to find books about dance or ones with movement. Set up a permanent display spot that highlights dance and movement literature (e.g., use a clear plastic book pocket to display a book and change weekly).

Principle Seven: ADAPT Curriculum and Instruction Models

Fourth graders wrote stories during an Aboriginal unit and gradually a dance emerged. Stressing "authenticity rather than the stereotype," the class learned about spatial and floor patterns and were able to notate their original dances. During a study of weather, later in the year, a dance showing children's feelings about cold, by such movements as shivering, freezing, and sliding was created. The class went on to study pulleys and levers, resulting in experimentation with body balance and the concepts of gravity, strength, energy, and force. A study of pollution yielded a pollution dance. Boys created a "Gazinta"

> math dance based on the operation of division. Teacher DeNette Garber concluded, "Virtually all of our movement activities evolve around some phase of the fourth grade curriculum whether it be language arts, aesthetics, human relations, science, history, math, or current events. These experiences have made me realize that creative movement is not a frill or an extra added attraction." (Fleming, 1990, p. 30)

Unit Structures. In Chapter 2, four different unit structures were explained for integration. Each of the units is based on one of four centres or bodies with nine legs. See Post It Page 2–2.

Unit topics to be explored through dance can be solicited from students (feelings, weather, fire, water, celebrations, cooking, hiking, weddings, birthday parties, funerals, shopping, work, recess) by asking them to list movements that correspond to a topic. Once they explore these movements in unison and then in small groups, they can plan a three-part "frozen shape–movements–frozen shape" dance using choice BEST elements. *Note:* Stinson (1988, p. 51) recommends staying away from the topic of "superheroes" because of the aggressive nature of their actions. Also, stereotyped movements such as sitting "Indian style" or dancing to "war dances" during Aboriginal studies should be avoided.

An adaptation of the more common perspective on units is to envision a unit with dance as the body. A unit might focus on (1) a dancer or choreographer, (2) a genre or form (jazz, ballet, tap), (3) a problem, theme, topic, or question (e.g., Why do people dance? How do dances emerge?), or (4) a particular book, poem, song, or dance (e.g. *Chin Chiang and the Dragon's Dance* by I. Wallace) Major concepts and skills in math, science, social studies, reading and language arts, and the other art forms would be used as support legs. Of course, in

Post It Page • 9-3

Teacher Habits for Using Dance as a Teaching Tool

1. Emphasize process over product.
2. Use descriptive feedback to focus attention on dance elements and concepts.
3. Assessment and evaluation includes student self-evaluation.
4. Guided lessons are needed before free dancing.
5. Ask students to show rather than tell.
6. Give freedom with structure.
7. Teacher questions should be open or fat.
8. You get what you ask for, so ask for variety.
9. Use student ideas.
10. Choose music that promotes creative, not stereotypical, movement.
11. Teach students the discipline of dance, i.e., how to control their bodies as they move.
    - Show that you are enthusiastic.
    - Expect movement and noise!
    - Structure lessons.
    - Teach basic rituals for getting attention, stop signals, transitions, and dividing into groups.
    - Teach ground rules by explaining, posting them, role playing, and games.
    - Teach how and why to concentrate and focus.
    - Rules are not worth much without consequences.

any integrated lesson or unit, all bodies and legs should be correlated with courses of study and standards to ensure substantive and focused study. Post It Page 5–6 is an example unit web for an author–artist study. Examine the ways dance is used.

Start Small and Grow. Rather than plan a whole unit on dance or even one with significant use of dance, teachers and students often feel much more comfortable if trying just one lesson (e.g., a lesson on body parts related to health or a lesson on the shapes we can make with our bodies on different levels related to body language and communication). The key is to make sure first attempts are successful, for you and for students. Another way to begin is to integrate energizing warm-ups to introduce the day or particular lessons (e.g., math lessons after lunch could start with counted movements). Plan short lessons of about fifteen minutes at first. If classroom management is an issue, begin with students staying at their desks or help them learn about movement in one spot (e.g., stick a coloured dot or piece of masking tape on the floor to designate each child's home spot or personal space).

Post It Page • 9-4

Annotated Examples of Dance-based Children's Literature

Ackerman, K. (1988). *Song and dance man.* Random House. (a grandpa relives his vaudeville days)

Archambault, J., Martin, B., & Ted Rand (1986). *Barn dance.* Henry Holt. (the animals of the farm gather together with a skinny little boy for a hoedown in the barn)

Barboza, S. (1992). *I feel like dancing: A year with Jacques d'Amboise and the National Dance Institute.* Crown. (three students spend a year with the Institute)

Bourdeau Waboose, J. (1999). *Firedances.* Toronto:Stoddart. (A Nishinawbe grandmother passes on dance and cultural heritage in a coming-of-age story)

Cleaver, E. (1980). *Petrouchka*. Macmillan of Canada. (Petrouchka, a puppet with a soul, fails in his amorous pursuit of a ballerina puppet and is fatally wounded by the ballerina's other suitor, but his spirit lives on)

Gauch, P., & Ichikawa, S. (1992). *Bravo, Tanya.* Philomel. (Tanya loves to dance ballet in the meadow with the music only she hears, but in ballet class she finds it difficult to dance with real music)

Jonas, A. (1989). *Color dance.* Greenwillow. (three dancers show how colours combine through an overlapping scarf dance)

Lobel, A. (1980). "The camel dances." *Fables.* A Scott Foresman Edition. (a camel loves to dance ballet and performs for her friends; through this she learns a valuable lesson)

McKissack, P. (1988). *Mirandy and Brother Wind.* Knopf. (Mirandy tries to capture the wind as her partner for a dance contest)

Patrick, D., & Ransome, J. (1993). *Red dancing shoes.* Tambourine Books. (a girl is given bright, shiny, red dancing shoes that allow her to dance many dances, until something happens and she gets them dirty)

Tennant, V. (1977). *On stage, please*. McClelland & Stewart. (a young girl pursues her dream to be a professional ballet dancer)

Wallace, I. (1984). *Chin Chiang and the dragon's dance.* Atheneum. (a boy gains his grandfather's respect when he performs the dragon's dance)

Waters, K., & Cooper, M. (1990). *Lion dancer: Ernie Wan's Chinese New Year.* Scholastic. (Ernie, a young boy, describes the Chinese New Year and his first Lion Dance performance)

Wood, A., and Rosekrans, H. (1986). *Three sisters.* Dial. (Dot, one of the three pig sisters, wants to be a dancer until she takes her first class)

Structuring Clear Lessons. By giving children clear language and a predictable lesson structure, they will have the skills to succeed and feel safer about taking risks. Direct instruction can be used to teach basic elements of BEST (body, effort, space, and time) using visual aids like charts, and lessons can be focused on just one or two dance elements so that students are able to go into some depth, becoming comfortable with the possibilities of each element. Dancing about images like happiness or sadness or inviting free dance before the elements are grasped can be stumbling blocks to student success. Students may simply get silly (humour may be used to cope) or even withdraw if they don't have the necessary tools. Adapting instructional models like direct or explicit instruction calls for a three-part lesson framework using the introduction, development, and conclusion introduced in Chapter 2. (See integrated arts lesson framework in Post It Page 2–1 and the example dance plan in Post It Page 9–5.) Here are a few pointers related to dance:

Introduction. Teach elements directly and creatively by naming the element, using visuals, and continuing to remind students about the focus element throughout the lesson. Try to relate the goals (elements focus) to real-life uses and contexts. Get in the habit of asking students for examples, rather than telling them, so that they think as much as the teacher.

Development (demonstration and practice guided by teacher feedback and coaching). This is a time for students to experiment and explore: Ask *how, what,* and *where* questions about the elements. Ask students to move in *place* and then in *space*. Try the movement with different body parts and then with different locomotor movements. Change levels, directions, the time and speed, and energy. Ask students to combine elements. For example, walk at a low level slowly or with energy. *Note:* Teachers need only *model* a movement to help clarify thinking, not to get students to simply imitate, except in the case of teaching specific folk or ethnic dance step sequences.

Conclusion (opportunities for students to "show they know" they have met the lesson goals). At this point students should be able to put what they've learned to artistic use in a simple form. If students are to create a dance for classmates to observe, structure is essential (e.g., a frozen shape–movements–frozen shape sequence is a *basic* structure students can use to create dances). This involves creating a beginning, middle, and end. Encourage students to build in changes in levels to make dances more interesting. Ask students to freeze the starting shape so that you and their peers can give descriptive positive feedback on what the shape communicates. Students can be asked to give each other feedback on the element focus and what the dance communicated after a dance sharing. Finally, closure is achieved and important assessment information can be gained from asking students to explain what was learned about the element dance in general, and other subject matter content in the lesson.

The Integrated Dance Lesson: Connections and Meaning Making. Dance "suggests vitality of fresh, interdisciplinary and expressive experiences for children . . . active participation, meaningful activity, total involvement, and allegiance to high standards" (Fleming, 1990, p. vii). Loretta Woolard (Richmond, Virginia) is a teacher experienced in integrating dance into science. In a unit on the sea, her second graders increased their vocabulary and writing when they danced the concepts of waves, shells, fish, gulls, and other aspects of sea life.

> [Children] became better aware of their own potential, discovered spatial relationships, and were able to handle themselves. . . . I now know that a reading experience involves more than just books and words. It involves the child's life and interest as a source, his mind for thinking, his voice for verbalization (stories, poems, songs), his hands for writing, and his whole body for a deeper understanding through creative movement and dance. A child must sense and respond for true learning and understanding. (Fleming, 1990, pp. 24–25)

The point of teaching is to help students create meaning for themselves—to become independent. A lesson that integrates dance begins with the assumption that important concepts and skills will be taught about a subject *and* about dance. The planning begins with selecting topics, themes, questions, and problems to investigate (see possible unit structures in Chapter 2). To use dance successfully, the lesson focus should be full of movement possibilities—actions and shapes should readily come to mind. Joyce Boorman describes the use of action and reaction relative to a theme of natural phenomenon in her book *Dance and Language Experiences with Children* (1973, p. 2).

> The first group of words was centered around two ideas: "The Wind and the Leaf" and "A Forest Fire". Before the children came to the auditorium for the first dance lesson, I wrote [action] words on the board in the following order:

If "Mr. Wind" was---	*then the leaves would be---*
whipping	*whirling, twirling, swirling*
hurrying	*lying, floating*
rushing	*trembling, frisking*
fading	*settling*
whispering	*floating, lingering*

The children worked initially with one or two words, for example, "whirling" and "settling", or "rushing" and "flying", until they felt both the action and the quality or texture of the words.

When dance is used to explore concepts in content and skill areas (e.g., math, science, language arts, and reading), the teacher needs to feel comfortable that all the disciplines involved, including dance, are used in respectful ways and not trivialized. For example, a circle–cycle dance created to a steady beat in a unit on the circulatory system can help students understand the feeling of the heart pumping and beating, the blood moving, and how the whole system operates on a cyclical basis. They can get a better understanding of the word *circulatory* from relating it to the feeling of a circle shape.

It is helpful to preplan lessons by first doing an exploration of the content concepts and skills through dance elements. Think of the BEST elements to create questions and directions for students (e.g., *"Make circles with your head, tongue, wrists, knee"*). Start with a specific direction and move on to *"Think of a way to show a circle that we haven't done yet."* Actually write out some questions and directions you'll use. Imagine yourself teaching the lesson and seeing how the students are responding.

Once movement possibilities have been squeezed from the topic or theme, it is time to plan the introduction, development, and conclusion of the lesson. See Post It Page 9–5 for an example plan for fifth grade health and science and dance. Teachers need to decide on whether they will expect a dance structure as a culmination or if they will just be using warm-ups or isolated dance strategies throughout a lesson.

The conclusion of the lesson involves students showing what they have learned by demonstrating movements, or having a *memory minute* for everyone to close their ideas and review the lesson, or a relaxation exercise to *preserve the aesthetics* of the lesson. Plans need to include strategies for transition, use of space, materials, and even ways to dismiss by groups (e.g., *"Your ticket out today is . . ."* or *"All those that . . . may 'slither' out for a reptiles lesson"*).

Post It Page 9–6 summarizes preplanning steps for an integrated dance lesson. Post It Page 9–7 shows an actual example. Post It Page 9–5 is a finished lesson plan for integrating health and dance.

Build Dances Around Ideas. Any idea can be related to dance by asking questions involving the BEST elements and then connecting elements (travelling moves in different shapes or at levels). Ideas are also given depth by use of contrast; ask students to do the opposite or show a non-example, for example, the sustained or continuous movements of the circulatory system versus the bound movements of the digestive system such as food being swallowed, moving in clumps.

Adapting Curriculum to Meet Individual Needs. A final consideration under adapting models for curriculum and instruction with focus on dance integration involves a return to thinking about the different adjustments teachers can make for students with special needs. The adaptations introduced in Chapter 2 (Post It Page 2–4) were to change the *place, amount, rate, target objectives, instruction, curriculum materials, utensils, levels of difficulty, assistance,* and *response.* Using these changes, lessons can be matched to students' ages or stages (e.g., older students may laugh a lot at first because they are unsure of themselves and conscious of changing bodies; laughing is a way people deal with problems). Amount and rate can be adjusted by starting with basic dance warm-ups and doing a thorough job of teaching the BEST elements, one at a time, so that students are comfortable. Target objectives, materials, and response may need to be adjusted for physically handicapped students; for example, wheelchair-bound students, with limited use of the body, might be given the role of beat keeper or be in charge of start and stop signalling.

Principle Nine: EXHIBIT Student Progress

When You Want an Audience. Using dance as a teaching tool involves planning for students to both "do and view." "The processes of creating, performing and appreciating dances and the skills, knowledge and understanding gained from such experiences, can be defined as *artistic education* in that the learner is coming to know more about the art form itself" (Smith-Autard, 1994, p. 268). For example, through concert viewing, students can develop a *discriminating* awareness of movement as an artistic medium. When there is a need for students to exhibit progress through performance, teachers can invite parents and grandparents or use the children themselves. By dividing the class in half and taking turns performing, students are put in both the "do and view" roles. Audience mem-

Post It Page • 9-5

Example: Integrated Dance and Health Lesson Plan (grade five)

Two-pronged Focus: (1) Circulatory system concepts and (2) dance elements
Student Objectives: Students should be able to:

1. Show dance phrases that express differing heartbeats (rhythms).
2. Show movement qualities that express changes in the circulatory system (e.g., flow).
3. Use body shapes and personal space to show heart's shapes and movement.
4. Maintain focus.
5. Work cooperatively in groups.

Teaching Procedure

Introduction: The teacher will:

Signal for attention and tell students to sit in personal space.

Remind about posted rules.

Use riddle routine (riddle on board).

Ask what they remember about heart and circulatory system. Use visual of circulatory system.

Show how to take pulse and move to beat. Use slit drum.

Ask "What if. . . ?" and "Show me. . . ?" beats and rhythms during rest, anger, etc.

Development

Read aloud fantasy journey and ask students to show with body shape and focus what is described (about heart changing rhythms).

Choral read and move to "Dr. Heart" chant to show heartbeat and blood flow. Repeat and increase rate.

Pause to ask about flow (sustained movement) and rhythm or beat (percussive).

Play "Tranquility" tape and ask students to create a sustained or percussive movement to go with it.

Group students to create a dance with a beginning–middle–end to show flow and beat. Challenge them to include creative use of the "circle."

Circulate and give descriptive feedback as students work.

Conclusion

Divide class so one-half observes while others dance.

Audience gives feedback about concentration, percussive versus sustained beats, and shapes (e.g., circles to represent cycle).

Repeat chant.

Ask what they learned.

Assessment and Evaluation: Observe students and use checklist with range of evaluation criteria from "clear" to "not present" based on objectives 1 to 5.

bers can be asked to give descriptive feedback after the performance so that they see their role as meaningful. This develops social skills and the ability to do analysis and evaluation. Of course, as with all art exhibitions, it is important to stress that there is no right nor wrong and that applauding is a part of the ritual. A variety of start and stop signals can be used to structure performances (e.g., say "curtain," "show time," "close your eyes," "positions," and "lights," as cues).

Videotapes of student dance compositions can be added to portfolio collections related to any topic under study to show how students are using movement to demonstrate learning. These tapes can serve as progress indicators of how students are using ideas like BEST or variations on the three-part dance to "show they know" about key concepts and skills in science, social studies, math, and language arts. In addition, students can re-view past tapes and do self-evaluations of how they have grown related to the use of dance.

Principle Ten: SPECIALISTS Are Important Resources

Collaboration. Dancers, dance educators, and physical educators are all potential persons to help integrate dance in a regular classroom. Teachers can begin a collaboration by showing an interest in using dance throughout the curriculum and by finding out what specialists are doing that could be used in the regular classroom. A positive way to begin collaboration of this kind is to ask to observe dance lessons. If there is a dance specialist in the school, she/he can be given lists of units, concepts, and skills to be taught during the month. Specialists can be asked to provide the same information to the classroom teacher so that both can look for possible links. Once a working relationship begins to develop, specialists can be asked to do special lessons with students that connect to classroom lessons. Classroom teachers need to expect to reciprocate.

Reassurance for Classroom Teachers: Common Problems

In the dance, even the weakest can do wonders.

Karl Gross

Any teacher who values creativity and movement can learn to integrate dance. Teachers who feel uncomfortable about dancing in front of students need to understand that this is not at all necessary to integrate dance throughout the curriculum. Students can be asked or directed to move in certain ways without any demonstration; this actually can cause students to do more creative problem-solving than if they were shown a specific step. After all, the goal of integrating dance is not to imitate the teacher.

Another problem that sometimes arises is with the word *dance* itself. While teachers and students occasionally feel uneasy using the term dance, we need to "call a spade a spade." Dance must be recognized as an aesthetic form along with music, visual art, drama, and film. By calling it *movement*, the aesthetic elements are discarded. Using the term *Creative Dance* is quite acceptable, as the elements being explored and the process of discovery and composition are intrinsic to the form of *Creative Dance.* Most people will accept that students must know how to move appropriately and that creative thinking is an important life skill to develop—what would any business be today without creative problem-solving?

A third concern is a lesson that flops. Most failures seem to occur because the teacher does not know what the specific thing is to be learned or when preparation or structure is lacking. By using a lesson plan framework, much of this problem can be alleviated. Such a framework includes (1) the arts elements to teach and the content area concepts and skills to be developed and (2) a clear introduction, development, and conclusion that organize the teaching and learning. Keep in mind that too many directions confuse students and that dance is kinesthetic—get students moving as soon as possible. Learning to integrate dance involves trial and error, and when something is not working, teachers should feel free to alter *strategies* in the lesson plan while maintaining the dance and other curricular focus. It is possible to be flexible but to be guided by basic beliefs about effective teaching, how children learn best, and the principles of arts integration.

Finally, the dance construction by the children should not be considered an absolute essential. Teachers who do not feel well prepared may confine the creative aspects of their teaching to other areas of movement exploration, such as more teacher-directed dance element exploration. Eventually, students spontaneously begin to construct dance sequences, if they are given experiences that focus on problem-solving through movement exploration, invention, and improvisation. "The culmination of the aesthetic in dance education is an 'intellectual' knowledge of dance from all aspects and across all the organizing strands, introducing critical, imaginative, appreciative, and perceptive faculties." (Bannon, 1997, p.28)

Conclusion

In this chapter, an introduction to integrating dance throughout the curriculum has been discussed with a focus on the role of the general classroom teacher. Rationale was presented for integrating dance *(why)*, information teachers need to know was reviewed *(what)*, and general principles for integrating dance were explained *(how)*. In Chapter 10, specific starter ideas for teaching dance basics and integrating dance throughout the curriculum are given. See the appendix Bibliography of Recommended Reading and Viewing for additional resources.

Post It Page • 9-6

Preplanning: Integrated Lesson with Dance

Start with one of four "bodies" for lessons: (1) problem/topic/theme/problem, (2) person, (3) core book, or (4) genre/form, and decide the content focus for the dance exploration.

Brainstorm movements related to:

- **Body:** parts, shapes, actions (nonlocomotor/on the spot and locomotor/travelling)
- **Effort:** space, timing, force, flow
- **Space:** personal, general; direction, pathways, levels, size, destinations, focus
- **Time:** speed, duration, rhythm, patterns/phrases, accent

Plan questions and directions: to cause "exploration" of BEST and concepts from target discipline (e.g., science). Think about lesson introduction, development, and conclusion.

Plan dance composition criteria: e.g., frozen shape (5 counts), movements (10 counts), shape (5 counts)

Make plan using *Integrated Plan Form* in Chapter 2: Post It Page 2–1 includes teaching strategies organized into introduction, development, conclusion.

Post It Page • 9-7

Example: Preplan for Integrated Lesson with Dance

Start with one of four "bodies" for lessons: *Themes = No one likes to feel powerless. We all like to be in control* (core book: *Where the Wild Things Are*).

Brainstorm movements related to:

- **Body**
- **Effort**
- **Space**
- **Time**

Focus on flow (bound versus free) and using concentration on speed (fast and slow) to develop feel of control (inside self).

Body: all parts, shapes doing nonlocomotor and locomotor with "powerless qualities" (e.g., floppy, jerky, uncertain).

Questions and directions to cause "exploration" of BEST and concepts from target discipline.

Ask how Max felt when he had to stay in his room—besides angry. Use your hand to show how you can control your foot without touching it, like there is an invisible string attached. Try using a finger to control your knee . . . your elbow. Bend over and hang loose, dangling your fingers and arms. Explore loose and controlled with body parts. Take steps forward and backward as if pulled by an invisible force. Walk across the room using an uneven rhythm that shows you are not in control. Collapse to floor level in a loose way. Move all body parts with lots of control and flow. How different does this feel? Start at head and move to feet doing controlled, sustained, and slow moves and then faster. Do same with controlled and bound, slow and then fast.

Dance composition criteria

In small groups, make a dance that compares powerlessness with self-control. Start with a frozen shape. Put five to ten actions in your dance. Have a frozen ending shape. Be sure to include different levels and shapes in your dance.

Go now to *Integrated Lesson Plan* framework form (Post It Page 2–1).

Activities:

Opening Vignette: What? Why? How?

Think about Mr. Moore's lesson. What did he teach about both dance and science? Why did he use the strategies he used? How did he cause the students to become active in the lesson?

Abstract a Movement

Think about an everyday movement (e.g., washing the dishes, combing your hair). Take a minute and explore it. Go beyond "pretending" to do dishes or whatever movement you choose. Instead, explore the movement potential itself, by moving using different body parts than would normally be used. Try doing the movement fast, then very slowly. Feel the essence of the movement.

Qualities of Movement

Rudolf von Laban (1879–1958) was a dancer and a movement scientist who studied the elements that create "qualities of movement." He discovered how mood is created by combining eight actions, using different degrees of effort and amounts of space. The eight are thrust, slash, float, glide, wring, press, flick, and dab. Each is made by movements that are either sustained or sudden, strong or light, direct or indirect. For example, wringing is a twisting and turning movement that must be sustained; it is strong and involves several body parts going in different directions (versus direct action toward a definite goal). Think like Laban and complete this movement analysis chart:

Action	Sudden or Sustained	Strong or Light	Direct or Indirect
Wring	Sustained	Strong	Indirect
Thrust			
Slash			
Float			
Glide			
Press			
Flick			
Dab			

Sign Language

Get a book of sign language like *Joy of Signing* (Riekehof, 1987) and make a list of ten signs you can use in your classroom. Students love to learn: very good, sit down, line up, listen, dance, funny, yes, no, partner, and other common "words" through this kinesthetic communication system.

Selected Teacher Resources

Alison, L. (1991). *A handbook of creative dance and drama*. Portsmouth, NH: Heinemann.

Bennett, J. P. (1995). *Rhythmic activities and dance*. Champaign, IL: Human Kinetics.

Bergman Drewe, S. (1998). *Creative dance: Enriching understanding*. Calgary, AB: Temeron Books.

Bergman Drewe, S. (1998). *Creative dance inspirations: Facilitating expression*. Calgary, AB: Temeron Books.

Choksy, Lois (1987). *120 singing games and dances for elementary schools*. Englewood Cliffs, NJ: Prentice Hall.

Creative movement: A step towards intelligence (1993). West Long Bran, NJ: Kultur (80-min. video).

Dance and grow (1994). 60-min. video. Scotch Plains, NJ: Dance Horizons.

Fleming, G. A. (1990). *Children's dance*. Reston, VA: American Alliance for Health, Physical Education, Recreation and Dance.

Gilbert, A. (1977). *Teaching the three Rs through movement experiences*. Minneapolis, MN: Burgess Publishers.

Gilbert, A. (1992). *Creative dance for all ages*. Reston, VA: National Dance Association.

Joyce, M. (1984). *Dance technique for children*. 1st ed. Palo Alto, CA: Mayfield Publishers.

Landalf, Helen (1997). *Moving the earth: Teaching earth science through movement for grades 3–6 (Young Actor Series)*. Lyme, NH: Smith & Kraus.

McGreevy-Nichols, S. (1995). *Building dances: A guide to putting movements together*. Champaign, IL: Human Kinetics.

Nachmanovitch, S. (1990). *Free play: The power of improvisation in life and the arts*. New York: G. P. Putnam's Sons.

Pica, R. (1995). *Experiences in movement with music, activities, and theory*. Albany, NY: Delmar.

Rowen, B. (1994). *Dance and grow: Developmental dance activities for three-through-eight-year-olds*. Pennington, NJ: Princeton Book Co.

Stinson, S. (1988). *Dance for young children: Finding the magic in movement*. Reston, VA: American Alliance for Health, Physical Education, Recreation and Dance.

Taylor, P. *Music for Creative Dance* (cassette titles: *Dreams and surprises*; *The moving environment*; *Zone zero*; *Dance links*; *Feet, fins and wings*; *Motor skills*; *Carols for dancing*). Don Mills, ON: Can. Ed. Media.

References

Web Sites

www.artsednet.getty.edu (Opening Doors to Arts Education from the Getty Education Institute for the Arts)

www.edu.gov.on.ca/eng/welcome.html (Ontario Curriculum Policy Documents)

Books, Articles and Papers

Anderson, C. (ed.) (1998). *This passion: For the love of dance.* Toronto, ON: Dance Collection Danse Press/es.

Bannon, F. (1997). "An aesthetic approach to dance education." In *Proceedings of the 1997 Conference of Dance and the Child: International; The Call of Forests and Lakes.* Kuopio, Finland: 28–36.

Baron, R. (Feb. 1997) Scientific thought in motion. Presentation at The Kennedy Center. Washington: DC.

Boorman, J. (1969). *Creative dance in the first three grades.* Don Mills, ON: Longman Canada.

Boorman, J. (1971). *Creative dance in grades four to six.* Don Mills, ON: Longman Canada.

Boorman, J. (1973). *Dance and language experiences with children.* Don Mills, ON: Longman Canada.

Ellfeldt, L. (1976). *Dance from magic to art.* Dubuque, IA: Wm. C. Brown Co.

Fisher-Stitt, N. S., & Warner, M. J. (1997). "Integration: Friend or foe of dance in the schools?" In Proceedings of the 1997 Conference of Dance and the Child: International; The Call of Forests and Lakes. Kuopio, Finland: 381–386.

Fleming, G. A., ed. (1990). *Children's dance.* Reston, VA: American Alliance for Health, Physical Education, Recreation and Dance.

Gardner, H. (1983). *Frames of mind.* New York: Basic Books, Inc.

Garrett, R. (1994). "The influence of dance on adolescent self esteem." In Proceedings of the 1994 Conference of Dance and the Child: International; Kindle the Fire. Sydney, Australia: MacQuarie University, 134–141.

Gilbert, A. (1992). *Creative dance for all ages.* Reston, VA: National Dance Association.

Greenhill, J. & Patrick, K. C.(1995). "Creative movement for everyone." *Dance Teacher Now*, November 1998.

Haselbach, B. (1994). "Dance and the fine arts: An interdisciplinary approach to dance education." In Proceedings of the 1994 Conference of Dance and the Child: International; Kindle the Fire. Sydney, Australia: MacQuarie University, 166–175.

Hill, R. (1978). "The importance of dance experiences and concepts in the aesthetic development of children." In *Keynote Addresses and Philosophy Papers: Dance and the Child.* Edmonton, AB: University of Alberta, 64–79.

Hunt, P. (1997). "The role of dance in producing ecological change." In Proceedings of the 1997 Conference of Dance and the Child: International; The Call of Forests and Lakes. Kuopio, Finland: 146–151.

Jay, D. (1991). "Effect of a dance program on the creativity of preschool handicapped children." *Adapted Physical Activity Quarterly,* 8, 305–16.

Joyce, M. (1994). *First steps in teaching creative dance to children,* 3rd ed. Mountain View, CA: Mayfield Publishing.

Morningstar, M. (1986). *Growing with dance: Developing through creative dance from ages two to six.* Heriot Bay, BC: Windborne Publications.

Murray, R. L. (1975). *Dance in elementary education: A program for boys and girls,* 3rd ed. New York: Harper & Row.

Pica, R. (1991). *Moving and learning.* Champaign, IL: Human Kinetics.

Purcell, T. (1994). *Teaching children dance: Becoming a master teacher.* Champaign, IL: Human Kinetics.

Riekehof, L. (1987). *The joy of signing,* 2nd ed. Springfield, MO: Gospel Publishing House.

Rossberg-Gempton, I. (1998). "Creative dance: Potentiality for enhancing psychomotor, cognitive, and social-affective functioning in seniors and children." *B.C. Dance Educators' Association Quarterly,* Fall 1998, 5.

Smith-Autard, J. (1994). "Expression and form in the art of dance in education." In Proceedings of the 1994 Conference of Dance and the Child: International; Kindle the Fire. Sydney, Australia: MacQuarie University, 268–283.

Stinson, S. (1988). *Dance for young children: Finding the magic in movement.* Reston, VA: American Alliance for Health, Physical Education, Recreation and Dance.

Waboose, J. B. (1999). (Ill. by C. J. Taylor). *Firedancers.* Toronto, ON: Stoddart Kids.

Children's Literature References

Baylor, B., Sears, B., & Longtemps, K. (1973). *Sometimes I dance mountains.* New York: Atheneum.

Cleaver, E. (1980). Petrouchka. Toronto, ON: Macmillan of Canada.

Isadora, R. (1976). *Max.* New York: Simon & Schuster.

Sendak, M. (1964). *Where the wild things are.* New York: Harper& Row.

Tennant, V. (1977). *On stage, please.* Toronto, ON: McClelland & Stewart.

Wallace, I. (1984). *Chin Chiang and the dragon's dance.* Toronto: Groundwood Books.

Dance Seed Strategies

Consultant:
Mary-Elizabeth Manley

Who can turn a child's mouth into a smile? A child's thoughts into a dream? Who can turn a child's walk into a dance?

A teacher.

In this chapter there are specific ideas to (1) get students ready for dance, (2) teach basic elements and concepts so that students can use dance as a learning tool, and (3) integrate dance throughout the curriculum. These seed strategies must be grown by developing them to fit student and curricular needs. Seeds can be selected to solve particular teaching and learning problems and can be adapted for students with special needs. The strategies are organized into the following sections, but many could be placed in several sections. Energizers and elements and concepts do *not* represent integration, as they stand, but are provided to ready students for creative work and teach dance concepts needed if dance is to be used as a way to make meaning.

I. Energizers and Warm-ups
II. Dance Concepts BEST Elements Activities
III. Connecting Dance to Other Curricular Areas
- Science
- Social Studies
- Math
- Reading and Language Arts

I. Energizers and Warm-ups

The purposes of energizers and warm-ups are to get the attention of students, actually warm up the body so that it is ready to dance, set mood, and stimulate creative problem-solving. Many build concentration and skills in following directions.

Watch My Hand Concentration. Partner students. One is the "hand" and the other must follow the partner's hand with his eyes. Leader should change levels and directions. At teacher's signal, partners reverse roles.

Hang Loose. Use an object to represent the concepts of "relaxed and tense" or "loose and tight" (e.g., scarf versus rock, piece of yarn versus pencil, rag doll versus Barbie doll). Call out a body part and ask students to make it tight and hard, then loose and soft.

No Words. Teacher uses only motions to tell students what to do: *"Come forward, turn, sit."* Students then get a partner and communicate what to do without words. Don't *show* your partner. Tell with your movements. Repeat without using hands. Afterward, discuss the role of gestures and movements in communication.

Stretches to Music. Direct students to slowly: *Inhale, reach up and overhead and to floor with knees bent. Exhale. Repeat to each side. Roll head and shoulders forward and backward, bend arms, do socket rolls, touch head to shoulders, touch knees, touch toes, sit and twist and bend, do slow windmills, toe presses, heel to toe slowly, clasp hands behind and stretch shoulders, spine stretches, squat and press forward (exhale), bend one leg and repeat (exhale).* Slow, nonrhythmic mood music can be used, and many CDs and tapes are available with nature sounds that work well.

Step In. This is a simple movement activity. Children form a circle and the teacher gives a series of movement directions. For example, *Take two steps in if you know the capital city of Newfoundland. Step back one if you know the name of the new Inuit territory.*

Weight Shift. Ask students to *"Move foot to foot (most basic locomotor step). Go smaller, larger, faster, slower. Expand to leap with body curved forward."*

Who Started the Motion. Players stand or sit in a circle. One player is sent from the room while another player is selected to be leader, who leads others through different motions, such as moving hands or tapping feet. Player who left the room comes back in and watches carefully to figure out who is starting the movements as the leader begins a new one.

Cumulative Name Game. Form a circle. The first individual says his or her name and makes a motion. The next person says the name and makes a motion and then everyone repeats the first person's name and motion. The process continues in a cumulative manner until it goes all around.

Hand Warm-up. Teacher directs everyone to make a fist and then show 1, then 2, then 3, then 4, and then 5 fingers. Repeat. Do other hand and then both. Change tempo.

Hug Yourself. Leader calls out body part to hug (e.g., hand hug, finger hug). Encourage creative thinking.

Head, Shoulders, Knees, and Toes. First practise singing the song by this title. Then repeat and ask students to stand in a circle and touch body parts as they are mentioned in the song. Do the movement sequence, dropping the name of one body part from the song each time until the entire sequence is hummed.

Then repeat adding in a body part to the song and sequence one at a time.

Follow the Leader. Students imitate actions or words of the leader. For example, move different body parts at different levels. Use the BEST elements for ideas.

"Simon Says" with Dance Elements. Play "Simon Says" using BEST elements (Post It Page 9–2) and Laban actions (e.g., bend, twist). For example, "Simon Says" use your body to show a circle. Relate to units (e.g., time lesson: move clockwise in a circle).

Body Touches. Do a rhythm or chant (e.g., "Touch your head, head, head . . . touch your toes, toes, toes), and ask students to do the appropriate movements.

Walk Different Ways. Ask children to walk in the following ways: in place slow and fast, forward, backward, and sideways. Work on posture and alignment: students walk freely as you call out tiny steps, giant steps, on heels, on tiptoe, in place, backward, forward, as lightly as possible (an element of force), or as slowly as possible (an element of time). Use scarves and students throw up scarves and must catch with different parts of the body as they walk. Can be done to music. Other materials: balls, hoops, ropes.

Freeze (self-control). Play music or use a tambourine and tell students to move in a specific way using space until the sound stops and they must freeze. When the music begins again, they are to move in their frozen shape. For example, "When drum begins, you are to walk in place to the beat."

Magic Shoes. Students should imagine they have on magic shoes that allow them to walk in special ways (e.g., on water, on air).

Body Directions. Say, *Show me "up" with your body, "down." How can you make your body go all the way up? All the way down? How high can you get? Show me halfway down. Make yourself so small I can hardly see you. Now as big as you can. Imagine your feet are glued to the floor. Move your body up and down now.*

Fantasy Journey (for concentration). Teacher tells or reads a story or series of movements. For example, *Put your feet into warm water and wiggle your toes. Now put your legs in and swish them around. Make circles in the water. You slip farther into the water and sway your hips back and forth. You are up to your waist. Slowly walk in place in the water. Feel the weight of the water. Now you raise your hands up out of the water and stretch them over your head. You jump up and down. Feel the water. You sink down up to your neck. Let your arms float on top of the water. Press your hands down in the water to your sides and then raise them up. Put your hands on your hips and twist, twist, twist. Now rotate your head forward, to left and back, then right and around again. Oops, the water splashes up your nose, so you wiggle your nose and blow the water from your lips. With your toes you pull the plug and the water begins to drain out. You shiver as it moves below your arm pits. As it reaches your thighs, you raise your knees up and down, up and down. Finally the water drains out. You twirl around and sit down.*

Spaghetti Freeze (for following directions). Students move in as many loose and relaxed ways as they can. Do these in one spot, varying the speed and levels. When the teacher gives a signal, students must freeze in a shape. Students can then be asked to give a one-liner about their shape (e.g., how they feel).

Five Shape Concentration. Goal is to create, number, and remember shapes. Teacher says "one" and each person makes the first shape. On "two," a second different shape is made. This continues through "five." Then the teacher calls numbers at random and students must do the shape they first made for that number.

Slow-motion Concentration. Each student picks an everyday movement and does it as slowly as possible. Groups can perform by dividing class in half, with audience half giving feedback on focus and concentration.

Circle Back Rub (relaxation). Form circle and each person puts hands on shoulders of person in front. Leader says "go" and each person rubs the back of the person in front. Leader says "switch" and all turn and do same for person behind them.

Lightning Concentration. Form circle and join hands. Teacher squeezes a rhythm to both the right- and left-hand partners and the rhythm is passed around the circle until it collides in one person. That person shouts "lightning" and becomes the leader.

Paranoia (concentration). Group spreads out to fill up space. On signal (e.g., drum beat), they all begin to walk around the room trying to fill up the space and leave no holes. The leader then calls "one" and everyone finds someone to follow around, not letting the person know he's being followed and still trying to fill up the whole space. Then the leader calls "two" and a second person is followed. Finally "three" is called. The leader then alternates numbers and everyone continually switches, filling up the space.

Popcorn. On signal, the group begins to walk around, filling up space. When leader signals "one," each person identifies a person to track with their eyes. Whenever they actually come near that person, they jump. Next the leader signals "two" and a second person must be tracked, while still tracking the first. When the second person is passed by, you must now freeze for a split second. Everyone is now walking around jumping and freezing. Finally, leader says "three," and a third person is now visually identified by each individual. When that person is passed, say "popcorn." Continue until the leader signals "freeze."

Breathing Warm-up. Slowly breathe in through your right nostril and out through your left. Breathe in slowly, becoming as high and large as you can and then slowly exhale and shrink as small as possible. Breathe in very slowly and exhale slowly, making a single sound. Group can choose to make same sound (e.g., one of short vowel sounds). Breathe in slowly with clenched teeth and out through your nose. Breathe to the rhythm of a piece of music. Put your hands on your abdomen and breathe in slowly and exhale slowly.

Wiggle and Giggle. Ask students to show how they can giggle with a foot, a knee, and on up the body to the head. Shaking and wiggling with controls (signals, numbers) helps students learn self-discipline and focus.

Energizers and Warm-ups for Cooperation

Add On. Groups of four to six form and stand in a line, side to side. At one end a person starts a movement and the next person picks it up and adds to it. The movement travels down the line until the end. The originator then moves to the end and a new inventor begins.

Movement Chain. Stand in a line or U shape. On signal, people on the two ends start a movement or a rhythm and send it around until it reaches the end. End people then go to the centre of the line, and new end people start new movements or rhythms.

Don't Cross the Line. Pairs face each other and hold on to shoulders. They imagine a line between them. Each starts pushing, but cannot cross the line. The goal is to push hard, but not push each other over. Repeat back to back or side to side.

Buddy Walk. Pairs are back to back, leaning against each other. First, they silently walk around the room. Then they try to sit on the floor and rise up again. Can be done side by side.

Back to Back Dancing. Pairs slightly lean against each other and begin dancing with music. Use something slow at first. Each must try to sense what movements to make to keep them together.

Shrink and Stretch. Group forms a circle stretching out so only fingertips touch and extending out as much as possible without losing touch. Leader signals "shrink," and the circle moves in and tries to take up as small a space as possible. Then leader says "stretch" again, and so forth.

Balloon Balance or Bust. Group joins hands and forms circle. Several balloons are thrown out and the object is to keep them in the air without dropping each other's hands.

Stuck Together. Pairs must hold a note card between their two body parts (e.g., head to head with card in between). Another card is then added, and so on, until one card falls. Can be done in small groups with one person in the centre and others joined to the one person with a card in between. When leader signals, centre person must move and group must try to follow without dropping cards.

No Holes. Group spreads out to fill up all available space. On signal (e.g., drum beat), everyone walks around trying to keep the space completely filled. When leader signals "stop," all must freeze. If there is a hole, someone must fill it up.

Body Count. Everyone walks around and fills up the space. Leader then calls out a combination (e.g., three heads and two hands). Students must work together to find others to create this combination of touching body parts.

Spider Web. Everyone in the group must be touching someone else in an appropriate spot. When leader signals to start, everyone moves slowly around the room, always touching someone (e.g., with a foot, hand, shoulder). When leader signals "stop," everyone must be touching (i.e., connected by the human web).

II. Dance Concepts and BEST Elements

These strategies and activities can be used after you have introduced the BEST dance elements.

Personal Space. Teacher directs students to find a personal spot. Students then explore their personal space, not moving from the spot, by making shapes at low, middle, and high levels.

Action Words Charts. Challenge students to find all the words they can that go in either the locomotor or nonlocomotor categories. Here are examples:

Locomotor: walk, run, leap, step, jump, hop, drag, slide, scoot, gallop, skip, crawl, creep, dart, dash, float, fly, glide, patter, pounce, prance, roll, sail, spin, stamp, swoop, tramp, slip.

Nonlocomotor: bend, stretch, twist, swing, rock, sway, collapse, curl, dodge, expand, explode, flop, grab, jerk, lean, lift, point, poke, pull, press, push, quiver, rise, shake, shiver, sink, sit, slap, squirm, strike, sway, tap, thrust, turn, wriggle, writhe.

Movement Words Card Sort. Ask students to call out ways to move. Write them on cards. Ask groups to sort the cards into locomotor and nonlocomotor. Next, ask students to list adverbs that qualify each (e.g., walk slowly, quickly, with force, directly, in a "shape," using a lot of space, in a rhythm).

Locomotor and Nonlocomotor Action Bingo. Give the definition of these dance concepts. Students cover the word on a bingo card. See Chapter 2 for "big bingo" idea.

Walk: shift weight from one foot to other with one foot always on the ground.

Run: same as walk, but there are moments when neither foot touches the ground.

Gallop: this is a step leap with the same foot always leading in an uneven rhythm.

Leap: like a run but you are in the air longer with both feet off the ground.

Skip: combines step and hop in an uneven rhythm, and the lead foot alternates.

Jump: weight changes from both feet to both feet.

Hop: requires weight change from one foot to the same foot.

Shake: trembling or vibration of whole body or body parts.

Bend: close up your joints.

Stretch: open up your joints.

Push: use your body to move against a resistance.

Pull: use your body away from a resistance.

Twist: rotate in a direction up to the body's limit.

Turn: spin around, whirl, and twirl.

Rise: come up to a higher level.

Sink: move down to a lower level.

Other action words to add include: zoom, slither, scatter, explode, crumple, melt, and tiptoe.

I'm Stuck. Students stand in personal space. Teacher narrates a series of sticky situations and students mime:

You are clapping your hands when they suddenly won't come apart. You work them to try to get them to separate. Finally, they pop apart and you reach up to scratch your face. Now your hand is stuck to your face. You are frustrated because you try different ways to pull your hand off, but it is hard. Blop! It comes off and you start to walk around when your left foot sticks solidly to the floor. This time you decide to make the best of it, and you move around all the ways you can with your left foot glued down. Variation: Follow up with writing about feelings.

Body Actions, Travelling and In Place. Use these activities as ways to practise types of moves and steps:

Leap: Pretend to leap over objects or use actual objects (e.g., a log or a rubber swimming pool).

Hop: Use a hoop. Students hop in and out. Hop all the way around the hoop. Change tempo.

Jump: Jump in the following ways: knee straight, landing and taking off only on balls of feet, with feet together, then apart, alternating these, landing on one foot, clicking heels together in air.

Run: Explore running with imagery. Ask the students to run on hot sand, to the finish line, playing basketball, to catch a bus, etc.

Slide: Slide as if the floor was slick, the floor was warm, you are tired, you are in a hurry.

Step hop: Clap a one–two beat with your hands and instruct students to step on beat one and hop on beat two. Then try it to music.

Stretch: Ask students to stretch like they are waking up, yawning; ask them how long they can stretch out, how wide.

Bend: Do bends from real life (e.g., to tie shoes, pet a dog, pick up a dime on the floor).

Sit: Have students practise sitting, kneeling, and lying down without the use of their hands.

Shake: Ask for images of shaking in real life and do (e.g., a bowl of jelly, a baby's rattle, piece of bacon sizzling on a pan, leaf in the wind, riding on a bumpy road).

Turn, twist, lift: Have students practise turning on feet. Do at different levels and speeds.

Rock and sway: Sway like the wind and then gradually increase the force of the sway so that it is more like rocking. Ask students to sway while walking, slowly, faster, larger, smaller, etc. (Pica, 1991).

Eight Laban Effort Actions. Practise these actions in various ways by asking students to use different body parts or amounts of energy or by changing the timing (sustained versus quick): *Punch, slash, wring, press, dab, flick, float, glide.* Ask students to try to lead with different parts of body (e.g., glide with your shoulder, flick with a hand, punch with a shoulder). Finally, give three Laban actions and ask students to create a dance with five movements. Dance can be in the three-part frozen shape–movements–shape sequence. Partner and have students teach each other their dances.

Shake It Up. On a signal, everyone shakes and wiggles a body part. When leader says "freeze," all must stop. Begin again. Ask students to give descriptive comments about body shapes when they freeze.

Movement Problems. Begin a movement such as arm swinging. Ask problem-solving questions like *"How can you make it smaller? Show me. Now larger. Move the swinging to whole body and then back to just arms. What are the effects of these movements?"* Have half the class do and others observe and then reverse. Ask fat questions like *"What did you see? How did it feel?"*

Across the Floor. Divide into groups and do as relay. Teacher calls a travelling action (e.g., walk, run, leap, jump, skip) or a combination, and when the student touches the "target," the next person goes.

Walks. Ask students to walk to a variety of drum beats (e.g., half-time, double-time, walk time, march time). Next, direct students to explore other aspects of walking by talking them through a sequence: *"Walk in place and then walk around the room without bumping into people. Cover the whole room. Walk with toes first. Walk as if you . . . just got a compliment, were just embarrassed, have a stomach ache, are worried, are expectant, have a heavy load, are in love!"* Encourage walks in low, medium, and high levels to music (e.g., Enya).

Imagination Walk. Line up the class and each takes a turn and walks to a destination as others observe and describe. Each must walk a *different way* to the other side of the room. Repeat and add energy, change time, use space and body differently, repeat phrases.

Jump–Turn–Freeze. Students walk around and keep an eye on one person. They should not follow the person. Next, add a second person and then, after a while, a third person to the list of others that each student is trying to watch. Students are to keep walking. Then say, *"When you pass the first person JUMP!"* Continue for a while and then add TURN for the second person and finally FREEZE for the third.

Levels (Space). Students create a shape and then freeze in low, middle, and high levels on a count or signal.

Pathways. Everyone spies a destination and then moves there in a straight pathway and back home, then a curvy pathway and back home, using as little space as possible, with stops and starts inserted, and so on.

Adopt a Dance. Each person chooses a movement or step and gives it a "unique touch." Sustain until you make eye contact with someone and then adopt their dance.

Dance Machine. Each student chooses a movement that can be repeated over and over. One student goes to the centre and begins to dance. One by one all "add on" by touching on some plane and repeating his or her movement until all are "one" machine with a variety of moving parts. Machine can be around an idea (e.g., a book or chapter in a book, a concept or feeling).

Pass It On. One person in the circle starts a movement and others imitate until the original movement gets all the way around to the starter. The next person to the right then begins a new movement, and so on. Do to music.

Four Corners Stations. Each group begins at a station with a movement problem (e.g., a warm-up station could have a tape of music or directions, stretch station, wiggle station, walk-in-place station). At signal, students rotate to next station.

String Shapes. Each person stands in elastic loop (one yard of tied together elastic). They then make movements while holding on to the elastic. Ask the children to then move to music while creating a variety of shapes with the elastic.

Responding to Accent. Clap a phrase accenting the first beat (e.g., think of "I love you" with accent on three different words). Clap the same phrase accenting the last beat. Children move to the phrase, showing the accent by a change of movement (after time element is taught).

Video Response. Watch a video (e.g., a musical with dance in it like *Anne of Green Gables*) that ties into a lesson's topic and has a dance connection. Have children watch for specific dance elements (BEST) and how they are used to communicate an idea or feeling. This can be a jigsaw cooperative learning activity.

Ribbon or Scarf Dancing. Tape about two feet of ribbon to the end of a dowel, creating a wand for each student. In a large space, allow students to experiment with dancing to music with the scarves or ribbons.

Shape Rope. In own space, hold rope up high and drop it. *Look at how rope landed. Make the same shape with your body.* Continue dropping the rope in different ways.

General Space. Use imaginary bubbles or hula hoops. Have students imagine that the hoops are big bubbles around them. Ask them to explore the limits of their hoops or bubbles. Now have them dance carefully without touching others' bubbles. Use drum or count to change time, space, energy.

Personal Space. Provide a carpet square or a hula hoop to represent personal space. Ask students to dance at low, medium, and high levels. Combine with force, time, and leading with different body parts (e.g., bend slowly leading with your shoulder).

Balancing Actions. Ask students to stand in their spots and explore balancing challenges (e.g., stand on one foot, on tip toes, twist), but while balancing a book on their heads.

Energy. Ask for images that create slow, strong, quick, weak, or light movement pictures. For example, *"What moves slowly and lightly?"* Compare and contrast movements.

Statues. Assume a shape. Change on signal to another shape. Say *"memorize your body."* Do at different speeds. Do three shapes and put together as a shape or statue dance. *Variation:* Move freely around the room until the teacher says *"freeze."* Students then stand still in a shape and do not move until the teacher says *"go."* Teacher should give descriptive comments on shapes (e.g., levels, space).

Movement Sentence Add On. Each person creates a sentence (e.g., three movements or steps) and next person adds on. Do in small groups.

What Did You See or Feel? Divide notebook paper into four sections. As each group presents its dance, the audience records impressions in one of the squares. After the dances, written comments are shared.

III. Connecting Dance to Other Curricular Areas

In this section there are examples of seed strategies that use dance to explore concepts and skills in science, social studies, math, and language arts. Courses of study and curriculum guides are useful in identifying dance material suitable in curricular areas, and topics for dance exploration can be solicited from students. To do the latter, ask students for dance ideas related to categories such as feelings, weather, fire, water, celebrations, cooking, hiking, weddings, birthday parties, funerals, shopping, work, and recess. Movements can be explored in unison and then in small groups. A culminating activity is for students to plan a dance with a beginning, middle, and end around an idea. The three-part freeze–move–freeze dance structure can be used as a starter.

Science Focus

- Natural world, systems of the body, seasons, weather, plants, animals, the environment, machines, electricity, magnets, space, gravity, and states of matter.
- Finding out how and why things happen in the world through careful observation, hypothesis making, and prediction.

Webbing. Choose any topic (see examples in Post It Page 10–1) and web all the kinds of movement associated with it. Use BEST dance elements to expand movements. Break into groups, and each group chooses one or several to explore by doing movement possibilities. Share with class.

Environmental Dance. Choose a category from Post It Page 10–1 to explore through movement using the principles in Chapter 6.

Environmental Walk. Explore how to walk in different places: beach on hot sand, deep sand, on an icy hilly walk, crowded city street, in a parade, up a steep hill. Discuss why walks must be changed.

Places to Sit. Experiment with the effect on the body on places to sit: on a bicycle, on a horse, on a swing, on an airplane, on a step, on a pillow. Make frozen sculptures and ask half the class to view and comment as they would for a museum display. Reverse roles. Combine with photos and art, for example, Rodin's *Thinker.*

Tool Dance. Explore movements associated with tools: shovel, vacuum, typewriter, saw. Next, label the different movements and discuss common movements.

Mechanical Movements. Brainstorm things that move in nonorganic ways (e.g., jerky moves of robot or computer). In pairs or small groups, show how to move different body parts at different levels using mechanical movements.

Post It Page • 10-1

Environmental Sources of Dance Making

Use webbing strategy to discover the many different movements associated with the topic. Then use BEST dance elements to expand on the movement ideas. Explore, then select the dance ideas that clearly reflect the topic. Have students shape the dance ideas in a sequence with a beginning, middle, and end.

Body systems: respiratory, circulatory, digestive, nervous

Body actions: eat, walk, run, hug, hop, skip, sit

Seasons and cycles: life cycles (e.g., butterfly)

Growing things: small to large movements, slow, sustained

Weather: contrasts in nature (e.g., force of tornado versus gentleness of a breeze)

Plants: sizes, shapes, ways they grow

Animals and insects: cats creep, stretch, sneak, roll, slink, ball up, leap

Places or environments: movements at beach, mountains, desert, prairie, tundra, ocean

Machines and mechanical actions: pulleys and levers, tools

Electricity and magnetic forces: north and south poles, pull, repel

Space and solar system: rotate, use of space, size, shape, pathways

Gravity: force, pull, weight

States of matter: solid, liquid, gas

Causes and effects: temperature, wind

Energy: fire, steam, solar, nuclear

Technology: computer, elevator

Inventions and objects: crepe paper, cotton balls, rope scarves, elastic

Dance Machines. Create a group dance based on BEST elements of machines, like the elevator, escalator, and computer. (See description of "machine" in Chapter 9.)

Science Insect Dances. Each student or group chooses an insect to explore through movement. Dance should include movements related to eating, life cycle, environmental changes, and their effects.

Real-life Sounds. Sounds of the body, city, nature, animals, machines, chants, rhymes ("Pease Porridge Hot"), familiar songs ("Row Row Row Your Boat"), and nonsense phrases ("Ziggety Zaggety Zap") can inspire movement. Children's names, names of provinces, cities, work chants ("heave heave ho, yo yo, heave heave ho") are also sources. Explore the rhythm, size, shape, and energy of sounds. Stress original movements that no ones else does.

Ordinary Objects Dance. Use common things like facial tissue, boxes, paper clips, ropes, and elastic bands to create a dance of inventions in which movement *with the object* is explored, not mimed.

States of Water. Students show through dance the molecular movement in a solid, liquid, or gas. Lead students through small-group explorations to move as if melting, condensing, evaporating, and so on. Explore changing from a solid to a liquid and then to a gas. Use different parts of the body, effort, space, and time. Finally, ask each group to create a freeze–move–freeze dance that shows they've learned about molecular movement and structure in the different states of water.

North Pole, South Pole Magnetic Force. Students try to walk as if the floor is a giant magnet. Then suggest that the ceiling is the magnet. Call out the pull on different body parts. Suggest they walk as if the body is an opposite pole of a magnet. How would it move?

Habitats. Ask students to choose an outdoor place or environment—forest, beach, mountains, prairie, tundra. Move imaginatively on or through the habitats. Consider creatures living in the environments and choose an endangered species. Explore all the ways it might move under different circumstances (tired, hungry, scared, threatened). Use "what if..." questions to explore all possibilities. Use children's literature for resource ideas, for example, *The Elders Are Watching*, to link environmental concerns, art and culture.

Heartbeat. Listen first to heartbeat and then take pulse. Students then move to their own heartbeats using a variety of shapes and ways of travelling through space. Ask "What if . . ." questions: *"You got really scared? tired?"*

Bird Flight. Students work in groups to create a dance based on different types of bird flight. Include the different formations (space and pathway) birds use, changes in speed and level, changes in leaders. Think about different body parts. Dance should have a beginning, middle, and end.

Weather Dance. All students are frozen in a shape. Weather changes are announced by narrator and they respond by changing levels and shapes for snow, light rain, and raging hailstorm. Begin by restricting movement to one spot and then encourage travelling. *Variation:* Convert to a relay dance in which all start frozen and then begin to move, one at a time, until all are moving. Then reverse the action. This works well if the weather event starts small and slow, escalates, slows, and stops.

Arts Alive. Make action come to life from a painting by creating a freeze, move, freeze dance. For example, use *Dempsey and Firpo* or *Stag at Sharkey's* by George Bellows and discuss balance, centre of gravity, momentum, muscles, use of light and shade.

Life Cycle. Students dance each phase of the life cycle of an animal, insect, or plant separately by using BEST elements. After each phase, have them put it together in a dance. Stress that movements can convey feelings. Sounds can be added.

Constellations. Start in frozen shapes of constellations in small groups and then move across night sky to night sounds. *Variation:* Small groups rotate in and out of the "stage" space or come in low, move to high formation, and back to low across the space.

Social Studies Focus

- Relationships among human beings, occupations, transportation, communities, governments, customs, cultures, holidays, and use of natural resources.
- History, geography (use of maps), civics (citizenship and government) or political science, economics, anthropology, and sociology.
- Investigations into cultural diversity and global understanding.
- Special questions: How did it used to be and why? Why is it like it is today? What can I do about it? Thinking processes: cause and effect, sequence, gather data, discover relationships, make judgments, draw conclusions and problem-solve about community issues (e.g., economic issues like school funding or values conflicts related to free speech).
- Use of primary source material like newspapers, art, music, diaries, letters, journals, books, and artifacts, rather than the use of textbooks and gathering data through interviews, surveys, and other investigatory strategies that historians and other social scientists use.

Post It Page 10–2 uses BEST to explore action in social studies.

Real-life Rituals. Brainstorm patterns of movement in life (greetings, farewells). Divide into pairs and explore the patterns with one another in a variety of ways using BEST elements.

Work Movements. Brainstorm all the ways people work: picking, washing, sweeping, raking, fixing. Each person creates a work dance based on a real or imaginary prop associated with work (e.g., broom). Music could be added. Dance should have a beginning, middle, and end.

Trio Dances (to develop community). Trios form and each develops a shape and dance phrase around a concept (e.g., loneliness). All group members teach their part to their group. The final dance consists of members doing the dances of all members in a sequence.

Ceremonies. Invent a ceremony related to daily life within the classroom. Create a dance to accompany it

Post It Page • 10-2

Social Studies: Topics with Movement Possibilities

Directions: Choose any topic and then experiment with all movement associated with it. Brainstorm and then explore BEST dance elements related to:

Holidays
Customs
Legends
Rituals
Population density
Directions
Land and water formations
Occupations
Everyday actions (cook, wash)
Economic development
Transportation
Communities
Governments
Cultures and diversity
Citizenship
Global understanding
Housing
Map skills and geography
Social interactions (sharing, cooperation, respect, trust)
Physical environment (e.g., use of natural resources)
Thinking skills: cause and effect, sequencing, gathering data, discovering relationships, making judgments, drawing conclusions.

Big Questions: "How did it used to be and why? Why is it like it is today and what can I do about it?"

and use high, medium, and low levels in the dance, for example, a start–the–day ceremony.

Military Movements. Use military actions to prompt thinking. Research actions used in different countries (e.g., pivot). Learn terms and actions like left flank, right, centre, offence and defence (Joyce, 1994).

Explore a Country or Province. Show terrain by changes in levels as narrator describes a tour of a place. Show the size of the province or country in relation to other countries or provinces as teacher calls them, for example, Prince Edward Island and Quebec. Use movement to show what you know about a place (products, industries, climate, or plant life) by interacting with them through dance and imagination.

Dance a Historical Event. Brainstorm actions that would have been part of a special event like the signing of the Nisga'a Treaty. Do in slow motion, changing rhythm and space. Create the mood of the moment with your body.

Holiday and Season Dances. Brainstorm movement qualities of Halloween characters (stiff movements of a skeleton) or create a "giving" dance for Thanksgiving (focus on rituals and feasts), or "loving shapes" to rhythms for Valentine's Day. Spring dances can focus on rising and stretching and other growing movements.

Current Events Dances. Use teachable moments: brainstorm dance possibilities. For example, the Olympic Games can inspire sports dances or dances related to the opening or closing event.

Multicultural Folktale Dance. Focus on an event in a folk tale, for example, Gerstein's *The Mountains of Tibet*: a man chooses his own country when he is offered a new life anywhere in the world.

Sports Dance. Create dances using sports actions. Have students plan warm-ups and then explore motions of the actual game. Try sequences in slow motion to create intrigue. They can play music to go with the movements and organize final explorations into a freeze–move–freeze dance.

Folk and Ethnic Dances. Discuss different ways dances have been used through the centuries (ceremonies, prayers, celebrations) and how the forms of dance have evolved, based on common movements used for expressive purposes. Teach a dance or some steps from another culture or time period. Discuss what is represented (rituals for marriage, weather, seasons). When teaching traditional dance steps, it helps to use an "I do, we do, you do" sequence: All face the same direction. Show the whole dance, then practice in unison until all have the basics. Involve children in the process of identifying step components and then join steps to create a whole work or even a new step. Steps do need to be mastered before doing the dance figures in which they are to be used. Mix up partners frequently so no one feels "stuck." (This process deviates from total teacher direction requiring only student imitation.)

Folk dances are usually appropriate for students eight years and up and can begin with short dances based on a dance step like *walk* in time to music, walk in a circle, forward and backward. Horas and kolas of the Middle East are basically a series of steps and variations on the steps performed without partners in a circle or open circle. Some demand challenging footwork. Common dances include the polka, waltz, schottische, and mazurka. *Variation:* Create original dances around the same topics. An example is the *Irish jig*. Begin by playing Irish folk tunes and or showing a video of Irish folk dancing (e.g., "Riverdance"). Ask open questions about the BEST elements and the feel of the dance. Then have students make their own jig using their feet and legs. Hands are held behind the back. Encourage them to step or tap to the beat, but create new steps, turns, and so on.

Reading and Language Arts Focus

- Reading, listening, speaking, written composition (including handwriting and spelling, grammar, usage, capitalization, and punctuation). Since reading and language arts are processes, they must be connected to a subject to have meaning, i.e., something to read and write about.
- Goal: *Create* meaning and enjoyment using print through thinking, at every level from memory to critical thinking or evaluation.
- The printed word and its components (letters, syllables, spelling patterns), how words combine to make phrases and sentences, and sentences combine to make paragraphs and other forms of discourse, from tongue twisters to novels.
- Types of words: antonyms and synonyms, parts of speech and figurative language (metaphor, idiomatic expressions).

Phonics Shapes. Ask students to make soft shapes for soft *c* and *g* words and hard shapes for hard *c* and *g*, for example, city, ceiling, giraffe; cat, can, go, gone. For short and long vowels, make sustained movements (vowels are continuous; when given a vowel make your body long or short when you hear the sound of a long or short vowel). Consonants can make "stop" sounds that can be danced using bound moves for *b, p, t,* hard *c, k, d,* hard *g, j, v* and sustained for consonants like *s, l, r, m, n*. For consonant blends, students can partner to show "blending." Vowel digraphs can be shown in pairs with one person becoming "silent."

Letters of the Alphabet. Students work in pairs to make letters; use high, medium, and low levels. Stress original ideas and ask students to explain their interpretations. *Variations*: Write letters with different body parts. Walk, jump, skip, hop letters in large or small patterns. Students make a shape of an object that starts with the letter. Do at different levels and speeds.

Rhyming Words. Give a spelling pattern (*-ack, -ick, -ot, -eek, -id, -op*). Read a poem that contains many words with the pattern or read a list, some of which should have the rhyming pattern. When students hear a word that rhymes with the pattern, they do a creative movement (e.g., make different shapes).

Syllables. Ask students to change BEST dance elements according to number of syllables. Say words aloud. For example, *"Hippopotamus has five syllables so make five shapes as I say each syllable."* Vary the elements (e.g., time, energy) during word repetitions.

Spelling. Teacher gives a word and students spell it by moving in a floor pattern to "write it" using a chosen pathway to shape the letters. *Variation:* Pairs call words to each other.

Antonyms. Brainstorm movement words and opposites, for example, smooth–jerky, tight–loose. Then (1) call a word and students do it at different levels and speeds, (2) call a word and students do its opposite, and (3) partner students with one person doing the word and the other its opposite. Use with different levels, qualities, and tempo.

Compare and Contrast. Contrast movements like heavy–light, tight–loose, explosive–smooth, up–down, and wide–narrow by asking students to jump all these ways. Compare ways to do the same movement: walk = stride, pace, shuffle, tramp.

Word a Day. Pick a movement word. Students try to squeeze the word for all its possible meanings by exploring it through movement and finding synonyms and related words (e.g., jump = bound, vault).

Word Walls and Webs. Develop and extend vocabulary through movement by asking students to be on the lookout for action and movement words in all their reading. Put up large paper on a wall. Ask students to add unusual words to the word wall web. At any point, these words can then be used for movement (e.g., slither, sneak, ambulate, dodge, drag, plod, saunter, amble, trot).

Cause–Effect. Pair students facing each other. One is the *cause* and the other is the *effect*. Cause moves and the effect must respond appropriately (e.g., if cause steps forward, effect must move to keep from being stepped on). Encourage creative effect responses.

Classification. Call out a category or way to classify a movement. Students explore all they can do in that category (e.g., low level, bending, twisting, reaching). *Variation:* Students take turns demonstrating three different actions and group must guess the category.

Parts of Speech. *Adverbs example:* Do locomotor/nonlocomotor movements/steps different ways (e.g., merrily, sadly). *Literature verbs:* select from a story, put on cards, explore different ways (e.g., run slowly, crawl sneakily). Combine into dances about a chapter or event in a story.

Gestures. Brainstorm everyday gestures used to greet each other or respond (e.g., wave, beckon, stop). Explore ways to perform gestures (e.g., fast, slow, different body parts, levels).

Tableaux. Get into small groups and use body shape and space to show a concept (e.g., grief, celebration, loneliness). Freeze in the shape.

Math Focus

- Daily living situations involving counting, measuring, probability, statistics, geometry, logic, patterns, functions, and numbers.
- Problem-solving through use of skills (raising questions and answering them, finding relationships and patterns).
- Concepts about numbers, operations, and concepts like bigger, longer, greater than, less than, three, four, even, and odd.
- The National Council of the Teachers of Mathematics (Canada and USA) and the Provincial Math Educators Associations encourage teachers to have children solve problems in many ways, focus on explaining and thinking, rather than just correctness, and using a hands-on approach.

Math is basically the study of quantitative relationships. Dance is also concerned with relationships among shape, time, and size. Through dance, students can come to understand basic math concepts like add, subtract, divide, and duration (second or minute). Higher-level math skills require sequential thinking, examining situations for important details and patterns. Dance also involves these types of thinking, so dance and math can reinforce one another.

Facts and Functions. Consider all the functions in math; include estimating, adding, subtracting, multiplying, dividing, patterns, geometric shapes, fractions, lines, and curves. Discover movement possibilities for each. Assign groups—students then decide at least three different ways to show one math concept through dance patterns.

Geometric Shapes (following directions). Everyone walks around filling up the space. When a leader calls out a shape, all freeze in that shape (circle, triangle, square). Leader should give feedback for unusual ideas (use of energy or space). *Variation:* Students partner to make the shape. Do also with letters of the alphabet.

Telling Time. Use masking tape to make a large clock on the floor. Children move around in the twelve-hour spaces by stretching arms to a person in the middle of the clock as a time is called by the teacher. Explore different times: recess time and lunch time and ways to move around (fast, slow, hop, slide).

Shape Dance. Many folk dances are done in a circle, square, or line. Invite a guest to teach one and relate it to the math concept. Challenge students to find other math ideas in the dance (e.g., counting, parallel lines, sequencing—first, second, third).

Get the Facts! Call out math problems for students to solve by jumping, hopping, or walking along a number line. Give a different way to move each time (fast, slow, low, halting, flowing). Sounds, chants, and instruments can be added.

Math Glue. Everyone moves around the room in slow motion. Teacher says "glue 2" and students find others to stick to in that number (everyone must keep moving in slow motion). Teacher then calls "unstick" and continues with a new number.

Twos and Threes. Teach number groups by calling out a way to move and giving the pattern. For example, *"Hop in twos with a pause after the two hops."* Make into dances of moves grouped into twos and threes.

Angle Dance. Students create a dance that illustrates angles (right, oblique). Each dance should have a beginning, middle, and end and can be locomotor or nonlocomotor. Use freeze, move, freeze form.

Math Dance. Students choreograph a dance to teach to others by creating instructions in math terms. For example, math hop = take two steps forward, slide right, hold for four counts, and hop three times.

Number Shapes. Teacher calls out a signal and students make their bodies into shapes of numbers. They may need to work together. Challenge them to make these shapes combining with time, space, and force.

References

Books

Joyce, M. (1994). *First steps in teaching creative dance to children.* (3rd ed.) Mayfield: Mountain View, CA.

Pica, R. (1991). *Moving and learning.* Champaign, IL: Human Kinetics.

Children's Literature

Bouchard, D., & Vickars, H. R. (1990). *The elders are watching.* Vancouver, BC: Raincoast Books.

Gerstein, M. (1987). *The mountains of Tibet.* New York: Harper and Row.

Integrating Music Throughout the Curriculum

I am music. I make the world weep, laugh, wonder and worship.

Goethe

CLASSROOM VIGNETTE

Bud the Spud

Mrs. Davis's grade four class was beginning a unit on Canadian geography. As soon as she pulled a potato out of her bag, Jessica laughed and said, "I know—Bud the Spud." A few of the boys chanted "It's Bud the Spud of the bright red mud, goin' down the highway smilin'" in a perfect imitation of Stompin' Tom's voice. By the end, there were smiles all around. The students in the class had become used to Mrs. Davis's strategy of introducing units of study through music. The previous week, she had put Stompin' Tom Connors's song "Bud the Spud" on a cassette in the listening station along with the book of the same title.

"Well, we might as well play it, I guess," was Mrs. Davis's response, and Andy, the helper of the day, went to turn on the tape. On his way, he asked, "Can we join in on the chorus?" Mrs. Davis replied "Sure," and they all listened and sang the parts they knew.

When it finished Adam asked, "Is that true about the OPP?"

Mrs. Davis: "What do you think?"
Dylan: "Is that song true? is the first thing we need to know."
Amber: "I bet there was a guy called Bud the Spud, but it was in the olden days."
Mrs. Davis: "What olden days do you mean?"
Amber: "When our parents were kids."
Lindsay: "Well, can we find out when Stompin' Tom wrote that song? Oh yeah, I remember, we can look at the recording date. Do you have the tape box here, Mrs. Davis?"
Mrs. Davis: "No. I'm sorry, I taped it at home. I'll bring it in tomorrow. Now, can you guess the first thing I'm going to ask you to do?"

Lots of hands go up and the following ideas are offered:

"Talk about where our bag of potatoes at home comes from?"

"Listen again and write down all the places in the song and find them on a map?"

"Tell you something new we learned from the song?"

"Tell you how many verses there were?"

"Write a new verse for the song?"

"Ask our parents if they know the song?"

"Tell you what kind of music that was?"

"Can we make home-made french fries?—oh, I guess the hot oil is too dangerous for school."

"Tell you what kind of potatoes we like best—oh yeah, and do a survey and a bar graph like we did for favourite colours?"

Mrs. Davis: "Boy, I can always trust you to give me some terrific ideas! Well, it was actually to listen again and write down all the places Stompin' Tom sings about. Thanks for rewinding, Andy. Are we ready?"
Jessie: "And then let's draw and cut out potatoes and stick them on the places on the big map."
Tyler: "French fries will win that survey. No contest!"

The tape begins and everyone starts to write. Many whispers of "How do you spell Charlottetown?"

Introduction

Where words leave off, music begins.

Heinrich Heine

Every child begins life immersed in the most basic element of music—rhythm. The steady beat of the mother's heart introduces the baby to patterned sound. Into the safe, suspended world of the womb also come outer world voices with unique rhythms and timbre. The unborn child responds, physically, to these external sounds, showing an innate desire to listen and learn. Early on the fetus reacts to phonemes (smallest sound units) like the percussive consonant sounds of */t/*, */p/*, and */f/*. Phonemic awareness later forms spoken language. As the growing child listens, the brain grows, absorbs, and makes connections that establish lifetime patterns. If the external world is rich in music, the brain's structure will reflect it. So, even before birth, children hear sounds in their brains. Eventually, these inner sounds become the foundation for learning to read as children connect them to the printed page and learn to conjure the *music of words* during silent reading.

Music—a sound so pleasant we continually seek out its beauty. We never seem to get enough. Once it was common to hear people sing, whistle, and make music going to work, at work, and at school. Workers sang in farm fields, musicians played on street corners, and families gathered around the piano after dinner. Then came television, tapes, CDs, and headsets. Somehow a notion developed that only a talented few should sing or play instruments. The rest were to listen.

Musical Development: Preferences and Tastes

Most children enter school with some background in music, and many have well-defined preferences. Musical taste seems to be established in early childhood and not easily altered (Schuckert and McDonald, 1968). Because the introduction to music usually occurs in powerful social contexts like singing with friends, listening to the radio as the family travels, or singing in church, the result is positive, even passionate, feelings attached to particular styles or genres of music. Music is of central importance in the world's cultures, but *how* it is important varies greatly. Personal musical tastes develop through the process of acculturation. Children whose parents sing to them and who hear many kinds of music are more likely to sing well and have diverse tastes. For example, some cultures expect every person to participate by singing or playing an instrument: In Polynesian culture singing in harmony is valued, and so many Polynesian children sing well. In the Vendan culture (Africa), each child's first rattles and bangs are celebrated and amplified by adults; parents convert baby's rhythms into music, in the same way North American parents expand babblings of "ma-ma" into "Mommy, yes, I am your mommy." Most cultures go further to use music in a range of important societal rituals (e.g., weddings, holidays) (Page, 1995).

In light of brain research, it is not surprising to learn that Mozart and Haydn grew up in musically fertile environments. Babies, the world over, babble the phonemes of the language around them, and children want to sing and hear comfortingly familiar music. We know a foreign language is best learned when the brain is still growing rapidly, and this is also true for the language of music. Conclusion? The elementary and middle school years need to be musically rich. Young children are more open to types of music—from classical to country—and it is what they hear the most that becomes what they like and value. The teaching implication is to take advantage of this openness to musical diversity by providing experiences with an eclectic range of styles, types, periods, and cultural music experiences. Such variety sustains interest, engenders a flexibility of attitude, and builds respect for the diverse expressions of people. From American jazz to African drums, the world is full of music for children to enjoy and learn.

Music Is Not Part of My Job

Classroom teachers have lost confidence in their abilities to use musical experiences and often claim a lack of resources. It is no longer common to see a piano in every classroom, and it is possible for pre-service teachers to take *no* music courses during pre-service years. Generalists and specialists have grown to believe in some places, the music teacher should solely be responsible for children's musical education, which contributes to the perception that music is an élite domain of the talented and well trained. Yet, in many cultures outside North America, there isn't this degree of separation between the talented and untalented; everyone is thought to have the ability to express feelings and to think through music. It is unfortunate for music *inside* North American schools to become segregated in a manner so unlike music *outside* school. Students miss much by not having music fully integrated into the curriculum.

Because inexperienced teachers and those with minimal music background may feel uncomfortable with the explicit teaching of musical literacy, it helps to view music integration as an experience to be offered, rather than a subject to be taught—there often is a specialist to do the latter. If music integration is conceived as a way to explore, test, and investigate ideas by connecting music to topics studied, the general classroom teacher usually feels more comfortable and specialists less threatened. In this view, the focus is on student participation and the process, not perfect singing or competence in playing an instrument. Another way of putting it is to consider that generalists are not teaching just for the aesthetic experience that music provides, but *through* it. Every child deserves to grow up with music woven into the full fabric of learning, not as an isolated event that happens every other Tuesday.

Why Should Classroom Teachers Integrate Music?

> *Most people will go to their graves with their song still in them.*
>
> Benjamin Disraeli

Throughout history, music has been used by every culture to share messages of inspiration, to tell stories, to pass on history, to inspire others, to glorify achievements, and to amuse, relax, and educate. Music is used to express love, anger, despair, and hope. Young adults use music to bond with peers and express individuality. Parents use music to comfort and communicate with infants and toddlers; they instinctively sing to babies, play music boxes, and rhythmically rock fussy children.

Recent research on connections between music and brain development, along with studies by educators, psychologists, and linguists on music's potential to stimulate intellectual development in children, has piqued the interest of both teachers and parents. A new industry of private music schools, such as Kindermusik Canada (Cambridge, Ontario), has sprung up as a result. Children's communication and perceptual skills are enhanced by early music experiences, and even unconscious listening gives a foundation for conscious listening—listening *is* a basis for learning. When young children use music to explore their environment, they engage in critical phonemic awareness experiences necessary to speak and read. (Current research in reading disabilities targets lack of phonemic [sound] awareness as a determining cause of problems; children who cannot hear distinct sound nuances have trouble decoding words.) Music making begins early with the babbling songs of babies, and babies can grow into children who use music to gather information and sort out feelings, ideas, and experiences.

Indeed, we now know a great deal, and yet it is still somewhat of a mystery how music affects us. It is clear that play and music arise from instincts to create, express, and experiment, so it isn't surprising that music raises students' interest in subject matter. It is also clear that experiences with listening to music and opportunities to respond to and perform it all stimulate imaginative thinking and sharpen problem-solving skills. Music is, in fact, one of the seven alternative ways of knowing counted as a distinct form of human intelligence (Howard Gardner). Post It Page 11–1 gives examples of current efforts to use music as a learning tool.

Reasons to Integrate Music

A man should hear a little music, read a little poetry, and see a fine picture everyday of his life.

Goethe

1. **Music is a significant part of life outside school.** Imagine a day without music. Out would go the

Post It Page • 11-1

News Bulletins — Music Research You Can Use

In one experimental study, 1200 elementary and high school students in Austrian and Swiss schools had five music classes per week, rather than the usual one or two, at the expense of math and language classes. After three years, they were as good in math and better in languages than their peers who had regular schedules with more math and language classes (Armstrong & Casement, 1977).

The College Board Entrance examinations reported that students with course work in music performance or the arts scored 59 points higher in verbal and 44 points higher in math on the 1995 SAT (Scholastic Achievement Test).

Seventy-eight preschool children who were exposed to eight months of music keyboard and singing lessons scored 34 percent higher on temporal-spatial reasoning tests than their peers. (Rauscher, Shaw, Levine, Wright, Dennis, & Newcomb, 1997)

A review of fifty-seven studies showed all the following were increased through arts experiences: self-concept, language, cognitive development, critical thinking, and social skills. Of special note was the positive effect of music participation on self-concept (Trusty & Oliva, 1994).

Music therapy has been found successful in illnesses ranging from anorexia or drug addiction to profound mental retardation (e.g., to help autistic children tolerate being touched). It triggers the release of endorphins, our body's natural opiates. It changes the brain waves (e.g., people with Parkinson's have had their walking become more rhythmic over a three-week period and gain more assured quality and cadence). (National Association for Music Therapy, 8455 Colesville, R. Suite 1000, Silver Spring, MD 20910, 301-589-3300) radio, our CDs, much of television. Life without music would be dull indeed. In addition to the spice music adds to life, music is an important career field. The direct economic impact of the arts and cultural industries sector in Canada, in terms of gross domestic product (GDP), when both direct and indirect economic impacts are taken into account, is almost $40 billion. The sector's labour force grew by 5.5 percent between 1989 and 1994; in contrast, the total employment in Canada decreased slightly over the same period. In 1993–94, 894,000 jobs (6.9 percent of employment) were directly associated with the sector, and almost 1.1 million jobs were associated with it directly and indirectly (Statistics Canada). We spend hundreds of millions each year on concerts, CDs, tapes, and music videos, making music more than an incidental component of our economy, and there are more than 100 orchestras in Canada that generate employment for thousands of people. The music recording industry in Canada has grown substantially over the last decade. Between 1990 and 1995, sound-recording exports grew by 324 percent (Statistics Canada). Music is big business.

Much of school motivation comes from the perception that what is learned is important to life beyond the school walls. Music is out there. We need to bring it in and make explicit how it is connected to life and learning. Music elements are so embedded in our lives we don't even think about how hard it would be to talk, read, or walk effectively without them. Think of the roles of rhythm, accent, and tempo in saying a simple sentence like "Turn out the lights." Is it "Turn out the lights," "Turn out the lights," "Turn out the lights," or a gentle whisper of "Turn out the li-i-i-ghts"? It's *all* in the music.

2. ***Music gets attention and is memorable.***

An educated Iatmul in New Guinea . . . knows between 10,000 and 20,000 clan names. . . . Part of the secret . . . is that he chants the names in a rhythmic way.

Armstong, 1993

Most teaching in the thousands of years of human history has happened through storytelling and song. Songs and chants with attractive rhythms, satisfying repetition, and unforgettable melodies have helped people remember lessons from the past and the tenets of their religions. Information and values are still passed along in hymns and military chants; during more recent human history, the power of song has been deftly used by advertisers to create jingles that haunt us—almost compelling us to buy products: "You deserve a break today, so get out and get away, at ______ ." We can't get the jingles, with their "get it—rent it—eat it—buy it" messages, out of our heads. Most of us have experienced this *mnemonic* force of music; for example, the alphabet is frequently learned through song and the number of days in each month remembered by the sing-song rhythms and rhymes in the poem "Thirty days hath September." At a more advanced level, math performance improved in a study in which one group studied math with a Mozart sonata (thought to activate particular regions in the brain) and scored an eight-point increase over the control group without music. (Contact the Music and Science Information Computer Archive at the University of California, Irvine, for details on this and other research studies: www.musica.uci.edu.)

Why is it easier to learn a song than a series of math facts? The brain is attuned to patterns and responds to rhythmic patterns in music, perhaps hearkening back to soothing rhythms in the womb. Learning through music can seem effortless, because the brain almost automatically picks up musical patterns, even when we are not conscious of it happening. Brain imaging technology now enables us to see how music stimulates areas of the brain inactive before a music experience. We are attracted to music and it draws our attention. It is widely known that time spent attending to a task is a major factor in learning, so if music can increase time on task, might it be an alternative to drug treatment for attention deficit? This area of research has yet to show conclusive results, but educators are certainly justified in experimenting with coupling music with learning to get extended attending—under pleasurable circumstances.

3. ***Music engages the affective with cognitive and psychomotor domains.***

Music is the shorthand of emotion.

Leo Tolstoy

Music therapy—the systematic use of music to aid in the treatment of disease or illness—has been an accepted medical treatment since the 1950s, but the healing, soothing properties of music have been known since drum beats were first pounded out in Africa. What do we do when we get in the car after a hard day's work? Turn on the radio or put in a favourite CD. Why? Early on we learn how music relaxes, gives energy, and alters perceptions of time and mood. Music can even change the state of consciousness; it is not uncommon for people to report *chromesthesia*—seeing colours or images as a result of musical sounds—and experience emotional cathartic effects like sobbing in response to music. Faster musical rhythms induce smiling, even laughing; endorphins, the bodies natural painkillers, are produced as a result. Listening to music causes changes in breath rate, pulse, blood pressure, pupillary muscle tone, and blood flow. Musical sounds charge the brain, activating areas in both hemispheres and stimulating whole-brain involvement. Business and industry use this power of music not only in advertising, but to increase attention and energy in the workplace. For example, music is intentionally used to create positive moods and a positive attitude to energize employees. Cognitive (thinking), affective (emotional), and psychomotor (body) responses are needed to function as whole persons and music provokes all three. Finally, music is a kind of intelligence, a way of knowing and expressing ideas and feelings. By integrating music, teachers help students become more well rounded and successful because they are drawing on additional avenues of learning.

4. ***Music solves problems.***

Music can assist in both solving and enduring problems by relaxing us. It can relieve stress, reduce pain awareness, and increase blood flow to stimulated areas of the body. Human existence is defined by the ways we cope with our problems, and music is often a part of wrenching moments like funerals, lost loves, and fear ("Whenever I feel afraid I whistle a happy tune"). We hum and rhythmically rock to give physical and mental solace and sing lullabies to calm cranky children. We sing or hum to ease the passing of time or to accompany work.

Teachers learn quickly to play soft, calm music to make transitions in the day or use faster rhythms to rouse students for a lesson requiring mental and physical energy. It is exciting to consider other creative ways to use music to solve problems in the classroom. From academic to discipline problems, music holds potential. For example, teachers who use warm-ups like clapping rhythms for students to echo entrain students to become one with the teacher's rhythm—and this gets attention. (*Entrainment* is the tendency for two rhythms or pulses to synchronize with each other, like the speed of speaking affects the listener's speed.) Using the concept of entrainment, teachers can use music to aid transition from high-energy activities to slower, more reflective ones or to energize students with fast-tempo music. The rhythms of the brain imitate external rhythms, and in this way music serves as a mood signal. Slower speaking can calm, just as slower music can, and a fast tempo causes children to entrain to a more active body response. Physically, we entrain with others as we walk together, pausing or adjusting our gaits. Everything from heart rate to brain waves entrains to the rhythms around us (Page, 1995; Armstrong, 1994).

5. ***Music bonds people.***

Music cures a lot of loneliness.

Anonymous

When we sing together, we are brought closer because collective musical experiences create bonds born of shared feelings. Singing classrooms are classrooms where the learning community is made strong through ancient powers of rhythm and sound. Group singing can be an inspiring ritual, as evident in the faces of children who may show joy not otherwise seen at school. Singing together weaves an invisible sound web of group spirit (Page, 1995). Community feeling grows through shared experience, and community building is often the focus of patriotic songs, folk songs, and humorous camp songs. Think of how it feels to sing "O Canada" at the start of a baseball game or to sing songs around campfires on chilly nights when everyone is brought into an envelope of one sound. Then there are the young lovers who bind themselves together with a trademark "our song" symbolic of shared feelings. Shared music is nonverbal communication that can bridge gaps between generations and mend fences among disparate groups. During World War II, at Christmas 1941, Allied and German soldiers, weary from fighting each other during the day, sang Christmas carols across the night.

6. ***Music is a vehicle for learning.***

Through song and music, students can increase general vocabulary, sight word knowledge, use of idiomatic expressions, oral fluency, visual tracking along a line, concentration, understanding of rhyme, rhythm, repetition, alliteration, and syllables, phonemic awareness, concepts of beginning–middle–end, sequence, diction, and parts of speech. Music is a communication symbol system that develops listening skills and, as previously discussed, listening is an important part of the motivation to learn. In addition, listening to music is a pleasant reinforcing experience, and *critical* listening (close listening to musical elements) develops attending skills. Music also develops important *learning rhythms,* like the word rhythms in reading necessary to achieve *fluency*—a pulse and phrasing that must be sustained or the message is not constructed.

7. ***Music triggers creative expression and develops discipline.***

There was once a teacher who taught her fourth graders to sing *"I've been working in this classroom all the live long day. I've been learning lots of new things just to pass the time away. Soon we'll hear the bell start ringing and out the door we'll go. Now it's time to get ready, clean up and go on home"* (tune: "I've Been Working on the Railroad"). At the end of each day they were energized to prepare to depart—always on a good note. That was a creative teacher, so different from the teacher who struggles daily to get chores done before dismissal.

Music can be a form of language play, but it also requires skill and discipline. To sing or play an instrument *well* demands attention, know-how, practice, and the desire to improve. Used creatively, music develops the kinds of thinking associated with creative problem-solving, like viewing ideas from a new perspective, and can develop group and independent work skills, such as cooperation and responsibility. Educators involved in the singing schools of Hungary feel music increases sensitivity, harmony, and cooperation because of its emotional appeal and the need for group work in choirs. On a simple level, the pairing of music with other tasks creates an opportunity for responding to common work in uncommon ways. Think of the songs the *voyageurs* sang as they paddled their canoe trading routes for thousands of miles across this country.

Music stimulates creativity because making music involves playing and experimenting with sounds and rhythms. For example, children readily create and adapt hand clap and jump rope rhymes. When teachers engage students in sound experiments, they stimulate the use of brain centres needed for elaborative, original, fluent, and flexible thinking. Why wouldn't teachers make use of the power of this natural creative-thinking motivator in the classroom?

8. ***Music can develop pride and identity.***

Alas for those who never sing, but die with their music in them.

Oliver Wendell Holmes

From early childhood we sing to discover ourselves. Music brings power to children because it gives a mode to express feelings and release energies and emotions in new and novel ways. Universal questions are asked in favourite songs, questions children would not otherwise be able to articulate (Page, 1995). Childhood ditties can express the ineffable ("Twinkle, twinkle little star, How I wonder what you are"). The "me" egocentrism of childhood eventually morphs into a world of "we" as children discover the importance of peers; song preferences change to a focus on relationships with others. Teenagers become passionate about "their music" as bodies and brains go through sweeping changes triggering unfamiliar feelings. During adolescence, music commonly becomes a means to express identity, a way to express or to associate emerging views of self with things deemed unique symbols of what is important. This use of music to define views and values continues throughout life. As self-identity develops, so do life patterns related to the motivation to learn. Pride is a powerful fuel

Guitar

for the learning engine. By learning a song or to play an instrument, children develop confidence, posture, and poise. Through musical achievements they gain insight into important connections between sustained effort and satisfaction. Perry's book *Let's Celebrate* is full of ideas for celebrating the holidays and festivals of many religious and cultural groups in Canada. When children feel proud and know that significant adults share pride in their hard work, it is more likely that self-discipline will grow and be transferred to other areas of life.

9. ***Music expresses culture and history.***

Without music life would be an error.

Nietzsche

So important is music to cultures that the act of music making is considered a gift—a gift of beauty through sound. West African cultures view music this way, and in North American culture it is a high tribute to have a song written especially for you. Music reveals cultural values, is used to celebrate triumphs, helps in the grieving process, expresses fears, gives hope, sustains traditions, and is integral to religion. Recorded history is replete with songs and music that tell stories of heroes, passions, and wars. Think of Tanglefoot's song "Secord's Warning" or Lightfoot's "The Wreck of the Edmund Fitzgerald." At a time in history, each tribe or cultural group had a unique musical identity. Today, diverse kinds of music represent the human family. In Canada we have become culturally diverse in our musical tastes and embrace every genre and style from folk to classical, rock and roll to rap. Celtic? Fiddle music?—all readily available at the local mall. Teachers who share the wondrous varieties of music and celebrate the unique music of cultures and ethnic groups are showing children that diversity is something to be respected and treasured.

10. ***Music gives enjoyment.***

People don't sing because they are happy, they're happy because they sing.

Goethe

Music is a form of celebration, and our children need more time to celebrate learning. Music is a form of beauty, and classrooms need all the beautifying they can get. When we help children tap into musical intelligence, we liberate them to make music and add beauty to their personal and shared worlds. Encouraging each child to find a special musical identity gives many options for using a special way of knowing and expressing, plus the possibility of feeling a joyous sense of freedom. This doesn't mean teachers should not let students know a particular *use* of music can be harmful. Music has power that can be used and abused; for example, excessive volume creates permanent auditory loss. Music can also provoke aggressive responses through rhythms and lyrics that are not school appropriate; teachers need to be direct in teaching how any art form that demeans a person or group is questionable. But back to the main point: music is fun and *fun* is fundamental to motivation to learn. Happy children learn better. One way to increase happiness is to sing.

11. ***Music can support learning throughout curricular areas.*** Singing naturally integrates the *language arts* of listening, speaking, and reading. To sing, we must hear in our heads, in the same way we must hear the music of words when reading silently: which words are to be stressed? what rate? volume? Singing also emphasizes clear enunciation of words, and because we usually sing *words,* vocabulary is built through singing. By pointing out lyrics on a large chart or the overhead, students make the speech-to-print match essential for reading.

When children learn to compose original songs, collect favourite songs (lyrics), and keep response journals of responses to songs and music, they are *writing,* another language arts area. Because of the patterned nature of music, it can be an assist in learning another aspect of writing, *spelling.* When we teach students how to tap out rhythms in words—"en-cy-clo-pedia" or sing the spelling of words, they can add an important study mnemonic to their learning repertoire. We can encourage students to create their own word melodies using the universal notes of G, E, and A or any tune. A simple strategy is to break into small groups and give each a word to spell using a melody. Remind them to use the music elements (rhythm, tempo, dynamics, etc.) to create their word melodies (see Post It Page 11–2). Afterward, ask if this helped and why, as a means of using action research to gauge the effects. Keep track of spelling performance to add statistical evidence to the experiment.

Several studies have documented the influence of music on *math.* For example, in one study university students who listened to Mozart increased their spatial reasoning. In another, preschoolers given eight months of keyboarding and singing outperformed children with no music on object assembly tasks requiring them to form mental images and move objects to reproduce the images (they showed enhanced long-term spatial reasoning) (Rauscher et al., 1995). Counting songs have long been a part of the early childhood curriculum, and for good reason: through the strategic use of music, teachers help improve skills in measuring, counting, graphing (the five-line staff is a graph), fractions, problem-solving, time, and spatial reasoning. See the music-based bibliography in the appendix for collections of math songs like Baker's *Raps and Rhymes in Maths* (songs about probability and time).

Music can support *science* learning in a number of ways. As one example, a unit on sound can include a study of how vibration enables us to sing or a musical instrument to play. Students can explore the nature of sound and learn about musical elements, such as the variety of timbres possible when an object is struck or is used to strike other objects—forks and knives or hands.

A key aspect of *social studies* is learning about diverse cultures. Music fits easily into this area because to understand a culture we must know what the members believe is important; music reveals values. Every culture produces music for similar purposes: to celebrate, mourn, relax, or unite a group. But each culture approaches music differently. While it is rare to hear singing in most work environments in Canada today, in many cultures and countries work songs are still an integral part of life. Music is considered critical to growing crops in areas of the world like West Africa, where songs and dances are believed to coax plants to grow (Page, 1995). Another cultural difference relates to our Western notion of an audience in one place and musicians in another (on a stage). This concept is foreign to cultures where everyone participates in music creation and everyone is both audience and performer. Happily, hundreds of high-quality multicultural materials are now available, including CDs and videos. (See the appendix.) Post It Page 11–5 lists some.

Another part of social studies is *history*. Studying the music of a time period can be an exciting introduction to a past era, with students learning the origins of songs like the "Huron Carol" or Stan Rogers's "The Northwest Passage." Students can analyze lyrics to discover purposes for which the songs were written, reflect on how composers felt, and learn how historic events even inspire music (e.g., "The Ship Titanic"). Music can be related to a unit focus, such as transportation systems (canal and railway songs), and students can discuss what causes particular music to endure for decades or centuries, bringing them right up to current events, like the continued fervour over Elvis and the passionate responses to anniversaries of his death.

What Does a Classroom Teacher Need to Know and Teach about Music to Use It as a Teaching Tool?

The woods would be very silent if no birds sang except those that sang best.

Henry David Thoreau

To begin to understand what a classroom teacher needs to know about and teach to integrate music with curricular areas, it is important to be familiar with current patterns of music study in schools. In elementary and middle school, special music classes focus on music's historical, social, and cultural role in life; communication through music by expressing, performing, and responding; and valuing music and developing an aesthetic sense of it. Topics include music elements, genre and styles, musical tastes, musicians, instruments (including the human voice), composers, and music of diverse cultures (songs and particular musical pieces). Also of importance is the role of beauty and emotion in music as a form of communication. Drawing from this foundation, here is a checklist of titles for folder tabs to organize information for music integration:

- Basic music elements and concepts used to create and think about music.
- Biographical and style information about musicians, composers, songwriters, and singers (e.g., the children's tape *Beethoven Lives Upstairs,* and other titles in the Classical Kids Series.
- Styles, forms, and genres of music (e.g., opera, jazz, country, classical, folk).
- Particular examples (e.g., actual songs on CD, tape, and collections of sheet music).
- Specific approaches or teaching strategies (e.g., ways to teach a song, Kodaly, Dalcroze).
- Poems, quotes, current news articles about music (e.g., collection of poems about music like Myra Cohn Livingston's *Call Down the Moon, Poems of Music* (1995)).
- Musical instrument information (e.g., types, history, pictures).
- Bibliographies of children's literature that is music related (e.g., *The Philharmonic Gets Dressed* by Karla Kuskin).

- Research articles about music integration and the mnemonic power of music.
- Music ethnography or world music of diverse cultures.
- Other possibilities: information about careers in music, music history, science or math of music, economics and music, psychology of music (e.g, music therapy).

Defining Music: When Does Sound Become Music?

> *It gives a soul to the universe, wings to the mind, flight to the imagination, a charm to sadness, gaiety and life to everything. It is the essence of order and leads to all that is good, just, and beautiful, of which it is the invisible, but nevertheless dazzling, passionate, and eternal form.*
>
> Plato on music

What is music? Simply put, it is sound organized in time and space. It is aural, kinesthetic, and cognitive and is dependent on our ears for perception. But what is the difference between sound and music? Consider an African drum beat and the patter of a baby's feet. Both sound patterns have the musical element of rhythm. Both evoke emotional response. But the drum beat is an *intentional* organization of sounds for the sake of making sound. The sounds evoke feelings and emotions through the use of rhythm, tempo, melody, harmony, pitch, and repetition. These basic components or elements are used to create images and ideas in a musical form. So, music can be thought of as "sound patterns over time *intended* to express moods, ideas, or feelings."

Music Elements That Help Define Music

While musical terms alone do not create music, classroom teachers need to understand and teach basic elements so that there is a common language to discuss music and concepts to use when exploring music creation. In other words, to integrate music, teachers and students need some tools of music. The caution is for teachers not to kill the joy and spirit of music through overanalysis of a song's elements. Later, in the *How* section and in Chapter 12, there are specific suggestions to teach musical concepts and terms as music is integrated throughout the curriculum.

Rhythm is movement of sounds through time. In songs the words usually match the rhythm. Try saying and clapping the words "happy birthday to you." Now do the same with "She'll be comin' round the mountain when she comes." Feel the difference in the rhythm? Everything we sing or say has a rhythm that can be varied by changing the tempo, beat, and accent.

Beat and accent have to do with the rhythmic pulse, like the steady beat of a clock ticking. The accent is where the strongest emphasis is placed, as in *one* two three, *one* two three.

Tempo is the speed, how fast or slow the music is.

Metre is the groupings of rhythms (e.g., triple metre = 3/4 (waltz) like "Happy Birthday").

Syncopation. Syncopated rhythms are uneven, as in jazz. The beat remains steady, however. Try to say "Charlie Parker Played Be Bop" by syncopating it to Charrrr-lie Parrr-ker Played Be Bop." (He was a great jazz saxophone player.)

Melody is the tune. It is a series (more than one) of musical tones or pitches falling into a recognizable pattern. Melodies may be based on major or minor scales. You do not need to know what a scale is to make a melody. When we sing words, they become melodies.

An octave is the distance between the first and last notes of our Western scales of eight notes (think of Do Re Mi Fa Sol La Ti Do) or between any pitched note and the next note with the same name (eight notes higher or lower). Most of our folk songs use the eight main notes of the Western scale. There are five other notes that come between the scale notes called sharps and flats, usually the black keys on a piano.

Pitch is the relative highness or lowness of tone high or low tones in the sound pattern.

Timbre (pronounced "tambur") is the same as tone colour and has to do with the unique qualities of a sound (e.g., voices or sounds made by plucking, beating, rattling, or blowing various instruments). In essence, any sound has a timbre that enables you to hear whether you've dropped your keys or a book. Children enjoy experimenting with all the timbres they can create with one body part (e.g., hands or objects like sticks or even a ruler).

Dynamics is the volume or relative loudness or softness of the sound. Dynamics give emotional intensity. The Italian words *forte, crescendo, piano,* and *pianissimo*, etc., appear in music to indicate dynamics or how loud the music should be played.

Texture is the layering of instruments and/or voices to create a thin or full feeling. Melodies, rhythms, and timbres can be combined to create different textures. Music made by an orchestra is an example of a full texture. We can create texture by combining voices, as in singing a round like "Frère Jacques."

Post It Page • 11-2

Music Elements That Help Define Music

Rhythm: movement of sounds through time (matches words not beat). Includes *beat or accent, tempo, metre, and syncopation.*

Melody (tune): a series (more than one) of musical tones falling into a pattern. Includes *Pitch.*

Timbre (tambur): tone colour or unique qualities of sound.

Dynamics: volume or relative loudness or softness of the sound; gives emotion.

Texture: layering of instruments and/or voices to create a thin or full feeling.

Harmony: the blending of sounds, e.g., chords; two or more pitches simultaneously.

Form: structure, shape, or distinct patterns. Related to *style* and *genre.*

Harmony is the blending of tones or sounds (e.g., chords). When two or more pitches are blended simultaneously, harmony is made. When we sing a round in several parts, we are producing vocal harmony.

Form is the structure, shape, or pattern of a piece of music or a song, for example, AB (binary form) like "Fish and Chips," ABA (ternary) like "Twinkle Twinkle Little Star," and ABACA (rondo form). The A's and B's are separate *themes.* It is the order of *repetition* that is the key and largely determines the form of a piece of music. Musical **styles** and **genre** are closely related to form (e.g., jazz versus opera).

Ostinato is simple rhythmic or melodic content repeated over and over to accompany a song. Post It Page 11–2 summarizes music elements.

Musical Instruments

Students want and need to create, explore, and imitate sounds. They enjoy activities involving discrimination, classification, sequencing, improvisation, and organization of sounds into songs and music. While classroom teachers may not be able to stock many kinds of instruments, there are many ways to explore sounds through a variety of "found," homemade, or inexpensive instruments. See, for example, Hopkins' *Making Simple Musical Instruments.* Instruments from different cultures can be demonstrated, shown in pictures, and heard on recordings, as students study uniqueness among peoples. Musical instruments include:

- Sound makers (sticks, stones, shakers)
- Percussion or rhythm instruments; anything that can be hit or struck, scraped, rubbed (tambourines, triangles, wood blocks, bells, maracas, finger cymbals, drums)
- Melody instruments to make tunes (bells, xylophone, tone bars, glasses of water, bamboo flutes, rubber bands, African kalimba)
- Harmony instruments (autoharp, guitar, piano, dulcimer)
- Orchestral and band (violins, trumpets, clarinets)

Composers, Genre, and Styles of Music Possible for Classroom Use

What Musical Genre and Styles Should Classroom Teachers Integrate? It would take more than one course in music history to become familiar with all the music that people have produced. Teachers who have such background start the process of integration with a definite advantage. But most teachers know more than they think they do. For example, you're probably familiar with a great deal of classical music from Bugs Bunny cartoons, and advertisers are always sneaking in a bit of Bach or Beethoven to sell a product. Films like *Platoon* and *Ordinary People* introduced millions to works of composers like Vivaldi and Pachelbel.

While some styles and genres overwhelm young children, one guideline is to use variety and consider appropriateness. The music specialist will usually be responsible for the sequential music curriculum, leaving the classroom teacher free to explore genre or types, including gospel, jazz, bluegrass, madrigal, Celtic, lullabies, opera, or barbershop according to preferences, student interests, and connections to curricular goals. Teachers new to music integration are encouraged to begin with genres and styles they know and enjoy so that they can transfer their enthusiasm to children. Once the integration begins, teachers can branch out and explore new types and styles, along with students. Post It Page 11–6 clarifies some of the eras or periods of music commonly used to classify Western *classical* (music considered to have lasting significance) music. (Note that classical is also used to label one of the periods.) Teachers should remember that exposure to non-Western music enlarges children's concept of what is "good" and that twentieth-century North American music has much to offer, too (the Latin music of the 1930s, big-band music of the 1940s, rock 'n' roll from the 1950s, punk rock and New Age in the 1980s, and country music in the 1990s).

The example works in Post It Page 11–6 are just that, examples, and are limited to Western culture. They are offered as a place to *begin* as teachers attempt to increase music background. Dates are included for those interested in plotting birthdays on a time line to go along with social studies. Celebrating specific birthdays of composers and other artists is also a routine teachers can use to integrate the arts throughout the school year.

Note: The terms *genre* and *style* are sometimes used interchangeably, but style generally refers to the distinctive way in which musical elements are used; for example, periods of musical development like the Baroque had a unique style. Style can even refer to media used to make music (e.g., keyboard style).

Composers. By introducing students to composers and their music, a real-person element is added to music. Children who listen to *"Beethoven Lives Upstairs,"* and read the picture book by the same title have an opportunity to know something of the idiosyncratic human being behind the famous music. Just as children become excited about book authors, they can come to identify with the troubles and triumphs of composers and other people who have made music an integral part of their lives. It is inspirational and comforting for children to realize they share many life experiences with famous composers and can create music, just as these individuals did. Of course, introducing children to a diversity of genres, styles, and composers of different racial, ethnic, and cultural backgrounds gives the opportunity to understand from additional perspectives and create in a wider array of forms and styles.

For ideas about genre, styles, composers, songs, and other potential questions about *what* to teach, you may want to consult *The Music Teacher's Book of Lists* (Ross and Stangl, 1997).

Songs Everyone Should Know

It's always touchy to start listing books or topics everyone should know about. That didn't stop the Music Educators National Conference in the United States from recommending songs they felt all Americans should know and treasure as part of their national common culture. See Post It Page 11–7. It includes folk songs, Negro spirituals, patriotic songs, a Jewish celebration song, a Japanese folk melody, and many old favourites of the twentieth century. In an informal survey at the Faculty of Education at Queen's University in Kingston, Ontario, these songs emerged as the Top Ten Songs Every Canadian Should Know.

1. "O Canada"
2. The "Hockey Night in Canada" theme
3. (tied) "The Wreck of the Edmund Fitzgerald" and "Land of the Silver Birch"
4. "This Land is Your Land"
5. "Farewell to Nova Scotia"
6. "The Maple Leaf Forever"
7. "You Are My Sunshine"
8. "Four Strong Winds"
9. (tied) "Amazing Grace" and "The Huron Carol"
10. (tied) "If I had a Hammer" and "Bud the Spud"

In addition, you may want to survey your own community and school and involve students in compiling a favourites list. Post It Page 11–3 includes favourite songs recommended by teachers and children from informal surveys.

Teachers Need Not Sing Well nor Read Music to Integrate Music

As in each of the other chapters, reassurance is offered to teachers about the importance of enthusiasm, willingness to learn, and ability to do creative problem-solving being more important to music integration than having a fine voice or music literacy. It is effective for teachers to take the risk to sing *with* and *to* students—

being able to read music or play an instrument do give an added dimension to integration efforts. These are desirable, *not necessary,* teacher attributes. A non-Western cultural perspective, where *everyone* is seen as an important music participant, rather than a passive listener, does much to help us consider how music can become an integral part of learning throughout the curriculum. To consider music as a natural extension of the human spirit is to accept its place in every discipline that examines people's courage, creativity, inventiveness, and resiliency. With all that said, Post It Page 11–8 on *reading music* is intended for those with absolutely no experience, but with a curiosity to know some basics.

Curriculum Guidelines

Canada does not have national standards for the arts. Many provinces have provincial standards, or curricular outcomes or guidelines. Teachers are expected to be familiar with these documents and follow the set curriculum. Unfortunately, some of these curricula assume that teachers have more musical knowledge than they actually have. How classroom teachers work with provincial curricula varies from province to province. Teachers can contact their board or district curriculum consultants for help and information.

How Can a Classroom Teacher Use Music as a Teaching Tool?

> *If you can talk, you can sing. If you can walk, you can dance.*
>
> Zimbabwe aphorism

Teachers don't need to be able to play an instrument to integrate music. They don't need to know how to *read* music, either. A teacher need not even know who Mozart was or what a fugue is. Classroom teachers can integrate music by using ideas like those discussed next. In so doing they will help students learn how music is another way to make meaning.

To begin with, think of music as another dimension of artistic and creative thinking and consider that all sound has music potential. Knowledge of basic musical elements, introduced previously, enables students to understand music better and can assist them in music making. There are special skills, like reading and notating music, that teachers can pursue with students or help those who are interested to get resources or mentors. Most critical to music integration is a positive attitude about being able to use music in meaningful ways throughout the curriculum.

Music Integration Checklist

Teaching and composing songs, as well as listening to curriculum-related music, make up the bulk of what a classroom teacher does when integrating music. Take a moment and do a self-assessment of strategies you would be comfortable using. Would you. . . .

- Teach songs from diverse cultures, for holidays, traditional ones and others that go with units? (See the appendices Music in Arts-Based Children's Literature and Recommended Reading and Viewing for resources. Students and their families are also wonderful sources of songs and music; consider *co-constructing* your curriculum with your class.)
- Help students learn songs that make up a *cultural repertoire,* including the songs that make up their own cultural repertoire? (See Post It Page 11–7.)
- Present songs and rhythmic activities for pure enjoyment (e.g., release of emotion and energy)?
- Use activities that support awareness of musical elements and concepts to help students use musical intelligences and develop vocabulary? (See ideas for teaching in Chapter 12.)
- Invite in guests to play instruments, sing, or share about unique aspects of music?
- Involve students in making and playing instruments as a means of *creative expression?*
- Play a variety of types of music to stretch students' concepts of the familiar?
- Sing with students to show you value all voices and are willing to risk sharing your own?
- Cooperate with the music specialist to integrate music throughout the school curriculum?
- Share your own musical tastes and preferences—not as what is best, but as a way of celebrating everyone's unique proclivities? (And encourage students to share, too?)
- Use music to introduce units, like *"Secord's Warning"* for the War of 1812?
- Offer music as a starter or as a response to a lesson? (For example, write a song about a topic or use music as a journal-writing, art, dance, or drama stimulus.)

Post It Page • 11-3

Favourite Songs

The following is a list compiled by surveying music teachers, classroom teachers, and children.

A-Hunting We Will Go
Alouette
Alphabet Song
The Ants Go Marching
Baby Bumble Bee
Bear Song
A Bear Went over the Mountain
Bingo
Camptown Races
Clementine
Do Your Ears Hang Low?
Down by the Bay
Down in the Valley
Eensy Weensy Spider
Farmer in the Dell
Found a Peanut
Go In and Out the Window
Good Night, Ladies
Grand Old Duke of York
Green Grass All Around
Have You Ever Seen a Lassie?
Head, Shoulders, Knees, and Toes
Hokey Pokey
Home on the Range
Hush Little Baby
I Know an Old Lady
If You're Happy
I'se the B'y
It Ain't Gonna Rain
It's a Small World
I've Been Working on the Railroad
Jack Was Every Inch a Sailor
Jingle Bells
John Brown's Body
Kookaburra
Kum-Ba-Ya
Land of the Silver Birch
Little Skunk's Hole
Little Tommy Tinker
London Bridge
Loopy Loo
Make New Friends
Michael Row Your Boat Ashore
Miss Mary Mack
Mud
My Bonnie Lies Over the Ocean
My Paddle's Keen and Bright
Oh, Chester
Oh Susanna
Old Hiram's Goat
Old MacDonald
Old Texas
On Top of Old Smoky/Spaghetti/Pizza
One Bottle of Pop
Over in the Meadow
Peanut Butter Song
Polly Wolly Doodle
Pop! Goes the Weasel
Puff the Magic Dragon
Rise and Shine
Row, Row, Row Your Boat
She'll be Comin' Round the Mountain
Simple Gifts
Six Little Ducks
Skip to My Lou
Sweetly Sings the Donkey
Take Me Out to the Ball Game
There's a Hole in the Bottom of the Sea
There's a Hole in the Bucket
This Old Man
Turkey in the Straw
Twinkle, Twinkle
Waltzing Matilda
Wheels on the Bus

- Connect chants and poetry with music? Help students understand that all reading of words involves adding musical elements to the print?
- Use music to set mood (e.g., to slow things down or speed up, to relax to make transition)?
- Teach basic concepts and skills (e.g., alphabet, counting through music)?
- Learn a few songs (with limited voice range and notes, e.g., sol, mi, la) for pitch matching, some action songs, and word rhyme songs (e.g., nursery rhymes)?

Music Approaches That Influence Integration

The human voice is the most readily available and most important musical instrument for children to explore . . . accompaniment can distract the children's attention from the musical elements of pitch, volume, and timbre, produced by the voice alone.

Zoltan Kodaly

In real life, music is everywhere, all day, every day—on the radio, in department stores, in the hums and whistles of people with whom we work. In regular classrooms music is often viewed as a pleasant, but expendable, aspect of the curriculum—significant music experiences are reserved for music class. But should music be confined to one special class in school, any more than music, outside school, is limited to concerts? If the answer is no, then one next step is to know some approaches *from* music class that can shed light on current integration efforts by helping generalists understand how specialists construct music curricula. The following brief summaries offer background on what music specialists do and what is appropriate when using music as a teaching and learning tool. A common thread in most is the *active* involvement of students in making and responding to music through movement. All these approaches connect music to a wide array of curricular areas, from language development to social studies. General classroom teachers can investigate each further by talking with specialists in their schools.

In the 1890s, Swiss educator Émile Jacques **Dalcroze** pursued a theory that control of balance and body movements, along with the use of the senses, prepared children to develop the attention and concentration skills necessary for school success. He believed sensory-based learning caused muscles to relax, while maintaining alertness, and helped learning channels to be open for concentration. Dalcroze called his method of teaching music *eurythmics*. In eurythmics, music and movement are inseparable, and the body is used as a natural instrument for the study of music. Dalcroze believed any musical idea could be transformed into movement and any movement could be translated into a musical idea. To start off, Dalcroze students "become" the music as they listen and move to it. Later they study musical symbols and instruments. It seems incredible that Dalcroze was dismissed from the Geneva Conservatory for encouraging students to remove shoes and experience the musical rhythms through movement. We have him to thank for helping advance the idea of body-kinesthetic learning widely accepted today.

Dalcroze was joined by Carl **Orff,** in Germany, in emphasizing links between music and movement. (Music and dance were not connected until the turn of the century, because music was considered high art, while dance was deemed common.) In the early part of the twentieth century, Orff developed the Orff music education program. He worked from the idea that feeling comes *before* understanding and stressed the thrill of music making with chants, rhythms, and language. The Orff approach uses rhymes and proverbs as a basis for teaching rhythm, phrasing, and musical expression. Orff's special instruments, which require little technical facility, are still used to enable children to experiment with musical sounds, perform in ensembles and improvise.

Zoltan **Kodaly,** Hungarian composer and early-childhood expert, believed singing should be the basis of a music program, and his work provided impetus for the *singing schools* in Budapest (Hungary is regarded as having one of the best music education programs in the world). He thought children should learn many simple songs, sing in tune, and do conscious listening activities to develop aural skills. Kodaly contended that children can learn complex musical ideas in game situations and that all children can become musically literate (reading and writing music) by developing concepts in experiential ways, rather than through rote teaching. Kodaly believed quality musical listening experiences enhance the ability to concentrate and focus and develop thinking skills. He reasoned that language development, reading ability, and coordination were developed when children learn to discriminate sound patterns in music. Kodaly's methods are based primarily on singing nursery songs and doing traditional circle games that include movement. Eventually, children learn musical terms and reading through folk songs. Musical skills are developed through a sequential curriculum so that children learn to sight read and sight sing. Kodaly used a system of hand signs to help children sing and *show* the notes of the scale: do = fist in knocking position; re = palm outstretched down and tilted up; mi = palm down; fa = thumb down; so = handshake; la = first two fingers and thumb make a U (downward); ti = point index finger up (see Choksy, 1974).

General Principles for Integration

In this chapter the concept of teaching *with, about, in,* and *through* the arts is applied to music integration using ten principles. Each principle contains general guidelines to help teachers think of how music integration can proceed. More specific starter ideas are available in Chapters 12 and 13. The latter includes ideas to integrate the arts with the arts.

Principle One: INFUSE the Art of Music

Infuse means to permeate or to cause to penetrate. Teachers can infuse music by creating an environment in which music is used throughout the day.

- Sing daily.
- Hold regular discussions about music-related topics, student interests, music in the news, and music related to units under study.
- Invite students to bring in tapes and CDs to share at the start of the day, during recess, or for silent reading and writing times.
- Invite guests to sing and play for the class; involve students in finding potential candidates.
- Create a class lending library of CDs and tapes, like a class library of books; ask parents to share tapes and check for PTA help in this project. Make tape/CD bags to take home with a book and activity. With young children, repeated reading of the lyrics, while listening to the song, is an excellent reinforcement for literacy skills.
- Keep music journals about how music is a part of life.
- Play mood music when students come in in the morning, after lunch, and at other points in the day where a change of mood is called for.
- Take advantage of teachable moments to point out rhythms of words; repeat poetry readings and discuss poems for their musical quality.
- Create songs by involving students in creating lyrics, using rhythm instruments, and improvising familiar melodies. These could be entirely original or based on other songs and pieces of music.

Principle Two: TEACH Music Elements and Concepts

Start a Materials Collection. Basic materials to begin to integrate music include musical instrument-making books, biographies of musicians, finger play books, chants and rhymes books, song collections, music-related children's literature, CDs and tapes, and

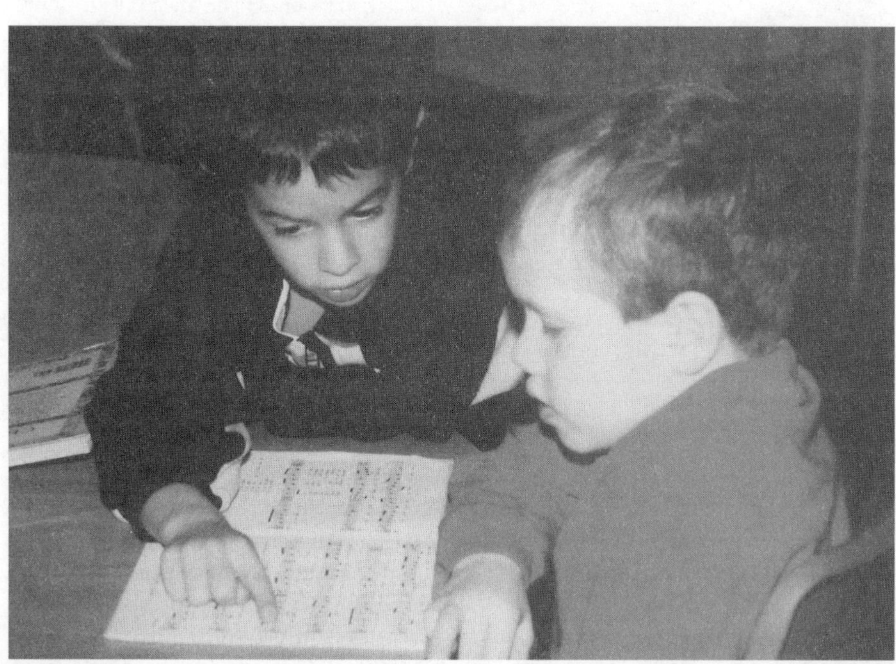

Reading Music

videos like *Vivaldi's Four Seasons* and *Beethoven Lives Upstairs*. Start a discography of music to use in units. See Post It Pages 11–9 and 11–10 for music ideas organized by unit topics.

Teach the Elements. In some provinces and school districts, classroom teachers have primary responsibility for teaching musical skills and elements. In other provinces and school districts, elementary schools have music specialists. Classroom teachers can teach or reinforce the basic concepts necessary for students to be successful with lessons involving music integration. For example, basic elements are needed to talk about the music of cultures under study. Elements are labels for words, and words contribute to general vocabulary development; so by teaching elements, students develop language and conceptual anchors to explore ways music can be thought about and created. Here is a sampling of strategies to develop concepts about elements. There are many more ideas in Chapter 12 under *Basic Elements and Musical Concepts.*

Display elements visually so that students have a permanent reference. See Chapter 2 for ideas.

Rhythm. Use the motivational power of children's names to explore rhythm. *Name rhythms:* Call a child's name and beat out the rhythm using syllable patterns and accent. Everyone echoes the rhythm. The teacher can also beat out the rhythm of a name and the *owner* must echo and becomes the leader. For example, "Virginia" would be three claps with the second accented. Be careful not to distort the natural rhythm of names. Relate this to poetry metre patterns. See the "word rhythms" in Post It Page 3–4.

Harmony. Singing rounds is one way to introduce harmony. See Post It Page 11–4. Easier than singing rounds is to have one group sing an ostinato (repeated pattern) while the other group sings the round in unison. For example, one group sings just the line "Row, row, row your boat" over and over while the other group sings the whole song. This works with any round. Choose one line of the round for one group to sing as an ostinato while the other group sings the whole song.

Principle Three: Teacher Habits

Before teaching anyone else, I must teach myself. . . .

Sylvia Ashton Warner

Teachers are people, and who you are as a person has a profound influence on how you teach. Probably the most powerful teacher habit for achieving music integration is to continue to grow musically by attending concerts, being involved in a choir, taking music lessons, or just being more active in the pursuit of making music more a part of your life through the use of tapes and CDs.

Make Music a Part of Life. Music is an important way all humans relieve stress and change their moods. Integration of music should be as much for the teacher as for the students. One teacher, Mrs. Engle, started playing music in her classroom in the mornings as she was getting ready for the day when she first began her teaching career in the 1950s. She played big-band music that she had loved as a teenager. One morning she was in a rush and had left a record on when her fifth graders came in. They were shocked at what the staid Mrs. Engle was listening to, but begged to hear more. Mrs. Engle was surprised the kids liked the "old stuff," but it became a routine to start the day with music. She retired after 42 years of teaching and credited much of her career longevity to using music to start, and often end, each day in her classroom.

This Too is Music. Musicians and non-musicians alike often have a narrow approach to music—what it is and how it is made. A truly inspiring and innovative book is Upitis's *This Too is Music.* Preservice teachers who read it frequently suggest that it should be required reading for all elementary school teachers.

Assess Students' Interests, Musical Abilities, and Preferences. Much can be learned about students' music background through conversations with them, observation, and talks with parents. An interest inventory can be the basis for action research on music integration in a classroom, for example, an inventory as a pre-test at the start of the year and a post-test at the end of the year to see changes in students' skills, knowledge, and attitudes toward learning and music. (See an example inventory in the Appendix.)

Select Quality Music. Children are inundated with music—in the car, on television and radio, in the supermarket. We need to ensure that music chosen for school gives exposure to music they would not otherwise listen to and be worth the time. Of course, *worthy music* is a subjective concept, but it is important for every teacher to use quality criteria; for example, if music lyrics are to be examined, then the words should be audible and clear. Some orchestral music can overwhelm students and elicit exaggerated responses. Use a music specialist as a resource, and consult the bibliographies in this chapter and in the appendix for help in finding quality music.

Set Mood with Music. Concertos by Bach or pieces like Pachelbel's *Canon* can be used to set mood and relax students as information about a topic is presented verbally. There is a great deal of current interest in using music in this manner and to set the stage for learning. Consider the use of music therapy, not in the clinical application, but using the concept of music as a motivator, to boost energy and good feelings about school. A listening station or centre with calming music can be used by individual students as needed or desired. Try the use of music to deal with anxiety; for example, have a sing-in or play music before tests to relax. Music can be used to create mood or give background for study and writing, too.

Use Music to Introduce. To use a piece of music to introduce units, begin by asking students to listen to a piece of music or examine lyrics and then speculate about what it means, how it feels, the values conveyed, and who wrote it and why. Do a repeated listening several times so that students develop skills for close listening. The class can be divided into groups to examine designated sections of the lyric.

Connect to Real Life. Focus on the goals of music integration—not to please an audience, but to attain personal enjoyment and emotional response; to understand how music is an expression of our humanity and culture, a way of understanding and expressing ourselves. Ask students to brainstorm reasons we use music (e.g., rituals). Discuss the harmful effects of some music (the typical teenager has 40% hearing loss—more than 90 decibels over time causes this). Ask students to log or web music in their lives in one day or imagine a single day without music. Do class scavenger hunts for places music happens and the types of music students can find. Regularly ask students to think of connections between songs and music and topics in math, science, and social studies. Cue them to use their musical intelligences. Finally, discuss how it affects a group when music is integrated. What effects does it have on motivation, attitude, and concentration?

Play with the "Music" of Reading or Talking. A teacher habit that connects music with learning to read and speak is to regularly practise reading and saying words and phrases in different ways. Take a moment to read aloud this sentence: *Sir John A. MacDonald was the very first Prime Minister of Canada*. Now, try again and change the dynamics (volume). Try again and change tempo (speed). Once more, and change pitch and tone. Finally, try changing the rhythm (group phrases differently and add a regular beat, e.g., 1–2–3–4). Students can have fun adding musical elements to words and will discover how words really convey very little without the added music. Take time to ask how different versions of the same sentence mean different things based on how the person interprets them through the added music elements. Discuss how different words, phrases, and sentences *feel* different based on how they are said and read. The habit of playing with the musical elements of language will increase reading comprehension and help students speak in more interesting ways and more effectively communicate what they want to say.

Use Descriptive, Nonjudgmental Feedback. Another important habit is to focus on specific information in response to student efforts. When students create, perform, or respond to music, give them feedback by commenting on musical elements. For example, *"You have great volume because you opened your mouth and have upright posture. You are breathing from your diaphragm!"* As mentioned in other chapters, praise *controls* others, while descriptive feedback liberates because it is clearer and less value-laden.

Sing with Students. Students do not mind if the teacher does not have a fine singing voice if genuine enthusiasm is expressed. Teachers can make the effort to sing with students and show enjoyment of the community built through group activity. Since classroom teachers are not perceived as music specialists, students accept their amateur efforts as simply a human being doing a natural thing—singing. With experience and commitment to music integration, teachers can learn to model how to sing without embarrassment and without being overly concerned about the Western notion that only the talented should sing out. Teachers should take heart in Thoreau's words about how the forest would be a very quiet place if only the birds who were the best singers did the singing.

Teach Songs. To learn a song, the singer must be motivated to learn and listen closely to hear specific pitches, grasp the tempo and underlying beat, and identify the rhythmic patterns. In addition, the singer must combine all this into a whole. Here are important guidelines:

- ***Consider the developmental levels of students*** and keep songs for younger students simple—easy lyrics, limited melody (not too high or too low), and a catchy beat.
- ***Combine singing with movement.*** Students need to see the teacher move to the song, as well, and

show appropriate facial expressions. Sign language can be used to add movement; see Riekehof's *Joy of Signing* or improvise hand signs or motions. Practise keeping a steady beat together by clapping or playing rhythm instruments, and use this as a basis for moving to singing together, doing rounds, and creating harmony later.

- ***Keep in mind that singing in tune is a developing skill.*** The common range for children is usually from about middle C up to G. If songs are pitched too high or low, they have trouble matching the pitch. Light voices travel much higher than heavy voices. Phillips' *Teaching Kids to Sing* is an excellent resource for teachers who want to encourage fine and healthy singing in children. Usually, students who sing out of tune are not hearing the notes clearly and may need to have a note or phrase isolated for practice. Use the amount of repetitions necessary for students to be successful in matching pitch. Ask students to hear the notes in their heads before they sing them. By taking time to teach careful, close listening, almost all children can learn to sing well. Even intermediate and middle school students, who have not done much singing, can learn to sing well if the teacher takes the time to work on listening carefully to the tune so that intonation is accurate. Don't despair if students aren't perfect singers immediately. Remind yourself and your students that singing in tune, like all important life skills, comes with practice.
- ***Start with songs they all know and like.*** There is a *Favourite Songs* list that teachers and children selected in Post It Page 11–3. In general, it is recommended that students learn to sing songs without accompaniment so that they learn to listen to themselves and rely on their voices. One easy way to begin is use "Call and response" songs because they are easy; students simply echo what the teacher sings (for example, "Old Hiram's Goat" and "Old Texas"). Begin with keeping a steady beat and clapping or snapping rhythms for students to echo. Students can also become leaders. Here is a favourite chant to use as a call and response: Teacher: *Acka lacka ching/* Students (echo)/T: *Acka lacka chow/* Students (echo)/ T: *Acka lacka ching ching chow chow/* Students (echo)/ T: *Booma lacka booma alack sis boom bah/* Students (echo)/ T: *Reading Reading/* Rah Rah Rah (substitute any phrase you want)/Students (echo).
- ***Sing daily and post lyrics after students hear songs.*** Use a chart or pocket chart to write the words large enough for all to see. Pocket charts enable one line to be put up at a time for focus. Sing songs to start the day and clean-up ("I've been working on the railroad"). Instead of giving directions, sing or chant directions; use the universal melody of "na na na na na"—think of the childhood taunt—and sing "Line up and go home."
- ***Teach new songs slowly, with many repetitions.*** Use nonsense syllables like "la," "ti" and "tah" to explore singing voice. Encourage students frequently and be supportive about their efforts. Remember, singing requires taking a risk. Tell them that everyone can sing well if they listen carefully and try their best. Music is a skill learned through the three Ps: practise, practise, practise. Neural pathways and muscle tone develop with multiple repetitions.
- ***Model, imitate, and repeat*** are the most typical techniques for teaching songs. Students should hear the whole song first, before seeing the lyrics, so that they experience the aesthetics of the music first. Use a whole–part–whole sequence technique mentioned for introducing all arts: experience the art form as a whole, then work on the skills or individual parts, and then put it all back together again. Give direct instruction line by line or phrase by phrase. Finally, sing the whole song several times to increase fluency and enjoyment. (Some music educators do recommend starting with the parts and building up to the whole song, rather than having students hear the whole to begin with.) Both whole-to-part and part-to-whole methods involve students in listening to a part of a song and then echoing the teacher as the bulk of the lesson. As parts are mastered, the song builds up until students can sing the entire song well. Post It Page 11–4 summarizes steps.

Include Listening Experiences, as Well as Making Music. Critical and creative music listening experiences are beneficial in many ways. Listening to music stimulates the right and the left hemispheres of the brain, emphasizes cognitive and affective processes, and enlarges us as whole persons. Because music is primarily an art form created for enjoyment, children need to experience music for the pleasure it brings; we need to give time to *just* listen and *just* sing. Even when students are to do critical thinking (analysis and evaluation) about a piece of music, it is helpful to let

Post It Page • 11-4

Teaching a Song

Rote Method

1. Motivate and stimulate interest. For example, give background on the song. (See *New Grove Dictionary of Music* for ideas.)
2. Sing the song or play a recording. The singing should be in your normal voice. The range should be appropriate for the students. Teacher enthusiasm is critical at this step, so show it.
3. Ask students to describe what they heard using music terms (e.g., repetitions, rhythm).
4. Echo sing. Teacher sings a line or phrase and students echo. Go through the whole song this way. Continue to build up the song by repeating previous phrases and adding new ones. If the song is difficult, slow down, but keep a steady beat. If there are unusual words, try doing the whole song echoically in a speaking voice the first time through. Repeat this step as much as necessary.
5. Display the song's lyrics on a chart, overhead, or pocket chart.
6. Sing through many times. Ask students for ideas on how they can improve and target an element (e.g., dynamics, enunciation).

Rounds

1. Use rote method to teach the whole round. Not all songs are rounds. If it is a round, it will be identified as such.
2. Sing the round in unison twice through while lightly tapping the steady beat on knees.
3. Divide the class into two groups. Play this game to help them learn how to listen to the other part: Group two chooses a word from the first two lines of the round and tells group one the selected word. Group one will begin the song first. Group two begins at the appropriate time. When group one hears group two sing the selected word, group one stops singing. Then the groups switch roles. This activity is a good antidote for the "plug-your-ears-and-shout" method of singing rounds.
4. When the groups can do the preceding activity easily, establish start and stop hand signals.
5. Start with two parts to keep it simple, have students tap the steady beat on knees while singing, always insisting that the groups listen to each other. Sing the round through twice.
6. Once they can sing softly in two parts listening to each other, try three and then four parts.

them experience the music as a whole, as an enjoyable art form, before breaking it down for study. There are strong connections between forms of listening and forms of oral expression, including singing. When students learn to listen closely, they sing better. When students have many opportunities to listen to a variety of music during morning routines and at other times, they gradually acquire more refined listening skills for identifying how pieces are alike and different and why we respond in so many different ways to music. Giving children a "listen for" (element, instrument, style or genre) and doing repeated listening to selections helps develop abilities to do close listening for critical thinking purposes. Try this: Once students are familiar with the various instrument themes in *Peter and the Wolf*, distribute cards with pictures of instruments, and ask children to hold up the card that corresponds with the instrument when they hear its timbre.

Stretch the Concept of the Familiar. People have a tendency to disdain the strange. If you are serious about teaching tolerance, flexibility, and respect for diversity and wish to use music as a tool in this endeavour, here are some suggestions. First, don't give students the chance to say they don't like unfamiliar music. Start right in and have them listen with a purpose—to instruments they hear, voices, the beat. Next, ask them to try to describe what they heard as best they can, not *evaluate* it for preferences, yet. Then, give students many opportunities to hear a piece over and over (at least three times, with different purposes each time) so that they become familiar with it. This simple strategy is effective in expanding musical taste. Make the strange familiar.

Involve Students with Special Needs. Lois Birkenshaw's book *Music for All: Teaching Music to People with Special Needs* is an invaluable resource for planning and adapting curriculum for students with special needs.

Principle Four: ENERGIZERS and Warm-ups

Prepare students for experiences that require risk taking and creative thinking by doing energizers and warm-ups that activate the brain, relax the body, and tap into interests. Since performing music is also a physical activity, the body often needs to be prepared as well. Energizers and warm-ups cause students to use both body and mind. In Chapter 12 there are many ideas to choose from—ones for teaching musical concepts and elements can also be used as energizers. There are also energizers and warm-ups in the other arts chapters that would be appropriate before music-related experiences, for example, drama verbal strategies and dance rhythm strategies. In general, think about doing song sharing, poems, chants, and rhythms that take only a few minutes and cause both mental and physical engagement.

Principle Five: USE Great Children's Literature Related to Music

Never has there been more high-quality children's literature available to integrate the arts. There is a plethora of children's literature devoted to music specifically and a variety of genres of music-related children's books (e.g., biographies of musicians). Children's literature can become the basis for a variety of lessons that integrate music. For example, Raffi's *Baby Beluga* is a much loved song, which can be used in the primary grades in a unit on sea mammals. *Charlie Parker Played Be Bop* is a striking picture book appropriate for any age. If it is read while playing a Charlie Parker tape or CD, it becomes a magical lesson and can lead to discoveries about genres, styles, and forms. Biographies are particularly important ways for students to get in-depth and personal accounts of individuals with whom they might identify. Biographies are valuable in both science and social studies to add the human element. For example, Krull's *The Lives of Musicians* gives short biographical pieces with interesting facts and a perspective on the historical period in which the musician lived. Plantamura's *Women Composers* is another important resource. Post It Pages 11–9 and 11–10 offer a sampling of titles focused on aspects of music and curricular topics. There are many more titles in the Arts-Based Children's Literature bibliography in the appendix.

Principle Six: ROUTINES

Putting particular routines and rituals in place early in the school year makes a substantial contribution to music integration and enables students to assume increasing responsibility. Once students understand the structure, they should be able to conduct, adapt, and suggest new routines, much like Mrs. Lucas's class did in the vignette in Chapter 2. See Chapter 2 under Routines for additional ideas. Here are some common ones to start music integration:

Use music to signal classroom events, like recess, lunch, or the end of day.

Have a composer of the day or week. A few facts about the composer and a musical piece or song can be shared in a morning routine. Students can select favourites from among several songs or pieces of music and display titles with "speech bubbles" around them telling facts or feelings about composers or the music.

Celebrate musicians' birthdays. Play the music the person is famous for to celebrate.

Use background music daily to set mood. Morning music and music played during art making and silent reading and writing times are easy routines to establish. Gentle folk music from diverse traditions or classical music works well. Remember, the rhythms of the brain tend to echo the rhythms of music, and the rhythms can enhance attention and learning (entrainment).

Collect and post music quotes and poems. Livington's *Call Down the Moon* is a lovely collection of poetry about music. Try a poem a day or a quote a day with this collection.

Set up an ongoing display of music-based children's books. Children can even be in charge of supplying a special section of the chalk tray with books they find about music. Once a spot is established, students will pick on helping supply displays.

Start the day with singing favourite songs that children know. Make song charts of songs and begin with a sing-in of ones they choose. If song charts are used, a few minutes can be used to examine the lyrics for language patterns being studied (adjectives, homophones, etc.).

Principle Seven: ADAPT Curriculum and Instruction Models for Music Integration

Music integration, based on the models and theories for thinking about curriculum and integration in Chapters 1 and 2, should include considerations about:

- Differentiating or individualizing lessons
- Students' interests and concerns
- Connections with life-centred issues
- Teaching for depth, not breadth
- Focusing on essential or universal human questions
- Themes versus topics
- Sources for unit and integrated lessons: provincial and local course of study or curriculum guides for science, social studies, reading, language arts, music
- The variety of integrated unit structures: basic unit types, six interdisciplinary design options, schoolwide topics, centres or stations related to themes
- Multiple intelligences lesson plan formats
- Integrating music with other arts
- Three-part teaching structure in lesson plans: introduction, development, and conclusion

You may wish to reread the general discussion of each of the above issues in Chapter 2. Here are applications of these ideas that apply specifically to music:

Make Lessons Appropriate to Age and Stage. Children progress through stages of musical experience. Even babies respond to music by bouncing and rocking. Preschoolers learn simple songs and love to play with sounds. By age 4, children can understand the concepts of rhythm, tempo, volume, and pitch and can create their own songs by improvising lyrics. Of course, children love songs that have suggested actions, like "Head, Shoulders, Knees, and Toes," and enjoy active engagement through fingerplays, using rhythm instruments, and creative movement or dance. Some children start school able to sing melodies and echo rhythms and melodies during call and response songs. Most children have established musical preferences. Classroom teachers have a lot to build on as they integrate music.

As teachers consider what's appropriate for the age and stage of students, it is important to begin with what children already know—start with strengths and interests. One example of this idea is integrating music with reading by asking children to dictate lyrics to a familiar song. Once the chart is created, it can then be read and reread. Sight words, phonic patterns, special spellings, and so on, can then be discussed as students play "I Spy" examples of language concepts they see or the teacher suggests a category, for example, all the words that begin with "B." This strategy can be adapted for more mature students by using songs of interest to them as the basis for teaching sentence structure (grammar), usage, alliteration, assonance, consonance, parts of speech, and the like.

Unit Structures. In Chapter 2, four different integrated unit structures were explained. Each unit is based on one of four centres or bodies with nine legs. See Post It Page 2–2. When integrating music, a teacher or team may plan integrated lessons and units using one or more of the traditional subject areas as the orientation for a unit. Another option is to choose a body or centre from the four other unit types: (1) author–artist, (2) genre or form, (3) problem, theme, topic, or question, or (4) single work (poem, book, song). For example, unit 1 could be a study of a musician, like Charlie Parker, using the book *Charlie Parker Played Be Bop* as a key resource material, with all the arts, as well as math, science, social studies, and reading and language arts as *legs* that would support the body—learning about a person, in this case. Music would be used as a learning tool in such a unit, just as any other leg. A unit might focus on a composer or singer, as well. The second unit type could be planned around a particular genre or form of music (gospel, folk, swing), and the third, which has a problem, theme, topic, or question (e.g., Why and how do people create music? What causes music styles to emerge?), is another option. Finally, a particular book, poem, or song could serve as the unit centre (e.g., Hesse's *Out of the Dust,* the 1998 Newbery Award winner, has significant themes about the importance of music in the life of a teenager enduring the Dust Bowl of the 1930s). Other songs the family might have sung would fit into such a unit, including occasions for music in the book (a funeral, wedding, work songs). Major concepts and skills in math, science, social studies, reading and language arts, and the other art forms would be used as support legs. Of course, in any integrated lesson or unit, all bodies and legs should be correlated with courses of study and standards to ensure substantive and focused study. Post It

Page 5–6 is an example integrated unit. Take a moment to examine the music ideas in it. See the arts-based bibliography and other bibliographies in this chapter for ideas about children's books.

Start Small and Grow. Rather than plan a whole unit on music or even one with significant use of music, try just one lesson (e.g., a lesson on the history of a familiar song, like "Row, Row, Row Your Boat"). The key is to make sure your first attempts are successful, for you and for your students. Begin by integrating energizing warm-ups to introduce the day or particular days for lessons. For example, teach a new song every Monday. Explore the language arts connections by using a song chart and the "I Spy" strategy in which students tell all the types of words and language structures they see in the song. Plan short mini-lessons of about ten to fifteen minutes at first.

Integrated Music Lessons. Clear lessons that integrate music begin with planning. Brainstorm about music connections (and other web legs) for one of the unit types. For example, a core book unit around Raschka's *Charlie Parker Played Be Bop* could develop the concept of jazz, as well as language arts concepts such as onomatopoeia, rhyme, and language repetition. The power of the book and listening to jazz are bound to make this a memorable learning experience because Charlie Parker was so full of energy and creativity. It's very helpful to use local and provincial curricula to get specific concept and skills ideas for teaching and to ensure that lessons are developing the competencies the school district expects. Another critical idea is to decide how lessons will be ordered in a unit—which will be taught first, second, third, and so on. The flow of lessons is established by thinking about how one will lead into another. For this reason, it is important to think about which lesson will be the introductory one and to plan a culminating lesson to wrap up each unit. The culminating lesson generally involves students in presenting projects worked on throughout a unit. For example, students might write their own jazz "scat" songs and present them to show that they understand syncopation and the use of nonsense words in jazz.

See the lesson format using a two-pronged focus and student objectives in Chapter 2, and refer to the detailed discussion about dividing the teaching strategies into introduction, development, and conclusion. Keep in mind that if students are expected to create a song, structure is very important; for example, adapt lyrics to a familiar tune or, in the case of the Charlie Parker book, write new words to use in place of be bop, fisk fisk, and other "scat" words. Plans need to include strategies for transition, use of space, materials, and even ways to dismiss groups: *"Your ticket out today is . . ."* or *"All those that can/know . . . may. . . ."* See Post It Page 2–1 for more information on lesson planning.

Guided Music and Language Lesson. Music and listening, speaking, reading, and writing are integrated in these special guided lessons led by the teacher. This is a special variation on the two-pronged plan format, but it still includes an introduction, development, and a conclusion. The instructional steps are *listen closely and think; predict; read; share; write; music response; publish.* These can be posted so that students can eventually guide small- or whole-group lessons. The *guided music and language arts lesson* teaching steps are outlined in Post It Page 11–11.

Integrate Music with Art, Dance, Drama, and Literature. Integrating the arts is about helping students discover the interrelationships that exist in our world and using their creative-thinking gifts to make meaning through all art forms. To achieve this goal, students need to be shown how all the arts share common aspects. Basic elements cut across art forms (rhythm, line, shape) and all art forms are created through the creative problem-solving process. We can ease students into the risk taking necessary to do higher-order thinking to create, perform, and respond in the arts by setting the stage with expectations. For example, begin to collect and share anecdotes about the struggles and failures most famous artists endure before achieving any measure of success. Share stories about the reactions to highly innovative ideas; Igor Stravinsky's *Rites of Spring* caused a riot when it was first played because it didn't conform to what people thought was good music. If students are shown how people are often uncomfortable with change or the unfamiliar, they can learn to be more open to difference and thus grow in flexibility and tolerance.

Use Music as a Mnemonic and as a Motivator for Content and Skill Learning. Throughout this chapter there are examples of how music can support learning across the curricular areas of science, social studies, math, and reading and language arts. Teachers can use the mnemonic power of music by putting information into raps or chants to sing math facts or spell words to a rhythm. See Dunleavy's *The Language Beat* and Cullen's *Solid Gold for Kids* for practical ideas. Rhythm instruments can be used to express ideas through music (e.g., use simple rhythm instruments with a poem or convey ideas learned in a unit on space or even as a means of learning parts of speech), and anytime students write original songs about content areas they are transforming information that entails elaborate thinking.

We are a multicultural country and we need to seek out every means to teach respect for the diversity of people. Songs, musical pieces, and instruments fit well into social studies because of the historical and cultural basis of music. Traditional songs and folk music, passed from generation to generation, help students understand the rules and values of a culture and see how there is a human inclination to create patterns. For example, German songs are often grouped into threes, while Australian songs frequently have beats grouped into twos and fours and are organized using eight notes. Japanese music is often based on a scale of five notes, rather than the eight-note scale used in Western cultures. Use the bibliographies in the appendix and at the end of the chapter to find collections like *Rise Up Singing!* a collection of folk songs including multicultural favourites like "Hava Nagila" (Hebrew round), "If I Had a Hammer," and "De Colores" (United Farm Workers folk song). Recordings can be purchased to go with the book (tapes and CDs). Campbell's *Roots and Branches* (1994) is another resource that includes background information and songs from more than twenty-five countries. It comes with a CD. See Post It Page 11–5, which is organized by cultures and countries. When music is used to explore concepts in content and skill areas (math, science, language arts, and reading), the teacher needs to feel comfortable that all the disciplines involved, including music, are used in respectful ways and not trivialized.

Listening Centres. Centres or stations with headphones are particularly useful in integrating music. Centres allow students to independently make music a part of their classroom lives. Tapes of environmental sounds can be available at a centre for classification and identification, or music can be selected for free listening. Various musical selections can be at a centre for children to listen to, along with information about the composers or as elaborations of ideas introduced in a lesson. Children can match musical selections with the correct composers as a follow-up to "close listening" done as a group to discern genre and style characteristics. Students can also be invited to go to listening centres during free time and use them as a source for selecting music to be played for the whole class to enjoy at the start of the day or other group times. This kind of exposure to music has the potential to spur a lifelong interest and further expand a child's musical tastes.

Principle Eight: TAKE Music-based Field Trips

When teachers think of music-related field trips, they often think first of visits to hear the local symphony or a special concert, and certainly these opportunities are pivotal in children's musical development. Many communities now have arts coordinators that contact schools to schedule trips and provide pre- and post-trip lesson ideas. The checklist for planning field trips in Chapter 2 will help prepare for such a trip. In addition, in Chapter 7 there are two ideas that apply to music-based field trips: the section on preparing students for live performances and the strategy of using *simulated mind trips* to take students mentally to places they cannot go physically. Both ideas are under the Take Field Trips section in that chapter.

If your community is not so fortunate, use the phone book and check the resources in the community. Meaningful field trips can be made to music stores or local universities, if preplanning is done with the speakers and a focus is set for the trip. For example, combine a lesson on running a business and music for a trip to a music store. Take your class to an orchestra, band, or choir rehearsal at a nearby secondary school. Arrange to have the students from your class sit among the choir, band, or orchestra, pairing each of your students with a singer or player. Then there are the easy field trips that are right there for all of us. Take time to tune in on the sounds of the world. Take listening walks with the class to collect sounds around the school, in the cafeteria, on the playground. Stop and listen closely to the sounds of the classroom or sounds outside the window. Stop and listen for a minute each day to body sounds and rhythms. Ask students to label sounds they hear as fast or slow or high or low. Describe and model sounds made with instruments, and ask students to describe them. Develop the concept of how sounds express emotions. Ask students to make sounds that are tired, happy, or fearful. In general, develop sensitivities to the role that sound plays in how they feel about a place. Schafer's *A Sound Education* is an imaginative collection of sound activities.

Principle Nine: EXHIBIT Student Progress

Both students and teachers need evidence that all the work put into music integration is paying off. Ideas mentioned for demonstrating how students have grown in both cognitive and affective areas include keeping portfolios of songs created and collected in anthologies, actual tapes students have made, checklists of progress made in using musical elements effectively, journal entries and other writing about music, and even tests—especially tests to show parents and administrators how music is connected to reading and language arts, math, science and social studies learning. While we'd like to have music considered valuable on its own, this is not the case in many communities and will not be the case anytime soon. By sharing student progress made through music integration, in all the forms mentioned, teachers are most likely to win over skeptics.

Principle Ten: SPECIALISTS Are Important Resources

Collaboration with specialists has been discussed in all previous chapters. Music integration can include the music teacher, local musicians, and others with the musical expertise classroom teachers may not possess. Consult the Specialists sections of earlier chapters, including the guidelines in Chapter 2 on artist residencies.

A developing speciality area in music that needs particular attention is the use of technology, especially the computer. Ten years ago teachers would not have considered looking to the technology world for help in music integration. What a difference a decade has made. While most music software is for music reading and history, music-computer specialists can show teachers how to involve students in creating original musical compositions with software. A sequencer is needed to program a background drum beat or harmony—toy stores sometimes have cheap ones that let you do things like get the three-note C major chord by just pressing the C note, one key. By pressing another button, the chord plays in different rhythms, from waltz to rock. Another button causes the sequencer to play bells, a piano, or a trumpet. Some allow taping of your own voice and play using its unique sounds. Musical software often requires a MIDI (musical instrument digital interface). A system which connects a keyboard, MIDI , computer and printer offers limitless possibilities. For example, it is possible to play music on a keyboard and have the computer generate in traditional music notation what has been played into it. Inexpensive MIDI can be purchased, and amplifiers or speakers are needed, also reasonably priced. There is software that does not require a MIDI or any amplification. A book that reviews music software is *The Musical PC*. CD-ROMs can now be purchased that allow students to see and hear orchestras playing, and you can press a button to get background information on composers or instruments. Social studies, math, reading, and language arts experiences are automatically integrated in this type of software experience. There is a large range of computer programs that teach musical skills. Technology-assisted instruction in Music (TAIM) has many benefits. One is that students learn privately, which eliminates performance anxiety. Students work at their own pace and choose as many repetitions of skill drills as they need. Technology-assisted instruction in Music is appropriate for skill building in rhythm and pitch-matching, ear training, reading traditional music notation, and theory. Try before you buy: *MiBAC Music Lessons* for MacIntosh and *Music Lab* for IBM.

A good national mail-order source is:

Saved by Technology
10 Breadalbane Street, Toronto, ON M4Y 1C3
tel: 416-928-6434
fax: 416-928-0262
E-mail: sales@savedbytech.com

Conclusion

This chapter is an introduction to *why* music should be integrated, *what* classroom teachers need to know and integrate about music, and the basic principles for integration (*how*). In the next chapter more specific ideas are given to teach the tools of music so that students can use it as a way of learning. There are starter strategies for integrating music throughout curricular areas.

Post It Page • 11-5

World Music Resources

Putumayo World Music, 324 Lafayette Street, 7th Floor, New York, NY 10012, www.putumayo.com. This series of recordings is widely available in Canadian stores. Title include:

A Native American Odyssey
Caribbean Party
Latino! Latino!
Islands
Women's Work
One World
A Celtic Collection
A World Instrumental Collection
Women of the World: Celtic
Women of the World: International
Kotoja: The Super Sawale Collection
World Dance Party
Reggae
African
World Vocal

Anderson, W. H. (ed.). (1991). *Teaching music with a multicultural approach.* Reston, VA: Music Educators National Conference.

Campbell, P. S. (1992). *Lessons from the world*. NY: Schirmer Books.

Fowler, C., Lawrence, V., & Gerber, T. (1994). *Music: Its role and importance in our lives*. New York: Macmillan/McGraw-Hill.

George, L. (1987). *Teaching the music of six different cultures.* World Music Press.

Jessup, L. (1988). *World music: A source book for teaching.* World Music Press.

Lederman, A. *Come from every way: Canadian songs for children*. Falcon Productions. A collection of songs about coming to Canada from all over the world.

Papp, C. (1988). *Follow the sunset: A beginning geography record with nine songs from around the world* (with tape or CD). Entomography Publications.

Present, G., & Present, S. (1986). *We all live together: Song & activity book and leader's guide.* Hal Leonard.

Titon, J. T. (ed.). (1996). *Worlds of music: An introduction to the music of the world's peoples.* New York: Schirmer Books.

Walter, C. (1995). *Multicultural music: Lyrics to familiar melodies and authentic songs.* T. S. Denison.

Africa

Atumpan, the talking drums of Ghana. UCLA (1964) 45 min. VHS. Shows carving of a set of drums for the Ashanti king. Available from UCLA or Original Music.

Bryan, A. (1991). *All night: All day: A child's first book of African-American spirituals.* Atheneum.

Connelly, B. (1997). *Follow the drinking gourd* (African American). Simon & Schuster.

Floyd, M. (arr.) (1991). *Folksongs from Africa.* Faber Music.

Mattox, C. (1990). *Shake it to the one that you love best: Play songs and lullabies from black musical tradition.* Warren Mattox.

Asia: China, Japan, and Korea

Arthur Barr (producer) (1982). *Discovering the music of Japan* (21 min. video). Instruments are introduced, plus background is provided. Performances of shakuhatchi, koto, and samisen.

Asian Cultural Centre for UNESCO (books, recordings on Asian music and culture), 6, Fukuromachi, Shinjuku-ku, Tokyo 162 Japan.

Chinese Information Service (information on Chinese music, art and history), 159 Lexington Ave., New York, NY 10016.

Chinese Music Society of North America, 2339 Charmingfare, Woodridge, IL 60517-2910.

Gritton, P. (arr.) (1991). *Folksongs from the Far East.* Faber Music.

Kinokuniya Bookstores (books and records on Japan and Japanese music and culture), 1581 Webster St., San Francisco, CA 94115.

Kodo: Heartbeat drummers of Japan (28 min. VHS) Kinetic Film and Video. Shows the training of the musicians who form Kodo, a Japanese taiko drum ensemble.

Australia

Australian Institute of Aboriginal Studies, Box 553 City P.O., Canberra, A.C.T., 2600 Australia.

Caribbean, Central and South America

Arthur Barr (producer) (1982). *Discovering the music of Latin America* (Video). Indian and Spanish elements in Latin American music.

Hawaii

Hawaiian musical instruments (slides and tape). Bishop Museum. Hawaiian instruments like the dog tooth rattle and the nose flute. Other materials are available from the Bishop Museum.

Hula Supply Center (musical instruments and hula supplies), 2346 King St., Honolulu, HI 96822.

Bishop Museum, Education Dept. (materials on music of the Pacific), P.O. Box 6037, Honolulu, HI 96818.

India

Arthur Barr (producer) (1982). *Discovering the music of India* (21 min. video). Music of the South (Carnatic) and North (Hindustani) are introduced, with explanations of melody and rhythm.

Folk musicians of Rajasthan (45 min. VHS). UCLA. Folk traditions of northeast India; includes songs, rituals, and dances.

Folk performers of India (45 min. VHS). UCLA. Nine views of Indian folk traditions; includes magic acts, puppetry, acrobatics, impersonation, and other acts accompanied by music.

God with a green face (16 mm). American Society for Eastern Art. Training and performances of the Kathakali dance drama of southern India. Available from the Center for World Music, San Diego State University.

Gritton, P. (arr.) (1993). *Folksongs from India.* Faber Music.

Indonesia

Indonesian dance drama (30 + min. VHS). UCLA Original Music. Balinese shadow play, the puppets of Java, a dance drama and Sundanese masked dances.

Serama's mask (25 min. video). Coronet Films and Video. A Balinese teenager practises traditional masked dances and carves a mask for a performance.

Israel and the Jewish Culture

Cindy Marshall Productions. *A life of song* (38 min. video). Yiddish folk songs by Ruth Rubin.

Tara Publications, 29 Derby Ave., Cedarhurst, NY 11516, specializes in Jewish music.

North American

Fowke, E. & Johnston, R. (1954). Folk songs of Canada (Vol. 1 & 2). Waterloo, ON: Waterloo Music.

Krull, Kathleen (collected and arranged) (1992). *Gonna sing my head off!: American folk songs for children.* Knopf.

Medearis, A. (1994). *Singing man.* Holiday House.

National Gallery of Art (1991). *An illustrated treasury of songs: Traditional American songs, ballads, folk songs, nursery rhymes.* Rizzoli International.

Raffi (1979). *Corner grocery store and other singable songs* (American/French) (tape or CD). Shoreline.

Sills, J. (1995). Canadiana: A collection of Canadian folk materials. Edmonton, AB: Black Cat Productions (through Oliver Music, 1-800-661-3613).

Zemach, H. (1984). *Sing children sing: Songs of Mexico* (with tape or CD). Caedmon.

American Folklore Society (publishes *Journal of American Folklore*), 1703 New Hampshire Ave., NW, Washington DC 20009.

Canadian Folk Music Society, 15 Julien St., Pointe Claire, Quebec, Canada.

Center for Intercultural Studies in Folklore and Oral History. American Folklife Society, University of Texas, Austin TX 78712.

Country Music Association, Inc. (information on country music and the country music industry), 7 Music Circle, Nashville TN 37203.

Country Music Foundation (publishes the *Journal of Country Music*), 700 16th Ave. S., Nashville, TN 37203.

Learning Corporation of America (film: *Black Music in America—From Then Till Now*), 711 Fifth Ave. New York, NY 10022.

Middle East

Arthur Barr (producer). *Discovering the music of the Middle East* (20 min. video). Covers several instruments and styles of music and discusses the spread of Islam.

Other Organizations

Canadian Society for Traditional Music, P.O. Box 65066, North Hill Post Office, Calgary, AB T2N 4T6, email leeders@nucleus.com, web site members.tripod.com/~sherretg/csmthome.htm

Multicultural Media, RR#3, Box 6655, Granger Road, Barre, Vermont 05641, tel: 802-223-1294, fax 802-229-1834, email mcm@multiculturalmedia.com

Music Educator's National Conference (MENC) (publishes *Music Educators Journal*), 1806 Robert Fulton Drive, Reston, VA 22091.

North American Institute for Canadian Music, Faculty of Music, University of Toronto, Toronto, ON M5S 1A1

Smithsonian Institution, Office of Folklife Programs, 955 L'Enfant Plaza SW, Suite 2600, Washington, DC 20560.

UNESCO: United Nations Educational, Scientific and Cultural Organization, 7 Place de Fontenoy 75700, Paris, France.

The World Music Institute (ethnic festivals, concert series, mail order for booklets and recordings), 48 West 27th St., #810, New York, NY 10001. email: Worldmus@aol.com

Sources for Books and Instruments

The Canadian Society for Traditional Music is an excellent site for links (web site: members.tripod.com/~sherretg/csmthome.htm).

Try also:

The Acoustic Guitar Store, Calgary. www.acousticguitar.net/other.html

Halifax Folklore Centre, 902-422-6350

Ottawa Folklore Centre, 613-730-2887

Soul Drums, Toronto, www.souldrums.com, 416-225-5295

Post It Page • 11-6

Western Art Music: Selected Periods, Composers, and Works

Baroque Era: 1600–1750 Ornate, elaborate, flamboyant, marked by strict forms

Bach (1685–1750), German: *Brandenburg Concerti* and *22 Preludes and Fugues*

Pachelbel (1653–1706), German: Canon in D Major

Vivaldi (1678–1741), Italian: *The Four Seasons*

Handel (1685–1759), German: *Messiah*, *Water Music*, and *Royal Fireworks Music*

Classical Era: 1750–1820 Music without pretense

Haydn (1732–1809), Austrian: Surprise Symphony, *The Seasons*

Mozart (1756–1791), Austrian: Operas (*The Magic Flute*), *Jupiter Symphony*, *Coronation Concerto* for piano, *A Little Night Music*

Beethoven (1770–1827), German: All nine of his symphonies

Romantic Era: 1820–1900 Often suggests a story or concept, dreamlike

Schubert (1792–1828), Austrian: *Unfinished Symphony*, "March Militaire"

Schumann (1810–1856), German: *Spring Symphony*, *Papillons* (butterflies)

Mendelssohn (1809–1847), German: *Songs without Words*, "Midsummer Night's Dream"

Chopin (1810–1849), Polish: All his piano works

Prokofiev (1891–1953), Russian: *Peter and the Wolf*

Strauss (1804–1849), Austrian: waltzes, "Blue Danube"

Liszt (1811–1886), Hungarian: *Hungarian Rhapsodies*

Puccini (1858–1924), Italian: Operas (*La Boheme, Tosca, Madame Butterfly*)

Tchaikovsky (1840–1893), Russian: *Swan Lake*, *The Sleeping Beauty*, *The Nutcracker*, "1812 Overture"

Brahms (1833–1897), German: *Hungarian Dances*

Wagner (1813–1883), German: Operas (*Tristan and Isolde, The Flying Dutchman, The Valkyries*)

Post-romantic Era: 1890–1930 Focuses more on mood or expression of inner experience than telling a story, experimentation with music "without melody"

Mahler (1860–1911), Bohemian: *Songs of the Wayfarer*, *The Song of the Earth*, *Symphony of a Thousand* (no. 8)

Debussy (1862–1918), French: *The Sea* (*La Mer*), *Prelude to the Afternoon of a Faun*, *Children's Corner Suites*

Stravinsky (1882–1971), Russian: *The Rite of Spring*, *The Firebird*, *Petrushka*, *The Soldier's Tale*

Shostakovitch (1906–1975), Russian: Symphony No. 5 in D minor, Piano Quintet

Post It Page • 11-7

Songs MENC* Thinks All Americans Should Know

Amazing Grace
America (My Country Tis of Thee)
America the Beautiful
Battle Hymn of the Republic
Blue Skies
Danny Boy
De Colores
Dona Nobis Pacem
Do-Re-Mi
Down by the Riverside
Frère Jacques
Give My Regards to Broadway
God Bless America
Green, Green Grass of Home
Havah Nagilah
He's Got the Whole World in His Hands
Home on the Range
If I Had a Hammer
I've Been Working on the Railroad
Let There Be Peace on Earth
Lift Ev'ry Voice and Sing
Michael (Row Your Boat Ashore)
Music Alone Shall Live
Oh! Susanna
Oh, What a Beautiful Mornin'
Over My Head
Puff the Magic Dragon
Rock-a My Soul
Sakura
Shalom Chaverim
She'll Be Comin' Round the Mountain
Shenandoah
Simple Gifts
Sometimes I Feel Like a Motherless Child
The Star Spangled Banner
Swing Low, Sweet Chariot
This Land Is Your Land
This Little Light of Mine
Yesterday
Zip-A-Dee-Doo-Dah
Over My Head

*Music Educators National Conference

Post It Page • 11-8

Reading Music—Simplified Quick Reference

1. Each note is represented by these letters of the alphabet: ABCDEFG (no note letters above G).
2. Notes are written on a *staff,* which has five lines and four spaces. Each line represents a note, as does each space. The staff looks like this:

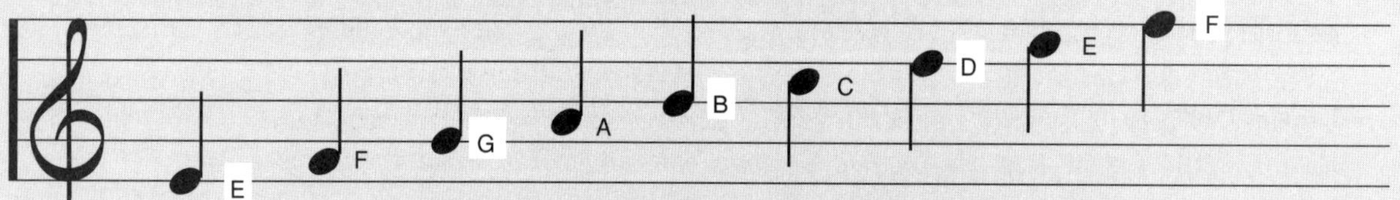

3. To remember the notes on the lines, the phrase *"Every Good Boy Does Fine"* can be used. For the notes in the spaces, use the acronym FACE. (Treble clef only)
4. If music has two staffs, one is for the higher notes and the other the lower notes. The top staff is the treble or G clef and has this special sign: 𝄞. The bottom staff is the bass or F clef and has this sign: 𝄢
5. On a piano, middle C is in the centre of the keyboard. To figure out the white notes on either side of it use the A–G sequence. The black keys are the sharps (#) and flats (*b*). A sharp raises a note a half-tone (makes it higher) and a flat lowers it a half-tone.
6. The staff is divided into measures or bars (vertical lines) and can have any combination of notes and rhythms. There are symbols for notes worth different counts or number of beats. For example,

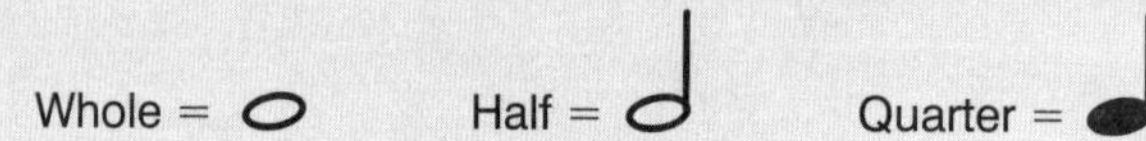

7. The time signature is two numbers (looks like a fraction) at the start of the staff that tells you the number of beats in a measure (bar) and what kind of note gets one beat, (e.g., 3/4 = 3 beats to a measure and the quarter note gets one beat.).

Post It Page • 11-9

Music-Based Literature by Musical Categories

Picture Books Based on Songs

Aliki. (1968). *Hush little baby*. Prentice Hall.

Bonne, R. (1961). *I know an old lady who swallowed a fly*. Scholastic.

Carle, E. (1993). *Today is Monday*. Philomel.

Connors, T. ("Stompin' Tom") & Jones, B. (1994). *Bud the spud*. Ragweed Press.

Connors, T. ("Stompin' Tom") & Jones, B. (1995). *Hockey night tonight*. Ragweed Press.

Hurd, T. (1987). *Mama don't allow*. Harper & Row.

Keats, E. J. (1987). *The little drummer boy*. Macmillan.

Kovalski, M. (1987). *The wheels on the bus*. Kids Can Press.

Langstaff, J. (1955). *Frog went a-courtin'*. Harcourt Brace.

Langstaff, J. (1974). *O, a-hunting we will go*. Athenaeum.

Raffi *Songs to Read* Series: *One light, one sun; Tingalayo; Wheels on the bus; Down by the bay; Five little ducks; Shake my sillies out; Baby beluga*. Random House.

Reid, B. (1993). *Two by two* (based on *Who Built the Ark?*). Scholastic.

Rosen, M., & Oxenbury, H. (1989). *We're goin' on a bear hunt*. Walker Books.

Seeger, P. (1986). (Ill. M. Hayes). *Abiyoyo*. Aladdin.

Spier, P. (1961).*The fox went out on a chilly night.* Doubleday.

Spier, P. (1967). *London Bridge is falling down*. Doubleday.

Staines, B. (1978). *All God's critter's got a place in the choir.* E. P. Dutton.

Winter, J. (1988). *Follow the drinking gourd.* Knopf.

About Orchestras and Bands

Hurd, T. (1987). *Mama don't allow*. Harper and Row.

Johnston, T. (1988). *Pages of music.* Putnam's.

Kuskin, K. (1982). *The Philharmonic gets dressed.* Harper & Row.

Sargent, R. (1968). *Peter and the wolf.* Lancelot Press.

Williams, V. (1984). *Music, music for everyone.* Greenwillow.

Musical Genre and Styles

Bryan, A. (1991). *All night: All day: A child's first book of African-American spirituals.* Atheneum.

Farb, P. (1970). *Yankee Doodle* (patriotic). Simon and Schuster.

Fleischman, P. (1988). *Rondo in C* (classical). Harper & Row.

Gray, M. (1972). *Song and dance man* (vaudeville). E. P. Dutton.

Hart, J. (1982). *Singing bee! A collection of favorite children's songs.* Lothrop Lee & Shepard.

Martin, B. (1986). *Barn dance!* (country). Henry Holt.

Papp, C. (1988). *Follow the sunset: A beginning geography record with nine songs from around the world* (lullabies) (tape or CD). Entomography Publications.

Raschka, C. (1992). *Charlie Parker played bee bop* (bee bop). Orchard Books.

Musical Instruments

Jenkins, E. (1989). *Rhythms of childhood* (with tape or CD). Smithsonian/Folkways.

Lohans, A., & Watson, M. (1996). *Nathaniel's violin*. Orca.

Wiseman, A. (1979). *Making musical things: Improvised instruments.* Scribner.

Careers in Music/Composers and Musicians

Fleischman, P. (1988). *Rondo in C.* Harper & Row.

Gmoser, L. (1997). *Great composers.* Smithmark.

Isadora, R. (1979). *Ben's trumpet* (jazz). Greenwillow.

Johnston, T. (1988). *Pages of music.* Putnam's.

Kenneth, G. (1967). *Louis Armstrong.* Children's Press.

Krull, K. (1993). *Lives of musicians.* Harcourt Brace Jovanovich.

Lionni, Leo (1979). *Geraldine, the music mouse.* Pantheon.

Mitchell, B., & Smith, J. (1988). *America, I hear you: A story about George Gershwin.* Carolrhoda.

Plantamura, C. (1994). *Women composers*. Bellerophon Books.

Williams, Vera B. (1984). *Music, music for everyone.* Greenwillow.

Post It Page • 11-10

Music-Based Literature: Artists and Recordings by Curricular Topic

Abilities and Disabilities

Corcoran, B. (1974). *A dance to still music.* Atheneum.

Keats, E. J. (1964). *Whistle for Willie.* Viking.

McCloskey, R. (1940). *Lentil.* Viking.

White, E. B. (1970). *The trumpet of the swan.* Harper & Row.

Animals

Collection of Brothers Grimm (1988). *The Bremen-town musicians.* McGraw-Hill.

Conover, C. (1976). *Six little ducks.* Crowell.

Hurd, T. (1987). *Mama don't allow: Starring Miles and the Swamp Band.* Harpercrest.

Karas, G. (1994). *I know an old lady who swallowed a fly.* Scholastic.

Keats, E. J. *Down in the Meadow*. Scholastic.

Langstaff, J. (1974). *O, a-hunting we will go*. Athenaeum.

Pearson, T. (1984). *Old MacDonald had a farm.* Dial.

Prokofiev, Sergei (1961). *Peter and the wolf.* F. Watts.

Raffi *Songs to Read* Series: *Five little ducks; Baby beluga*. Random House.

Reid, B. (1993). *Two by two*, (based on *Who Built the Ark?*). Scholastic.

Rojankovsky, F., retold by J. Langstaff (1955). *Frog went a-courtin'.* Harcourt Brace.

Rosen, M., & Oxenbury, H. (1989). *We're goin' on a bear hunt*. Walker Books.

Spier, P. (1961). *The fox went out on a chilly night.* Doubleday.

Steig, W. (1994). *Zeke Pippin.* HarperCollins.

White, E. B. (1970). *The trumpet of the swan.* Harper & Row.

Creativity and Imagination

Isadora, R. (1979). *Ben's trumpet* (jazz). Greenwillow.

Rylant, C. (1988). *All I see.* Orchard Books.

Cumulative and Repetitive Stories

Dodd, M. (1988). *This old man.* Houghton Mifflin.

Emberley, B. (1967). *Drummer Hoff.* Simon and Schuster.

Karas, G. (1994). *I know an old lady who swallowed a fly.* Scholastic.

Knight, H. (1981). *Hilary Knight's the twelve days of Christmas.* Macmillan.

Martin, B. (1989). *Chicka chicka boom boom.* Simon and Schuster.

Raffi (1987). *Down by the bay.* Crown Publishers.

Zemach, H. (1966). *Mommy, buy me a China doll.* Follett.

Dance and Movement

Gray, M. (1972). *Song and dance man.* E. P. Dutton.

Isadora, R. (1976). *Max.* Macmillan.

Martin, B. (1986). *Barn dance!* Henry Holt.

Raffi Songs to Read Series: *Wheels on the bus*; *Shake my sillies out.* Random House.

Seeger, M. (1987). *American folk songs for children* (with tape or CD). Cambridge Rounder.

Fairy and Folk Tales

Collection of Brothers Grimm (1988). *The Bremen-Town musicians.* McGraw-Hill.

Lewis, R. (1991). *All of you was singing.* Atheneum.

Prokofiev, Sergei (1961). *Peter and the wolf.* F. Watts.

Whitehead, P. (1989). *The Nutcracker.* Stoneway Books.

Families and Friends

Gray, M. (1972). *Song and dance man.* E. P. Dutton.

Griffin, H. (1986). *Georgia music.* Greenwillow.

Pinkwater, D. (1991). *Doodle flute.* Macmillan.

Williams, Vera B. (1984). *Music, music for everyone.* Greenwillow.

Holidays

Johnston, T. (1988). *Pages of music* (Christmas). Putnam's.
Keats, E. J. (1987). *The little drummer boy* (Christmas). Aladdin Books.
Whitehead, P. (1989). *The Nutcracker* (Christmas). Stoneway Books.
Yolan, J. (1991). *Hark! A Christmas sampler.* Putnam's.

Humour

Scieszka, J. (1993). *Your mother was a neanderthal.* Viking.

Nursery Rhymes and Lullabies

Aliki. (1968). *Hush little baby*. Prentice Hall.
dePaola, T. (1984). *Mary had a little lamb.* Holiday House.

Social Studies

Connors, T. ("Stompin' Tom") & Jones, B. (1994). *Bud the Spud*. Ragweed Press.
Winter, J. (1988). *Follow the drinking gourd* (slavery). Knopf.

Sound Effects

McGovern, A. (1992). *Too much noise.* Demco Media.
Spier, P. (1990). *Crash! Boom! Bang!* Doubleday.

Sports

Isadora, R. (1976). *Max.* Macmillian.

Toys

Whitehead, P. (1989). *The Nutcracker.* Stoneway Books.
Zemach, H. (1966). *Mommy, buy me a China doll.* Follett.

Musical Artists That Record for Children

Susan Aglukark
Peter Alsop
Linda Arnold
Heather Bishop
Kim and Jerry Brodey
Tom Chapin
Charlotte Diamond
Jack Grunsky
Ella Jenkins
Kids on the Block
Anne Murray
Eric Nagler
Hap Palmer
Tom Paxton
Fred Penner
Peter, Paul, and Mary
Raffi
Rosenshontz
Pete Seeger
Sharon, Lois and Bram
Marlo Thomas and Friends
Bill Usher
The Weavers

Post It Page • 11-11

Guided Music and Language Arts Lesson

Two-pronged Focus: (1) Choose from music elements and key concepts and (2) specify reading and language arts skills and concepts; see courses of study for help.

Objectives: By the end of the lesson, students should be able to. . . (list specific music and language arts outcomes here).

Teaching Procedure: The teacher will ask students to. . .

◆ **Introduction**

L *Listen closely and think:* Say, "Listen to . . . (a piece of music for a set period of time) to hear and feel everything it is about. No talking at this stage."

P *Predict:* Next, ask students to write predictions about what the composer is trying to communicate. With younger children the teacher can scribe on a chart or the overhead.

◆ **Development**

R *Read:* Read about the musician and/or the work. Teachers may read to the students.

S *Share:* Ask students to share their predictions about the work, whether they were confirmed or rejected in the reading material. This can be done in pairs, small groups, or whole group.

◆ **Conclusion**

W *Write:* Students do a writing response. Provide students with examples of different writing forms to choose from; see Post It Page 4–2. Focus writing on important ideas learned about the music or composer.

M *Music:* Give students options of ways to respond to the lesson, using the musical intelligence (see Post It Page 12–2).

P *Publish:* Student responses are "made public" through displays, oral sharing and singing, and book making (e.g., class big book).

Activities:

Musical Identity

Take five minutes to reflect on the music you enjoy. What is special about the music you like? How is your musical identity different from your friends'? your students'?

Musical Genres, Styles, and Composers

Divide a sheet of paper into two columns. List all the genres or styles you can think of on one side and composers you know on the other. Take five more minutes and talk with another person to expand the list. Discuss how you both came to know the genres, styles, and composers listed.

Integrated Music Lesson

Select a piece of music-based children's literature from a Post It Page in this chapter. Use it and a course of study from a school district to web *what* could be taught with it about music (concepts, skills, attitudes), and *what* could be taught about language arts and reading with the book. From the *whats* branch off to *hows* (strategies to use to teach).

Recommended Teacher Resources

Books about Music Teaching and Learning

Ashworth-Bartle, J. (1998). *Lifeline for children's choir directors.* Toronto, ON: Gordon V. Thompson.

Birkenshaw, L. (1974). *Music for fun, music for learning* (3rd ed.). Toronto, ON: Holt, Rinehart and Winston.

Birkenshaw, L. (1989). *Come on everybody, let's sing.* Toronto, ON: Gordon V. Thompson (Warner Chappell).

Birkenshaw-Fleming, L. (1993). *Music for all: Teaching music to people with special needs.* Toronto, ON: Gordon V. Thompson.

Campbell, P. (1994). *Roots and branches.* Danbury, CT: World Music Press (with CD).

Campbell, P., & Scott-Kassner, C. (1995). *Music in childhood: From preschool through the elementary grades.* New York: Schirmer.

Choksy, L., Abramson, R., Gillespie, A., & Woods, D. (1986). *Teaching music in the twentieth century.* Englewood Cliffs, NJ: Prentice Hall.

Cullen, Louise. (1995). *Solid gold for kids: Musical energizers!* Scarborough, ON: Prentice Hall Ginn.

Hammond, Susan. *Classical kids teacher's notes.* Available from The Children's Group, 1400 Bayly St., Suite 7, Pickering, ON L1W 3R2. Tel: 905-831-1995.

Mills, J. (1991). *Music in the primary school.* Cambridge: Cambridge University Press.

Schafer, M. (1992). *A sound education.* Indian River, ON: Arcana Editions. Order by mail: Arcana Editions, Indian River, ON K0L 2B0.

Upitis, R (1990). *This too is music.* Toronto, ON: Heinemann.

Wood, D. (1982). *Move, sing, listen, play.* Toronto, ON: Gordon V. Thompson.

Collections of Songs and Fingerplays

Birkenshaw, L. (1974). *Music for fun, music for learning* (3rd ed.). Toronto, ON: Holt, Rinehart and Winston.

Birkenshaw, L. (1989). *Come on everybody, let's sing.* Toronto, ON: Gordon V. Thompson (Warner Chappell).

Campbell, P. (1994). *Roots and branches.* Danbury, CT: World Music Press (with CD).

Choksy, L. & Brummitt, D. (1987). *120 singing games and dances for elementary schools.* Toronto, ON: Prentice-Hall.

Fallis, L. (1982). *Seasons and themes: Songs, activities, and musical playlets.* Waterloo, ON: Waterloo Music.

Fowke, E. (1969). *Sally go round the sun.* Toronto, ON: McClelland & Stewart.

Fowke, E., & Mills, A. (1984). *Singing our history.* Toronto, ON: Doubleday Canada.

Fowke, E., & Morrison, B. (1972). *Canadian vibrations.* Toronto, ON: Macmillan (Good selection of songs for older students).

Glazer, T. (1992). *Eye winker, Tom Tinker, chin chopper: Fifty musical fingerplays.* New York: Doubleday.

Gordon, S. (1984). *Songs to sing and sing again.* Available from 25 Belsize Dr., Toronto, ON M4S 1L3.

Jenkins, E. (1989). *You'll sing a song and I'll sing a song* (Tape or CD). Washington, DC: Smithsonian.

Metropolitan Museum of Art Staff. (1989). *Go in and out the window: An illustrated songbook for young people.* New York: Henry Holt.

Metterson, E. (1969). *This little puffin.* Hammondsworth, UK: Puffin.

Pinel, S., Mason, E., & Hardie, M. (1989). *Musique, s'il vous plaît.* Toronto, ON: Berandol.

Raffi. (1981). *Singable songbook.* Toronto, ON: Chappell.

Raffi. (1983). *Baby beluga book.* Toronto, ON: McClelland & Stewart.

Richards, M. H. (1985). *Let's do it again! The songs of ETM.* Richards Institute of Music Education and Research, 149 Corter Madera Road, Portola Valley, CA 94025.

Seeger, M. (1987). *American folk songs for children.* Cambridge: Rounder.

Sharon, Lois, & Bram. (1980). *Elephant jam.* Toronto, ON: McGraw-Hill Ryerson.

Wood, D. (1982). *Move, sing, listen, play.* Toronto, ON: Gordon V. Thompson.

Classroom Music Series

Canada is...Music
4 Volumes: 1–2, 3–4, 5–6, and 7–8.
Teacher guides and recordings available for each level.
Classroom texts for all levels except 1–2.
Gordon V. Thompson (Warner Chappell Music Canada Ltd.)
85 Scarsdale Rd., Unit 101
Don Mills, ON M3B 2R2
tel: 416-445-3131

Musicanada
4 Volumes 3–6.
Teacher's guide, classroom texts, and recordings available at all levels.
Holt, Rinehart and Winston of Canada Ltd.
tel: 1-800-387-7278

MusicBuilders (This is out of print but still widely available in schools and resource centres. Some excellent material, but be selective.)
K–6.
Teacher's Manual and Records come as a set for each level.
No classroom texts.

Musictime (Lois Birkenshaw)
Canadian Supplement to Silver Burdett.
2 volumes: K–3 and 4–6.
Classroom texts, teacher guides, and recordings.
GLC Silver Burdett.

Professional Organizations for Teacher Development

Canadian Music Educator's Association
Department of Elementary Education
University of Alberta
551 Education Building South
Edmonton, AB T6G 2G5
tel: 403-492-4273, ext. 241
fax: 403-492-7622

Dalcroze Society of Canada
Wendy Taxis
R.R.4 Roseneath, ON K0K 2X0
tel: 905-352-2515

Education through Music (ETM)
The Richards Institute
Geraldine McGeorge
P.O. Box 1240, Chatham, ON N7M 5R9
tel: 519-674-2555

Kodaly Society of Canada
cnet.unb.ca/achn/Kodaly/
This site gives information on the Kodaly system of music education. It includes teacher resources, publishers, information on summer institutes, publications, and research.

Music for Children–Carl Orff Canada
www.orffcanada.ca
This site contains information about Carl Orff, the Carl Orff Canada organization, Regional Chapters, workshops, national conferences, and teacher training courses.

Sources for Instruments and Music

Brocklin Toys (excellent Canadian-made bells on dowelling—catalogue available)
R.R. #3, Middleton, NS
tel: 905-825-4218

Empire Music
8553 Main Street,
Vancouver, BC V5X 3M3
empire@empire.music.com
tel: 1-800-663-5979

Fogarty Music Inc.
netcomsolution-ont.com/fogmusic.shtml
45 Brisbane Rd. Unit #1, Downsview, ON
M3J 2K1
tel: 416-663-3994
fax: 416-663-3715

Long and McQuade
www.long-mcquade.com
They have stores in Surrey, Vancouver, Port Coquitlam, Victoria, Calgary, Edmonton, Saskatoon, Regina, Winnipeg, Oshawa, Scarborough, North York, Toronto, Windsor, Brampton.

Royal Conservatory of Music
273 Bloor St. W., Toronto, ON M5S 1W2
tel: 416-408-2824

Waterloo Music Co.
3 Reginal St., Waterloo, ON N2J 4A5
tel: 1-800-563-9683

Warner Chappell Music Canada Ltd
85 Scarsdale Rd., Suite 101, Don Mills, ON M3B 2R2
tel 416-227-0566

Music Education Web Sites

A good beginning site with links to many others is Educational Resources in the Fine Arts www.cln.org/subjects/fine.html (Curriculum resources, instructional materials, and theme pages).

Others:
home.earthlink.net/~upnup/link.htm (mainly for links)
www.bpm.on.ca/ (folk music resources)
www.interlog.com/~cpreal/coma.html (Canadian On-Line Musicians Association)

Books and Articles

Armstrong, A. & Casement, C. (1977). *The child and the machine.* Toronto, ON: Key Porter.

Armstrong, T. (1994). *Multiple intelligences in the classroom.* Alexandria, VA: ASCD.

Armstrong, T. (1993). *7 Kinds of smart.* New York: Penguin.

Birkenshaw-Fleming, L. (1993). *Music for all: Teaching music to people with special needs.* Toronto: Gordon V. Thompson.

Campbell, P. (1994). *Roots and branches.* Danbury, CT: World Music Press. (with CD).

Choksy, L. (1974). *The Kodaly method.* Englewood Cliffs, NJ: Prentice Hall.

Cullen, L. (1995). *Solid gold for kids: Musical energizers!* Scarborough, ON: Prentice Hall Ginn.

Dunleavy, D. (1992). *The language beat.* Markham, ON: Pembroke.

Fowke, E. (1969). *Sally go round the sun.* Toronto, ON: McClelland & Stewart.

Gardner, H. (1993). *Multiple intelligences: The theory in practice.* New York, NY: Basic Books.

Hart, A., & Mantell, P. (1993). *Kids make music!* Charlotte, VT: Williamson.

Metterson, E. (1969). *This little puffin.* Hammondsworth, UK: Puffin.

Page, N. (1995). *Sing and shine on! A teacher's guide to multicultural song leading.* Portsmouth, NH: Heinemann.

Perry, C. (1987) *Let's celebrate: Canada's special days.* Toronto, ON: Kids Can Press.

Philips, K. H. (1992). *Teaching kids to sing.* New York: Schirmer.

Rauscher, F. S., G. & Ky, K. (1995). "Listening to Mozart enhances spatial-temporal reasoning: Towards a neurophysiological basis." *Neuroscience Letters,* 185, 44–47.

Rauscher, F. S. G. et al. (1997). "Music training causes long-term enhancement of preschool children's spatial–temporal reasoning." *Neurological Research,* 19, 208.

Riekehof, L. (1978). *Joy of signing.* Springfield, MO: Gospel Publishing House.

Ross, C., & Stangl, K. (1994). *The music teacher's book of lists.* West Nyack, NY: Parker.

Schafer, M., (1992) *A sound education.* Indian River, ON: Arcana Editions. Order by mail: Arcana Editions, Indian River, ON K0L 2B0

Statistics Canada. *Focus on Culture,* Vol. 8, No. 2 (Summer 1996), p. 6.

Trusty, J., & Oliva, G. (1994). "The effects of arts and music education on students' self-concept." *Update: Applications of Research in Music Education,* 13(1), 23–28.

Upitis, R (1990) . *This too is music* . Toronto: Heinemann.

Children's Literature

Baker, A., & Baker, J. (1991). *Raps & rhymes in maths.* Portsmouth, NH: Heinemann.

Hesse, K. (1997). *Out of the dust.* New York: Scholastic.

Hill, S. (1990). *Raps and rhymes.* New York: Penguin.

Hopkins, B. (1995). *Making simple musical instruments.* Asheville, NC: Lark Books.

Krull, K. (1993). *The lives of the musicians: Good times, bad times (and what the neighbors thought).* San Diego: Harcourt, Brace, Jovanovich.

Kuskin, K. (1982). *The philharmonic gets dressed.* New York, NY: Harper and Row.

Livington, M. (1995). *Call down the moon: Poems of music.* New York, NY: M.K. McElderry Books.

Nichol, B. (1994). *Beethoven lives upstairs.* New York: Orchard Books.

Plantamura, C. (1994). *Woman composers.* Santa Barbara: Bellerophon Books.

Raschka, C. (1992). *Charlie Parker plays be bop.* New York: Orchard Books.

Music Seed Strategies

This chapter contains specific ideas for integrating music throughout the curriculum. The ideas are seeds or kernels to stimulate thinking about creative ways to meet student needs and reach curricular goals. It is important to select and adapt these starter ideas to the ages, stages, and interests of students and change them to suit lessons and units. The strategy seeds are organized into sections, but many fit in more than one section. The sections on *energizers and elements and concepts* do *not* represent an integrated focus, but are provided to help teach the tools students need to do integrated thinking with music throughout curricular areas. For ideas about integrating music with other arts areas, consult Chapter 13.

I. Energizers and Warm-ups
II. Basic Musical Concepts and Elements
III. Connecting Music to Curricular Areas
- Science
- Social Studies
- Math
- Reading and Language Arts

I. Energizers and Warm-ups

Louise Cullen's book *Solid Gold for Kids: Musical Energizers!* is a wonderful source of energizers and warm ups—highly recommended!

Tongue Twisters. Warm up for singing songs by doing tongue twisters. See more examples in Chapter 8. Here is one for singing: *Tip of the tongue, the teeth, and the lips.* Say it three to five times.

Bingo Scavenger Hunt. Set up a bingo-type page with musical categories in each box. (Put the categories on the board and have students write them at random in the boxes.) Possible categories are musical genre and styles, composers, singers, musical instruments, musical elements, and particular songs. At a signal, students get up and begin to talk with others to find the names of people who know about the items in the boxes (e.g., a student who likes reggae). The goal is to write down the names of other students until the search results in bingo—across, down, diagonally.

Clap Phrases. *Record* student suggestions of favourite poems or songs on the board. Then, instead of singing the songs, simply clap the rhythm. On a simpler level, clap sentences: *"Hello, how are you?"*

Echoing Rhythms. This is an attention getter to increase focus and concentration. A leader claps, slaps, snaps, or clicks a series of rhythms that are echoed by the rest of the class. Use children's names by dividing them into syllables and giving an accent: Clau′ di a. This is adaptable to special phrases or topics like days of the week, months of the year, animal names, or plants.

Question and Answer Songs. Many songs involve people asking and answering questions, for example, "Baa Baa Black Sheep." Divide the class in half and direct one-half to sing questions and other half the answers.

Join In. Assemble students in four or five groups to listen to a musical selection. Challenge each group to create a simple movement pattern involving clapping hands, patting knees, and tapping their feet as the music is played again. Then stop the music. Have group 1 do their movements when the music starts. Keep adding more groups until all groups are doing their movements.

Musical Memories (concentration). Tell students to close their eyes and imagine different sounds as sounds are described (crickets chirping, wind chimes, jingle bells, a robin singing, someone singing "Twinkle Twinkle Little Star" played on a piano, a baby babble singing). Give students time to create the images.

Time and Tempo. Explore time and tempo with music by asking children to move at different speeds in response to music. Use slow, fast, staccato (choppy), or legato (smooth) or music that has accelerando (gets faster, e.g., "Beep Beep," the little Nash Rambler song).

Group Rhythm Mirror (concentration and focus). Group forms a circle with an IT in the middle who begins a rhythm or movement. Others must mirror. IT passes the rhythm on by staring at one person, who slowly takes over and changes places with IT. The class observes and begins to mirror the new rhythms and actions when they feel the exchange is complete.

Rhythm Wave. Group sits or stands in a circle. When leader says "begin," everyone makes their own rhythm using hands, feet, or voice. Slowly, by listening to each other, the group becomes one rhythm. Then individuals slowly begin their own new rhythms and a new group rhythm emerges.

Exchange. Two lines are formed on opposite sides of the room. The first pair at one end starts. Each person in the pair claps a repeated rhythm pattern and walks toward her partner. As they pass, the two exchange rhythms. Then the next pair goes and on down the line. Use simple rhythm patterns.

"Head, Shoulders, Knees, and Toes." First, sing the song through. Then sing and add motions. Practise singing the song together at a slow tempo. Finally, ask students to stand in a circle and do movements as they sing, gradually substituting a body part with hums, but continuing the actions: touch head, touch shoulders, touch knees, touch toes, and so on.

Shoe Beat. Everyone sits in a circle and removes one shoe. They agree on a song to sing together during which shoes are passed, left to right, and held. Begin by passing shoes to the right on the steady beat. Students can say "pick up, pass, pickup, pass" as they perform the actions. Then try simple variations (e.g., pick up, tap, tap, pass)

Knock and Respond Rhythms (attention getters). When someone knocks on a door to the rhythm "da–da da–da-da," we know to reply "da-da." In partners, one student claps a short pattern and the other responds with a short reply. If the response includes a rhythmic impulse from the question, it will sound more complete and be easier to remember.

Rhythms Circle. Stand in a circle and with one person as IT. IT creates any rhythmic phrase desired and it is passed around the circle to the right until it returns to IT. The person to IT's right then becomes IT.

Improvised Songs. Collect songs that invite additional verses like "If you're happy and you know it," "The more we are together," "Aikendrum," and "Down by the Bay." This type of song has a structure which remains the same, while portions of the song are replaced. Putting whole sets of new words to known tunes (copycat songs) can be confusing for young children; the practice destroys the special relationship between tune and words.

Word Choirs. Ask for volunteers to form a choir line. Give them a topic like happiness. When a leader points to each student, he must say or sing a word or make a sound related to the topic. For example, students say "play, laugh, love" for happiness. Create directing signals for students to say or sing their words or sounds and hold or sing at different pitches. Students can learn to conduct the word choirs, and they can be about current units—growing things, other cultures, and similar.

Rainstorm Simulation. This is a rhythm activity. Sit in a circle with eyes closed. A leader begins by rubbing hand palms together. Person to right picks it up until the whole class is participating. Then the leader switches to finger snaps and that moves around the circle. Next is thigh slaps, then foot stomps. Reverse the order to show the storm dying out.

II. Basic Musical Concepts and Elements

Note: The ideas described here are means to *achieve* integration and do *not* constitute integration, if used in isolation or never connected to other areas of the curriculum.

A Sound Education. Canadian composer and music educator Murray Schafer has published a collection of innovative listening activities called *A Sound Education*, available by mail from Arcana Editions, Indian River, ON, K0L 2B0. Along with his other books, *Rhinoceros in the Classroom* and *Earcleaning*, Schafer's *A Sound Education* provides ideas and activities that are challenging and worthy of teachers' and students' time and attention—most highly recommended!

Hum Melodies. Choose a song that the children know. Hum the first line. If they don't guess it, keep humming the song until someone guesses. Everyone sings the words as soon as they know the song chosen. Then have one of the children take a turn humming a song. Example songs are "I've Been Working on the Railroad" and "Row, Row, Row Your Boat."

Sing the Scales. Warm up voices by singing scales, with or without the do-re-mi syllables. Borrow the Suzuki idea and sing "Mississippi hot dog" on each note of the scale.

Kazoo Melodies. A leader plays a melody on a kazoo and the others must imitate it on kazoos. Make kazoos from combs by folding paper over them or use empty candy boxes.

Environment Sounds (pitch). Listen to sounds in the environment; it's a good idea to tape record common ones. Ask children if the sounds are high or low or in between high and low. Examples are a door bell, mixer, and computer hum.

Guess Who (timbre). In a group, tell children to close their eyes and someone will be tapped on the shoulder. Whoever is tapped says a word, like "hello." The others guess who spoke. Each time a correct response is given, ask *"How did you know who spoke?"* The answer will be related to the uniqueness of the person's voice. Repeat the activity. In a following session, play the game again, but have the children *sing* "hello." Stress how each person's speaking voice is unique, and so is the singing voice.

Name That Instrument (timbre). Have children experiment with various rhythm instruments to become familiar with their sounds. Then ask them to close their eyes as each instrument is played. Stress that each instrument has a unique sound, even though some may sound similar to each other. *Variation:* Use a tape or CD of orchestral instruments or other music instruments (guitar, banjo).

Dynamics Dial. Dynamics has to do with volume. Make a volume dial out of cardboard or use an old clock. Label "soft" to "loud" on the dial with the musical symbols *pp* (very soft), *p* (soft), *mp* (medium soft), *mf* (medium loud), *f* (loud), *ff* (very loud), *mfz* (loudest). Have children sing a familiar song or talk as someone turns the dial or volume button. The children should sing or speak according to what the dial reads. For example, if the dial said "pp," children sing or talk very, very softly. *Variation:* Use hand signals to slow dynamics.

Conducting Dynamics. Use with musical instruments children have made or purchased ones (Orff or other rhythm instruments). Ask them to play very softly, softly, loudly, and very loudly. Challenge students to start softly and gradually play louder (*crescendo*), and vice versa (*decrescendo*). One child can then be conductor. The other children play louder as the conductor raises her hands and softer as she lowers her hands. Have the conductor try fast raising of hands to practise sudden dynamic changes.

Sound Effects Textured Story. Read a story (cumulative stories work well and sound stories in Chapter 8), and then assign repetitive words or sound effects for children to perform on cue. For example, every time the word "hen" is heard, children say "cluck cluck cluck" or strike triangles. Involve everyone; sounds can be made by the whole group or individuals. Record results to show textured *layers* throughout the story as sounds enter and re-enter.

"Thick and Thin" Voices (texture). Use poems or stories and assign different numbers of children to participate in solo and choral readings or parts. Ask the children how it sounds when more people are reading compared to less. This should produce "thicker" and "thinner" sounding stories. Repeat the activity using singing voices. Relate to using individual versus multiple instruments by playing recordings of the same song performed as a solo and performed by a choir.

Canons and Rounds (harmony). First, practise *speaking* rounds. Students can also sing along with a tape that features rounds. Once they can sing with a recording, they are ready to sing on their own. Movements can be created for each line and performed while singing, once the singing is confident. For help in teaching and singing rounds, see Post It Note 11–4.

Picture Form. Play a variety of musical works. Discuss repetitive patterns and similar and contrasting sections. Select a simple song for discussion. Ask each student to raise his or her right hand when the first line or phrase is heard. Label this A and draw a picture of an object that begins with the letter A. Have children raise the same hand if the next line is similar and draw another A object on the board. If the line is different, have them raise their left hands and draw an item that begins with the letter B. Continue until there is a complete picture to represent all the phrases. Sing the song again and have children raise appropriate hands as symbols are designated. For example, "Mary Had a Little Lamb" would be "ABAC."

Repeat a Beat. Make a sound and repeat it a number of times: tap the window, click your tongue, slap your leg, or repeat a syllable (dum dum dum). Tell children to listen carefully. Then they repeat the sound exactly. Let the children take turns making a sound while others listen and repeat the pattern.

Spoken Rounds with Ostinati. Children first memorize a poem. Explain the concept of ostinato (something repeated over and over). Then ask one group to recite the poem, while another group recites an ostinato (a line or word that repeats over and over). The ostinato may be a line they have created, the title of the poem, or a selected line from the poem. When children have practised the last two activities, break the class into three groups. Two groups perform the poem as a spoken round, while the third group performs the ostinato. An example poem is Dennis Lee's "A Sasquatch from Saskatchewan" (*Garbage Delight*). Repeat the first line as an ostinato. *Variation:* Use rhythm instruments to create osinati.

Space and Line Walk (notation). Make a large musical staff on the floor (masking tape). Children "walk" scales or simple songs on the staff. Everyone says or sings notes touched as they walk. *Variation:* Throw bean bags on lines or spaces of the staff and name the notes.

Critical Listening. This helps students hear notes, phrasing, and rhythm. Choose a jingle from a commercial or use a familiar melody. Sit in a circle and ask each student to sing only one syllable. Go around the circle until it is blended. *Variation:* Use whole words or phrases to help students hear ostinati (repetition).

Instruments Centre. Create a learning centre for students to explore the use of instruments. Collect or ask parents to donate old guitars and drums. This is a popular centre during inside recess. In primary classrooms, store instruments on shelves rather than a box if possible. Trace the outline of each instrument on a shelf, so each instrument has its own place. Then it is easy and fun to put instruments away. In junior and intermediate classrooms, store instruments in separate boxes for each category (e.g. shakers, metals, drums)

Sound Box. For volume control in younger grades, create a sound box. Use a large cardboard container (stove or refrigerator box from an appliance store), cut a door and window, and set out a tray of instruments inside. Limit the number of children to two at a time.

Graphic Notation. Find everyday items—"found sounds" that make music. Even use body parts. The goal is for students to write music for each sound. First, pairs choose two found sound instruments and decide ways to notate (make symbols for) timbre, pitch, and volume. For example, jingle bells might be small dots to show the high, light sound. Next, write the numbers 1 to 8 across the top of the paper and the names of instruments or sounds down the left margin. Next, put symbols for each instrument under the numbers to show when each should be played. When both are to be played, place them under the same number. Loudness can be shown by drawing a symbol larger or smaller. Pairs then perform.

Music Concentration (notation). Draw traditional music symbols and different kinds of notes on the chalkboard, for example, quarter, half, and whole notes. Players take turns naming each symbol and remembering it. Students then close their eyes while a symbol is erased. They open their eyes and try to guess what symbol was erased. As more are erased, the students are to name the most recent deletions, as well as the previous ones. Correct answers are reinforced by writing the answer back on the board.

Musical Notation. Use a favourite children's song to introduce musical notation. First, speak the lyrics while clapping the rhythm. Decide where long, short, and silent sounds occur in the song. Ask children to invent symbols to record musical sounds. Write or draw melodies using circles, squares, or lines for notes. The symbols should show if the melody goes up or down and if the notes are long or short in time; for example, use small circles for short notes and large circles for long notes. Chant the lyrics again while pointing to the symbols. Ask the children again how to represent high and low sounds in the melody, as well as symbols for rhythm. Repeat and then ask children to create symbols to address tempo and dynamics. Sing the complete song while pointing to the symbols.

Body Parts Sound Compositions (notation and composition). Ask children to demonstrate sounds that can be made with their hands, fingers, feet, tongue, lips, cheeks, slapping, and other body parts. Students work in pairs to create a composition using various combinations.

Jives (rhythm). Hand and body jives allow children to explore rhythm with their body parts. Examples include "Shimmy, Shimmy Cocoa Puff" and "Hambone." Basically, you slap and brush your hands to a rhythm. See Mattox's *Shake It to the One That You Love Best* and Dunleavy's *Language Beat.*

Two-part Rhythm. One group chants and claps a steady beat to the nursery rhyme "Hot Cross Buns," while another groups chants "One a penny two a penny" as an ostinato over and over.

Italian Experiments (tempo, dynamics). Students can quickly learn the effect of speed on singing or on any task and can expand their vocabularies to incorporate a bit of Italian using this activity. A metronome is needed. Put the following tempos on a chart, set the metronome, and sing a familiar song at each tempo, for example, *"Row, row, row your boat"* Ask students to discuss changes in pitch, enunciation, and so on.

Largo = broad (40–60 beats per minute)
Lento = slow (60–66 bpm)
Adagio = at ease (66–76 bpm)
Andante = walking (76–108 bpm)
Moderato = moderate (108–120 bpm)
Allegro = quick/happy (120–168 bpm)
Presto = very fast (168–200 bpm)
Prestissimo = fast as possible (200–208)

Variation: Extend creative thinking by playing examples of accelerando (e.g., Ravel's *Bolero*). Try singing any song using accelerando. Add dynamics changes like *crescendo* and *decrescendo* (get louder and get softer) or use *staccato* (choppy) and *legato* (very smooth).

Musical Instrument Categories. Collect orchestral instrument pictures from magazines and put on cards. Ask children if they know family members whose voices are alike and discuss how people have similar voices, but unique voice sounds, too; this is also true for instruments. Show pictures of instruments grouped in families (percussion, strings, woodwind, and brass). Shuffle cards and have children group them by similar sound. Reinforce efforts based on sound groupings (some may group by size, material, etc.). Explain how instruments are grouped by (1) sound similarity, (2) the way they are played, and (3) the material from which they are made.

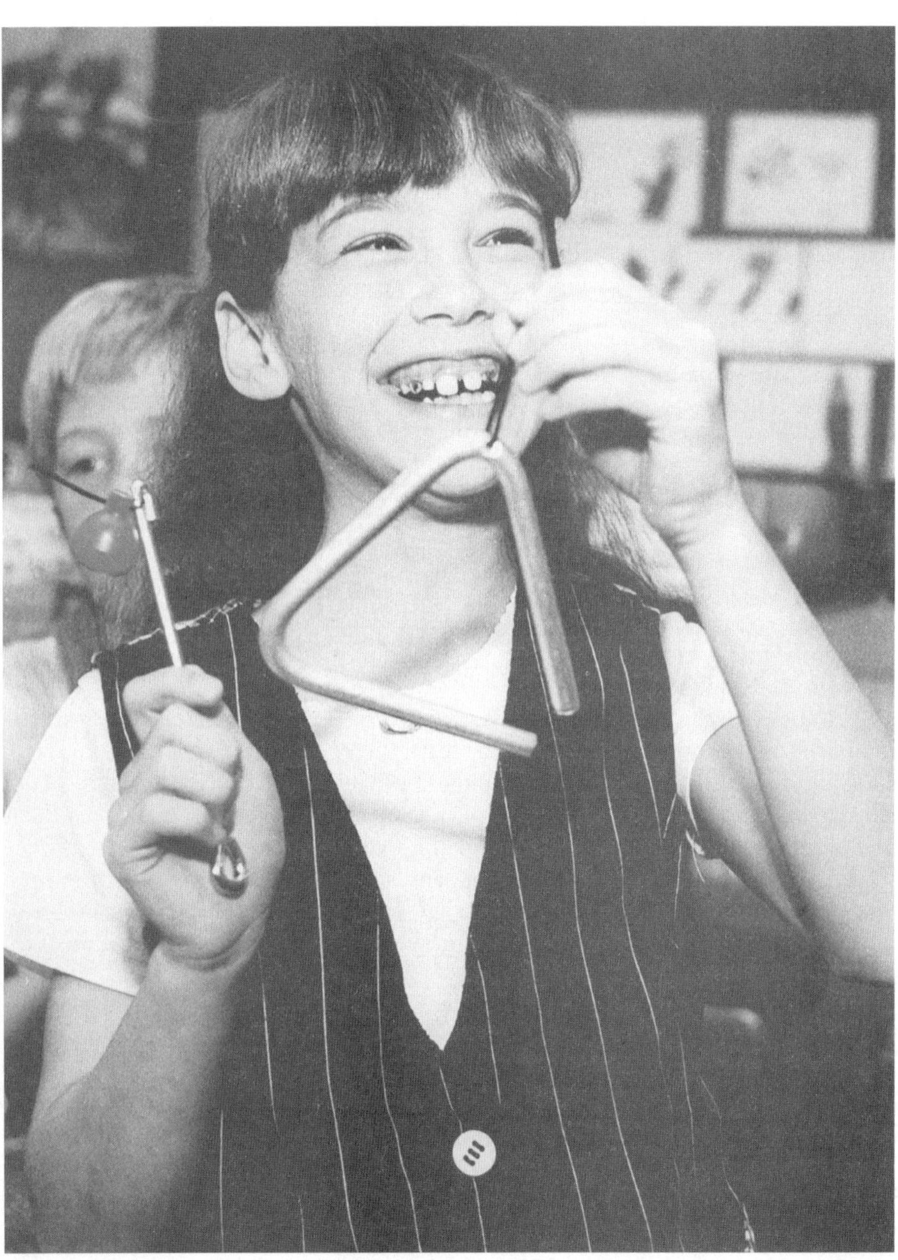

Rhythm Instruments

Instrument Rummy. Make a deck of fifty-two cards, with pictures of instruments from the four groups (above) replacing the four groups of face cards. Each player gets five cards. Place remaining cards on the table. The object is to acquire sets of four common instruments (string, brass, woodwind, and percussion). The first player draws from the pile and chooses to keep the card or discard it face up. The player with the most instrument sets at the end is the winner.

Homemade Jam. Have a jam session with instruments students have made. Put on music and play along. *Variation:* Create a parade using all the instruments made. (Titles of instrument-making books can be found in the appendix under Arts-Based Children's Literature.)

Playing Instruments. In the younger grades, it works well to have class sets (one for each child) of the four basic instruments: shaker, drums, sticks, and bells. For sticks, cut 3/4 inch dowelling in 30 cm lengths. Children can sand the ends. Commercial rhythm band sticks are as long as five-year-olds' arms. Imagine trying to play sticks as long as your arms! Cut commercial rhythm sticks in half, sand the cut ends, and you'll have twice as many pairs. Large plastic ice cream containers without their lids and turned upside down work well for drums. Children can make the shakers using film canisters. Bells are more difficult and expensive to make. Order some from Brocklin Toys (tel: 905-825-4218) and then use them as a pattern to create enough for your class. One way of using the instruments that sounds pleasant and doesn't go out of control is to pass out all the sticks first, and tap sticks together while you chant "Hickory, dickory dock" or sing "This is the way we play our sticks" (to the tune of "Here we go round the Mulberry Bush"). Gather up the sticks and pass out the drums. Good songs for drums are "Baa baa black sheep" and "The bear went over the mountain." Repeat with bells ("Are you sleeping," "Ride a cock horse") and shakers (Raffi's "Shake my sillies out").

Musical-Style Party. Have a party where everyone comes dressed as a country, jazz, rock, opera, or other type of musician. Students may choose a specific musician, such as Elvis Presley or Louis Armstrong. *Variation:* Invite students to imitate a favourite musical artist by lip syncing Elvis Presley, Whitney Houston, Alvin and the Chipmunks, Garth Brooks, The Beatles, Disco groups, etc. (Combine with the "Style Party" above.)

Music Response Options. Students can use their musical intelligences to respond to a book or unit of study using a variety of activities. There are many ideas on Post It Page 12–2.

III. Connecting Music to Curricular Areas

Webbing

Choose any topic and web all the kinds of music associated with it. Break into groups and each group chooses one or several to explore in depth. Share with class.

Science Focus

- Natural world, systems of the body, seasons, weather, plants, animals, the environment, machines, electricity, magnets, space, gravity, and states of matter.
- Finding out how and why things happen in the world through careful observation, hypothesis making, and prediction.

Metamorphoses. Groups of students choose an example of a metamorphosis in nature (egg-tadpole-frog, a volcano). They create a piece using instruments and vocal sounds to depict the metamorphosis.

Vibration Study. Vibrations pass through the eardrum, hammer, and stirrups, and the fluid in the cochlea and are sent as an electrical nerve signal to the brain. We also hear sounds because sound is conducted through our bones. Ask students to cover their ears and hum to hear the sound coming through the bones.

Singing Coathangers. Tie one end of an arm's-length piece of string to the hook of a wire coat hanger. Press the other end of the string to the hard bone right in front of the ear opening. With the free hand, tap the bottom of the coat hanger with a pencil. Analyze the phenomenon.

Tuning Forks. Teach children how to use a tuning fork. Tap the fork end hard against knee and press the stick end to the bone in front of the ear opening.

Bird Song Survey. In the spring, go on a listening-closely walk to find bird songs. Tape each song and match with bird pictures on return to class. Discuss the differences in melodies, pitches, rhythms, and the like, and the different timbres of each bird. Listen to a bird song tape or CD. One example is *Know Your Bird Songs, A Northword Nature Guide*, available from Northward Press, Box 1360, Minoqua, WI 54548 (tel: 1-800-726-6784). *Variation:* Use musical notation to write down bird songs or ask a music teacher to help do so. Students can also write lyrics to bird songs, similar to the "bob white" we use to make the quail song.

Body Parts Rap. Use the body parts to create a chant or rap, for example, "Two Hundred Bones" (tap each bone to the rhythm as it is mentioned):

> The skull is the head bone, head bone, head bone. The skull is the head bone, head bone, YEAH!
>
> Ribs, vertebrae, pelvis, pelvis. Ribs, vertebrae, pelvis, BONES!
>
> Clavical–collar bone, scapula–shoulder bone.
>
> Two hundred bones, bones, bones, bones (do in decrescendo—get softer).
>
> Humerus, radius–ulna are arm bones, arm bones. Humerus, radius–ulna are arm bones, Yeah! Femur, tibia–fibula are leg bones, leg bones. Femur, tibia–fibula are leg bones, Yeah!
>
> Two hundred bones in the body, body. Two hundred bones in the body, Yeah!

Science Symphonies. Many pieces of music celebrate or are intended to describe aspects of our world or universe. Start collecting examples to listen to and discuss what they depict through tempo and timbre of instruments. Examples are Holst's *The Planets*, Rimsky-Korsakov's *Flight of the Bumblebee*, Grofe's *Grand Canyon Suite*, and the theme to *2001: A Space Odyssey.*

Science and Sound. Explore acoustics by inviting a speaker from a sound system company, or invite a conductor to speak and show a score (which is a graph of frequencies, intensities, and volume changes).

Nature Soundscapes. Each group selects a natural environment (e.g., rainforest, lakeshore, first-growth forest, arctic tundra). After researching the chosen environment, each group creates a soundscape using voices, found sounds, and instruments.

Songs about the Environment. Listen to and sing songs about the environment, for example,"Song of the Land," *Arctic Rose*, Susan Aglukark; "Garbage No No No," *Let's Help This Planet*, Kim & Jerry Brody; If A Tree Falls," *The Earth Day Album*, Bruce Cockburn; "This Pretty Planet," *Family Tree*, Tom Chapin.

Musical Season Stories. Play seasonal music without words and mime events from the season. For a spring story, students may mime a flower blossoming. Afterwards, students may also practise writing about the process of a flower growing from a tiny seed sprout. Vivaldi's *The Four Seasons* is a piece of classical music that can be used.

Musical Weather Reports and Songs. What would a rainy day sound like? towering cumulus clouds? thunder and lightning? a hurricane? Instruct students to create and present weather reports in which the meteorologist makes the sounds as the type of weather is mentioned. *Variation:* Write or find songs about the weather that could be used to introduce or conclude weather reports. Poetry can also be used.

Social Studies Focus

- Relationships among human beings, occupations, transportation, communities, governments, customs, cultures, holidays, and use of natural resources.
- History, geography (use of maps), civics (citizenship and government) or political science, economics, anthropology, and sociology.
- Investigations into cultural diversity and global understanding.
- Special questions: How did it used to be and why? Why is it like it is today? What can I do about it? Thinking processes: cause and effect, sequence, gather data, discover relationships, make judgments, draw conclusions and problem-solve about community issues (e.g., economic issues like school funding or values conflicts related to free speech).
- Use of primary source material like newspapers, art, music, diaries, letters, journals, books, and artifacts, rather than the use of textbooks, and gathering data through interviews, surveys, and other investigatory strategies that historians and other social scientists use.

Sing Canadian Folk Songs. These songs depict a historical event or way of life:

> "Northwest Passage" (Stan Rogers)
>
> "Wreck of the Edmund Fitzgerald" (Gordon Lightfoot)
>
> "Beothuk Song" (David Campbell)
>
> "Les Raftsmen"
>
> "The Chesapeake and Shannon"
>
> "The Buffalo Hunt"
>
> "Un Canadien Errant"
>
> "The Ballad of the Bluenose"
>
> "Cape Breton Coal"
>
> "Ballad of Terry Fox"

"Ballad of the Frank Slide"
"Lumber Camp"
"Shantyman's Life"
"The Whale"
"Squid-Jiggin' Ground"
"The Ballad of Springhill"
"Ocean Ranger"
"Way up the Ucletaw"

Canadian artists who write and sing songs about historical and current events include Ian Tyson, Susan Aglukark, Connie Kaldor, Stan Rogers, Stompin' Tom Connors, Tanglefoot, and Gordon Lightfoot.

Music and Culture. Explore a culture by listening to its music. Ask students to generate a list of questions. Prompt with examples like

- Why is music created in the culture?
- Who makes the music?
- How is music made? What instruments are used?
- When is music made?
- What kind of music is made? How is it different from other music?
- How has music in the culture changed over time?

See Campbell's *Roots and Branches* for resources.

Multicultural Song Book. Students can collect songs from different cultures and countries by making notebooks of lyrics and music and tapes. Begin with music from the cultural heritage of students in your class. Encourage students to invite musicians from their own cultural community to visit your classroom and perform for your students. *Variation:* Each student selects one country or culture for which to find songs and music.

How Instruments Began. Use this idea with a unit on the early human history. Explain how our ancestors did not have instruments like we have today and had to create music from their feelings, experiences, and materials available. Music was made by plucking, blowing, and striking these first instruments. Instruments have been found that were made from bones, rocks, wood, and shells. Invite students to design an instrument that requires plucking, blowing, or striking using a familiar item in their environment. *Variation:* Each student researches an instrument played in the manner of the one he made and presents findings.

Music Current Events. Ask students to find clippings of stories related to music. Set aside time to share "Music in the News."

Multicultural Music and Dances. Integrate the music and dance of each culture and time period studied by analyzing how songs are historical records of how people felt, thought, and acted. Possibilities abound: Celtic music, First Nations music, folk music of the 1960s and 1970s, songs of Newfoundland, western cowboy songs. Students can come to understand how music helps create identity and explore a people's values and passions as expressed in a song.

Song Sources. Review purposes of songs and various song types (lullabies, work songs, sea chanties, spirituals, patriotic songs, etc.). Ask for examples of social and historical events that use certain types of songs, like birthdays. Read a book about a historical event and allow children to suggest various types of songs that the characters in the book might sing, play, or compose. Ask them to tell why. This is also a good time to share picture books that are based on songs, e.g., *Follow the Drinking Gourd* (Winter). Discuss how some historical songs were work songs ("I've Been Working on the Railroad") that are now sung for enjoyment or other purposes.

History Time Line. Play a musical selection from different musical periods (Middle Ages, Renaissance, Baroque, Classical, Romantic, and Twentieth Century). After studying each period, create a poster featuring magazine cutouts of corresponding art work, clothing, architecture, dances, or theatrical productions from each period. When completed, display the posters. Discuss how art reflects societal changes, as well as the materials and technology available in a given time or area. *Variation:* Read about composers of different time periods and place contributions on the time line. Add other significant events (composers' birthdays, song or music events).

Class Community Songs. Write or sing class songs to build community. For example, create a class anthem or write songs to celebrate people, seasons, or special events, like Secretary's Day.

History Through Music. Find songs and music that reflect the environment and times, for example, music or songs about specific historical events and values (Tanglefoot's *Secord's Warning*), or examine a song of a period to discover the attitudes and values of the time.

Introduce a Time Period. Play music to introduce a social studies unit. Play music of the period and ask, *What do you hear?* and *What does it tell you about this time?*

Reading and Language Arts Focus

- Reading, listening, speaking, written composition (including handwriting and spelling, grammar, usage, capitalization, and punctuation). Reading and language arts are processes that must be connected to a subject to have meaning, that is, something to read and write about.
- Goal: *Create* meaning and enjoyment using print through thinking, at every level from memory to critical thinking or evaluation.
- The printed word and its components (letters, syllables, spelling patterns), how words combine to make phrases and sentences, and sentences combine to make paragraphs and other forms of discourse, from tongue twisters to novels.
- Types of words: antonyms and synonyms, parts of speech, and figurative language (metaphor, idiomatic expressions).

An excellent Canadian resource is Deborah Dunleavy's *The Language Beat.*

Guided Music and Language Arts Lessons. See the special steps in this type of integrated lesson in Post It Page 11–11.

Teaching Language Arts Skills with Songs. Post It Page 12–1 gives ways to use songs to teach reading, writing, speaking, and listening skills.

Musician Expert. Students pick a musician and do any number of the following activities to become an expert on the person and his or her work. Any of these can culminate in class oral presentations.

- **Collection:** start finding and saving other works by the person (e.g., tapes, CDs, sheet music).
- **Ape the greats:** use the mood, style, and techniques of music and songs as a frame for students to create adaptations (e.g., add verses, write new lyrics, own adapted work).
- **Update:** make or find a modern-day version of the work (e.g., *Hooked on Classics* versions of the classics).
- **Guests and experts:** invite a local musician, singer, professor, or conductor to speak about a musician or his or her music, or interview a person.
- **Concert:** go to one! Write a review.
- **Musician's studio:** visit the place where a musician works (e.g., a concert hall). Ask to shadow the person for a day.
- **Music show:** have an event to display the musician's work and students' work together. Set up classroom stations to listen to tapes or CDs.
- **Mini display:** in the hall, classroom, or special place in the school. Include works by famous musicians and students' works (e.g., compositions, pictures, information about the musician).
- **Vary it:** do another version of a piece of music (e.g., use just a part of a song or piece of music to play or sing; write different lyrics to a song).

Compose an Opera. Introduce children to opera using books like Englander's *Opera! What's All the Screaming About?,* Price's *Aida: A Picture Book for All Ages,* or Rosenberg's *Sing Me a Song: Metropolitan Opera's Book of Opera Stories for Children,* and listen to opera examples. Mennotti's *Amahl and the Night Visitors* on CD or video is an accessible opera for children. Then choose a familiar story or a folktale. Compose and find songs for each main scene. When words from the story are changed into a form to be sung, they are called a *libretto.* Children can use familiar tunes or compose new ones. Songs can be sung without accompaniment, or instruments or taped music can be added. Lead characters can sing their dialogue, or some parts may be spoken.

Songwriting. Use these basic steps to show students how to write their own songs. This is an adaptation of a strategy for teaching students to read and write, called the *language experience approach,* in which students work under the guidance of a teacher and then work independently.

1. Choose a topic (e.g., long division in math).
2. Brainstorm words and feelings related to the topic. The teacher or a student can serve as a recorder using a chart, board, or the overhead projector. Ideas can be webbed.
3. Students organize ideas. Phrases can be dictated to the teacher as she scribes or students can work in small groups.
4. Lyrics are put in an order and students decide the form, rhythm, melody, tempo, etc. For example, will there be a background beat? rhythm instruments? Which lines or words are to be repeated? How fast, slow? What melody? (If students just use the universal melody, the three notes G, E, A, they can make many songs. They all know this because it is the taunt used world wide: Na na na na na.) Let students know that composers often repeat melodies (listen to pieces to discover this).

Post It Page • 12-1

Reading and Language Arts Skills to Teach with Songs

Directions: Make song charts by printing lyrics on poster board or chart paper. Overhead transparencies can also be used so that students can clearly see the lyrics.

- **Echoic reading** of lyrics to work on echoing oral expression elements (volume, rate, tone, pitch, pause, stress and emphasis).
- **Repeated reading** of lyrics to build reading fluency.
- **Speech-to-print match** made by pointing at lyrics and lines as they are sung.
- **Put each song line on a sentence strip.** Students must put them in the song's order.
- **Students can write out songs** they already know by heart to practise composing, spelling, and handwriting.
- **Singing a word** is another way of stretching its sounds to help with phonemic awareness.
- **Words in songs can be cut apart** and students can sort them into categories (parts of speech, alphabetically, number of syllables).
- **Turn songs into big books** by giving each child or a group a line to illustrate and making a page for each line.
- **Word finds.** Students find sight words or word patterns (silent *e*, *r*-controlled, phonograms, etc.) in lyrics and highlight or circle the target words.
- **Write new verses or song adaptations.** *Example:* "Down by the Bay." Add any name and rhyming words to make new verses.
- **Song books.** Students make a favourite song into an individual book by illustrating each line of the song. See book-making options in Chapter 6.
- **Song anthologies.** Students collect favourite songs in a notebook or file. These can be bound and given as gifts.

5. Make final revisions.
6. Perform: make a tape, do live sharing, make visuals (e.g., transparencies of lyrics) to accompany.

If you are interested in additional material on songwriting, a good resource is Wiggins's *Composition in the Classroom: A Tool for Teaching*. See the bibliography for more resources, including books about rap music.

Echo Me. Use this activity to explore oral interpretation using the musical concepts of dynamics, pitch, tempo, beat, accent, and rhythm. Recite the alphabet or a nursery rhyme in your normal manner. Repeat and talk very fast or very slow, use a high-pitched voice or deep, bass voice. Break everything into distinct separate syllables, or put the accent on every third word, or similar. Challenge students to echo you exactly. For example, "Mary had a little lamb" could become a mystery or a proclamation simply by varying the delivery. Also try different dialects and foreign accents.

Have a Hootananny. Have weekly sing-alongs from a song collection made by students. Add new songs to the list as they find new favourites. Put some of the lyrics on posters or transparencies and invite students to make their own song books by copying choice songs. Fluency is increased by doing repeated readings or singing of lyrics.

Have a Campfire. Build a fake campfire out of logs and sticks with a flashlight inside. Make a class list of favourite camp songs, have a few groups prepare skits, turn out the lights, and have a campfire.

Finger Plays and Songs. There are many finger plays and songs that can be used to develop vocabulary, reading skills, sequencing, rhyming, and of course musical form (e.g., "Five Little Squirrels" and "Five Green and Speckled Frogs").

Musical Response Journals. Students can keep journals and write in them while listening to a certain selection of music. They may choose to write a story that suits the type of music or a description or write about feelings or images stimulated by the music.

Sing the Vowels. Professional singers practise by singing vowels, because vowels are sounds made with the throat loose and open, allowing more sounds to come out. Consonants stop sounds. For example, in a speaking voice: "Happy birthday to you." In a singing voice: "Haa py Birrrthday to yououou." Children can learn about the sounds of vowels and consonants by singing. This is particularly helpful with students who have trouble hearing individual sounds, since this stretches sounds and increases phonemic awareness.

Read All About It

- The life of the musician or singer (biographical information: birth, death, marriage, children, friends)
- Who and what most influenced the artist
- Time period in which the artist lived
- Country or countries where the artist lived
- Style in which the artist worked or school of art to which the artist belonged
- Influence the artist had on the world of music (what the artist is known for)
- Other artists of that period
- Particular work the artist did (e.g., the most famous or controversial)
- Criticism about the artist and his or her work

Write All About It

- Letter to the musician
- Letter to the music publishing company to request information about a song, piece, or the musician
- Biographical sketch of the musician
- Story in a modern setting that includes the music
- Description of the music or song
- Report on the customs of the time of the artist
- Report on the clothing styles of the time of the artist
- Story about how the work came to be
- Report about the period of time
- Play or poem about the musician's life
- Comparison of the work of two musicians
- Time line of the musician's work
- Book for children about a musician, style, or genre of music

Music Dictionary. Students make their own dictionary of musical elements, concepts, song titles, and composers. Use wallpaper to make covers and encourage students to illustrate entries.

Song Charts. Teach reading with song charts made by putting lyrics on poster board or large newsprint. Use sticky notes on the charts to cover certain words for practice at figuring out concealed parts. Cut apart charts and use song line strips in a pocket chart or make big song books from the charts. *Variation:* Give each student or group a line from a song to illustrate for a class big book on the song.

Class Song Books. Create class anthologies of favourite songs, composer fact sheets, song fact sheets, and even riddles about music. For example, brainstorm ideas and make a chart of kids' favourite songs. Have each child sign up to write up the lyrics and research the song. Sing or read from the book each week. Have students make individual song books, song collections, or tape collections to go with their interests and needs (e.g., moods, study music).

Musical Poetry. Use chants, street rhymes, and jump rope rhymes for language arts. Encourage students to make up their own movements and add rhythm instruments (see collections like Cole and Calmenson's *"Miss Mary Mack"*).

Song Scavenger Hunts. Use songs as content to find language patterns, or conduct a week-long hunt to find songs in certain categories (e.g., ones with lots of B words, with rhyme, alliteration, about books).

Experts. Students choose to do research on a musical instrument or music in a particular culture. They then make a presentation to the class on their findings.

Put It to Music. Find appropriate music to play as favourite poems or stories are read.

Compare and Contrast. Compare recorded performances of the same composition, for example, *Peter and the Wolf.* Use a Venn diagram to note differences and similarities.

Culture and Language Through Song. Teach students to sing a familiar song in the language of the country under study (e.g.,"Frère Jacques" or "Allouette" for France).

Math Focus

- Daily living situations involving counting, measuring, probability, statistics, geometry, logic, patterns, functions, and numbers.
- Problem-solving through the use of skills (raising questions and answering them, finding relationships and patterns).
- Concepts about numbers and operations and concepts like bigger, longer, greater than, less, three, four, even, and odd.
- The National Council of the Teachers of Mathematics (U.S.A. and Canada) and the Provincial Math Educators Associations encourage teachers to have children solve problems in many ways, to focus on explaining and thinking, rather than just correctness, and to use a hands-on approach.

Number songs.
"5 Little Monkeys," *One Elephant Deux Eléphants,* Sharon, Lois & Bram.

"This Old Man, He Played One," *Baby Beluga*, Raffi.

"Let's Do the Number Rumba," *Rise and Shine*, Raffi.

"Inchworm," *There's A Hippo in My Tub*, Anne Murray.

"Star Shining," "Number Number One," One *Elephant. Deux Eléphants,* Sharon, Lois & Bram.

Rhythm and Sound Math. Students use rhythm instruments or body sounds to present addition and subtraction problems. For example, pairs present with student A = 2 beats and student B = 4 bells. Class responds with six claps or snaps.

Fraction Pies. Since music is rhythmically based on subdivisions of time into fractions, students can cut pies into fractions using musical notation. For example, pies could be divided into half with a picture of a half-note in each slice.

Counting Songs and Chants. Teach counting songs and chants to help students learn this skill (e.g., "One potato, two potato" songs like "The Ants Go Marching" (also good for marching to a one–two beat). See the arts-based bibliography under "Music" for book titles.

Shape Composition. Students need fifteen to twenty geometric paper shapes (multiple numbers of three to five different shapes cut ahead, or they can cut triangles, squares, circles, and diamonds). Review shape names. In groups, students lay out a pattern they like and then decide on a sound for each shape. Rhythm instruments may be used. Groups rehearse and then perform their composition (e.g., square = drum, circle = shaker). Think of how this pattern would sound:

Post It Page • 12-2

Music Responses

Directions: Use these ideas to respond to a book or area of study.

Sing it, rap it. Choose an important part of the story or event to put to music (sing it, rap it).

Background music read aloud. Choose a part and add rhythm instruments or music.

Match instruments. List musical instruments associated with characters, parts of the plot, the setting, or a topic (e.g., a plant or animal).

Diagram the story plot. Choose musical elements to recreate the action. For example, show rising action with faster rhythm and climax with loud music.

Rhythm plus. Make a list of special words and phrases. Put them to a rhythm or even create a melody. Think about which words or phrases could be repeated over and over (ostinato).

Opera. Make the story into an opera. Rewrite words so they can be sung (libretto).

Jingle writing. Write an advertising jingle to sell the book.

Sound collage. List all the sounds in the book. Make a sound collage by recreating the sounds and organizing them on a tape.

Singing words. Practise reading the story or a section aloud, adding music elements to make the print sing (e.g., change dynamics, tempo, or pitch).

References

Books

Campbell, P. (1994). *Roots and branches.* Danbury, CT: World Music Press. (with CD).

Cullen, L. (1995). *Solid gold for kids: Musical energizers!* Scarborough, ON: Prentice Hall Ginn.

Dunleavy, D. (1992). *The language beat.* Markham, ON: Pembroke.

Schafer, M. (1992). *A sound education.* Indian River, ON: Arcana Editions. Order by mail: Arcana Editions, Indian River, ON K0L 2B0

Wiggins, J. (1991). *Composition in the classroom: A tool for teaching.* Reston, VA: Music Educators National Conference.

Children's Literature

Cole, J., & Calmenson, S. (1990). *"Miss Mary Mack" and other children's street rhymes.* Long Beach, CA: BeechTree Books.

Englander, R. (1983). *Opera! What's all the screaming about?* New York: Walker.

Lee, D. (1977). *Garbage delight.* Toronto, ON: Macmillan Canada.

Mattox, C. (1990). *Shake it to the one you love best: Play songs and lullabies from the black musical tradition.* El Sobrante, CA: Warren Mattox.

Price, L. (1990). *Aida: A picture book for all ages.* San Diego: Harcourt Brace Jovanovich.

Rosenberg, J. (1989). *Sing me a song: Metropolitan Opera's book of opera stories for children.* New York: Thames & Hudson.

Winter, J. (1988). *Follow the drinking gourd.* New York: Knopf.

Integrating the Arts with the Arts: Strategy Seed Ideas

13

An ulcer is an unkissed imagination taking its revenge for having been jilted. It is an unwritten poem, it's an undanced dance, it's an unpainted watercolor. It is a declaration that a clear spring of joy has not been tapped and that it must break through muddling on its own.

John Ciardi, poet

This book has focused on integrating the arts with curricular areas other than the arts. And yet this is not the only important integration plan. The arts have much in common with one another and are often used in concert, so it is important to consider ideas for integrating the arts *with each other.* This chapter offers starter ideas to do so. There are ten possible combinations when using any two of the five arts. Of course, more than two can be integrated at a time, and several could be integrated with other curricular areas, making the number of combinations large and the results rich in creative possibilities. The following seed ideas are presented to trigger creative thinking and are best used after becoming familiar with individual arts areas and principles of integration. See the previous chapters on the five separate art forms for *why, what,* and *how* to integrate the arts. Here are ten combinations of strategies in the order they will appear:

I. Literature and Art (LA)
II. Art and Drama (ADr)
III. Drama and Dance (DrD)
IV. Dance and Music (DM)
V. Music and Literature (ML)
VI. Literature and Drama (LDr)
VII. Drama and Music (DrM)
VIII. Music and Art (MA)
IX. Art and Dance (AD)
X. Dance and Literature (DL)

Overall Focus of the Arts

These strategy seeds dovetail with the main aims of the arts, which include studying the historical, social, and cultural roles of each art form in our lives; communication through art forms by expressing, performing, and responding; and valuing the arts and developing an aesthetic sense. Topics include the basic elements of each art form, media, genre, artists, and products (paintings, plays). The unique focus of each art form is summarized below to give clarity about purposes for arts activities and to encourage development of other integrating arts with arts ideas.

- *Literature focus:* Respond to and produce writing of all forms and genre, from the tongue twister to the novel. Artistic use of elements such as character, plot, and theme and style elements like alliteration and onomatopoeia. Learn about authors and artists. Share and perform literature (e.g., oral interpretation of poetry). *Also see Chapter 4.*
- *Art focus:* Art elements, artists, works of art, art forms, subject matters, styles, history of art, artistic tastes, art making (media and techniques), art in our lives, the art of other cultures, and art galleries. *Also see Chapter 6.*
- *Drama focus:* Drama elements and skills, actors and acting, plays, playwriting, forms, styles, history, drama and theatre in our lives, and the theatre and drama of other cultures. *Also see Chapter 8.*
- *Dance focus:* Dance elements, dancers, choreographers, folk and popular dances, genre or forms, styles, history of dance, preferences, dance making, music in our lives, and the dance of other cultures. *Also see Chapter 10.*
- *Music focus:* Elements, musicians, songs, musical compositions, genres or music forms, styles, history of music, musical tastes, music making with voice and instruments, music in our lives, and the music of other cultures. *Also see Chapter 12.*

I. Literature and Art (LA)

Art-Based Books. The appendix has a list of children's literature about doing and viewing art, as well as learning about artists and art history. There are books in every genre, from biography to folktales.

Reading Picture Book Art. These general guidelines about using picture books supplement ideas in Chapters 3 through 6.

1. *Teach art elements so that students have words to think and talk with.* In Chapter 5 each of the elements, types of media, techniques, and styles are explained. See the Post It Pages (Post It Pages 5–4, 5–7, 5–8, and 5–9) in Chapter 5 for a summary.
2. *Take time to "decode" the art in picture books.* Use magnifying glasses and paper tubes to isolate and examine the artist's use of line, colour, and other art elements, as well as the media, style, and mood. *How* would the book be different if the art wasn't included or was in a different style (e.g., cartoon versus impressionistic)?

3. *Compare the art in different versions of the same story.* Many folk tales, such as "Cinderella," "Jack and the Beanstalk," and "Little Red Riding Hood," are available in picture book form. Gather many versions and do big Venn diagrams on bulletin board paper.
4. *Ape the greats.* Using creative problem-solving (Chapter 1), students can experiment with various media and styles used by artists of children's books. In addition, students can try out formats of books (e.g., pop-ups, shape books).
5. *Plan author–artist centred units.* By examining an entire body of artwork produced by artists like Maurice Sendak, Ann Blades, or Barbara Reid, students can become versed in the concept of style, grow to love various styles, and understand the creative process through an up-close, personal look. Aesthetic development occurs as preferences form, beginning with exposure. Students can't like what they don't know.

Picture Book Detectives. Children are more attuned to details than adults and will enjoy doing "look closely" activities with magnifying glasses to discover the small, surprising aspects of the visual art in picture books. For example, artists may insert repeated "side notes" (Chris Van Allsburg puts his dog in most books). Have children explore a book to find what the art tells about the

- *Setting* (where and when)
- *Characters* (especially body shapes and parts such as hands and faces; also look for how the characters change in the art from the beginning to the end of the book)
- *Plot* (the pictures may show events not in the text, even subplots or asides, as in Gilman's *Something from Nothing*, or foreshadow events and create tension with hints and clues)
- *Style* (use of exaggeration, humour, how mood is created with colour, shape, line)
- *Point of view* (where does the viewer enter the picture?)

In addition, books can be examined to find (1) where the story is extended through art or just illustrates the text and (2) picture book parts (endpapers, gutters, borders, double-page spreads, where the story begins in the art) can be studied. Questions such as *"what does the artist do that surprises you?"* and *"how does the book feel and why?"* help children discover aesthetic differences by comparing two books in terms of details that artists use and the amount of action or movement in the art. The subtle is significant, and a well-placed bit of line can say volumes.

Mini Museum. Students need a sturdy box to create a display of collected items that relate to a book, story, or poem. Items may be made or found that connect to characters, setting, and theme. Museum tags are added to items with a title, approximate date, and material for each. Set up museums as stations to be visited by groups, with "creators" serving as "docent" guides to talk about the items.

Wanted Posters. After showing examples of Wanted Posters and portraits, each student selects a book character and creates a poster. A portrait is drawn by examining the general shape of the face and measuring distances between eyes, nose, mouth, etc. At the bottom of the poster, students write a description of the character, the place and time last seen, and a contact person. Rewards or other notifications may be added. (Parts of the text may be reread for accurate details.)

Literature Quilts. Each student is given a square of paper (large origami works well) on which he or she uses choice art materials and style to respond to a book everyone has read, a favourite book, an author–artist study, or a genre. Squares are glued on to large, black bulletin board paper. (Use chalk to mark placement until they are glued and then wipe the chalk off.) Make a border by rolling long paper and cutting into slices with a paper cutter. Cut sliced minirolls to make a pattern when it unrolls (just like cutting paper doll strips). Glue onto the quilt, display, and discuss what the quilt shows.

Sketch-to-Sketch. (Harste, Short, & Burke, 1988) Students interpret what happened to characters and the roles each played by making sketch drawings (quick rough drawings). Each character might be sketched in several different story actions to summarize the events. Students present their drawings to explain interpretations and discuss how others saw things differently and why. Drawings can be compared and contrasted.

Quickdraws (Tompkins, 1997). Before reading, students draw for a few minutes about a topic that relates to the upcoming book. The drawing activates visual imagery. They then use these images while reading to confirm, reject, and modify their ideas—this is active meaning construction.

Sketch Books. Each child has a sketch book to sketch in before, during, or after reading or listening to literature. Sketch book responses can be brought to literature discussions to organize sharing. Prompts for sketches include characters, setting, most exciting points, special objects or symbols, plot, theme, and even style sketches related to special words. Sketches can also be used as a stimulus for writing (e.g., choose a sketch to write a poem or paragraph about).

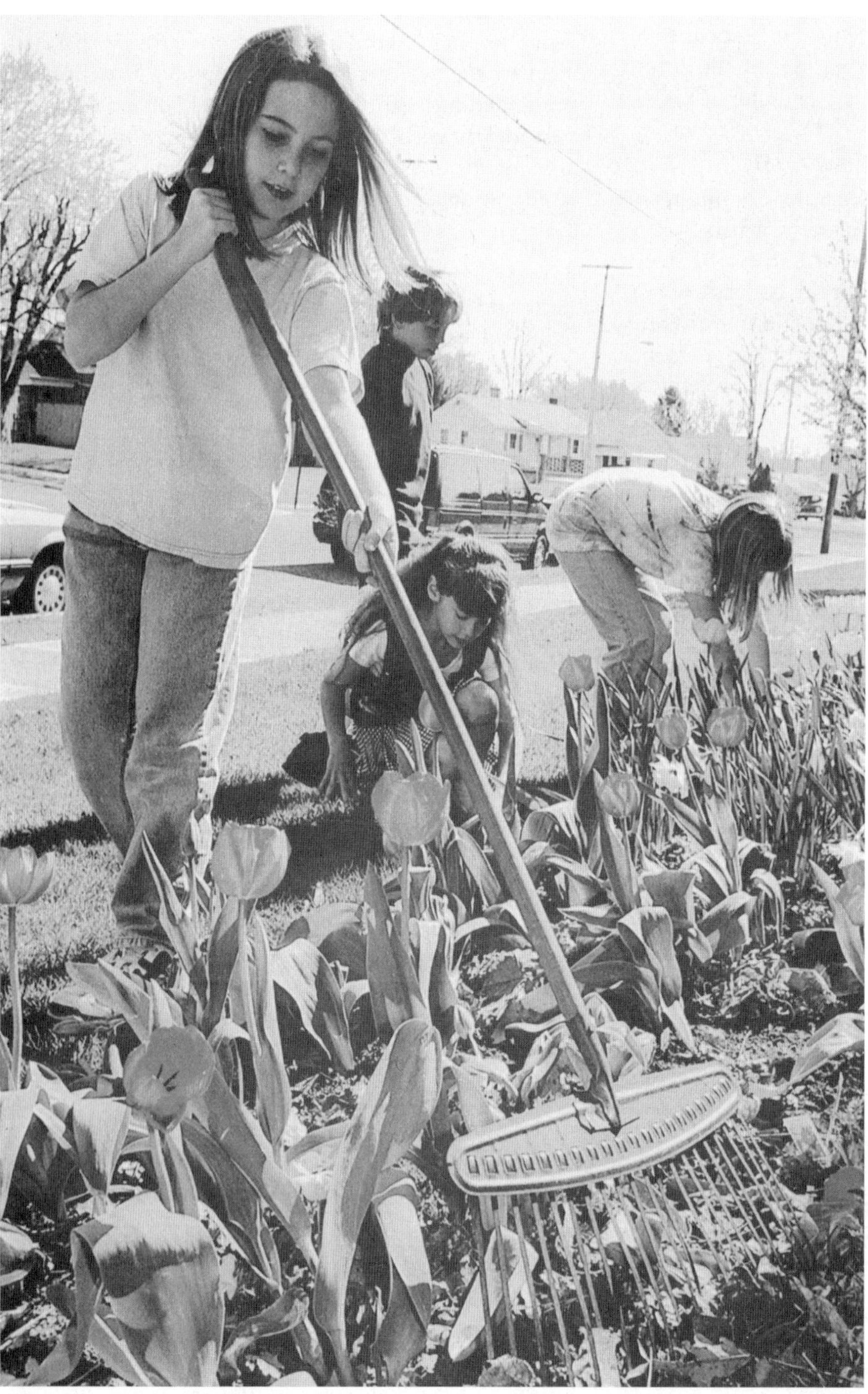

Working in Monet's Garden

Poem Match. Students find or write a poem that connects to a work of art. See *Things to Write and Say from A to Z* in Post It Page 4–2. In addition, see the *poem patterns* in Post It Page 3–4 and a special section on poetry in Chapter 4. Art and poetry can be shared in docent talks and displayed together in a class museum.

Art Story Map. Provide students with portraits, landscapes, and nonrepresentational art (e.g., abstract) to choose from. Students write or tell a story using portraits for characters, a landscape for the setting, and an abstract work for a story problem. Remind them to establish the problem quickly and be descriptive about the setting and characters. Share stories with art displayed.

Story Board. When picture book artists write books, they often begin with a story board—brief sketches or mock-ups of how the finished book might look. Students can make a series of drawings (in order) that tell a story and glue them on a poster board to create a story board about any book.

Art Prewrite. Students create any type of art or collect art (postcards, magazine pictures, sculptures, pottery) to use as topics for writing and then "squeeze" art for writing ideas by brainstorming and webbing ideas. Any of the *things to write and say from A to Z* in Post It Page 4–2 can be used as writing forms (caption, letter, list).

Art *Media* Literature Responses. Making art is an important way for students to respond to any book or poem they've read. Art can also accompany any writing that students produce. For example, after reading a story students can create the following (see Post It Page 5–7 for additional media options):

- Book (pop-up, accordion, big books, mini-books, sewn book)
- Collage—objects (wallpaper, tissue, torn or cut construction paper) glued on
- Craft—handcrafted items like pottery, weaving, quilt square, or whole quilt
- Drawing—with pencil, charcoal, marker, pen and ink, crayon
- Enlargement—use overhead projector to blow up a favourite book picture and outline on large paper. Complete art by using tempera, watercolour, collage, etc.
- Fibre art—use fabrics and yarn
- Fresco—paint on wet plaster so that paint becomes a part of the material
- Mixed media—paper, wire, paint, fabric, all used in one artwork
- Mobile—3D art that moves
- Painting—tempera, acrylic, watercolour, oil
- Pastel—oil-based chalk art
- Print—pull a print or stamp with found objects, woodcuts, linoleum
- Rubbing—paper is placed on objects and crayon, marker, etc., are used to bring up images
- Sculpture—3D art made from wood clay, metal, found objects, plaster, paper mâché

Art *Subject Matter* Literature Responses. Students can respond to important ideas in any piece of literature by creating art with one of these subject matters that connects to the book: landscape (outdoor scene in the story); portrait (a character in the story); cityscape (view of a city in the story); interior (inside a room or building in the story); seascape (a view of a body of water in the story); still life (nonliving objects in the story arranged on a surface); abstract (colour, shape, line, and texture are the focus and are used to express images and feelings).

Visual Poetry. Create shape or concrete poetry written in the shape of the subject of the poem. See Corcett's "November," Morton's "Tomato," and MacKinnon's "Why/because," all in Booth's collection of Canadian poems for children, *Til All the Stars Have Fallen.*

Masks: Six Dramatic Roles. According to Temple (1991), story characters fill one or more of six roles, and characters may also change roles. These roles can be used to create masks and puppets throughout the year:

1. The Lion Force: main character
2. The Sun or Object: what the Lion Force wants
3. Mars, the Rival: tries to keep the Lion Force from getting what she or he wants
4. Moon, the Helper: helps Lion Force achieve desired goals
5. Earth, the Receiver: benefits from Lion Force's actions
6. Libra, the Judge: decides if Lion Force may have the Sun or Object

II. Art and Drama (ADr)

Sculpting. In pairs or groups of four, one person becomes the clay to be sculpted. The others then sculpt the person into specific emotions, concentrating on body shape and levels.

One Liner Tableau. Students recreate, in tableau, scenes from photographs, portraits, cartoon strips, and the like. A *series* or cartoon strip can also be performed. Tableaux can be created for scenes before or after a scene in a painting or photo to stimulate creative thinking. After students are "set," teacher taps them one by one and each says a one liner of what they are thinking or feeling. *Variation:* When they are tapped, students come to life, do one action, and then freeze. *Note:* Large, old picture frames can be used to "pose" for drama tableaux and to take pictures of children posing inside the frames.

Storytelling. Ask students to create stories about a piece of art or several pieces (e.g., two portraits, a landscape, and an abstract work can set up characters, setting, and problem for a good story).

Experts. Cover half of painting or ask groups to choose a section on which to focus (e.g., foreground, background). Small groups serve as "experts" on their section and report to the whole group after small-group time.

One Minute After. Ask students to imagine what happened one minute after a piece of art was finished. Divide into groups and allow students to plan a scene. Groups then present to the whole class.

Art Auction. Students prepare information about works of art to "sell" the works. Each student then takes a turn at selling and auctioning his art. Give each a sum to spend at the art auction.

Partner Sculptures. Partners take turns sculpting each other by imitating famous character poses or sculptures (e.g., Rodin's *The Thinker*). *Variation:* Half of the class assumes the pose of a famous sculpture while the other half pretends to be museum visitors who tour in pairs and use dialogue to show what they see, how they feel, and who they are.

Pretend to Paint. Students imagine they have very tiny paintbrushes and not much space to paint. Narrate a pantomime in which you tell them to keep painting, but the size of the brush and the space keeps getting bigger and bigger. Music can be used to accompany this (e.g., "The Blue Danube" waltz).

Listen and Draw. Partner students and give one person a secret object. They sit back to back and one describes the object while the other tries to draw it as described. Encourage students to tell size, shape, and colour and focus on use of visual details.

Photographs. Class pretends to pose in a group photograph that might happen or have happened in a piece of literature (e.g., the family at the fair in *Charlotte's Web*). Students decide about the composition, background, and so on. Pose and freeze. Ask students to each give a one-liner of their thoughts as they pose at this moment in the story.

Statues. Look at famous statues and discuss their emotions and why statues exist. Look closely to see how different parts of the body are arranged. Students assume the pose of a statue and, when tapped, each says a one-liner about what he or she is thinking or feeling.

III. Drama and Dance (DrD)

Dance Freeze. After learning dance elements, put on music without lyrics (new age, jazz or classical) and allow students to free dance. When the music stops, they freeze and each gives a one-liner about a dance element they are using.

Dance in Character. Students think about a famous person or character and how each might dance. When a signal is given, students dance in character. Divide the class in half so that one-half can observe and comment. Reverse.

Musicals and Dance. Watch a musical (e.g., *Oklahoma*) and discuss how dance is used. What does dance communicate about the story and characters that would be missing without the dance?

Verbal Dance. Students create a freeze–move–freeze dance, but actually "talk" as they dance. For example, "low level, low level, flick fingers, flick toes, jump, jump, twirl, high level, punch, shrink, collapse."

Dance a Story. Stories abound with characters and situations with movement potential. If the art medium is to be dance, and not drama, only the essence of the character or situation is used. A literal movement translation results in mime (drama), not dance. Stories can be danced or mimed; both call for targeting a particular event or image, rather than a whole story. An example that combines dance and drama is McCulley's *Mirette on a High Wire*. (Put a strip of masking tape on the floor. Groups take turns balancing in many different ways: one foot, tiptoes along the line—dance movements exploration. Those waiting mime the crowd watching and reacting.)

Balance Mime. Brainstorm when balance is important (e.g., walking on a wall, crossing a creek on stepping stones). Mime situations. Ask half of class to be observers and give feedback. Reverse.

Ball Bounce. Narrate a mime in which students start bouncing a small ball (e.g., a tennis ball). Change to a beach ball, basketball, and so on. Tell them to show the size and hardness of the ball with their bodies. Change speeds.

IV. Dance and Music (DM)

Dance and Movement Songs. There are many action or movement songs, singing games, and song dances available. Raffi, Fred Penner, and other Canadian recording artists have produced movement-oriented song collections on tape and CD for children. Special songs with dances include twist music, hokey pokey, chicken dance, and the pony.

Mood Setting for Dance. Use music to relax students before engaging them in movement. Allow them to move or not move. Example artists are Enya and Natalie McMaster.

Repeated Listening to Choreograph a Dance. Play a piece of music and ask students to listen closely to the tempo, mood, and rhythm. Discuss and repeat listening. Brainstorm ways to show the important parts of the music with dance. As a whole or in small groups, create a dance to go with the music. Devise a symbol system to note how to perform the dance (e.g., circles, lines, and squares to show movements).

Sound to Motion. Make different sounds (with rhythm instruments, bells, etc.) to stimulate creative thinking. Ask students to show the motion that each suggests (e.g., strong? high? low? direction?).

Dynamics! Use a drum, finger cymbals, and other percussion instruments. Ask students to change the size of their body actions according to the sound (e.g., loud makes large movements). Using different instruments helps students understand how timbre can change and still have a loud or soft sound.

Dancin'

Dancing Songs. Many songs are naturally connected to movement (e.g., "The grand ole Duke of York, He had ten thousand men, He marched them up to the top of the hill and marched them down again"). Collect such songs and invite students to add the movements suggested. See the bibliographies for both dance and music in the appendix for ideas. *Variation:* Ask students to create movements to accompany a round. Then perform the round with movement in several parts. Sometimes it can work to have the students form three concentric circles, one to each part. The inner circle begins, then the middle circle, and finally the outer circle.

Dancing Animals. Play various types of music for children to dance to. Encourage them to warm up by moving to the music as different animals, concentrating on using animal moves at all the different levels and using a variety of body parts.

Body Melody Match. Select a familiar song. As children sing or listen to the song, lead them in moving up or down in a personal space to illustrate the shape of the melody. Point out that their bodies may move to show the melodic pattern.

Create a Folk Dance. Select a favourite folk song and ask groups to create movements for one line. (Use BEST elements from Chapter 9 to involve arms and feet.) Sing the song with each performing his or her line.

Cooperative Musical Chairs. Remove chairs, as in the traditional version, but all must find a place to sit when the music stops and help each other do so! No one is eliminated.

Sign Language. Teach songs in sign language or add signs to any song. See Riekehof's *The Joy of Signing.*

Someone Else's Dance. Contrast how creative problem-solving feels with mimicking dance steps modelled by the teacher. Play a familiar piece (e.g., "Dance of the Flowers"). Teach specific movements by modelling and asking them to imitate (use BEST from Chapter 9 to invent five to six dance movements). Ask the students to repeat the dance three to four times until they can do it in unison. Next, play another piece of music and ask students to invent their own movements. To keep this simple, do another piece that might suggest flowers or plants (e.g., Enya's "Trees"). Ask students to practise, and then split the class in half to do performances. The audience half then gives descriptive feedback. After both halves have performed, ask about the differences between the two ways to learn to "dance" to music.

V. Music and Literature (ML)

Music-based Books. The appendix has a list of music-based children's literature. There are books in every genre, from biography to folktales, including books about making and listening to music.

Musical Literature. Read books to children that are based on music or a song and have them "sing" the story. A variation would be to read stories that are from ballets, such as "The Nutcracker," while playing the music from the ballet in the background.

Operettas. An opera is a story told with music or song. Students can create an opera for a story they know, such as a fairy tale. For example, use the "Three Little Pigs" and have students choose characters, props and costumes, and melodies to sing the story. Teach students how to write cues in dramatic opera form (e.g., *Enter Big Bad Wolf, shifting eyes from side to side* or *Trees (chorus) sing*).

Onomatopoeia Poems. Create sound poems by using objects and rhythm instruments. Begin by exploring sounds to make with different objects. Work in small groups to plan a five-line poem that builds from one sound up to five sounds. Decide which sound will be line 1, which two sounds will be line 2, etc. Encourage thinking about rhythm patterns, accent, tempo, and dynamics. Students rehearse their sound poems, present them, and then write them down using onomatopoeic words. For example,

Ding
Bang Bang
Shush Shush Shush
Rattle Rattle, Clap Clap
Ding Bang Shush Rattle Donk

Poetry Collections. Collect poems about music (e.g., Shel Silverstein's "Ourchestra"). Display on posters or create individual or class anthologies. Perform poems with rhythm instruments.

Artist Studies. Do units based on biographies of composers, singers, and musicians—even instrument inventors.

Song Story. Students select a song and brainstorm who might have written it and why. Work in groups to write a story that explains how the song came to be. *Variation:* Students can research song origins using references such as the *New Grove's Dictionary of Music.*

Word Rhythms. Find examples of the following five phrase patterns in names of classmates, song lyrics, place names, and so on. Each of the patterns can also be played with rhythm instruments.

1. Iambic = dah DAH: *Do what?* (Iambic pentameter = 5 iambs *"I like to eat my peas without a fork."*)
2. Trochaic = DAH dah: *Rudy, Eileen*
3. Anapestic = dah dah DAH: *Virginia*
4. Dactylic = DAH dah dah: *Claudia* (double dactyl = *Gloria Zittercoff*)
5. Spondaic = DAH DAH: *Go there.*

VI. Literature and Drama (LDr)

Drama-Based Books. The appendix has a list of drama and theatre-based children's literature. There are books in every genre, from biography to fiction, including books about doing and viewing drama and theatre.

Puppet Shows. Students can plan the story adaptation, stage, and props to make a story come to life. For example, write a Reader's Theatre script (see Chapter 8). Help students map out the story using events in the beginning, middle, and end. Then decide who will make each character, scenery, and so on. In Chapter 4 there are several types of puppets to adapt to story characters. Stages can be made by using a push rod in a doorway to hang a curtain. Presentations can also be made using the overhead projector (shadow puppets). Rather than memorize a script, encourage improvisation. As with all performances, a rehearsal is important to practise with puppets and oral expression.

Choral Reading. Choral reading invites experimentation with words and the use of vocal elements (volume, rate, tone, pitch, pause, stress, and emphasis) to build fluency. Options include (1) leader reads a line and class echoes, (2) leader reads a section and class reads a refrain in the story or inserted for dramatic effect, (3) solo readers read sections and whole group reads the rest, or (4) two groups take turns reading a section. (See the *poetry alive* strategies in Post It Page 4–4.) Do repeated readings for fluency.

Tableau. (freeze frame). Students choose a *key moment* (not a complete scene) from a piece of literature. In small groups, they plan facial expressions, body shapes, use of space, and so on, to create a frozen scene. Each group takes a turn to perform. The rest shut their eyes and when the tableau group says "curtain," they open their eyes and begin to "look closely" to describe all they see. The focus is on describing details and not just guessing the scene. *Variation:* All groups do the same key moment. Compare and contrast.

Story Drama. A play can be created from any story with no scripts to memorize. Start with quality stories with lots of action and believable characters. Dialogue can be improvised during the story playing using these steps: (1) Read or tell a story and tell students to listen for dialogue, special words, and refrains and to get the gist of the story. (2) Afterward, review the plot and proceed to cast, adding characters, and even crowds so that all can participate. Plan sound effects, music, and the space to be used. At desks? Create open space? (3) Decide who is to narrate and how to start and end the drama (e.g., will the teacher take a role?). (4) Play the story drama with the teacher coaching. If there are problems in the replaying (e.g., if students don't know when or how to end), assume a character role and facilitate, or be the narrator and tell a conclusion with students following your lead.

Round Robin Retellings. This is a creative retelling variation in which a known story is retold from another character's point of view. Sit in a circle to retell. Begin with one person telling a line, and move around the circle until the full story has been retold. For example, retell *Cinderella* from a stepsister's viewpoint.

Read Arounds (adapted from Tompkins & McGee, 1993). After reading a story, each student chooses just one sentence from the story and rehearses to read it aloud. Each student then reads the line using the oral expression elements of volume, rate, tone, pitch, pause, stress, and emphasis to convey the interpretation of meaning. Afterward students discuss why they chose their lines (e.g., the special sound or sense in the passage). *Variation:* Use each line to make a class big book with each page having one line and art.

Poetry Sharing. See Post It Page 4–4 for a dozen ways to share poetry.

Reader–Responder. Do in partners, usually with a poem. Reader reads one line and responder orally improvises by saying whatever comes to mind. Continue throughout the poem. For example, reader: "Jack and Jill went up the hill." Responder: "I wonder how high the hill was."

Poem Mimes. Mime possibilities exist in many poems. For example, Bogart's "Poems can give you" (in Booth's *Til All the Stars Have Fallen*) is about what a poem can do for you. Students mime as the poem is read (narrative mime), leaving silent spaces for movement if desired. For example, Wadley's "My toboggan and I carve winter," Miriam Waddington's "Laughter," and Lysyk's "The north wind," all from Booth's *Til All the Stars Have Fallen,* are examples of poems with rich drama and movement possibilities.

Character Meetings. Each child chooses a character from a book or story everyone knows. They then partner and have conversations, in character, about their lives, problems, and so on. Invite pairs to share highlights of conversations with the whole class. *Variations:* (1) Use in social studies with historical characters; (2) at a signal, characters freeze and audience suggests an emotion. When conversation begins again, characters must use the suggested emotion.

Planning Character Improvisation. Read a story or book and stop after the conflict is introduced. Break into groups to discuss these questions: *What does the character want or need (goals or motives)? What is the problem or conflict? What stands in the way of the character getting what he or she wants? What actions can the character take to deal with the problem (plot)? Where might the character be (place)? What might the character say (e.g., a one liner about the problem)?* These are the same categories contained in a literature storymap. *Note:* It helps to give students a planning sheet with the questions and permit work in groups to plan a scene with a beginning, middle, and end to deal with the questions. A good way to structure is to plan a one-liner about the problem to end the scene.

Reader's Theatre. See guidelines and examples in Chapter 8.

Rhyme Change. Nursery rhymes and other chants and poems are adaptable to word play activities. Use these as verbal warm-ups and to stimulate creative thinking, for example, "Hickory Dickory Dock, A mouse ran up my . . ." (students supply rhyme). Do all the vowel sounds for phonemic awareness development: "Hickory Dickory Dack . . . ," Hickory Dickory Deck . . . ," and so on.

Nursery Rhyme Mime. Sing or recite nursery rhymes. Divide into groups and have each group plan which rhyme to say and mime, or just mime, for others to guess.

VII. Drama and Music (DrM)

Mime and Action Songs. There are numerous songs with actions to mime as the group sings, for example, "If You're Happy and You Know It." *Variation:* Write your own with actions (e.g., if you're happy and you know it laugh out loud, smile a while, show your teeth, grin a lot). Other examples: "Shake My Sillies Out," "Grand Old Duke of York," "My Hat It Has Three Corners," and "This Old Man, He Played One." See the music chapter and Arts-Based Bibliography for more.

Singing Commercials. Divide students into teams and give each a magazine with picture advertisements. Teams create a song to promote the product in their picture. They may select from familiar tunes or write lyrics to an original tune. Teams then present their commercial jingles.

Interviews. Students work in groups to list questions to ask musicians, songwriters, conductors, and so on. Guests are invited to class, and students act as interviewers to find out answers to their questions.

I Heard It First. Brainstorm a list of songs that are famous: Hallelujah chorus, "Four Strong Winds," "The Huron Carol," and the like. Students then break into small groups and plan a scene about the first time the music or song was ever heard by an audience and their reactions. Scenes should have a beginning, middle, and end.

Hum Groups. Put the names of four song titles on slips of paper. Repeat the titles until you have enough for everyone. Students draw a slip and on a signal must sing or hum the melody and try to find others in their group with the same melody. Use songs they know, for example, "Row, Row, Row Your Boat."

VIII. Music and Art (MA)

Make Rhythm Instruments. Many resource books show ways to make rhythm instruments that can be painted and decorated. For example, place papier mâché over a light bulb, let it dry, and then tap it to break the inner light bulb. Paint and you have a shaker. Rainsticks can be made by inserting toothpicks up and down a wrapping paper tube (it helps to make the holes ahead for the students with a drill). Fill tubes with rice or small beans and plug the ends. Sticks can then be painted or covered with collage materials.

Foot Painting. Put on music and ask students to listen to its rhythm and mood. Spread out a large paper, like long bulletin board paper. Use shallow trays of tempera; be sure to have students roll up pant legs. Start with a choice of a few colours. Students create art by painting with their feet to the music.

Draw to Music. Listen to music about a topic (e.g., *Grand Canyon Suite*). Write or draw to the music and then share how the music communicated messages about the topic.

Musical Mobiles. Make mobiles from old silverware or other objects that will create music as they move. Use string or wire to tie objects to a stick, pipe, or hanger.

Illustrate a Song. Each child chooses a favourite song to illustrate, or the whole class can do the same song to find all the ways one song could be interpreted. Students could create a group mural of a song, or songs can be cut apart, line by line, with children working on illustrating their part. By assembling all the art, the entire song is then depicted (e.g., "Jack was Ev'ry Inch a Sailor" will work).

Finding Musical Elements in Art. After teaching the elements of music, use a piece of art to ask students to find these same elements. For example, folk art and folk music can be compared. Find rhythm in art, texture, tempo, style aspects, and dynamics (areas that are louder or softer).

Media Show and Sound Compositions. Students prepare a sound and art presentation around a choice topic, for example, friends, animals, feelings, weather, culture, or country. They may work in groups or pairs to find a piece of music to play as they present art on transparencies or on an easel as the song is played. Art could be student made or "found art." This could also be done as a computer slide show.

IX. Art and Dance (AD)

> *When one looks at the image of a rising arch or tower in architecture or at the yielding of a tree bent by the storm, one receives more than the information conveyed by the image. . . . The body of the viewer reproduces the tensions of swinging and rising and bending so that he himself matches internally the actions he sees being performed outside. And these actions . . . are ways of being alive, ways of being human.*
>
> Arnheim, 1989, p. 26

Art Dance Connection. Much of art is movement (e.g., draw, paint, and art and dance elements parallel). Dance can awaken the kinesthetic sense and put feelings into motion. Students can dance a painting or paint the dances they create. The kinesthetic centre of dance can motivate children to want to move, and the need to express through movement can extend to scribbling, drawing, and painting. Relate the dance elements to other art forms so that students see connections and develop structures for thinking. For example, explore shape in art and dance by painting to music on big paper. Find line, pattern, rhythms, images expressed in art, music, and so on. Movement possibilities include explorations of lines, directions, and the use of shape.

Art in Motion. Show artwork with physical motion in it. Discuss how motion is shown and why a particular step is sometimes "frozen" by the artist (e.g., which part of a sneeze would you depict?). Explore as a dance with movements before and after: Freeze–move–freeze–move–freeze sequence.

Sound Movement Collages. Sounds of the body, city, nature, animals, machines, children's names, and names of provinces and cities can all suggest movement. Brainstorm a category with students and then stretch it for movement possibilities. Encourage them to think of the shape, size, rhythm, and energy, of the words. Break into groups and ask each group to make a collage (an assemblage of items pasted or glued together) of sounds and movement. Groups can then create a freeze–move–freeze dance and perform. This activity could be followed by a visual art collage interpretation of the same topics danced.

Sculpture or Architecture Dances. Display pieces of sculpture or pictures of buildings or furniture. Ask about space, curves, and movements and how each might move if it came to life. Ask students to show the size, energy, and flow with their bodies.

Artists That Move. Set up a station with art books or assign students to locate art that includes movement (e.g., Matisse and Degas). Discuss how artists show movement through line, shape of body, and use of space.

Dance a Painting. Display a reproduction and ask students to brainstorm all the shapes, movements, and emotions (note the word "motion" in this word). Direct attention to the foreground, middle ground, and background in subjects like landscape, seascape, and still life. Divide into small groups. Each group decides a way to dance the painting, using a beginning–middle–end structure. The goal is not to merely mime, but to stretch for ideas: What movements came *before* this moment in the art, *during, after,* what is just outside the subject matter (e.g., other people, movements)? After students prepare, take turns presenting. Background or mood music can be added.

Paint a Dance. Use large paper to capture a dance after doing it. This can begin on a small scale with just painting or drawing certain movements (e.g., curved lines, circles, shaking, turning).

Magic Wand. Display a full-length portrait, like a narrative scene from history with several figures in it. Students assume figures' positions. When touched by a magic wand, they move in ways the figure might move. Coach them to become conscious of how to bend and walk, the use of curved and straight lines, and positive and negative space. Leader can add emotions: "Move as if you are in a hurry."

Body Painting. Pretend each body part is a paintbrush and explore a variety of brushstrokes (e.g., broad and sweeping, quick and short, slow and thick).

Negative and Positive Space. On signal, students make body shapes. Start with "fixed spot" shapes before locomotor. Stress the use of different levels. At freeze signal, all stop and look for "holes" in people's body shapes, made with arms, legs, or fingers. Ask students to squint to see hole shapes—the negative space. *Variation:* Do as partners. Person A makes a shape with holes (negative space) in it and person B then makes a shape that interacts with the negative space.

Emotion or Colour Dance. Small groups decide on three actions to show an emotion or colour and the order and times that each will be repeated.

X. Dance and Literature (DL)

Dance-based Children's Books. See the appendix for a bibliography of dance-based literature. There are books in every genre, from biography to folk tales, and books about *doing* dance and dancers. Any literature, however, that includes movement or movement imagery has potential use with dance.

Character Dance. Any character in a story or book can be explored through dance by considering all the ways a character might move. For example, how would Wilbur in *Charlotte's Web* move if he was happy? hungry? afraid? tired? How is his movement different from Charlotte's or Templeton's? How does body shape show something about a character?

Character Walk. Each person walks around the room as a famous person or character, varying normal level, posture, rhythm, and gait. When leader says "change," each person tries another walk variation.

Theme Dance. Any theme from a poem or book can be danced by first brainstorming all the ways to express the theme with body parts, movements, energy, and use of space and time. For example, the theme that courage comes out of fear can be danced in a frozen shape, movements, and frozen shape three-part dance planned and performed by small groups, who will each present a very different interpretation.

Key Topic Dance. Make a list of important words or topics in a poem or book. Brainstorm all the movements, shapes, levels, and energy that could be used to convey the topic. Give small groups the choice of a topic or word to plan a dance or a series of creative movements to express it.

Dance Poetry. A poem about dance can be read as students move creatively to express its meaning. For example, encourage showing different ways to use the body and space to express the joy of dance in these poems: Wadley's "My toboggan and I carve winter," Miriam Waddinton's "Laughter," McLaren's "Field in the Wind," and Lysyk's "The north wind," all from Booth's *Til All the Stars Have Fallen.* Put poems about dance on poster board to make charts.

Line by Line. Read a poem to students. Then give each student or group a line from the poem. They then explore all the movement possibilities of the line (e.g., the rhythm of the words, the emotions expressed, the images). The poetry can then be danced line by line as a narrator reads, or groups can each plan to perform just one line.

Write about a Dance. After any dance, students can write about what they did and felt. The BEST elements can give focus to the writing. The writing could be in the form of a story, informational piece, or even a poem (e.g., a couplet or diamante about the dance). For example,

Shapes
Round Angled
Changing Size and Levels
Dance Shapes Show Feelings
Frozen Moving Forms
Pointed Curvy
Shapes

Characters Alive! Use a painting or picture from a book with several characters in it. Groups of students become the characters by posing as a frozen picture.

They then "come alive" and do three dance moves consistent with the characters. Coach students to do locomotor moves and use low, medium, and high levels. Finally, they return to their original frozen positions.

References

Books

Arnheim, R. (1989). *Thoughts on art education.* Los Angeles: CA: Getty Center for Education in the Arts.

Harste, J., Short, K., & Burke, C. (1988). *Creating classrooms for authors.* Portsmouth, NH: Heinemann.

Riekehof, L. (1978). *The joy of signing.* Springfield, MO: Gospel Publishing House.

Temple, C. (1991). Seven readings of a folktale: Literary theory in the classroom. *New Advocate,* 4, 29.

Tompkins, G. (1997). *Literacy for the 21st century.* Upper Saddle River, NJ: Prentice Hall.

Tompkins, G., & McGee, L. (1993). *Teaching reading with literature: Case studies to action plans.* New York: Merrill.

Children's Literature References

Booth, D. (ed.). (1989). *Til all the stars have fallen: Canadian poems for children.* Toronto, ON: Kids Can Press.

Gilman, P. (1992). *Something from nothing.* New York: Scholastic.

McCully, E. A. (1992). *Mirette on the high wire.* New York: G. P. Putnam's Sons.

Raffi (1987). *Shake my sillies out.* New York: Crown.

White, E. B. (1952). *Charlotte's web.* New York: Harper.

Assessment in the Arts

14

Introduction

Assessment in the arts is full of paradox. Walter Pitman, former MP, MPP, and university president, is one of Canada's wisest and most knowledgeable advocates for the arts. In a recent book he makes the following observation:

> [The] belief in the lack of standards in arts instruction has a long history emerging from many decades of trivialization of the arts in North American society. Yet there is surely no fragment of our lives in which we expect such obeisance to the gods of quality as in our experience with the arts. We accept incompetence on our shopping trips, mediocrity in any number of services we request at the gas pump or bank counter, but we demand excellence when we attend a theatre, a concert hall and dance studio or an art gallery.... The local newspaper may provide nothing but flattery and hyperbole in its coverage of sports, business and professional activities, but even small-town symphonies and theatres receive the critical assessment and intense evaluation normally accorded to a doctoral dissertation. (p. 116)

Therein lies one paradox: arts may be regarded as trivial and yet, in the real world of arts in performance and exhibition, the arts are assessed according to the highest standards. Within education, at the secondary school level, the same paradox exists. It is acknowledged by students and teachers that high school arts courses are some of the most demanding and rigorous courses, and yet universities in Canada routinely disregard grades in secondary school arts courses even for entrance into their own fine arts programs. Within this context of paradox, what goals and strategies are appropriate for arts assessment in elementary schools?

Arts Assessment in Elementary Schools

In elementary schools, a wide discrepancy exists among provinces, and among school jurisdictions, in arts curriculum and assessment policies. The thoughtful teacher in the elementary classroom has always had questions and concerns about assessment in the arts. Those questions and concerns reveal the teacher's regard for the artistic sensibilities of each child, and for appropriate ways to encourage development without killing the artistic spirit of the child. We all know someone who stopped singing as a young child after a music teacher told him or her to mouth the words. We all know people who decided they couldn't "do art" after a whole year in which the teacher never once selected their artwork to "put up" in the classroom. How then are we to address the challenge of assessment in the arts, in ways that encourage development, without doing injury to the artistic self in each child?

Signs of Our Times

Teachers of the arts often end a disagreement by saying "Well, our methods may be different but our goals are the same." However, we are living in a time of such transition now that teachers' goals are not the same, in fact they can be fundamentally different from one anothers'. Without entering into a lengthy explanation of this time of transition from modern to postmodern thought, some sign posts are helpful. This list is simplistic, but it can point to how this transition is affecting schools, teaching, and education.

Modern	*Postmodern*
Students and teachers value: certainty, scientifically proven knowledge, security, information	Students and teachers value: living with paradox and ambiguity; practical knowledge, imagination, flexibility
Teacher owns the knowledge	Students and teachers own knowledge, and this knowledge is unique to the particulars of their own classroom dilemmas and complexities
Students get knowledge from teachers	Students and teachers learn from their interactions with one another, from resources, and from their environment
Curriculum is set	Students and teacher develop curriculum
Challenges to teacher are threatening	Challenges to teacher are required for teacher to perform role in interactive process
Teachers "cover" curriculum	Students learn how to learn

"While there is much debate as to what the postmodern is, it signals both the proliferation of ... differences and the sense that we live between the no longer and the not yet, a time when formerly comfortable holds on making sense of the world no longer suffice"

(Lather and Ellsworth, 1996, p 70). Living well within the postmodern moment becomes learning to live well with these contradictory and competing expectations and demands placed upon us from within the classroom and from outside forces. It is a time for us, as teachers, to look closely at our own practice and learn to trust what comes out of the particulars, letting go of more generalized calls for one kind of classroom practice or another (because they no longer work). We construct our own sense of things, we trust that certain things can be true to our practice while knowing that these things are not necessarily the Truth. (For helpful explanations of this transition in education and assessment, two excellent and readable articles are Wolf, Bixby, Clemmitt, & Gardner's (1991) "To use their minds well: New forms of student assessment" and Doll's (1993) "An educational vision.")

Edwin Gordon's (1984) dictum that "You should be able to measure what you expect your students to learn" represents the modernist view of assessment. Doll's (1993) suggestion that "evaluation would be a negotiary process within a communal setting for the purpose of transformation" (p.174) represents a postmodern view. The roles that teachers and students assume determine the role of assessment. No matter where individual teachers or provincial ministries of education are along this transition continuum, the writing on the wall is clear: "The focus of assessment today is shifting to the student; teachers are expected to use observational skills to a greater degree than previously in this century; furthermore, assessments should be appropriate, be an integral part of the curriculum, be ongoing and involve students" (Hanley, 1992). Even in provinces with arts curriculum grading expectations beginning in grade one, teachers can exercise their judgement in adapting curricular and assessment expectations in a responsible way.

Principles of Arts Assessment

1. Every child is an artist. Picasso once said, "Every child is an artist. The problem is how he [sic] remains an artist once he grows up." Each child's artistic growth is the most important consideration for assessment in the arts at the elementary level. In order to ensure that each child's artistic growth remains the prime consideration, teachers can first ask about every arts activity and assessment practice: "Will this enhance the artistic life of this student?" or "Does this have the potential to damage the artistic life of this student?" They can then choose only the enhancing activities.
2. Assessment must be rich in context, respect diversity, encourage different ways of exhibiting different strengths, and develop the abilities of self-assessment. Assessment strategies are rich in context when they take place over time in the student's daily environment (e.g., checklist observations of the same child involved in classroom musical activity at four different times over a two-month period). Some ways to respect diversity include offering choice of activity and having students share their own cultural arts experiences and knowledge with the class. Examples of ways in which students can exhibit different strengths include portfolios, audio and video tapes of out-of-school arts activity, and chosen modes of performance. Self-assessment is a skill that students develop through experience. Beginning in kindergarten, arts assessment can have a large self-assessment component.

Assessment is generally considered to be the process of gathering information to *plan for* meaningful instruction for students, evaluation as a value judgement placed on work, and grading as the attaching of a symbol to the results of evaluation. However, because of some differences in how people understand the meanings of the three terms, in this chapter only the word *assessment* is used.

Assessment Strategies

For strategies particular to each art form, see the sections in Chapters 3, 5, 7, 9, and 11 called "Exhibit student progress." The additional strategies presented in this chapter can be adapted for each art form. With Saskatchewan Education's permission, this chapter borrows liberally from their excellent resource documents, *Saskatchewan Arts Education Curriculum Guides.*

Assessing Process and Products

Although there are several types of endeavours in arts education, they are placed in the two following categories for the purpose of establishing appropriate assessment strategies: process and product.

Process. When assessing each student's learning *processes* in the arts, teachers can observe

- all arts activities and projects in progress
- the actual process of creative problem-solving
- individual, pair, and group work in progress
- portfolios, including rough drafts and notes
- notebooks and sketchbooks
- ongoing visual and written journal entries

- use of computers and other technology
- video and audio cassettes of student work in progress
- student reflection

Assessment techniques to use include anecdotal records, observation checklists, portfolios, conferences, analysis of audio and video records, and self-assessment.

Product. When assessing each student's *products or presentations* in the arts, teachers can observe

- collective and individual arts projects and presentations
- portfolios
- audio and video tapes
- contract criteria
- the student's previous products or presentation
- students' reflections

Possible assessment techniques include anecdotal records, observation checklists, tests (e.g., recorder playing) portfolios, conferences, self-assessment, and analysis of audio and video records.

Assessment techniques

Anecdotal records. Teachers keep ongoing records in various ways. Some jot down comments on sticky notes as they observe the student's activity and then date and file them in folders for each child at the end of the day. Some use more structured forms; see Samples 5, 6, and 8 at the end of the chapter.

Observation checklists. Samples 1, 2, and 3 provide many ideas for checklist criteria for both process and product.

Conference. Talking with individual students about their work gives them a chance to explain aspects of their thinking and process that you may not understand. Questions like those in Sample 10 (What is the most interesting thing about what you did? What was the main problem you had to solve while you were working? What would you do differently if you were to experience this activity or project again?) are effective conference questions.

Analysis of audio and video records. See sections following on *Documentation* and *Establishing criteria for assessing documented data.*

Self-assessment. When we ask students to self-assess, we must provide them with appropriate criteria, and we must value, respect, and count their assessment, even if we disagree with it. See examples 4, 10, 11, and 12. Students require help with this skill. Begin with a specific project or task, for example, recorder playing. Create the assessment criteria with the children, then do a self-assessment on your own work as an example. Student and teacher can assess using the same criteria and scale and then compare and discuss assessments.

Tests. Tests must actually test what they claim to test. Pitman (1998) relates the story of a motor mechanics teacher who revealed that his students were failing the test on dismantling a car engine, yet every one of them could actually do it efficiently. Tests can be appropriate assessment strategies for arts knowledge and skills if they are frequent and informal, to meet the assessment principle of being rich in context, and if they are identified (e.g., *rhythmic notation test* rather than *music test,* or *elements of drama test* rather than *drama test*). See Sample 13, "Week Four Recorder Playing Test."

Documentation

Documentation is a key element in supporting the assessment strategies suggested above. Documentation takes attention, time, and some money. The Reggio Emilia schools in Italy are some of the best models of appropriate and effective arts-based education in which young children are encouraged to express themselves through many "languages" or modes of expression, including words, movement, drawing, painting, sculpture, shadow play, collage, and music (Edwards, Gandini & Forman, 1993). One recommendation in Reggio Emilia schools is that all schools find ways to provide "Documentations" for classroom teachers. The only practical way to have help with documentation in Canadian schools is through classroom volunteers. We can advertise for parent and grandparent volunteers to photograph or videotape and audiotape children. Educational assistants and student teachers can also fulfil this role.

No elementary teacher has time to do rich assessment of every aspect of every child's development in the arts. Teachers can choose assessment programs appropriate to their own class, curriculum, and philosophy (i.e., a teacher might choose to assess a few aspects in depth and report on only those, or decide to structure self-evaluation activities and report only those). It is most important and helpful to parents and students if reporting is specific and detailed. Effective documentation routines provide those specific details.

Photography and video and audio taping. You need a foolproof camera ready with film, preferably one with autofocus and flash in order to "catch things on the fly."

A cassette recorder with an internal microphone is most convenient, or a small mike. Book the school video camera and tripod for two hours one morning a week. Label all films and tapes before you use them. Speak date, time, and students' names onto video or audio tape at beginning of each taping episode.

- photograph: projects, art work, art work in process, drama tableaux
- audio tape:
  - individual, small group, and class performances
  - individual children reading, telling stories, singing, playing instrument
- practices for performance
- videotape:
  - individual, group, and class performances
  - group work in process (drama, music, dance, visual art)
  - individual children for a ten or fifteen minute segment of arts classes. (Keep a class list for video purposes, have the video operator focus on one child for ten minutes, then switch to another child for ten minutes. Ten minutes per child is a good balance between what a more expanded time of tape might reveal about the child, and the amount of videotape the teacher can actually examine. One volunteer can videotape six children in an hour, one morning a week, resulting in one hour of video for a teacher to watch per week.)

Portfolios. Portfolios can be collections of students' work chosen by students and/or teachers, with contributions by students and/or teachers. Contents may include:

- artwork
- sketch books and idea keepers
- favourite visual images, e.g., pictures cut from magazines
- photographs of student working
- audio and video tape of student activity
- list of songs the student knows
- list of dances the student knows or has created
- list of music the student has listened to
- list of books read
- drawings or paintings of music, dance, or drama experiences
- student records (visual or written) of artist visits, field trips, performances
- original work in each of the arts
- journals or selected journal entries

Sketch books and idea keepers. Artists, particularly visual and literary artists, keep sketch books or idea journals. Lund (1994) describes one way of encouraging children to have and record ideas. Idea keepers are folders containing both plain and lined paper for students of any age to draw and write about things that are important to them. Lund created a specific "idea keepers" time on Tuesday mornings from nine to ten. At the start of the idea keepers program, the teachers needed to provide examples and stimulation for the "having of ideas." While the class was involved in a botany unit, the idea keeper sessions started with five-minute introductory activities in which they planted bulbs, made drawings of their bulb's growth in botanical sketchbooks, read about Monet's garden, or looked at paintings and photographs of Monet's garden. Over time, students took ownership of idea keeper time and used it in diverse and individual ways.

Establishing Criteria for Assessing Documented Data

Provincial and board curricular guidelines provide expected outcomes, goals, and/or standards. Teachers balance those guidelines or mandates with their own practical knowledge, convictions, and experience. Some teachers choose to work in depth in a few curricular topics, others try to "cover" the suggested curriculum. Teachers have both the freedom and responsibility to make appropriate and responsible choices about how they will alter the given curriculum or create curriculum for their own context, and how they will assess student's processes and products.

As well as the criteria in provincial and board curricular guidelines, the three lists of sample criteria (see Samples 1, 2, and 3 at the end of the chapter) are sources of possible criteria. It is important that students have a role in selecting criteria as well. A set of four or five criteria is sufficient. Selected criteria can be used in checklists (see Samples 1, 2, and 7), rubrics (see Sample 9), analyses of audio and video records, assessment of portfolios, self-assessment, and in other strategies.

Making Aesthetic Value Judgments

Standards of excellence will vary from person to person, depending on the person's experience and knowledge, but there are some common criteria. Beardsley (1950) carefully examined many kinds of criteria for assessing performance and creative work. Only three criteria emerged from Beardsley's critical examination as defensible and appropriate (he eliminated other criteria such as humour and passion as not necessary or not fundamental). The three are intensity, complexity, and unity. Too much of any of these attributes is as undesirable as too little. For each person there is an optimal amount, but probably everyone requires some element of each of the three. Let's look at each one in terms of a stage play.

Intensity: Was there substance, energy, vigour, power, profundity? To what degree?

Complexity: Was there conflict, were there several layers of meaning, surprises, ambiguity, twists in plot? To what degree?

Unity: Did it make sense? Was there progression, a development that made all the parts ultimately hang together?

These three criteria are useful when teachers are required to make value judgments of student work.

Rating Process and Product

Rubrics (see samples 4, 5, and 8) and three-point scales (samples 3, 4, 7, and 8) are sufficient in almost every case. Students in the junior and intermediate grades need to know specifically what constitute the criteria and rating system.

For children in kindergarten and the primary grades, appropriate arts experiences involve play, exploration, and communication. The arts are one of the voices or languages of childhood. Observation, documentation, and anecdotal reporting can be appropriate. Grading is not appropriate at the primary level in the arts. Young children do not have the capacity to understand that a low grade in any of the arts means that the child did not meet grade-level expectations. The child only hears that he or she cannot sing, dance, or do art or drama. Children's artistic selves can sustain life-long damage through the practice of grading in the arts at the primary level. Here, as in all decisions regarding assessment, the goals of arts education should determine assessment practices. The danger, in some jurisdictions, is that assessment expectations will determine goals and curriculum. It is easy to test whether children can write rhythm notation, or draw musical symbols, or write key signatures. If teachers are required to give grades, they teach things that can be graded. If students know that their creative work is to be graded, they will produce work that they think the teacher will value. They are not likely to take risks, or allow their imagination to push the boundaries of the assignment. The most important goals of arts education cannot be tested, for example, the development of a life-long disposition towards making music and making art; an attitude of curiosity and acceptance of unfamiliar dance, drama, music, and visual arts; the ability to use one's voice and body language to enhance communication; and the ability to imagine the "as if" worlds of others' environments and cultures (Greene, 1995). These dispositions and attitudes are formed in the early years and last a lifetime.

Some will argue that even though grading may not be appropriate for creative work, that it is appropriate for skills and knowledge in the arts. In that case, it is the responsibility of the teacher to be clear about what the grade represents (e.g., colour theory: A, *not* Art: A, music notation: B, not Music: B) If grades are mandated at the primary level, one option is to give every child the highest possible grade, acknowledging that it makes a travesty of the inappropriate mandate to grade and at the same time knowing that a good grade sends an important message to every child that he or she is *good* in the arts. Helping children feel that they are good in the arts may well be the most important goal and outcome in arts education for young children.

Summary

Two important and long-lasting benefits of effective assessment in the arts are the ability to clearly judge our own performance with courage and compassion, and the ability to base decisions on personal standards. The ultimate assessment of teachers' and students' development in the arts may well be our ability to use the arts for our personal well-being and for the well-being of all life on this planet. If we keep these long-term benefits in mind when we create our assessment models, we will not go wrong.

Thanks to Martin Schiralli and Gary Rasberry at the Faculty of Education, Queen's University, for their contributions to this chapter.

Sample 1 Checklist for Evaluating Students' Responses to Arts Expressions

Examples of Possible Criteria						
Offers first impressions about the arts expression.						
Contributes to discussion and other activities that elicit student responses.						
Uses observation skills when giving descriptions of the arts expression.						
Demonstrates critical thinking when analyzing the work.						
Is able to make observations and comparisons and identify significant factors appropriate to the work.						
Applies prior learning to personal responses.						
Uses appropriate vocabulary.						
Analyzes based on the evidence found in the work.						
Uses knowledge obtained through analysis to interpret the work.						
Identifies images, sensations, or ideas evoked by the arts expression.						
Considers several interpretations.						
Offers personal perspectives and interpretations of the work.						
Researches and gathers background information about the arts expression.						
Demonstrates reflective thinking.						
Supports opinions based on information and evidence found in the work.						
Shows interest in arts discussions.						
Challenges self.						
Describes whether, how, and why first impressions may have changed after critical thinking and/or discussion.						
Contributes ideas when working in groups.						
Works cooperatively if working in a group.						
Works independently.						
Comments:						

This form may be used to assess students or one student on different dates.

Source: Reprinted from Saskatchewan Education (1994) *Arts Education: A Curriculum Guide for Grade 6* with permission.

Sample 2 Checklist or Rating Scale for Evaluating Creative Processes

Examples of Possible Criteria						
Contributes ideas to explore the theme or concept.						
Contributes to discussion and brainstorming activities.						
Extends the theme or concept(s) in a new direction.						
Develops one aspect of theme or concept(s) in detail.						
Transfers knowledge of the theme or concept into personal artworks.						
Explores several ideas.						
Takes risks by exploring something new to him or her.						
Shows interest in the arts experience.						
Shows commitment toward the experience of creating.						
Challenges self.						
Describes what did and did not work in personal experience.						
Identifies what he or she would like to change in order to improve the arts expression.						
Describes what his or her own arts expression means personally.						
Maintains awareness of personal intentions in arts expression.						
Shows concentration in arts experiences.						
Discusses why choices were made.						
Describes images, sensations, or ideas evoked by the arts experience.						
Contributes ideas when working in groups.						
Works cooperatively within the group.						
Works independently.						

Comments:

This form may be used to assess students or one student on different dates.

Source: Reprinted from Saskatchewan Education (1994) *Arts Education: A Curriculum Guide for Grade 6* with permission.

Sample 3 Checklist for Evaluating Creative Expression

Student's Name: ________________________________ Date: ____________________

	Often	Sometimes	Seldom
Contributes ideas to explore the theme or concept.	☐	☐	☐
Contributes to brainstorming activities.	☐	☐	☐
Extends the theme in a new direction.	☐	☐	☐
Develops one aspect of the theme in detail.	☐	☐	☐
Transfers knowledge of the theme or concept into his or her artworks.	☐	☐	☐
Explores several ideas.	☐	☐	☐
Takes risks by exploring something new to him or her.	☐	☐	☐
Shows interest in the arts experience.	☐	☐	☐
Shows commitment toward the experience of creating.	☐	☐	☐
Challenges himself or herself.	☐	☐	☐
Describes what did and did not work in his or her arts experience.	☐	☐	☐
Identifies what he or she would like to change in order to improve the arts expression.	☐	☐	☐
Describes what his or her own arts expression means personally.	☐	☐	☐
Maintains awareness of his or her intentions in arts expressions.	☐	☐	☐
Shows concentration in arts experiences.	☐	☐	☐
Discusses why choices were made.	☐	☐	☐
Describes images and sensations evoked by the arts experience.	☐	☐	☐
Contributes ideas when working in groups.	☐	☐	☐
Works cooperatively within the group.	☐	☐	☐
Works independently.	☐	☐	☐

Source: Reprinted from Saskatchewan Education (1991). *A Curriculum Guide for Grade 2* with permission.

Sample 4 Student Self-evaluation Form for Drama

Name:______________________________ Date: ______________

	Seldom	Sometimes	Often
1. Contributed my ideas to the drama work.			
2. Encouraged others positively as we worked.			
3. Gave direction to the work.			
4. Followed the direction of others.			
5. Helped to make decisions and solve problems.			
6. Was committed to the drama and the roles I assumed.			
7. Took risks by exploring something new to me.			

8. What did I contribute to the process?

9. What is the most interesting thing about what I did?

10. What decisions did I have to make while we were working and how did I try to solve the problems I face?

11. What have I learned from this particular experience and how could I apply what I've learned to other drama projects and everyday life?

Source: Reprinted from Saskatchewan Education (1994) *Arts Education: A Curriculum Guide for Grade 6* with permission.

Sample 5 Anecdotal Record-Keeping Form for a Dance Lesson

Dance Lesson: Date:

Students' Names	Criterion/Objectives		
	Had a definite beginning, middle, and ending	Used high, medium, and low levels	Showed concentration and serious involvement
Geri			
Mark			
LeAnne			
Kent			
Carla			

Special Comments:

Source: Reprinted from Saskatchewan Education (1991). *A Curriculum Guide for Grade 2* with permission.

Sample 6 Rating Scale Form or Checklist

Foundational Objective(s): Date:

- examine sources of ideas for dance making, make connections between ideas and dance expressions, and use dance for personal expression
- develop an understanding of the elements of dance and the principles of composition and apply this understanding to all their dance experiences

	Criterion/Objectives			
Students' Names	Uses starting-points as inspiration for improvisation and movement exploration	Works effectively in large and small groups	Is becoming familiar with choreographic forms	Applies knowledge of the elements of dance
Wayne				
Laurie				
Françoise				
Myles				
Carol				

Other Comments:

Source: Reprinted from Saskatchewan Education (1994) *Arts Education: A Curriculum Guide for Grade 6* with permission.

Sample 7 Anecdotal Record-Keeping Form for a Dance Lesson

Foundational Objective(s): Date:

- Develop an understanding of the elements of music and principles of composition and discover how these can be manipulated
- Examine the work of various musicians and composers

	Criterion/Objectives						
Students' Names	Is able to discuss the elements of music	Manipulates the elements of music to improve own compositions	Uses form purposefully in compositions	Distinguishes among various styles of music	Recognizes the historical, social, and environmental factors that influence composers		
Lynda	M	N	N	M	M		
Michelle	E	M	M	E	M		
Alonso	M	M	M	E	E		
Elaine	E	E	M	M	M		
Sarah	N	N	N	M	M		
Greg	M	N	M	M	N		
Joelle	E	M	M	M	E		
etc.							

Rating Key

☐ N = Needs Improvement
M = Meeting Expectations Or ☐ 1–5 Or ☐ Checklist
E = Exceeding Expectations

Source: Reprinted from Saskatchewan Education (1994) *Arts Education: A Curriculum Guide for Grade 6* with permission.

Sample 8 Anecdotal Record-keeping Form and Rating Scale for Visual Art

Student's Name: Date:

Foundational Objective(s):

- examine sources of ideas for art making, make connections between ideas and visual art works, and generate ideas for personal expression
- develop an understanding of the elements of art and principles of design and learn to apply this understanding to their expressions and responses to works of art
- develop critical thought and learn to support their interpretations and opinions when responding to art

Criteria/Objectives	Comments	Ratings
Increase their understanding of the contributions of Saskatchewan and Canadian artists, including Aboriginal artists, to the field of visual art		
Continue to determine and explore appropriate media, technology, forms, and methods for visual expression		
Investigate how visual artists use symbols and other means to convey meaning		
Identify and explore environmental, historical, and social factors that influence visual artists and their work		
Support opinions and interpretations for particular types of art based on evidence found in the work		
Reflect on how the elements of art, principles of design, images and techniques used convey meaning in works of art		

Other Comments:

Rating Key

☐ N = Needs Improvement
M = Meeting Expectations Or ☐ 1–5
E = Exceeding Expectations

Source: Reprinted from Saskatchewan Education (1991). *A Curriculum Guide for Grade 2* with permission.

Sample 9 Creating an Original Canadian Landscape

	Beginning	Developing	Competent	Powerful
Creates a sense distance	Uses one or more conventions for creating 3-D on 2-D picture plane. Sense of depth not evident.	Uses one or more conventions for creating 3-D on 2-D picture plane. Although depth is evident, the effect is not consistent.	Uses several conventions for creating depth. Result is consistent, effective, and successful.	Uses several conventions for a highly convincing sense of depth.
Uses elements and principles of design to portray characterful trees, part of the Canadian landscape	Attempts to use one or more elements, but with little impact. Trees are not harmonious with the landscape.	One or more elements and principles are evident in development of tree images. Trees may not be consistent with creation of depth in the picture plane.	Trees are effectively portrayed with deliberate use of the elements and principles of design. Trees are a harmonious part of the landscape.	Demonstrate thoughtful, creative use of a number of elements and principals for powerful, characterful portrayal of trees. Trees enhance the landscape, contributing to sense of depth in the picture plane.
Creates an original, imaginative landscape image	Image may have few ideas. It may be unrelated to the landscape theme.	Some original ideas are evident in the portrayal of the landscape.	Image is original, reflecting thoughtful inclusion of imaginative ideas for a successful portrayal of landscape.	Image is unique, a highly original and powerful portrayal of landscape.
Skill development	Some colour mixing is evident, but there may be muddy colours. Brush strokes are not varied nor executed with skill for achievement of desired effect.	A range of mixed colours is evident. Some deliberate use of colour for the achievement of special effects. Various textures through brush strokes are used with varying success.	A range of colour is mixed and used competently, for the creation of various special effects. Brush strokes are used skilfully to create appropriate textures.	A wide range of colour is achieved through skillful mixing. Application of colour shows a range of skillful and imaginative brushstrokes that enhance the image.

Source: Reprinted from Neale, Aileen (1997). "Beginning with the end in view: criterion-referenced assessment in an elementary visual arts class." *British Columbia Art Teachers Association (BCATA) Journal for Art Teachers,* 37(1), 5–10 with permission.

Sample 10 Self-Evaluation Form

Name: Date:

Project/Activity Description:

1. What was the most interesting or challenging thing about what I did?

2. What was the main problem that I had to solve while I was working?

3. How did I try to solve the problem?

4. What have I learned from this particular project?

5. What sort of effort did I put into the work?

6. If working in a group, what did I contribute to the process or the product?

7. If I were to experience this project or activity again, what would I change or do differently?

8. What other project/experience might grow out of the one I just completed?

Source: Reprinted from Saskatchewan Education (1994) *Arts Education: A Curriculum Guide for Grade 6* with permission.

Sample 11 Focus on Evaluation

Second-Term Music Evaluation

Student's Name: ______________________________ Date: ____________________

This second term we have begun to explore more advanced musical concepts such as texture, unity and contrast, and the rondo form. We have made chord charts and used them to play accompaniments on the autoharp. We have improvised melodies and demonstrated the form of a song through a dance. We have also begun to assess our own work. This sheet is a continuation of this self-evaluation.

1. So far this year in music class I have learned:

2. I understand the following musical concepts better than before:

3. I can do the following musical activities better than before:

4. I have contributed to the class by:

5. Of all the activities we have done this term I would select the following as my best work:

   Explain why:

6. In the next term I want to improve:

Source: Reprinted from Harley, B. (1994). "Assessment Exchange: Student self-evaluation." *Canadian Music Educator,* 35(5), 7 –10 with permission.

Sample 12 Visual Art Self-Evaluation

Name: ______________________________

Block: ______________________________

Title of work: ______________________________

Description

Describe your project in detail. Pretend that the reader will not actually see your work but will form a visual image from your written description. ______________________________

____

____

Intent

What guidelines were you given? What visual problems were you attempting to solve? What objectives were you attempting to meet? ______________________________

____

____

Evaluation of Intent

Were you able to meet both your own and the class objectives? If you were not, explain where the problems occurred. ______________________________

____

Growth

What new materials, techniques, or vocabulary did you encounter? What new imagery did you explore?

____

____

Effort

Did you work every period? If not, please explain. Did you make use of your class time? Explain. Did you work outside class time? When? How long? How would you rate your effort?

____

____

Completion

Do you feel your work is complete? What might you do differently if you had more time or unlimited supplies? Please be specific.

____

____

Success

What specifically do you like about your work? Why? What did you learn from this work?

____

____

____

____

Source: Reprinted from Scarr, Margaret (1990). "Self evaluation for secondary arts students, why bother?" *British Columbia Art Teacher Association [BCATA] Journal for Art Teachers,* 30(2), 5–8 with permission.

Sample 13 Recorder Playing Assessment for Grade Four #13

Part one: Interview about process

If students understand that this part is not graded, they will be more likely to answer freely. Ask students what they have discovered in their playing that makes it easier or sound better. Ask how much the child enjoys playing recorders. If the answer is *not much*, ask if there is anything that would help him or her be able to enjoy it. Ask if they ever play the recorder at home for pleasure. Do they try to play songs they know that they haven't played at school? Do they play songs they hear in their head?

Part two: performance

Student chooses performance piece. Explain the scale for each element. The student and the teacher can both assess his or her playing using the scale and then compare and discuss their ratings..

Melody:	Completely accurate	Close to accurate	Not accurate
Rhythm:	Completely accurate	Close to accurate	Not accurate
Tone:	Pleasant	OK	Harsh
Overall effect:	The listener responds with great pleasure	With satisfaction	With some anxiety
Level for the child:	Difficult	Moderate	Easy

Teacher and student agree on grade if one is required. Using 3, 2 or 1 for numerical equivalent in rating scale, maximum points = 15

References

Beardsley, M. C. (1950). *Practical Logic.* New York: Prentice Hall.

Doll, W. (1993). *A post-modern perspective on curriculum.* New York: Teacher's College Press.

Edwards, C., Gandini, L., & Forman, G. (1993). *The hundred languages of childhood: The Reggio Emilia approach to early childhood education.* Norwood, NJ: Ablex.

Gordon, E. (1984). *Learning sequences in music.* Chicago, IL: GIA Publications.

Greene, M. (1995). *Releasing the imagination: Essays on education, the arts, and social change.* San Fransisco, CA: Jossey-Bass.

Hanley, B. (1992). "Student assessment in music education: Report on a research project for the British Columbia ministry of Education." *Canadian Music Educator* 33(5), 19–24.

Lund, P. (1994). "Idea keepers: Young children's drawings and writing." *Visual Arts Research* 20(1), 20–34.

Pitman, W. (1998). *Learning the arts in an age of uncertainty.* North York, ON: Arts Education Council of Ontario.

Saskatchewan Education. (1991). *Arts education: A curriculum guide for grade 2.*

Saskatchewan Education. (1994). *Arts education: A curriculum guide for grade 6.*

Wolf, D., Bixby, J., Glenn, J., & Gardner, H. (1991). "To use their minds well: New forms of student assessment." In G. Grand (ed.), *Review of research in education* (pp. 31–74). Washington: American Educational Research Association.

Further Reading

Books and Articles

Beatty, R. (1992). "Evaluation in music education: An Ontario perspective." *Canadian Music Educator* 33(5), 35–36.

Brandt, R. (1987). "On assessment in the arts: A conversation with Howard Gardner." *Educational Leadership* 45(4), 30–34.

Bresler, L. (1994). "Zooming in on the qualitative paradigm in art education: Educational criticism, ethnography, and action research." *Visual Arts Research* 20(1), 1–19.

Carlin, J. L. (1996). "Using videotape as an assessment tool in elementary music classrooms." *The B.C. Music Educator* 39(1), 31–33.

Cartwright, P. (1989). "Assessment and examination in arts education: Teachers talking." In M. Ross (ed.), *The Claims of feeling: Readings in aesthetic education.* 283–311.

Eisner, E. (1985). *The art of educational evaluation.* London: Falmer.

Gallas, K. (1994). *The languages of learning: How children talk, write, dance, draw, and sing their understanding of the world.* New York: Teacher's College Press.

Gilbert, L. (1990). "Aesthetic development in music: An experiment in use of personal construct theory." *British Journal of Music Education* 7(3), 173–190.

Hanley, B. (1994). "Assessment exchange: Student self-evaluation." *Canadian Music Educator* 35(5), 7–10.

Knight, S. (1992). "Evaluation-Alpha and omega." *Canadian Music Educator* 33(5), 25–32.

Lather, P. & Ellsworth, E. (1996). "This issue: Situated pedagogies — classroom practices in postmodern times." *Theory Into Practice* 35(2), 70–71.

Noddings, N. (1992). *The challenge to care in schools: An alternative approach to education.* New York: Teacher's College Press.

Roberts, B. (1994). "Assessment in music education: A cross-Canada study." *Canadian Music Educator* 35(5), 3–6.

Upitis, R. (1990). *This too is music.* Portsmouth, NH: Heinemann.

Willingham, L. (1993). *Classroom assessment and evaluation in the arts.* Scarborough, ON: Scarborough Board of Education.

Willingham, L. (1993). "Evaluating musical growth in an authentic context." *The Recorder* 37(4), 11–21.

Winner, E., Davidson, L., & Scripp. L. (eds.). (1992). *Arts propel: A handbook for music.* Boston: Harvard Project Zero and Educational Testing Service.

Zimmerman, E, (1994). "How should students' progress and achievements in art be assessed? A case for assessment that is responsible to diverse students' needs." *Visual Arts Research* 20(1), 29–35.

Questions Often Asked

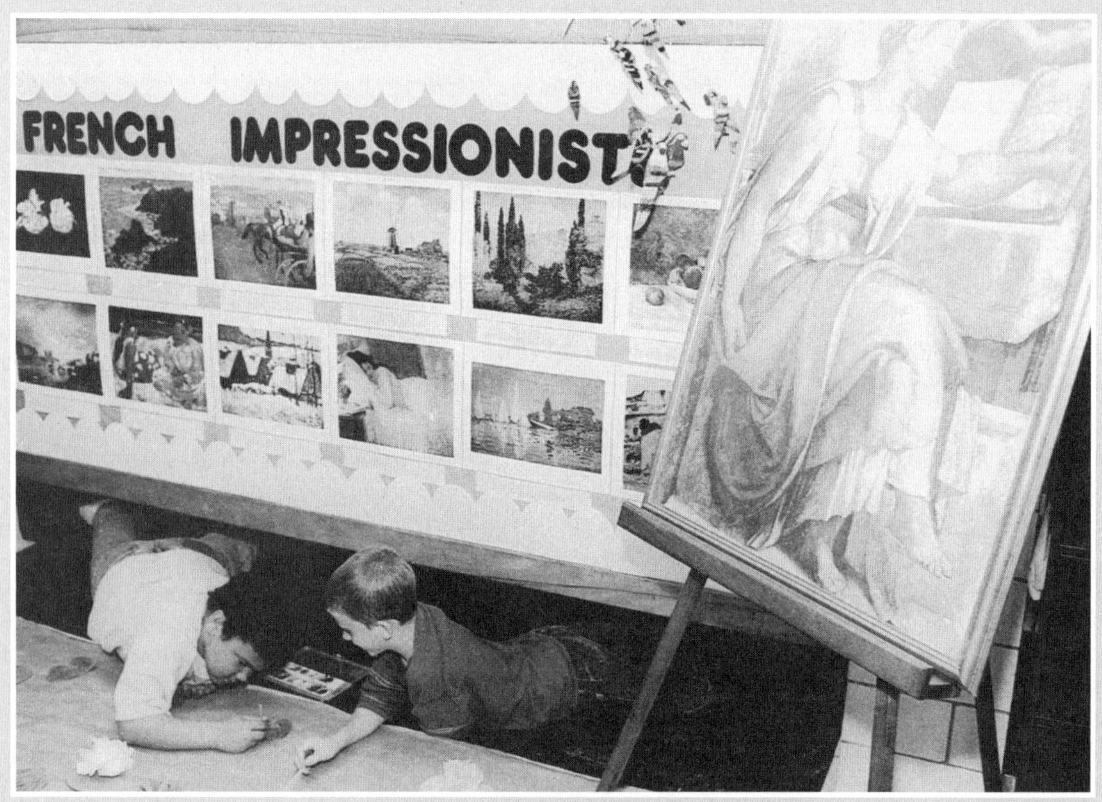

The arts should become a basic part of the K–12 curriculum, not simply for their intrinsic value as a course of study—to help all children and young adults to interpret their world, better understand history—but also for their contribution to students' mastery of other basic areas of the curriculum.

Larson, p. 167, 1997

This final chapter includes questions that frequently arise on the journey to more holistic learning through integrating literature and the arts throughout the curriculum. Many of the answers are provided as food for thought from teachers who are still on the journey.

1. **Aren't the arts diluted in an integrated program?** Arts-based classrooms cannot substitute for specialized classes students should have. Integrating the arts into classrooms is intended to *expand* arts experiences. Communities are sometimes even more ready to support taxes for arts specialists *after the arts have been integrated* into general classrooms. The arts speak for themselves when allowed to become an *integral* part of school—not just extras. When children clamour for more arts experiences that require the knowledge and skills of specialists, parents listen.

2. **What about art for art's sake? Shouldn't the arts be valued because they are—not because they fix social or academic problems?**

Perhaps one day we will hear the news that researchers have shown how the study of reading and mathematics can make us all better artists.

Playwright Alan Brody, in Larson, 1997, p. 111

There are those that look askance at the practical use of the arts and bewail any view of the arts as fixits for the economy or to solve drug problems. Some think integrating the arts means lowering of standards and decry efforts of those outside the arts community who view the arts as repositories of practical knowledge and skills. Others actually seem to want an "inner circle" of specialists who control access to the arts and, therefore, culture. Unfortunately, an élitist attitude contributes to isolation of the arts from everyday people, who often believe creativity is the province of a few, talented recipients of years of special training. It is no wonder, when schools experience financial exigency, the solution is frequently to cut areas felt to be unrelated to the majority of students. The arts seem alien, apart, out there, on "gallery walls or in concert halls."

3. **What about censorship of the arts (e.g., children's literature)?** What is offensive to one person is beautiful to the next. Censorship attempts seem to be on the rise, and any art form is vulnerable. Why? Art is dangerous. It intentionally provokes thought and emotional response—that's why Hitler banned books. Across the country, complaints related to the arts have been voiced, including challenges to teachers who use children's literature, visual art, and dance. For example, these books have all been accused of the following: Willhoite's *Daddy's Roommate* for condoning homosexuality, Lionni's *Swimmy* (1963) for promoting communism, Sendak's *In the Night Kitchen* (1970) because of nudity in the art, Silverstein's *The Giving Tree* (1973) for being antifeminist, a poem in Silverstein's *A Light in the Attic* about a girl making a milkshake by shaking a cow for suggesting humans engage in sex with animals, Speare's *Witch of Blackbird Pond* for promoting witchcraft, and Steig's *Sylvester and the Magic Pebble,* which was the subject of attack by a police association because police are depicted as pigs in the book. Traditional folktales, especially original versions, are replete with violence causing some to object—they believe children should only be given sugar-coated reading. Any work that deals with religion, sex, nudity, violence, or the occult or uses profanity is particularly prone to complaint. For more information, see "When the Censor Comes" (www.efc.ca/pages/chronicle/whattodo.html).

Every school should have a policy for evaluating and selecting books and other art materials (prints, videos, etc.) and a procedure for handling grievances. It is helpful to include a requirement for complaints to be made in writing, with reasons and a signature. Then, if parents object, teachers can follow the policy. School boards need to also allow parents to opt for "substitute" experiences (e.g., books on the same unit topic), but parents do not have the right to prohibit all children from using materials obtained under the school's selection policy. Usually, school boards stand behind teachers who use good children's literature or any art considered high-quality. It behooves teachers to make sure materials and activities fit the course of study, are appropriate to students' developmental levels, and are defensible. Use recommended book lists, such as the Governor General's Award for Children's Literature, the Canadian Library Association Awards, and the Caldecott and Newbery awards lists (see Appendix B), and be sensitive to the community's values. Call each parent at the beginning of the year, introduce yourself, and explain how you'll be using rich arts experiences throughout the year (for most teachers that's about five calls a night for one week). Have reasons ready. Build an open relationship and encourage parents to visit the class. Most parents want their children to be happy and successful, so if you have the research and good results to show that your approach is working, most will be satisfied. People generally call for censorship because they feel threatened and because they don't have all the facts. Share facts, listen to complaints, and see what facts parents have and what other information is needed.

4. **What about parents who object to dancing for religious reasons or ones who think religious books or art about religion has no place in public schools?** The concern over dance arises because the word "dance" has come to convey sexual images. It is important to provide information to parents *before* beginning to integrate dance. If the word "dance" is inflammatory, call it "movement" or "kinesthetic learning," which is being honest and politically astute.

   As far as religion in public schools is concerned, there is no law against teaching *about* religions or religious groups, but public school teachers *cannot* proselytize students regarding a religious point of view. Units on Native Americans, Jews and the Holocaust, Japan, and so on, including study of the religions of these groups, are common; it is difficult to understand any culture without studying its religious views.

5. **How do you grade and evaluate things students do in the arts?** It is important to distinguish among *grades, evaluation,* and *assessment.* Assessment is the process of gathering information to *plan for* meaningful instruction for students. Evaluation is a value judgment placed on work, and grading is attaching a symbol to the results of evaluation. Most of us would prefer not to give grades at all, but that is not always feasible. It is recommended that teachers *not* grade everything, but give descriptive feedback on progress made during practices. When work in the arts is to be graded, students need to know evaluation criteria before they begin. A grading rubric can be useful and simply describes what each grade means, specifically. A checklist of tasks, based on concept and skill goals, can be given so that students can independently track activities they're doing to reach goals. It is also important to discuss what makes quality work. After much exploration and practice, evaluation and grading can happen without destroying students' interest, but this is a delicate area. See Chapter 1 for *creativity squelchers.*

6. **Is assessment necessary in the arts?** Yes. Assessment is the process of gathering information to plan appropriate instruction, so it is as needed in the arts as it is in other curricular areas. Effective assessment focuses on strengths and needs, not just on problems, process, or products, and is authentic, multifactored, and continuous. We need to collect data from a variety of sources, especially through observing students all year long and noting needs and strengths. Some teachers use a clipboard to lay out sticky notes so that observations can be easily jotted down and transferred to student folders. It is also important to be clear about the purpose of gathering assessment data and what the information is to be used for. Decisions need to be made about the kinds of information to be collected and how they will be collected. Students also need to learn to self-assess.

7. **Isn't integrating the arts a lot more work? I liked the ideas of whole language, literature-based instruction, and portfolio assessment, but now I'm exhausted.** Teachers who enjoy using the arts and see the results in student achievement and motivation are energized by accomplishing important goals in different ways, often made easier because students *want* to be involved.

8. **How do I find the time to "integrate the arts" with all the other expectations (e.g., inclusion, proficiency tests)?** The arts are not to be integrated *in addition to* the present curriculum. Integration involves using time differently. Research supports use of the arts to get students to academic proficiency *more efficiently* than traditional approaches, and students enjoy themselves more! Those involved in inclusion are learning about alternative approaches to teaching reading, writing, science, social studies, and math. Teaching *with, about, in,* and *through* the arts is a powerful alternative approach.

9. **What if my school is not using the integrated arts philosophy?**

> *The problems of the world cannot possibly be solved by skeptics or cynics whose horizons are limited by the obvious realities. We need men who can dream of things that never were.*
>
> John F. Kennedy

Start to share ideas with one or two teachers and your principal. Journal articles and research tidbits (see the *News Bulletins*) can be circulated. Copy the Post It Pages and share. Suggest to staff development committees that workshops be provided on arts integration. Contact local arts agencies to see what they presently offer. Keep in mind we retain

- 10% of what we read
- 20% of what we hear
- 30% of what we see
- 50% of what we hear and see together
- 70% of what we see, hear, and say
- 90% of what we see, hear, say, and do (drama, dance, make art, sing, write) (Fauth, 1990, pp. 159–87)

10. How can I feel more creative and help my students to get away from wanting to "copy"? Is it really possible to teach creativity?

A mind once stretched by imagination never regains its original dimensions.

Anonymous

Do this activity to see how to activate creative thinking: Line a group up and explain that each will be asked to walk across the room in a way different from everyone else. Start with one person and go down the line. Afterward, discuss how everyone was able to accomplish this "creative" task so easily. Next, here are two children's books that show the values of creative thinking. Use them with adults and children: *The Big Orange Splot* by Daniel Pinkwater and *Imogene's Antlers* by David Small. Discuss the importance of not copying, but "data gathering" from sources and then "doing your own thing." Try the creativity strategies described in Chapter 1 (and the rest of the book). Repeat them one at a time until they become second nature. For example, try using brainstorming in social studies and science to discuss problems. Keep adding a few strategies at a time. Tell students what you are doing and put up posters about what they can try. Consider setting aside ten minutes of class time each week to discuss how everyone is creative; ask students to discover specific examples by talking with friends, parents, and other relatives. Finally, invite artists and others to class to speak about how they create.

11. What if I have a very limited budget? How can I get the materials I would need ? You don't need a lot of expensive materials. Push back the desks and use the strategies in this book, along with children's literature and other current teaching materials. Check out *more* library books that are arts-based, and spruce up the room with art (some public libraries lend reproductions). Playing background music at the start of the day means bringing in a CD player. Eventually, you'll want to have a wider range of art materials like those recommended in Chapter 5, but to start off, use what's on hand and investigate free community resources such as museums that provide docent-led tours. The public library may have staff to do storytelling. Survey teachers to ask what they know and can do in music, art, drama, dance, literature, poetry, and storytelling. Ask about spouses' talents and others they know who would be willing to share (e.g., seniors in the community). There are many capable people out there just waiting to be asked.

12. Why are the arts specialists the first teachers to be cut when there is a budget crunch? Don't school administrators and board members know the arts research?

A dramatic revolution in cognitive understanding began in the 1970's. Research now substantiates what some teachers and parents already knew intuitively—that the arts are critical to learning.

Murfee, 1995

It is interesting to trace how the arts became dispensable extras. But surveys show most parents now think the arts are as important as reading, writing, math, science, and social studies and favour cuts in administration or sports to pay for arts classes (Harris, 1992). There is a growing consensus among educational policymakers and parents that the arts should be an integral part of education, but support is built on information. Not everyone has had access to the kind of research in the *News Bulletins* of this book. The 1997 booklet *Making the Case for Arts Education* provides a summary of research and trends in arts education and is available from the Ontario Arts Council by e-mail (info@arts.on.ca).

13. Doesn't direct instruction in the arts interfere with natural creative development? Guided or direct instruction helps children to attain skills, learn to use particular tools, and discover important patterns they will not be likely to find independently. Explicit instruction gives children the confidence to take risks and try new things because they have some know-how. Guided instruction does need to be short and followed by time to experiment to explore creative variations.

14. Doesn't emphasizing "beauty" focus on looks and appearance when we should focus on more substantial aspects of people and the world?

You may find yourself driving along a highway when you suddenly pass a vista that catches your breath. You stop the car, get out for just a few minutes, and behold the grandeur of nature. This is the arresting power of beauty, and giving in to that sudden longing of the soul is a way of giving it what it needs. Discussions of beauty can sometimes sound ethereal and philosophical, but from the soul viewpoint beauty is a necessary part of ordinary life. Every day we will find moments when the soul glimpses an occasion for beauty, if only passing a store window and stopping for a second to notice a beautiful ring or an arresting pattern in a dress.

Thomas Moore, *Care of the Soul*, pp. 277–278.

15. How do you begin to collaborate with special teachers of the arts? Begin by asking to sit in on their classes to learn about the arts. Ask about sharing a list of unit topics and skills each of you will address during a semester, and see where there are natural connections. Start slowly and build a respectful relationship that acknowledges that each of you has a different expertise to bring to the common goal of teaching children.

16. How can a teacher who is not artsy integrate the arts? What if I have little or no background in the arts? Almost everyone has more background than they think they do. Think about what you do know and can do in music, art, drama, dance and movement, literature, and poetry. Start small, maybe with a one-minute arts routine like those described in Chapter 2. Read journal articles like those in the bibliography in the appendix and watch recommended videos.

Integrating the arts is about good teaching and is based on brain-based learning. You need not be a dancer, singer, visual artist, or actor to use this research. You do need a basic knowledge of key concepts, principles, techniques, and tools in each of the arts disciplines and a solid foundation in research on child development and learning theory (see Vygotsky, Piaget, Gardner, Maslow, etc., in Chapter 1). Finally, it is necessary for a teacher to be committed to integrating the arts. Enthusiasm and passion are hard to fake and are major determiners in the success of children in any classroom. Ginott (1985) said it best when he reminded teachers to say to themselves

> I am the decisive element in the classroom. It is my personal approach that creates the climate. It is my daily mood that makes the weather. As a teacher, I possess tremendous power to make a child's life miserable or joyous. I can be a tool of torture or an instrument of inspiration. I can humiliate, humor, hurt or heal. In all situations, it is my response that decides whether a crisis will be escalated or de-escalated and a child humanized or dehumanized.

Conclusion

The arts are unique ways humans understand and respond—ways we communicate by receiving and expressing information. They are outgrowths of culture, emotions, values, experiences, and history, created because everyday words are inadequate. As disciplines, the arts are work—brain and body work—that offer unusual perspectives, tools, and techniques to liberate feelings and ideas locked up inside a person. This book has been about tapping a vast potential of the arts to impact learning by giving classroom teachers background to teach *with, about, in,* and *through* the arts.

But great teaching involves more than savoir faire. The goal is not to do what was done *to* you, but to transcend our own teachers by using research, theory, curriculum models, and strategies to create an individual teaching style based on a personal philosophy. For meaningful arts integration, this philosophy needs to address beliefs about an aesthetic learning environment, the power of belief and expectation, giving students freedom to fail, meaning making about important life-centred issues, the use of teacher demonstration, active learning, opportunities to apply and practice, developing student independence and responsibility, ensuring progress through success, focusing on intrinsic motivation, and the essential role of creative problem-solving in learning. We need teachers who will invent, discover, adapt, and twist ideas to solve learning problems, not simply repeat the methods of past generations. We need teachers who believe for every problem there are multiple solutions—the best of which may seem bizarre because they are so creative. But as Dr. Seuss put it, "If you can see things out of whack, you can see things in whack." Of course, this requires risk taking—moving out of a zone of comfort and being willing to experience a degree of dissonance, imperatives for creative thinking. It is the teacher's own knowledge, strategy repertoire, enthusiasm, humour, creativity, and passion that are forces powerful enough to change a child's universe by creating the "what if? classroom." Change the child and we change the future.

References

Books

Fauth, B. (1990). Linking the visual arts with drama, movement, and dance for the young child. In Stinson, J., *Moving and learning for the young child.* Reston, VA: American Alliance for Health, Physical Education, Recreation, and Dance.

Harris, L. (1992). *Americans and the Arts VI/Nationwide Survey of Public Opinion.* Americans for the Arts.

Larson, G. (1997). *American canvas.* Washington, DC: National Endowment for the Arts.

Moore, T. (1992). *Care of the soul.* New York, NY: HarperCollins.

Murfee, E. (1995). *Eloquent evidence: Arts at the core of learning.* Washington, DC: President's Committee on the Arts & Humanities and the National Assembly of State Arts Agencies with the National Endowment of the Arts.

Children's Literature

Pinkwater, D. (1993). *The big orange splot.* New York: Scholastic.

Silverstein, S. (1981). *A light in the attic.* New York: Harper & Row.

Silverstein, S. (1973). *The giving tree.* New York: Harper & Row.

Small, D. (1985). *Imogene's antlers.* New York: Crown.

Speare, E. (1958). *Witch of Blackbird Pond.* Boston: Houghton Mifflin.

Steig, W. (1969). *Sylvester and the magic pebble.* New York: Little Simon.

Appendix A: Arts-Based Children's Literature

Note: The Children's Literature Web Guide (www.vcalgary.ca/~dkbrown/) has a bibliography of books with artistic protagonists.

Art

Making Art

Adkins, J. (1975). *Inside: Seeing beneath the surface.* New York: Walker.

Albenda, P. (1970). *Creating painting with tempera.* New York: Van Nostrand.

Arnosky, J. (1982). *Drawing from nature.* New York: Lothrop.

Baumgardner, J. (1993). *60 Art projects for children: Painting, clay, puppets, paints, masks, and more.* New York: Clarkson Potter.

Belloli, A., & Godard, K. (1994). *Make your own museum.* Boston: Houghton Mifflin.

Blegvad, E. (1979). *Self-portrait: Eric Blegvad.* Reading, MA: Addison Wesley.

Bolognese, D., & Thornton, R. (1983). *Drawing and painting with the computer.* New York: Franklin Watts.

Carle, E. (1974). *My very first book of colors.* New York: Crowell.

Emberly, E. (1991). *Ed Emberly's drawing book: Make a world.* Boston: Little, Brown.

Fine, J., & Anderson, D. (1979). *I carve stone.* New York: Crowell.

Fischer, L. E. (1986). *The papermakers.* Boston: David Godine.

Galate, L. (1980). *A beginner's guide to calligraphy.* New York: Dell.

Gibbons, G. (1987). *The pottery place.* San Diego: Harcourt Brace Jovanovich.

Graham, A., & Stoke, D. (1983). *Fossils, ferns, and fish scales: A handbook of art and nature projects.* New York: Four Winds.

Haldane, S. (1988). *Painting faces.* New York: Dutton.

Hauser, J. (1995). *Kids' crazy concoctions: 50 mysterious mixtures for art & craft fun.* Charlotte, VT: Williamson.

Hoban, T. (1974). *Circles, triangles, and squares.* New York: Macmillan.

Hoban, T. (1983). *Round & round & round.* New York: Greenwillow.

Hoban, T. (1986). *Shapes, shapes, shapes.* New York: Greenwillow.

Hyman, T. S. (1981). *Self-portrait: Trina Schart Hyman.* Reading, MA: Addison Wesley.

Irvine, J., & Reid, B. (1987). *How to make pop-ups.* New York: William Morrow.

Joe, E. (1978). *Navajo sandpainting art.* Tucson, AZ: Treasure Chest.

Kinney, J., & Kinney, C. (1976). *23 Varieties of ethnic art and how to make each one.* New York: Atheneum.

Kohl, M. (1989). *Mudworks.* Bellingham, WA: Bright Ring.

Kohl, M., & Gainer, C. (1991). *Good earth art: Environmental art for kids.* Bellingham, WA: Bright Ring.

Marks, M. (1972). *OP-tricks: Creating kinetic art.* Philadelphia: Lippincott.

Muller, B. (1987). *Painting with children.* Edinburgh, Scotland: Floris Books.

Pluckrose, H. (1989). *Crayons.* New York: Watts.

Reid, B. (1989). *Playing with plasticine.* Longbeach, CA: Beechtree Books.

Sakata, H. (1990). *Origami.* New York: Japan Publishers, U.S.A.

Smith, R. (1987). *The artist's handbook: Complete guide to tools, techniques, and materials of painting, drawing and printing.* New York: Knopf.

Solga, K. (1992). *Make sculptures.* Cincinnati: North Light Books.

Stangl, J. (1986). *Magic mixtures.* Carthage, IL: Teaching Aids.

Striker, S. (1984). *The anti-coloring book.* New York: Holt, Rinehart & Winston. One of a series including *The circus anti-coloring book* and *The newspaper anti-coloring book.*

Takahama, T. (1988). *Quick and easy origami.* New York: Japan Publications.

Terzian, A. (1993). *The kids' multicultural art book: Art & craft experiences from around the world.* Charlotte, VT: Williamson.

Webb, P. H., & Corby, J. (1991). *Shadowgraphs anyone can make.* New York: Running Press.

Weiss, P., & Giralla, S. (1976). *Simple printmaking*. New York: Lothrop.

Zemach, M. (1978). *Self-portrait: Margot Zemach*. Reading, MA: Addison Wesley.

Art as Part of the Book's Theme

Aardema, V. (1985). *Bimwilli and the Zimwi*. New York: Dial Books.

Aardema, V. (1967). *Who's in rabbit's house?* New York: Dial Books.

Abby Aldrich Rockefeller Folk Art Center (1991). *The folk art counting book*. New York: Abrams.

Ackerman, K. (1990). *Araminta's paint box*. New York: Atheneum.

Alcott, L. M. (1994). *Little women*. Boston: Little, Brown.

Alexander, L. (1982). *Kestrel*. New York: Dutton.

Alexander, M. (1995). *You're a genius* BLACKBOARD BEAR. Cambridge, MA: Candlewick Press.

Allen, C. (1991). *The rug makers*. Austin, TX: Steck-Vaughn.

Allington, R. (1979). *Colors*. Milwaukee, WI: Raintree Press.

Allison, B. (1991). *Effie*. New York: Scholastic.

Angelou, M. (1994). *My painted house, my friendly chicken*. New York: Clarkson-Potter.

Anholt, L. (1994). *Camille and the sunflowers*. Hauppauge, NY: Barron's Educational Series.

Anno, M. (1989). *Anno's faces*. New York: Philomel Books.

Asch, F. (1985). *Bear shadow*. New York: Simon & Schuster.

Asch, F. (1981). *Bread and honey*. New York: Parents Magazine Press.

Asch, F. (1978). *Sand cake*. New York: Parents Magazine Press.

Asch, F. (1995). *Water*. New York: Harcourt Brace Jovanovich.

Ata, T., & Moroney, L. (1989). *Baby rattlesnake*. San Francisco: Children's Book Press.

Baker, A. (1994). *Brown rabbit's shape book*. New York: Larouse Kingfisher.

Baker, A. (1994). *White rabbit's color book*. New York: Larouse Kingfisher.

Baker, J. (1991). *Window*. New York: Puffin Books.

Baker, J. (1987). *Where the forest meets the sea*. New York: Greenwillow.

Bang, M. (1985). *The paper crane*. New York: Greenwillow.

Barrett, P., & Barrett, S. (1972). *The line Sophie drew*. New York: Scroll.

Bartalos, M. (1995). *Shadow Willie*. New York: Viking.

Bedard, M. (1992). *Emily*. New York: Doubleday.

Blood, C., & Link, M. (1990). *The goat in the rug*. New York: Aladdin-Macmillan.

Bouchard, D. (1993). *The elders are watching*. Golden, CO: Fulcrum.

Brenner, B. (1989). *The color wizard*. New York: Bantam Books.

Brown, M. (1984). *There's no place like home*. New York: Parents Magazine Press.

Bulla, C. (1987). *The chalk box kid*. New York: Random House.

Burke-Weiner, K. (1992). *The maybe garden*. New York: Beyond Worlds Publications.

Burns, M. (1994). *The greedy triangle*. New York: Scholastic.

Bush, T. (1995). *Grunt, the primitive cave boy*. New York: Crown.

Byars, B. (1978). *The cartoonist*. New York: Viking.

Canning, K. (1979). *A painted tale*. New York: Barron's.

Carle, E. (1992). *Draw me a star*. New York: Philomel Books.

Carle, E. (1984). *The mixed-up chameleon*. New York: Crowell.

Carle, E. (1974). *My very first book of shapes*. New York: Harper & Row.

Carle, E. (1972). *The secret birthday message*. New York: Harper Trophy.

Carlstrom, N. W. (1992). *Northern lullaby*. New York: Philomel Books.

Carrick, D. (1985). *Morgan and the artist*. New York: Clarion.

Castaneda, O. S. (1993). *Abuela's weave*. New York: Lee & Low.

Cazet, D. (1993). *Born in the gravy*. New York: Orchard Books.

Cazet, D. (1986). *Frosted glass*. New York: Bradbury Press.

Christiana, D. (1990). *Drawer in a drawer*. New York: Farrar, Straus, & Giroux.

Church, V. (1971). *All the colors around me*. Chicago: Afro-American Press.

Clark, A. N. (1957). *The little Indian basket maker*. Chicago: Melmont.

Clark, A. N. (1955). *The little Indian pottery maker*. Chicago: Melmont.

Clement, C. (1986). *The painter and the wild swans*. New York: Pied Piper-Dial.

Coerr, E. (1986). *The Josefina story quilt*. New York: Harper Trophy.

Cohen, J. (1995). *Why did it happen?* New York: William Morrow.

Cohen, M., & Hoban, L. (1980). *No good in art.* New York: Greenwillow.

Cole, B. (1989). *Celine.* New York: Farrar, Straus, & Giroux.

Cooney, B. (1982). *Miss Rumphius.* New York: Viking Penguin.

Coville, B. (1991). *Jeremy Thatcher, dragon hatcher.* Harcourt Brace Jovanovich.

Craven, C., & dePaola, T. (1989). *What the mailman brought.* New York: Putnam.

Demarest, C. L. (1995). *My blue boat.* New York: Harcourt Brace.

de Paola, T. (1991). *Bonjour, Mr. Satie.* New York: Putnam.

de Paola, T. (1973). *Charlie needs a cloak.* Englewood Cliffs, NJ: Prentice Hall.

de Trevino, E. B. (1965). *I, Juan de Pareja.* New York: Farrar, Straus, & Giroux.

Dewey, A. (1995). *The sky.* New York: Green Tiger Press.

Dillon, L., & Dillon, D. (1994). *What am I?* New York: Blue Sky Press.

Dixon, A. (1994). *Clay.* New York: Garrett Educational.

Dobrin, A. (1973). *Josephine's imagination.* New York: Scholastic.

Druscher, A. (1992). *Simon's book.* New York: Lothrop, Lee & Shepard.

Dubelaar, T., (1992). *Looking for Vincent.* New York: Checkerboard Press.

Dunrea, O. (1995). *The painter who loved chickens.* New York: Farrar, Straus, & Giroux.

Ernst, L. C. (1986). *Hamilton's art show.* New York: Lothrop.

Feiffer, J. (1993). *The man in the ceiling.* New York: HarperCollins.

Fitzhugh, L. (1964). *Harriet the spy.* New York: Harper & Row.

Fox, P. (1988). *The village by the sea.* Orchard Books.

Freeman, D. (1987). *Norman the doorman.* New York: Viking Penguin.

French, F. (1977). *Matteo.* New York: Oxford University Press.

Gibbons, G. (1987). *The pottery place.* New York: Harcourt Brace Jovanovich.

Goffstein, M. B. (1980). *An artist.* New York: Harper & Row.

Goffstein, M. (1985). *An artist's album.* New York: Harpercrest.

Goffstein, M. (1986). *Your lone journey: Paintings.* HarperCollins.

Grifalconi, A. (1990). *Osa's pride.* Boston: Little, Brown.

Harwood, P. A. (1965). *Mr. Bumba draws a kitten.* Minneapolis: Learner Publications.

Heyer, M. (1986). *The weaving of a dream.* New York: Puffin.

Hort, L. (1987). *The boy who held back the sea.* New York: Dial Books.

Isadora, R. (1988). *The pirates of Bedford Street.* New York: Greenwillow.

Isadora, R. (1991). *Swan lake.* New York: Putnam.

Isadora, R. (1977). *Willaby.* New York: Macmillan.

Jarrell, R. (1964). *Bat poet.* New York: Macmillan.

Jenkins, J. (1992). *Thinking about colors.* New York: Dutton.

Johnson, C. (1955). *Harold and the purple crayon.* HarperCollins.

Keats, E. J. (1962). *The snowy day.* New York: Viking.

Kesselman, W., & Cooney, B. (1980). *Emma.* New York: Doubleday.

Knox, B. (1993). *The great art adventure.* New York: Rizzoli.

Koch, K., and Farell, K. (1985). *Talking to the sun.* New York: Metropolitan Museum of Art.

Konigsburg, E. L. (1975). *Second Mrs. Giaconda.* New York: Atheneum.

Leaf, M. (1987). *Eyes of the dragon.* New York: Lothrop, Lee & Shephard.

Lobel, A. (1980). *Fables.* New York: Harper & Row.

Lobel, A. (1968). *The great blueness and other predicaments.* New York: Harper & Row.

MacAgy, D., and E. (1978). *Going for a walk with a line.* New York: Doubleday.

Markun, P. M. (1993). *The little painter of Sabana Grande.* New York: Bradbury Press.

Martin, B. (1992). *Brown bear, brown bear, what do you see?* New York: Henry Holt.

Mayers, F. (1991). *The ABC: Museum of Fine Arts, Boston.* New York: Abrams.

Mayers, F. (1991). *The ABC: Museum of Modern Art, New York.* New York: Abrams.

Mayhew, J. (1989). *Katie's picture show.* New York: Bantam Books.

McPhail, D. (1978). *The magical drawings of Mooney B. Finch.* New York: Doubleday.

Minarik, E. (1968). *A kiss for Little Bear.* New York: Harper & Row.

Mori, K. (1993). *Shizuko's daughter.* New York: Henry Holt.

Munsch, R. (1992). *Purple, green and yellow.* Toronto: Annick Press.

O'Kelley, M. L. (1983). *From the hills of Georgia: An autobiography in paintings.* Boston: Atlantic Monthly.

O'Neal, Z. (1985). *In summer light.* New York: Viking Kestrel.

O'Neal, Z. (1980). *Language of goldfish.* New York: Viking.

Parr, L. (1991). *A man and his hat.* New York: Philomel Books.

Paterson, K. (1990). *The tale of Mandarin ducks.* New York: Lodestar.

Paulsen, G. (1988). *Island.* New York: Franklin Watts.

Paulsen, G. (1991). *Monument.* New York: Delacorte Press.

Peet, B. (1989). *Bill Peet: An autobiography.* Boston: Houghton Mifflin.

Picard, B. L. (1966). *One is one.* New York: Henry Holt.

Pilkey, D. (1990). *Twas the night before Thanksgiving.* Orchard Books.

Pinkwater, D. (1993). *The big orange splot.* New York: Scholastic.

Polacco, P. (1997). *In Enzo's splendid gardens.* New York: Philomel.

Polacco, P. (1988). *The keeping quilt.* New York: Simon & Schuster.

Reiner, A. (1990). *A visit to the art galaxy.* New York: Green Tiger Press.

Rockwell, A. (1993). *Mr. Panda's painting.* New York: Macmillan.

Rodari, F. (1991). *A weekend with Picasso.* New York: Rizzoli.

Rylant, C. (1982). *When I was young in the mountains.* New York: E. P. Dutton.

Sanford, J. (1991). *Slappy Hooper: The world's greatest sign painter.* New York: Warner.

Schick, E. (1987). *Art lessons.* New York: Greenwillow.

Small, D. (1987). *Paper John.* New York: Farrar, Straus, & Giroux.

Spier, P. (1978). *Oh, were they ever happy!* New York: Doubleday.

Spilka, A. (1964). *Paint all kinds of pictures.* New York: Hill and Wang.

Sutcliff, R. (1978). *Sun Horse, Moon Horse.* New York: Dutton.

Tallarico, T. (1984). *I can draw animals.* New York: Simon & Schuster.

Testa, F. (1982). *If you take a paintbrush: A book of colors.* New York: Dial.

Trevino, E. (1965). *I, Juan de Pareja.* New York: Farrar, Straus, & Giroux.

Tuyet, T. (1987). *The little weaver of Thai-Yen village.* Emeryville, CA: Children's Book Press.

Wadell, M., & Langley, J. (1988). *Alice the artist.* New York: Dutton.

Watson, W. (1994). *The fox went out on a chilly night.* New York: Lothrop, Lee & Shepard.

Wilhelm, J. (1988). *Oh, what a mess.* New York: Random House.

Williams, V. B. (1986). *Cherries and cherry pits.* New York: Greenwillow.

Xiong, B. (1989). *Nine-in-one, Grr, Grr.* Emeryville, CA: Children's Book Press.

Art History and Appreciation

Alcron, J. (1991). *Rembrandt's beret.* New York: Tambourine Books.

Ball, J. A., & Conant, C. *Georgia O'Keefe-painter of the desert.* The Rosen Publishing Group.

Bearden, R., & Henderson, H. (1972). *Six black masters of American art.* Osceda, WI: Zenith Books.

Behrens, J. (1977). *Looking at the beasties.* Chicago: Children's Press.

Behrens, J. (1982). *Looking at children.* Chicago: Children's Press.

Blanquet, C. (1994). *Miro: Earth and sky. Art for children.* Chelsea House.

Blizzard, G. (1992). *Come look with me: Exploring landscape art with children.* Charlottesville, VA: Thomasson-Grant.

Bohn-Ducher, M., & Cook, J. (1991). *Understanding modern art.* London: Osborn House.

Bolton, L. (1970). *The history and techniques of the great Masters: Gaugin.* Edison, NJ: Booksales.

Bonafoux, P. (1987). *Van Gogh: The passionate eye.* New York: Abrams.

Bonafoux, P. (1991). *A weekend with Rembrandt.* New York: Rizzoli International.

Boutan, M. (1995). *Van Gogh: Art activity pack* and *Monet.* San Francisco: Chronicle Books.

Brown, L. K., & Brown, M. (1986). *Visiting the art museum.* New York: Dutton.

Burdett, L. (1995). *A child's portrait of Shakespeare.* Buffalo, NY: Blackmoss Press.

Cachin, F. (1991). *Gaughin: The quest for paradise.* New York: Abrams.

Ceserani, G. P,. & Ventura, P. (1983). *Grand constructions.* New York: Putnam's Sons.

Chapman, L. *Discover Art. Vol. 1–6.* Worchester, Mass: Davis Publishing.

Chase, A. E. (1966). *Looking at art.* New York: Crowell Company.

Collins, D. R. (1989). *The country artist: A story about Beatrix Potter.* Minneapolis: Carolrhoda.

Collins, P. L. (1972). *I am an artist.* Brookefield, CT: Millbrook Press.

Conner, P. (1982). *Looking at art: People at home.* New York: Atheneum.

Conner, P. (1982). *Looking at art: People at work.* New York: Atheneum.

Contempre, Y. (1978). *A Sunday afternoon on the Island of Jatte.* Paris: Dululot.

Craft, R. (1975). *Brueghel's the fair.* New York: J. B. Lippincott.

Crespi, F. (1995). *A walk in Monet's garden.* Canada: Little, Brown & Co.

Cummings, P. (1992). *Talking with artists.* New York: Bradbury.

Cummings, R. (1982). *Just imagine: Ideas in painting.* New York: Scribner.

Cummings, R. (1979). *Just look: A book about paintings.* New York: Scribner.

Davidson, M. B. (1984). *A history of art.* New York: Random House.

Deem. G. *Art school: An homage to the masters.* San Francisco: Chronicle Books.

Dobrin, A. (1975). *I am a stranger on earth: The story of Vincent Van Gogh.* New York: Warne.

Drucker, M. (1991). *Frida Kahlo: Torment and triumph in her life and art.* New York: Bantam.

Elderfield, J. (1978). *The cut-outs of Henry Matisse.* New York: George Brogiller.

Epstein, V. S. (1978). *History of women artists for children.* Denver, Colorado: VSE Publisher.

Galli, L. (1996). *Mona Lisa: The secret of the smile.* New York: Bantam Doubleday Dell.

Gardner, J. M. (1993). *Henry Moore: From bones and stones to sketches and sculptures.* New York: Four Winds.

Gates, F. (1982). *North American Indian masks: Craft and legend.* New York: Walker.

Gherman, B. (1986). *Georgia O'Keefe.* New York: Atheneum.

Glubok, S., & Nook, G. (1972). *The art of the New American.* New York: Macmillan.

Greenberg, J., & Jordan, R. (1991). *The painter's eye: Learning to look at contemporary American Art;* (1993) *The sculptor's eye: Looking at contemporary American art.* New York: Delacorte Press.

Greenfield, H. (1991). *Marc Chagall.* New York: Abrams.

Harrison, P. (1995). *Claude Monet.* New York: Sterling.

Hart, T. (1993). *Michelangelo.* Hauppuage, NY: Barron's Educational Series.

Highwater, J. (1978). *Many smokes, many moons: A chronology of American Indian history through Indian art.* New York: Lippincott.

Holmes, B. (1979). *Enchanted worlds: Pictures to grow up with.* New York: Universal Press.

Isaacson, P. M. (1993). *A short walk around the pyramids and through the world of art.* New York: Knopf.

Janson, H. W., & Janson, A. F. (1992). *History of art for young people.* New York: Abrams.

Kennet, F., & Measham, T. (1979). *Looking at paintings.* New York: Van Nostrand Reinhold.

Kinghorn, H., Badman, J., & Lewis-Spicer, L. (1998). *Let's meet famous artists.* Minneapolis, MN: T. S. Denison.

Klein, M., & Klein, N. (1972). *Kalbe Kollwitz: Life in art.* New York: Holt, Rinehart & Winston.

Krull, K. (1995). *Lives of the artists: Masterpieces, messes, and what the neighbors thought.* San Diego: Harcourt Brace.

Lepscky, A. (1984). *Pablo Picasso.* Woodbury, NY: Barron's.

LeTord, B. (1995). *A blue butterfly: A story about Claude Monet.* New York: Bantam Doubleday Dell.

Luchner, L., & Kaye, G. (1971). *A child's story of Vincent van Gogh.* Morristown, NJ: Silver Burdett.

McLanathan, R. (1991). *Leonardo da Vinci.* New York: Abrams.

Messinger, L. M. (1991). *For our children.* Burbank, CA.: Disney Press (to benefit Pediatric AIDS Foundation).

Messinger, L. M. (1988). *Georgia O'Keefe.* New York, NY: Thomas and Hudson.

Meyer, S. (1990). *Mary Cassatt.* New York: Abrams.

Milande, V. (1995). *Michelangelo and his times.* New York: Henry Holt.

Mondays, G. (1975). *Norman Rockwell's Americana ABC.* New York: Dell.

Muhlberger, R. (1993). *What makes a Monet a Monet?* New York: Viking.

Munthe, N., & Kee, R. (1983). *Meet Matisse.* Boston: Little, Brown.

Nelson, M. (1972). *Maria Martinez.* New York: Dodd Mead.

Newlands, A., & National Gallery of Canada Staff (1989). *Meet Edgar Degas.* New York: Harper.

O'Neal, Z. (1986). *Grandma Moses: Painter of rural America.* New York: Viking Kestrel.

Peppin, A. (1980). *The Usborne story of painting.* Tulsa, OK: EDC Publishing.

Peter, A. (1974). *Paul Gaugin.* (Art for Children). New York: Doubleday.

Pluckrose, H. (1987). *Crayons.* New York: Watts.

Price, C. (1977). *Arts of clay.* New York: Scribner.

Priess, B. (1981). *The art of Leo and Diane Dillion.* New York: Ballantine.

Proddow, P. (1979). *Art tells a story: Greek and Roman myths.* New York: Doubleday.

Provenson, A., & Provenson, M. (1984). *Leonardo da Vinci: The artist, inventor, scientist in three-dimensional, movable pictures.* New York: Viking.

Raboff, E. (1987 and 1988). Art for Children Series: *da Vinci; Rembrandt; Renoir; Matisse; Michelangelo; Raphael; Velasquez; van Gogh.* New York: Lippincott.

Raboff, E. (1982). *Marc Chagall.* Garden City, NY: Doubleday.

Raboff, E. (1982). *Pablo Picasso.* Garden City, NY: Doubleday.

Raboff, E. (1982). *Paul Klee.* Garden City, NY: Doubleday.

Richardson, J. (1993). *Inside the museum: A children's guide to the Metropolitan Museum of Art.* New York: Metropolitan Museum of Art: Abrams.

Richmond, R. (1992). *Children in art.* Nashville, TN: Ideals Children's Books.

Rockwell, A. (1971). *Paintbrush and peace pipe: The story of George Catlin.* New York: Atheneum.

Rodari, F. (1991). *A weekend with Picasso.* New York: Rizzoli International.

Schwartz, L. (1992). *Rembrandt.* New York: Abrams.

Sills, L. (1989). *Inspirations: Stories about women artists.* Nills, IL: Whitman.

Skira-Venturi, R. (1990). *A weekend with Renoir; A weekend with Degas.* New York: Rizzoli.

Strand, M. (1986). *Rembrandt takes a walk.* New York: Clarkson.

Sturgis, A. (1994). *Introducing Rembrandt.* Boston: Little, Brown.

Sullivan, C., ed. (1989). *Imaginary gardens: American poetry and art for young people.* New York: Abrams.

Swain, S. (1988). *Great housewives of art.* New York: Penguin.

Tobias, T. (1974). *Isamu Noguchi: The life of a sculptor.* New York: Crowell.

Turner, R. (1991). *Georgia O'Keefe.* Boston: Little, Brown.

Venezia, M. (1988–1991). Getting to Know the World's Great Artists Series: *Picasso; Rembrandt; van Gogh; da Vinci; Mary Cassatt; Edward Hopper; Monet; Botticelli; Goya; Paul Klee; Michelangelo.* Chicago: Children's Press.

Ventura, P. (1984). *Great painters.* New York: Putnam.

Ventura, P. (1989). *Michelangelo's world.* New York: Putnam.

Waldron, A. (1991). *Claude Monet.* New York: Abrams.

Walker, L. (1994). *Roy Lichenstein: The artist at work.* New York: Dutton Lodestar.

Walters, A. (1989). *The spirit of Native America: Beauty and mysticism in American Indian art.* San Francisco: Chronicle.

Waterfield, G. (1982). *Looking at art: Faces.* New York: Atheneum.

Winter, J. (1991). *Diego.* New York: Knopf.

Woolf, F. (1993). *Picture this century: An introduction to twentieth-century art.* New York: Doubleday.

Woolf, H. (1989). *Picture this: A first introduction to paintings.* New York: Doubleday.

Yenawine, P., & Museum of Modern Art (1991). Series on Modern Art: *Colors; Lines; Shapes; Stories.* New York: Delacorte Press.

Zhensun, A., & Low, A. (1991). *A young painter: The life and paintings of Wang Yani, China's extraordinary artist.* New York: Scholastic.

Photography

Allen, M., & Rotner, S. (1991). *Changes.* New York: Macmillan.

Arnold, C. (1991). *Snake.* New York: Morrow.

Barrett, N. (1988). *Pandas.* New York: Watts.

Bauer, J. (1995). *Thwonk!* New York: Dutton.

Behrens, J. (1986). *Fiesta.* San Francisco: Children's Book Press.

Brenner, B. (1973). *Bodies.* New York: Dutton.

Brown, T. (1987). *Chinese New Year.* New York: Henry Holt.

Brown, T. (1986). *Hello, Amigos.* New York: Henry Holt.

Burton, J. (1991). *See how they grow series: Kitten; Puppy.* New York: Lodestar.

Cobb, V. (1990). *Natural wonders.* New York: Lothrop.

Cornish, S. (1974). *Grandmother's pictures.* Freeport, ME: Bookstore Press.

Cousteau Society Series. (1992). *Dolphins; Penguins; Seals; Turtles.* New York: Simon & Schuster.

Doubilet, A. (1991). *Under the sea from A to Z.* New York: Crown.

Eye Openers Series. (1991). *Baby animals; Jungle animals; Pets; Zoo Animals.* New York: Aladdin.

Feeney, S. (1980). *A is for aloha.* Honolulu: University Press of Hawaii.

Feeney, S. (1985). *Hawaii is a rainbow.* Honolulu: University Press of Hawaii.

Goldsmith, D. (1992). *Hoang Auk: A Vietnamese-American boy.* New York: Holiday House.

Hewett, J. (1990). *Hector lives in the United States now: The story of a Mexican-American child.* New York: Lippincott.

Hirschi, R. (1991). *Fall.* New York: Dutton.

Hirschi, R. (1990). *Spring.* New York: Dutton.

Hirschi, R. (1990). *Winter.* New York: Dutton.

Hoban, T. (1990). *Exactly the opposite.* New York: Greenwillow.

Hoban, T. (1985). *A children's zoo.* New York: Greenwillow.

Hoban, T. (1985). *Is it larger? Is it smaller?* New York: Greenwillow.

Kuklin, S. (1991). *How my family lives in America.* New York: Bradbury.

Lehrman, F. (1990). *Loving the earth: A sacred landscape book for children.* Berkeley, CA: Celestial.

Marshall, J. P. (1989). *My camera at the zoo.* Boston: Little, Brown.

Meltzer, M. (1986). *Dorothea Lange: Life through the camera.* New York: Puffin.

Miller, M. (1991). *Whose shoe?* New York: Greenwillow.

Morris, A. (1989). *Bread, bread, bread.* New York: Lothrop, Lee, & Shepard.

Morris, A. (1989). *Hats, hats, hats.* New York; Lothrop, Lee, & Shepard.

Morris, A. (1990). *Loving.* New York: Lothrop, Lee, & Shepard.

Oliver, S. (1990). *My first look at seasons.* New York: Random House.

Rauzon, M. (1992). *Jungles.* New York: Doubleday.

Ricklin, N. (1988). *Grandpa and me.* New York: Simon & Schuster.

Robbins, K. (1991). *Bridges.* New York: Dial.

Schlein, M. (1990). *Elephants.* New York: Aladdin.

Schlein, M. (1990). *Gorillas.* New York: Aladdin.

Steichen, E. (1985). *The family of man.* New York: Museum of Modern Art.

Waters, K., & Slorenz-Low, M. (1990). *Lion dancer: Earnie Wan's Chinese New Year.* New York: Scholastic.

Wilkes, A. (1991). *My first green book.* New York: Knopf.

Drama

Doing Drama (includes pantomime and verbal activities)

Aardema, V. (1975). *Why mosquitoes buzz in people's ears.* New York: Dial.

Adoff, A. (1981). *Outside/inside poems.* New York: Lothrop, Lee & Shepard.

Ahlberg, J., & Ahlberg, A. (1986). *The jolly postman's or other people's letters.* Boston: Little, Brown.

Alexander, L. (1992). *The fortune tellers.* New York: Dutton.

Alexander, S. (1980). *Whatever happened to Uncle Albert?: And other puzzling plays.* New York: Houghton Mifflin/Clarion Books.

Bailey Babb, K. (1990). *Beginning readers theatre: Presentation masks and scripts for young readers.* Denver, CO: Skipping Stone Press.

Barchers, S. (1993). *Reader's theatre for beginning readers.* Englewood, CO: Teacher Ideas Press.

Bayer, J. (1984). *My name is Alice.* New York: Dial.

Bemelmens, L. (1939). *Madeline.* New York: Viking Penguin.

Bennett, J. (collected) (1987). *Noisy poems.* New York: Oxford University Press.

Berger, B. (1984). *Grandfather Twilight.* New York: Philomel.

Blos, J. (1984). *Martin's hats.* New York: William Morrow.

Bodecker, N. M. (1974). *"Let's marry," said the cherry.* New York: Atheneum.

Boiko, C. (1981). *Children's plays for creative actors: A collection of royalty-free plays for boys and girls.* Boston: Plays, Inc.

Boiko, C. (1985). *Children's plays for creative actors: A collection of royalty free plays for boys and girls.* Boston: Plays, Inc.

Bradley, A. (1977). *Paddington on stage.* Boston: Houghton Mifflin.

Cameron, P. (1961). *"I can't," said the ant.* New York: Coward-McCann.

Caras, R. (1977). *Coyote for a day.* New York: Windmill Books.

Carle, E. (1969). *The very hungry caterpillar.* New York: Philomel/Putnam.

Carlson, B. W. (1982). *Let's find the big idea.* Nashville: Abingdon.

Carlson, B. W. (1973). *Let's pretend it happened to you.* Nashville: Abingdon.

Carroll, L. (1989). *Jabberwocky.* New York: Abrams.

Cauley, L. B. (retold) (1979). *The ugly duckling.* New York: Harcourt Brace Jovanovich.

Chaconas, D. (1970). *The way the tiger walked.* New York: Simon & Schuster.

Charlip, R. (1980). *Fortunately.* New York: Four Winds Press.

Chess, V. (1979). *Alfred's alphabet walk.* New York: Greenwillow.

Cole, J. (1987). *The magic schoolbus inside the earth.* New York: Scholastic.

Collins, M. (1976). *Flying to the moon and other strange places.* New York: Farrar, Straus, & Giroux.

Corbett, S. (1984). *Jokes to tell your worst enemy.* New York: E. P. Dutton.

Cunningham, J. (1970). *Burnish me bright.* New York: Pantheon.

Day, A. (1985). *Good gog, Carl.* New York: Green Tiger Press.

de Paola, T. (1979). *Charlie needs a cloak.* Englewood Cliffs, NJ: Prentice Hall.

Dunn, S. (1990). *Crackers and crumbs. Chants for whole language.* Portsmouth, NH: Heinemann.

Eastman, P. D. (1960). *Are you my mother?* New York: Random House.

Emberley, B. (1967). *Drummer Hoff.* Englewood Cliffs, NJ: Prentice Hall.

England, A. W. (1990). *Theatre for the young (Modern Dramatists).* New York: St. Martin's Press.

Fraser, P. (1982). *Puppets and puppetry: A complete guide to puppetmaking for all ages.* New York: Stein & Day.

Gag, W. (1928). *Millions of cats.* New York: Coward-McCann.

Galdone, P. (1968). *The Bremen town musicians.* New York: McGraw-Hill.

Georges, C., & Cornett, C. (1986). *Reader's theatre.* Aurora, NY: Developers of Knowledge.

Gerke, P. (1996). *Multicultural plays for children: Grades K–3 (Young Actors Series), Vol. 1.* Lyme, NH: Smith & Kraus.

Gerke, P. (1996). *Multicultural plays for children: Grades 4–6 (Young Actors Series), Vol. 2.* Lyme, NH: Smith & Kraus.

Gerstein, M. (1984). *Roll over!* New York: Crown.

Gibbons, G. (1985). *Lights! Camera! Action! How a movie is made.* New York: Crowell.

Goffstein, M. (1987). *An actor.* New York: Harper & Row.

Grimm, J., & Grimm, W. *Rumpelstiltskin.* (Several editions)

Guarino, D. (1991). *Is your mama a llama?* New York: Scholastic.

Hackbarth, J. (1994). *Plays, players, and playing: How to start your own children's theater company.* Colorado Springs, CO: Piccadilly Books.

Haley, G. (1970). *A story—A story.* New York: Atheneum.

Haskins, J. (1982). *Black theater in America.* New York: Crowell.

Heide, F. P. (1971). *The shrinking of treehorn.* New York: Holiday House.

Hutchins, P. (1976). *Don't forget the bacon.* New York: Greenwillow.

Jennings, C. (1988). *Plays children love: A treasury of contemporary & classic plays for children, Vol. 2.* New York: St. Martin's Press.

Jennings, C. A., & Harris, A. (1981). *Plays children love: A treasury of contemporary and classic plays for children.* Garden City, NY: Doubleday.

Jennings, C. A., & Harris, A., eds. (1988). *Plays children love, Vol. 2.* New York: St. Martin's Press.

Johnson, C. (1955). *Harold and the purple crayon.* New York: Harper & Row.

Juster, N. (1989). *A surfeit of smiles.* New York: William Morrow.

Kahl, V. (1955). *The duchess bakes a cake.* New York: Scribner's.

Kamerman, S. (1988). *The big book of Christmas plays: 21 modern and traditional one-act plays for the celebration of Christmas.* Boston: Plays, Inc.

Kamerman, S. (1989). *The big book of comedies: 25 one-act plays, skits, curtain raisers, and adaptations for young people.* Boston: Plays, Inc.

Kamerman, S. (1991). *The big book of folktale plays: One-act adaptations of folktales from around the world, for stage and puppet performance.* Boston: Plays, Inc.

Kamerman, S. (1994). *The big book of large-cast plays: 27 one-act plays for young actors.* Boston: Plays, Inc.

Kamerman, S. (1996). *Big book of skits: 36 short plays for young actors.* Boston: Plays, Inc.

Kase-Polisini, J. (1989). *Drama as a meaning maker.* Lanham, MD: University Press of America.

Keats, E. J. (1964). *Whistle for Willie.* New York: Viking.

Keller, C. (1985). *Astronauts: Space jokes and riddles.* New York: Simon & Schuster.

Kellogg, S. (1971). *Can I keep him?* New York: Dial.

Kline, S. (1993). *Who's Orp's girlfriend?* New York: Putnam's.

Knight L. M. (1990). *Readers theatre for children: Scripts and script development.* Englewood, CO: Teachers Idea Press.

Kuskin, K. (1982). *The philharmonic gets dressed.* New York: Harper & Row.

Laughlin, M. K., & Latrobe, K. H. (1990). *Reader's theatre for children.* Englewood, CO: Teacher Ideas Press.

Malkin, M. (1979). *Training the young actor: An idea book (for students from seven to fourteen).* South Brunswick, Australia: Barnes.

Martin, J. (1997). *Out of the bag: The paper bag players book of plays.* New York: Hyperion.

McDermott, B. (1976). *The Golem: A Jewish legend.* Philadelphia: Lippincott.

McGovern, A. (1967). *Too much noise.* Boston: Houghton Mifflin.

McGowan, D. (1997). *Math play!* Charlotte, VT: Williamson.

McNulty, F. (1979). *How to dig a hole to the other side of the world.* New York: Harper & Row.

Miller, H. (1971). *1st plays for children.* Boston: Plays, Inc.

Munsch, R. (1980). *The paper bag princess.* Toronto: Annick Press.

Murray, B. (1995). *Puppet and theater activities: Theatrical things to do and make.* Honesdale, PA: Boyds Mills Press; distributed by St. Martin's Press.

Numeroff, L. J. (1985). *If you give a mouse a cookie.* New York: Harper & Row.

Parish, P. (1963). *Amelia Bedelia.* New York: Harper & Row.

Pollock, J. (1997). *Side by side: Twelve multicultural puppet plays (School Library Media, No. 13).* Lanham, MD: Scarecrow Press.

Rey, H. A. (1941). *Curious George.* Boston: Houghton Mifflin.

Rosenfeld, S. (1970). *A drop of water.* Irvington-on-Hudson, NY: Harvey House.

Ross, L. (1975). *Mask-making with pantomime and stories from American history.* Lothrop, Lee & Shepard.

San Souci, R. (1989). *The talking eggs.* New York: Dial.

Scieszka, J. (1989). *The true story of the 3 little pigs by A. Wolf.* New York: Viking.

Scull, M. (1990). *The skit book: 101 skits for kids.* Hamden, CN: Linnet Books.

Sendak, M. (1963). *Where the wild things are.* New York: Harper & Row.

Seuss, Dr. (1940). *Horton hatches the egg.* New York: Random House.

Seuss, Dr. (1961). *The Sneetches.* New York: Random House.

Sharmat, A. (1989). *Smedge.* New York: Macmillan.

Shaw, E. (1971). *Octopus.* New York: Harper & Row.

Small, D. (1985). *Imogene's antlers.* New York: Crown.

Smith, M. (1996). *The Seattle Children's Theatre: Seven plays for young actors (Young Actors Series).* Lyme, NH: Smith & Kraus.

Stanley, D., & Venneman, P. (1992). *Bard of Avalon: The story of Shakespeare.* New York: Morrow.

Steptoe, J. (1987). *Mufaro's beautiful daughters.* New York: Lothrop, Lee & Shepard.

Stevenson, J. (1977). *"Could Be Worse!"* New York: William Morrow.

Stone, R. (1975). *Because a little bug went ka-CHOO!* New York: Random House.

Straub, C. (1984). *Mime for basic beginners.* Boston: Plays, Inc.

Swortzell, L. (1997). *Theatre for Young Audiences: Around the World in 21 Plays.* New York: Applause.

Thaler, M. (1974). *Magic letter riddles.* New York: Scholastic.

Thayer, E. L. (1988). *Casey at the bat.* Boston: Godine.

Tolstoy, A. (1968). *The great big enormous turnip.* New York: Franklin Watts.

Tresslet, A. (1964). *The mitten.* New York: Lothrop, Lee & Shepard.

Tripp, V. (1994). *Addy's theater kit: A play about Addy for you and your friends to perform.* Middletown, WI: Pleasant Co.

Tripp, V. (1994). *Felicity's theater kit: A play about Felicity for you and your friends to perform.* Middletown, WI: Pleasant Co.

Tripp, V. (1994). *Kirsten's theater kit: A play about Kirsten for you and your friends to perform.* Middletown, WI: Pleasant Co.

Tripp, V. (1994). *Molly's theater kit: A play about Molly for you and your friends to perform.* Middleton, WI: Pleasant Co.

Tripp, V. (1994). *Samantha's theater kit: A play about Samantha for you and your friends to perform.* Middleton, WI: Pleasant Co.

Turkle, B. (1976). *Deep in the forest.* New York: E. P. Dutton.

Ungerer, T. (1986). *Crictor.* New York: Harper & Row.

Van Allsburg, C. (1984). *The mysteries of Harris Burdick.* Boston: Houghton Mifflin.

Van Allsburg, C. (1986). *The stranger.* Boston: Houghton Mifflin.

Viorst, J. (1972). *Alexander and the terrible, horrible, no good, very bad day.* New York: Atheneum.

Walsh-Bellville, C. (1986). *Theater magic: Behind the scenes at a children's theater.* Minneapolis: Carolrhoda Books.

Westcott, N. B. (1988). *The lady with the alligator purse.* Boston: Little, Brown.

White, M. (1993). *Mel White's Readers Theatre anthology: Twenty-eight all-occasion readings for storytellers.* Colorado Springs, CO: Meriwether.

White, W. (1997). *Speaking in stories: Resources for Christian storytellers.* Minneapolis: Augsburg.

White, W. (1986). *Stories for telling: A treasury for Christian storytellers.* Minneapolis: Augsburg.

Wiesner, D. (1991). *Tuesday.* New York: Clarion.

Winter, P. (1976). *The bear and the fly.* New York: Crown.

Winther, B. (1992). *Plays from African tales.* Boston: Plays, Inc.

Wolf, A. (1993). *It's show time!: Poetry from the page to the stage.* Asheville, NC: Poetry Alive!

Wood, A. (1985). *King Bidgood's in the bathtub.* New York: Harcourt Brace Jovanovich.

Young, E. (1989). *Lon Po Po: A Red-Riding Hood story from China.* New York: Philomel.

Zemach, M. (1976). *It could always be worse.* New York: Farrar, Straus, & Giroux.

Drama as Part of the Book's Theme

Berenstain, S., & Berenstain, J. (1986). *The Berenstain bears get stage fright.* New York: Random House.

Booth, C. (1992). *Going live.* New York: Scribner's.

Boyd, C. (1994). *Fall secrets.* New York: Puffin Books.

Brandenberg, F. (1977). *Nice new neighbors.* New York: Scholastic.

Brown, M. (1983). *Arthur's April fool.* New York: Little, Brown.

Byars, B. (1992). *Hooray for the Golly sisters!* New York: Harper Children's Books.

Cohen, M. (1985). *Starring first grade.* New York: Greenwillow.

Coville, B. (1987). *Ghost in the third row.* New York: Bantam.

dePaola, T. (1978). *The Christmas pageant.* Houston, TX: Winston Press.

dePaola, T. (1979). *Flicks.* New York: Harcourt Brace Jovanovich.

dePaola, T. (1983). *Sing, Pierrot, sing: A picture book in mime.* NY: Harcourt Brace Jovanovich.

de Regniers, B. (1982). *Picture book theatre: The mysterious stranger and the magic spell.* San Francisco: (Seabury Press) Harper & Row.

Freeman, D. (1970). *Hattie: The backstage bat.* New York: Viking Press.

Fujikawa, G. (1981). *The magic show.* New York: Grosset and Dunlap.

Gerrard, R. (1992). *Jocasta Carr: Movie star.* New York: Farrar, Straus, & Giroux.

Giff, P. (1984). *The almost awful play.* New York: Viking.

Giff, P. (1992). *Show time at the Polk St. school.* New York: Delacorte Press.

Greydanus, R. (1981). *Hocus pocus, magic show!* Mahwah, NJ: Troll.

Grimm, J., and LeCain, E. (illus). (1978). *The twelve dancing princesses.* New York: Viking.

Holabird, K. (1984). *Angelina and the princess.* New York: C. N. Potter.

Howard, E. (1991). *Aunt Flossie's hats (and crab cakes later).* Boston: Houghton Mifflin.

Kroll, S. (1986). *The big bunny and the magic show.* New York: Holiday House.

Kroll, S. (1988). *Looking for Daniela: A romantic adventure.* New York: Holiday House.

Leedy, L. (1988). *The bunny play.* New York: Holiday House.

Lepscky, I. (1989). *William Shakespeare.* New York: Barron's Educational Series.

Marshall, E. (1981). *Three by the sea.* New York: Dial.

Marshall, J. (1993). *Fox on stage.* New York: Dial.

Martin, A. M. (1984). *Stage fright.* New York: Holiday House.

McCully, E. A. (1992). *Mirette on the high wire.* New York: Putnam's.

Morley, J. (1994). *Entertainment: Screen, stage, and stars.* New York: Franklin Watts.

Robinson, B. (1972). *The best Christmas pageant ever.* New York: Harper & Row.

Sendak, M. (1960). *The sign on Rosie's door.* New York: Harper & Row.

Thee, C. (1994). *Behind the curtain.* New York: Workman.

Tryon, L. (1992). *Albert's play.* New York: Atheneum.

Dance

Doing Dance

Barlin, A. (1993). *Goodnight toes!: Bedtime stories, lullabies, and movement games.* Pennington, NJ: Princeton Book Co.

Bennett, J. (1995). *Rhythmic activities and dance.* Champaign, IL: Human Kinetics.

Brady, Martha (1997). *Dancing hearts: Creative arts with books kids love.* Golden, CO: Falcrum.

Esbensen, B. (1995). *Dance with me.* New York: HarperCollins.

Krementz, J. (1976). *A very young dancer.* New York: Dell.

LaPrise, L. (1996). *The hokey pokey.* New York: Simon & Schuster.

Southgate, M. (1996). *Another way to dance.* New York: Delacorte.

Weiwsan, J. (1993). *Kids in motion: A creative movement and song book.* Milwaukee, WI: Hal Leonard.

Dance in a Book's Theme

Ackerman, K., & Gammell, S. (1988). *Song and dance man.* New York: Knopf.

Asch, F. (1993). *Moondance.* New York: Scholastic.

Auch, M. (1993). *Peeping beauty.* New York: Holiday House.

Baylor, B. (1973). *Sometimes I dance mountains.* New York: Scribner's.

Berenstain, S., & Berenstain, J. (1993). *The Berenstain bears gotta dance!* New York: Random House.

Binford, D. (1989). *Rabbits can't dance!* Milwaukee, WI: Gareth Stevens.

Bornstein, R. (1978). *The dancing man.* New York: Seabury Press.

Carter, A. (1989). *The twelve dancing princesses.* New York: Lippincott.

Daly, N. (1992). *Papa Lucky's shadow.* New York: Margaret K. McElderry Books.

Esbensen, B. J. (1995). *Dance with me* (poems). New York: HarperCollins.

Edwards, R. (1994). *Moles can dance.* Cambridge, MA: Candlewick Press.

Elliot, D. (1979). *Frogs and the ballet.* Ipswich, MA: Gambit.

Freeman, D. (1996). *A rainbow of my own.* New York: Viking.

French, V. (1991). *One ballerina two.* New York: Lothrop.

Gauch, P. (1989). *Bravo, Tanya.* New York: Putnam's.

Gauch, P. (1989). *Dance, Tanya.* New York: Philomel Books.

Getz, A. (1980). *Humphrey the dancing pig.* New York: Dial.

Giannini, E. (1993). *Zorina ballerina.* New York: Simon & Schuster.

Gray, L. M. (1995). *My Mama had a dancing heart.* Orchard Books.

Greene, C. (1983). *Hi, clouds.* Chicago: Children's Press.

Hoff, S. (1994). *Duncan the dancing duck.* New York: Dial.

Holabird, K. (1992). *Angelina dances.* New York: Random House.

Hollinshead, M. (1994). *Nine days wonder.* New York: Philomel.

Hurd, E. (1965). *The day the sun danced.* New York: Harper & Row.

Hurd, E. (1982). *I dance in my red pajamas.* New York: Harper & Row.

Isadora, R. (1980). *My ballet class.* New York: Greenwillow.

Keats, E. J. (1962). *The snowy day.* New York: Viking.

Komaiko, L. (1992). *Aunt Elaine does the dance from Spain.* New York: Doubleday.

Kuklin, S. (1989). *Going to my ballet class.* New York: Macmillan.

Landry, A. (1964). *Come dance with me.* New York: Heineman.

Lasky, K. (1994). *The solo.* New York: Macmillan.

Lionni, L. (1963). *Swimmy.* New York: Pantheon.

Lowery, L. (1995). *Jitter with bug.* Boston: Houghton Mifflin.

Marshall, J. (1990). *The cut-ups carry on.* New York: Viking.

Mathers, P. (1991). *Sophie and Lou.* New York: HarperCollins.

Martin, B. (1970). *The wizard.* New York: Holt, Rinehart and Winston.

Mayer, M. (1971). *The queen always wanted to dance.* New York: Simon & Schuster.

McCully, E. A. (1990). *The evil spell.* New York: Harper & Row.

McPhail, D. (1985). *The dream child.* New York: E. P. Dutton.

Medearis, A. S. (1991). *Dancing with the Indians.* New York: Holiday House.

Mott, E. C. (1996). *Dancing rainbows: A pueblo boy's story.* New York: Cobblehill Books/Dutton.

Myers, W. (1972). *The dancers.* New York: Parents Magazine Press.

Noll, S. (1993). *Jiggle, wiggle, prance.* New York: Puffin Books.

Oxenbury, H. (1983). *The dancing class.* New York: Dial.

Patrick, D. L. (1993). *Red dancing shoes.* New York: Tambourine.

Richardson, J. (1987). *Clara's dancing feet.* New York: Putnam's.

Rockwell, A. (1971). *The dancing stars: An Iroquois legend.* New York: Crowell.

Scheffrin-Falk, G. (1991). *Another celebrated dancing bear.* Scribner's.

Schroeder, A. (1989). *Ragtime turnpie.* Boston: Little, Brown.

Schumaker, W. (1996). *Dance!* Niles, IL: Harcourt Brace Jovanovich.

Sendak, M. (1962). *Alligators all around.* New York: Harper & Row.

Sendak, M. (1963). *Where the wild things are.* New York: Harper & Row.

Shannon, G. (1982). *Dance sway.* New York: Greenwillow.

Shannon, G. (1982). *Dancing the breeze.* New York: Greenwillow.

Simon, C. (1989). *Amy, the dancing bear.* New York: Doubleday.

Skofield, J. (1984). *Nightdances.* New York: Harper & Row.

Spinelli, E. (1993). *Boy, can he dance!* New York: Four Winds Press.

Wallace, I. (1984). *Chin Chang and the Dragon's Dance.* New York: Atheneum.

Waters, K. & Slovenz-Low, M. (1990). *Lion dancer: Earnie Wan's Chinese New Year.* New York: Scholastic.

Wood, A. (1986). *Three sisters.* New York: Dial.

Zion, G., and Graham, M. (1951). *All falling down.* New York: Harper & Row.

Dance History and Appreciation

Alice in wonderland in dance (videorecording) (1993). New York: V.I.E.W. Video.

Anderson, H. C. (1991). *The red shoes.* New York: Simon & Schuster.

Bailey, D. (1991). *Dancing.* Milwaukee: Raintree Press.

Barboza, S. (1992). *I feel like dancing: A year with Jacques D'Amboise and the National Dance Institute.* New York: Crown.

Bottner, B. (1979). *Myra.* New York: Macmillan.

Cinderella: A dance fantasy. (1993). New York: V.I.E.W. Video.

Dood, C., & Soar, S. (1988). *Ballet in motion: A three-dimensional guide to ballet for young people.* New York: Lippincott.

Fonteyn, M. (1989). *Swan Lake.* San Diego: Gulliver.

Gross, R. B. (1980). *If you were a ballet dancer.* New York: Dial.

Haskins, J. (1990). *Black dance in America: A history through its people.* New York: Crowell.

Hoffman, E. T. (1984). *The Nutcracker.* New York: Crown.

Isadora, R. (1991). *Swan Lake.* New York: Putnam's.

Klein, N. (1983). *Baryshnikov's Nutcracker.* New York: Putnam.

Schick, E. (1992). *I have another language, the language is dance.* New York: Macmillan.

Sorine, S. R. (1981). *Our ballet class.* New York: Knopf.

Usborne's starting ballet. Usborne Publishing.

Verdy, V. (1991). *Of swans, sugarplums, and satin slippers: Ballet stories for children.* New York: Scholastic.

Werner, V. (1992). *Petrouchka.* New York: Viking.

Music

Making Music

Adams, P. (1975). *This old man.* New York: Grossett and Dunlap.

Aliki (1974). *Go tell Aunt Rhody.* New York: Macmillan.

Aliki (1968). *Hush, little baby.* New York: Prentice-Hall.

Axelrod, A. (1991). *Songs of the Wild West.* Metropolitan Museum of Art. New York: Simon & Schuster.

Bangs, E. (1976). *Yankee Doodle.* New York: Parents Magazine Press.

Bantok, N. (1990). *There was an old lady.* New York: Viking Penguin.

Barbareski, N. (1985). *Frog went a-courting.* New York: Scholastic.

Bierhorst, J. (1979). *A cry from the earth: Music of the North American Indians.* New York: Atheneum.

Bolam, K., & Bolam, J. (arr.) (1992). *Folksongs from Eastern Europe.* London: Faber Music.

Bolam, K., & Gritton, P. (arr.) (1993). *Folksongs from the Caribbean.* London: Faber Music.

Brett, J. (1990). *The twelve days of Christmas.* New York: Putnam's.

Bryan, A. (1991). *All night, all day: A child's first book of African-American spirituals.* New York: Atheneum.

Bunting, J. (1980). *My first recorder and book.* New York: Barron's.

Campbell, P., et al (1994). *Roots and branches.* Danbury, CT: World Music Press (with CD).

Child, L. (1987). *Over the river and through the woods.* New York: Scholastic.

Cole, J., & Calmenson, S. (1991). *The eentsy, weentsy spider: Fingerplays and action rhymes.* New York: Mulberry Books.

Cooney, B., & Griego, M. C. (1981). *Tortillitas para Mama and other nursery rhymes.* New York: Henry Holt.

Coonover, C. (1976). *Six little ducks.* New York: Crowell.

Corp, R. (arr.) (1993). *Folksongs from Ireland.* London: Faber Music.

Corp, R. (arr.) (1992). *Folksongs from North America.* London: Faber Music.

Corp, R. (arr.) (1991). *Folksongs from the British Isles.* London: Faber Music.

Cracre, L. (1989). *Arroz con leche: Popular songs and rhymes from Latin America.* New York: Scholastic.

Currie, S. (1992). *Music in the Civil War.* Cincinnati: Betterway Books.

de Regniers, B. (1970). *Catch a little fox.* New York: Seabury.

Disney Press (1991). *For our children.* Burbank, CA: Disney Press.

Emberly, B. (1969). *London Bridge is falling down.* New York: Prentice Hall.

Emberly, B. (1969). *One wide river to cross.* New York: Prentice Hall.

Emberly, B. (1969). *Simon's song.* New York: Prentice Hall.

Fiarotta, N. (1993). *Music crafts for kids: The how-to book of music discovery.* New York: Sterling.

Floyd, M. (arr.) (1991). *Folksongs from Africa.* London: Faber Music.

Garson, E. (compiled) (1968). *The Laura Ingalls Wilder songbook.* New York: Harper & Row.

Gauch, P. (1978). *On to Widecombe Fair.* New York: Putnam's.

Gill, M., and Pliska, G. (1993). *Praise for the singing: Songs for children.* Boston: Little, Brown.

Girl Scouts of U.S.A. (1980). *Canciones de nuestra cabana: Songs of our cabana.* New York: Girl Scouts.

Glass, P. (1969). *Singing soldiers: A history of the Civil War in song.* New York: Grosset & Dunlap.

Glazer, T. (1980). *Do your ears hang low? Fifty more musical fingerplays.* New York: Doubleday.

Glazer, T. (1990). *The Mother Goose songbook.* New York: Doubleday.

Glazer, T. (1982). *On top of spaghetti.* New York: Doubleday.

Glazer, T. (1988). *Tom Glazer's treasury of songs for children.* New York: Doubleday.

Griego, F. M. (1980). *Tortillas para Mama.* New York: Holt, Rinehart, & Winston.

Gritton, P. (arr.) (1991). *Folksongs from the Far East.* London: Faber Music.

Gritton, P. (arr.) (1993). *Folksongs from India.* London: Faber Music.

Hart, A. (1993). *Kids make music! Clapping & tapping from Bach to rock.* Charlotte, VT: Williamson.

Hazen, B. (1973). *Frere Jacques.* Philadelphia: Lippincott.

Hoban, T. (1973). *Over, under, through and other spatial concepts.* New York: Macmillan.

Houston, J. (1972). *Song of the dream people: Chants and images of the Indians and Eskimos of North America.* New York: Atheneum.

Jeffers, S. (1974). *All the pretty horses.* New York: Scholastic.

Keats, E. J. (1972). *Over in the meadow.* New York: Scholastic.

Kellogg, S. (1976). *Yankee Doodle.* New York: Parents' Magazine Press.

Kennedy, J. (1983). *Teddy Bear's picnic.* San Marcos, CA: Green Tiger Press.

Kent, J. (1973). *Jack Kent's twelve days of Christmas.* New York: Parents' Magazine Press.

Kidd, R., and Anderson, L. (1992). *On top of Old Smokey: Collection of songs and stories from Appalachia.* Nashville, TN: Ideals Children's Books.

Knight, H. (1981). *The twelve days of Christmas.* New York: Macmillan.

Koontz, R. (1988). *This old man: The counting song.* New York: Putnam's.

Kovalski, M. (1987). *The wheels on the bus.* Boston: Little, Brown.

Krull, K. (1989). *Songs of praise.* San Diego: Harcourt Brace Jovanovich.

Langstaff, J. (1974). *Oh, a hunting we will go.* New York: Atheneum.

Leedy, L. (1988). *The bunny play.* New York: Holiday House.

Livingston, M. (1986). *Earth songs.* New York: Holiday House.

Livingston, M. (1986). *Sea songs.* New York: Holiday House.

Magers, P. (1987). *Sing with me animal songs.* New York: Random House.

McNally, D. (1991). *In a cabin in a wood.* New York: Cobblehill Dutton.

National Gallery of Art (1991). *An illustrated treasury of songs: Traditional American songs, ballads, folk songs, nursery rhymes.* New York: Rizzoli International.

Oram, H., Davis, C., & Kitamura, S. (1993). *A creepy-crawly song book.* New York: Farrar, Straus, & Giroux.

Parker, R. (1978). *Sweet Betsy from Pike: A song from the Gold Rush.* New York: Viking.

Paterson, A. B. (1972). *Waltzing Matilda.* New York: Holt, Rinehart, & Winston.

Peek, M. (1987). *The balancing act: A counting song.* New York: Clarion.

Peek, M. (1988). *Mary wore her red dress and Henry wore his green sneakers.* Boston: Houghton Mifflin.

Peek, M. (1981). *Roll over! A counting song.* Boston: Houghton Mifflin.

Poddany, E. (1967). *The cat in the hat songbook: 19 Seuss-songs for beginners.* New York: Random House.

Quakenbush, T. C. (1975). *The man on the flying trapeze.* Philadelphia: Lippincott.

Quackenbush, T. C. (1973). *She'll be coming 'round the mountain.* New York: Dial.

Rae, M. M. (1989). *The farmer in the dell.* New York: Scholastic.

Raffi (1987). *Down by the bay.* New York: Crown.

Raffi (1989). *The Raffi everything grows songbook.* New York: Crown.

Rounds, G. (1989). *Old MacDonald had a farm.* New York: Holiday House.

Seeger, P. (1989). *Abiyoyo.* New York: Scholastic.

Silberg, J. (1989). *My toes are starting to wiggle! and other easy songs for circle time.* Overland Park, KS: Miss Jackie Music Co.

Spier, P. (1961). *The fox went out on a chilly night.* New York: Doubleday.

Spier, P. (1967). *London Bridge is falling down.* New York: Doubleday.

Stanley, L., ed. (1992). *Rap, the lyrics: The words to rap's greatest hits.* New York: Penguin.

Toop, D. (1991). *Rap attack 2: African rap to global hip hop.* London: Serpent's Tail.

Walter, C. (1995). *Multicultural music: Lyrics to familiar melodies and authentic songs.* Minneapolis: T. S. Denison.

Walther, T. (1981). *Make mine music.* Boston: Little, Brown.

Warren, J. (1991). *Piggyback songs for school.* Everett, WA: Warren Publishing.

Wessells, K. (1982). *The golden songbook.* New York: Golden.

Westcott, N. (1980). *I know an old lady who swallowed a fly.* Boston: Little, Brown.

Westcott, N. (1989). *Skip to my Lou.* Boston: Little, Brown.

Williams, V. (1988). *Music, music for everyone.* New York: Morrow.

Winter, J. (1988). *Follow the drinking gourd.* New York: Knopf.

Wirth, M. (comp.) (1983). *Musical games, finger plays, and rhythmic activities for early childhood.* West Nyack, NY: Parker Publishing.

Wiserman, A. (1979). *Making musical things.* New York: Scribner.

Yokum, J. (1986). *The lullaby songbook.* San Diego: Harcourt Brace Jovanovich.

Yolen, J. (1992). *Jane Yolen's Mother Goose songbook.* Honesdale, PA: Caroline House/Boyds Mills.

Yolen, J. (1989). *The lap-time song and play book.* San Diego: Harcourt Brace Jovanovich.

Making Instruments

Doney, M. (1995). *Musical instruments.* New York: Franklin Watts.

Elliott, D. (1984). *Alligators and music.* Boston: Harvard Common Press.

Fiarotta, N. (1995). *Music crafts for kids: The how-to book of music discovery.* New York: Sterling.

Hawkinson, J. (1969). *Music and instruments for children to make, vol. 1.* Chicago: A. Whitman.

Hopkin, B. (1995). *Making simple musical instruments.* Asheville, NC: Lark Books.

Palmer, H. (1990). *Homemade band: Songs to sing: Instruments to make.* New York: Crown.

Wilt, J. (1978). *Listen!: 76 listening experiences for children, including 60 rhythm and musical instruments to make and use.* Waco, TX: Creative Resources.

Music as Part of Book's Theme

Alexander, L. (1970). *The marvelous misadventures of Sebastian.* New York: Dutton.

Ambrus, V. (1969). *Seven skinny goats.* San Diego: Harcourt Brace Jovanovich.

Angell, J. (1982). *Buffalo nickel blues band.* New York: Bradbury.

Baer, G. (1989). *Thump, thump, rat-a-tat-tat.* New York: Harper & Row.

Bang, M. (1985). *The paper crane.* New York: Greenwillow.

Baylor, B., & Himler, R. (1982). *Moon song.* New York: Scribner's.

Birdseye, T., & Bammell, S. (1988). *Airmail to the moon.* New York: Holiday House.

Blake, Q. (1991). *All join in.* Boston: Little, Brown.

Bodecker, N. M. (1981). *The lost string quartet.* New York: Atheneum.

Bottner, B. (1987). *Zoo song.* New York: Scholastic.

Boynton, S. (1979). *Hester in the wild.* New York: Harper & Row.

Brandt, K. (1993). *Pearl Bailey with a song in her heart.* Mahwah, NJ: Troll.

Brett, J. (1991). *Berlioz the bear.* New York: Putnam's.

Brooks, B. (1986). *Midnight hour encores.* New York: Harper & Row.

Buffett, J., & Buffett, S. J. (1988). *The jolly man.* New York: Harcourt Brace Jovanovich.

Bunting, B., & Zemach, K. (1983). *The travelling men of Ballycoo.* New York: Harcourt Brace Jovanovich.

Burningham, J. (1984). *Granpa.* New York: Crown.

Byars, B. (1985). *The glory girl.* New York: Puffin Books.

Card, O. S. (1980). *Songmaster.* New York: Dial.

Carle, E. (1996). *I see a song.* New York: Scholastic.

Carlson, N. (1983). *Loudmouth George and the cornet.* Minneapolis: Carolrhoda.

Clement, C. (1988). *The voices of the wood.* New York: Penguin.

Crews, D. (1983). *Parade;* (1982) *Carousel.* New York: Greenwillow.

de Paola, T. (1983). *Sing, Pierrot, sing.* San Diego: Harcourt Brace Jovanovich.

Duder, T. (1986). *Jellybean.* New York: Viking.

Dupasquier, P. (1985). *Dear Daddy.* New York: Bradbury.

Edwards, P. K., & Alisson, D. (1987). *Chester and Uncle Willoughby.* Boston: Little, Brown.

Fleischman, P., & Wentworth, J. (1988). *Rondo in C.* New York: Harper & Row.

Freeman, L. (1953). *Pet of the Met.* New York: Viking.

Gilson, J. (1979). *Dial Leroi Rupert, DJ.* New York: Lothrop.

Gioffre, M. (1985). *Starstruck.* New York: Scholastic/Apple.

Goffstein, M. (1977). *Two piano tuners.* New York: Farrar, Straus, & Giroux.

Goffstein, M. B. (1972). *A little Schubert.* New York: Harper & Row.

Greenfield, E. (1988). *Nathaniel talking.* New York: Writers & Readers.

Grimm, J., & Grimm, W. (E. Shub & J. Domanska, trans.) (1980). *The Brementown musicians.* New York: Greenwillow.

Haas, I. (1981). *The little moon theatre.* New York: Atheneum.

Haley, G. E. (1984). *Birdsong.* New York: Crown.

Hantzig, D. (1989). *Pied Piper of Hamlin.* New York: Random House.

Hasley, D., & Gammel, S. (1983). *The old banjo.* New York: Macmillan.

Hedderwick, M. (1985). *Katie Morag and the two grandmothers.* London: Bodley Head.

Hentoff, N. (1965). *Jazz country.* New York: Harper & Row.

Hilgartner, B. (1986). *A murder for Her Majesty.* New York: Harper & Row.

Hill, D. (1978). *Ms. Glee was waiting.* New York: Atheneum.

Hoban, R. (1976). *A bargain for Frances.* New York: Harper & Row.

Hoffman, E. T., & Sendair, M. (1984). *The Nutcracker.* New York: Crown.

Hogrogian, N. (1973). *The cat who loved to sing.* Palmer, AK: Aladdin.

Hughes, S. (1983). *Alfie gives a hand.* New York: Mulberry Books.

Jeffers, S. (1974). *All the pretty horses.* New York: Macmillan.

Johnson, J. W. (1976). *God's trombones.* New York: Viking Penguin.

Johnston, T. (1988). *Pages of music.* New York: Putnam's.

Keats, E. J. (1971). *Apt. 3.* New York: Macmillan.

Keller, C. (compiled) (1985). *Swine lake: Music and dance riddles.* New York: Prentice Hall.

Kherdian, D., & Hogrogian, N. (1990). *The cat's midsummer jamboree.* New York: Putnam's.

Kidd, R. (1988). *Second fiddle: A sizzle & splat mystery.* New York: Lodestar Books.

Komaiko, L., & Westman, B. (1987). *I like music.* New York: Harper & Row.

Krementz, J. (1991). *Very young musician.* New York: Simon & Schuster.

Kroll, S., & Lobel, A. (1988). *Looking for Daniela.* New York: Holiday House.

Lasker, D. (1979). *The boy who loved music.* New York: Viking.

Leodhas, S. N., & Hogrogian, N. (1965). *Always room for one more.* New York: Henry Holt.

Lionni, L. (1979). *Geraldine, the music mouse.* New York: Random House.

Lisle, J. T. (1986). *Sirens and spies.* New York: Bradbury.

Lobel, A. (1966). *The troll music.* New York: Harper & Row.

MacLachlan, P. (1988). *The facts and fictions of Minna Pratt.* New York: Harper & Row.

Marshall, J. (1973). *George and Martha: Encore.* Boston: Houghton Mifflin.

Martin, B., & Rand, T. (1988). *Up and down on the merry-go-round.* New York: Henry Holt.

Martin, B., Archambaut, J., & Endicott, J. (1988). *Listen to the rain.* New York: Henry Holt.

Martin, B., Archambault, J., & Rand, T. (1986). *Barn dance.* New York: Henry Holt.

Maxner, J., & Joyce, W. (1989). *Nicholas Cricket.* New York: Harper & Row.

Mayer, M. (1974). *Frog goes to dinner.* New York: Scholastic.

McCaffrey, A. (1976). *Dragonsong.* New York: Macmillan.

McCloskey, R. (1940). *Lentil.* New York: Viking Penguin.

Menotti, G., & Lemieux, M. (1986). *Amahl and the night visitors.* New York: Morrow.

Newton, S. (1983). *I will call it Georgie's blues.* New York: Viking.

Old, W. (1996). *Duke Ellington: Giant of jazz.* Hillside, NJ: Enlsow.

Paterson, K. (1985). *Come sing, Jimmy Jo.* New York: Dutton.

Paulsen, G. (1985). *Dogsong.* New York: Bradbury.

Peyton, K. M. (1971). *The Pennington Series.* New York: Crowell.

Plume, I. (1980). *The Bremen-Town musicians.* New York: Harper & Row.

Purdy, C. (1994). *Mrs. Merriwether's musical cat.* New York: Putnam's.

Raschka, C. (1992). *Charlie Parker played be bop.* New York: Orchard.

Ray, M. L. (1994). *Pianna.* San Diego: Harcourt Brace Jovanovich.

Rayner, M. (1993). *Garth pig steals the show.* New York: Dutton.

Rylant, C., & Gammell, S. (1985). *The relatives came.* New York: Morrow.

Schick, E. (1977). *One summer night.* New York: Greenwillow.

Schick, E. (1984). *A piano for Julie.* New York: Greenwillow.

Schroeder, A., & Fuchs, B. (1989). *Ragtime tumpie.* Boston: Little, Brown.

Sendak, M. (1981). *Outside over there.* New York: Harper & Row.

Shannon, G. (1981). *The piney woods peddler.* New York: Morrow.

Shannon, G., Aruego, J., & Dewy, A. (1981). *Lizard's song.* New York: Greenwillow.

Sharmat, M. (1991). *Nate the great and musical note.* New York: Dell.

Showell, E. (1983). *Cecilia and the blue mountain boy.* New York: Lothrop.

Skofield, J., & Gundersheimer, D. (1981). *Night dances.* New York: Harper & Row.

Stecher, M. (1980). *Max the music maker.* New York: Lothrop.

Steig, W. (1994). *Zeke Pippin.* New York: HarperCollins.

Stevens, B. (1990). *Handel and the famous sword swallower of Halle.* New York: Philomel.

Stevermer, C. (1992). *River rats.* New York: Harcourt Brace Jovanovich.

Stock, C. (1988). *Sophie's knapsack.* New York: Lothrop.

Taylor, S. (1985). *All-of-a-kind family.* New York: Dell.

Thomas, I. (1981). *Willie blows a mean horn.* New York: Harper & Row.

Treschel, G. (1992). *The lute's tune.* New York: Doubleday.

Turkle, B. (1968). *The fiddler of High Lonesome.* New York: Viking.

van Kampen, V., & Eugen, I. C. (1989). *Orchestranimals.* New York: Scholastic.

Voight, C. (1983). *Dicey's song.* New York: Atheneum.

Walter, M. (1989). *Mariah loves rock.* New York: Macmillan.

Walter, M. P., & Tomes, M. (1980). *Ty's one-man band.* New York: Scholastic.

Wharton, T. (1991). *Hildegard sings.* New York: Farrar, Straus, & Giroux.

Wildsmith, B. (1988). *Carousel.* New York: Knopf.

Williams, V. B. (1983). *Something special for me.* New York: Greenwillow.

Wood, A., Woo, A., & Wood, D. (1988). *Elbert's bad word.* New York: Harcourt Brace Jovanovich.

Yolen, J. (1983). *Commander Toad and the big black hole.* New York: Putnam's.

Yorinks, A., & Egielski, S. (1988). *Brave, Minsky!* New York: Farrar, Straus, & Giroux.

Zolotow, C., & Tafuri, N. (1982). *The song.* New York: Greenwillow.

Music History and Appreciation

The adventures of Peer Gynt: A puppet production (videorecording) (1995). Los Angeles, CA: Laser Light Video.

Ammons, M. (1995). *Music A.D. 450–1995.* Mark Twain Media: Carson-Dellosa Publishing.

Anderson, D. (1982). *The piano makers.* New York: Pantheon.

Arnold, C. (1985). *Music lessons for Alex.* New York: Clarion.

Autexier, P. (1992). *Beethoven, the composer as hero.* New York: Abrams.

Bain, G., & Leather, M. (1986). *The picture life of Bruce Springsteen.* New York: Franklin Watts.

Bayless, K., & Ramsey, M. (1990). *Music: A way of life for the young child.* New York: Merrill.

Berliner, D. C. (1961). *All about the orchestra and what it plays.* New York: Random House.

Bierhorst, J. (1979). *A cry from the earth: Music of the North American Indians.* New York: Four Winds.

Brighton, C. (1990). *Mozart: Scenes from the childhood of the composer.* New York: Doubleday.

Busnar, G. (1979). *It's rock and roll.* New York: Julian Messner.

Bye, L. D. (1988). *Students' guide to the great composers: A guide to music history for students.* Pacific, MO: Bayside Press.

Bye, L. D. (1986). *Mel Bay's student's guide to music theory: A book of music fundamentals.* Pacific, MO: Parker Publishing.

Bye, L. D. (1985). *Students' musical dictionary.* Pacific, MO: Bayside Press.

Carnival of the animals: A puppet production (videorecording) (1996). Los Angeles, CA: Laser Light Video.

Commins, D. B. (1961). *All about the symphony orchestra and what it plays.* New York: Random House.

Deitch, K. M. (1991). *Leonard Bernstein: America's maestro.* Lowell, MS: Discovery Enterprises.

Downing, J. (1990). *Mozart tonight.* New York: Julian Messner.

Emberely, R. (1989). *City sounds.* Boston: Little, Brown.

Emberely, R. (1980). *Jungle sounds.* Boston: Little, Brown.

Englander, R. (1983). *Opera! What's all the screaming about?* New York: Walker.

English, B. L. (1980). *You can't be timid with a trumpet.* New York: Lothrop.

Fonteyn, M. (1987). *Swan Lake.* New York: Harcourt Brace.

Fornatale, P. (1987). *The story of rock n' roll.* New York: Morrow.

Gass, I. (1970). *Mozart: Child wonder, child composer.* New York: Lothrop.

Glass, P. (1969). *Singing soldiers: A history of the Civil War in song.* New York: Grosset & Dunlap.

Greene, C. (1992). *John Philip Sousa, the marching king.* Chicago: Children's Press.

Greens, C. (1992). *Johann Sebastian Bach: Great man of music; Ludwig Van Beethoven, musical pioneer.* Chicago: Children's Press.

Haas, I. (1977). *The Maggie B.* New York: Atheneum.

Hargrove, J. *Pablo Casals.* Chicago: Children's Press.

Hart, M. (1990). *Drumming at the edge of magic: A journey into the spirit of percussion.* New York: Harper & Row.

Haskins, J. (1987). *Black music in America.* New York: Crowell.

Haskins, J. (1986). *Diana Ross: Star supreme.* New York: Puffin.

Hayes, A. (1995). *Meet the marching Smithereens.* San Diego: Harcourt Brace Jovanovich.

Hayes, A. (1991). *Meet the orchestra.* San Diego: Harcourt Brace Jovanovich.

Helprin, M., & Van Allsburg, C. (1990). *Swan lake.* Boston: Houghton Mifflin.

Hughes, L. (1982). *Jazz.* New York: Watts.

Jones, K. M. (1994). *The story of rap music.* Brookfield, CN: Millbrook Press.

Kendall, C. W. (1985). *More stories of composers for young musicians.* Edwardsville, IL: Toadwood.

Kendall, C. W. (1993). *Stories of women composers for young musicians.* Edwardsville, IL: Toadwood.

Lasker, D., & Lasker, J. (1979). *The boy who loved music.* New York: Viking.

Lepsky, I. (1982). *Amadeus Mozart.* New York: Baron's Educational Series.

Lillegard, D. (1987). *Woodwinds.* Chicago: Children's Press.

Mann, W. (1982). *James Galway's music in time.* Englewood Cliffs, NJ: Prentice Hall.

McKissack, P. (1991). *Louis Armstrong: Jazz musician.* Hillside, NJ: Enslow.

Meyerowitz, J. (narrator) (1993). *George Balanchine's The Nutcracker.* Canada: Little, Brown, & Co.

Mitchell, B. (1987). *Raggin': A story about Scott Joplin; America, I hear you: A story about George Gershwin.* Minneapolis, MN: Carolrhoda.

Monceaux, M. (1994). *Jazz: My music, my people.* New York: Knopf.

Monjo, F. N., & Brenner, F. (1975). *Letters to Horseface: Being the story of Wolfgang Amadeus Mozart's journey to Italy.* New York: Viking.

Mundy, S. (1980). *The Usborne story of music.* Tulsa, OK: EDC Publishers.

The Nutcracker: A puppet production (videorecording) (1995). Los Angeles: Laser Light Video Productions.

Parker, J. (1995). *I wonder why flutes have holes and other questions about music.* New York: Kingfisher.

Peter and the wolf: A puppet production (videorecording) (1995). Los Angeles: Laser Light Video Productions.

Pillar, M. (1992). *Join the band!* New York: HarperCollins.

Previn, A., Ed. (1983). *Andre Previn's guide to the orchestra.* New York: Putnam's.

Price, L. (1990). *Aida: A picture book for all ages.* San Diego: Harcourt Brace Jovanovich.

Prokofiev, S. *Peter and the wolf* (book and cassette). New York: Knopf.

Rosenberg, J. (1989). *Sing me a song: Metropolitan opera's book of opera stories for children.* New York: Thames & Hudson.

Sabin, F. (1990). *Mozart, young music genius.* Mahwah, NJ: Troll.

Sabin, L. (1992). *Ludwig van Beethoven: Young composer.* Mahwah, NJ: Troll.

San Souci, R. (retold) (1992). *The firebird.* New York: Dial.

Schaff, P. (1980). *The violin close up.* New York: Four Winds.

Schonberg, H. (1981). *The lives of the great composers.* New York: W. W. Norton.

Schulman, J. (adap.) (1991). *Story of the Nutcracker* (cassette). New York: HarperCollins.

Simon, C. (1992). *Seizi Owaza: Symphony conductor.* Chicago: Children's Press.

Simon, H. W. (1989). *100 Great operas and their stories.* New York: Doubleday.

Spier, P. (1973). *The star-spangled banner.* New York: Doubleday.

Stevens, B. (1983). *Ben Franklin's glass harmonica.* Minneapolis: Carolrhoda.

Stevens, B. (1991). *Handel and the famous sword swallower of Halle.* New York: Philomel.

Suggs, W. W., & Arno, E. (1971). *Meet the orchestra.* New York: Macmillan.

The Swan Lake story (videorecording) (1993). New York: V.I.E.W. Video.

Tames, R. (1991). *Frederick Chopin.* New York: Franklin Watts.

Terkel, S. (1975). *Giants of jazz.* New York: Crowell.

Thompson, W. (1991; 1993). *Pyotr Ilyich Tchaikovsky; Claude Debussy; Franz Schubert; Wolfgang Amadeus Mozart; Ludwig van Beethoven; Joseph Haydn.* New York: Viking.

Venezia, M. (1995). *Aaron Copland;* (1994) *George Gershwin;* (1995) *George Handel.* Chicago: Children's Press.

Ventura, P. (1989). *Great composers.* New York: Putnam's.

Weil, L. (1989). *The magic of music.* New York: Holiday House.

Weil, L. (1982). *Wolferl: The first six years in the life of Wolfgang Mozart.* New York: Holiday House.

Wildlife symphony (video) (1993). Pleasantville, NY: Reader's Digest.

Wilson, R. (1991). *Mozart's story.* London: A. & C. Black.

Wolff, V. E. (1991). *The Mozart season.* New York: Henry Holt.

Zin! Zin! Zin!: A violin (video) (1996). Lincoln, NE: The Library.

Appendix B: Award-Winning Children's Literature*

CANADIAN AWARDS

Governor General's Literary Awards

(Governor General's Awards for Children's Literature)

The award was established in 1975 as the Canada Council Children's Literature Prize. Up to four prizes are awarded annually by the Canada Council in each of the following categories: text in an English-language book, text in a French-language book, illustrations in an English-language book, illustrations in a French-language book. Initially, awards were presented for best writing, but awards for illustration were added in 1977–78. The award honours Canadian citizens creating books for young people.

The Canada Council Children's Literature Prize

1975 Text – ***Shantymen of Cache Lake*** by B. Freeman

1976 Text – ***The Wooden People*** by M. Paperny

1977 Text – ***Listen for the Singing*** by J. Little

1978 Text – ***Hold Fast*** by K. Major
Illustration – ***A Salmon for Simon*** by A. Blades (Text: B. Waterton)

1979 Text – ***Days of Terror*** by B. Smucker
Illustration – ***The Twelve Dancing Princesses*** by L. Gal (Text: J. Lunn)

1980 Text – ***The Trouble with Princesses*** by C. Harris
Illustration – ***Petrouchka*** by E. Cleaver

1981 Text – ***The Guardian of Isis*** by M. Hughes
Illustration – ***Ytek and the Arctic Orchid: An Inuit Legend*** by H. Woodall (Text: G. Hewitt)

1982 Text – ***Hunter in the Dark*** by M. Hughes
Illustration – ***ABC/123: The Canadian Alphabet and Counting Book*** by V. Van Kampen

1983 Text – ***The Ghost Horse of the Mounties*** by S. O'Huigin
Illustration – ***The Little Mermaid*** by L. Gal (Text: M. Crawford Maloney)

1984 Text – ***Sweetgrass*** by J. Hudson
Illustration – ***Lizzy's Lion*** by M.-L. Gay (Text: D. Lee)

1985 Text – ***Julie*** by C. Taylor
Illustration – ***Murdo's Story*** by T. Gallagher (Text: M. Scribe)

1986 Text – ***Shadow in Hawthorn Bay*** by J. Lunn
Illustration – ***Have You Seen Birds?*** by B. Reid (Text: J. Oppenheim)

Governor General's Literary Awards

In 1986 this award was renamed the Governor General's Award for Children's Literature.

English-Language Awards

1987 Text – ***Galahad Schwartz and the Cockroach Army*** by M. Nyberg
Illustration – ***Rainy Day Magic*** by M.-L. Gay

1988 Text – ***The Third Magic*** by W. W. Katz
Illustration – ***Amos's Sweater*** by K. LaFave (Text: J. Lunn)

1989 Text – ***Bad Boy*** by D. Wieler
Illustration – ***The Magic Paintbrush*** by R. Muller (Text: R. Muller)

1990 Text – ***Redwork*** by M. Bedard
Illustration – ***The Orphan Boy*** by P. Morin (Text: T. M. Mollel)

1991 Text – ***Pick-Up Sticks*** by S. Ellis
Illustration – ***Doctor Kiss Says Yes*** by J. Fitzgerald, (Text: T. Jam)

1992 Text – ***Hero of Lesser Causes*** by J. Johnston
Illustration – ***Waiting for the Whales*** by R. Lightburn (Text: S. McFarlane)

1993 Text – ***Some of the Kinder Planets*** by T. Wynne-Jones
Illustration – ***Sleep Tight, Mrs. Ming*** by M. Levert (Text: S. Jennings)

1994 Text – ***Adam and Eve and Pinch-Me*** by J. Johnston
Illustration – ***Josepha: A Prairie Boy's Story*** by M. Kimber (Text: J. McGugan)

1995 Text – ***The Maestro*** by T. Wynne-Jones
Illustration – ***The Last Quest of Gilgamesh*** by L. Zeman (Text: L. Zeman)

1996 Text – ***Ghost Train*** by P. Yee
Illustration – ***The Rooster's Gift*** by E. Beddows (Text: P. Conrad)

1997 Text – ***Awake and Dreaming*** by K. Pearson
Illustration – ***The Party*** by B. Reid (Text: B. Reid)

1998 Text – ***The Hollow Tree*** by J. Lunn
Illustration – ***A Child's Treasury of Nursery Rhymes*** by K. MacDonald Denton (Selected by K. MacDonald Denton)

*P = primary ages 4–8; I = intermediate; I–U and U = young adult ages 13+.

The Canadian Library Association Book of the Year for Children

Presented by the Canadian Library Association since 1947, this award recognizes the most distinguished children's book published that year by a Canadian citizen. Beginning in 1954, an additional award was created for a French-language book.

English-language awards:

1947 *Starbuck Valley Winter* by R. Haig-Brown,
1948 *Kristi's Trees* by M. Dunham
1949 No Award
1950 *Franklin of the Arctic* by R. S. Lambert
1951 No Award
1952 *The Sun Horse* by C. A. Clark
1953 No Award
1954 *Mgr. de Laval* by E. S. J. Gervais
1955 No Awards
1956 *Train by Tiger Lily* by L. Riley
1957 *Glooskap's Country* by C. Macmillan
1958 *Lost in the Barrens* by F. Mowat
1959 *The Dangerous Cove* by J. F. Hayes
1960 *The Golden Phoenix* by M. Barbeau & M. Hornyansky
1961 *The St. Lawrence* by W. Toye
1962 No English language award.
1963 *The Incredible Journey* by S. Burnford
1964 *The Whale People* by R. Haig-Brown
1965 *Tales of Nanabozho* by D. Reid
1966 *Tikta' Liktak* by J. Houston
The Double Knights by J. McNeal
1967 *Raven's Cry* by C. Harris
1968 *The White Archer* by J. Houston
1969 *And Tomorrow the Stars* by K. Hill
1970 *Sally Go Round the Sun* by E. Fowke
1971 *Cartier Discovers the St. Lawrence* by W. Toye
1972 *Mary of Mile 18* by A. Blades
1973 *The Marrow of the World* by R. Nichols
1974 *The Miraculous Hind* by E. Cleaver
1975 *Alligator Pie* by D. Lee
1976 *Jacob Two-Two Meets the Hooded Fang* by M. Richler
1977 *Mouse Woman and the Vanished Princess* by C. Harris
1978 *Garbage Delight* by D. Lee
1979 *Hold Fast* by K. Major
1980 *River Runners: A Tale of Hardship and Bravery* by J. Houston
1981 *The Violin Maker's Gift* by D. Kushner
1982 *The Root Cellar* by J. Lunn
1983 *Up to Low* by B. Doyle
1984 *Sweetgrass* by J. Hudson
1985 *Mama's Going to Buy You a Mockingbird* by J. Little
1986 *Julie* by C. Taylor
1987 *Shadow in Hawthorn Bay* by J. Lunn
1988 *A Handful of Time* by K. Pearson
1989 *Easy Avenue* by B. Doyle
1990 *The Sky is Falling* by K. Pearson
1991 *Redwork* by M. Bedard
1992 *Eating Between the Lines* by K. Major
1993 *Ticket to Curlew* by C. Barker Lottridge
1994 *Some of the Kinder Planets* by T. Wynne-Jones
1995 *Summer of the Mad Monk* by C. Taylor
1996 *The Tiny Kite of Eddie Wing* by M. Trottier
1997 *Uncle Ronald* by B. Doyle
1998 *Silverwing* by K. Oppel

Canadian Library Association Young Adult Book Award

The award was established in 1980 and is awarded annually by the Canadian Library Association for the best work of creative literature (novel, play, or poetry) for young adults. The author must be a Canadian citizen and the book must be published in Canada.

1981 *Far from Shore* by K. Major
1982 *Superbike* by J. Brown
1983 *Hunter in the Dark* by M. Hughes
1984 *The Druid's Tune* by O. R. Melling
1985 *Winners* by M.-E. Lang Collura
1986 *The Quarter-Pie Window* by M. Brandis
1987 *Shadow in Hawthorn Bay* by J. Lunn
1988 *January, February, June or July* by H. Fogwell Porter
1989 *Who Is Frances Rain?* by M. Buffie
1990 *Bad Boy* by D. Wieler
1991 *The Leaving* by B. Wilson
1992 *Strandia* by S. L. Reynold
1993 *There Will Be Wolves* by K. Bradford
1994 *Nobody's Son* by S. Stewart
1995 *Adam and Eve and Pinch-Me* by J. Johnson
1996 *The Maestro* by T. Wynne-Jones
1997 *Takes: Stories for Young Adults* edited by R.P. MacIntyre
1998 *Bone Dance* by M. Brooks

The Amelia Frances Howard-Gibbon Illustrator's Award

Awarded since 1971 by the Canadian Library Association, this medal honours excellence in children's illustration in a book published in Canada. The award must go to a citizen or resident of Canada. Unless otherwise indicated, the author is also the illustrator.

1971 ***The Wind Has Wings*** edited by M. A. Downie and Barbara Robertson, illustrated by E. Cleaver

1972 ***A Child in Prison Camp*** by S. Takashima

1973 ***Au Delà du Soleil/Beyond the Sun*** by J. de Roussan

1974 ***A Prairie Boy's Winter*** by W. Kurelek

1975 ***The Sleighs of My Childhood/Les Traineaux de Mon Enfance*** by C. Italiano

1976 ***A Prairie Boy's Summer*** by W. Kurelek

1977 ***Down by Jim Long's Stage: Rhymes for Children and Young Fish*** by A. Pittman, illustrated by P. Hall

1978 ***The Loon's Necklace*** by W. Toye, illustrated by E. Cleaver

1979 ***A Salmon for Simon*** by B. Waterton, illustrated by A. Blades

1980 ***The Twelve Dancing Princesses*** by L. Gal

1981 ***The Trouble with Princesses*** by D. Tait

1982 ***Ytek and the Arctic Orchid: An Inuit Legend*** by H. Woodall

1983 ***Chester's Barn*** by L. Climo

1984 ***Zoom at Sea*** by T. Wynne-Jones, illustrated by D. Nutt

1985 ***Chin Chiang and the Dragon's Dance*** by I. Wallace

1986 ***Zoom Away*** by T. Wynne-Jones, illustrated by K. Nutt

1987 ***Moonbeam on a Cat's Ear*** by M.-L. Gay

1988 ***Rainy Day Magic*** by M.-L. Gay

1989 ***Amos's Sweater*** by J. Lunn, illustrated by K. LaFave

1990 ***Til All the Stars Have Fallen: Canadian Poems for Children*** selected by D. Booth, illustrated by K. MacDonald Denton

1991 ***The Orphan Boy*** by T. M. Mollel, illustrated by P. Morin

1992 ***Waiting for the Whales*** by R. Lightburn, illustrated by S. McFarlane

1993 ***The Dragon's Pearl*** by J. Lawson, illustrated by P. Morin

1994 ***Last Leaf First Snowflake to Fall*** by L. Yerxa

1995 ***Gifts*** by J. E. Bogart, illustrated by B. Reid

1996 ***Just Like New*** by A. Mason, illustrated by K. Reczuch

1997 ***Ghost Train*** by P. Yee, illustrated by H. Chan

1998 ***The Party*** by B. Reid

Elizabeth Mrazik-Cleaver Canadian Picture Book Award

Established in 1986 by the National Library of Canada and the International Board on Books for Young People in memory of children's book illustrator Elizabeth Mrazik-Cleaver (1932–1985). The award is presented annually, unless no book is judged deserving of the award, to a Canadian children's book illustrator whose work on a new book is deemed both original and worthy.

1986 ***By the Sea: An Alphabet Book*** by A. Blades

1987 ***Have You Seen Birds?*** by B. Reid (Text: J. Oppenheim)

1988 ***Can You Catch Josephine?*** by S. Poulin

1989 ***Night Cars*** by E. Beddows (Text: Teddy Jam)

1990 ***The Name of the Tree*** by I. Wallace (Text: C. Baker Lottridge)

1991 ***The Orphan Boy*** by P. Morin (Text: T. Mollel)

1992 ***Waiting for the Whales*** by R. Lightburn (Text: S. McFarlane)

1993 ***Two by Two*** by B. Reid

1994 ***Last Leaf First Snowflake to Fall*** by L. Yerxa

1995 ***Josepha: A Prairie Boy's Story*** by M. Kimber (Text: J. McGugan)

1996 ***Selina and the Bear Paw Quilt*** by J. Wilson (Text: B. Smucker)

1997 ***Ghost Train*** by H. Chan (Text: P. Yee)

1998 ***Rainbow Bay*** by P. Milleli (Text: S. Hume)

The Geoffrey Bilson Award for Historical Fiction for Young People

Established in 1988 in memory of respected historian and children's author Geoffrey Bilson, the annual prize of $1,000 has been made possible by the Canadian children's publishing industry. It is awarded to a Canadian author for an outstanding work of historical fiction for young people by the Canadian Children's Book Centre.

1988 ***Lisa*** by C. Matas

1989 ***Mystery in the Frozen Lands*** by M. Godfrey

Rachel's Revolution by D. Perkyns

1990 ***The Sky is Falling*** by K. Pearson

1991 *The Sign of the Scales* by M. Brandis

1992 No award given

1993 ***Ticket to Curlew*** by C. B. Lottridge

1994 ***The Lights Go on Again*** by K. Pearson

1995 *The Dream Carvers* by J. Clark

1996 ***Rebellion: A Story of Upper Canada*** by M. Brandis

1997 *To Dance at the Palais Royale* by J. McNaughton

Mr. Christie's™ Book Award

Sponsored by Christie Brown & Co., a division of Nabisco Brands Ltd., the award was established in 1990 to encourage the development and publishing of high-quality Canadian children's books and to stimulate children's desire to read. Books must be created by a Canadian author and/or illustrator. At present, there are three categories in both English and French.

English Awards:

1990 Illustration – ***The Name of the Tree*** by I. Wallace (Text: C. Lottridge)
Text – ***The Sky is Falling*** by K. Pearson

1991 Illustration – ***The Story of Little Quack*** by K. Macdonald Denton (Text: B. Gibson)
Text – ***Covered Bridge*** by B. Doyle

1992 Illustration – ***Zoe* Board Books** (*Zoe's Rainy Day, Zoe's Snowy Day, Zoe's Windy Day, Zoe's Sunny Day*) by B. Reid
Text – ***The Ice Cream Store*** by D. Lee

1993 Illustration – ***A Prairie Alphabet*** by Y. Moore (Text: J. Bannatyne-Cugnet)
Text (Ages 8 and under) – ***There Were Monkeys in My Kitchen*** by S. Fitch
Text (Ages 9–14) – ***The Story of Canada*** by J. Lunn and C. Moore

1994 Ages 7 and under – ***Brewster Rooster*** by B. Lucas

Ages 8–11 – ***A Little Tiger in the Chinese Night*** by S. N. Zhang

Last Leaf First Snowflake to Fall by L. Yerxa
Ages 12 and over – ***Ran Van the Defender*** by D. Wieler

1995 Ages 7 and under – ***Thor*** by W. D. Valgardson, author; A. Zhang, illustrator

Ages 8–11 – ***A Pioneer Story*** by B. Greenwood; H. Collins, illustrator
Ages 12 and over – ***Out of the Blue*** by S. Ellis

1996 Ages 7 and under – ***How Smudge Came*** by N. Gregory, author; R. Lightburn, illustrator
Ages 8–11 – ***Jacob Two-Two's First Spy Case*** by M. Richler
Ages 12 and over – ***The Dream Carvers*** by J. Clark

1997 Ages 7 and under – ***The Fabulous Song*** by D. Gillmor, author; M.-L. Gay, illustrator
Ages 8–11 – ***Discovering the Iceman*** by S. Tanaka and L. McGaw
Ages 12 and over – ***Uncle Ronald*** by B. Doyle

1998 Ages 7 and under – ***Biscuits in the Cupboard*** by B. Nichol, author; P. Beha, illustrator

Ages 8–11 – ***The House of Wooden Santas*** by K. Major, I. George, and N. Pratt
Ages 12 and over – ***Silverwing*** by K. Oppel

Information Book Award

This award was established in 1987 by the Children's Literature Roundtables of Canada and is awarded for an outstanding information book for children ages 5 to 15, written in English by a Canadian citizen, and published in Canada during the previous year.

1987 ***Looking at Insects*** by D. Suzuki.

1988 ***Let's Celebrate*** by C. Parry.

1989 ***Exploring the Sky by Day*** by T. Dickinson.

1990 ***Wolf Island*** by C. Godkin.

1991 ***Hands On, Thumbs Up*** by C. Gryski.

1992 ***A Tree in a Forest*** by J. Thornhill.

1993 ***The Story of Canada*** by J. Lunn, C. Moore, and A. Daniel.

1994 ***On the Shuttle: Eight Days in Space*** by B. Bondar with Dr. R. Bondar

Cowboy: A Kid's Album by L. Granfield

1995 ***A Pioneer Story: The Daily Life of a Canadian Family in 1840*** by B. Greenwood (H. Collins, illustrator)

1996 ***In Flanders Fields: The Story of the Poem*** by L. Granfield (J. Wilson, illustrator)

1997 ***On Board the Titanic*** by Shelley Tanaka (K. Marschall, illustrator)

1998 ***The Buried City of Pompeii*** by S. Tanaka (G. Ruhl, illustrator)

AMERICAN AWARDS

THE RANDOLPH CALDECOTT MEDAL for the most distinguished picture book for children published in the United States during the preceding year. Sponsored by American Library Association.

1938 ***Animals of the Bible, A Picture Book*** by H. D. Fish. Illus. by D. Lathrop (P). HONORS: *Seven Simeons: A Russian Tale* (Trad., P), *Four and Twenty Blackbirds* (Trad., P).

1939 ***Mei Li*** by T. Handforth (Realism, P). HONORS: *The Forest Pool* (Realism, P), *Wee Gillis* (Realism, P), *Snow White and the Seven Dwarfs* (Trad., P), *Barkis* (Realism, P), *Andy and the Lion* (Fant., P).

1940 ***Abraham Lincoln*** by I. Aulaire & E. P. d'Aulaire (Biog., P). HONORS: *Cock-a-Doodle-Doo* (Animal realism, P), *Madeline* (Realism, P), *The Ageless Story* (Bible, P).

1941 ***They Were Strong and Good*** by R. Lawson (Biog., P). HONORS: *April's Kittens* (Realism, P).

1942 ***Make Way for Ducklings*** by R. McCloskey (Animal Fant., P). HONORS: *An American ABC* (Alphabet, P), *In My Mother's House* (Info., P), *Paddle-to-the-Sea* (Info., P), *Nothing at All* (Animal Fant., P).

1943 ***The Little House*** by V. Burton (Fant., P). HONORS: *Dash and Dart* (Realism, P), *Marshmallow* (Realism, P).

1944 ***Many Moons*** by J. Thurber. Illus. by L. Slobodkin (Modern folktale, P). HONORS: *Small Rain: Verses from the Bible* (Bible, P), *Pierre Pigeon* (Realism, P), *The Mighty Hunter* (Fant., P), *A Child's Good Night Book* (Realism, P), *Good Luck Horse* (Trad., P).

1945 ***Prayer for a Child*** by R. Field. Illus. by E. Jones (Realism, P). HONORS: *Mother Goose: Seventy-Seven Verses with Pictures* (Trad., P), *In the Forest,* (Fant., P), *Yonie Wondernose* (Realism, P), *The Christmas Anna Angel* (Modern folktale, P).

1946 ***The Rooster Crows*** selected and Illus. by M. and M. Petersham (Mother Goose rhymes, P). HONORS: *Little Lost Lamb* (Realism, P), *Sing Mothers Goose* (Nursery songs, P), *My Mother Is the Most Beautiful Woman in the World* (Trad., P), *You Can Write Chinese* (Info., P).

1947 ***The Little Island*** by G. MacDonald. Illus. by L. Weisgard (Fant., P). HONORS: *Rain Drop Splash* (Info., P), *Boats on the River* (Info., P), *Timothy Turtle* (Animal Fant., P), *Pedro, the Angel of Olvera Street* (Realism, P), *Sing in Praise: A Collection of the Best Loved Hymns* (Info., P).

1948 ***White Snow, Brite Snow*** by A. Tresselt. Illus. by R. Duvoisin (Realism, P). HONORS: *Stone Soup: An Old Tale* (Trad., P), *McElligot's Pool* (Fant., P), *Bambino the Clown* (Realism, P), *Roger and the Fox* (Realism, P), *Song of Robin Hood* (Trad., I-U).

1949 ***The Big Snow*** by B. and E. Hader (Animal realism, P). HONORS: *Blueberries for Sal* (Realism, P), *All Around the Town* (Alphabet, P), *Juanita* (Realism, P), *Fish in the Air* (Fant., P).

1950 ***Song of the Swallows*** by L. Politi (Realism, P). HONORS: *America's Ethan Allen* (Biog., P), *The Wild Birthday Cake* (Realism, P), *The Happy Day* (Animal Fantasy, P), *Henry—Fisherman* (Realism, P), *Bartholomew and the Oobleck* (Modern folktale, P).

1951 ***The Egg Tree*** by K. Milhous (Realism, P). HONORS: *Dick Wittington and His Cat* (Trad., P), *The Two Reds* (Fantasy P), *If I Ran the Zoo* (Fant., P), *T-Bone, the Baby-Sitter* (Realism, P), *The Most Wonderful Doll in the World* (Realism, P).

1952 ***Finders Keepers*** by Will (pseud. for W. Lipkind). Illus. by Nicolas (N. Mordvinoff) (Modern Folktale, P). HONORS: *Mr. T. W. Anthony Woo* (Modern Folktale, P), *Skipper's John's Cook* (Realism, P), *All Falling Down* (Info., P), *Bear Party* (Animal Fant., P), *Feather Mountain* (Modern folktale, P).

1953 ***The Biggest Bear*** by L. Ward (Realism, P). HONORS: *Puss in Boots* (Trad., P), *One Morning in Maine* (Realism, P), *Ape in a Cape: An Alphabet of Odd Animals* (Alphabet, P), *The Storm Book* (Info., P), *Five Little Monkeys* (Animal Fant., P).

1954 ***Madeline's Rescue*** by L. Bemelmans (Realism, P). HONORS: *Journey Cake, Ho!* (Trad., P), *When Will the World Be Mine?* (Animal Fant., P), *The Steadfast Tin Soldier* (Modern folktale, P), *A Very Special House* (Fant., P), *Green Eyes* (Animal Fant., P).

1955 ***Cinderella, or the Little Glass Slipper*** by C. Perrault. Trans. and Illus. by M. Brown (Trad., P). HONORS: *Book of Nursery and Mother Goose Rhymes* (Nursery rhymes, P), *Wheel on the Chimney* (Realism, P), *The Thanksgiving Story* (Hist. fiction, USA, P).

1956 ***Frog Went A-Courtin',*** retold by J. Langstaff. Illus. by F. Rojankovsky (Trad., P). HONORS: *Play with Me* (Realism, P), *Crow Boy* (Realism, P).

1957 ***A Tree Is Nice*** by J. Udry. Illus. by M. Simont (Info., P). HONORS: *Mr. Penny's Race Horse* (Animal Fant., P), *1 is One* (Counting, P), *Anatole* (Animal Fant., P), *Gillespie and the Guards* (Realism, P), *Lion* (Animal Fant., P).

1958 ***Time of Wonder*** by R. McCloskey (Realism, P). HONORS: *Fly High, Fly Low* (Animal Fant., P), *Anatole and the Cat* (Animal Fant., P).

1959 ***Chanticleer and the Fox*** by Chaucer. Adapted and Illus. by B. Cooney (Trad., P). HONORS: *The House That Jack Built* ("La Maison Que Jacques a Batie"): A Picture Book in Two Languages (Info., P), *What Do You Say, Dear? A Book of Manners for All Occasions* (Fant., P), *Umbrella* (Realism, P).

1960 ***Nine Days to Christmas*** by M. Ets and A. Labastida. Illus. by M. Ets (Realism, P). HONORS: *Houses from the Sea* (Info.P), *The Moon Jumpers* (Realism, P).

1961 ***Baboushka and the Three Kings*** by R. Robbins. Illus. by N. Sidjakov (Trad., P). HONORS: *Inch by Inch* (Animal Fant., P).

1962 ***Once a Mouse,*** retold by M. Brown (Trad., P). HONORS: *The Fox Went out on a Chilly Night* (Trad., P), *Little Bear's Visit* (Animal Fant., P), *The Day We Saw the Sun Come Up* (Info., P).

1963 ***The Snowy Day*** by E. J. Keats (Realism, P). HONORS: *The Sun Is a Golden Earring* (Modern folktales, P–I), *Mr. Rabbit and the Lovely Present* (Animal Fant., P).

1964 ***Where the Wild Things Are*** by M. Sendak (Fant., P). HONORS: *Swimmy* (Animal Fant., P), *All in the Morning Early* (Trad., P), *Mother Goose and Nursery Rhymes* (Trad., P).

1965 ***May I Bring a Friend?*** by B. de Regiers. Illus. by B. Montresor (Fant., P). HONORS: *Rain Makes Applesauce* (Fant., P), *The Wave* (Trad., P–I), *A Pocketful of Crickets* (Realism, P).

1966 ***Always Room for One More*** by S. Nic Leodhas (pseud. for L. Alger). Illus. by N. Hogrogian (Trad., P). HONORS: *Hide and Seek* (Realism, P.), *Just Me* (Realism, P), *Tom Tit Tot* (Trad., P).

1967 ***Sam, Bangs and Moonshine*** by E. Ness (Realism, P). HONORS: *One Wide River to Cross* (Bible, P).

1968 ***Drummer Hoff,*** adapted by B. Emberley. Illus. by Ed Emberley (Trad., P). HONORS: *Frederick* (Animal Fant., P), *Seashore Story* (Realism, P), *The Emperor and the Kite* (Mod. folktales, P).

1969 ***The Fool of the World and the Flying Ship: A Russian Tale*** by A. Ransome. Illus. by U. Shulevitz (Trad., P). HONORS: *Why the Sun and the Moon Live in the Sky: An African Folktale* (Trad., P).

1970 ***Sylvester and the Magic Pebble*** by W. Steig (Animal Fant., P). HONORS: *Goggles* (Realism, P), *Alexander and the Wind-up Mouse* (Animal Fant., P), *Pop Corn and Ma Goodness* (Modern folktale, P), *Thy Friend, Obadiah* (Hist. fic., New England, 1700s, P), *The Judge: An Untrue Tale* (Modern folktales, P).

1971 ***A Story, A Story: An African Tale*** by G. Haley (Trad., P). HONORS: *The Angry Moon* (Trad., P), *Frog and Toad Are Friends* (Animal Fant., P), *In the Night Kitchen* (Fant., P).

1972 ***One Fine Day*** by N. Hogrogian (Traditional, P). HONORS: *If All the Seas Were One Sea* (Trad., P), *Moja Means One: Swahili Counting Book* (Counting, P), *Hildilid's Night* (Modern folktale, P).

1973 ***The Funny Little Woman,*** retold by A. Mosel. Illus. by Dutton (Trad., P). HONORS: *Hosie's Alphabet* (Alphabet, P–I), *When Clay Sings* (Info., P), *Snow-White and the Seven Dwarfs* (Trad., P), *Anansi the Spider: A Tale from the Ashanti* (Trad., P).

1974 ***Duffy and the Devil,*** retold by H. Zemach. Illus. by M. Zemach (Trad., P). HONORS: *Three Jovial Huntsmen* (Trad., P), *Cathedral: The Story of Its Construction* (Info., I–YA).

1975 ***Arrow to the Sun,*** adapted and Illus. by G. McDermott (Trad., P). HONORS: *Jambo Means Hello: Swahili Alphabet Book* (Alphabet, P).

1976 ***Why Mosquitoes Buzz in People's Ears,*** retold by V. Aadema. Illus. by L. and D. Dillon (Trad., P). HONORS: *The Desert Is Theirs* (Info., P), *Strega Nona* (Trad., P–I).

1977 ***Ashanti to Zulu: African Traditions*** by M. Musgrove. Illus. by L. and D. Dillon (Info., P–I). HONORS: *The Amazing Bone* (Fant., P), *The Contest* (Trad., P), *Fish for Supper* (Realism, P), *The Golem: A Jewish Legend* (Trad., P–I), *Hawk, I'm Your Brother* (Realism, P–I).

1978 ***Noah's Ark*** by P. Spier (Bible/Wordless, P). HONORS: *Castle* (Info., ages 8–YA), *It Could Always Be Worse* (Trad., P).

1979 ***The Girl Who Loved Wild Horses*** by P. Goble (Trad., P). HONORS: *Freight Train* (Inform. Concept, P), *The Way to Start a Day* (Info., P–I).

1980 ***Ox-Cart Man*** by D. Hall. Illus. by B. Cooney (Hist. fic., New England, 1800s, P–I). HONORS: *Ben's Trumpet* (Realism, P), *The Treasure* (Trad., P), *The Garden of Abdul Gasazi* (Fant., P).

1981 ***Fables*** by A. Lobel (Animal Fant., P). HONORS: *The Bremen-Town Musicians* (Trad., P), *The Grey Lady and the Strawberry Snatcher* (Fant./wordless, P), *Mice Twice* (Animal Fant., P), *Truck* (Concept, P).

1982 ***Jumanji*** by C. VanAllsburg (Fant., P). HONORS: *A Visit to William Blake's Inn: Poems for Innocent and Experienced Travelers* (Biog./Poetry, I), *Where the Buffaloes Begin* (Trad., ages P), *On Market Street* (Alphabet, P), *Outside Over There* (Fant., I).

1983 ***Shadow*** by B. Cendrars. Trans. and Illus. by M. Brown (Trad., I). HONORS: *When I Was Young in the Mountains* (Realism, P–I), *A Chair for My Mother* (Realism, P).

1984 ***The Glorious Flight: Across the Channel with Louis Bleriot*** by A. and M. Provensen (Hist. fic., France, 1909, P–I). HONORS: *Ten, Nine Eight* (Counting, P), *Little Red Riding Hood* (Trad., ages P–I).

1985 ***Saint George and the Dragon,*** adapted by M. Hodges. Illus. by T. S. Hyman (Trad., P–I). HONORS: *Hansel and Gretel* (Trad., P), *The Story of Jumping Mouse* (Trad., P–I), *Have You Seen My Duckling?* (Animal Fant., P).

1986 ***The Polar Express*** by C. Van Allsburg (Fant., P–I). HONORS: *The Relatives Came* (Realism, P–I), *King Bidgood's in the Bathtub* (Fant., P–I).

1987 ***Hey, Al*** by A. Yorinks. Illus. by R. Egielski (Fant., P–I). HONORS: *The Village of Round and Square Houses* (Trad., P–I), *Alphabatics* (Alphabet, P), *Rumpelstiltskin* (Trad., P–I).

1988 ***Owl Moon*** by J. Yolen. Illus. by J. Schoenherr (Realism, P). HONORS: *Mufaro's Beautiful Daughters* (Trad., P–I).

1989 ***Song and Dance Man*** by K. Ackerman. Illus. by S. Gammell (Realism, P–I). HONORS: *Free Fall* (Fant./Wordless, P–I), *Goldilocks and the Three Bears* (Modern Folktale, P), *Mirandy and Brother Wind* (Trad., P–I), *The Boy of the Three-Year Nap* (Trad., P–I).

1990 ***Lon Po Po: A Red Riding Hood Story from China.*** Trans. and Illus. by E. Young (Trad., P). HONORS: *Hershel and the Hannukkah Goblins* (Modern folktale, P–I), *The Talking Eggs* (Trad., P–I), *Bill Peet: An AutoBiog* (Biog., P–I), *Color Zoo* (Concept, P).

1991 ***Black and White*** by D. Macaulay (Mystery, P–I). HONORS: *Puss 'n Boots* (Trad., P), *"More, More, More" Said the Baby: 3 Love Stories* (Realism, P).

1992 ***Tuesday*** by D. Wiesner (Fant./Wordless, P–I). HONORS: *Tar Beach* (Multicultural, African-American, P–I).

1993 ***Mirette on the High Wire*** by E. McCully (Realism, P–I). HONORS: *Seven Blind Mice* (Modern folktale, P–I), *The Stinky Cheese Man and Other Fairly Stupid Tales* (Modern folktale, P–I), *Working Cotton* (Realism, African-American, P–I).

1994 ***Grandfather's Journey*** by A. Say (Biog., P–I). HONORS: *Peppe the Lamplighter* (Realism, P–I), *In the Small, Small Pond* (Pattern, P), *Owen* (Animal Fant., P), *Raven: A Trickster Tale from the Pacific Northwest* (Trad. Native American, P), *Yo! Yes?* (Realism/ Multicultural, P-I).

1995 ***Smoky Night*** by E. Bunting. Illus. by D. Diaz (Realism/Multicultural, P). HONORS: *Swamp Angel* (Modern Folktale, P–I), *John Henry* (Trad., P–I), *Time Flies* (Wordless, P–I).

1996 ***Officer Buckle and Gloria*** by P. Rathmann (Cont. Fiction, P). HONORs: *Alphabet City* (Concept [alphabet], P), *Zin! Zin! Zin!: A Violin* (Inform. [Music instruments], P–I), *The Faithful Friend* (Fant., P–I), *Tops & Bottoms* (Fant., P).

1997 ***Golem*** by D. Wisniewski (Legend, P–I). HONORS: *Hush!: A Thai Lullaby* (Contemp. Fic, P), *The Graphic Alphabet.* (Concept [alphabet], P), *The Paperboy,* (High Fant., P), *Starry Messenger* (Biog. [Galileo], P–I).

1998 ***Rapunzel*** by P. O. Zelinsky (Folktale, P). HONORS: *Harlem: A Poem* (Poetry, I–U), *The Gardener* (Hist. Fic. [Depression], P), *There Was an Old Lady Who Swallowed a Fly* (High Fant., P).

THE JOHN NEWBERY MEDAL for the most distinguished contribution to children's literature published during the preceding year. Presented by the American Library Association.

1922 ***The Story of Mankind*** by H. W. Van Lonn (Info., U). HONORS: *The Great Quest* (Hist. fiction, New England, 1826, U), *Cedric the Forester* (Hist. fic., England, 1200s, U), *The Old Tobacco Shop* (Fant., U), *The Golden Fleece and the Heroes Who Lived before Achilles* (Trad. Fant., U), *Windy Hill* (Realism, I–U).

1923 ***The Voyages of Doctor Doolittle*** by H. Lofting (Fant., I).

1924 ***The Dark Frigate*** by C. Hawes (Hist. fic., England, 1600s, I–U).

1925 ***Tales from Silver Lands*** by C. Finger. Illus. by Paul Honore (Trad. Fant., I–U). HONORS: *Nicholas* (Fant., Little people, I–U), *Dream Coach* (Fant., I-U).

1926 ***Shen of the Sea*** by A. Chrisman. Illus. by E. Hasselriis (Fant., Literary tale, I–U). HONORS: *The Voyagers* (Trad./Info., I–U).

1927 ***Smoky, the Cowhorse*** by W. James (Animal realism, I–U).

1928 ***Gay-Neck, The Story of a Pigeon*** by D. Mukerji. Illus. by B. Artzybasheff (Animal realism, I–U). HONORS: *The Wonder Smith and His Son* (Trad. Fant., Ireland, I–U), *Downright Dencey* (Hist. fic., New England, 1812, I–U).

1929 ***The Trumpeter of Krakow*** by E. Kelly. Illus. by A. Pruszynska (Hist. fic., Poland, 1400s, U). HONORS: *The Pigtail of Ah Lee Ben Loo* (Fant./poetry, I–U), *Millions of Cats* (Pict. book; Fant., P), *The Boy Who Was* (Hist. fic., Italy through 3000 years, I–U), *Clearing Weather* (Hist. fiction, USA, 1787, U), *The Runaway Papoose* (Realism/Multicultural, I–U), *Tod of the Fens* (Hist. fic., England, 1400s, U).

1930 ***Hitty: Her First Hundred Years*** by R. Field. Illus. by D. Lathrop (Hist. Fant., I-U). HONORS: *The Tangle-Coated Horse and Other Tales: Episodes from the Fionn Saga* (Trad., I-U), *Vaino: A Boy of New Finland* (Hist. fic., Finland, 1920s, U), *Pran of Albania* (Realism, U), *The Jumping-off Place* (Realism, I-U), *A Daughter of the Seine* (Biog., U), *Little Blacknose* (Fant., I-U).

1931 ***The Cat Who Went To Heaven*** by E. Coatsworth. Illus. by L. Ward (Fant., I-U). HONORS: *Floating Island* (Fant., I), *The Dark Star of Itza* (Hist. fic., Mayan Empire, U), *Queer Person* (Hist. fic./Multicultural, Native American, I-U), *Mountains Are Free* (Hist. fic., Switzerland, U), *Spice and the Devil's Cave* (Hist. fic., Portugal, 1400s, U), *Meggy McIntosh* (Hist. fic., Scotland, USA, 1775, I-U), *Garram the Hunter: A Boy of the Hill Tribes* (Realism, Africa, I-U), *Ood-Le-Uk, the Wanderer* (Realism, Alaska, U).

1932 ***Waterless Mountain*** by L. Armer. Illus. by S. Armer (Realism/Multicultural, Native Am., I-U). HONORS: *The Fairy Circus* (Fant., P-I), *Calico Bush* (Hist. fic., USA, 1743, I-U), *Boy of the South Seas* (Realism, I-U), *Out of the Flame* (Hist. fic, France, 1500s, I-U), *Jane's Island* (Realism, I-U), *The Truce of the Wolf and Other Tales of Old Italy* (Trad. Fant., I-U).

1933 ***Young Fu of the Upper Yangtze*** by E. Lewis. Illus. by K. Wiese (Realism, U). HONORS: *Swift Rivers* (Hist. fic., USA, 1835, U), *The Railroad to Freedom* (Biog., U), *Children of the Soil* (Realism, I-U).

1934 ***Invincible Louisa: The Story of the Author of "Little Women"*** by C. Meigs (Biog., I-U). HONORS: *The Forgotten Daughter* (Hist. fic., Italy, 2nd century B.C., U), *Swords of Steel* (Hist. fic., USA, 1859, U), *ABC Bunny* (Picture book, Fant./Alphabet, P), *Winged Girl of Knossos* (Hist. fic., Ancient Greece, U), *New Land* (Realism, I-U), *The Apprentice of*

Florence (Hist. fic., Italy, 1400s, U), *The Big Tree of Bunlahy: Stories of My Own Countryside* (Fant., I-U), *Glory of the Seas* (Hist. fic., USA, 1850s, U).

1935 ***Dobry*** by M. Shannon. Illus. by A. Katchamakoff (Realism, I-U). HONORS: *The Pageant of Chinese History* (Info., U), *Davy Crockett* (Biog., U), *A Day on Skates: The Story of a Dutch Picnic* (Realism, P).

1936 ***Caddie Woodlawn*** by C. Brink. Illus. by K. Seredy (Hist. fic., USA, 1860s, I-U). HONORS: *Honk: The Moose* (Realism, I-U), *The Good Master* (Realism, I-U), *Young Walter Scott* (Biog., U), *All Sails Set* (Hist. fic., USA, 1851, U).

1937 ***Roller Skates*** by R. Sawyer. Illus. by V. Angelo (Realism, I-U). HONORS: *Phoebe Fairchild: Her Book* (Hist. fic., New England, 1830s, I-U), *Whistler's Van* (Realism, I-U), *The Golden Basket* (Realism, P-I), *Winterbound* (Realism, U), *Audubon* (Biog., U), *The Codfish Musket* (Hist. fic., USA, 1780s, U).

1938 ***The White Stag*** by K. Seredy (Trad., ages 10-YA). HONORS: *Bright Island* (Realism, U), *Pecos Bill* (Trad., I-U), *On the Banks of Plum Creek* (Hist. fiction, USA, 1870s, I-U).

1939 ***Thimble Summer*** by E. Enright (Realism, I-U). HONORS: *Leader by Destiny: George Washington, Man and Patriot* (Biog., U), *Penn* (Biog., U), *Nino* (Realism, I-U), *"Hello, the Boat!"* (Hist. fict., USA, 1817, I-U), *Mr. Popper's Penguins* (Animal fant., I-U).

1940 ***Daniel Boone*** by J. Daughtery (Biog., I-U). HONORS: *The Singing Tree* (Hist. fic., Eastern Europe, 1910s, I-U), *Runner of the Mountain Tops* (Biog., U), *By the Shores of Siver Lake* (Hist. fic., USA, 1880s, I-U), *Boy with a Pack* (Hist. fic., USA, 1837, I-U).

1941 ***Call It Courage*** by A. Sperry (Realism, I-U). HONORS: *Blue Willow* (Hist. fic., USA, 1930s, I-U), *Young Mac of Fort Vancouver* (Hist. fic., Canada, early 1800s, U), *The Long Winter* (Hist. fic., USA, 1800s, I-U), *Nansen* (Biog., U).

1942 ***The Matchlock Gun*** by W. Edmonds. Illus. by P. Lantz. (Hist. fic., Colonial America, 1757, I-U). HONORS: *Little Town on the Prairie* (Hist. fic., USA, 1881, I-U), *George Washington's World* (Info./Biog., I-U), *Indian Captive: The Story of Mary Jemison* (Hist. fic., USA, 1750s, I-U), *Down Ryton Water* (Hist. fict., England, Netherlands, 1600s, U).

1943 ***Adam of the Road*** by E. Gray. Illus. by R. Lawson (Hist. fict., England, 1290s, I-U). HONORS: *The Middle Moffat* (Realism, I-U), *"Have You Seen Tom Thumb?"* (Biog., U).

1944 ***Johnny Tremain*** by E. Forbes. Illus. by L. Ward (Hist. fic., Boston, 1770s, U). HONORS: *These Happy Golden Years* (Hist. fic., USA, 1880s, I-U), *Fog Magic* (Modern Fant., I-U), *Rufus M.* (Realism, I-U), *Mountain Born* (Animal Realism, I-U).

1945 ***Rabbit Hill*** by R. Lawson (Animal Fant., P-I). HONORS: *The Hundred Dresses* (Realism, P-I), *The Silver Pencil* (Realism, ages 10-YA), *Abraham Lincoln's World* (Info./Biog., U), *Lone Journey: The Life of Roger Williams* (Biog., U).

1946 ***Strawberry Girl*** by L. Lenski (Hist. fic., Florida, early 1900s, I-U). HONORS: *Justin Morgan Had a Horse* (Animal Realism, I-U), *The Moved-Outers* (Multicultural, I-U), *Bhisma, the Dancing Bear* (Realism, I-U), *New Found World* (Info., ages 10–YA).

1947 ***Miss Hickory*** by C. Bailey. Illus. by R. Gannett (Fant./toys, P-I). HONORS: *The Wonderful Year* (Realism, I-U), *The Big Tree* (Info., I-U), *The Heavenly Tenants* (Fant., I-U), *The Avion My Uncle Flew* (Realism, U), *The Hidden Treasure of Glaston* (Hist. fic., England, 1172, U).

1948 ***The Twenty-one Balloons*** by W. Pene duBois (Fant., I-U). HONORS: *Pancakes—Paris* (Realism, ages 8–11), *Li Lun, Lad of Courage* (Realism, I-U), *The Quaint and Curious Quest of Johnny Longfoot, The Shoe-King's Son* (Trad., I-U), *The Cow-Tail Switch, and Other West African Stories* (Trad., I-U), *Misty of Chincoteague* (Animal realism, horse, I-U).

1949 ***King of the Wind*** by M. Henry. Illus. by W. Dennis (Hist. fic., Morocco, Europe, 1700s, I-U). HONORS: *Seabird* (Info., I-U), *Daughter of the Mountains* (Realism, I-U), *My Father's Dragon* (Fant., P-I), *Story of the Negro* (Info., U).

1950 ***The Door in the Wall*** by M. de Angeli (Hist. fic., England, 1300s, I-U). HONORS: *Tree of Freedom* (Hist. fic., USA, 1780s, I-U), *The Blue Cat of Castle Town* (Trad., U), *Kildee House* (Realism, I-U), *George Washington* (Biog., I-U), *Song of the Pines* (Hist. fic., USA, 1850s, U).

1951 ***Amos Fortune, Free Man*** by E. Yates. Illus. by N. Unwin (Biog., I-U). HONORS: *Better Known as Johnny Appleseed* (Biog., U), *Gandhi, Fighter without a Sword* (Biog., U), *Abraham Lincoln, Friend of the People* (Biog., I-U), *The Story of Appleby Capple* (Fant., P).

1952 ***Ginger Pye*** by E. Estes (Realism, I-U). HONORS: *Americans before Columbus* (Info., U), *Minn of the Mississippi* (Info., P-I), *The Defender* (Realism, I-U), *The Light at Tern Rock* (Realism, P-I), *The Apple and the Arrow* (Biog., I-U).

1953 ***Secret of the Andes*** by A. Clark. Illus. by J. Charlot (Realism/Multicultural, Native American, I-U). HONORS: *Charlotte's Web* (Animal fant., P-I), *Moccasin Trail* (Hist. fic., USA, 1830s, U), *Red Sails to Capri* (Hist. fic., Italy, 1826, I-U), *The Bears on*

Hemlock Mountain (Hist. fic., USA, 1800s P-I), *Birthdays of Freedom* (Info./Biog., U).

1954 ***And Now Miguel*** by J. Krumgold. Illus. by J. Charlot (Hist. fic., New Mexico, 1940s, I-U). HONORS: *All Alone* (Realism, I-U), *Shadrach* (Animal realism, I-U), *Hurry Home, Candy* (Animal realism, I-U), *Theodore Roosevelt, Fighting Patriot* (Biog., I-U), *Magic Maize* (Realism, I-U).

1955 ***The Wheel on the School*** by M. DeJong. Illus. by M. Sendak (Realism, I-U). HONORS: *The Courage of Sarah Noble* (Hist. fic., USA, 1707, I-U), *Banner in the Sky* (Hist. fic., Europe, 1860s, I-U).

1956 ***Carry on, Mr. Bowditch*** by J. Latham (Biog., U). HONORS: *The Golden Name Day* (Realism, I-U), *The Secret River* (Fant., P-I), *Men, Microscopes, and Living Things* (Info., U).

1957 ***Miracles on Maple Hill*** by V. Sorensen. Illus. by B. and J. Krush (Realism, I-U). HONORS: *Old Yeller* (Animal realism, I-U), *The House of Sixty Fathers* (Hist. fic., China, 1940s, I-U), *Mr. Justice Holmes* (Biog., I-U), *The Corn Grows Ripe* (Realism, I-U), *The Black Fox of Lorne* (Hist. fic., Scotland, 10th century, I-U).

1958 ***Rifles for Watie*** by H. Keith. Illus. by P. Burchard (Hist. fic., USA, 1860s, I-U). HONORS: *The Horescatcher* (Realism, U), *Gone-Away Lake* (Realism, I-U), *The Great Wheel* (Hist. fict., USA, 1890s, I-U), *Tom Paine, Freedom's Apostle* (Biog, U).

1959 ***The Witch of Blackbird Pond*** by E. Speare (Hist. fic., USA, 1860s, I-U). HONORS: *The Family under the Bridge* (Realism, I-U), *Along Came a Dog* (Animal realism, I-U), *Chucaro: Wild Pony of the Pampa* (Animal realism, I-U), *The Perilous Road* (Hist. fic., USA, 1860s, I-U).

1960 ***Onion John*** by J. Krumgold. Illus. by S. Shimin (Realism, I-U). HONORS: *My Side of the Mountain* (Realism, U), *America Is Born* (Info., I-U), *The Gammage Cup* (Fant., little people, I).

1961 ***Island of the Blue Dolphins*** by S. O'Dell (Hist. fic., USA, 1800s, Multicultural/Native-American, I-U). HONORS: *America Moves Forward* (Info., I-U), *Old Ramon* (Realism, I-U), *The Cricket in Times Square* (Animal Fant., P-I).

1962 ***The Bronze Bow*** by E. Speare (Hist. fic., Jerusalem, 1st century A.D., U). HONORS: *Frontier Living* (Info., I-U), *The Golden Goblet* (Hist. fic, Ancient Egypt, I-U), *Belling the Tiger* (Fant., P-I).

1963 ***A Wrinkle in Time*** by M. L'Engle. (pseud. for Leclaire Alger). (Fant., I-U). HONORS: *Thistle and Thyme* (Trad. Fant., I-U), *Men of Athens* (Biog, U).

1964 ***It's Like This, Cat*** by E. Neville (Realism, I-U). HONORS: *Rascal* (Animal realism, I-U), *The Loner* (Realism, I-U).

1965 ***Shadow of a Bull*** by M. Wojciechowska (Realism, I-U). HONORS: *Across Five Aprils* (Hist. fic., USA, 1860s, U).

1966 ***I, Juan de Pareja*** by E. de Trevino (Biog., I-U). HONORS: *The Black Cauldron* (Fant., quest, I-U), *The Animal Family* (Fant., U), *The Noonday Friends* (Realism, I-U).

1967 ***Up a Road Slowly*** by I. Hunt (Realism, I-U). HONORS: *The King's Fifth* (Hist. fic., Spain, 1500s, I-U), *Zlateh the Goat and Other Stories* (Fant., I-U), *The Jazz Man* (Realism, I-U).

1968 ***From the Mixed-up Files of Mrs. Basil E. Frankweiler*** by E. L. Konigsburg (Realism, I-U). HONORS: *Jennifer, Hecate, Macbeth, William McKinley, and Me, Elizabeth* (Realism, I-U), *The Black Pearl* (Realism, I-U), *The Fearsome Inn* (Fant., I-U), *The Egypt Game* (Realism, I-U).

1969 ***The High King*** by L. Alexander (Fant., hero-quest, I-U). HONORS: *To Be a Slave* (Info., U), *When Shlemiel Went to Warsaw and Other Stories* (Fant., I-U).

1970 ***Sounder*** by W. Armstrong. (Hist. fic., Southern USA, early 20th cent., U). HONORS: *Our Eddie* (Realism, U), *The Many Ways of Seeing: An Introduction to the Pleasure of Art* (Info., I-U), *Journey Outside* (Fant., U).

1971 ***Summer of the Swans*** by B. Byars (Realism, U). HONORS: *Kneeknock Rise* (Fant., I-U), *Enchantress from the Stars* (Fant., sci. fict., U), *Sing Down the Moon* (Hist. fic., USA, 1860s, U).

1972 ***Mrs. Frisby and the Rats of NIHM*** by R. O'Brien (Animal Fant., I-U). HONORS: *Incident at Hawk's Hill* (Hist. fic., Canada, 1870/Animal realism, I-U), *The Planet of Junior Brown* (Realism, U), *The Tombs of Atuan* (Fant., quest, I-U), *Annie and the Old One* (Picture book; Realism/Multicultural, Native-American, I-U), *The Headless Cupid* (Realism, mystery, I-U).

1973 ***Julie of the Wolves*** by J. George (Realism/Multicultural, Native American, U). HONORS: *Frog and Toad Together* (Picture book; Animal Fant., P), *The Upstairs Room* (Hist. fic., Holland, 1940s, I-U), *The Witches of Worm* (Realism, I-U).

1974 ***The Slave Dancer*** by P. Fox (Hist. fict., USA, Africa, 1840s, U). HONORS: *The Dark Is Rising* (Fant., quest, I-U).

1975 ***M. C. Higgins, the Great*** by V. Hamilton (Realism/Multicultural, African American, U). HONORS: *Figgs & Phantoms* (Realism, U), *My Brother Sam is Dead* (Hist. fict., Colonial America, 1700s, I-U), *The Perilous Guard* (Hist. fic., England, 1558, U), *Philip Hall Likes Me. I Reckon Maybe* (Realism/Multicultural, African American, I-U).

1976 ***The Grey King*** by S. Cooper (Fant., hero-quest, U). HONORS: *The Hundred Penny* (Realism/ Multicultural/African-American, I-U), *Dragonwings* (Hist. fic., San Francisco, 1903–1909/Multicultural, Chinese American, U).

1977 ***Roll of Thunder, Hear My Cry*** by M. Taylor (Hist. fic., Mississippi, 1934/Multicultural/African American, I-U). HONORS: *Abel's Island* (Animal Fant., I-U), *A String in the Harp* (Fant., I-U).

1978 ***The Bridge to Terabithia*** by K. Paterson (Realism, I-U). HONORS: *Anpao: An American Indian Odyssey* (Trad. fantasy/Muticultural, Native American, I-U), *Ramona and Her Father* (Realism, P-I).

1979 ***The Westing Game*** by E. Raskin (Realism, mystery, I-U). HONORS: *The Great Gilly Hopkins* (Realism, I-U).

1980 ***A Gathering of Days: A New England Girl's Journal, 1830–32*** by J. Blos (Hist. fic., New England, 1830s, U). HONORS: *The Road from Home: The Story of an Armenian Girl* (Hist. fic., Turkey, Greece, 1907–24, U).

1981 ***Jacob I Have Loved*** by K. Paterson (Hist. fic., USA, 1940s, U). HONORS: *The Fledging* (Fant., I-U), *A Ring of Endless Light* (Fant./Science fiction, I-U).

1982 ***A Visit to William Blake's Inn: Poems for Innocent and Experienced Travelers*** by N. Willard. Illus. by A. and M. Provensen (Picture book/Poetry, I-U). HONORS: *Ramona Quimby, Age 8* (Realism, P-I), *Hungary, 1939–1944* (Hist. fic., U).

1983 ***Dicey's Song*** by C. Voigt (Realism, I-U). HONORS: *The Blue Sword* (Fant., quest, U), *Dr. DeSoto* (Picture book/Animal Fant., P), *Graven Images* (Fant., I-U), *Homesick: My Own Story* (Biog., I-U), *Sweet Whispers, Brother Rush* (Fant./Multicultural, African-American, U).

1984 ***Dear Mr. Henshaw*** by B. Cleary (Realism, I-U). HONORS: *The Sign of the Beaver* (Hist. fic., Colonial America, I-U), *A Solitary Blue* (Realism, I-U), *Sugaring Time* (Info., I-U), *The Wish Giver* (Fant., I-U).

1985 ***The Hero and the Crown*** by R. McKinley (Fant., quest, U). HONORS: *Like Jake and Me* (Picture book; Realism, P-I), *The Moves Make the Man* (Realism, Multicultural/African American, U), *One-Eyed Cat* (Realism, I-U).

1986 ***Sarah, Plain and Tall*** by P. MacLachlan (Hist. fic., USA western frontier, 1800s, I-U). HONORS: *Commodore Perry in the Land of the Shogun* (Info., I-U), *Dogsong* (Realism, Multicultural/Native American, U).

1987 ***The Whipping Boy*** by S. Fleischman. (Hist. fic., Medieval England, I-U). HONORS: *On My Honor* (Realism, I-U), *Volcano: The Eruption and Healing of Mount St. Helens* (Info., I-U), *A Fine White Dust* (Realism, I-U).

1988 ***Lincoln: A PhotoBiog*** by R. Freedman (Biog., I-U). HONORS: *After the Rain* (Realism, U), *Hatchet* (Realism, I-U).

1989 ***Joyful Noise: Poems for Two Voices*** by P. Fleischman (Poetry, I-U). HONORS: *In the Beginning: Creation Stories from Around the World* (Trad. Fant., I-U), *Scorpions* (Realism/Multicultural/African American, Hispanic American, U).

1990 ***Number the Stars*** by L. Lowry (Hist. fic., Denmark, 1940s, I-U). HONORS: *Afternoon of the Elves* (Realism, I-U), *Shabanu, Daughter of the Wind* (Realism, U), *The Winter Room* (Realism, U).

1991 ***Maniac Magee*** by J. Spinelli (Realism, I-U). HONORS: *The True Confessions of Charlotte Doyle* (Hist. fiction, England, USA, 1830, I-U).

1992 ***Shiloh*** by P. Naylor (Animal realism, I-U). HONORS: *Nothing but the Truth* (Realism, I-U), *The Wright Brothers: How They Invented the Airplane* (Info./Biog, I-U).

1993 ***Missing May*** by C. Rylant (Realism, U). HONORS: *The Dark-Thirty: Southern Tales of the Supernatural* (Modern Fant./Ghost stories/African American, I-U), *Somewhere in Darkness* (Realism, African American, IU), *What Hearts* (Realism, U).

1994 ***The Giver*** by L. Lowry (Modern Fant., I–U). HONORS: *Crazy Lady* (Realism, I–U), *Dragon's Gate* (Hist. fic., China, USA West, 1860s, U), *Eleanor Roosevelt: A Life of Discovery* (Biog., I–U).

1995 ***Walk Two Moons*** by S. Creech (Realism, Native American, ages 11–14). HONORS: *Catherine, Called Birdy* (Hist. fic., England, 1200s, I–U), *The Ear, the Eye, the Arm* (Modern Fant., U).

1996 ***The Midwife's Apprentice*** by K. Cushman (Hist. fic., medieval Eng., I–U). HONORS: *What Jamie Saw* (Fiction, child abuse, I–U), *The Watsons Go to Birmingham—1963* (Hist. fic., African American, I–U), *Yolonda's Genius* (Contemp. Fic., I), *The Great Fire* (Info., Chicago's Fire, I–U).

1997 ***The View from Saturday*** by E. L. Konigsburg (Contemp. fic, I). HONORS: *A Girl Named Disaster* (Contemp. fic., I–U), *The Moorchild* (Fant., I), *The Thief* (Fant., P–I), *Belle Prater's Boy* (Contemp. Fic., I–U).

1998 ***Out of the Dust*** by K. Hesse (Contemp. fic., I–U). HONORS: *Lily's Crossing* (Hist. Fic., I–U), *Ella Enchanted* (Fant., I–U), *Wringer* (Contemp. fic., I–U).

Appendix C: Arts Organizations, Addresses, and Internet Sites

In Canada:

Canadian Conference of the Arts
804 – 130 Albert Street,
Ottawa, ON 7PM 5G4.
Tel: (613) 234-2742
Fax: (613) 234-7556

Canadian Society for Education through Art
675 Samuel-de-Champlain
Boucherville, QC J4B 6C4
Tel: (514) 655-2435
Fax: (514) 655-4379

Canadian Music Educators Association
Department of Elementary Education
University of Alberta
551 Education Building South
Edmonton, AB T6G 2G5
Tel: (403) 492-4273, ext. 241
Fax: (403) 492-7622

Music for Children—Carl Orff Canada
www.orffcanada.ca
This site contains information about Carl Orff, the Carl Orff Canada organization, Regional Chapters, workshops, national conferences, and teacher training courses.

Kodaly Society of Canada
cnet.unb.ca/achn/Kodaly/
This site gives information on the Kodaly system of music education. It includes teacher resources, publishers, information on summer institutes, publications, and research.

Dalcroze Society of Canada
Wendy Taxis
R.R.#4 Roseneath, ON K0K 2X0
Tel: (905) 352-2515

Early Childhood Music Association (ECMA)
Wing-tee Hai
93 Annette Street
Toronto, ON M6P 1N7

Education Through Music (ETM)
The Richards Institute
Geraldine McGeorge
P.O. Box 1240
Chatham, ON N7M 5R9
Tel: (519) 674-2555

In the United States:

American Alliance for Theater and Education (AATE)
c/o Arizona State University Theater Department
P.O. Box 872002
Tempe, AZ 85287-2002
www.aate.com
e-mail: aate.info@asu.edu

American Arts Alliance
805 15th St., N.W.
Suite 500
Washington, DC 20005
Telephone: (202) 289-1776
Fax: (202) 371-6601
web site: www.artswire.org/~aaa/

Principal advocate for America's professional nonprofit arts organizations.

Americans for the Arts
www.artsusa.org/index.html
1 East 53rd St. NY, NY 10022
Tel: (212) 980-4857

Resource and leadership development, information services, public awareness and education.

Dance USA
www.danceusa.org
1156 15th Street NW, Suite 820
Washington, DC 2005
(202) 628-0144

Getty Center for Education in the Arts
www.getty.edu
1200 Getty Center Drive
Los Angeles, CA 90049
(310) 440-7300

Dedicated to improving arts education in the nation's K–12 public schools. The Center is one of the J. Paul Getty Trust's seven divisions. The Center coordinates partnerships among arts agencies and schools and disseminates information about art education programs.

Harvard Project Zero
Harvard Graduate School of Education
Longfellow Hall, 13 Appian Way
Cambridge, MA 002138
(617) 495-4342
tzweb.harvard.edu

International Society for the Performing Arts
17 Purdy Avenue, P.O. Box 909
Rye, NY 10580
Telephone: (914) 921-1550
Fax: (914) 921-1593
www.ispa.org

An international network dedicated to advancing the field of the performing arts.

Kennedy Center Performing Arts Centers & Schools: Partnerships in Education
Kennedy Center for the Performing Arts
Washington, DC 20566
(202) 416-8000

Coalition of statewide, nonprofit organizations working in partnership to support policies, practices, and partnerships that ensure that the arts are woven into the fibre of American education.

Lincoln Center Institute for the Arts in Education
Lincoln Center for the Performing Arts, Inc.,
70 Lincoln Center Plaza, 7th Floor
New York, NY 10023-6594
www.lincolncenter.org/institut
Telephone: (212) 875-5535
Fax: (212) 875-5539

The Institute was created to fulfill a commitment to aesthetic education as an important part of learning through educational partnerships with school districts. *Institutes in the following cities:* Albany, Binghamton, Buffalo, New York City, Rochester, Syracuse, and Utica, NY; Philadelphia, PA; Wilmington, DE; Nashville and Memphis, TN; Bowling Green, OH; Lincoln, NE; Houston, TX; Tulsa, OK; San Diego, CA; and Melbourne, Australia.

Music Educators National Conference (MENC)
www.menc.org
1806 Robert Fulton Drive
Reston, VA 20191
(703) 860-4000

National Art Education Association (NAEA)
1916 Association Drive
Reston, VA 20191–1590
(703) 860-8000
www.naea_reston.org
e-mail: naea@dgs.dgsys.com

Comprises nearly 15,000 art educators and anyone concerned about quality art education.

National Assembly of State Arts Agencies (NASAA)
www.nasaa-arts.org

Each of the 50 states has an arts agency to support excellence in and access to the arts by supporting established and emerging artists and arts organizations.

National Dance Association
1900 Association Drive
Reston, VA 22091
(703) 476-3421

National Endowment for the Arts
1100 Pennsylvania Avenue NW
Washington, DC 20506
(202) 682-5426

NEA's web site is divided into (1) "arts.community"—a hyperlinked periodical with features and news about the arts; (2) "Guide to the National Endowment for the Arts," an overview of the grant-making programs; a hyperlinked list of state and regional arts organizations is also available; and (3) "Arts Resource Center," which includes a catalogue of publications (some free), contact information for a broad range of national arts service organizations, and a library of online publications.

OPERA America
www.operaam.org

1156 15th Street NW, Suite 810
Washington, DC 20005
(202) 293-4466

Its fundamental mission is to promote opera. Provides resources on arts education leadership and professional development, as well as resources of interest to administrators, performers, and educators.

Internet Web Sites on the Arts

See also resource sections at ends of chapters

Arts Edge
The Kennedy Center's web site for lesson plans and other resources.
artsedge.kennedy-center.org

The Art Teacher Connection
Encouraging Innovation in Art Education through Technology
www.inficad.com/~arted/
For Art and classroom teachers

ArtsEdNet
The Getty Center's extensive curriculum, lesson plans, and resources.
www.artsednet.getty.edu

ArtsNet
Arts management and cultural diversity resources.
artsnet.heinz.cmu.edu

Arts Education in Public Elementary and Secondary Schools
Surveys and support.
artsedge.kennedy-center.org/db/nea/survey.html

The Arts for Kids
www.stemnet.nf.ca/CITE/arts.htm
The Arts Theme Pages from Gander Academy, Newfoundland. Themes for elementary students include Instruments of the Orchestra, Classical Composers, Origami, and Kinder Art.

Arts Resource Connection
Minnesota's Center for Arts Education Arts Resource Connection.
www.mcae.k12.mn.us/art_connection/art_connection.html

Arts Wire: The New York Foundation for the Arts
www.artswire.org
Arts Wire is a national computer-based communications network for the arts community.

Association for the Advancement of Arts Education (information page)
www.aaae.org/aboutaaae.html

Association for the Advancement of Arts Education: Connections
www.aaae.org/

Association for the Advancement of Arts Education: Other Web Links
www.aaae.org/othersites.html

Basic Art Lessons
home.att.net/~tisone/lessonpg1.htm
Lesson series for grades 2–12 include Pencil, Black Pen Drawing Lessons, Adding Coloured Marker, Collage, Mixing Paint, and Art History.
Each lesson lists the materials required, the steps (along with appropriate graphics), and resources.

Bell's & Blue Web'n
www.kn.pacbell.com/wired/bluewebn/

The Canadian Youth Virtual Gallery
cap.unb.ca/achn/cyvg
Features the work of kids across Canada.

CanTeach – Fine Arts
persweb.direct.ca/ikhan/elementary/finearts.html
persweb.direct.ca/ikhan/index.html
This site for Canadian teachers has links to resources and lesson plans for drama, dance, music, and visual arts.

Cartoon Corner
www.cartooncorner.com/index.html
Learn how to draw cartoons, get drawing tricks, and find out what cartoonists do. For grades 2–12

Crayola Arts Education
Share ideas, lesson plans, news on arts advocacy.
www.crayola.com

The Drama Teachers Resource Page
www3.sk.sympatico.ca/erachi/index.html
Mainly IS lesson plans but some for elementary. Also articles on costume, props, set design, lighting, and scenic painting as well as other drama links.

Educational Resources in the Fine Arts
www.cln.org/subjects/fine.html
Curriculum resources, instructional materials, and theme pages.

Education Survey
www.aaae.org/caesumm-p.html

The Educational Theatre Association (ETA)
Teaching production.
www.etassoc.org

Elementary Art
www2.gov.pe.ca/educ/lester/educator/elementary/art.html
Links to lessons and resources for elementary (grades K–6) art teachers.

Elementary Arts Education
www.sasked.gov.sk.ca/schools/n_lakes/rbl/elementary.art.html
Includes lesson plans and general resources

The Foundation Center
Guides to grant and research writing.
www.fdcenter.org

GeoCities the Tropics
Vast information on museums, art styles and periods, art education and advocacy.
www.geocities.com/thetropics/1009/index.html

The Incredible Art Department
Student work, cartoons, lesson plans, links, news, jobs, chat rooms, awards.
www.in.net/~kenroar/

Infusion Program
aspin.asu.edu?~rescomp/targeted/augusta.html

KODAK Picture
www.kodak.com/digitalImaging/pictureThis/picThisHome.shtml (Send email postcards)

Learning in Motion's Top Ten List
www.learn.motion.com/lim/links/linkmain

A Lifetime of Color
www.sanford-artedventures.com/index.html
Topics include Create Art, Study Art, Play Art Games, Teach Art, and Newsletter. Activities and lesson plans included. For grades K–12

Minnesota Center for Arts Education
Resources, links, lessons.
www.mcae.k12.mn.us/

National Art Education Association
www.arts.arizona.edu/arted/12-1-arted.html
Links to art education sites for art educators, artists, and administrators.

National Endowment for the Arts
arts.endow.gov.

Origami
tqjunior.advanced.org/5402/
This site, developed by middle school students, is the 1999 Junior Thinkquest winner. Includes A History of Origami, Uses and Benefits, Terms, Symbols and Tips, Origami and Peace, Poems about Origami, Fun Activities, and Resources.

Puppetry Theme Page
www.cln.org/themes/puppetry.html
Includes resources, lesson plans, and many links.

Reader's Theatre Online Canada
loiswalker.com/catalog/index.html
Provides scripts to print, copy, and use in the classroom, for students in grades K–12.

Stage Hand Puppets
www3.ns.sympatico.ca/onstage/puppets/
This is the home page of Performing Puppets, a Canadian company. The Activity Page has links to Performance Tips, Ventriloquism, Paper Puppets, and Scrap Puppets!

Stained Glass Theme Page
www.cln.org/themes/stainedglass.html
Includes links to images, historical information, patterns, and techniques.

Strings, Springs and Finger Things.
A New Puppet Collection at the Canadian Museum of Civilization
www.civilization.ca/membrs/arts/ssf/ssf00eng.html
Learn about different types of puppets.

Theatre Education Literature Review
www.aaae.org/theatre/thfront.html

Theatre Education Literature Review Cont'd:
www.aaae.org/theatre/theatre5.html

CHILDREN'S LITERATURE INTERNET SITES

Below is a small sample of the approximately 600,000 web sites that focus on some aspect of children's literature. Not only do sites "come and go," but sites regularly update their information and revise their offerings. The content of the sites described in this appendix is accurate as of February 1999.

It is important to remember that once a site is accessed, one can easily link to other sites that provide additional information and references.

1. The following are excellent starting points for surfing the web for children's literature sites. Each leads to more specific information.

Carol Hurst's Children's Literature Site
www.carolhurst.com
Hurst's site contains a collection of reviews of excellent children's books and uses a three-star system to rate the books: recommended, highly recommended, and outstanding. Professional materials published by Hurst offer ideas about themes, curriculum, and other books and services.

The Children's Literature Web Guide
www.acs.ucalgary.ca/~dkbrown/
This is the most comprehensive Internet site on children's literature. D. K. Brown's popular site includes resources for teachers, parents, storytellers, writers, and illustrators. A few examples of the subpages located in the Children's Literature Web Guide include Web Traveller's Toolkit: Essential Kid Lit Websites, Conferences Bulletin Board, Children's Literature Organizations on the Internet, Lots of Lists: Recommended Books, and Children's Publishers and Booksellers on the Internet.

Fairossa Cyber Library: Children's Literature
www.dalton.org/libraries/fairrosa/
Visitors to this site can access several other links including articles about children's literature, book lists, book reviews, information about authors and illustrators, and other children's literature web sites.

How Novel!: Canadian Young Adult Literature
192.197.206.5/novel/index.html
This online resource, produced by the Saskatoon Public Library, features information on Canadian

fiction written for readers aged 12–18 and focuses on materials written from 1985 to present.

2. The following sites focus on resource, reference, and bibliographic materials about children's literature.

The Canadian Children's Book Centre
www3.sympatico.ca/ccbc/
The Canadian Children's Book Centre was formed to promote and encourage reading, writing, and illustrating of Canadian children's books. The web site contains information about the CCBC, Our Choice (book recommendations), reviews, and recommended links.

Canadian Children's Literature Service: National Library of Canada
www.nlc-bnc.ca/services/eelec.htm
This site provides information about Canadian children's literature award-winning books, Canadian authors and illustrators, and Internet sites that pertain primarily to Canadian children's literature.

Children's Literature: A Library Timesaver—S.F.U. Libraries
www.lib.sfu.ca/kiosk/finlayso/childlit.htm
This site lists useful children's literature reference books and describes the research steps for accessing children's literature resources by discussing a number of frequently asked questions on the topic.

Children's Literature Reference
mahogany.lib.utexas.edu/Libs/PCL/child/
An electronic bibliography of children's references to guide visitors to basic resources in the area of children's literature. Topics include awards and honours, classics, authors and illustrators, genres, teacher resources, suggested web sites, reviews and criticisms, and electronic journals.

Internet Resources for Children's Literature
www.unisa.edu.au/library/internet/pathfind/childlit.htm
This guide is designed to assist visitors in finding electronic resources and contains useful starters such as "AskERIC," Children's Bookwatch, Fairrosa's Cyberlibrary, and Canadian Children's Literature Service Collection Electronic Products. This site also provides connections to discussion lists such as KidLit and Childlit, newsgroups, and links to electronic journals such as the Canadian Review of Materials.

3. The following sites are developed specifically to offer links to other sites that provide information on Children's Literature.

Around the Net
www.macabees.ab.ca/net.html
This site claims to have identified the best sites that feature information about Canada, Canadian authors, and Canadian literature. Some of the recommended sites include The Canadian Children's Book Centre, Children's Literature Web Guide, CCL: Canadian Children's Literature, and The National Library of Canada: Forthcoming Books.

Children's Literature: Suggested Web Sites Worth Visiting
www.lib.utexas.edu/Libs/PCL/child/sites.html
This site provides links to children's literature under the following categories: Associations and Discussion Lists; Children's Literature Information Sites; Electronic Books and Serials on the Web; Indexes, Abstracts, and Internet Searching Aids; Libraries; and Sites Especially for Kids.

4. The following sites deal with specific issues or special topics in children's literature.

Classics in Children's Literature
www.scils.rutgers.edu/special/kay/classics.html
This site encourages the visitor to read or reread books that have achieved classic status in children's literature. Some books are completely reproduced online. Visitors are invited to consider whether these works appeal to and are of interest to today's young people or whether these books should be retained as historical artifacts.

Dealing With Sensitive Issues Using Children's Literature
www.scils.rutgers.edu/special/kay/issues.html
This site lists books that identify sensitive issues in regards to inclusion, multiculturalism, and gender. It also provides guidelines and resources to refer to when dealing with sensitive issues in children's literature.

Multicultural Book Review Homepage
www.isomedia.com/homes/jmele/homepage.html
This home page allows visitors to link to reviews of multicultural books and to other multicultural web sites.

NICHCY A Guide to Children's Literature and Disability
www.kidsource.com/NICHCY/literature.html
This site is intended to assist parents/guardians, teachers, and other professionals in identifying books that are written about or include characters who have a disability. Books are categorized by age group or grade level appropriateness. This site also includes a guide to other children's literature selections about particular disabilities.

Appendix D: Interest Inventory

Arts for Life Interest Inventory

Name__________________ Nickname________________ Birthday________________ Favourite Colour _______________

What are your favourite

- foods?
- sports?
- toys?
- TV shows?
- movies?
- things about school? your least favourite?
- book?
- songs? music?

1. Do you have any pets?
2. What do you enjoy doing with your family?
3. What books have you read that you enjoyed?
4. What do you do well?
5. How do you like to spend your free time? What hobbies do you have?
6. Where have you travelled?
7. If you could be anywhere right now, where would you be?
8. Do you belong to any clubs or organizations?
9. Do you play or would you like to play a musical instrument?
10. Do you like to draw?
11. Do you like to dance? What dances do you know?
12. Have you ever been to a library? a museum?
13. Have you ever been in a play? watched a play?
14. Do you read the newspapers or magazines at home?
15. What things have you written? Any poetry?
16. What types of art do you like? photography___ puppets___ weaving___ drawing___ charcoal___ pastels/chalk___ pen and ink___ painting___ acrylics___ watercolour___ print making___ woodcuts___ sculpture___ paper___ collage___ papier mâché___ mobiles___ diorama___ carving___ felt tip markers___
17. Who do you admire? Why?
18. Do you like to pretend?
19. Do you like storytelling?
20. What makes you laugh? How do you make other people laugh?
21. Do you own any art?
22. If you could meet an artist (musician, visual artist, dancer, actor, writer), who would it be? Why? What three questions would you ask him or her?
23. If you could visit any country, which one would it be? Why?
24. Would you like to visit an art gallery___ museum___? go to a play___ concert___?
25. If you had the opportunity to create a work of art, what would you use? What would it be about?
26. What type of literature do you enjoy? picture books___ poetry___ fables___ folk tales___ fairy tales___ myths___ legends___ epics___ historical fiction___ science fiction___ realistic fiction___ informational___ autobiographies___ biographies___
27. If you could read a biography or autobiography about an artist, which one would it be?
28. If you could write a book, what would it be about?
29. What would you like to know more about or be able to do?

Appendix E: Creating a Positive Classroom Environment

Post It Page

Setting the Environment

Create an inviting classroom environment. Consider your room a living room and bring in rugs, art, and music.

Really be the teacher you would want for yourself. Model what you expect in the way of attitude, courtesy, respect, and enthusiasm for learning. Listen to students using "active listening" techniques.

Enjoy the kids and let them know it. Tell them they are the best! Laugh with students and share humour with them. No sarcasm. Start with a riddle, cartoon, or poem related to the lesson. Write down specific positive behaviours on post-its and give them to students to keep in a "positive post-its" folder. Put students' names on the board for positive contributions to class.

A few rules or consequences are necessary. Post them. Start out firm and allow students to "earn" more and more freedom. Examples: I Care rules. (Focus on respect and courtesy. Be a model!) Involve students in making rules (e.g., role play: "Show me how you'll look when you are really listening" and "In groups of three, show me a scene of showing respect").

Teach using the principle of variety. Change methods and integrate the arts!

Explain the real-life connections between school and school work.

Do give choices within limits (e.g., "When you finish . . . you can either . . . or . . .").

Interest and attention are essential! Research results show that interest accounts for as much as twenty-five times the variance in student success. Get attention before starting a lesson. Use signals (e.g., a rhythm, secret word, chant, sign language). Stop during the lesson if you don't have attention and state your expectation in a direct, business-like way (e.g., "I need . . .").

Set up classroom routines. Assign jobs and responsibilities for running the class. Have a predictable routine (e.g., opening of class with poem, song, riddle, or cartoon). Post a daily agenda. Tell students the focus and goals of lessons.

Cause students to believe you know important things. Let students know you read books, like to dance, sing, or draw. No one wants to be around blah know-nothing people who can't do anything and seem to have few interests. Ask open or fat questions to get more thought and participation (e.g., "What did you learn about. . . ?" versus "Who was the main character?").

Intrinsic motivation is more important than concrete rewards. The research is clear: extrinsics can harm interest. Use stickers and stamps sparingly and only as "symbols" of hard work. Focus on learning for its own worth and how it relates to the real world. If you use extrinsic reinforcers, remember they must: (1) be intermittent and phased out as soon as possible, (2) be focused on privileges students want versus "things," (3) show students they are making progress toward the reinforcer. Use frequent daily or hourly points to start out with, rather than some vague "certificate" at the end of the week.

Proximity. Stand or sit close and circulate around the room as you teach. Vary the pattern to give each child a chance to be close to you. "Yardstick": walk about three steps toward a non-listener and he will usually be brought back to the lesson or stand between one or more students making a disturbance. Use the two-finger touch technique or touch a student's paper or desk as you walk around to focus attention on it.

Let students sit where they want until they show they cannot learn in that spot. Show them how to establish personal space.

Expect that students will have bad days, too. Give a coupon for turning in homework late one time per grading period. Allow use of the "pass" option during questioning.

Send silent signals to student. Use sign language to praise, nod your head, make eye contact.

Post It Page

Intervention Strategies

Ignore a behaviour unless it interferes with the learning of others. Follow up with a private conference with the student who perpetually is a problem. Some teachers keep a camera handy to take pictures (even if there isn't always film in it).

Never threaten, but if you make a promise, carry it out. Be consistent.

Talk to repeat offenders individually and privately. Focus the conference on what you observed, what you expect and why, and ask, "What can you do to solve your problem?" Do not humiliate since you wouldn't want this done to you. Set behaviour goals.

Encourage shy or hesitant speakers. Nod your head "yes" and smile as they speak.

Remember to start fresh each day. Greet children and make them feel welcome. Be positive at the start and throughout each day. Prevent problems by displaying an enthusiastic "can-do, will-do, want-to-do" attitude.

Volume (teacher's) should be lowered or use silence and pauses to get attention.

Elevate students with descriptive feedback versus praise. Say, "John, you have three different colours on your quilt piece so far" (praise just controls and may be empty).

Never get in the habit of casually discussing problems of students with other teachers. This is unprofessional and may put unfair labels on kids. Never talk about a student in front of other students—as if they aren't listening.

Time outs away from the group should include a chance to return to the group when they can follow the rules. Before allowing a child to leave time out, ask what rule was broken and discuss how the child will behave the next time if confronted with a similar situation.

Institute consequences that are hierarchical and appropriate. A warning is a courtesy we all appreciate. Take away one minute of recess at a time, instead of a whole recess. Never assign sentence writing as a consequence because this makes writing seem like a punishment! Do not allow some students to "get away" with not doing their share of cleanup or not taking responsibility after an activity in the classroom. Loss of privilege is appropriate here.

On the spot assistance: Make eye contact, move toward the student, and state your expectation (e.g., "Joe, I want you to sit in your chair and start writing"). Give THE EYE. Attack the problem, not the person. Mention names as you teach (e.g., "This morning Pat was saying she thought . . . and now . . ."). Say a child's name before asking a question to help them "tune in."

Negative remarks don't solve problems. "Stop talking and get back to work" (negative) versus "Susan, what do you need to do and how can I help you do it?" (positive).

State what you want children TO DO versus NOT TO DO. Instead of "Don't talk," say "Listen." Address the group as a first step: "There are people who are talking who need to listen."

Appendix F: Bibliography of Recommended Reading and Viewing

This bibliography is in addition to the references that appear at the ends of chapters. Films and videos are given in the last section on this appendix.

The Arts (General)

Altieri, J. L. (1995). Pictorial/oral and written responses of first grade students: Can aesthetic growth be measured? *Reading Horizons,* 35(4), 273–286.

Anderson, T. (Mar./Apr. 1995). Rediscovering the connection between the arts: Introduction to the symposium on interdisciplinary arts education. *Arts Education Policy Review,* 10–12.

Anderson, W. M., & Lawrence, J. E. (Sept. 1982). Approaches to allied arts. *Music Educator's Journal,* 69(1), 31–35.

Barrie, J. (1986). G. H. Bantock's conceptualization of the relationship between the expressive arts and education. *Journal of Aesthetic Education,* 20(2), 41–50.

Best, D. (1974). *Expression in movement and the arts.* London: Lepus.

Bloom, B. (1956). *Taxonomy of educational objectives.* New York: Longman.

Boyer, E. (1995). *The basic school: A community for learning.* Princeton, NJ: Carnegie Foundation for the Advancement of Teaching.

Brandt, R. (Dec./Jan. 1987/88). On assessment in the arts: a conversation with Howard Gardner. *Educational Leadership,* 30–34.

Brewer, C. B., & Campbell, D. (1991). *Rhythms of learning.* Tucson, AZ: Zephyr Press.

Broudy, H. S. (1977). How basic is aesthetic education? or is it the fourth *r*? *Language Arts,* 54, 631–37.

Casey, M. B., & Tucker, E. (October 1994). Problem-centered classrooms. *Kappan,* 139–43.

DeMille, R. (1981). *Put your mother on the ceiling: Children's imagination games.* Santa Barbara, CA: Santa Barbara Press.

Edwards, B. (1979). *Drawing on the right side of the brain.* Los Angeles: Jeremy P. Tarcher.

Eisner, E. (1983). *Beyond creating.* Los Angeles: Getty Center for Education in Art.

Epstein, T. (March 1994). Sometimes a shining moment: High-school students' representations of history through the arts. *Social Education,* 136–141.

Farrell, G. (May 1991). Drawbridges and moats: The arts and the middle school classroom. *Middle School Journal,* 28–29.

Feeney, S., & Moravcik, E. (1987). A thing of beauty: aesthetic development in young children. *Young Children,* 42(6), 7–15.

Fisher, L. (June 1994). The arts curriculum. *Curriculum Leader,* 1–7.

Fowler, C. (Nov. 1994). Strong arts, strong schools. *Educational Leadership,* 4–9.

Galda, L. (1984). Narrative competence: Play, storytelling and story comprehension, in A. Pellegrini and T. Yawkey (eds.), *The development of oral and written language in social contexts* (pp. 105–117). Norwood, NJ: Ablew.

Gallas, K. (Feb. 1991). Arts as epistemology: Enabling children to know what they know. *Harvard Educational Review,* 61(1), 40–50.

Gardner, H. (1989). *To open minds: Chinese clues to the dilemma of contemporary education.* New York: Basic Books.

Gardner, H. (1989). Zero-based arts education: An introduction to ARTS PROPEL. *Studies in Art Education,* 71–83.

Gibbs, N. The EQ factor. *Time.* October 25, 1995, 60–68.

Gingrich, D. (1974). *Relating the arts.* New York: Center for Applied Research in Education.

Ginsberg, H., & Opper, S. (1969). *Piaget's theory of intellectual development.* Englewood Cliffs, NJ: Prentice Hall.

Goleman, D. (1995). *Emotional intelligence: Why it can matter more than IQ.* New York: Bantam.

Gopher://gopher.ed.gov.1001/00/initiatives/goals/overview/file (Internet).

Gowan, J. C. (1967). *Creativity: Its educational implications.* San Diego: Knapp.

Gowan, J. C. (1972). *Development of the creative individual.* San Diego: Knapp.

Greene, A. (1995). Schools, communities, and the arts: a research compendium. Morrison Institute for Public Policy School of Public Affairs, Arizona State University and National Endowment for the Arts.

Hamblen, K. (Sept. 1985). Developing aesthetic literacy through contested concepts. *Art Education,* 19–24.

Hanna, J. L. (Apr. 1992). Connections: arts, academics and productive citizens. *Kappan,* 601–607.

Hoyt, L. (Apr. 1992). Many ways of knowing: Using drama, oral interactions, and the visual arts to enhance reading comprehension. *Reading Teacher,* 45(8), 580–84.

Khattri, N., Kane, M., & Reeve, A. (Nov. 1995). How performance assessments affect teaching and learning. *Educational Leadership,* 80–83.

Lazear, D. (1991). *Seven ways of knowing.* Palatine, IL: Skylight Publishers.

Lazear, D. (1992). *Seven ways of teaching.* Palatine, IL: Skylight Publishers.

Lee, M. A. (June 1993). Learning through the arts. *Journal of Physical Education, Recreation, and Dance,* 42–46.

MacGregor, R. (Nov. 1992). A short guide to alternative assessment practices. *Art Education,* 34–38.

Manebur, D. (Mar. 1994). Assessment as a classroom activity. *Music Educators Journal,* 23–47.

Oddleifson, E. (Feb. 1994). What do we want our schools to do? *Kappan,* 446–451.

Ohio's model competency based program. Comprehensive arts education (1996). Columbus, OH: State Department of Education.

Olshansky, B. (Sept. 1995). Picture this: An arts-based literacy program. *Educational Leadership,* 44–47.

Parnes, S. (1966). *Creative behavior guidebook.* New York: Scribner's.

Remer, J. (1990). *Changing schools through the arts.* New York: American Council for the Arts.

Schaefer, C. (1973). *Developing creativity in children: An idea book for teachers.* Buffalo, NY: Developers of Knowledge.

Slywester, R. (Dec./Jan. 1993/1994). What the biology of the brain tells us about learning. *Educational Leadership,* 46–51.

Sukraw-Ebert, J. (Jan. 1988). Arts not apart, but a part. *Principal,* 11–14.

Tardif, T. Z., with Sternberg, R. J. (1988). What do we know about creativity? In R. J. Sternberg (ed.), *The nature of creativity.* New York: Cambridge University Press, 429–40.

Torrance, E. P. (1970). *Encouraging creativity in the classroom.* Dubuque, IA: W. C. Brown.

Warner, S. (1989). *Encouraging the artist in your child.* New York: St. Martin's Press.

Integration of the Arts

Aaron, J. (May 1994). Integrating music with core subjects. *Music Educators Journal,* 33–36.

Alejandro, A. (Jan. 1994). Like happy dreams—integrating visual arts, writing, and reading. *Language Arts,* 12–21; 71.

Altieri, J. L. (Sept. 1991). Integrating literature and drama. *Reading Teacher,* 45, 74–75.

Amdur, D. (May 1993). Arts and cultural context: A curriculum integrating discipline-based art education with other humanities subjects at the secondary level. *Art Education,* 12–19.

Anderson, W., & Lawrence, J. (1991). *Integrating music into the classroom,* 2nd ed. Belmont, CA: Wadsworth.

Beane, J. (Apr. 1995). Curriculum integration and the disciplines of knowledge. *Kappan,* 616–22.

Burnaford, G. (July 1994). The challenge of integrated curricula. *Music Educators Journal,* 44–47.

Cardarelli, A. F. (1979). *Twenty-one ways to use music in teaching the language arts.* Evansville, IN: Indiana State University, ed 176 268.

Dean, J., & Gross, I. (Apr. 1992). Teaching basic skills through art and music. *Kappan,* 613–618.

Donlan, D. (Oct. 1974). Music and the language arts curriculum. *English Journal,* 63(7), 86–88.

Dunn, P. (Mar./Apr. 1995). Integrating the arts: Renaissance and Reformation in arts education. *Arts Education Policy Review,* 32–37.

Friedlander, J. L. (Nov./Dec. 1992). Creating dances and dance instruction—an integrated-arts approach. *Journal of Physical Education, Recreation, and Dance,* 49–52.

Gardner, H., & Boix-Mansilla, V. (Feb. 1994). Teaching for understanding—within and across the disciplines. *Educational Leadership,* 14–18.

Gilbert, A. G. (1977). *Teaching the three Rs through movement experiences.* Minneapolis: Burgess.

Irwin, R., & Reynolds, J. K. (Mar./Apr. 1995). Integration as a strategy for teaching the arts as disciplines. *Arts Education Policy Review,* 13–19.

Kalb, V. (Summer 1990). Curriculum connections: Literature—helping children experience the arts. *School Library Media Journal,* 249–50.

Katz, S., & Thomas, J. (1992). *Teaching creatively by the working word: Language, music, and movement.* Englewood Cliffs, NJ: Prentice Hall.

Ross, E. (1994). *Using children's literature across the curriculum.* Bloomington, IN: Phi Delta Kappa.

Roucher, N., & Lovano-Kerr, J. (Mar./Apr. 1995). Can the arts maintain integrity in interdisciplinary learning? *Arts Education Policy Review,* 20–25.

Scheinfield, D., & Steele, T. (Jan. 1995). Expressive education: Arts-integrated learning and the role of the artist in transforming the curriculum. *New Art Examiner,* 22–27.

Silva, C., & Delgado-Larocco, E. L. (Oct. 1993). Facilitating learning through interconnections: A concept approach to core literature units. *Language Arts,* 70, 469–474.

Slay, J., & Pendergast, S. (May 1993). Infusing the arts across the curriculum: A South Carolina school lifts students' self-esteem through arts study. *School Administrator,* 32–35.

Thompson, K. (Nov. 1995). Maintaining artistic integrity in an interdisciplinary setting. *Art Education,* 39–44.

Weisskopf, V. (1981). Art and science. *Leonardo,* 14(3), 238–42.

Williams, D. (1995). *Teaching mathematics through children's art.* Portsmouth, NH: Heinemann.

Children's Literature

Benton, M. (Spring 1995). From 'A rake's progress' to 'Rosie's walk': Lessons in aesthetic reading. *Journal of Aesthetic Education,* 29, 33–46.

Brozo, W. (1988). Applying the reader response heuristic to expository text. *Journal of Reading,* 32, 140–55.

Cohen, D. (1968). The effect of literature on vocabulary and reading achievement. *Elementary English,* 45, 209–213; 217.

Cullinan, B. (ed.). (1992). *Invitation to read: More children's literature in the reading program.* Newark, DE: International Reading Association.

Devescovi, A., & Baumgartner, E. (1993). Joint-reading a picture book: Verbal interaction and narrative skills. *Cognitive Instruction,* 11(3/4), 299–323.

Dishner, E., Bean, T., Readance, J., & Moore, D. (eds.). *Reading in the content areas: Improving classroom instruction,* 2nd ed. Dubuque, IA: Kendall/Hunt.

Fallen, J. R. (Mar. 1995). Children's literature as a springboard to music. *Music Educator's Journal,* 81, 24–27.

Forte, I., & Schurr, S. (1995). *Using favorite picture books to stimulate discussion and encourage critical thinking.* Nashville, TN: Incentive Publications.

Funk, H. D., & Funk, G. D. (Spring 1992). Children's literature: An integral facet of the elementary school curriculum. *Reading Improvement,* 29, 40–44.

Galda, L., & Kiefer, B. (Feb. 1991). Children's books: Accent on art. *Reading Teacher,* 44(6), 406–414.

Glazer, J. (1997). *Introduction to children's literature,* 2nd ed. Englewood Cliffs, NJ: Prentice Hall.

Hancock, M. R. (Dec. 1993). Exploring the meaning-making process through the content of literature response journals: A case study investigation. *Research in the Teaching of English,* 27, 335–68.

Hara, K. (Spring 1995). Teacher-centered and child-centered pedagogical approaches in teaching children's literature. *Education,* 115, 332–38.

Hennings, D. G. (1992). *Beyond the read aloud: Learning to read through listening to and reflecting on literature.* Bloomington, IN: Phi Delta Kappa.

Hillman, J. (1995). *Discovering children's literature.* Englewood Cliffs, NJ: Prentice Hall.

Johnson, P. H., et al. (July 1995). Assessment of teaching and learning in "literature-based" classrooms. *Teaching Education,* 11, 359–71.

Johnson, T., & Louis, D. (1987). *Literacy through literature.* Portsmouth, NH: Heinemann.

Jones, H. J., et al. (Winter 1994/1995). A themed literature unit versus a textbook: A comparison of the effects on content acquisition and attitudes in elementary social studies. *Reading Research and Instruction,* 34, 85–96.

Kiefer, B. (1995). *The potential of picturebooks: From visual literacy to aesthetic understanding.* Upper Saddle River, NJ: Prentice Hall.

Krening, N. (1992). Authors of color: A multicultural perspective. *Journal of Reading,* 36(2), 124–29.

Lamme, L. L. (Apr. 1979). Song picture books—A maturing genre of children's literature. *Language Arts,* 56(4), 400–407.

Lamme, L. L. (Dec. 1990). Exploring the world of music through picture books. *Reading Teacher,* 44(4), 294–300.

Lukens, R. (1990). *A critical handbook of children's literature,* 4th ed. Glenview, IL: Scott, Foresman/Little, Brown Higher Education.

Madura, S. (Oct. 1995). The line and texture of aesthetic response: Primary children study authors and illustrators. *Reading Teacher,* 49, 110–118.

McCabe, A. (1996). *Chameleon readers: Teaching children to appreciate all kinds of good stories.* New York: McGraw-Hill.

McCord, S. (1995). *The storybook journey: Pathways to literacy through story and play.* Upper Saddle River, NJ: Prentice Hall.

Miller-Hughes, K. A. (Dec. 1994). Making the connection: Children's books and the visual arts. *School Arts,* 94, 32–33.

Mitchell, F. (Dec. 1990). Introducing art history through children's literature. *Language Arts,* 67, 839–46.

Norton, D. (1995). *Through the eyes of a child: An introduction to children's literature,* 4th ed. Upper Saddle River, NJ: Prentice Hall.

Ogle, D. (1986). K–W–L: A teaching model that develops active reading of expository text. *Reading Teacher,* 39, 564–70.

Pantaleo, S. (1995). What do response journals reveal about children's understandings of the working of literary texts? *Reading Horizons,* 36(1), 76–93.

Peterson, R., & Eeds, M. (1990). *Grand conversations: Literature groups in action.* New York: Scholastic.

Richards, P. O. (Sept. 1994). Thirteen steps to becoming a children's literature expert. *Reading Teacher,* 48, 90–91.

Rose, L. (1996). *Developing intelligences through literature: Ten theme-based units for growing minds.* Tucson, AZ: Zephyr Press.

Rostankowski, C. (Fall 1994). A is for aesthetics: Alphabet books and the development of the aesthetic in children. *Journal of Aesthetic Education,* 28, 117–27.

Rothlein, L., & Meinbach, A. M. (1996). *Legacies: Using children's literature in the classroom.* New York: HarperCollins.

Sipe, L. R. (Sept. 1993). Using transformations of traditional stories: Making the reading–writing connection. *Reading Teacher,* 47, 18–26.

Slaughter, J. P. (Summer 1994). The readers respond—a key component of the literary club: Implementing a literature-based reading program. *Reading Improvement,* 31, 77–86.

Smardo, F. (Apr. 1984). Using children's literature as a prelude or finale to music experiences with young children. *Reading Teacher,* 37(8), 700–705.

Stewig, J. (1988). *Children and literature,* 2nd ed. Boston: Houghton Mifflin.

Van Kraayenoord, C. E., & Paris, S. G. (Mar. 1996). Story construction from a picture book: An assessment activity for young learners. *Early Childhood Research Quarterly,* 11, 41–61.

Art

Anderson, T. (Nov. 1981). Wholes and holes: Art's role in holistic education. *Art Education,* 36–39.

Arnold, A. (Winter 1995). Opening windows to stories through art. *Journal of Youth Services in Libraries,* 8, 204–207.

Baumgardner, J. M. (1993). *60 art projects for children.* New York: Clarkson Potter.

Beattie, D. K. (Mar. 1994). The mini-portfolio: Locus of a successful performance examination. *Art Education,* 14–18.

Blandy, D., Pancsofar, E., & Mockensturm, T. (Jan. 1988). Guidelines for teaching art to children and youth experiencing significant mental/physical challenges. *Art Education,* 60–66.

Caldwell, H., & Moore, B. (1991). The art of writing: Drawing as preparation for narrative writing in the primary grades. *Studies in Art Education,* 32(4), 207–219.

Chalmers, F. G. (Sept. 1987). Beyond current conceptions of discipline-based art education. *Art Education,* 58–61.

Chertok, B., Hirshfield, G., & Rosh, M. (1992). *Meet the masterpieces.* New York: Scholastic.

Clark, R. (1998). *An Introduction to Art Education.* London. ON: Plan B Books (142 Chestnut Hill, London, ON N6K 4J6, tel: 519-641-4551).

Clark, R. (1994). *Art Eucation: A Canadian Perspective.* Toronto: Ontario Society for Education through Art (ISBN: 0-698237-0-).

Dalke, C. (Nov. 1984). There are no cows here: Art and special education together at last. *Art Education,* 6–9.

Englebaugh, D. (1994). *Art through children's literature: Creative art lessons for Caldecott books.* Englewood, CA: Teacher Ideas Press.

Evans, J., & Moore, J. E. (1992). *How to teach art to children.* Monterey, CA: Evan Moor.

Gainer, R. S. (Nov./Dec. 1983). At home in art. *Childhood Education,* 102–109.

Galda, L. (Mar. 1993). Visual literacy: Exploring art and illustration in children's books. *Reading Teacher,* 46(6), 506–16.

Godfrey, R. (Apr. 1992). Civilization, education, and the visual arts: A personal manifesto. *Kappan,* 596–600.

Greco, R. (Dec. 1996/Jan. 1997). Introducing art history through children's literature. *Reading Teacher,* 50, 365.

Greer, W. D. (1984). Discipline-based art education: Approaching art as a subject of study. *Studies in Art Education,* 25(4), 212–218.

Hamblen, K. (1987). What general education can tell us about evaluation in art. *Studies in Art Education,* 28(4), 246–50.

Hart, K. (1988). *I can draw: Ideas for teachers.* Portsmouth, NH: Heinemann.

Herberholz, B., & Hanson, L. (1995). *Early childhood art.* Madison, WI: Brown and Benchmark.

Herberholz, D., & Herberholtz, B. (1994). *Artworks for elementary teachers: Developing artistic and perceptual awareness.* Madison, WI: Brown and Benchmark.

Herman, G. (1992). *Kinetic kaleidoscope: Exploring movement and energy in the visual arts.* Tucson, AZ: Zephyr Press.

Hurwitz, A., & Day, M. (1995). *Children and their art: Methods for the elementary school.* Orlando, FL: Harcourt Brace.

Jefferson, B. (1964). The color book craze. *Bulletin F.* Washington, DC: Association for Childhood Education International.

Linderman, M. G. (1990). *Art in the elementary school: Drawing, painting, and creating for the classroom.* Ames, IA: William C. Brown.

Massey, S., & Darst, D. (1992). *Learning to look: A complete art history and appreciation program for grades K–8.* Englewood Cliffs, NJ: Prentice Hall.

Parrott, J. (1986). Developing excellence through curriculum in art. *Journal of Aesthetic Education,* 20(3), 69–80.

Perkins, D. N. (Dec./Jan. 1987/88). Art as an occasion of intelligence. *Educational Leadership,* 36–42.

Rowe, G. (1987). *Guiding young artists: Curriculum ideas for teachers.* Melbourne: Oxford University Press.

Seely, C., & Hurwitz, A. (May 1983). Developing language through art. *School Arts,* 20–22.

Simpson, J. (Jan. 1996). Constructivism and connection making in art education. *Art education,* 53–59.

Smith, N. (1993). *Experience and art: Teaching children to paint.* New York: Teachers College Press.

Smout, B. (Feb. 1990). Reading, writing, and art. *Reading Teacher,* 430–31.

Stover, L. (Sept. 1988). What do you mean, we have to read a book for art class? *Art Education,* 8–13.

Wachowiak, F., & Clements, R. (1993). *Emphasis art: A qualitative art program for elementary and middle schools.* New York: HarperCollins.

Drama

Barchers, S. (1993). *Reader's theatre for beginning readers.* Englewood, CO: Teacher Ideas Press.

Bray, Errol (1995). *Playbuilding: A guide for group creation of plays with young people.* Portsmouth, NH: Heinemann.

Collins, R. (1997). Storytelling: Water from another time. *Drama Teacher,* 5(2), 6.

Comeaux, P. (Winter 1994). Performing poetry: Centering the language arts program. *Contemporary Education,* 77–81.

Cottrell, J. (1987). *Creative drama in the classroom, grades 1–3 and 4–6.* Lincolnwood, IL: National Textbook Company.

Fennessey, S. (Sept. 1995). Living history through drama and literature. *Reading Teacher,* 49, 16–19.

Flynn, R., & Carr, G. (Jan. 1994). Exploring classroom literature through drama: A specialist and a teacher collaborate. *Language Arts,* 38–43.

Fox, M. (1987). *Teaching drama to young children.* Portsmouth, NH: Heinemann.

Hackbarth, J. (1994). *Plays, players, and playing: How to start your own children's theater company.* Colorado Springs, CO: Piccadilly Books.

Harmon, R. (1994). *Teaching a young actor: How to train children of all ages for success in movies, TV, and commercials.* New York: Walker.

Harp, B. (May 1988). Is all of that drama taking valuable time away from reading? *Reading Teacher,* 938–40.

Heathcote, D., & Bolton, G. (1995). *Drama for learning.* Portsmouth, NH: Heinemann.

Heinig, R. B. (1987). *Creative drama resource book for kindergarten through Grade 3* and *Creative drama resource book for Grades 4 through 6.* Englewood Cliffs, NJ: Prentice Hall.

Heller, P. (1995). *Drama as a way of knowing.* Galef Institute. York, ME: Stenhouse.

Henderson, L. C., & Shanker, L. C. (1978). The use of interpretive dramatics versus basal reader workbooks. *Reading World,* 17, 239–243.

Landy, R. (1986). *Drama therapy: Concepts and practices.* Springfield, IL: Charles C Thomas.

Laughlin, M. K., & Latrobe, K. H. (1990). *Reader's theatre for children.* Englewood, CO: Teacher Ideas Press.

Livo, N., & Rietz, S. (1987). *Storytelling activities.* Littleton, CO: Libraries Unlimited.

McDonald, M. R. (1986). *Twenty tellable tales: Audience participation folktales for the beginning storyteller.* New York: Wilson.

Martinez, M. G. (May 1993). Motivating dramatic story reenactments. *Reading Teacher,* 46, 682–88.

Mazor, R. (Mar. 1978). Drama as experience. *Language Arts,* 55(3), 328–33.

O'Neill, C., Lambert, A., Linell, R., & Warr-Wood, J. (1977). *Drama guidelines.* Portsmouth, NH: Heinemann.

Ross, E., & Roe, B. (Jan. 1977). Creative drama builds proficiency in reading. *Reading Teacher,* 383–87.

Sawyer, R. (1942). *The way of the storyteller.* New York: Viking.

Scher, A., & Verrall, C. (1981). *One hundred plus ideas for drama.* Portsmouth, NH: Heinemann.

Scher, A., & Verrall, C. (1987). *Another one hundred plus ideas for drama.* Portsmouth, NH: Heinemann.

Spolin, V. (1963). *Improvisation for the theatre.* Evanston, IL: Northwestern University Press.

Spolin, V. (1986). *Theatre games for the classroom: A teacher's handbook.* Evanston, IL: Northwestern University Press.

Stewig, J. (1983). *Informal drama in the elementary language arts program.* New York: Teachers College Press.

Verriour, P. (1985). Face to face: Negotiating meaning through drama. *Theory into Practice,* 24(3), 181–86.

Wagner, B. J. (Mar. 1979). Using drama to create an environment for language development. *Language Arts,* 56(3), 268–74.

Wagner, B. J. (Jan. 1988). Research contents: Does classroom drama affect the arts of language? *Language Arts,* 65(1), 46–54.

Ward, W. (1981). *Stories to dramatize.* New Orleans: Anchorage Press.

Way, B. (1981). *Audience participation: Theatre for young people.* Boston: W. H. Baker.

White, M. (1993). *Mel White's readers theatre anthology: Twenty-eight all-occasion readings for storytellers.* Colorado Springs, CO: Meriwether.

Wolf, A. (1993). *It's show time!: Poetry from the page to the stage.* Asheville, NC: Poetry Alive!

Dance

Allen, B. (Nov./Dec. 1988). Teaching training and discipline-based dance education. *Journal of Physical Education, Recreation, and Dance,* 65–69.

Barlin, A. L. (1979). *Teaching your wings to fly: The nonspecialist's guide to movement activities for young children.* Santa Monica, CA: Goodyear.

Barlin, A. L., & Greenberg, T. (1980). *Move and be moved: A practical approach to movement with meaning.* Los Angeles: Learning through Movement.

Benzwie, T. (1988). *A moving experience: Dance for lovers of children and the child within.* Tucson, AZ: Zephyr Press.

Boorman, J. (1969). *Creative dance in the first three grades.* Toronto: Longman Canada.

Exiner, H., & Lloyd, P. (1973). *Teaching creative movement.* Sydney: Angus & Robertson.

Exiner, H., & Lloyd, P. (1987). *Learning through dance: A guide for teachers.* Melbourne, Australia: Oxford University Press.

Griss, S. (Feb. 1994). Creative movement: A language for learning. *Kappan,* 78–80.

Kane, K. A. (May 1994). Stories to help students understand movement. *Strategies,* 7, 13–17.

Lee, A. (1985). *A handbook of creative dance and drama.* Portsmouth, NH: Heinemann.

Lee, P. (Feb. 1994). To dance one's understanding. *Kappan,* 81–82.

Mettler, B. (1980). *The nature of dance as a creative art activity.* Tucson, AZ: Mettler Studio.

National Dance Association (1990). *Guide to creative dance for the young child.* Reston, VA: National Dance Association.

Pesetsky, S., & Burack, S. (1984). *Teaching dance for the handicapped: A curriculum guide.* Lansing, MI: Michigan Dance Association.

Preston-Dunlop, V. A. (1980). *Handbook for dance in education,* 2nd ed. Estover, Plymouth, England: Macdonald & Evans.

Schwartz, V., Ed. (Nov./Dec. 1989). A dance for all people. *Journal of Physical Education, Recreation, and Dance,* 49–64.

Silk, G. (Nov./Dec. 1989). Creative movement for people who are developmentally disabled. *Journal of Physical Education, Recreation, and Dance,* 56–58.

Werner, P., ed. (Dec. 1974). Movement, music, and children's literature. *Physical Education,* 31(4), 216–18.

Willis, C. (May/June 1995). Creative dance—how to increase parent and child awareness. *Journal of Physical Education, Recreation, and Dance.*

Witkin, K. (1978). *To move, to learn.* New York: Schocken Books.

Zirulnik, A., & Abeles, J., eds. (1985). *Resource lists for children's dance.* Lansing, MI: Michigan Dance Association.

Music

Ameigh, T. (Jan. 1993). Learn the language of music through journals. *Music Educators Journal,* 30–32.

Bennett, P., & Bartholomew, D. (1997). *Songworks I: Singing in the education of children.* Belmont, CA: Wadsworth.

Best, H. (Nov. 1992). Music curricula in the future. *Arts Education Policy Review,* 2–7.

Bibbins, P. (July 1993). More than music: A collaborative curriculum. *Music Educators Journal,* 23–26.

Boshkoff, R. (Oct. 1991). Lesson planning the Kodaly way. *Music Educators Journal,* 30–34.

Campbell, D. (1997). *The Mozart effect.* New York: Avon.

Collett, M. J. (Nov. 1991). Read between the lines: Music as a basis for learning. *Music Educators Journal,* 42–45.

Davidson, L. (May 1990). Tools and environments for musical creativity. *Music Educators Journal,* 47–51.

Deither, B. (Dec. 1991). Using music as a second language. *English Journal,* 72–76.

Goodkin, D. (July 1994). Diverse approaches to multicultural music. *Music Educators Journal,* 39–43.

Grant, J. M. (1995). *Shake, rattle & learn.* York, ME: Stinhouse Publishers.

Judy, S. (1990). *Making music for the joy of it.* Los Angeles: Jeremy P. Tarcher.

Kaplan, D. (Jan. 1985). Music in the classroom: A new approach. *Learning,* 13(5), 28–31.

Lehman, P. (Mar. 1993). Why your school needs music. *Arts Education Policy Review,* 30–34.

Levene, D. (1993). *Music through children's literature: Theme and variations.* Englewood, CO: Teacher Ideas Press.

Livo, N. J. (April 1975). Multiply music with books and add art. *Elementary English,* 52(4), 541–44.

Lynch, S. (1994). *Classical music for beginners.* New York: Writers and Readers.

Manins, S. (Mar. 1994). Bridge building in early childhood music. *Music Educators Journal,* 37–41.

Mann, R. (Mar. 1979). The effect of music and sound effects on the listening comprehension of fourth grade students. Paper presented at the Annual Convention of the Association for Educational Communications and Technology. New Orleans.

Markel, R. (1983). *Music for your child: A complete guide for parents and teachers.* New York: Facts on File.

McGirr, P. I. (Winter 1994/1995). Verdi invades the kindergarten: Using song picture books. *Childhood Education,* 71, 74–79.

Merritt, S. (1990). *Mind, music, and imagery: 40 exercises using music to stimulate creativity and self-awareness.* New York: NAL/Plume.

Miller, A., & Coen, D. (Feb. 1994). The case for music in the schools. *Kappan,* 459–61.

Nash, G., & Repley, J. (1990). *Music in the making: Optimal learning in speech, song, instrument instruction, and movement for grades K–4.* Van Nuys, CA: Alfred.

Painter, W. (1989). *Musical story hours: Using music with storytelling and puppetry.* Hamden, CT: Library Professional Publications.

Phillips, K. (Sept. 1993). A stronger rationale for music education. *Music Educators Journal,* 17–19.

Present, G. (1986). *We all live together: Song & activity book and leader's guide.* Milwaukee, WI: Hal Leonard Publishing.

Reaser, D. (Mar. 1993). Let's speak music! *Education Digest,* 66–68.

Seeger, A. (May 1992). Celebrating the American music mosaic. *Music Educators Journal,* 26–29.

Shaffer, G. (Sept. 1982). Music teaches poetry, poetry teaches music. *Music Educator's Journal,* 69(1), 40–42.

Speake, C. (Feb. 1993). Create an opera with elementary students. *Music Educators Journal,* 22–6.

Stover, L. (Oct. 1989). Read a book for music class? Are you serious? *Music Educators Journal,* 76(2), 48–52.

Warner, L. (Jan./Feb. 1982). 37 music ideas for the nonmusical teacher. *Childhood Education,* 58(3), 134–37.

Whitaker, N. (July 1994). Whole language and music education. *Music Educators Journal,* 24–28.

Videography

American storyteller video series (1987). New York: H. W. Wilson.

Art education in action (1994) (video, 112 min.). Los Angeles: J. Paul Getty Trust.

The art of learning (1993) (video, 46 min). Santa Monica, CA: Getty Center for Education in the Arts.

Arts for life (1990) (video, 15 min.). J. Paul Gerry Trust. Excellent rationale for arts integration.

The arts and children: A success story (video, 15 min.). Goals 2000 Arts Education Partnership. Motivational video on why the arts should be integrated. Classroom examples and interviews.

Art's place (1994). Princeton, NY: Films for the Humanities, Inc. Series of children's videos on art.

The arts: Tools for teaching (1994) (video). Washington, DC: John F. Kennedy Center for the Performing Arts.

Artscape (1994). Princeton, NY: Films for the Humanities, Inc. Series of children's videos on art.

Aurand Harris demonstrating playwriting with children (1983) (24 min. video). Edward Feil Production. Cleveland, OH. 44103. Teaching playwriting to fifth and sixth graders.

Brighten your road (1986). Allen, TX: KLM Teaching Resources.

Creative beginnings (1991) (video, 59 min). New York: Ambrose Video Publishing, Inc.

Creative movement: A step towards intelligence (1993) (video, 80 min.). West Long Branch, NJ: Kultur.

Creativity: A way of learning (video, 11 min.). NEA Distribution Center, Academic Bldg., Saw Mill Rd., West Haven, CT 06516 Explores how to encourage creativity.

Dance and grow (1994) (video, 60 min.). Dance Horizons.

Dorothy Heathcote talks to teachers (1973). Northwestern University (62 min: two parts on drama).

Drama with the kindergarten (1987) (video). Tempe, AZ: Arizona State University. Three drama approaches.

Introduction to creative drama & improvisation (1990). Indianapolis: DVC, Inc.

Humor in music: What is a melody? (1993). New York: Sony Classical (113 min.).

Literary visions (1992). South Burlington, VT: Annenberg/CPB Collection (5 vol., 30 min./each).

The lively art of picture books (1957). Weston Woods (57 min.; older, but a classic piece).

Master class (1992). Columbia University Media and Society Seminars Collection. PBS Video. West Tisbury, MA: Vineyard Video.

Max made mischief: An approach to literature (1977) (video, 30 min.). University Park, PA: Pennsylvania State AV Services.

One of a Kind (film, 58 min.). Phoenix Films, Inc., 470 Park Ave. South, New York, NY, 10016. Use of puppets. Troubled child gains emotional release. Good for special education.

Playing: Pretending spontaneous drama with children (film, 20 min.). Community Services Dept., Pittsburgh Child Guidance Center, 201 De Soto St., Pittsburgh, PA., 15213.

Picture thoughts (1994) (video). Columbia, MD: Hamilton Associates.

Poetry is words that I sing! (1988) (video, 30 min.). Berkeley: University of California Extension Media Center.

The role of art in general education (1988) (video). Los Angeles: Getty Center for Education in the Arts.

Statues hardly ever smile (film, 25 min.). Brooklyn Museum, Eastern Parkway and Washington Ave., Brooklyn, NY, 11238. Creative drama in a museum.

Teaching in and through the arts (1995) (video, 25 min.). Santa Monica, CA: Getty Center for Education in the Arts. Classroom examples, elementary through high school, are shown.

Three looms waiting (52 min. film). BBC. Distributed by Time-Life Films, 43 W. 16th St., New York, NY, 10016 Dorothy Heathcote working with children.

Traditional expressions. Santa Cruz, CA: Multi-Cultural Communications, Inc. Several multicultural art projects are demonstrated, including mask making and aboriginal dot painting.

What do you see? (video, 25 min). The Art Institute of Chicago.

What is Kodaly music education? An historical overview (1992). Wellesley, MA: KCA (48 min.).

What's a good book? (1982) (video, 27 min.). Weston, CT: The Studios.

Why are the arts essential to education reform? (1993) (video). Los Angeles: J. Paul Getty Trust.

Why man creates (film, 25 min.). Pyramid Films, Box 1048, Santa Monica, CA 90406.

Appendix G

Post It Page

Six National Standards for Visual Arts K-8*

Overall focus: Create, express, and respond through visual media, expression of feelings and emotions, new ways of communicating and thinking, application of knowledge to world problems, historical and cultural investigation, and evaluation and interpretation of the visual world.

1. **Understanding and applying media, techniques, and processes.** Example activities: Communicate ideas and experiences through visual art. Use materials safely.
2. **Using knowledge of structures and functions.** Example activities: Explain messages art conveys and what an artist does to convey messages.
3. **Choosing and evaluating a range of subject matter, symbols, and ideas.** Example activities: Explain possible content for artwork and ways to show meaning in different ways.
4. **Understanding the visual arts in relation to history and cultures.** Example activities: Examine how aspects of culture and history are expressed in works of art.
5. **Reflecting upon and assessing the characteristics and merits of their work and the work of others.** Example activities: Explain purposes for art and how people's experiences influence their art.
6. **Making connections between visual arts and other disciplines.** Example activities: Find similarities and differences between visual art and other disciplines. Use visual art throughout the curriculum to make meaning.

---

*Content Standards (material printed in bold type) excerpted from the *National Standards for Arts Education,* published by Music Educators National Conference (MENC). Copyright (c) 1994 by MENC. Reproduced with permission. The complete *National Standards* and additional materials relating to the *Standards* are available from Music Educators National Conference, 1806 Robert Fulton Drive, Reston, VA 20191 (telephone 800-336-3768).

Post It Page

The National Standards for Theater K–8*

Overall focus: Learn about life, pretend and assume roles, social development, interact with peers, bring stories to life, direct one another, improvisation, writing, acting, designing, comparing forms, analyzing, evaluating, understanding the world (history, cultures).

1. *Script writing by planning and recording improvisations based on personal experience and heritage, imagination, literature and history (k–4) and by creation of improvisations and scripted scenes based on personal experience and heritage, imagination, literature, and history (5–8).* Example activities: Create classroom dramatizations. Improvise dialogues to tell a story.
2. *Acting by assuming roles and interacting in improvisations (k–4) and by developing basic acting skills to portray characters who interact in improvised and scripted scenes (5–8).* Example activities: Clearly describe characters. Use concentration and body and vocal elements to express characters. Dramatize personal stories.
3. *Designing by visualizing and arranging environments for classroom dramatizations (k–4) and by developing environments for improvised and scripted scenes (5–8).* Example activities: Use art media and techniques to make settings. Organize materials for dramatic play.
4. *Directing by planning classroom dramatizations (k–4) and by organizing rehearsals for improvised and scripted scenes (5–8).* Example activities: Plan a class play. Use drama elements and skills. Play the roles of director, writer, designer, and actor.
5. *Researching by finding information to support classroom dramatizations (k–4) and by using cultural and historical information to support improvised and scripted scenes (5–8).* Example activities: Find literature to adapt for classroom drama (books, poems, songs, any material usable for plays). Research time periods and cultures for dramatic material.
6. *Comparing and connecting art forms by describing theater, dramatic media (such as film, television, and electronic media) and other art forms (k–4). Comparing and incorporating art forms by analyzing methods of presentation and audience response for theater, dramatic media (such as film, television, and electronic media) and other art forms (5–8).* Example activities: Compare how the different arts communicate ideas. Describe visual, aural, oral, and kinetic elements of theater.
7. *Analyzing and explaining personal preferences and constructing meanings from classroom dramatizations and from theater, film, television, and electronic media productions (k–4). Analyzing, evaluating, and constructing meanings from improvised and scripted scenes and from theater, film, television, and electronic media productions (5–8).* Example activities: Evaluate performances using specific criteria. Explain characters' wants and needs.
8. *Understanding context by recognizing the role of theater, film, television, and electronic media in daily life (k–4). Understanding context by analyzing the role of theater, film, television, and electronic media in the community and other cultures (5–8).* Example activities: Web ideas for why theatre is created. Attend performances and discuss what is learned about culture, history, and life from theatre.

---

*Content Standards (material printed in italic type) excerpted from the *National Standards for Arts Education,* published by Music Educators National Conference (MENC). The complete *National Standards* and additional materials relating to the standards are available from Music Educators National Conference, 1806 Robert Fulton Drive, Reston, VA 20191 (800-336-3768).

Post It Page

Seven National Standards for Dance*

Overall focus: Develop self-image, self-expression, and discipline, body awareness, movement exploration, and creative problem-solving, appreciation of self and others, cooperation and collaboration, use of musical rhythms, performing for an audience, respect for diversity, and celebration of humanity and cultures.

1. **Identifying and demonstrating movement elements and skills in performing dance.** Example activities: Perform locomotor movements, create shapes, personal space, pathways, move to beat and tempo, show concentration, describe actions and dance elements.
2. **Understanding choreographic principles, processes, and structures.** Example activities: Create dances with a beginning, middle, end structure. Improvise and create new movements. Use partner skills like leading and copying. Create dance phrases.
3. **Understanding dance as a way to create and communicate meaning.** Example activities: Explain how dance is different from sports and everyday gestures. Discuss what a dance is communicating. Present original dances and explain their meanings.
4. **Applying and demonstrating critical and creative thinking skills in dance.** Example activities: Find multiple solutions to movement problems. Observe two different dances and discuss differences and similarities. Apply esthetic criteria to observed dances. Demonstrate appropriate audience etiquette.
5. **Demonstrating and understanding dance in various cultures and historical periods.** Example activities: Perform folk dances. Share dances from own heritage. Put dance into historical periods based on style and elements. Analyze for values conveyed.
6. **Making connections between dance and healthful living.** Example activities: Set personal goals for a dancer. Discuss healthy practices. Create and use dance warm-ups.
7. **Making connections between dance and other disciplines.** Example activities: Create a dance to explain a concept from another discipline. Respond to dance by making a painting, song, or writing about messages it conveys.

---

*Content *Standards* (material printed in bold type) excerpted from *National Standards for Arts Education,* published by Music Educators National Conference (MENC). Copyright (c) 1994 by MENC. Reproduced with permission. The complete *National Standards* and additional materials relating to the *Standards* are available from Music Educators National Conference, 1806 Robert Fulton Drive, Reston, VA 20191 (800-336-3768).

Post It Page

The National Standards for Music K-8*

Overall focus: creating, performing, responding to music (sing, play instrument, move to music, create own music, read and notate, listen to, analyze, evaluate, understand historical and cultural heritage (i.e., basic human expression)

1. **Singing, alone and with others, a varied repertoire of music.** Example activities: Learn songs from different cultures, traditional North American songs, songs from different genres (lullabies, gospel, rounds, work songs). Observe conductor's cues during singing (change dynamics, sing expressively, use appropriate posture and rhythm).
2. **Performing on instruments, alone and with others, a varied repertoire of music.** Example activities: Echo short rhythms (clap, stamp, etc.). Play rhythm instruments while others sing.
3. **Improvising melodies, variations and accompaniments.** Example activities: Use "sounds" to create songs with a beginning, middle, and end. Improvise rhythm and ostinato accompaniments.
4. **Composing and arranging music within specific guidelines.** Example activities: Make and use instruments with songs. Find background music to go with poetry or literature readings.
5. **Reading and notating music.** Example activities: Recognize 2/4, 3/4, and 4/4 meter signatures. Read pitch (do re mi . . .) with hand signals.
6. **Listening to, analyzing, and describing music.** Example activities: Do close critical listening to identify music elements and characteristics of styles and genre.
7. **Evaluating music and music performances.** Example activities: Explain personal preferences and why using musical terms.
8. **Understanding relationships between music, the other arts, and disciplines outside the arts.** Example activities: Compare and contrast concepts across art forms (texture, line, rhythm). Connect ways music intersects with reading and language arts, science, social studies, and math.
9. **Understanding music in relation to history and culture.** Example activities: Explain how music expresses cultural and history. Investigate musical careers. Use appropriate audience behaviour.

---

*Content standards (material printed in bold type) excerpted from the *National Standards for Arts Education,* published by Music Educators National Conference (MENC). Copyright © 1994 by MENC. Reproduced with permission. The complete *National Standards* and additional materials relating to the *Standards* are available from Music Educators National Conference, 1806 Robert Fulton Drive, Reston, VA 20191 (800-336-3768).

Index